Applied Economic Forecasting using Time Series Methods

Applied Economic Forecasting using Time Series Methods

Eric Ghysels
University of North Carolina, Chapel Hill, United States

Massimiliano Marcellino
Bocconi University, Milan, Italy

OXFORD
UNIVERSITY PRESS

OXFORD
UNIVERSITY PRESS

Oxford University Press is a department of the University of Oxford. It furthers the University's objective of excellence in research, scholarship, and education by publishing worldwide. Oxford is a registered trade mark of Oxford University Press in the UK and in certain other countries.

Published in the United States of America by Oxford University Press
198 Madison Avenue, New York, NY 10016, United States of America.

Library of Congress Cataloging-in-Publication Data
Names: Ghysels, Eric, 1956- author. | Marcellino, Massimiliano, author.
Title: Applied economic forecasting using time series methods / Eric Ghysels
    and Massimiliano Marcellino.
Description: New York, NY : Oxford University Press, [2018]
Identifiers: LCCN 2017046487 | ISBN 9780190622015 (hardcover : alk. paper) |
    ISBN 9780190622039 (epub)
Subjects: LCSH: Economic forecasting–Mathematical models. | Economic
    forecasting–Statistical methods.
Classification: LCC HB3730 .G459 2018 | DDC 330.01/51955–dc23 LC record
    available at https://lccn.loc.gov/2017046487

9 8 7 6 5 4 3
Printed by Sheridan Books, Inc., United States of America

Contents

Part II   Forecasting with Time Series Models

Part III   TAR, Markov Switching, and State Space Models

Part IV   Mixed Frequency, Large Datasets, and Volatility

Preface

Economic forecasting is a key ingredient of decision making both in the public and in the private sector. Governments and central banks, consumers and firms, banks and financial institutions base many of their decisions on future expected economic conditions or on the predictions of specific indicators of interest such as income growth, inflation, unemployment, interest rates, exchange rates, earnings, wages, oil prices, and so on. Unfortunately, economic outcomes are the realization of a vast, complex, dynamic and stochastic system, which makes forecasting very difficult and forecast errors unavoidable. However, forecast precision and reliability can be enhanced by the use of proper econometric models and methods, like those we present in this book.

We wish to satisfy an audience including both undergraduate and graduate students willing to learn basic and advanced forecasting techniques, and researchers in public and private institutions interested in applied economic forecasting. For this reason, the book is divided into four parts. In Part I, the first chapter provides a brief review of basic regression analysis, followed by two chapters dealing with specific regression topics relevant for forecasting, such as model mis-specification, including structural breaks, and dynamic models and their predictive properties. The fourth chapter, on the topic of forecast evaluation and combination, is the first exclusively dedicated to forecasting. The material in Part I could be used in the senior year of an undergraduate program for students who have a strong interest in applied econometrics, or as an introduction to economic forecasting for graduate students and researchers from other disciplines.

Part II of the book is devoted to time series models, in particular univariate autoregressive integrated moving average (ARIMA) models and vector autoregressive (VAR) models. Specifically, Chapter 5 deals with ARIMA models, Chapter 6 with VAR models, Chapter 7 with cointegration and error correction (ECM) models, and Chapter 8 with Bayesian methods for VAR analysis. The material progressively becomes better suited for master level and/or PhD level classes, in particular the chapters on cointegration and Bayesian VARs. Models considered in Part II are also common tools for practical forecasting in public and private institutions.

Parts III and IV of the book contain a collection of special topics chapters. Each chapter is self-contained, and therefore an instructor or researcher can pick and choose the topics she or he wants to cover. Part III deals mainly with modeling parameter time-variation. Specifically, Chapter 9 presents Threshold and Smooth Transition Autoregressive (TAR and STAR) models, Chapter 10 Markov switching regime models, and Chapter 11 state space models and the Kalman filter, introducing, for example, models with random coefficients and dynamic factor models.

Part IV deals with mixed frequency data models and their use for now-casting in Chapter 12, forecasting using large datasets in Chapter 13 and, finally, volatility models in Chapter 14.

Each chapter starts with a review of the main theoretical results to prepare the reader for the various applications. Examples involving simulated data follow, to make the reader familiar with application using at first stylized settings where one knows the true data generating process and one learns how to apply the techniques introduced in each chapter. From our own teaching experience we find this to be extremely useful as it creates familiarity with each of the topics in a controlled environment. The simulated examples are followed by real data applications - focusing on macroeconomic and financial topics. Some of the examples run across different chapters, particularly in the early part of the book. All data are public domain and cover Euro area, UK, and US examples, including forecasting US GDP growth, default risk, inventories, effective federal funds rates, composite index of leading indicators, industrial production, Euro area GDP growth, UK term structure of interest rates, to mention the most prominent examples.

The book is mostly software neutral. However, for almost all the simulated and empirical examples we provide companion *EViews*® and *R* code. The former is mostly - but not exclusively - a menu driven licensed software package whereas the latter is an open source programming language and software environment for statistical computing and graphics supported by the

R Foundation for Statistical Computing.[1]. We provide code and data for all the simulated and empirical examples in the book on the web.[2] Moreover, all the tables and figures appearing in the book were produced using *EViews*®.

As the title suggests, this book is an *applied* time series forecasting book. Hence, we do not have the pretense to provide the full theoretical foundations for the forecasting methods we present. Indeed, there are already a number of books with thorough coverage of theory. The most recent example is the excellent book by Elliott and Timmermann (2016) which provides an in-depth analysis of the statistical theory underlying predictive models, covering a variety of alternative forecasting methods in both classical and Bayesian contexts, as well as techniques for forecast evaluation, comparison, and combination. Equally useful and complimentary are the many standard econometrics textbooks such as Hendry (1995), Judge, Hill, Griffiths, Lütkepohl, and Lee (1988), Stock and Watson (2009), Wooldridge (2012), and the many graduate time series textbooks such as Box and Jenkins (1976), Clements and Hendry (1998), Diebold (2008), Hamilton (1994), or Lütkepohl (2007), among others.

We should also highlight that this book is an applied *time series* forecasting book. As such, we will not discuss forecasting using economic theory-based structural models, such as Dynamic Stochastic General Equilibrium (DSGE) models, see, e.g., Del Negro and Schorfheide (2013) for an exhaustive overview and references. Typically, these structural models are better suited for medium- and long-horizon forecasting, and for policy simulations, while time series methods work better for nowcasting and short-term forecasting (say, up to one-year ahead).

This book would not have been completed without the invaluable and skillful help of a number of our current and former TAs and RAs. Special thanks go to Cristina Angelico, Francesco Corsello, Francesco Giovanardi, Novella Maugeri, and Nazire Özkan who helped with all the simulation and empirical examples throughout the entire book, as well as Hanwei Liu who wrote the *R* codes. Their contributions to the book were invaluable. We would also like to thank many cohorts of undergraduate, master, and PhD

---

[1]Please visit the web page http://www.eviews.com for further information on *EViews*® and *R* programming language Wikipedia web page https://en.wikipedia.org/wiki/R_ (programming_language).

[2]Please visit our respective webpages www.unc.edu/~eghysels or www.igier.unibocconi. it/marcellino to download the code and data.

students who took courses based on the materials covered in the book at Bocconi University and at the University of North Carolina, Chapel Hill and the Kenan-Flagler Business School.

We are also grateful to a number of coauthors of papers on the topics covered in the book. In particular, Eric Ghysels would like to thank Lucia Alessi, Elena Andreou, Jennie Bai, Fabio Canova, Xilong Chen, Riccardo Colacito, Robert Engle, Claudia Foroni, Lars Forsberg, Patrick Gagliardini, René Garcia, Clive Granger, Andrew Harvey, Jonathan Hill, Casidhe Horan, Lynda Khalaf, Andros Kourtellos, Virmantas Kvedaras, Emanuel Moench, Kaiji Motegi, Denise Osborn, Alberto Plazzi, Eric Renault, Mirco Rubin, Antonio Rubia, Pedro Santa-Clara, Pierre Siklos, Arthur Sinko, Bumjean Sohn, Ross Valkanov, Cosmé Vodounou, Fangfang Wang, Jonathan Wright, and Vaidotas Zemlys (and Massimiliano of course!). Massimiliano Marcellino would like to thank Knut-Are Aastveit, Angela Abbate, Elena Angelini, Mike Artis, Anindya Banerjee, Guenter Beck, Stelios Bekiros, Ralf Burggemann, Andrea Carriero, Roberto Casarin, Todd Clark, Francesco Corielli, Sandra Eickmeier, Carlo Favero, Laurent Ferrara, Claudia Foroni, Giampiero Gallo, Ana Galvão, Pierre Guérin, Jerome Henry, Christian Hepenstrick, Kristin Hubrich, Oscar Jorda, George Kapetanios, Malte Knüppel, Hans-Martin Krolzig, Danilo Leiva-Leon, Wolfgang Lemke, Helmut Lütkepohl, Igor Masten, Gian Luigi Mazzi, Grayham Mizon, Matteo Mogliani, Alberto Musso, Chiara Osbat, Fotis Papailias, Mario Porqueddu, Esteban Prieto, Tommaso Proietti, Francesco Ravazzolo, Christian Schumacher, Dalibor Stevanovic, Jim Stock, Fabrizio Venditti, and Mark Watson (and Eric of course!).

Several colleagues provided useful comments on the book, in particular Frank Diebold, Helmut Lütkepohl, Serena Ng, Simon Price, Frank Schorfheide, and Allan Timmermann. Of course, we remain responsible for any remaining mistakes or omissions.

Finally, we would like to thank our families for their continuous support and understanding. We forecast a quieter and more relaxed "Life after the Book," but as all forecasters, we could be proven wrong.

Eric Ghysels, Chapel Hill, United States
Massimiliano Marcellino, Milan, Italy

Part I

Forecasting with the Linear Regression Model

Chapter 1

The Baseline Linear Regression Model

1.1 Introduction

The most common model in applied econometrics is the linear regression model. It also provides the basis for more sophisticated specifications, such as those that we will consider in the following chapters. Hence it is useful to start with a short overview about the specification, estimation, diagnostic checking and forecasting in the context of the linear regression model. More detailed presentations can be found, for example, in Hendry (1995), Judge, Hill, Griffiths, Lütkepohl, and Lee (1988), Marcellino (2016), Stock and Watson (2009), Wooldridge (2012), among others.

The chapter is structured as follows. In Section 1.2 we introduce the basic specification and assumptions. In Section 1.3 we discuss parameter estimation. In Section 1.4 we consider measures of model fit. In Sections 1.5 and 1.6 we derive, respectively, optimal point and density forecasts. In Section 1.7 we deal with parameter testing and in Sections 1.8 and 1.9 with variable selection. In Section 1.10 we evaluate the effects of multicollinearity. In Sections 1.11 and 1.12 we present examples based on, respectively, simulated and actual data. Section 1.13 explores some features of time lags in the context of forecasting with the baseline linear regression model. Section 1.14 concludes the chapter.

3

1.2   The basic specification

We are interested in assessing the explanatory power of a set of k variables, grouped into X, for the variable y. For example, we may want to study what explains the behavior of the short term interest rate or of inflation for a given country. For the former variable, candidate regressors to be included in X are measures of the output gap and of inflationary pressures, since these are the typical drivers of the decisions of central banks, whose policy rate is in turn a key determinant of the short term interest rate. For inflation, we may want to consider cost push factors, such as unit labor costs and the prices of intermediate inputs and energy, though inflation expectations can also matter if they affect the wage bargaining process and the price determination mechanism.

From a statistical point of view, both the elements of X and y are stochastic processes, namely, collections of random variables, for which we have a set of realizations, X_t and y_t, $t = 1, \ldots, T$. Continuing the previous example, we can collect data on inflation and the short term interest rate over a given temporal period, for example 1970 to 2012, at a given frequency t, e.g., each month or each quarter, or even each day, or even perhaps each minute for the interest rate. In the following we will not explicitly distinguish between a random variable and its realization, unless necessary for clarity. Note also that some of the variables in X can be deterministic, for example X can include an intercept or a linear trend.

If we assume that the explanatory variables X have a linear impact on the dependent variable y, we can write the model as follows:

$$y_t = X_{1t}\beta_1 + X_{2t}\beta_2 + \ldots X_{kt}\beta_k + \varepsilon_t, \qquad (1.2.1)$$

$t = 1, \ldots, T$. Moreover, β_i is a parameter related to the explanatory power of X_{it}, $i = 1, \ldots, k$. More precisely, as the model in (8.2.4) implies $E[y_t | X_{1t}, X_{2t}, \ldots, X_{kt}] = X_{1t}\beta_1 + X_{2t}\beta_2 + \ldots X_{kt}\beta_k$, β_i measures the change in the expected value of y_t when there is a marginal change in X_{it}, and the other Xs are kept constant. Finally, ε_t is an error term capturing the part of y_t that is not explained by the variables in X_t. Formally, it is $\varepsilon_t = y_t - E[y_t | X_{1t}, X_{2t}, \ldots, X_{kt}]$.

If we group y_t and ε_t, $t = 1, \ldots, T$, into the $T \times 1$ vectors y and ε respectively, $\beta_1, \ldots, \beta_k$ into the $k \times 1$ vector β, and $X_{1t}, \ldots, X_{kt}$, $t = 1, \ldots,$

T, into the $T \times k$ matrix X, we can rewrite the linear regression model as

$$\underset{(T \times 1)}{y} = \underset{(T \times k)(k \times 1)}{X\beta} + \underset{(T \times 1)}{\varepsilon} . \qquad (1.2.2)$$

We make a few additional assumptions on the model in (1.2.2), most of which will be relaxed later on:

Assumption 1.2.1 (Linear Regression Assumptions). The linear regression model defined in equation (1.2.2) satisfies the following assumptions:

LR1 $E(\varepsilon) = 0$,

LR2 $E(\varepsilon\varepsilon') = \sigma^2 I_T$,

LR3 X is distributed independently of ε,

LR4 $X'X$ is non singular,

LR5 X is weakly stationary.

The assumptions LR1 through LR5 are typically known as "weak assumptions." The first assumption says that the expected value of the error term should be equal to zero, namely, on average the model should provide a correct explanation for y, which is a basic ingredient of a reasonable model. Assumption 1.2.1 - LR2 states that the matrix of second moments of the errors (which is also equal to their variance covariance matrix given Assumption 1.2.1 - LR1) is diagonal. This implies that the variance of the error term is stable over time (homoskedasticity), and that the errors are uncorrelated over time (no correlation). The requirement that X is distributed independently of ε, in Assumption 1.2.1 - LR3, is needed to guarantee good properties for the simplest parameter estimator, as we will see in the next section. Assumption 1.2.1 - LR4 is typically referred to as lack of perfect multicollinearity, and it is concerned with regressor redundancy and the identifiability of all the β parameters. Actually, consider the case where $k = 2$ and $X_1 = X_2$. The matrix $X'X$ in this case has dimensions 2×2, but its rank is equal to one, and it can be easily shown that we can only identify (namely, recover from the available information) $\beta_1 + \beta_2$ but not both β_1 and β_2 separately. Assumption 1.2.1 - LR5 is instead concerned with the amount of temporal persistence in the explanatory variables, and basically requires that if each element of X is affected by a shock, the resulting effects on that element (and on y) are not permanent. A more precise definition of weak stationarity will be given in Chapter 5, and a treatment of the linear model without this assumption in Chapter 7.

To conclude, it is worth highlighting three additional implicit assumptions on the model in (1.2.2). First, all the relevant explanatory variables are included in the model (there are no omitted variables and no redundant variables). Second, linearity, which means that the model is linear in the parameters β. Hence, a model with x_{1t}^2 as an explanatory variable remains linear, while a model where y depends on x_{it}^β is no longer linear. Finally, stability of the β parameters over time, namely the relationship between y and X does not change over the sample under analysis. This is an important assumption which will be discussed at length later.

1.3   Parameter estimation

The model in (1.2.2) can still not be used for forecasting since we do not know the values of the parameters in β (and σ^2). To address this issue, we need to define an estimator for the parameters, namely, a function of the random variables X and y that is informative about the true β (and σ^2). Substituting the random variables X and y in the expression for the estimators with their realizations, we will then obtain an estimate for β (and σ^2).

Several estimators for the parameters of the linear regression model are feasible but, if we assume for the moment that X is deterministic, from the Gauss Markov theorem, we know that the best linear unbiased estimator (BLUE) for β is

$$\underset{k \times 1}{\hat{\beta}} = (X'X)^{-1}X'y. \tag{1.3.1}$$

This is the so-called ordinary least squares (OLS) estimator, which can be derived as the minimizer with respect to β of $\varepsilon'\varepsilon = \sum_{t=1}^{T} \varepsilon_t^2 = \sum_{t=1}^{T}(y_t - X_t\beta)^2$, where X_t is a $1 \times k$ vector containing $X_{1t} \ldots X_{kt}$.

The OLS estimator is unbiased because

$$E(\hat{\beta}) = \beta, \tag{1.3.2}$$

which means that if we could draw a very large number of samples from y, each of dimension T, and for each sample j we computed $\hat{\beta}_j$ using the formula in (1.3.1), the average across the many samples of $\hat{\beta}_j$ would be equal to β. The OLS estimator $\hat{\beta}$ is the best linear unbiased estimator since it is the most precise in the class of the linear unbiased estimators for β. In other words, $\hat{\beta}$ has minimal variance in the class of estimators that are obtained as a linear combination of the $y_1, \ldots, y_T$. Minimum variance, more formally, means that the difference between the variance covariance matrix of $\hat{\beta}_j$ and that of another linear unbiased estimator is negative definite. This is a convenient property since it implies that we are using optimally the available information, in the sense of obtaining the most precise estimator for the parameters β. Specifically, it is

$$Var(\hat{\beta}) = \sigma^2 (X'X)^{-1}, \tag{1.3.3}$$

where the k elements on the main diagonal of this $k \times k$ matrix contain $var(\hat{\beta}_j)$, $j = 1, \ldots, k$, and the off-diagonal elements report the covariances among the elements of $\hat{\beta}$. Note that we can rewrite $var(\hat{\beta})$ as

$$Var(\hat{\beta}) = \frac{\sigma^2}{T} \left(\frac{X'X}{T} \right)^{-1}$$

While estimators are random variables, estimates are just numbers, and since in general $X'X/T$ converges to a matrix when T diverges while σ^2/T goes to zero, it is

$$\lim_{T \to \infty} Var(\hat{\beta}) = 0.$$

This finding, combined with the unbiasedness of $\hat{\beta}$, implied that the OLS estimator is consistent for β, meaning that when the size of the sample size T gets very large $\hat{\beta}$ gets very close to the true value β (more formally, $\hat{\beta}$ converges in probability to β).

Let us now use $\hat{\beta}$ to construct the residuals

$$\hat{\varepsilon}_t = y_t - X_t \hat{\beta}, \tag{1.3.4}$$

and collect $\hat{\varepsilon}_t$, $t = 1, \ldots, T$, into the $T \times 1$ vector $\hat{\varepsilon}$. The residuals are related to the errors but different. Specifically, they are:

$$\hat{\varepsilon} = (I - X(X'X)^{-1}X')\varepsilon.$$

We can use the residuals to construct an estimator for the variance of the errors σ^2 as

$$\hat{\sigma}^2 = \hat{\varepsilon}'\hat{\varepsilon}/(T-k), \tag{1.3.5}$$

where we normalize by the degrees of freedom $(T - k)$ instead of the sample size (T) to achieve unbiasedness of $\hat{\sigma}^2$, namely,

$$E(\hat{\sigma}^2) = \sigma^2.$$

If, in addition to the assumptions stated above, we are also willing to maintain that the errors are normally distributed, so that

$$\varepsilon \sim N(0, \sigma^2 I_T), \tag{1.3.6}$$

then the distribution of the OLS estimator is:

$$\sqrt{T}(\hat{\beta} - \beta) \sim N\left(0, \sigma^2 \left(\frac{X'X}{T}\right)^{-1}\right), \tag{1.3.7}$$

$$(T - k)\hat{\sigma}^2/\sigma^2 \sim \chi^2(T - k), \tag{1.3.8}$$

and $\hat{\beta}$ and $\hat{\sigma}^2$ are independent. Adding normality to the assumptions LR1 - LR5 gives what are usually called "strong assumptions."

Similar results regarding the distribution of the parameter estimators hold when (some of) the elements of X are stochastic but uncorrelated with ε and the sample size T is very large (we say that the results hold asymptotically).

Note that the size of the estimated coefficients depends on the unit of measurement of the variables. For example, if we divide each element of X by 10, each element of β will be multiplied by 10. Hence, the magnitude of the estimated coefficients by itself should not be interpreted as an indicator of the importance of the associated regressors.

To conclude, we should mention that as the regression model is a not a structural equation, we should not assign a structural interpretation to the estimated parameters. Significant parameters simply indicate that the associated variables have explanatory and, hopefully, forecasting power for the target variable.

1.4   Measures of model fit

A model that fits well in sample, such that the errors are "small," is not necessarily a good forecasting model. Actually, the model could be too "tailored" for the particular estimation sample and therefore lose explanatory power beyond the specific sample. On the other hand, a model with a poor in sample fit rarely forecasts well. In this sense, it is convenient to examine measures of in sample model fit prior to forecasting, though this should not be the unique forecast selection criterion.

A common measure of model fit is the coefficient of determination, R^2, that compares the variability in the dependent variable y with that in the model (OLS) residuals $\hat{\varepsilon}$. The better the model, the smaller the latter with respect to the former. More precisely, R^2 is defined as

$$R^2 = 1 - \frac{\hat{\varepsilon}'\hat{\varepsilon}}{y'y} = \frac{\hat{y}'\hat{y}}{y'y} \tag{1.4.1}$$
$$= 1 - \frac{\sum_{t=1}^{T}\hat{\varepsilon}_t^2}{\sum_{t=1}^{T}y_t^2} = \frac{\sum_{t=1}^{T}(y_t - X_t\hat{\beta})^2}{\sum_{t=1}^{T}y_t^2}$$

where

$$\hat{y} = X\hat{\beta} \tag{1.4.2}$$

is the model fit. Hence, it is $0 \le R^2 \le 1$, with $R^2 = 0$ when $\hat{\varepsilon}'\hat{\varepsilon} = y'y$, namely the model has no explanatory power, and $R^2 = 1$ if the fit is perfect.[1]

It is possible to show that it is also

$$R^2 = Corr(y, \hat{y})^2,$$

meaning that the better the model fit the closer the correlation between actual and expected y according to the model.

A problem with the coefficient of determination is that it is monotonically increasing with the number of explanatory variables, meaning that a model with many regressors will always generate a higher R^2 than a model with a subset of them, even when the additional variables in the larger model are useless. Hence, it is convenient to introduce a modified version of R^2 that corrects this problem. The adjusted R^2 is defined as

$$\overline{R}^2 = 1 - \frac{\hat{\varepsilon}'\hat{\varepsilon}/(T-k)}{y'y/(T-1)} = 1 - \frac{\sum_{t=1}^{T}\hat{\varepsilon}_t^2/(T-k)}{\sum_{t=1}^{T}y_t^2/(T-1)}, \tag{1.4.3}$$

---

[1]Note that R^2 is based on a decomposition of y into two orthogonal components, $\hat{y}$ (the fit) and $\hat{\varepsilon}$ (the residual). OLS estimation guarantees orthogonality of fit and residuals, $\hat{y}'\hat{\varepsilon} = 0$, but this is not necessarily the case with other estimation methods. Moreover, an intercept should be included in the model to make sure that $0 \le R^2 \le 1$.

where k is number of regressors and T the sample size. Adding explanatory variables to the model has a double effect on $\overline{R}^2$: it decreases $\hat{\varepsilon}'\hat{\varepsilon}$, but it also decreases $T - k$, so that the overall impact on $\overline{R}^2$ will be positive only if the former effect dominates the latter, namely, if the added variables have sufficiently good explanatory power for y. Comparing (1.4.1) and (1.4.3), it is easy to show that $\overline{R}^2 \leq R^2$.

Information criteria provide an alternative method for model evaluation. They combine model fit with a penalty related to the number of model parameters. The idea is to penalize models with many explanatory variables, reaching a compromise between fit and parsimony of the specification. Information criteria will be discussed in details in the context of the dynamic linear model in Chapter 3; see also Chapter 5 on ARMA models.

The coefficient of determination and information criteria are both useful to compare alternative models for the same dependent variable. It is unfortunately not possible to define a generic threshold for them and decide which model is good. For example, a value of $R^2 = 0.1$ (i.e., 10%) can be very good for a model for a variable while very bad for another one. In particular, volatile variables such as equity returns are hard to be explained, and even harder to forecast, but even a low explanatory power can be useful, for example, to design an appropriate trading strategy. A polar opposite example would involve persistent variables, such as interest rates, which are instead easier to explain, but the model could add very little beyond the information contained in the past of the dependent variable.

1.5   Constructing point forecasts

We are interested in forecasting y_{T+h}, the value the dependent variable will take in period $T+h$, given the linear regression model in (1.2.2), with parameters estimated as in (1.3.1), assuming for the moment we know the future values of the regressors, i.e., X_{T+h}. We want to show that the best linear unbiased forecast of y_{T+h} is

$$\hat{y}_{T+h} = \underset{1 \times k}{X_{T+h}} \; \underset{k \times 1}{\hat{\beta}}, \tag{1.5.1}$$

in the sense of producing minimum forecast error variance and zero mean forecast error (forecast unbiasedness), where the forecast error is

$$e_{t+h} = y_{T+h} - \hat{y}_{T+h}. \tag{1.5.2}$$

Let us consider the set of linear predictors characterized by a $1 \times T$ vector l' applied to the data such that

$$y_{T+h} - l'y = (X_{T+h} - \underset{1 \times T}{l'} \underset{T \times k}{X}) \underset{k \times 1}{\beta} + \varepsilon_{T+h} - l'\varepsilon.$$

Taking expectations yields

$$E(y_{T+h} - l'y) = (X_{T+h} - l'X)\beta,$$

so that unbiasedness of the forecast (namely, zero mean forecast error) requires $l'X = X_{T+h}$.

Assuming that this condition is satisfied, the variance of the forecast error coincides with the second moment:

$$E(y_{T+h} - l'y)^2 = E(\varepsilon_{T+h} - l'\varepsilon)^2 = \sigma^2 (1 + l'l).$$

We want to find the vector l which minimizes this quantity, or just $l'l$, subject to the constraint $l'X = X_{T+h}$. To that end, we construct the Lagrangian function:

$$\mathcal{L} = l'l - \underset{1 \times k}{\lambda'} (X'l - X'_{T+h}),$$

whose derivatives with respect to l and λ are:

$$\underset{T \times 1}{\partial \mathcal{L}/\partial l} = 2l - X\lambda,$$

$$\underset{k \times 1}{\partial \mathcal{L}/\partial \lambda} = X'l - X'_{T+h}.$$

Therefore, the first order conditions can be written as:

$$\begin{bmatrix} \underset{T \times T}{2I} & \underset{T \times k}{-X} \\ \underset{k \times T}{X'} & \underset{k \times k}{0} \end{bmatrix} \begin{bmatrix} \underset{T \times 1}{l} \\ \underset{k \times 1}{\lambda} \end{bmatrix} = \begin{bmatrix} 0 \\ X'_{T+h} \end{bmatrix}$$

so that the optimal solutions, denoted l^* and λ^*, are

$$\begin{bmatrix} l^* \\ \lambda^* \end{bmatrix} = \begin{bmatrix} 1/2\, I - 1/2\, X(X'X)^{-1}X' & X(X'X)^{-1} \\ -(X'X)^{-1}X' & 2(X'X)^{-1} \end{bmatrix} \begin{bmatrix} 0 \\ X'_{T+h} \end{bmatrix},$$

and the optimal point forecast is indeed

$$\hat{y}_{T+h} = l^{*'}y = X_{T+h}(X'X)^{-1}X'y = X_{T+h}\hat{\beta}. \tag{1.5.3}$$

Moreover, the associated forecast error (which is unbiased by construction) is

$$e_{T+h} = X_{T+h}(\beta - \hat{\beta}) + \varepsilon_{T+h}, \tag{1.5.4}$$

and its variance can be computed as

$$E(y_{T+h} - \hat{y}_{T+h})^2 = E\left(X_{T+h}(\beta - \hat{\beta}) + \varepsilon_{T+h}\right)^2 = \tag{1.5.5}$$

$$= \sigma^2(1 + \underset{1 \times k}{X_{T+h}} \underset{k \times k}{(X'X)^{-1}} \underset{k \times 1}{X'_{T+h}}).$$

This expression is useful to understand which elements increase the variance of the forecast error and hence decrease the precision of the forecast. Forecast uncertainty, according to (1.5.5), is due to the variance of the error term in the model for y, σ^2, and the variance of the parameter estimator, $var(\hat{\beta}) = \sigma^2(X'X)^{-1}$.

There are, however, other important elements that increase forecast uncertainty. First, in general, the future values of the explanatory variables X_{T+h} are not known and have to be replaced by forecasts themselves. These forecasts can be obtained from external sources, such as values provided by other forecasters, or by extending the model to explain the X variables as well. Second, in practice, the explanatory variables to be inserted in the model for y are also unknown, so that we may be using an incomplete or too large set of regressors. This raises the important issue of variable selection. Third, the relationship between the explanatory variables and y could be non-linear and/or could change over time, which requires to go beyond the linear model with stable parameters that we have considered so far. We will consider all these issues one by one in due time.

A few final comments are worth making. First, we have derived the optimal linear forecast assuming that we want an unbiased forecast error with minimum variance. If we change the loss function, the optimal forecast will also change. The choice of the loss function should be based on the specific application and end use of the forecasts. For example, for a central bank the cost of under-predicting inflation may be very different from over-predicting it. Therefore, the bank may well use an asymmetric loss function where negative forecast errors (over-predicting inflation) have a larger weight than positive ones. In this case the optimal forecast can be biased and quite different from the expression given in (1.5.1). Additional details on this issue can be found, e.g., in Granger (1999), Artis and Marcellino (2001), Elliott, Komunjer, and Timmermann (2008), among others.

Second, note that we have used a similar loss function for the derivation of the OLS estimator and of the optimal linear forecast. If the forecast loss function is different from the mean squared error, we might use a comparable loss function also at the estimation stage, which of course would produce a different type of parameter estimator, see, e.g. Elliott, Komunjer, and Timmermann (2008).

Third, the empirical counterpart of the theoretical second moment of the forecast error (our loss function) is called Mean Squared Forecast Error (MSFE), and it is often used as a goodness of measure of a forecast, see Chapter 4 for more details.

Finally, and as mentioned, the forecast in (1.5.1) is optimal if the assumptions underlying the model are valid. If, for example, the errors of the linear model are not i.i.d., this should be taken into proper consideration in the derivations. We will revisit this issue in the next chapters.

1.6 Interval and density forecasts

A point forecast for a given variable, like that in (1.5.1), is certainly interesting but there can be situations where it is not sufficient, and the entire density of the variable is of interest. Consider for example the case of a central bank with an inflation target of 2%. Knowing that the optimal forecast for inflation is, say, 1.8% is interesting, but the bank may also want to know what is the probability that inflation will be above 2% or what is the interval that with a pre-assigned probability contains the future value of inflation. To address both question, we need to construct a density forecast.

Let us assume that Assumptions 1.2.1 LR1 - LR5 are valid, the sample size T is large and in addition the error term in (1.2.2) has a normal distribution. From the definition of the forecast error $e_{T+h} = y_{T+h} - \hat{y}_{T+h}$ (see (1.5.2)), it follows that

$$\left(\frac{y_{T+h} - \hat{y}_{T+h}}{\sqrt{\text{Var}(e_{T+h})}} \right) \sim N(0,1),$$

which implies

$$y_{T+h} \sim N(\hat{y}_{T+h}, \text{Var}(e_{T+h})). \tag{1.6.1}$$

The latter is the expression for the density forecast of y_{T+h}. In finite samples, it is only an approximation since we are basically treating the parameters as known (we are assuming that T is large). If instead we want to explicitly consider that we are using parameter estimators for β and σ^2 and the sample is finite, then the standardized forecast error has a Student t distribution with $T - k$ degrees of freedom, as well as y_{T+h} in (1.6.1).

The density forecast can be used to assign probabilities to specific events of interest concerning the future behavior of the variable y. For example, if y is inflation, with the formula in (1.6.1) we can compute the probability that inflation in period $T + h$ will be higher than 2%.

Another use of the forecast density is to construct interval forecasts for y_{T+h}. A $[1 - \alpha]$ % forecast interval is represented as

$$\hat{y}_{T+h} - c_{\alpha/2}\sqrt{\operatorname{Var}(e_{T+h})}; \hat{y}_{T+h} + c_{\alpha/2}\sqrt{\operatorname{Var}(e_{T+h})}, \qquad (1.6.2)$$

where $c_{\alpha/2}$ is the $(\alpha/2)$ % critical value for the standard normal density (or from the Student t density in the case of estimated parameters and small samples). For example, a 95% confidence interval is given by

$$\hat{y}_{T+h} - 1.96\sqrt{\operatorname{Var}(e_{T+h})}; \hat{y}_{T+h} + 1.96\sqrt{\operatorname{Var}(e_{T+h})}. \qquad (1.6.3)$$

For example, if y is again inflation, the optimal linear point forecast is $\hat{y}_{T+h} = 2$, and $\operatorname{Var}(e_{T+h}) = 4$, the formula implies that a 95% interval forecast for inflation in period $T+h$ is $[-1.92, 5.92]$. As in the case of the density forecast, the interval forecast is also only approximate with finite estimation samples.

The interpretation of the interval forecast is the following. Suppose that we could generate a very large number of samples of data for y and X, each of size $T + h$, and for each sample construct the interval forecast for y_{T+h} as in (1.6.2). Then, in $[1 - \alpha]$ % of the samples the realization of y_{T+h} will fall in the interval described in (1.6.2). A more common interpretation is that there is a $[1 - \alpha]$ % probability that the future realization of y_{T+h} will fall in the interval in (1.6.2). Hence, continuing the example, there is a 95% probability that inflation at $T + h$ will be lower than 5.92 and higher than -1.92. However, strictly speaking, only the former interpretation of the confidence interval is correct.

Note that density forecasts and confidence intervals can also be constructed with different assumptions on the distribution of the error term, though the derivations are more complex. Moreover, as long as the distribution of the error is symmetric, the density (and the interval forecasts) will be centered around the optimal point forecast that coincides, as said, with the future expected value of the dependent variable, conditional on the available information set.

Finally, both forecast densities and interval forecasts tell us more about (inflation) risk, a topic we will also discuss in further detail in later chapters.

1.7 Parameter testing

Let us consider again the linear regression model

$$y_t = X_{1t}\beta_1 + X_{2t}\beta_2 + \dots X_{kt}\beta_k + \varepsilon_t, \tag{1.7.1}$$

or, in compact notation,

$$y = X\beta + \varepsilon, \tag{1.7.2}$$

and assume that Assumptions 1.2.1 LR1 - LR5 and (1.3.6) hold, so that we are under strong assumptions.

So far we have maintained that all the relevant explanatory variables are included in the model for y, and all the irrelevant ones are excluded, in the sense that $\beta_i \neq 0$, $i = 1, \dots, k$, and $\beta_j = 0$ for $j > k$. However, one of the main practical problems in modeling and in forecasting is to include the proper set of regressors in the model for the variable of interest. Hence, we need statistical tools that help us decide whether a specific variable should be included or excluded from the model. A key instrument is hypothesis testing, which naturally can be applied to also verify more general hypotheses on the model parameters, as we now briefly review.

A testing problem has four main ingredients:

1. The hypothesis of interest, often labeled null hypothesis and indicated by H_0, which is typically a statement about what we believe true about a specific parameter or group of them. For example, $H_0 : \beta_1 = 0$ in (1.7.1) or $H_0 : \beta = 0$ in (1.7.2), where the latter means $\beta_1 = 0, \dots, \beta_k = 0$ jointly.

2. The alternative hypothesis, which is what we believe holds true when the null hypothesis is rejected, is indicated by H_1. For example, $H_1 : \beta_1 < 0$ or $H_1 : \beta \neq 0$, where the latter means that at least one β parameter is different from zero in (1.7.1). When the alternative hypothesis contains an inequality the test is said to be one-sided, while it is two-sided when H_1 is expressed as "different from."

3. The test statistic, which is a random variable that must be informative about the null hypothesis, and whose distribution under the null hypothesis must be known (i.e., not dependent on unknown parameters). For example, if we are interested in testing the null hypothesis $\beta_1 = 0$ versus the alternative hypothesis $\beta_1 < 0$, we may think of using the OLS estimator of β_1, $\hat{\beta}_1$, as the test statistic. $\hat{\beta}_1$ satisfies the first characteristic, since it is definitely informative about β_1 as we have seen above. However, from (1.3.7), the distribution of $\hat{\beta}_1$ depends on σ^2, which is not known, and therefore $\hat{\beta}_1$ cannot be used as a test statistic.

4. A decision rule that tells us, based on the value of the test statistic, whether to accept or reject the null hypothesis. In practice, we define a rejection region as a set of values such that if the realization of the test statistic falls in this region, we reject the null hypothesis.

Let us now consider the problem of testing the null hypothesis $\beta_i = c$ versus the alternative hypothesis $\beta_i < c$, where c is a generic value and $i = 1, \ldots, k$. We have seen that $\hat{\beta}_i$ is not a proper test statistic. However, we can use the t-statistic, or t-stat, defined as

$$t - stat = \frac{\hat{\beta}_i - c}{\sqrt{\widehat{var}(\hat{\beta}_i)}}, \tag{1.7.3}$$

where $\widehat{var}(\hat{\beta}_i)$ is the ith element on the diagonal of

$$\widehat{var}(\hat{\beta}) = \hat{\sigma}^2 \left(\frac{X'X}{T} \right)^{-1},$$

and $\hat{\sigma}^2$ is defined in (1.3.5).

It can be shown that, under H_0,

$$t - stat \sim t(T - k), \tag{1.7.4}$$

where $t(T - k)$ is a Student t distribution with $T - k$ degrees of freedom. Under the alternative hypothesis $\beta_i < c$, the t-statistics will be negative, the more so the further away we are from the null hypothesis. Hence, the rejection region will include low enough values of the t-statistic. But how low?

Formally, we need to define the significance level of the test, α, which is the maximum probability of rejecting the null hypothesis when it is true (often called type I error). For a one-sided test with $H_1 : \beta_i < c$, we then find t_α, the $\alpha\%$ critical value from the left tail of the distribution under H_0 of the test statistic, and we reject if the test is lower than t_α. In our case, t_α is the $\alpha\%$ critical value from the $t(T-k)$ distribution, namely, that value that has α % of probability to its left according to the $t(T-k)$ distribution. The choice of α is left to the user, but typical values are 1%, 5%, and 10%, meaning that in general we want a small probability of type I error.[2]

What happens instead if we change the alternative hypothesis to H_1 $\beta_i \neq 0$? We can still use the t-stat as defined above for this two-sided test, but we need to use a different rejection rule. Actually, now under the alternative hypothesis the t-stat can be either positive or negative, depending on the value of c. Hence, we reject when the absolute value of the t-stat is far enough from zero. More specifically, we reject when $|t - stat| > t_{\alpha/2}$, where $t_{\alpha/2}$ is the $(\alpha/2)$ % critical value from the right (or left) tail of the $t(T-k)$ distribution.

When the hypothesis of interest is $\beta_i = 0$, a case labeled significance testing since we are checking whether variable x_i is significant for explaining y, we proceed in exactly the same way. In particular, the test statistic is

$$t - stat = \frac{\hat{\beta}_i}{\sqrt{\widehat{var}(\hat{\beta}_i)}}, \tag{1.7.5}$$

and the rejection region depends on the chosen alternative hypothesis, which can be either $\beta_i \neq 0$ or $\beta_i < 0$ or β_i ¿ 0.

An alternative decision rule can be sometimes useful, in particular when using standard econometric software. Typically, the software reports the probability, under the null hypothesis, that the absolute value of the test statistic is larger than the realized value of the statistic. This quantity is called p-value and it is formally defined, in the case of the t-stat, as

$$p - value = prob_{H_0}(|t - stat| > a), \tag{1.7.6}$$

or

$$p - value = prob_{H_0}(t - stat > a) + prob_{H_0}(t - stat < -a),$$

---

[2]The case where the alternative hypothesis is $\beta_i > c$ is similar.

where a is the realization of the t-stat. Hence, if the p-value is smaller than α, it means that the t-stat is either very positive or very negative, and therefore we can reject the null hypothesis.

Let us now consider the composite null hypothesis $H_0 : \beta = c$ in (1.7.2), meaning $\beta_1 = c_1, \ldots, \beta_k = c_k$ jointly. For testing H_0 we can use the F-statistic, or F-stat, defined as

$$F - stat = \frac{(\hat{\beta} - c)' X' X (\hat{\beta} - c)}{k \hat{\sigma}^2} = \frac{(\hat{\beta} - c)' \widehat{var}(\hat{\beta})^{-1} (\hat{\beta} - c)}{k} \qquad (1.7.7)$$

and the expression for $\hat{\sigma}^2$ is provided in (1.3.5).

It can be shown that when H_0 is true it is

$$F - stat \sim F(k, T - k),$$

where $F(k, T - k)$ indicates an F-distribution (the ratio of two independent χ^2 distributions) with k and $T - k$ degrees of freedom.

Since the F-stat is a quadratic form, it can only take positive values. Hence, the alternative hypothesis can only be two-sided, namely, $H_1 : \beta \neq c$. We reject the null hypothesis when the realized value of the F-stat is larger than the critical value F_α, where F_α is in the right tail of the $F(k, T - k)$ distribution and has α % of probability in the right tail. Alternatively, we reject the null hypothesis when the p-value of the F-stat is smaller than α.

To conclude, we need to define the power of a test-statistic. It is the probability that the test will reject the null hypothesis when it is false. In general we would like to use test-statistics whose actual size is close to the nominal value, α, and as powerful as possible. It can be shown that in general the t-stat and the F-stat satisfy these requirements, though the actual power will depend on how large is the sample size and how far the parameter values are from those assumed under the null hypothesis.

1.8   Variable selection

As mentioned, one of the main practical problems in modeling and in forecasting is to include the proper set of regressors in the model for the variable of interest. Hence, in practice models can have omitted variables, and redundant ones. Let us briefly summarize the consequences of these two issues at the modeling stage, and then we will discuss the implications for forecasting.

If we include redundant variables in the model, namely regressors whose associated true coefficient is zero, the parameter estimators remain consistent. Hence, in large samples the estimated coefficients of the redundant variables will be close to zero, and t- and F-statistics for their significance will provide the right answer. However, in small samples it can be more problematic to detect which regressors are redundant, and their inclusion in the model can increase estimation uncertainty, and therefore also forecast uncertainty.

If instead we omit relevant explanatory variables from the model for y, it can be shown that the OLS estimators are in general biased, and they do not converge to the true parameter values even in very large samples. In addition, the omitted variables will enter as part of the error term, lowering the model fit and possibly invalidating the Assumptions 1.2.1 LR1-LR3. All these negative effects can naturally lower the quality of the forecasts. Therefore, omitting regressors is in general a more serious problem than including redundant variables.

An exception to this general rule is when either the coefficient of a variable is different from zero but close to it or the associated parameter estimator is very imprecise. In this case, the bias induced by omitting this variable can be dominated by the increased parameter estimation precision, thus yielding forecasts with an overall lower variance. See Clements and Hendry (1998, Chap. 12) for a theoretical derivation of this result and more precise conditions for its validity.

The aforementioned issues pertaining to variable omission suggest that a top-down modeling strategy that starts from a general model and tries to reduce it by deleting non-significant regressors is more promising than a bottom-up approach where a small model is progressively extended. The former approach is also often called general to specific, and the latter specific to general.

Reducing a general model is not a simple task, in particular when the sample size is not very large. In that case, the number of parameters will likely be fairly large compared with the number of observations, implying that parameter estimators will be rather imprecise, making it difficult to assess the significance of the single regressors. In addition, simplifying the model is a sequential specification procedure that can be conducted in several alternative ways. For example, we could decide to start by dropping the least significant regressor according to the outcome of a t-stat with a given level α, then re-estimate the model and drop again the least significant regressor, and continue untill all the retained regressors are significant. However, this procedure has a few drawbacks: first, it is very difficult to determine its overall probability of type I error, due to the use of sequential testing; second, if we choose a too high value of α we could keep redundant regressors, while with a too low value we could omit relevant regressors; third, if we deleted non-significant variables in groups rather than one by one, using F-statistics, we might end up with a different model; fourth, the final model could possibly not satisfy the Assumptions LR1 - LR5 in 1.2.1 even though the starting general model did; finally, manually the procedure may require a lot of time though it can be rather easily coded, see also Section 2.9.

An alternative approach to model specification is based on information criteria, as already described (and discussed in more detail in Chapter 5). In this case we need to select a specific criterion, compute it for each possible model (including different variables), and select the one that optimizes the criterion. Different criteria can yield different outcomes in terms of preferred models. However, the main defect of this approach is that it can be very time demanding, since we need to consider a total of 2^k models, where k is the number of explanatory variables in the general model. For example, with 10 regressors in the general model we should consider a total of 1024 alternative reduced models, while with 20 regressors the number becomes 1,048,576.

The reduction of a large general model based either on testing or on information criteria can be, as we have seen, very demanding. Economic theory should be used to restrict the starting set of variables under consideration, but often this is not sufficient to substantially reduce the number of potentially relevant regressors. Hence, specific automated procedures have been designed for this case, and we will review some of them in the next section.

To conclude, we should mention that while the general to specific modeling approach seems more promising from a statistical point of view, the specific to general method can be a good idea when the specific model is theory driven, and already works quite well. For example, theory suggests that aggregate private consumption should be driven by aggregate income and wealth, and possibly its own past values in the presence of habit persistence, so one may start with a specification that includes these explanatory variables only, and check whether it is appropriate and produces good forecasts, or instead the model is not satisfactory and requires the inclusion of additional explanatory variables.

1.9 Automated variable selection procedures

A few researchers, including Hoover and Perez (1999) and Hendry and Krolzig (2005), studied ways to automate the general-to-specific (GETs) model selection procedure, often associated with the London School of Economics methodology to econometric analysis. As we have discussed, the GETs methodology, starting from a general statistical model, exploits standard testing procedures to reduce its complexity by eliminating statistically insignificant variables and checking that the resulting model satisfies the underlying assumptions by means of diagnostic tests. The software Autometrics, Doornik (2009), permits a practical implementation, and the forecasts from the resulting models seem to be rather good, see also Castle, Doornik, and Hendry (2011).

Alternative techniques for model reduction can be classified into hard- and soft-thresholding rules, see, e.g., Bai and Ng (2008). Under hard-thresholding, a regressor is selected according to the significance of its correlation coefficient with the target. Typically, only regressors whose correlation with the target is above a given threshold are selected as predictors. The obvious shortcoming of this selection criterion is that it only takes into account the bivariate relationship between the target variable and each regressor, without accounting for the information contained in other regressors. As a result, hard-thresholding tends to select highly collinear targeted predictors and, as we will see in the next section, this can complicate parameter estimation.

Soft-thresholding rules, on the contrary, order and select the (N) regressors on the basis of a minimization problem of the following form:

$$\min_{\beta} \Phi(RSS) + \lambda\Psi(\beta_1, \ldots, \beta_j, \ldots, \beta_N),$$

where as usual RSS indicates the Residual Sum of Squares of a regression of the target on the N regressors. The parameter λ, which is a Lagrange multiplier, governs the shrinkage (the higher λ, the higher the penalty for having extra regressors in the model), while Φ and Ψ are functions of, respectively, the RSS and the parameters (β) associated with the N regressors. Clearly, the cross-correlation among the regressors is taken into consideration explicitly when minimizing this loss function.

Depending on the functional form of Φ and Ψ, different thresholding rules are obtained. We now discuss some of the most common ones, namely,

Forward Selection regressions (FWD), Least angle regressions (LARS), Least Absolute Shrinkage Selection Operator (LASSO), and Elastic net estimator (NET). We refer, e.g., to Bai and Ng (2008) and Bulligan, Marcellino, and Venditti (2015) for more details and empirical applications. Other variable selection methods are surveyed and applied in, e.g., Kapetanios, Marcellino, and Papailias (2014).

1.9.1   Forward selection (FWD)

Suppose a researcher wants to study the forecasting relationship between a target variable y and a large set of covariates X. A good starting point is to identify the regressor that shows the highest correlation with the target, say x_1. At this point Forward Selection (FWD) consists of regressing y on x_1, storing the residuals ($\hat{\varepsilon}_1$), and then looking for the covariate in the X information set with the highest correlation with this residual, say x_2. The residual $\hat{\varepsilon}_1$ is projected onto x_2, a new residual $\hat{\varepsilon}_2$ is stored, and the covariate mostly correlated with $\hat{\varepsilon}_2$ is next identified. The procedure continues until all the variables in the information set have been ranked, or it can be stopped when a given criterion is satisfied, e.g., the adjusted R^2 in a regression of y on the selected regressors is above a given threshold.

The philosophy behind FWD is exactly the opposite of that behind hard-thresholding. While the latter can select a large number of regressors very correlated with each other, Forward Selection tends to keep fewer variables, as orthogonal as possible to each other.

1.9.2   Least angle regressions (LARS)

The LARS (Least Angle Regression) algorithm, devised by Efron, Hastie, Johnstone, and Tibshirani (2004), starts as Forward Selection, by identifying the covariate that has the highest correlation with the target. Like in FWD, the largest step in the direction of this covariate x_1 is taken until a new predictor x_2 has as much correlation with the current residual. After this step, however, LARS proceeds equiangularly between x_1 and x_2 rather than orthogonally as in Forward Selection. After k steps, there are k variables in the active set. If the algorithm is stopped here, the coefficients of the remaining N - k regressors are all set to zero. The desired shrinkage can therefore be seen as a stopping rule for k.

Efron, Hastie, Johnstone, and Tibshirani (2004) show that the LARS algorithm encompasses other popular shrinkage methods, including Forward Selection itself, LASSO and the Elastic Net, to which we turn next.

1.9.3 LASSO and elastic net estimator (NET)

Least Absolute Shrinkage Selection Operator (LASSO) can be obtained in the LARS algorithm by imposing at each step of the algorithm a restriction on the sign of the correlation between the new candidate regressor and the projection along the equiangular direction in the previous step. To get some intuition on how the procedure works, let us start again from step 1, when the variable which is most correlated with the target enters the active set of regressors. Suppose that this correlation is positive. In selecting the second variable for the active set, LARS is agnostic on the sign of the correlation between the target and the new variable. If one imposes that the sign of this correlation must not switch, the LASSO regression is obtained.

LASSO can also be related to the RIDGE estimator, which is a constrained OLS estimator that penalizes overfitting. Given M regressors, RIDGE coefficients are obtained by solving the following minimization problem

$$\min_{\beta} RSS + \lambda \sum_{j=1}^{M} \beta_j^2,$$

where RSS is again the Residual Sum of Squares. The Lagrange multiplier λ governs the shrinkage: the higher λ, the higher the penalty for having extra regressors in the model.

LASSO introduces a slight but important modification of the penalty function of the RIDGE regressor, which, rather than being a quadratic function shows a kink at zero:

$$\min_{\beta} RSS + \lambda \sum_{j=1}^{M} |\beta_j|.$$

This modification implies that, unlike in the RIDGE setup, in LASSO some regression coefficients are set exactly at zero. This is a convenient feature in particular when many potential regressors are considered, as for example in applications with big data (see Chapter 13 for further discussion on the topic).

The Elastic Net (NET) estimator is a refinement of LASSO, and it is the solution to the following minimization problem:

$$\min_{\beta} RSS + \lambda_1 \sum_{j=1}^{M} |\beta_j| + \lambda_2 \sum_{j=1}^{M} \beta_j^2.$$

Shrinkage under NET depends on two tuning parameters, λ_1 and λ_2. Bai and Ng (2008) show that it suffices to apply a variable transformation to reformulate the NET as a LASSO problem, which can be therefore obtained through the LARS algorithm.

The more sophisticated estimators we have presented in general cannot be computed analytically, but the proper minimization problems can be solved numerically. See, for example, Hastie, Tibshirani, and Friedman (2008) for a discussion of the theoretical properties of the estimators. The parameters λ, or λ_1 and λ_2, that control the amount of shrinkage, are often selected via cross-validation. In a first step, a training sample is used to estimate the model for various values of λ; to compute a loss function of interest, e.g. the MSFE; and choose the value of λ, which minimizes the loss. In a second step, a new sample is used to compute the loss function for the selected values of λ, checking that the choices also produce good results outside the training sample.

Empirically, there is no clear-cut ranking of the forecasting performance of these alternative estimation algorithms, so in practical applications a few of them can be compared over a training sample and the best one used to estimate the parameters to be used over the forecast sample. This approach is another example of the "cross-validation" principle in the statistical literature.

1.10   Multicollinearity

We have so far maintained Assumption 1.2.1 LR4 that is concerned with regressor redundancy and the identifiability of all the β parameters in the regression model. As a counter-example, we have considered the case where $k = 2$ and $X_1 = X_2$. The matrix $X'X$ in this case has dimension 2×2 but its rank is equal to one. Since the model becomes

$$
\begin{aligned}
y_t &= \beta_1 x_{1t} + \beta_2 x_{2t} + \varepsilon_t \\
&= (\beta_1 + \beta_2)x_{1t} + \varepsilon_t,
\end{aligned}
\tag{1.10.1}
$$

we can only identify (namely, recover from the available information) $\beta_1 + \beta_2$ but not β_1 and β_2 separately. Technically, the first order conditions used to derive $\hat{\beta}_1$ and $\hat{\beta}_2$ admit an infinite number of solutions, while the solution for $\widehat{\beta_1 + \beta_2}$ is unique.

The case in the previous example is extreme, but in empirical applications, in particular with persistent macroeconomic variables, it can indeed happen that some of the explanatory variables are highly, though not perfectly, correlated. This still makes it difficult to separately identify all the β parameters, and it is reflected in large standard errors for the associated OLS estimators (since their variance covariance matrix is given by $\sigma^2(X'X)^{-1}$ and the determinant of $X'X$ is close to zero).

Hypothesis testing can also be affected by multicollinearity. The large estimation uncertainty will often lead to not rejecting the null hypothesis even when it is false, hence lowering the power of test statistics. In particular, significant coefficients could turn out to be not statistically different from zero. Intuitively, if X_1 and X_2 are highly correlated, we can by mistake say that X_1 is not relevant given that it is anyway well approximated by X_2. For the same reason, variable selection is complicated by the presence of multicollinearity.

It is in principle possible to check for perfect multicollinearity by testing whether the rank of $X'X$ is full or not. However, in practice it is more common to assess the extent of cross correlation among pairs of regressors. This check typically provides a good indication of possible high multicollinearity problems, though it can miss cases where the pattern of multicollinearity is more complex than bivariate, for example X_1 could be a linear combination of X_2 and X_3.

In terms of remedies, when high correlation among regressors is a temporary feature, extending the sample under analysis can alleviate the problem. For example, several real regressors could move together during a specific expansionary or recessionary phase, but if we use a sample including several business cycles, their overall correlation can be much lower.

When instead high correlation is not sample specific but related to the characteristics of the explanatory variables, either re-parameterizing the model, as for example in (1.10.1), or summarizing the highly similar regressors can work. Principal components are often used to reduce the number of highly correlated regressors. They are particular linear combinations of the original k regressors with the property of being orthogonal to each other and ordered according to their overall explanatory power for the original regressors, so that the first principal component explains the largest fraction of the variability of all the Xs. For example, as we mentioned, Hard-thresholding could end up with a large set of selected explanatory variables, each of them highly correlated with the target variable and with all the other selected variables. Hence, rather than using all the selected variables for forecasting y we could only exploit their first principal component. More details can be found in Chapter 13.

Multicollinearity is particularly problematic for structural analysis, where identification of each single component of the β parameter vector is relevant to assess the contribution of each explanatory variable. From a forecasting point of view, it is less of a problem as long as the main goal is to produce the best, in the mean square forecast error sense, forecast for the y variable. Consider for example the model in (1.10.1). The optimal forecast for y_{T+h} can be written either as

$$\hat{y}_{T+h} = \hat{\beta}_1 x_{1T+h} + \hat{\beta}_2 x_{2T+h},$$

or as

$$\hat{y}_{T+h} = \left(\widehat{\beta_1 + \beta_2}\right) x_{1T+h},$$

and in this sense multicollinearity is not an issue. However, for interpreting the forecast, for example to assess the relative role of x_{1T+h} and x_{2T+h} as determinants of $\hat{y}_{T+h}$, multicollinearity represents an issue also in a predictive context.

1.11   Example using simulated data

In this example we use simulated data to illustrate in a controlled environment parameter estimation, testing, and model selection. The forecasting procedure is discussed as well.

1.11.1   Data simulation procedure

We start with a brief discussion of the data generating process (DGP), which will also be further used for the examples in Chapters 2 - 4. For this reason, the DGP will be a bit more general – i.e., not a static linear regression model. Why do we start with a more general model? It will allow us to examine

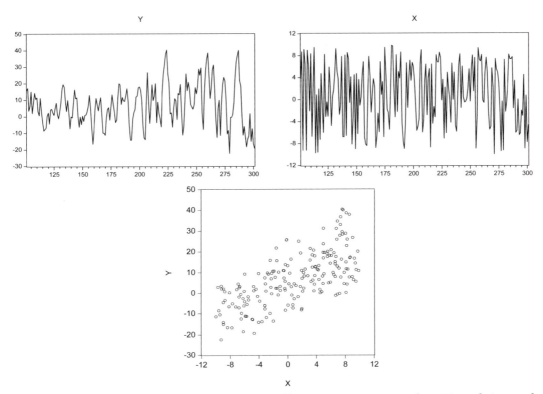

Figure 1.11.1: *Simulated dependent variable y, regressor x, and scatter plot y and X*

what happens when we estimate various models, starting with a static linear regression which will be de facto the wrong model. More specifically, the DGP is the following:

$$y_t = 1 + D_t + D_t x_t + x_t + 0.5 x_{t-1} + 0.5 y_{t-1} + \varepsilon_t \qquad (1.11.1)$$

where $y_t = \ln(Y_t)$ is the dependent variable, x_t is the independent variable, lags of $\ln(Y_t)$ and x appear also as explanatory variables, D_t is a dummy variable that determines a change in the intercept and in the coefficient of x_t, and ε_t is i.i.d. distributed as $N(0,1)$.[3] The total sample consists of 501 observations – the first observation is introduced to manage the lag of the

---

[3]Dummy variables and their use to allow for parameter changes are discussed in section 2.5 in Chapter 2.

dependent variable in the DGP. We discard the first 101 observations to prevent starting value effects, and divide the rest of the sample in 2 parts:

- Estimation sample: observations 102 - 301

- Forecasting sample: observations 302 - 501

The estimation sample is used to estimate and test model specifications while in the forecasting sample we evaluate the predictive performance of alternative model specifications. The dummy variable is equal to 1 for the observations from 202 to 501 and 0 otherwise.

Linear regression model

Figure 1.11.1 represents the temporal evolution of y and x, and a scatter plot of both y and x.

From the scatter plot we can see that there seems to be a linear relation between y and x. In particular, we observe that an increase in x is associated with an increase in y. To strengthen our hypothesis let us evaluate the correlation between y and x. The correlation is significantly high and positive, equal to 0.6729.

	Coefficient	Std. Error	t-Statistic	Prob.
BETA(0)	5.380	0.667	8.072	0.000
BETA(1)	1.491	0.117	12.801	0.000
R-squared	0.453	Mean dep var		6.695
Adjusted R-squared	0.450	S.D. dep var		12.560
S.E. of regression	9.314	Akaike IC		7.311
Sum squared resid	17176.480	Schwarz IC		7.344
Loglikelihood	-729.086	Hannan-Quinn		7.324
F-statistic	163.861	DW stat		0.955
Prob(F-statistic)	0.000			

Table 1.11.1: *Baseline linear regression model for the sample: 102 - 301*

The baseline linear regression model we consider is the following:

$$y_t = \beta_0 + \beta_1 x_t + \varepsilon_t, \tag{1.11.2}$$

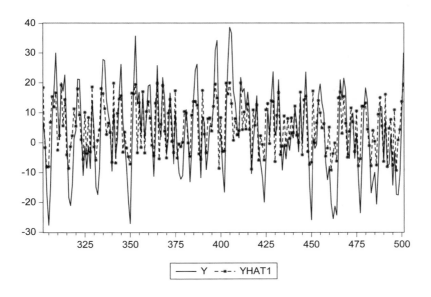

(a) ACTUAL y SERIES AND FORECAST $yhat1$.

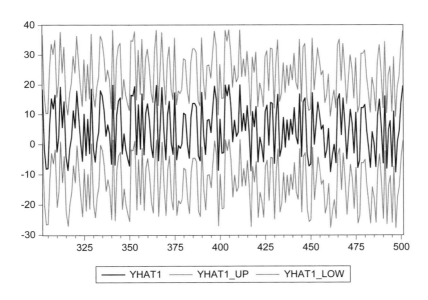

(b) CONFIDENCE INTERVAL UPPER AND LOWER
BOUNDS

Figure 1.11.2: *Plot of actual y series, linear model forecast yhat1, and yhat1_up and yhat1_low series of forecasts' 95% approximate forecast interval upper and lower bounds respectively*

From Table 1.11.1 we see that the coefficient for x is positive and significantly different from 0 at the 5% confidence level. Since we know the actual value of the coefficient because we are using simulated data, we can also compare it with the value of the estimated coefficient. In the DGP the coefficient of x is equal to 1. The estimated coefficient is equal to 1.491, which is significantly different from 1, $(t - stat = (\hat{\beta}_1 - 1)/SE_{\hat{\beta}_1} = 4.2181)$. This result is not surprising as the econometric model we are using is rather different from the DGP.

The equation output in many software packages – such as *EViews* – provides additional information about the model performance. In the chapter we have discussed several measures of model fit. Let us start with the coefficient of determination R^2. For the baseline linear model the R-squared is equal to 45.283 %, while the adjusted R-squared is equal to 45.01 %. *EViews* presents in the standard regression output also information criteria, another type of measures of model fit, such the Akaike Information Criterion (AIC) and the Schwarz Criterion. Those measures are mostly used for model selection purposes and will be discussed in later chapters.

	Forecasting Method	
	Static	*Recursive*
RMSE	9.7426	9.5705
MAFE	8.0798	7.9432

Table 1.11.2: *Baseline linear regression model forecasting performance*

Let us now consider the forecasting performance over the 302 - 501 sample of the simple linear regression model we have estimated. Figure 1.11.2 presents the forecast series and the approximate 95% forecast intervals computed as in equation (1.6.3) (Panel (b)) and the actual series against the forecasts (Panel (a)). When computing the forecast described above, we assume that the model coefficients are computed over the entire estimation sample and then kept fixed over the forecast sample. We call this scheme static. We also assume that the future values of the regressors x are known.

To take into account the possibility of parameter time variation, we can compute a recursive forecast where the model is estimated over an expanding estimation sample (one observation is added each time), and the forecasts are computed with the recursively estimated parameters. Hence, the method requires the following steps:

1. Estimate the model for a given estimation sample.

2. Compute (one-step-ahead) forecasts using the estimated coefficients from step 1.

3. Add one observation to the estimation sample and go to step 1 again.

Figure 1.11.3 presents the forecasts obtained from the recursive forecast procedure using 102 - 301 as first estimation sample and progressively expanding it by one observation. To evaluate the model forecasting performance we use two most common measures: the Root Mean Square Forecast Error (RMSE) and the Mean Absolute Forecast Error (MAFE), see Chapter 4 for further details. Table 1.11.2 presents these for static and recursive forecasts, indicating a mild preference for the latter.

In the next empirical examples we will repeat the same steps (model specification, estimation, and forecasting) but use real economic data.

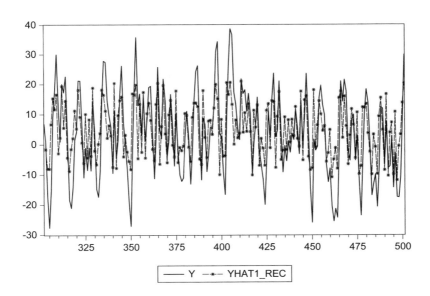

Figure 1.11.3: *Plot of actual y series and yhat1_rec which presents the forecasts obtained from a recursive forecast procedure*

1.12   Empirical examples

Three empirical examples are considered. The first two cover forecasting Gross Domestic Product (GDP), for respectively the Euro area and the United States. The third and final example deals with forecasting default risk spreads.

1.12.1   Forecasting Euro area GDP growth

In this empirical example, we illustrate the formulation, estimation, parameter testing and model selection using simple linear regressions without dynamics. We will also illustrate how to produce short term forecasts using such models. At the outset we should stress again that more structural models can be better suited for medium- and long-run forecasting.

Let us first talk about the data. We consider both hard and soft data. For hard data, we use GDP and industrial production (IPR) of Euro area 17 countries (EA17), an inflation measure – the monthly rate of change of the Harmonized Index of Consumer Prices (HICP), as well as the Eurostoxx data downloaded from the Eurostat website. Both GDP and IP data are seasonally adjusted. For soft data, we use the Economic Sentiment Indicator (ESI) of the Euro area downloaded from the Directorate General for Economic and Financial Affairs of the European Commission (DG-ECFIN) website.[4] The data of GDP, IP, and Eurostoxx are quarterly. As the survey data and the growth rate of the HICP are monthly, we aggregate them to their quarterly values (see Chapter 12 for methods to directly handle mixed frequency data). 111

We compute the quarterly aggregates as averages across the months in a quarter. We consider growth rate of the above variables in this example, except for HICP which is already a growth rate. We compute the quarterly growth rate as the first difference of the variables in natural logarithm multiplied by 100.

Throughout this example, we denote the variables using the following notations:

- y_t is the quarterly EA17 GDP growth

---

[4]In general the DG-ECFIN provides an excellent source of Euro area macroeconomic data such as the series used in this book, see http://ec.europa.eu/economy_finance/index_en.htm.

- ipr_t is the quarterly EA17 IP growth

- sr_t is the quarterly growth rate of the Eurostoxx (stock returns)

- su_t is the quarterly growth rate of the EA ESI

- pr_t is the quarterly aggregate of the monthly growth rate of the EA17 HICP (inflation rate)

We first consider the sample period from 1996Q1 to 2013Q2. The early 90's saw first major troubles in the managed exchange rate system – the EMS – with Italy and the UK leaving the EMS. Then many structural and policy changes, related to the adoption of the Maastricht Treaty for the introduction of the single currency, took place. Hence, we prefer to start our analysis in 1996, at the cost of losing estimation efficiency due to the rather short sample.

Figure 1.12.1 shows the plots of the above variables. It is clear from the graph that all series exhibit a dip around the end of 2008 and the beginning of 2009, most pronounced in the growth rate of GDP, IP, and survey data. Interestingly the dips in GDP growth and IP growth appear to lag the dips in stock returns, growth rate in the sentiment indicator, and inflation rate by one quarter. It may imply that the contemporaneous value of IP growth is more useful in explaining GDP growth, while the lag values of the other three variables are more informative about GDP growth. In this chapter, we focus on baseline regression model without dynamics. Details of dynamic models will be discussed in Chapter 3.

Model estimation, parameter testing and model/variable selection

Our interest here is first to illustrate the power of the regressors in explaining GDP growth, via significance tests applied to the estimated parameters, as well as the measures of model fit. As we noted before, the regression model is not a structural equation, and therefore we should not assign a structural interpretation to the estimated parameters. Significant parameters simply indicate that there is a statistical relationship that links the dependent variables to the dependent one in-sample, and hopefully out-of-sample as well.

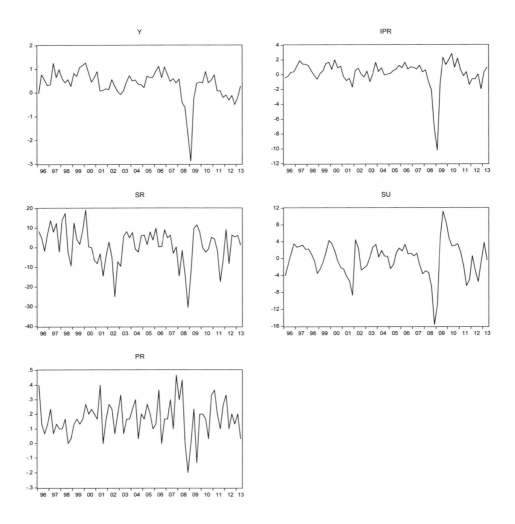

Figure 1.12.1: *Plots of the quarterly growth rates of Euro area GDP (Y), indus-trial production (IPR), economic sentiment indicator (SU), Eurostoxx stock index (SR), and the quarterly aggregates of the monthly growth of harmonized index of consumer prices (PR).*

We will also illustrate some automated variable selection procedures. We proceed by estimating the following linear regression models analogous to equation (1.2.2). To separate the role of the intercept, we denote it via the parameter α. We start with three cases in which the regressors X_t vary.

$$y_t = \alpha + X_t\beta + \varepsilon_t \tag{1.12.1}$$

- Case 1 (Model 1): $X_t = (ipr_t,\ su_t,\ pr_t,\ sr_t)$

- Case 2 (Model 2): $X_t = (ipr_t,\ su_t,\ sr_t)$

- Case 3 (Model 3): $X_t = (ipr_t,\ su_t)$

Variable	Coefficient	Std. Error	t-Statistic	Prob.
C	0.331	0.060	5.489	0.000
IPR	0.336	0.029	11.618	0.000
SU	-0.034	0.015	-2.239	0.029
PR	-0.388	0.305	-1.272	0.208
SR	0.012	0.005	2.181	0.033
R-squared	0.801	Mean dep var		0.350
Adjusted R-squared	0.789	S.D. dep var		0.629
S.E. of regression	0.289	Akaike IC		0.425
Sum squared resid	5.435	Schwarz IC		0.586
Loglikelihood	-9.881	Hannan-Quinn		0.489
F-statistic	65.338	DW stat		1.438
Prob(F-statistic)	0.000			

Table 1.12.1: *Estimation output for Model 1 for sample: 1996Q1 - 2013Q2*

Table 1.12.1 presents the estimation results for Model 1. Negative signs are found on the estimated parameters for the change of ESI and the inflation rate, contrary to economic intuition. This result can be due either to collinearity among the regressors or to model mis-specification. The reported t-statistics for individual two-sided significance tests show that the null hypothesis of an insignificant parameter can be rejected at the 5% significance level for all variables except pr_t. Excluding the inflation rate from the set of regressors and re-estimating the model results in the output shown in Table 1.12.2. While the IP growth remains highly significant, exclusion of the inflation rate results in less significant parameters on the change of ESI and stock returns, with the stock returns being the most insignificant in this case. Table 1.12.3 shows the estimation output when we further exclude stock returns from the list of regressors. It can be seen once again that IP growth still remains highly significant but the explanatory power of the change of ESI has been weakened. In addition to the individual significance tests, the F-statistic and the corresponding p-value for testing joint (model) significance of all the explanatory variables apart from the intercept are also reported as part of the estimation output. It is clear that the null hypothesis can be rejected at standard significance levels for all the three models.

Variable	Coefficient	Std. Error	t-Statistic	Prob.
C	0.269	0.036	7.481	0.000
IPR	0.326	0.028	11.683	0.000
SU	-0.029	0.015	-1.981	0.052
SR	0.010	0.005	1.892	0.063
R-squared	0.796	Mean dep var		0.350
Adjusted R-squared	0.787	S.D. dep var		0.629
S.E. of regression	0.291	Akaike IC		0.421
Sum squared resid	5.571	Schwarz IC		0.550
Loglikelihood	-10.742	Hannan-Quinn		0.472
F-statistic	85.774	DW stat		1.434
Prob(F-statistic)	0.000			

Table 1.12.2: *Estimation output for Model 2 for sample: 1996Q1 - 2013Q2*

The lower parts of the three tables present some summary statistics. The reported R^2 of the three models seem to be relatively high in general, with values around 0.8. The issue of the monotonic increase in the value of R^2 with number of explanatory variables can be observed by comparing the reported statistics across the three models. Having the largest set of regressors among the three, Model 1 appears to have the highest R^2. Besides, Model 1 also appears to have the highest $\overline{R}^2$, but the difference with the other models is diminished.

Variable	Coefficient	Std. Error	t-Statistic	Prob.
C	0.282	0.036	7.806	0.000
IPR	0.323	0.028	11.384	0.000
SU	-0.014	0.013	-1.114	0.269
R-squared	0.785	Mean dep var		0.350
Adjusted R-squared	0.778	S.D. dep var		0.629
S.E.of regression	0.296	Akaike IC		0.445
Sum squared resid	5.873	Schwarz IC		0.542
Loglikelihood	-12.590	Hannan-Quinn		0.484
F-statistic	122.169	DW stat		1.338
Prob(F-statistic)	0.000			

Table 1.12.3: *Estimation output for Model 3 for sample: 1996Q1 - 2013Q2*

Variable	Coefficient	Std. Error	t-Statistic	Prob.
C	0.501	0.082	6.101	0.000
IPR	0.326	0.075	4.377	0.000
SU	-0.023	0.024	-0.976	0.335
PR	-0.732	0.403	-1.815	0.077
SR	0.010	0.005	1.776	0.084
R-squared	0.524	Mean dep var		0.564
Adjusted R-squared	0.475	S.D. dep var		0.355
S.E. of regression	0.257	Akaike IC		0.228
Sum squared resid	2.578	Schwarz IC		0.431
Loglikelihood	-0.019	Hannan-Quinn		0.303
F-statistic	10.715	DW stat		1.940
Prob(F-statistic)	0.000			

Table 1.12.4: *Estimation output for Model 1 for sample: 1996Q1 - 2006Q4*

As mentioned in Section 1.4, the information criteria provide an alternative way to evaluate model fit. They measure the fit of models while at the same time penalize those with many explanatory variables. Although details of information criteria will be presented in Chapter 3, we can examine here the outcome while briefly mentioning that the preferred models are those with the lowest values. The tables report values of three information criteria: Akaike Information Criterion (AIC), Schwarz Criterion (BIC), and Hannan-Quinn Criterion (HQ), and models with smaller values of the criteria are preferred.

Variable	Coefficient	Std. Error	t-Statistic	Prob.
C	0.388	0.055	7.018	0.000
IPR	0.310	0.076	4.068	0.000
SU	-0.016	0.024	-0.683	0.499
SR	0.008	0.006	1.413	0.166
R-squared	0.483	Mean dep var		0.564
Adjusted R-squared	0.445	S.D. dep var		0.355
S.E. of regression	0.264	Akaike IC		0.264
Sum squared resid	2.796	Schwarz IC		0.426
Loglikelihood	-1.802	Hannan-Quinn		0.324
F-statistic	12.474	DW stat		1.938
Prob(F-statistic)	0.000			

Table 1.12.5: *Estimation output for Model 2 for sample: 1996Q1 - 2006Q4*

It turns out that the three information criteria do not always agree with each other in telling which model is best. Model 1 appears to have the largest values of all the reported information criteria, though marginally. Model 2 appears to have the smallest values of both AIC and HQ, though its SC is slightly larger than that of Model 3. Based on the value of the criteria and the fact that, if we set the significance level at 10%, all its estimated parameters are statistically significant, we can prefer Model 2.

Variable	Coefficient	Std. Error	t-Statistic	Prob.
C	0.410	0.054	7.602	0.000
IPR	0.297	0.076	3.884	0.000
SU	-0.002	0.022	-0.071	0.943
R-squared	0.458	Mean dep var		0.564
Adjusted R-squared	0.431	S.D. dep var		0.355
S.E. of regression	0.268	Akaike IC		0.267
Sum squared resid	2.936	Schwarz IC		0.389
Loglikelihood	-2.873	Hannan-Quinn		0.312
F-statistic	17.293	DW stat		1.854
Prob(F-statistic)	0.000			

Table 1.12.6: *Estimation output for Model 3 for sample: 1996Q1 - 2006Q4*

Forecasting

We now continue our empirical illustration by performing a forecasting exercise. We first split our full sample period 1996Q1 to 2013Q2 into an estimation sample that covers 1996Q1 to 2006Q4, and a forecast evaluation period that covers 2007Q1 to 2013Q2. We then re-estimate Models 1, 2, and 3 over the shorter estimation sample.

Tables 1.12.4, 1.12.5, and 1.12.6 present the estimation results. Comparing them with those presented in Tables 1.12.1, 1.12.2, and 1.12.3 which use the full sample, it can be seen that the values of the R^2 and $\overline{R}^2$ are much lower than before. Moreover, two out of three information criteria now seem to prefer Model 1. Moreover, the ESI becomes less significant. This is perhaps not surprising as the estimation sample now excludes the recent recession and survey data have been found to have more explanatory power during the recession than when the economy is relatively stable.

Note that there is evidence, as shown in Table 1.12.4, that the inflation rate has stronger individual significance in explaining GDP growth than the survey data over this sample period than when we consider the full sample (as shown in Table 1.12.3). We name the model that includes this set of regressors (IPR, PR, SR) as Model 4.

We now perform a forecasting exercise. To illustrate the importance of the choice of regressors, we consider forecasts using Models 1 through 4.

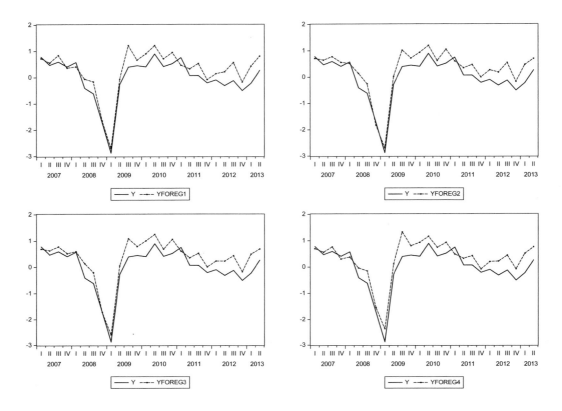

Figure 1.12.2: *Plots of forecasted GDP growth series produced by the four models against the actual GDP growth over the forecast evaluation period 2007Q1 to 2013Q2*

Figure 1.12.2 presents the plots of the $\hat{y}$ forecasts produced by the four models, conditioning on the true values of the future explanatory variables and the estimated parameters up to 2006Q4, against the actual y. It can be seen that the GDP growth forecasts all track the actuals, though the discrepancies between the predicted and the actual values tend to be in general larger post-2009Q2. The forecasts produced by the four models also seem to predict the big dip in 2009Q1 quite well, particularly the forecasts from Model 1 and Model 2, but less so for Model 4. Although details of forecast evaluation will be discussed in Chapter 4, we present some basic forecast evaluation statistics here in order to illustrate the importance of the choice of regressors included in a forecast model. Specifically, Table 1.12.7 reports the Root Mean Squared Forecast Error (RMSFE) and the Mean Absolute Forecast Error (MAFE) associated with the forecasts. The top panel reports static forecasts. The values of both RMSFE and MAFE show that Models 1 and 2 are comparable, while forecasts produced by Model 4 seem to be the least accurate, with the value of both the RMSFE and MAFE being the largest. Since survey data are not included in Model 4, this outcome provides indication that they do contain more useful information at the time of recession. So excluding such a regressor penalizes the accuracy of the forecasts.

	Model 1	*Model* 2	*Model* 3	*Model* 4
		Static forecasts		
RMSFE	0.3839	0.3783	0.3949	0.4153
MAFE	0.3275	0.3316	0.3442	0.3642
		Recursive forecasts		
RMSFE	0.3600	0.3511	0.3559	0.3730
MAFE	0.2987	0.3067	0.3102	0.3174

Table 1.12.7: *Forecast evaluations Models 1 - 4.*

One important point worth mentioning about the above forecasting exercise is that for each model, the forecasts for the entire evaluation period are computed using the coefficients from the regression estimated over the estimation sample 1996Q1 to 2006Q4, even though the actual observation of GDP growth is used for the forecast produced each period. That is, estimation is done only once and there is no updating of the values of the estimated parameters.

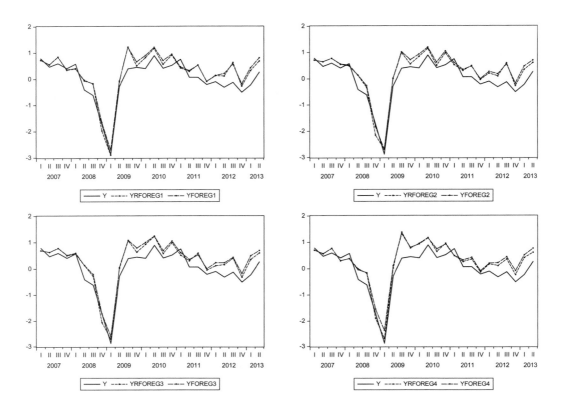

Figure 1.12.3: *Plots of the static and recursive one-step ahead forecasts of GDP growth by the four models against the actual GDP growth over the evaluation period 2007Q1 to 2013Q2 (Key: YRFOREx is the series of one-step ahead recursive forecast from Model x. YFOREx is the series of static forecast from Model x)*

As we will discuss in Chapter 2, there is no reason to believe the relationships between GDP growth and the regressors remain constant over time. One way to compute forecasts by taking into account the possible changing relationships is to update the estimated parameters at each point in time when a forecast is to be produced – as we did in the previous subsection. One can re-estimate the forecasting model by including the up-to-date data when a forecast is to be produced. For example, when computing the one-step ahead forecast for 2007Q1, we estimate the model using data from 1996Q1 to 2006Q4. The one-step ahead forecast for 2007Q2 is then computed using the parameter estimated using data from 1996Q1 to 2007Q1, and so on. We called this forecasting strategy recursive forecast. We now re-compute the one-step ahead forecasts for the four models using the recursive forecasting strategy.

Figure 1.12.3 shows the plots of the recursive forecasts alongside the static forecasts against the actual series. We also re-compute the evaluation statistics for these one-step ahead recursive forecasts, presented in the lower panel of Table 1.12.7. Comparing these statistics with those presented in the top panel, it can be seen that the forecast accuracy has generally been improved, likely signaling instability in the relationship between GDP growth and the explanatory variables during the crisis period.

1.12.2   Forecasting US GDP growth

In this empirical example, we illustrate the same procedures but focusing on modeling and forecasting the US GDP growth series using both hard and soft data as explanatory variables. For hard data, we use industrial production (IPR), the consumer prices index (PR), and the S&P500 index (SR). For soft data, we use the Michigan University consumer sentiment index for the United States, downloaded from the St. Louis Federal Reserve Bank website (SU). Soft and hard data are quarterly.[5]

We first consider the sample period that covers 1985Q1 to 2013Q4. As mentioned in the case of the Euro area, the estimation sample should be as long as possible, but also homogeneous when working under the assumption of stable model parameters. As monetary policy in the United States changed substantially in the early 1980s, and the phenomenon known as the Great Moderation (a major reduction in the volatility of many macroeconomic variables) took place in the same period, we prefer to start our empirical analysis in 1985, even though the time series for the variables that we consider are available much earlier.

Figure 1.12.4 shows the plots of the above variables. It is clear from the graph that all series exhibit a dip around the end of 2008 and the beginning of 2009, corresponding to the worst quarters of the financial crisis.

---

[5]In general the St. Louis Fed provides an excellent source of United States macroeconomic data such as the series used in this book, see https://fred.stlouisfed.org/.

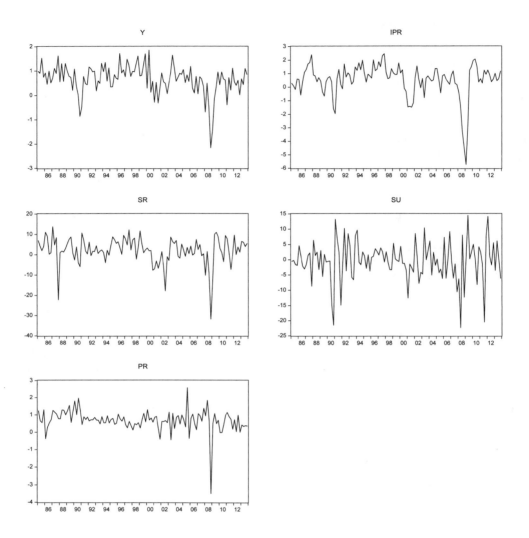

Figure 1.12.4: *Quarterly US GDP growth, IP growth, S&P 500 returns, CSI growth, CPI inflation.*

Model estimation, parameter testing, and model/variable selection

As in the previous example for Euro area GDP, our interest here is first to illustrate the power of the regressors in explaining GDP growth, via significance tests on estimated parameters, as well as measures of model fit. We proceed by estimating again a static linear regression model as in equation (1.12.1), with the same three alternative sets of regressors.

In Table 1.12.8 we report some summary statistics related to model fit. According to the R^2 and adjusted R^2, the best model is the first one. Other

	Model 1	Model 2	Model 3
R^2	0.533	0.522	0.508
$\overline{R}^2$ (adjusted R^2)	0.516	0.510	0.499
AIC	1.131	1.137	1.149
SC	1.250	1.232	1.220
HQ	1.180	1.175	1.178

Table 1.12.8: *Full sample measures of fit*

criteria, such as the AIC, SC, and HQ are not consistent. We know that the lower is the value of the criteria the "better" is the model. The minimum for AIC corresponds to Model 1. At the same time SC is minimized for Model 3 and HQ is lowest for Model 2. The differences are however small, so that we do not expect major differences in the forecasting performance of the models.

Forecasting

The next step is forecasting. To evaluate the forecasting performance we first split our sample period 1985Q1 to 2013Q4 into an estimation sample that covers 1985Q1 to 2006Q4, and a forecast evaluation period that covers 2007Q1 to 2013Q4. Tables 1.12.9, 1.12.10, and 1.12.11 present the estimation output of the models over the estimation sample.

Comparing these estimation results with those for the full sample, it can be seen that the values of the R^2 and $\overline{R}^2$ are even more similar for three models. According to R^2 Model 1 is "better," but $\overline{R}^2$ prefers Model 3. This conclusion is consistent with other criteria: AIC, SC, and HQ are lowest for Model 3.

As discussed in previous examples, to take into account possible changes in the coefficients we can use recursive forecasts, similar to the procedure described in the previous example. To compare the forecasts we use again two main criteria: RMSFE and MAFE, reported in Table 1.12.12. As we

Variable	Coefficient	Std. Error	t-Statistic	Prob.
C	0.579	0.088	6.586	0.000
IPR	0.310	0.049	6.328	0.000
SU	0.013	0.009	1.403	0.164
PR	-0.015	0.095	-0.153	0.879
SR	0.003	0.009	0.313	0.755
R-squared	0.387	Mean dep var		0.778
Adjusted R-squared	0.357	S.D. dep var		0.493
S.E. of regression	0.395	Akaike IC		1.036
Sum squared resid	12.956	Schwarz IC		1.176
Loglikelihood	-40.572	Hannan-Quinn		1.092
F-statistic	13.096	DW stat		2.028
Prob(F-statistic)	0.000			

Table 1.12.9: *Estimation output Model 1 for sample: 1985Q1 - 2006Q4*

can see from the table below Model 3 has the highest value of RMSFE and MAFE while Model 1 is best according to both criteria. Moreover, as is the case for the Euro area, statistics associated with the recursive forecasts are lower, suggesting also in this case the possibility of parameter instability associated with the financial crisis.

	Model 1	Model 2	Model 3
Static forecasts			
RMSFE	0.547	0.541	0.549
MAFE	0.417	0.414	0.418
Recursive forecasts			
RMSFE	0.524	0.529	0.546
MAFE	0.385	0.402	0.412

Table 1.12.12: *Forecast evaluation statistics of static and recursive forecasts*

Variable	Coefficient	Std. Error	t-Statistic	Prob.
C	0.569	0.058	9.827	0.000
IPR	0.310	0.049	6.376	0.000
SU	0.013	0.009	1.509	0.135
SR	0.003	0.009	0.306	0.761
R-squared	0.387	Mean dep var		0.778
Adjusted R-squared	0.365	S.D. dep var		0.493
S.E. of regression	0.393	Akaike IC		1.013
Sum squared resid	12.960	Schwarz IC		1.126
Loglikelihood	-40.584	Hannan-Quinn		1.059
F-statistic	17.659	DW stat		2.026
Prob(F-statistic)	0.000			

Table 1.12.10: *Estimation output Model 2 for sample: 1985Q1 - 2006Q4*

1.13   A hint of dynamics

Throughout this chapter we always aligned the timing of y_t and X_t in the regression equation

$$y_t = \alpha + X_t\beta + \varepsilon_t \qquad (1.13.1)$$

For example in the GDP regressions we used series ipr_t, su_t, pr_t, and sr_t which were contemporaneous to the quarter t GDP growth we want to forecast. This means that we have the regressors available when we forecast GDP. In practice that may not be the case as there may be publication lags.

While we are entering into dynamic regression territory, we will provide a simple example of how one can still use the classical regression model with the following specification:

$$y_t = \alpha + X_{t-1}\beta + \varepsilon_t \qquad (1.13.2)$$

where we shift back the regressors from t to $t-1$. In Chapter 2 Section 2.6 we will discuss data timing issues, and in Chapter 3 we will refer to the equation similar to the one appearing above as the Leading Indicator model (see in particular equation (3.2.6)). Shifting the regressors one period back implies that the regressors are more likely available when performing one-step ahead forecasts. This timing choice also reduces potential problems of endogeneity, see Section 2.7 for details.

Variable	Coefficient	Std. Error	t-Statistic	Prob.
C	0.576	0.053	10.931	0.000
IPR	0.309	0.048	6.404	0.000
SU	0.015	0.008	1.912	0.059
R-squared	0.386	Mean dep var		0.778
Adjusted R-squared	0.372	S.D.dependent var		0.493
S.E. of regression	0.391	Akaike IC		0.992
Sum squared resid	12.974	Schwarz IC		1.076
Loglikelihood	-40.633	Hannan-Quinn		1.026
F-statistic	26.726	DW stat		2.010
Prob(F-statistic)	0.000			

Table 1.12.11: *Estimation output Model 3 for sample: 1985Q1 - 2006Q4*

1.13.1   Revisiting GDP forecasting

We refit the GDP growth prediction equations using the specification in (1.13.1) instead of regression (1.12.1). To evaluate the forecasting performance we split again the sample period 1985Q1 to 2013Q4 into an estimation sample that covers 1985Q1 to 2006Q4, and a forecast evaluation period that covers 2007Q1 to 2013Q4. Table 1.13.1 reports the estimation sample measures of fit. Compared to the results in Table 1.12.8 we see an overall degeneration of the model fits. That is not too surprising as the regression model now relates next quarter's GDP growth with current quarter IPR, SU, PR, or SR as opposed to current GDP growth. Nevertheless, in relative terms Model 1 stays the best overall in the new dynamic setting.

	Model 1	Model 2	Model 3
R^2	0.310	0.304	0.248
$\overline{R}^2$	0.286	0.285	0.235

Table 1.13.1: *Estimation sample measures of fit*

In the contemporaneous quarter regression setting we learned from Table 1.12.12 that Model 1 remains the best one out-of-sample. That is no longer the case in the new dynamic setting as the results reported in Table 1.13.2

reveal. The more parsimonious Model 2, while inferior to Model 1 in-sample, is the superior one out-of-sample according to both RMSFE and MAFE criteria, whether using static or recursive forecasting schemes.

	Model 1	Model 2	Model 3
Static forecasts			
RMSFE	0.726	0.711	0.785
MAFE	0.515	0.492	0.528
Recursive forecasts			
RMSFE	0.713	0.702	0.724
MAFE	0.502	0.476	0.485

Table 1.13.2: *Forecast evaluation statistics of static and recursive forecasts*

Figure 1.13.1 illustrates the forecast performance by plotting the recursive out-of-sample 95% approximate confidence intervals and the realized growth rate. We observe again the financial crisis quarter 2008Q4 where the realized growth rate drops below the forecast interval.

1.13.2   Forecasting default risk

We focus on modeling and forecasting default risk as measured by the Bank of America Merrill Lynch US High Yield Master II Option-Adjusted Spread which we denote OAS.[6] Unlike the previous two examples, we have data sampled at a monthly frequency. As candidate regressors, we select the following set of series: (a) the Chicago Board Options Exchange (CBOE) Volatility Index, denoted VIX, (b) the surveys of consumers, University of Michigan, consumer sentiment index, denoted by SENT, (c) the ISM Manufacturing: purchasing managers index, PMI, and finally (d) the monthly returns, in percentage points, of the S&P 500 Index.

We consider a sample from January 1998 to December 2015 – which includes the Great Recession. Figure 1.13.2 plots all the aforementioned

---

[6]Details about the series can be found at https://research.stlouisfed.org/fred2/series/BAMLH0A0HYM2.

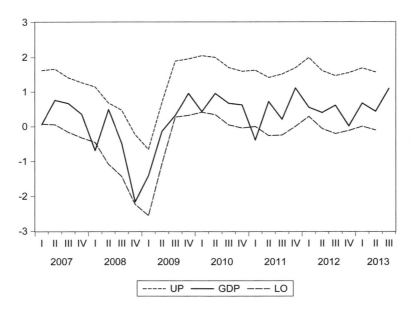

Figure 1.13.1: *Recursive GDP growth forecasts and 95% confidence intervals Model 2*

series – showing the unusual events following the Lehman bankruptcy in September 2008. We start with the following four single regressor regressions:

- Model 1: $OAS_t = \alpha + \beta_1\, VIX_{t-1} + \varepsilon_t$

- Model 2: $OAS_t = \alpha + \beta_1\, SENT_{t-1} + \varepsilon_t$

- Model 3: $OAS_t = \alpha + \beta_1\, PMI_{t-1} + \varepsilon_t$

- Model 4: $OAS_t = \alpha + \beta_1\, SP500_{t-1} + \varepsilon_t$

The output for models 1 - 4 appears in Tables 1.13.3 through 1.13.6. From the results we observe that previous month's VIX index is the best single predictor for default risk with a R^2 of almost 67%. The VIX is a forward-looking variable as it reflects the option market implied expectation of 22-day ahead volatility of the S&P500 stock market index. In other words, the VIX_{t-1} gives us the option market participant's expectation at the end of month $t-1$ of next month's – i.e., t - market volatility. Financial market variables often have this forward-looking feature and therefore are popular candidate regressors in a forecasting regression equation. This becomes even

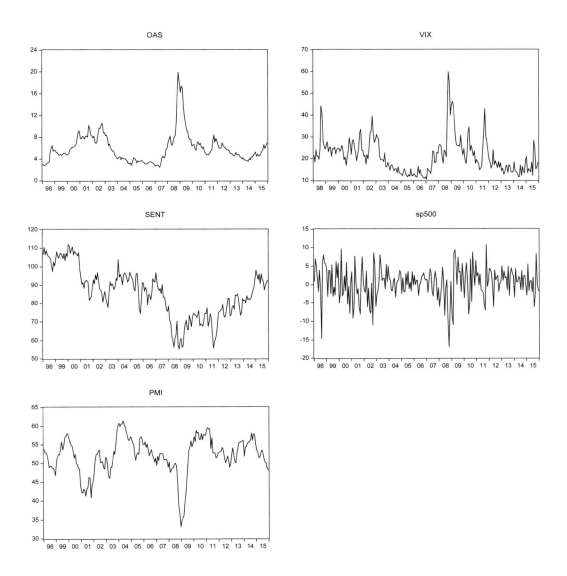

Figure 1.13.2: *Monthly OAS, VIX, SENT, SP500, and PMI.*

more appealing once we start adding the fact that such series are typically available at weekly, daily, or even higher frequencies – a feature which will be important once we cover mixed frequency regression models in Chapter 12.

Variable	Coefficient	Std. Error	t-Statistic	Prob.
C	0.054	0.310	0.175	0.861
VIX(-1)	0.280	0.014	20.549	0.000
R-squared	0.665	Mean dep var		6.008
Adjusted R-squared	0.663	S.D. dep var		2.792
S.E. of regression	1.621	Akaike IC		3.813
Sum squared resid	559.543	Schwarz IC		3.844
Loglikelihood	-407.894	Hannan-Quinn		3.826
F-statistic	422.245	DW stat		0.566
Prob(F-statistic)	0.000			

Table 1.13.3: *Estimation output for Model 1*

Variable	Coefficient	Std. Error	t-Statistic	Prob.
C	13.753	1.093	12.588	0.000
SENT(-1)	-0.090	0.013	-7.178	0.000
R-squared	0.195	Mean dep var		6.008
Adjusted R-squared	0.191	S.D. dep var		2.792
S.E. of regression	2.512	Akaike IC		4.689
Sum squared resid	1343.743	Schwarz IC		4.720
Loglikelihood	-502.074	Hannan-Quinn		4.702
F-statistic	51.520	DW stat		0.122
Prob(F-statistic)	0.000			

Table 1.13.4: *Estimation output for Model 2*

The estimated slope for Model 1 has the anticipated sign, namely it is positive – hence increased (expected) volatility implies higher default risk. The PMI index, while not market-based, also has a forward-looking nature as it is an indicator of the economic health of the manufacturing sector. It is based on four major indicators: new orders, inventory levels, production supplier deliveries, and the employment environment. It is therefore not surprising that Model 3 also does well, albeit not as good as the VIX. The slope coefficient is negative and significant in Model 3 – which is also anticipated

Variable	Coefficient	Std. Error	t-Statistic	Prob.
C	26.267	1.414	18.579	0.000
PMI(-1)	-0.389	0.027	-14.397	0.000
R-squared	0.493	Mean dep var		6.008
Adjusted R-squared	0.491	S.D. dep var		2.792
S.E. of regression	1.993	Akaike IC		4.226
Sum squared resid	845.780	Schwarz IC		4.257
Loglikelihood	-452.306	Hannan-Quinn		4.239
F-statistic	207.259	DW stat		0.239
Prob(F-statistic)	0.000			

Table 1.13.5: *Estimation output for Model 3*

Variable	Coefficient	Std. Error	t-Statistic	Prob.
C	6.108	0.180	34.009	0.000
SP500(-1)	-0.220	0.040	-5.488	0.000
R-squared	0.124	Mean dep var		6.008
Adjusted R-squared	0.120	S.D. dep var		2.792
S.E. of regression	2.620	Akaike IC		4.773
Sum squared resid	1462.058	Schwarz IC		4.805
Loglikelihood	-511.145	Hannan-Quinn		4.786
F-statistic	30.114	DW stat		0.263
Prob(F-statistic)	0.000			

Table 1.13.6: *Estimation output for Model 4*

as increasing the health of the economy means lesser default risk. The two other models 2 and 4, based on respectively consumer sentiment and stock returns, perform relatively poorly in comparison. Note that both models also feature negative slopes, again as expected.

We also consider all variables at once in the following regression - which we label Model 5:

$$OAS_t = \beta_0 + \beta_1 VIX_{t-1} + \beta_2 SENT_{t-1} + \beta_3 PMI_{t-1} + \beta_4 sp500_{t-1} + \varepsilon_t$$

According to the results reported in Table 1.13.7 all regressors are signifi-

Variable	Coefficient	Std. Error	t-Statistic	Prob.
C	15.899	1.413	11.251	0.000
VIX(-1)	0.183	0.014	12.697	0.000
SENT(-1)	-0.048	0.007	-7.205	0.000
PMI(-1)	-0.186	0.021	-8.772	0.000
SP500(-1)	-0.044	0.021	-2.055	0.041
R-squared	0.798	Mean dep var		6.008
Adjusted R-squared	0.794	S.D. dep var		2.792
S.E. of regression	1.267	Akaike IC		3.335
Sum squared resid	337.300	Schwarz IC		3.413
Loglikelihood	-353.483	Hannan-Quinn		3.366
F-statistic	207.239	DW stat		0.754
Prob(F-statistic)	0.000			

Table 1.13.7: *Estimation output for Model 5*

cant, and the adjusted R^2, almost 80%, is greater than any of the individual regressor models 1 - 4.

We re-estimate all the regressions for a shorter sample from Jan. 1998 to Dec. 2007 and produce forecasts out-of sample for the period Jan. 2008 until Dec. 2015. We then compute the in-sample regression statistics and the out-of-sample RMSFE for each of the regression models. The empirical results appear in Table 1.13.8. The in-sample fits align again with the out-of-sample performance. The findings suggest a Model 6, however, where we drop the SENT regressor. The results appear in the lower panel of Table 1.13.8. We observe that the R^2 remains roughly equal (and therefore the adjusted one, not reported, increases) but that the model performs not as well out-of-sample. The takeaway from this example is that while SENT appears to be a borderline significant regressor in-sample, it helps reduce forecasting errors out of sample. Part of that is explained by the fact that the parameter estimate for the SENT regressor for the full sample, reported in Table 1.13.7, is highly significant.

	Coefficient	Std Error	t-Statistic	R^2	RMSFE static
Models 1 - 4					
C	0.799	0.437	1.831		
VIX(-1)	0.222	0.020	11.067	0.509	2.040
C	7.159	1.964	3.646		
SENT(-1)	-0.019	0.021	-0.906	0.007	3.340
C	19.787	1.815	10.903		
PMI(-1)	-0.277	0.035	-7.963	0.350	2.620
C	5.457	0.186	29.401		
SP500(-1)	-0.156	0.044	-3.567	0.097	3.370
Model 5					
C	11.868	1.924	6.168	0.628	1.450
VIX(-1)	0.172	0.022	7.818		
SENT(-1)	-0.025	0.014	-1.844		
PMI(-1)	-0.146	0.032	-4.632		
SP500(-1)	-0.064	0.030	-2.107		
Model 6					
C	10.667	1.829	5.831	0.617	1.820
VIX(-1)	0.160	0.021	7.543		
PMI(-1)	-0.164	0.030	-5.405		
SP500(-1)	-0.070	0.030	-2.333		

Table 1.13.8: *Default risk models: In-sample and out-of-sample results*

1.14 Concluding remarks

The linear regression model reviewed in this chapter is the backbone of many forecasting techniques. In the next chapters we will expand the basic regression setting discussed so far. First, mis-specification analysis will be discussed, followed by dynamic extensions of regression models. The latter will also be a bridge towards time series models, both univariate and multivariate.

Chapter 2

Model Mis-Specification

2.1 Introduction

When Assumptions 1.2.1 - LR1 - LR5 hold, we showed in Chapter 1 that OLS estimators are consistent, efficient, and asymptotically normally distributed. In this chapter instead we will try to understand what happens if each of these hypotheses is violated, how we can assess if the hypotheses hold or not, and what we can do if they do not. In Sections 2.2 - 2.4 we will consider residual heteroskedasticity and serial correlation, in Section 2.5 we will deal with parameter instability, while in Section 2.6 we will allow the regressors to be correlated with the error term, in Sections 2.7, 2.8, and 2.9 we present examples based on, respectively, simulated and actual data. In Section 2.10 we present some concluding remarks. As with the previous chapter, more detailed presentations can be found, for example, in Hendry (1995), Judge, Hill, Griffiths, Lütkepohl, and Lee (1988), Marcellino (2016), Stock and Watson (2009), Wooldridge (2012), among others.

2.2 Heteroskedastic and correlated errors

The linear regression model with k explanatory variables can be written in compact notation as

$$\underset{T \times 1}{y} = \underset{T \times k}{X} \underset{k \times 1}{\beta} + \underset{T \times 1}{\varepsilon}, \tag{2.2.1}$$

Assumption 1.2.1 LR2 is actually a combination of:

Assumption 2.2.1 (Linear Regression Assumptions). In the regression model in equation (2.2.1):

LR2a The errors ε are homoskedastic, i.e., $\text{Var}(\varepsilon_i) = \sigma^2$, $i = 1, \ldots, T$,

LR2b The errors ε are uncorrelated, i.e., $corr(\varepsilon_t, \varepsilon_{t-j}) = 0$, $j = 1, \ldots$

Suppose now that there is heteroskedasticity, i.e., $\text{Var}(\varepsilon_i) = \sigma_i^2$, $i = 1, \ldots$ $,T$. In words, this amounts to say that the error variance changes with the different observations. For example, if y_i is the volume of sales from a given firm and the explanatory variable is the firm size, it is probable that the variability of sales will increase with the firm size, which will be reflected in an heteroskedastic error term. Similarly, consumption or investment's variability may rise with, respectively, disposable income or the profit level. There can also be specific periods where the volatility of the shocks hitting the economy increases, such as during financial crises.

The errors can also be correlated over time, i.e., $corr(\varepsilon_t, \varepsilon_{t-j}) \neq 0$. More specifically, let us consider the case of first order serial correlation, $\varepsilon_t = \rho\varepsilon_{t-1} + u_t$. For example, if ε_t is a labor productivity shock, due to the introduction of new technologies or to a legislative reform, typically it will be positively correlated over time. Additionally, if we omit a relevant explanatory variable which is also correlated across time, a part of its effect on the dependent variable will show up in the error term, resulting in serial correlation.

A simple way to formalize heteroskedasticity and serial correlation within the linear model is by changing the representation of the error's variance-covariance matrix from $\sigma^2 I$ to simply Ω, a $T \times T$ matrix that for the moment we treat as known. For example, if errors are uncorrelated but their variance changes across observations, Ω will be:

$$\Omega = \begin{bmatrix} \sigma_1^2 & 0 & \cdots & 0 \\ 0 & \sigma_2^2 & & \vdots \\ \vdots & & \ddots & 0 \\ 0 & \cdots & 0 & \sigma_T^2 \end{bmatrix}. \tag{2.2.2}$$

Instead, if the errors display first order serial correlation and $\varepsilon_t = \rho\varepsilon_{t-1} + u_t$, $u_t \overset{iid}{\sim} (0,\sigma_u^2)$, then we have:

$$\Omega = \sigma_u^2/(1-\rho^2) \begin{bmatrix} 1 & \rho & \rho^2 & \cdots & \rho^{T-1} \\ \rho & 1 & \rho & & \vdots \\ \rho^2 & \rho & & & \rho^2 \\ \vdots & & & \ddots & \rho \\ \rho^{T-1} & \cdots & \rho^2 & \rho & 1 \end{bmatrix}. \tag{2.2.3}$$

When Assumptions 2.2.1 - LR2a-LR2b are substituted with

$$\text{Var}(\varepsilon) = \Omega, \tag{2.2.4}$$

the resulting model is known as the generalized linear model.

Let us now examine what are the consequences of violating the assumptions of homoskedastic and uncorrelated errors for the properties of the OLS estimator. First, it turns out that the OLS estimator is no longer efficient, as there exists another unbiased estimator with a lower variance, which is called the Generalized Least Squares (GLS) estimator. We will derive its formulation later in the section. Second, $\hat{\beta}_{OLS}$ is still consistent but the formula for its variance covariance matrix requires modifications. Moreover, consistency is lost when the model is dynamic and the errors are serially correlated, as we will see in more details in the next section. Third, in general, the variance estimator $\hat{\sigma}_{OLS}^2 = \hat{\varepsilon}'\hat{\varepsilon}/(T-k)$ will be biased and inconsistent, since it was derived imposing $\text{Var}(\varepsilon) = \sigma^2 I$ while in this case $\text{Var}(\varepsilon) = \Omega$. Fourth, since the formula for the variance of $\hat{\beta}_{OLS}$ is no longer valid, the standard versions of the confidence intervals and of the $t-$ and $F-$tests, which rely on the variance of $\hat{\beta}_{OLS}$, are no longer valid.

There are four types of remedies to the aforementioned problems.

1. Improve the model specification when there is evidence that there are problems like omitted variables or model instability. For example, using a dynamic rather than a static model, namely, allowing for lags of the dependent variable as explanatory variables, typically reduces or eliminates serial correlation problems. We will study dynamic models in the next chapter.

2. Make appropriate transformations of the variables so that the modified model displays homoskedasticity, and possibly uncorrelated errors. For example, working with variables in logarithms (when positive valued) typically reduces the extent of the heteroskedasticity. Similarly, working with variables expressed in growth rates instead of levels can reduce error autocorrelation.

3. Change the method to compute the variance estimator for $\hat{\beta}_{OLS}$. Indeed, it is still possible to conduct appropriate inference based on $\hat{\beta}_{OLS}$ since it is in general consistent, but it is crucial to find a proper estimator for its variance. The Heteroskedasticity and Autocorrelation Consistent (HAC) variance estimator exploits this fact (see e.g., White (1980) and Section 2.3). Nevertheless, if the residuals properties are related to other forms of model mis-specification, such as omitted variables or unaccounted parameter changes, then $\hat{\beta}_{OLS}$ will be inconsistent and using the HAC correction for its standard errors will not really solve the problem.

4. Change the estimation method to GLS, as discussed in the next subsection. However, a similar comment on the effects of model mis-specification as in the case of the HAC variance estimator applies.

2.2.1   The Generalized Least Squares (GLS) estimator and the feasible GLS estimator

Since the error covariance matrix Ω is positive definite, there exists an invertible matrix H such that

$$H\Omega H' = I.$$

Hence

$$\Omega = H^{-1}(H')^{-1} = (H'H)^{-1}$$

For example, in the case of heteroskedastic errors, with the covariance matrix given by (2.2.2), the H matrix will have the following form:

$$H = \begin{bmatrix} 1/\sigma_1 & 0 & \cdots & 0 \\ 0 & 1/\sigma_2 & & \vdots \\ \vdots & & \ddots & 0 \\ 0 & \cdots & 0 & 1/\sigma_T \end{bmatrix}.$$

If instead the errors display first order autocorrelation, their covariance matrix is (2.2.3) and it is possible to show that H takes the form:

$$H = \begin{bmatrix} \sqrt{1-\rho^2} & 0 & \cdots & 0 \\ -\rho & 1 & 0 & \vdots \\ 0 & -\rho & 1 & 0 \\ 0 & & \cdots & -\rho & 1 \end{bmatrix}.$$

Let us consider again the linear model (2.2.1):

$$y = X\beta + \varepsilon$$

where now $\mathrm{Var}(\varepsilon) = \Omega$. If we multiply both sides by H we obtain

$$Hy = HX\beta + H\varepsilon$$

or

$$\tilde{Y} = \tilde{X}\beta + \tilde{\varepsilon} \tag{2.2.5}$$

where

$$E(\tilde{\varepsilon}\tilde{\varepsilon}') = H\Omega H' = I.$$

In practice, we have transformed the dependent and explanatory variables such that model (2.2.5) features homoskedastic and uncorrelated errors, while leaving the parameters β unchanged.

It is now possible to use OLS in the transformed model (2.2.5), hence obtaining the GLS estimator:

$$\hat{\beta}_{GLS} = (\tilde{X}'\tilde{X})^{-1}\tilde{X}'\tilde{Y} = (X'\Omega^{-1}X)^{-1}X'\Omega^{-1}Y. \tag{2.2.6}$$

Let us describe the properties of the GLS estimator:

1. $\hat{\beta}_{GLS}$ is unbiased as:

$$E(\hat{\beta}_{GLS}) = E((\tilde{X}'\tilde{X})^{-1}\tilde{X}'\tilde{Y}) = \beta + E((\tilde{X}'\tilde{X})^{-1}\tilde{X}'E(\tilde{\varepsilon})) = \beta.$$

2. The variance of $\hat{\beta}_{GLS}$ is:

$$Var(\hat{\beta}_{GLS}) = E(\hat{\beta}_{GLS} - \beta)(\hat{\beta}_{GLS} - \beta)' = (X'\Omega^{-1}X)^{-1}.$$

3. $\hat{\beta}_{GLS}$ is efficient, being the unbiased linear estimator with the lowest variance, as it is possible to show by simply applying the Gauss Markov Theorem to the transformed model (2.2.5).

4. $\hat{\beta}_{GLS}$ is consistent: it is unbiased and its variance goes to zero as the number of observations goes to infinity.

5. The asymptotic distribution of $\hat{\beta}_{GLS}$ is normal,

$$\hat{\beta}_{GLS} \overset{a}{\sim} N(\beta, (X'\Omega^{-1}X)^{-1}).$$

It is then possible to use the same inference methods as in the standard linear regression model, substituting $\hat{\beta}_{OLS}$ with $\hat{\beta}_{GLS}$, using where needed the variance of $\hat{\beta}_{GLS}$, and assuming the sample size is large enough.

6. Finally, if $\Omega = \sigma^2 I$, then $\hat{\beta}_{GLS} = \hat{\beta}_{OLS}$.

So far we have assumed that the variance covariance matrix of the errors, Ω, is known, although this is practically never the case and Ω has to be estimated. In particular, the GLS estimator would not be an actual estimator if it was dependent on all the unknown parameters of Ω. The GLS estimator where the Ω matrix is substituted by its estimator $\hat{\Omega}$ takes the name of Feasible GLS (FGLS) estimator:

$$\hat{\beta}_{FGLS} = (X'\hat{\Omega}^{-1}X)^{-1}X'\hat{\Omega}^{-1}Y.$$

Estimation of the Ω matrix is not simple, since in general it consists of $T(T+1)/2$ distinct unknown elements while the number of observation is only T. For this reason, one needs to impose some a priori restrictions on Ω. In the case of heteroskedastic errors, a common assumption one can make is that the variance only takes two (or a limited number of) values, say σ_1^2 and σ_2^2. Similarly, when the errors are serially correlated, one can assume a first order structure, $\varepsilon_t = \rho\varepsilon_{t-1} + u_t$, so that only ρ and σ_u^2 need to be estimated.

Let us take the case of heteroskedasticity. Assuming that the variance is equal to σ_1^2 in a first subsample of length T_1 while it becomes σ_2^2 in a second subsample of length T_2, we can estimate both σ_1^2 and σ_2^2 using the standard

OLS formula applied separately in each subsample. The resulting $\hat{\Omega}$ will be:

$$\hat{\Omega} = \begin{bmatrix} \hat{\sigma}_1^2 & \cdots & 0 & 0 & \cdots & 0 \\ & \ddots & & & \vdots & \vdots \\ 0 & \cdots & \hat{\sigma}_1^2 & 0 & \cdots & 0 \\ 0 & \cdots & 0 & \hat{\sigma}_2^2 & \cdots & 0 \\ \vdots & & \vdots & & \ddots & \\ 0 & \cdots & 0 & 0 & \cdots & \hat{\sigma}_2^2 \end{bmatrix} \qquad (2.2.7)$$

In the case of serially correlated errors, one can estimate by OLS the original regression model and use the resulting residuals $\hat{\varepsilon}_t$ to estimate the model $\hat{\varepsilon}_t = \rho\hat{\varepsilon}_{t-1} + u_t$. Then, the OLS estimators of ρ and $\text{Var}(u_t)$, $\hat{\rho}$ and $\hat{\sigma}_u^2$, can be used to build $\hat{\Omega}$ as:

$$\hat{\Omega} = \frac{\hat{\sigma}_u^2}{1-\hat{\rho}^2} \begin{bmatrix} 1 & \hat{\rho} & \hat{\rho}^2 & \cdots & & \hat{\rho}^{T-1} \\ \hat{\rho} & 1 & \hat{\rho} & \cdots & & \vdots \\ \hat{\rho}^2 & \hat{\rho} & & & & \hat{\rho}^2 \\ \vdots & & & & & \hat{\rho} \\ \hat{\rho}^{T-1} & & \cdots & \hat{\rho}^2 & \hat{\rho} & 1 \end{bmatrix}. \qquad (2.2.8)$$

Note that since we used a regression of y on X to obtain $\hat{\Omega}$, $\hat{\Omega}$ and ε are in general correlated. This implies that the FGLS estimator is biased in small samples, since

$$E\left[(X'\hat{\Omega}^{-1}X)^{-1}X'\hat{\Omega}\varepsilon\right] \neq 0 \Rightarrow E(\hat{\beta}_{FGLS}) \neq \beta. \qquad (2.2.9)$$

Moreover, $\hat{\beta}_{FGLS}$ is no longer a linear estimator, as y is also used for the estimation of $\hat{\Omega}$, and it is not necessarily the minimum variance estimator. However, $\hat{\beta}_{FGLS}$ remains a consistent estimator, $\hat{\beta}_{FGLS} \to \beta$, and asymptotically it has the same properties as $\hat{\beta}_{GLS}$ (provided a consistent estimator for Ω is used).

In terms of forecasting, it can be shown that the optimal (in the MSFE sense) h-steps ahead forecast is

$$\hat{y}_{T+h} = x_{T+h}\hat{\beta}_{GLS} + W'\Omega^{-1}\hat{\varepsilon}, \qquad (2.2.10)$$

where $W = E(\varepsilon_{T+h}, \varepsilon)$, which is a $1 \times T$ vector containing as elements $E(\varepsilon_{T+h}, \varepsilon_t) \,\forall\, t = 1, \ldots, T$, see, e.g., Granger and Newbold (1986, p. 191). For this formula to be applicable, Ω and W must be replaced by their (consistent) estimators.

Hence, if $E(\varepsilon_{T+h}, \varepsilon) = 0$ (no correlation in the errors), the difference with respect to the optimal forecast from Chapter 1 is only in the use of $\hat{\beta}_{GLS}$ instead of $\hat{\beta}_{OLS}$. Otherwise, we need to add an extra term to the forecast $(W'\Omega^{-1}\hat{\varepsilon})$, since current errors matter, being correlated with future (unobserved) errors.

2.3   HAC estimators

In this subsection we deal with the estimation of variances in settings where we do not specify a (parametric) model for the process involved, often referred to as Heteroskedasticity and Autocorrelation Consistent (HAC) variance estimators.

We consider two situations. The first situation is the estimation of $\hat{\Omega}$ without imposing some parametric model for heteroskedasticity. The approach is often called in econometrics White standard errors named after White (1980). With heteroskedasticity, the regression errors ε_i are independent, but have distinct variances σ_i^2, $i = 1, \ldots, T$. Then $\Omega = diag(\sigma_1^2, \ldots, \sigma_T^2)$, and $\hat{\sigma}_i^2$ can be estimated with $\hat{\varepsilon}_i^2$, yielding $\hat{\Omega} = diag(\hat{\varepsilon}_1^2, \ldots, \hat{\varepsilon}_T^2)$. It can then be shown that using an expression for $\text{Var}(\hat{\beta}_{OLS})$ similar to $(X'X)^{-1}X'\hat{\Omega}X(X'X)^{-1}$ instead of $\hat{\sigma}^2(X'X)^{-1}$ yields White's estimator, often referred to as a heteroskedasticity consistent estimator. MacKinnon and White (1985) suggest various small sample improvements, namely if we characterize $\hat{\Omega} = diag(\hat{\omega}_1^2, \ldots, \hat{\omega}_T^2)$, then the following estimators can be defined:

$$\hat{\omega}_i = \frac{T}{T - k}\hat{\varepsilon}_i^2$$

$$\hat{\omega}_i = \frac{\hat{\varepsilon}_i^2}{1 - h_i}$$

$$\hat{\omega}_i = \frac{\hat{\varepsilon}_i^2}{(1 - h_i)^2} \tag{2.3.1}$$

where h_i is the ith diagonal element of the matrix $X(X'X)^{-1}X'$.

For some applications – several considered later in the book – we are interested in the unconditional variance $\text{Var}(\varepsilon_t)$, where ε_t features autocorrelation of unknown form. In fact this analysis is often cast in a more general multivariate settings where ε is a vector (think of the errors for a system of multiple equations). We will present the vector case, with the scalar ε_t being a straightforward simplification. The generic procedure is usually referred to as Heteroskedasticity and Autocorrelation Consistent (HAC) variance estimation.

Let us define $\hat{\Gamma}_{j,T} = (1/(T-j)) \sum_{t=j+1}^{T} \hat{\varepsilon}_t \hat{\varepsilon}'_{t-j}$. Then, we can consider the following estimator for $var(\varepsilon_t)$, which we will denote by $\hat{V}_T$:

$$\hat{V}_T = \hat{\Gamma}_{0,T} + \left[\sum_{j=1}^{T-1} w_{j,T} (\hat{\Gamma}_{j,T} + \hat{\Gamma}'_{j,T}) \right] \qquad (2.3.2)$$

where $w_{j,T}$ is a weighting scheme, also known as kernel. Starting with **?**, Newey and West (1987), and **?**, different choices for the weights w have been suggested in the econometrics literature. Andrews (1991) provides a general framework of choosing the weights by kernel functions with automatic bandwidth selection.[1] In particular, $w_{j,T} = k(j, b_T)$ with kernel functions typically of the Bartlett type (Bartlett (1955)), Parzen-type (Parzen (1957)) or Quadratic Spectrum (QS) (Epanechnikov (1969), Priestley (1962), Andrews (1991)). The bandwidth b_T, is a positive valued parameter which determines how many $\hat{\Gamma}_{j,T}$ are included in the HAC estimator with the Bartlett and Parzen kernels, whereas the kernel function determines their weights. Andrews (1991) shows that the QS weights are optimal in a mean squared error sense. An extensive Monte Carlo study reported in Newey and West (1994) finds that the choice of the kernel function is not as critical as is the choice of the bandwidth in determining the finite sample properties.

Consistency of the HAC estimator requires that b_T tends to infinite as sample size T grows. Andrews (1991) shows that the optimal bandwidth has to grow at rates $O(T^{1/3})$ for Bartlett and $O(T^{1/5})$ for Parzen and QS. The details of the kernel functions and bandwidth appear in the table below.

---

[1]The long run variance is equal to $2\pi f(0)$, i.e., 2π times the spectral density at frequency zero. The estimation of spectral density has been considered in Parzen (1957) (scalar case) and Hannan (1970) (multivariate case).

Bartlett, Parzen and Quadratic Spectral (QS) kernels

Kernel	$w_{j,T}$	Optimal Bandwith
Bartlett	$k(j, b_T) = \max{(1 - a_j, 0)} \quad a_j = j/(1 + b_T)$	$O(T^{1/3})$
Parzen	$k(j, b_T) = \begin{cases} 1 - 6a_j^2 + 6a_j^3 & \text{for} \quad 0 \le a_j \le 1/2 \\ 2(1 - a_j)^3 & \text{for} \quad 1/2 < a_j \le 1 \\ 0 & \text{otherwise} \end{cases}$	$O(T^{1/5})$
QS	$k(j, b_T) = \frac{25}{12\pi^2 d_j^2} \left(\frac{\sin(m_j)}{(m_j)} - \cos(m_j) \right)$ $d_j = j/b_T \quad m_j = 6\pi d_j/5$	$O(T^{1/5})$

Finally, it is often recommended to use a mixture of parametric models and HAC estimators to obtain better estimates of $\hat{V}_T$ (see e.g., Den Haan and Levin (2000) and Section 6.3 for further discussion).

2.4   Some tests for homoskedasticity and no correlation

We have seen that when the hypotheses on the errors in the linear regression model are violated, many complications arise for the estimation procedures. Hence, it is convenient to check the validity of the assumptions, and in this section we will consider some tests for homoskedasticity and absence of correlation.[2]   We will consider procedures that are implemented in standard econometrics packages, such as *Eviews, Matlab*, and *R* or can be easily computed.

The main problem is that the errors are unobservable. However, it is possible to proxy them with the estimated residuals, although with due caution. A first heuristic method to check for homoskedasticity is to plot $\hat{\varepsilon}_i^2, i = 1, \dots, T$, where as usual we indicate with $\hat{\varepsilon}$ the residuals of the OLS

---

[2]A more detailed analysis appears in standard econometric textbooks, such as Hendry (1995), Judge, Hill, Griffiths, Lütkepohl, and Lee (1988), Stock and Watson (2009), Wooldridge (2012), among others.

regression, $\hat{\varepsilon} = y$ - $X'\hat{\beta}_{OLS}$. If the variability of $\hat{\varepsilon}_i^2$ changes substantially over time (or across observations) this might be a sign of heteroskedasticity.

There also exist more rigorous testing procedures, and we will now consider first the Goldfeld-Quandt test, and then the Breusch-Pagan-Godfrey and White tests for homoskedasticity.

The null hypothesis of the Goldfeld-Quandt test is that errors are homoskedastic, namely, $H_0 : \sigma_i^2 = \sigma^2$. The alternative is $H_1 : \sigma_i^2 = cz_i^2$, $c > 0$, that is to say that the variance increases with the explanatory variable z. The test can be performed in three steps.

First, the sample observations (y_i, x_i), $i = 1, \ldots, T$, are ranked according to the values of z_i, so that the lowest values of x_i are in the first part of the sample.

Second, the d central observations of the re-ordered sample are excluded (e.g. 20% of the sample, or $d = 0.2T$), and the remaining observations are divided in two subsamples of size $(T - d)/2$.

Finally, for each subsample one computes the Residual Sum of Squares $RSS = \sum \hat{\varepsilon}_i^2$, and constructs the following ratio:

$$GQ = \frac{RSS_2}{RSS_1}, \tag{2.4.1}$$

where RSS_j refers to subsample $j = 1$ and 2. Assuming that all the other hypotheses on the regression model hold, including normally distributed errors, under the null hypothesis the test statistic GQ is distributed as $F(p, p)$, where $p = [(T - d)/2]$- k degrees of freedom, since both the numerator and the denominator are distributed as two independent χ_p^2. The intuition behind the Goldfeld-Quandt test is that if the error variance is constant, the value of the numerator and the denominator of (2.4.1) should be similar, hence the statistic should fall within the acceptance region of the null distribution. On the contrary, if the variance increases with z_i, the test statistic should grow in size and fall within the rejection region. The standard form of the test is unilateral, therefore if one wants to assume that under H_1 the variance decreases with the values of z_i, one simply has to consider the slightly modified test statistic RSS_1/RSS_2.

The Breusch-Pagan-Godfrey test for homoskedasticity assumes that the null hypothesis is $H_0 : \sigma_i^2 = \sigma^2$. Under the alternative there is an unknown relationship between the errors' variance and one or a set of variables Z, i.e. $H_1 : \sigma_i^2 = \gamma + \delta Z_i$, where possibly $Z = X$. The test is conducted in the following way.

First, using the OLS residuals $\hat{\varepsilon}$ one regresses the squared residuals on Z:

$$\hat{\varepsilon}_i^2 = \gamma + \delta Z_i + v_i. \tag{2.4.2}$$

Second, one computes the Breusch-Pagan-Godfrey (BPG) test as:

$$BPG = TR^2, \tag{2.4.3}$$

where R^2 is simply the coefficient of determination of regression (2.4.2), and T is the sample size. Under the null hypothesis, and the basic assumptions of the linear regression model, asymptotically $BPG \sim \chi_q^2$, where q is the dimension of Z. The intuition behind this test is that under the null, R^2 should be quite low.

White's homoskedasticity test assumes the null hypothesis $H_0 : \sigma_i^2 = \sigma^2$, while the alternative is $H_1 : \sigma_i^2 = f(X_i, Z_i)$, with f some unknown function. The test goes as follows.

First, we run the regression (assuming for simplicity that X and Z are scalar):

$$\hat{\varepsilon}_i^2 = \gamma_0 + \gamma_1 X_i + \gamma_2 Z_i + \gamma_3 X_i^2 + \gamma_4 Z_i^2 + \gamma_5 X_i Z_i + v_i \tag{2.4.4}$$

Then, similar to the BPG test, we compute the White's statistic (W) as: W= TR^2 for regression (2.4.4). Note that, in the event of multiple regressors or elements in Z, we take all linear, quadratic and cross-product terms. Under the null, the asymptotic distribution is again χ_q^2, where q is the number of regressors (other than the constant) in the above regression.

Let us consider now testing for no serial correlation in the errors. One of the most famous testing procedures in econometrics is the Durbin-Watson (DW) test for no serial correlation. The null hypothesis is $H_0 : \varepsilon_t$ *uncorrelated*, while the alternative is first order correlation, i.e. $H_1 : \varepsilon_t = \rho\,\varepsilon_{t-1} + u_t$, $\rho \neq 0$. The test statistic is based on the OLS residuals:

$$DW = \frac{\sum_{t=2}^{T}(\hat{\varepsilon}_t - \hat{\varepsilon}_{t-1})^2}{\sum_{t=1}^{T}\hat{\varepsilon}_t^2} \approx 2 - 2\hat{\rho}. \tag{2.4.5}$$

Hence $0 \leq DW \leq 4$, with $DW \approx 2$ under the null.

Despite its popularity, this test has many limitations. First, under the null H_0 the test statistic DW has a non-standard distribution, thereby forcing the user to look at specifically tabulated critical vales. Second, it is not possible to use it with dynamic specifications. Finally, the alternative hypothesis is too specific, as the user might be interested in detecting also serial correlation of a order higher than one. Therefore, the DW statistic is often used as an informal first check for model's performance: when it substantially departs from the value of 2 it is considered as a first sign of errors' serial correlation.

An alternative method amending for such weaknesses is based on the Lagrange Multipliers (LM) principle, see for example Spanos (1987) for technical details. The LM test, also called the Breusch-Godfrey test, is based on the null hypothesis $H_0 : \varepsilon_t$ *uncorrelated*, while the alternative is $H_1 : \varepsilon_t$ *correlated up to order* m, where m is user-specified. Defining

$$\hat{r}_j = \frac{\sum_{t=j+1}^{T} \hat{\varepsilon}_t \hat{\varepsilon}_{t-j}}{\sum_{t=1}^{T} \hat{\varepsilon}_t^2}, \tag{2.4.6}$$

for $j = 1, \ldots, m$, the test statistic is:

$$LM = T \left(\sum_{j=1}^{m} \hat{r}_j^2 \right). \tag{2.4.7}$$

Under H_0, LM is asymptotically distributed as χ_m^2, assuming again that all the other model assumptions hold. There is no fixed rule for the choice of m : when there is no theoretical reason to assume something specific a priori, one can try with different alternatives. Behind this test there is the argument that, if errors are uncorrelated, also the residual sample autocorrelations should be low, resulting in values of $\hat{r}_j$ close to zero for $j = 1, \ldots, m$. On the other hand, if there is positive or negative autocorrelation in the errors, the test statistic should be high; clearly this implies that the test is unidirectional.

2.5 Parameter instability

One of the biggest problems in econometrics, and in particular in forecasting, is the assumption of stable model parameters. The presence of several institutional modifications, changes in economic policy, introduction of new products and production methods, the process of globalization, etc. are all possible sources of parameter instability.

Moreover, also rare events like wars, terrorist attacks, commodities price hikes, and financial market crashes could cause parameter instability, even if only temporarily. Outliers, i.e., extreme values of either the dependent variable or the regressors, can cause problems similar to parameter instability.

In this section we will evaluate what happens in the context of the linear regression model when parameters may not be constant over time (or across observations in the case of cross-sectional data), and what are the implications for forecasting. Next, we will discuss simple tests and methods to detect parameter instability, and the use of dummy variables as a remedy. Models with time-varying parameters are considered in more details in the third part of the book.

2.5.1 The effects of parameter changes

Let us reconsider equation (8.2.4) and allow for time-varying parameters:

$$y_t = X_{1t}\beta_{1t} + X_{2t}\beta_{2t} + \ldots X_{kt}\beta_{kt} + \varepsilon_t, \tag{2.5.1}$$

Then, we have so far imposed the following:

Assumption 2.5.1 (Linear Regression Assumptions). The linear regression model defined in equation (2.5.1) satisfies:

LR6 The parameters are stable across time, $\beta_{it} = \beta_i \ \forall \ i$ and t.

Let us consider now a specification where the dependent variable y depends on k regressors contained in the matrix X and suppose that at time T_1 a potentially destabilizing event happens. To simplify notation we will denote a sample by its end-point, i.e. the sample ending with T_1 will simply be denoted by observations $t \in \mathcal{T}_1$. The second sample is running from $t = T_1 + 1, \ldots, T$ has T_2 observations and the elements $t \in \mathcal{T}_2$. The model can be rewritten as:

$$y_t = X_t\beta_1 + \varepsilon_{1t} \quad t = 1, \ldots, T_1 \text{ or } t \in \mathcal{T}_1, \tag{2.5.2}$$

$$y_t = X_t\beta_2 + \varepsilon_{2t} \quad t = T_1 + 1, \ldots, T \text{ or } t \in \mathcal{T}_2, \tag{2.5.3}$$

$$\begin{bmatrix} \varepsilon_{1t} \\ \varepsilon_{2t} \end{bmatrix} \overset{iid}{\sim} N\left(\begin{bmatrix} 0 \\ 0 \end{bmatrix}, \begin{bmatrix} \sigma_1^2 I_{T_1} & 0 \\ 0 & \sigma_2^2 I_{T_2} \end{bmatrix} \right). \tag{2.5.4}$$

Let us suppose that, by mistake, we assume that the parameters are constant, that is to say:

$$y_t = X_t\beta + u_t \quad \forall \ 1 \leq t \leq T, \tag{2.5.5}$$

$$u_t \overset{iid}{\sim} N(0, \sigma_u^2).$$

Then, it can be easily shown that the OLS estimators $\hat{\beta}$ and $\hat{\sigma}_u^2$ are biased and inconsistent.

The implications of unaccounted parameter instability for forecasting are also important. The use of inconsistent parameter estimators, such as $\hat{\beta}$, to construct forecasts of future values of y is clearly suboptimal.

The presence of parameter instability in the forecast sample is also problematic. To illustrate this point, let us assume that $\mathcal{T}_1$ is the estimation sample and $\mathcal{T}_2$ the forecast sample. Abstracting from parameter estimation issues and assuming that future values of X_t are known, the optimal forecast made in $\mathcal{T}_1$ for y_t over $t \in \mathcal{T}_2$ is

$$\hat{y}_t = X_t \beta_1.$$

The actual values are instead:

$$y_t = X_t \beta_2 + \varepsilon_{2t},$$

so that the forecast errors are:

$$e_t = X_t(\beta_2 - \beta_1) + \varepsilon_{2t}.$$

Therefore, the larger the change in β the larger the forecast error (and the MSFE). A similar point holds if the parameters change during the forecast sample rather than at its start. Empirically, parameter change is one of the major sources of forecast failure.

In summary, both for parameter estimation and for forecasting, it is crucial to assess whether the model parameters are stable, and if not, to take proper measures.

2.5.2 Simple tests for parameter changes

In order to build an appropriate testing procedure, let us consider the following sets of hypotheses:

$$H_0' : \beta_1 = \beta_2 , \quad H_0'' : \sigma_1^2 = \sigma_2^2, \tag{2.5.6}$$
$$H_1' : \beta_1 \neq \beta_2 , \quad H_1'' : \sigma_1^2 \neq \sigma_2^2. \tag{2.5.7}$$

and where $H_0 = H_0' \cup H_0''$. It is convenient to consider two separate cases, according to whether the number of observations in the second subsample period T_2 is greater or smaller than the number or regressors k.

Case 1: $T_2 > k$

In this case it is possible to estimate both models (2.5.5) on the whole set of observations, and the two models (2.5.2) and (2.5.3) in the respective subsamples $\mathcal{T}_1$ and $\mathcal{T}_2$. The result will be three sets of residuals and the respective residuals sum of squares (RSS), denoted by RSS_T, RSS_{T_1}, and RSS_{T_2}.

The Chow test for the null hypothesis $H_0' : \beta_1 = \beta_2 | H_0''$ is

$$CH_1 : \left(\frac{RSS_T - RSS_{T_1} - RSS_{T_2}}{RSS_{T_1} + RSS_{T_2}}\right) \cdot \frac{T - 2k}{k} \underset{H_0}{\sim} F(k, T - 2k), \qquad (2.5.8)$$

where $T = T_1 + T_2$ and the rejection region is unilateral. Behind this test there is the argument that if parameters are stable, then RSS_T will probably be similar to $RSS_{T_1} + RSS_{T_2}$, while in the case of instability we expect that $RSS_T > RSS_{T_1} + RSS_{T_2}$.

It is important to stress that the null hypothesis for CH_1 is built on the simplifying assumption that the variance remains constant across the two subsamples, actually as we have seen it is $H_0' : \beta_1 = \beta_2 | H_0''$. If this was not the case, then the test would by biased towards rejection of the null $\beta_1 = \beta_2$ because RSS_T would be greater than $RSS_{T_1} + RSS_{T_2}$ by construction. Hence, it is very important also to make sure that the variance remains constant across subsamples. Therefore, we would like to test:

$$H_0'' : \sigma_1^2 = \sigma_2^2 \quad \text{against} \quad H_1'' : \sigma_1^2 < \sigma_2^2. \qquad (2.5.9)$$

The test statistic is now

$$CH_2 = \frac{\hat{\sigma}_2^2}{\hat{\sigma}_1^2} = \frac{RSS_{T_2}}{RSS_{T_1}} \frac{T_1 - k}{T_2 - k} \underset{H_0''}{\sim} F(T_2 - k, T_1 - k). \qquad (2.5.10)$$

Since it can be shown that CH_1 and CH_2 are independent, it is convenient to first use CH_2 to verify the variance stability and then to apply CH_1 to assess the regression parameters' stability. For further details, see e.g. Judge, Hill, Griffiths, Lütkepohl, and Lee (1988, p. 363).

Note that the null of the CH_2 test is the same as the null of the homoskedasticity tests we analyzed in the previous section. Hence, it is possible to apply those same tests also in this context. On top of that, once we find evidence of heteroskedasticity, it is always possible to try to apply some model transformation which amends for this problem, as we did for the GLS estimator. For example, in model (2.5.2)-(2.5.3) this transformation could simply consist in dividing the variables by σ_1 in the first subsample and by σ_2 in the second one (or by their sample estimators $\hat{\sigma}_1$ and $\hat{\sigma}_2$). It would be then safe to apply the CH_1 test and assess parameters' stability in the transformed model.

Case 2: $T_2 < k$

In this case there are not enough degrees of freedom to estimate model (2.5.3). The null $H_0' : \beta_1 = \beta_2 | H_0''$ must then be tested through a different test, which is:

$$CH_3 : \left(y_2 - X_2\hat{\beta}_1\right)' \frac{[I + X_2(X_1'X_1)^{-1}X_2']^{-1}}{\hat{\varepsilon}_1'\hat{\varepsilon}_1} \left(\underset{T_2 x 1}{y_2 - X_2\hat{\beta}_1}\right) \frac{T_1 - k}{T_2}$$

$$\underset{H_0}{\sim} F(T_2, T_1 - k).$$

This time the rejection region is in the right tail of the distribution. Here, y_2 - $X_2\hat{\beta}_1$ is the forecast error resulting from the use of $X_2\hat{\beta}_1$ to predict y_2, and actually it is the optimal predictor in the case in which X_2 is known while the model parameters are not. On the other hand, the term

$$\left(\left[I + X_2\left(X_1'X_1\right)^{-1}X_2'\right]^{-1} / \hat{\varepsilon}_1'\hat{\varepsilon}_1\right)(T_1 - k)$$

is an estimator of the forecast errors' covariance matrix. If the null hypothesis holds, forecast errors are small, and so is the test statistic CH_3, while the opposite happens if parameters change in the subsample T_2.

It is also possible to rewrite the CH_3 test in terms of residuals sum of squares as:

$$CH_3 = \left(\frac{RSS_T - RSS_{T_1}}{RSS_{T_1}}\right)\frac{T_1 - k}{T_2} \underset{H_0}{\sim} F(T_2, T_1 - k). \tag{2.5.11}$$

When $T_2 < k$ there is an appropriate test for testing variance stability, i.e. $H_0'' : \sigma_1^2 = \sigma_2^2$ against $H_1'' : \sigma_1^2 < \sigma_2^2$. The test statistic is now

$$CH_4 : \frac{\left(y_2 - X_2\hat{\beta}_1\right)'\left(y_2 - X_2\hat{\beta}_1\right)}{\hat{\sigma}_1^2} \underset{H_0''}{\overset{a}{\sim}} \chi^2(T_2). \tag{2.5.12}$$

The rationale is that since the numerator is an estimator for $T_2\sigma_2^2$ when the parameters are stable, under H_0'' the statistic CH_4 should roughly be equal to the size of the second subsample T_2. Note that both the numerator and denominator of CH_4 are based on $\hat{\beta}_1$, hence they are not independent. Therefore, the distribution of CH_4 is not F-shaped as before, but under the null hypothesis it is asymptotically behaves as a chi-square which is written as $\overset{a}{\underset{H_0}{\sim}} \chi^2(k)$, with k the degrees of freedom.

Finally, all the Chow tests we have discussed require the specification of the date of the parameter change. If this is not known with certainty, we can compute the tests for a set of possible candidate break dates, and then take the maximum (or supremum) of the resulting set of statistics. Unfortunately, the max-Chow test does not have a standard distribution, so that the proper critical values must be tabulated using simulation methods, see for example Andrews (1993) and Andrews and Ploberger (1994). Moreover, while the procedures we have discussed so far allow for a single break point, similar tests are available for multiple break points, possibly at unknown dates, see e.g., Bai and Perron (1998), (2003a), (2003b), Rossi (2012), and Section 2.5.5 for more details and references.

2.5.3   Recursive methods

An easier alternative to sophisticated versions of the Chow tests in the presence of unknown break points is recursive estimation, which can be helpful in determining if and when there is a break. The general form of the recursive OLS estimator underlying the recursive forecasts we have discussed in Chapter 1 is:

$$\hat{\beta}_t = \left(\underset{k \times t}{\bar{X}'_t \bar{X}_t} \right)^{-1} \underset{t \times 1}{\bar{X}'_t \bar{y}_t} \qquad t = T_0, T_0 + 1, \ldots, T \qquad (2.5.13)$$

where $T_0 > k$ and the matrices $\bar{X}'_t$ and vectors $\bar{y}_t$ contain the first t observations for the regressors X and the dependent variable y. The corresponding estimator for the variance of $\hat{\beta}_t$ is

$$var\left(\hat{\beta}_t \right) = \hat{\sigma}_t^2 \left(\underset{k \times t}{\bar{X}'_t \bar{X}_t} \right)^{-1} \qquad (2.5.14)$$

with

$$\hat{\sigma}_t^2 = (\bar{y}_t - \bar{X}_t \hat{\beta}_t)'(\bar{y}_t - \bar{X}_t \hat{\beta}_t)/(T - k). \qquad (2.5.15)$$

Plotting the recursive estimators of the parameters $\hat{\beta}_t$, $t = T_0, T_0 + 1$, ..., T with their confidence bands can prove useful in detecting potential parameter instability. If β is constant over time, then $\hat{\beta}_t$ should quickly settle down to a common value. Conversely, if for example the true model was (2.5.2) and (2.5.3), then we would expect to see $\hat{\beta}_t$ starting very close to β_1 and, after having trespassed $t = T_1 + 1$, to get closer and closer to β_2. The point in time when the change starts to be evident is a good candidate as the date of the structural change, when no a priori information is available.

Small changes in model parameters or changes happening at the beginning or at the end of the sample are much more difficult to detect with these type of methods (as well as with more sophisticated procedures).

Formal tests for parameter instability can be computed from the one-step ahead recursive residuals, which correspond to one-step ahead forecast errors, given by:

$$\tilde{\varepsilon}_t = \left(y_t - X_t \hat{\beta}_{t-1} \right) = \varepsilon_t + X_t(\beta - \hat{\beta}_{t-1}) \qquad (2.5.16)$$

with

$$\hat{\beta}_{t-1} = \left(\underset{k \times (t-1)}{\bar{X}_{t-1} \, \bar{X}_{t-1}} \right)^{-1} \underset{(t-1) \times 1}{\bar{X}'_{t-1} \, \bar{y}_{t-1}} \qquad (2.5.17)$$

and

$$\tilde{\sigma}_t^2 = Var(\tilde{\varepsilon}_t) = (1 + X_t(\bar{X}'_{t-1}\bar{X}_{t-1})^{-1}X'_t)\sigma^2. \qquad (2.5.18)$$

The standardized recursive residuals can be defined as:

$$\tilde{\omega}_t = \tilde{\varepsilon}_t / \tilde{\sigma}_t, \qquad t = k+1, \ldots, T \qquad (2.5.19)$$

Brown, Durbin, and Evans (1975) propose a CUSUM statistic:

$$CUSUM_t = \sum_{j=k+1}^{t} \frac{\tilde{\omega}_j}{\tilde{\sigma}_{\omega,T}} \qquad (2.5.20)$$

where $\tilde{\sigma}_{\omega,T}^2 = (T-k)^{-1} \sum_{t=k+1}^{T}(\tilde{\omega}_t - \bar{\omega})^2$. Under the null hypothesis that $\beta_{k+1} = \ldots = \beta_T$, $CUSUM_t$ has mean zero and variance that is proportional to $t - k - 1$.[3] The CUSUMSQ statistic is defined as:

$$CUSUMSQ_t = \frac{\sum_{j=k+1}^{t} \tilde{\omega}_j^2}{\sum_{j=k+1}^{T} \tilde{\omega}_j^2} \qquad (2.5.21)$$

---

[3]Ploberger and Krämer (1992) show that the CUSUM statistic can be computed with OLS instead of recursive residuals.

Under the null of parameter stability, the $CUSUMSQ_t$ statistic has an asymptotic $\chi^2(t)$ distribution.

Finally, it is worth noting that even a single outlier may result into a change in the recursive estimator and, more importantly, in a large recursive residual and therefore affect CUSUM type statistics.

2.5.4 Dummy variables

Once the presence of parameter instability or outliers is detected, one of the simplest remedies we can put forth is augmenting the linear model with specific binary variables, which are usually called dummy variables. These are variables which take value zero for the whole sample except during the periods of structural change or for outlying observations, when they are set equal to one.

To illustrate the use of dummy variables, let us take as a reference a simple model for the aggregate consumption function and assume that a negative shock like a war, a credit crunch or simply an increase of pessimism takes place. We want to show how to take into account these negative events in the consumption function, through dummy variables.

The basic consumption model is

$$c_t = \beta_1 + \beta_2 inc_t + \varepsilon_t,$$

where c indicates consumption and inc income. Let us insert a dummy variable D_t taking value one during credit crunch times and zero for the remaining part of the sample. There are three possible ways in which the dummy variable can be inserted in the model:

M1: Structural change in autonomous consumption

$$c_t = \beta_1 + \alpha D_t + \beta_2 inc_t + \varepsilon_t$$

M2: Structural change in the marginal propensity to consume

$$c_t = \beta_1 + \beta_2 inc_t + \gamma D_t inc_t + \varepsilon_t$$

M3: Structural change in both the autonomous consumption and in the marginal propensity to consume

$$c_t = \beta_1 + \alpha D_t + \beta_2 inc_t + \gamma D_t inc_t + \varepsilon_t$$

We focus on model M3 which has a more general form and accounts for structural changes in both the intercept and slope of the consumption function. Another formulation for model M3 is:

$$c_t = \begin{cases} \beta_1 + \beta_2 inc_t + \varepsilon_t, & t \notin credit\ crunch \\ \gamma_1 + \gamma_2 inc_t + \varepsilon_t, & t \in credit\ crunch \end{cases} \tag{2.5.22}$$

where $\gamma_1 = \beta_1 + \alpha$ and $\gamma_2 = \beta_2 + \gamma$. With this formulation we want to stress that the use of dummy variables as additional regressors in the basic model ultimately results in specifying a model with time-varying parameters.

Let us now turn the attention to a permanent structural change. Let us assume, for example, that at time t_0 there is a permanent shift in the marginal propensity to consume. The model could then be specified as

$$c_t = \beta_1 + \beta_2 inc_t + \beta_3(inc_t - inc_{t_0})D_t + \varepsilon_t \tag{2.5.23}$$

$$D_t = \begin{cases} 1\ if\ t \geq t_0 \\ 0\ if\ t < t_0 \end{cases} \tag{2.5.24}$$

In this case there are no discontinuities in expected consumption, as in t_0 we have

$$\beta_1 + \beta_2 inc_{t_0} = \beta_1 - \beta_3 inc_{t_0} + \beta_2 inc_{t_0} + \beta_3 inc_{t_0} \tag{2.5.25}$$

Using dummy variables, we can also rewrite model (2.5.2)-(2.5.3) as a single equation. Assuming that the error variance is constant, it is:

$$y_t = \beta_1 X_t + \gamma_2 D_t X_t + \varepsilon_t, \tag{2.5.26}$$

with $\beta_2 = \beta_1 + \gamma_2$ and

$$D_t = \begin{cases} 1\ if\ t > T_1 \\ 0\ if\ t \leq T_1 \end{cases} \tag{2.5.27}$$

It can be shown that an F−test for the null hypothesis $\gamma_2 = 0$ in (2.5.26) is exactly equivalent to the CH_1 test in (2.5.8). Under the null, the F−statistic has an $F(k, T-2k)$ distribution, since the model has $2k$ regressors k of which are being tested for significance.

When the variance is also changing across sub-periods

$$Var\ (\varepsilon_t) = \begin{cases} \sigma_1^2, & if\ t \leq T_1 \\ \sigma_2^2, & if\ t > T_1 \end{cases} \tag{2.5.28}$$

the model (2.5.26) can be reformulated as

$$
\begin{aligned}
y_t/((1 - D_t)\sigma_1 + D_t\sigma_2) \; = \; & \beta_1 X_t/((1 - D_t)\sigma_1 + D_t\sigma_2) + \gamma_2 D_t X_t/ \\
& ((1 - D_t)\sigma_1 + D_t\sigma_2) + u_t \qquad (2.5.29)
\end{aligned}
$$

where $u_t = \varepsilon_t/((1 - D_t)\sigma_1 + D_t\sigma_2)$, $\mathrm{Var}(u_t) = 1$. As a consequence, model (2.5.29) embeds a structural change in the variance, despite having homoskedastic errors.

So far we have used binary dummy variables that were meant to capture instantaneous structural changes, for example from β_1 to β_2. When the structural change is more gradual, but its shape is still known, dummies can take more general forms, such as

$$
D_t = \begin{cases} 1/(1 + \exp(\mu t)) & \text{if } t \geq t_0 \\ 0 & \text{if } t < t_0 \end{cases} \qquad (2.5.30)
$$

In more complex models, this gradual structural change may be driven by a specific regressor, as for example in

$$
D_t = \begin{cases} 1/(1 + \exp(\mu Z_t)) & \text{if } Z_t \geq Z_0 \\ 0 & \text{if } Z_t < Z_0 \end{cases} \qquad (2.5.31)
$$

In these cases, the model becomes non-linear and a proper estimation method is required, typically non-linear least squares (NLS). Models of this type will be considered in the third part of the book.

In case our sample contains multiple outliers or breaks, it is possible to amend their effects by adding a dummy variable for each outlier or break, even if the extent of multicollinearity increases with the number of added dummies.

As a final remark, we note that the use of dummy variables assumes that both the date of the break and the shape of parameter change are known. When this is not the case, more general modeling tools are needed. We will introduce models with general patterns of parameter time variation in Part III of the book.

2.5.5   Multiple breaks

The dummy variables in the previous subsection assumed that the breakpoints were known. What if we neither know how many breaks there are nor when they occur (if there is at least one breakpoint)? We describe now a procedure proposed by Bai and Perron (1998) to determine the number of breaks and their location. We consider a standard multiple linear regression model as in equation (8.2.4) estimated over a sample of T observations:

$$y_t = X_{1t}\beta_1 + X_{2t}\beta_2 + ...X_{kt}\beta_k + \varepsilon_t.$$

Suppose now that among the regressors, $X_{1t} \ldots$, X_{kt} we identify a k_1-dimensional set X_t^c which is not subject to potential structural change, whereas the remainder k_2-dimensional set called Z_t might be affected by parameter instability, where $k = k_1 + k_2$. If all the regressors are considered then $X_t = Z_t$, and the test procedure will apply to all variables. In some cases we might only consider that the parameter associated to a particular regressor (say X_{jt} - possibly the intercept) is changing through time, in which case we isolate it into Z_t with $k_2 = 1$.

We have a sample of size T periods and consider m potential breaks, producing $m + 1$ sample segments with stable parameters which we will call for convenience regimes. For the observations T_j, $T_j + 1 \ldots$, $T_{j+1} - 1$ in regime j we have the regression model

$$y_t = X_t^c\beta + Z_t\alpha_j + \varepsilon_t, \qquad (2.5.32)$$

for regimes $j = 0, \ldots, m$. The above equation is characterized by: (1) a set of breakpoints $T_m = T_1, \ldots, T_m$, and (2) a set of corresponding parameters θ_m ($\beta, \alpha_0 \ldots, \alpha_m$). Consider the LS minimization for a given m across all possible breakpoints T_m and associated parameter vector θ_m. This means solving a least squares problem that can be numerically quite involved as the number of comparison models increases rapidly in both the sample size T and the number of breaks m.[4]

One procedure proposed by Bai and Perron (1998) is a test for equality of the α_j across regimes, or put differently the null hypothesis of no breaks against the alternative of m breaks. More specifically, we consider the null hypothesis $H_0 : \alpha_0 = \ldots = \alpha_m$ and the associated $F-$statistic:

$$F_m(\hat{\alpha}) = \frac{1}{T}\left(\frac{T - (m + 1)k_2 - k_1}{mk_2}\right)(R\hat{\alpha})'(R\hat{V}(\hat{\alpha})R')^{-1}(R\hat{\alpha}) \quad (2.5.33)$$

---

[4]Practical algorithms for computing the global optimizers for multiple breakpoint models are outlined in Bai and Perron (2003a).

where $\hat{\alpha} = (\hat{\alpha}_0 \ldots, \hat{\alpha}_m)$ and $(R\hat{\alpha})' = (\alpha'_0 - \alpha'_1, \ldots, \alpha'_{m-1} - \alpha'_m)$ and $\hat{V}(\hat{\alpha})$ is the estimated variance matrix of $\hat{\alpha}$.

So far we assumed that the number of breaks m is pre-specified. In cases where m is not known, we may test the null of no structural change against an unknown number of breaks up to some upper-bound m^*. This type of testing is sometimes termed double maximum since it involves optimization both for a given m and across various values of the test statistic for $m \leq m^*$. The resulting statistics is sometimes referred to as $supF_m$.

In all cases, we are dealing with non-standard asymptotic distributions, whether it is for the F_m or $SupF_m$ statistics. Bai and Perron (2003b) provide critical value and response surface computations for various trimming parameters (minimum sample sizes for estimating a break), numbers of regressors, and number of breaks.

2.6   Measurement error and real-time data

This section is devoted to analyzing the consequences for OLS estimation when Assumption 1.2.1 - LR3 is violated, namely, the explanatory variables X are stochastic and not distributed independently of ε. We will also discuss reasons why independence may fail, focusing on the case of real-time data that is relevant in a forecasting context. By real-time data we refer to a situation where an indicator is at first published in preliminary form, with subsequent revisions being released. For example, GDP for quarter T can be released in preliminary form (so called flash estimates) as soon as 30 days into the next quarter $T + 1$ and updated frequently thereafter up to several years later (see e.g., Ghysels, Horan, and Moench (2017) for details). When nowcasting (see Chapter 12) and short term forecasting is involved, econometricians will generally use the information available at the time of forecasting. Hence, the econometrician is bound to use real-time data.

Let us assume that $E(\varepsilon|X) \neq 0$, so that ε and X are correlated. Then, the OLS estimator for β is biased:

$$E(\hat{\beta}) = \beta + E_{f(\varepsilon,X)}[(X'X)X'\varepsilon] = \beta + E_{f(x)}[(X'X)X']E_{f(\varepsilon|X)}(\varepsilon|X) \neq \beta,$$

where $f(\varepsilon, X)$ denotes the joint density of the regressors and the error term, whereas $f(\varepsilon)$ and $f(\varepsilon|X)$ are, respectively, the marginal and conditional densities. Furthermore, both $\hat{\beta}$ and $\hat{\sigma}^2$ are inconsistent. Inconsistency results from the fact that $\text{plim}(X'\varepsilon/T) \neq 0$ in the following expressions, where plim denotes the limit in probability:

$$\hat{\beta} = \beta + (X'X)^{-1}X'\varepsilon = \beta + \left(\frac{X'X}{T}\right)^{-1}\frac{X'\varepsilon}{T}$$

$$\overset{T\to\infty}{\longrightarrow} \beta + (\Sigma_{XX}^{-1})\text{plim}\frac{X'\varepsilon}{T} \neq \beta,$$

$$\hat{\sigma}^2 = \frac{\hat{\varepsilon}'\hat{\varepsilon}}{T-k} = \frac{\varepsilon'[I - X(X'X)X']\varepsilon}{T-k}$$

$$= \left[\frac{\varepsilon'\varepsilon}{T} + \frac{\varepsilon'X}{T}\left(\frac{X'X}{T}\right)^{-1}\frac{X'\varepsilon}{T}\right]\frac{T}{T-k}$$

$$\overset{T\to\infty}{\longrightarrow} \sigma^2 + \text{plim}\frac{\varepsilon'X}{T}(\Sigma_{XX}^{-1})\text{plim}\frac{X'\varepsilon}{T} \neq \sigma^2.$$

A typical condition causing the violation of Assumption 1.2.1 - LR3 is the presence of measurement error in the regressors. This is a common occurrence in economics, as the theoretical definition of a variable and its empirical counterpart are seldom perfectly matched. Typical examples include the natural rate of unemployment, potential output, and expectations in general. Even the most commonly used variables like GDP and the inflation rate are difficult to measure exactly. And data revisions is another possible source of measurement error.

Let us illustrate the issue using the following example. The model is:

$$y = X\beta + \varepsilon \quad \text{with} \quad Cov(X, \varepsilon) = 0 \tag{2.6.1}$$

but the observed regressors are

$$X^* = X + v,$$

where v represents the measurement error and has the following properties:

$$E(v) = 0 , \quad Var(v) = \sigma_v^2 I , \quad Cov(X, v) = 0 , \quad Cov(\varepsilon, v) = 0. \tag{2.6.2}$$

We can think of X as the final release of a given variable and of X^* as a preliminary release. For example, GDP is one among many macroeconomic variables that are released in preliminary form and then revised in subsequent releases.

If we rewrite the regression model in terms of observable variables we have:

$$Y = X^*\beta + \varepsilon - v\beta = X^*\beta + u,$$

so that $Cov(X^*, u) \neq 0$ and the OLS estimator for β, $\hat{\beta} = (X^{*\prime}X^*)^{-1}X^{*\prime}y$, is not consistent.

Let us now assess what happens when the dependent variable y is measured with error (v), while the regressors are independent of (or at least uncorrelated with) the error term. Let us suppose that

$$y^* = y + v, \tag{2.6.3}$$

with

$$E(v) = 0, \ \ Var(v) = \sigma_v^2, \ \ Cov(X, v) = 0, \ \ Cov(\varepsilon, v) = 0.$$

The model cast in terms of observables is now

$$y = y^* - v = X\beta + \varepsilon \ \ \text{or} \ \ y^* = X\beta + \varepsilon + v.$$

Since $Cov(X, \varepsilon + v) = 0$, the OLS estimator, $\hat{\beta} = (X'X)^{-1}X'y^*$, remains consistent. However, its variance increases to $(\sigma_u^2 + \sigma_v^2)E(X'X)^{-1}$, resulting in a loss of efficiency.

Another relevant case where the regressors can be correlated with the error term is when in dynamic models the errors are correlated across time. We will consider this situation in the next chapter.

2.7 Instrumental variables

Given the above discussion, we need to find an estimator that amends the loss of consistency of the OLS estimator when the regressors are correlated with the error term. Let us assume there exist q variables Z with the following properties:

$$
\begin{aligned}
\text{plim } Z'\varepsilon/T &= 0, \\
\text{plim } Z'X/T &= \Sigma_{ZX}, \\
\text{plim } Z'Z/T &= \Sigma_{ZZ}.
\end{aligned}
\tag{2.7.1}
$$

These properties require the variables Z to be (at least asymptotically) uncorrelated with the error term, while being correlated with the k explanatory variables X and having an asymptotic second order moments matrix.

Variables with these properties are called Instrumental Variables (IV). The number of instrumental variables, q, must be at least equal to the number of regressors correlated with the error term. Let us suppose for simplicity that $q = k$.

The IV estimator has the following formulation:

$$\hat{\beta}_{IV} = (Z'X)^{-1} Z'y.$$

We can easily derive the estimator $\hat{\beta}_{IV}$ as follows. Let us multiply by Z' both sides of the model

$$y = X\beta + \varepsilon,$$

obtaining:

$$Z'y = Z'X\beta + Z'\varepsilon.$$

If we assume that (2.7.1) also holds in finite samples, so that $Z'\varepsilon = 0$, we have

$$Z'y = Z'X\hat{\beta}_{IV} \Rightarrow \hat{\beta}_{IV} = (Z'X)^{-1} Z'y.$$

This is an example of method of moments estimator, in the sense that $\hat{\beta}_{IV}$ is obtained by imposing a population moment restriction (namely $E(z_t'\varepsilon_t) = 0$, with z_t the set of instruments for t) that has the empirical counterpart $Z'\varepsilon = 0$.[5] The properties of $\hat{\beta}_{IV}$ are the following:

- $\hat{\beta}_{IV}$ is consistent:

$$
\begin{aligned}
\hat{\beta}_{IV} &= (Z'X)^{-1} Z'y = \beta + (Z'X)^{-1} Z'\varepsilon \\
&= \beta + \left(\frac{Z'X}{T}\right)^{-1} \left(\frac{Z'\varepsilon}{T}\right) \xrightarrow{T\to\infty} \beta + \Sigma_{ZX}^{-1} \cdot 0 = \beta.
\end{aligned}
$$

- Its asymptotic variance is:

$$
\begin{aligned}
Var\left(\hat{\beta}_{IV}\right) &= E\left[\left(\hat{\beta}_{IV} - \beta\right)\left(\hat{\beta}_{IV} - \beta\right)'\right] \\
&= E\left[(Z'X)^{-1} Z'\varepsilon\varepsilon' Z (Z'X)^{-1}\right] \xrightarrow{T\to\infty} \frac{\sigma^2}{T}\Sigma_{ZX}^{-1}\Sigma_{ZZ}\Sigma_{ZX}^{-1}.
\end{aligned}
$$

- The asymptotic distribution of $\hat{\beta}_{IV}$ is given by:

$$\sqrt{T}\left(\beta - \hat{\beta}_{IV}\right) \overset{a}{\sim} N(0, \sigma^2\Sigma_{ZX}^{-1}\Sigma_{ZZ}\Sigma_{ZX}^{-1}).$$

---

[5]See for example Hansen (1982) and Hall (2005) for more elaborate discussions about method of moment estimators.

It is important to note that $Var(\hat{\beta}_{IV})$ decreases if Σ_{ZX} grows in size. Hence, we prefer instruments highly correlated with the regressors X (and not with the error ε) since this increases the precision of the IV estimator. Clearly, the challenge is always finding such instruments.

It is also worth pointing out that $Var(\hat{\beta}_{IV}) \geq Var(\hat{\beta}_{OLS})$.[6] Hence, if the regressors are correlated with the error, $\hat{\beta}_{OLS}$ is inconsistent while $\hat{\beta}_{IV}$ is consistent. However, if the regressors are uncorrelated with the error, $\hat{\beta}_{OLS}$ is more efficient than $\hat{\beta}_{IV}$ (which remains consistent). Therefore, in order to select the most appropriate estimator, we would like to test the null hypothesis of no correlation between the regressors and the error term.

We can use the following statistic, proposed by Hausman (1978) and known as the Hausman test:

$$H = (\hat{\beta}_{IV} - \hat{\beta}_{OLS})'(Var(\hat{\beta}_{IV}) - Var(\hat{\beta}_{OLS}))^{-1}(\hat{\beta}_{IV} - \hat{\beta}_{OLS}) \underset{H_0}{\overset{a}{\sim}} \chi^2(k).$$

Intuitively, under the null hypothesis the two estimators will be very similar in large samples, since they are both consistent, while under the alternative hypothesis they will be different since $\hat{\beta}_{OLS}$ is not consistent. Hence, the test is one-sided.

The use of the IV estimator is not so common in a forecasting context, while it is widespread for structural analysis (possibly after some generalizations, typically referred to as generalized method of moments estimators, GMM). A possible explanation is that, even if $\hat{\beta}_{OLS}$ is inconsistent, it still minimizes the sum of squared residuals. Since the latter is usually related to the sum of squared forecast errors, $\hat{\beta}_{OLS}$ could still produce a good MSFE. However, when structural models are used for forecasting, sometimes IV related parameter estimators (such as the two-stage least square estimator, TSLS) are adopted.

2.8   Examples using simulated data

In Chapter 1 we considered the baseline linear regression models estimated by OLS, measures of model fit, parameter tests, and forecasting properties. We know that OLS estimators are BLUE (best linear unbiased estimator) if the conditions of the Gauss-Markov theorem (GMT) are satisfied. The following are the conditions:

---

[6]Where the inequality holds in a matrix sense, meaning that the difference between $Var(\hat{\beta}_{IV})$ and $Var(\hat{\beta}_{OLS})$ is a positive semi-definite matrix.

F-statistic	7.577	Prob.F(1,198)		0.006
Obs*R-squared	7.372	Prob. Chi-Sq(1)		0.007
Scaled explained SS	5.715	Prob. Chi-Sq(1)		0.017
Variable	Coefficient	Std.Error	t-Statistic	Prob.
C	82.648	7.625	10.839	0.000
X	3.669	1.333	2.753	0.006
R-squared	0.037	Mean dep var		85.882

Table 2.7.1: *Breusch-Pagan-Godfrey homoskedasticity test*

- Linearity: the dependent variable is assumed to be a linear function of the variables in the model.

- Homoskedasticity and lack of correlation: the error term has constant variance ($Var(\varepsilon_t) = \sigma^2$) and is uncorrelated ($Cov(\varepsilon_i, \varepsilon_j) = 0$ for $i \neq j$).

- No collinearity: the regressors are not perfectly collinear (the rank of $X'X$ is full)

In addition, the errors are required to be normally distributed for the OLS estimators to have a finite sample normal distribution, which also justifies the finite sample distribution of the $t-$ and $F-$statistics. Furthermore, model parameters are implicitly assumed to be stable over time, and the regressors, when stochastic, to be uncorrelated with the error term.

We will check whether these conditions are satisfied in the basic static regression model used in the simulated example of Chapter 1, and propose remedies when they are not. Given the DGP used to simulate the data (reported in Chapter 1), we a priori expect several assumptions to be violated.

Homoskedasticity   To test the null hypothesis of homoskedasticity, we perform two tests: the Breusch-Pagan-Godfrey (BPGT) test and the White test (WT), described in the previous sections. Under the alternative hypothesis of BPGT, the variance of the residuals depends on the values of the independent variables. The outcome of the test, described in Table 2.7.1, leads to rejection of the null hypothesis for the BPGT test. Table 2.8.1 also presents the output for the WT test and, in line with BPGT, we can reject the null hypothesis.

F-statistic	4.304	Prob.F(2,197)		0.015
Obs*R-squared	8.373	Prob. Chi-Sq(2)		0.015
Scaled explained SS	6.491	Prob. Chi-Sq(2)		0.039
Variable	Coefficient	Std.Error	t-Statistic	Prob.
C	73.928	11.489	6.435	0.000
X^2	0.270	0.266	1.015	0.312
X	3.537	1.339	2.642	0.009
R-squared	0.042	Mean dep var		85.882

Table 2.8.1: *White heteroskedasticity test*

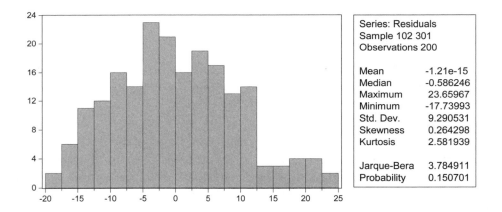

Figure 2.8.1: *Normality test: Histogram*

No Serial Correlation The next step is to check if the residuals are not serially correlated. There are two main diagnostic tests that can be used, as we noted earlier in this chapter: the Durbin-Watson (DW) statistic and

F-statistic	18.882	Prob. F(4,194)		0.000
Obs*R-squared	56.045	Prob. Chi-Sq(4)		0.000
Variable	Coefficient	Std.Error	t-Statistic	Prob.
ALPHA(1)	-0.003	0.572	-0.005	0.996
ALPHA(2)	-0.032	0.101	-0.314	0.754
RESID(-1)	0.492	0.072	6.807	0.000
RESID(-2)	0.097	0.080	1.213	0.227
RESID(-3)	-0.025	0.081	-0.306	0.760
RESID(-4)	-0.087	0.073	-1.190	0.235
R-squared	0.280	Mean dep var		-0.000

Table 2.8.2: *Breusch-Godfrey LM test*

the Breusch-Godfrey Lagrange Multipliers (LM) test. The null hypothesis of the Durbin-Watson test is no serial correlation, the alternative is first order correlation, i.e., $H_1 : \varepsilon_t = \rho\varepsilon_{t-1} + u_t$, $\rho \neq 0$. The DW statistic is reported in the estimation output by default, shown in Table 1.11.1, and in this case it is equal to 0.9545, much lower than the theoretical value under the null hypothesis, which is 2. This provides informal support against the null hypothesis, meaning that the evidence suggests the errors are autocorrelated. The LM test permits one to choose the serial correlation order under the alternative hypothesis. The results of the LM test, using a lag order equal to 4, reported in Table 2.8.2, suggest to reject no correlation, in line with the DW statistic.

Normality   Some descriptive information about normality of the error term is provided by the histogram of the residuals. The resulting graph is displayed in Figure 2.8.1. The figure also reports descriptive statistics on the residuals, and the Jarque-Bera (JB) statistic for the null hypothesis of normality against a generic alternative of non normality of the errors. Both the histogram and the JB test do not suggest to reject the null hypothesis of normal residuals (at the usual significance levels). Moreover, the estimated values of the residual skewness and kurtosis are, respectively, 0.2643 and 2.5819, close to the theoretical values of 0 and 3 for a standard normal variable.

Parameter Stability   An underlying assumption of the linear regression model is parameter stability.   To test whether the model parameters are constant for the whole estimation sample against the alternative of a break in a specific date, we can apply the Chow breakpoint or the Chow forecast tests, depending on whether or not the break date is such that we can re-estimate the model in both the pre- and the post-break samples (see the theory part for more details). Moreover, we can compute a set of recursive statistics, based on the recursive residuals, the one-step ahead forecast errors, and the recursive coefficients. These are particularly useful when the break date is unknown.

We start with the Chow breakpoint test, which evaluates whether there is significant difference between the sum of squared residuals obtained from the full sample, and adding the sum of squared residuals from the pre- and post-break samples. We consider three possible alternative breakpoints, corresponding to $t = 151$ or $t = 201$ or $t = 251$.

All the three test outcomes, reported in Table 2.8.3, lead to rejection of the null hypothesis at the 5% confidence level.

Chow Breakpoint Test: 151 Equation Sample: 102 301			
F-statistic	12.536	Prob.F(2,196)	0.000
Log likelihood ratio	24.074	Prob. Chi-Sq(2)	0.000
Wald Statistic	25.071	Prob. Chi-Sq(2)	0.000
Chow Breakpoint Test: 201 Equation Sample: 102 301			
F-statistic	27.779	Prob.F(2,196)	0.000
Log likelihood ratio	49.912	Prob. Chi-Sq(2)	0.000
Wald Statistic	55.558	Prob. Chi-Sq(2)	0.000
Chow Breakpoint Test:251 Equation Sample: 102 301			
F-statistic	14.526	Prob.F(2,196)	0.000
Log likelihood ratio	27.643	Prob.Chi-Sq(2)	0.000
Wald Statistic	29.051	Prob. Chi-Sq(2)	0.000

Table 2.8.3: *Chow breakpoint tests*

To illustrate the implementation of the Chow forecast statistic, let us assume that we want to test for a break at observation 301 (so that we have only one observation in the second subsample and we are in the case $T_2 < k$). The outcome is reported in Table 2.8.4. For example, the *EViews* software reports two test statistics for the Chow forecast test. The first one is the F−statistic, which is based on comparing the residuals sum of squares of the full sample and the first subsample, as shown in equation (2.5.11). The second test statistic is the Likelihood Ratio (LR) test that compares the maximum log likelihood function from the basic model and the same model augmented with a dummy for each observation in the post-break sample. The LR test statistic is asymptotically χ^2 distributed with degrees of freedom equal to the number of dummies. It turns out that stability at the end of the estimation sample (observation 301) is rejected at the 10% significance level.

Test predictions for observations from 301 to 301			
	Value	df	Probability
F-statistic	3.714	(1, 197)	0.055
Likelihood ratio	3.735	1	0.053

Table 2.8.4: *Chow forecast test*

The main criticism of the Chow tests is that the breakpoint should be known in advance. When this is not a realistic assumption, we can either implement more sophisticated procedures that also estimate the most likely break date (for example the Andrews (1993) and Bai and Perron (1998) tests), or we can use recursive methods.

When we implement Bai-Perron sequential test to determine the optimal breaks in a model regressing Y on the breaking variables C and X we find the results reported in Table 2.8.5.[7]

The Bai-Perron test detects breaks in the intercept for observations 146, 207, 237, 268. At the same time the null hypothesis of no breaks in X is rejected for observations 146, 176, 207, 237, 268. In this case we know the DGP and the fact that there is a single break in observation 201, so that the outcome of the Bai and Perron test is incorrect, likely due to the rather short sample available and size of the break.

The graphs of the recursively computed OLS estimates of the model parameters are displayed in Figure 2.8.2, with observations starting from 101

---

[7]Bai-Perron tests of 1 to m globally determined breaks. Break selection have the following settings: Highest significant, Trimming 0.15, Max. breaks 5, Sig. level 0.05.

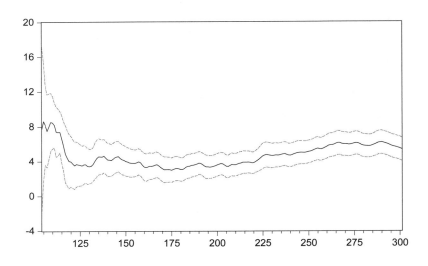

(a) RECURSIVE α_1 ESTIMATES $\pm$ 2 S.E.

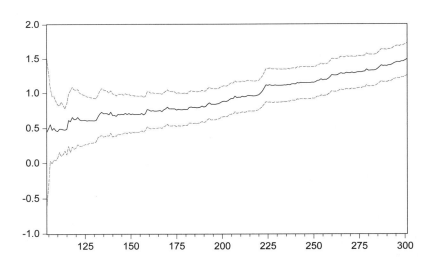

(b) RECURSIVE α_2 ESTIMATES $\pm$ 2 S.E.

Figure 2.8.2: *Recursive estimation*

since for the simulated data we skip the first 100 generated data points). In the presence of parameter instability, there should be significant time-variation in the plots. Indeed, we observe some relevant movement for both recursively estimated coefficients.

Variable	Coefficient	Std. Error	t-Statistic	Prob.
102-145 – 44 obs				
C	4.523	1.212	3.733	0.000
X	0.701	0.193	3.622	0.000
146-175 – 30 obs				
C	0.841	1.452	0.579	0.563
X	0.750	0.256	2.931	0.004
176-206 – 31 obs				
C	3.990	1.462	2.730	0.007
X	1.368	0.264	5.185	0.000
207-236 – 30 obs				
C	9.152	1.516	6.038	0.000
X	1.800	0.277	6.496	0.000
237-267 – 31 obs				
C	10.900	1.558	6.999	0.000
X	1.926	0.291	6.616	0.000
268-301 – 34 obs				
C	3.302	1.360	2.428	0.016
X	2.360	0.237	9.946	0.000

Table 2.8.5: *Bai and Perron breakpoint test*

Dummy variables An easy way to model structural breaks or parameter instability is by introducing dummy variables. From the DGP, we know that the model parameters indeed change after $t = 200$. The recursive analysis and Bai-Perron tests did not spot this date. But since we know the DGP we can define a dummy variable whose value is 0 when $t < 201$ and 1 afterwards. We then add the dummy to the starting model, which becomes:

$$y = \alpha_0 + \beta_1 D + \alpha_1 x + \beta_2 D x + u,$$

	Coefficient	Std. Error	t-Statistic	Prob.
ALPHA(0)	3.673	0.837	4.390	0.000
BETA(1)	3.221	1.187	2.714	0.007
ALPHA(1)	0.884	0.141	6.279	0.000
BETA(2)	1.316	0.208	6.320	0.000
R-squared	0.571	Mean dep var		6.695
Adjusted R-squared	0.564	S.D. dep var		12.560
S.E. of regression	8.290	Akaike IC		7.088
Sum squared resid	13468.600	Schwarz IC		7.154
Log likelihood	-704.768	Hannan-Quinn		7.114
F-statistic	86.940	DW stat		1.029
Prob(F-statistic)	0.000			

Table 2.8.6: *Model with dummy variable*

	Forecasting Method	
	Static	*Recursive*
RMSFE	10.1278	9.6421
MAFE	8.3141	7.9382

Table 2.8.7: *Forecasting performance model with dummy variable*

so that we can control for a change in both the intercept and the coefficient of x.

Estimation results, presented in Table 2.8.6, indicate that both β_1 and β_2 are statistically significant at the 5% level.

Since we know the DGP, we can also check if the estimated coefficients are significantly different from the true parameter values. The results are as follows:

- For $\alpha(0)$, $t-stat = \frac{3.6728-1}{0.8366} = 3.19$, for $\alpha(1)$, $t-stat = \frac{0.8841-1}{0.1408} = -0.82$

- For $\beta(1)$, $t-stat = \frac{3.2213-1}{1.1869} = 1.87$, for $\beta(2)$, $t-stat = \frac{1.3156-1}{0.2082} = 1.52$

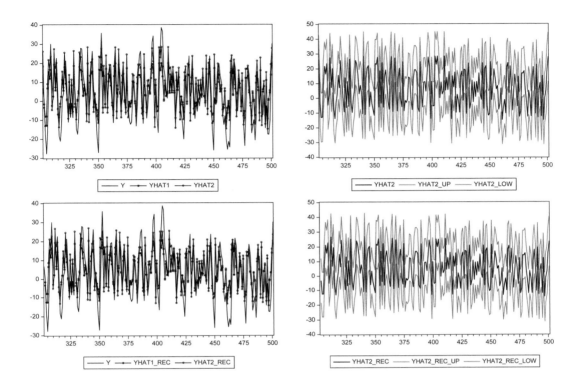

Figure 2.8.3: *Dummy regression: Simple and recursive forecasts vs forecast of the simple OLS regression*

Hence, at the 5% confidence level, the last three parameters are not different from the true values, but the first one is. This is likely due to the remaining mis-specification of the model.

The final step is the forecast computation and evaluation. As in the previous chapter, we use 102 - 301 as estimation sample and 302 - 501 as forecast sample. We want to assess the effects of ignoring the parameter break on the model forecasting performance. The forecasts from the models with and without the dummies are presented in Figure 2.8.3, while Table 2.8.7 reports the RMSFE and MAFE. It turns out that the dummies do not improve forecasts and this is due to the fact that mis-specification is still present, since as we know the DGP features dynamic effects.

2.9 Empirical examples

In Chapter 1, we have used the Euro area GDP example to illustrate the estimation, parameter testing, model selection based on model fit, and some variable selection procedures. We also showed the impact of the choice of indicator variables on forecast accuracy. As discussed at the beginning of this chapter, the estimation of the models in Chapter 1 is based on a set of assumptions. It is important for these assumptions to hold, as otherwise, the OLS estimators will no longer be consistent and efficient. This, in turn, can result in less accurate forecasts produced by a mis-specified model.

2.9.1 Forecasting Euro area GDP growth

Using again the Euro area GDP example, we now illustrate the use of some mis-specification tests, discuss how to improve the specification, and consider the forecasting performance of the improved models.

F-statistic	0.798	Prob. F(3,66)		0.499
Obs*R-squared	2.451	Prob. Chi-Sq(3)		0.484
Scaled explained SS	1.930	Prob.Chi-Sq(3)		0.587
Variable	Coefficient	Std.Error	t-Statistic	Prob.
C	0.075	0.013	5.617	0.000
IPR	0.009	0.010	0.851	0.398
SU	-0.005	0.005	-0.976	0.333
SR	0.002	0.002	1.283	0.204
R-squared	0.035	Mean dep var		0.080

Table 2.9.1: *Breusch-Pagan-Godfrey test for heteroskedasticity.*

Homoskedasticity   Let us focus on the Model 2 formulation for Euro area GDP growth that, from Chapter 1, is:

$$y_t = \beta_0 + \beta_1 ipr_t + \beta_2 su_t + \beta_3 sr_t + \varepsilon_t,$$

and consider the full sample period 1996Q1 to 2013Q2. The estimation results were reported in Table 1.12.2, and we now proceed with testing for homoskedasticity of the residuals. The Breusch-Pagan-Godfrey test output is shown in Table 2.9.1. The null hypothesis is $H_0 : \sigma_i^2 = \sigma^2$, i.e., homoskedasticity, against the alternative that there is an unknown relationship between the error variance and one or a set of regressors (or function thereof).

F-statistic	0.510	Prob.F(9,60)		0.861
Obs*R-squared	4.977	Prob. Chi-Sq(9)		0.836
Scaled explained SS	3.920	Prob. Chi-Sq(9)		0.917
Variable	Coefficient	Std.Error	t-Statistic	Prob.
C	0.058	0.022	2.710	0.009
IPR	0.009	0.018	0.486	0.629
IPR2	0.000	0.006	0.021	0.983
IPR*SU	-0.001	0.010	-0.120	0.905
IPR*SR	0.000	0.004	0.086	0.932
SU	-0.004	0.008	-0.471	0.639
SU2	0.001	0.002	0.696	0.489
SU*SR	-0.001	0.001	-0.667	0.507
SR	0.002	0.003	0.708	0.482
SR2	0.000	0.000	1.103	0.275
R-squared	0.071	Mean dep var		0.080

Table 2.9.2: *White test for heteroskedasticity.*

Under the null hypothesis, the statistic follows a χ^2 distribution with as many degrees of freedom as the number of regressors in the test equation. The null hypothesis cannot be rejected at 1%, 5%, and 10% significance levels, indicating no heteroskedasticity in the residuals. Table 2.9.2 presents the output of the White test. The null hypothesis of the White test is the same as that of the Breusch-Pagan-Godfrey test. The test equation can be formulated as regressing the squared residuals on all the regressors and, possibly, all their cross-products. Our example here includes all possible cross-products. The White test statistic is also reported as *Obs*R-squared* and it is asymptotically distributed as χ^2 with as many degrees of freedom as the number of parameters in the test equation except the constant. Once again, the null hypothesis of homoskedasticity cannot be rejected at conventional significance levels.

F-statistic	3.664	Prob.F(2,64)		0.031
Obs*R-squared	7.191	Prob. Chi-Sq(2)		0.028
Variable	Coefficient	Std.Error	t-Statistic	Prob.
C	0.002	0.035	0.051	0.960
IPR	-0.015	0.028	-0.520	0.605
SU	0.005	0.014	0.333	0.740
SR	-0.002	0.005	-0.346	0.731
RESID(-1)	0.230	0.124	1.858	0.068
RESID(-2)	0.199	0.133	1.493	0.140
R-squared	0.103	Mean dep var		0.000

Table 2.9.3: *Serial correlation LM test with* $m = 2$

F-statistic	4.439	Prob.F(3,63)		0.007
Obs*R-squared	12.214	Prob. Chi-Sq(3)		0.007
Variable	Coefficient	Std.Error	t-Statistic	Prob.
C	0.003	0.034	0.090	0.929
IPR	-0.029	0.028	-1.035	0.305
SU	0.013	0.014	0.883	0.381
SR	-0.003	0.005	-0.612	0.542
RESID(-1)	0.180	0.122	1.476	0.145
RESID(-2)	0.165	0.130	1.267	0.210
RESID(-3)	0.301	0.128	2.340	0.022
R-squared	0.174	Mean dep var		0.000

Table 2.9.4: *Breusch-Godfrey serial correlation LM test with* $m = 3$

No Serial Correlation We now move on to investigate the absence of serial correlation in the residuals of Model 2. The diagnostic tests we consider
are the Durbin-Watson (DW) test and the Breusch-Godfrey LM test. The
null hypothesis of the Durbin-Watson test is no correlation, against the al-
ternative of first order correlation, i.e., $H_1 : \varepsilon_t = \rho \varepsilon_{t-1} + u_t$, $\rho \neq 0$. The DW

test statistic is reported in the estimation output by default and, from Table 1.12.2, it is 1.433661, a borderline value. While the DW test is for testing serial correlation of first order under the alternative, higher order correlation can be allowed by the LM test. Tables 2.9.3 and 2.9.4 present the LM test with correlation of orders 2 and 3. The reported statistic (*Obs*R-squared*), is computed as T times R^2 from the test equation and it is asymptotically χ^2_m distributed, where $m = 2$ or $m = 3$ in our case. The null hypothesis is rejected by both tests at the 5% significance level, indicating that the residuals are serially correlated. Hence, the model does not fully capture the dynamic evolution of the dependent variable, and adding some lagged regressors could improve the model specification, as we will see in the next chapter.

Normality Normality of the errors, though not required for the OLS estimators to be BLUE, is necessary for them to have a normal distribution in finite samples, and for the $t-$ and $F-$statistics to have, respectively, a $t - Student$ and F distribution in finite samples. Moreover, as we discussed, violation of normality can be due to outliers and structural breaks, which affect more severely the OLS estimators.

To assess whether normality holds, we can start by plotting an histogram of the Model 2 residuals. Figure 2.9.1 reports the required histogram and a set of statistics on the residuals of Model 2. Specifically, there is also the Jarque-Bera statistic for the null hypothesis of normal errors, whose distribution is $\chi^2(2)$, and the corresponding p-value. It turns out that the null hypothesis of normality cannot be rejected at conventional significance levels.

Parameter stability Continuing with Model 2, we now illustrate some procedures, including the Chow breakpoint test, the Chow forecast test, and some recursive methods that look into the recursive residuals, the one-step ahead forecast errors, and the recursive estimators of the coefficients. We proceed by first using the Chow breakpoint test, which requires to specify the assumed break date and then to estimate Model 2 over the entire sample period, and then separately for the pre- and post-break subsamples. The test statistic is based on whether there is significant difference in the sum of squared residuals obtained over the full sample and that obtained by summing the RSS over the two subsamples. In principle, we should first test that the error variance does not change over the two subperiods, but since we did not reject homoskedasticity we take the variance to be constant. We illustrate the use of this test by investigating whether parameter instability or structural breaks exist in two occasions within our full sample period: the early 2000s economic recession that affected the European Union mostly around 2001 - 2002, and the recent 2007/2008 financial crisis. Specifically, we carry out three separate tests for single breakpoints in, respectively, 2001Q1, 2001Q2, and 2007Q3.

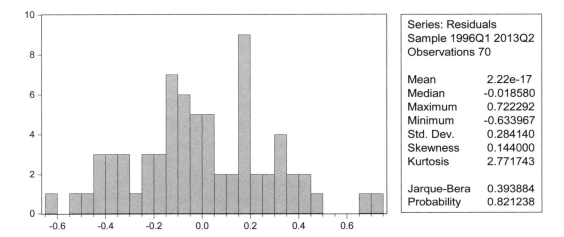

Figure 2.9.1: *Histogram of the errors in Model 2*

Tables 2.9.5 and 2.9.6 present the two tests for whether there is a structural change in the parameters in 2001. The CH_1 test statistic, see equation (2.5.8), has an F distribution. The null hypothesis of the Chow breakpoint test is $H_0' : \beta_1 = \beta_2 \mid H_0''$, meaning no break or structural change in the parameters at the specific date. At the 5% significance level, the null hypothesis of no break in 2001Q1 cannot be rejected, but the hypothesis of no break at 2001Q2 can be rejected. Hence, we have evidence that the relationship between Euro Area GDP growth and the indicators in Model 2 has changed before and after 2001Q2. Table 2.9.7 presents the same test but with 2007Q3 as the break date. The outcome shows a clear rejection of no breakpoint also at that time.

F-statistic	2.045	Prob. F(4,62)	0.099
Log likelihood ratio	8.674	Prob. Chi-Sq(4)	0.070
Wald Statistic	8.179	Prob. Chi-Sq(4)	0.085

Table 2.9.5: *Chow breakpoint test: Breakpoint in 2001Q1*

F-statistic	3.513	Prob. F(4,62)	0.012
Log likelihood ratio	14.301	Prob. Chi-Sq(4)	0.006
Wald Statistic	14.053	Prob. Chi-Sq(4)	0.007

Table 2.9.6: *Chow breakpoint test: Breakpoint in 2001Q2*

F-statistic	7.617	Prob. F(4,62)	0.000
Log likelihood ratio	27.980	Prob. Chi-Sq(4)	0.000
Wald Statistic	30.467	Prob. Chi-Sq(4)	0.000

Table 2.9.7: *Chow breakpoint test: Breakpoint in 2007Q3*

In the above Chow breakpoint tests, the number of observations in the post-break subsample (T_2) is larger than the number of parameters k. However, when the latter is larger than the former, there are not enough degrees of freedom for estimation. In these situations, we can use the Chow forecast test, as discussed in section 2.5.

	Value	df	Probability
F-statistic	3.115	(4,62)	0.021
Likelihood ratio	12.819	4.000	0.012

Table 2.9.8: *Chow Forecast Test: Breakpoint in 2012Q3.*

Suppose we are interested in whether there is a breakpoint in 2012Q3, close to the end of our full sample. Let us examine two versions of test statistics for the Chow forecast test. The first is the $F-$statistic that compares the residuals sum of squares of the full sample and the first subsample, as shown in equation (2.5.11). The second is the LR test that compares the maximum log likelihood function from the basic model and a model augmented with one dummy for each post-break observations. The LR test statistic is asymptotically χ^2 distributed with as many degrees of freedom as the number of added dummy variables. The outcome of the tests, shown in Table 2.9.8, leads to rejection of the null of no break in 2012Q3 at the 5% level.

Variable	Coefficient	Std.Error	t-Statistic	Prob.
1996Q1 - 1998Q3 – 11obs				
C	0.499	0.104	4.777	0.000
IPR	0.431	0.147	2.930	0.005
SU	-0.037	0.048	-0.759	0.452
SR	-0.023	0.010	-2.371	0.022
1998Q4 - 2001Q1 – 10obs				
C	0.840	0.135	6.212	0.000
IPR	-0.045	0.131	-0.344	0.732
SU	0.082	0.051	1.602	0.116
SR	0.008	0.011	0.743	0.461
2001Q2 - 2004Q2 – 13obs				
C	0.280	0.063	4.461	0.000
IPR	0.251	0.126	1.998	0.052
SU	-0.027	0.034	-0.773	0.444
SR	0.011	0.009	1.307	0.198
2004Q3 - 2008Q1 – 15obs				
C	0.341	0.122	2.793	0.008
IPR	0.390	0.142	2.745	0.009
SU	0.022	0.037	0.599	0.552
SR	0.002	0.011	0.222	0.825
2008Q2 - 2010Q4 – 11obs				
C	-0.051	0.094	-0.544	0.589
IPR	0.273	0.034	7.992	0.000
SU	0.016	0.034	0.462	0.646
SR	-0.015	0.017	-0.893	0.376
2011Q1 - 2013Q2 – 10obs				
C	0.044	0.081	0.537	0.594
IPR	0.280	0.079	3.541	0.001
SU	0.005	0.030	0.162	0.872
SR	0.000	0.012	0.036	0.972

Table 2.9.9: *Estimation output of Model 2 with breaks detected with the Bai and Perron breakpoint test.*

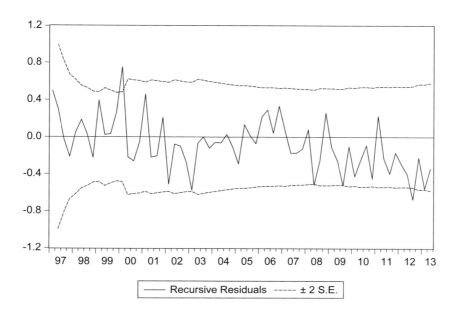

Figure 2.9.2: *Plot of recursive residuals with* $\pm 2 \times$ *s.e. confidence bounds.*

The Chow-type tests provide indication of whether structural changes in parameters have occurred at a specific point in time. The major criticism of such tests is that prior knowledge about the break dates is required. In some cases, such as the recent financial crisis, it is perhaps possible to pinpoint relatively precise dates when breaks are likely. However, there is also a need for tests that allow for the detection of structural changes without a pre-specified break date.

Bai and Perron (1998) describe procedures for identifying the multiple breaks. When we implement the Bai-Perron sequential test to determine the optimal breaks in Model 2, we find the results reported in Table 2.9.9.[8] The Bai-Perron test detects breaks in 1998Q4, 2001Q2, 2004Q3, 2008Q2, and 2011Q1.

As an alternative, recursive estimation can provide useful information, as we now illustrate again taking Model 2 as an example. We plot the recursive residuals in Figure 2.9.2, together with the plus and minus 2 times standard error bands. Evidence of parameter instability is found when the recursive

---

[8]Bai-Perron tests of 1 to m globally determined breaks Break selection have the following settings: Highest significant, Trimming 0.15, Max. breaks 5, Sig. level 0.05.

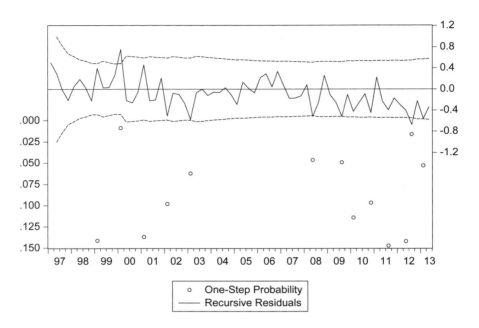

Figure 2.9.3: *One-step forecast test*

residuals are outside the bands. From the plot, the main deviations are in 2000Q1, soon after the introduction of the euro, and 2012Q3, though the residuals are mostly negative after 2007 which is also worrying as the model systematically over-estimates GDP growth.

Next we compute the one-step forecast test, which is simply a plot of the recursive residuals as in Figure 2.9.2, together with the points whose associated p-value is less than the 15% significance level. Based on the plot in Figure 2.9.3, and assuming a 5% significance level, evidence of parameter instability can be detected in 2000Q1, 2008Q2, 2009Q3, and 2012Q3.

Finally, we consider the recursively estimated coefficients, labeled as $C(1)$ to $C(4)$ in Figure 2.9.4, corresponding to the coefficients of the constant term, IP growth, growth in the ESI, and stock returns, respectively. In the presence of parameter instability, there should be significant variation in the evolution of the estimators. We observe some more marked changes prior to 2002, but this could be just due to the small sample available. There is also some movement around 2008Q3 and 2008Q4, in coincidence with the financial crisis.

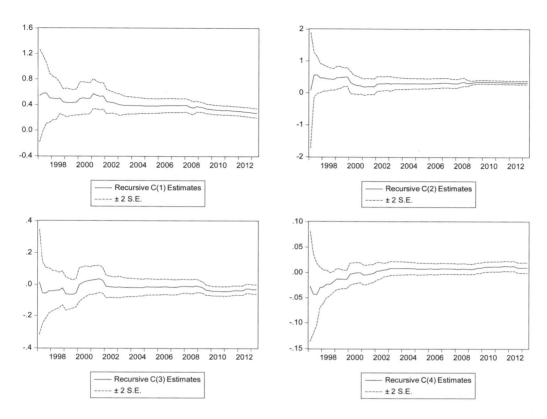

Figure 2.9.4: *Plots of recursive coefficients alongside the $\pm 2 \times$ s.e. confidence bounds*

Dummy variables As discussed in section 2.5, one way to accommodate structural breaks (or correct for outliers) is to include dummy variables in the model. Here we illustrate the use of these dummies, and then examine their impact on the forecast accuracy. The parameter stability analysis provided evidence for some possible breaks since the second half of 2007, in coincidence with the financial crisis and the resulting the Euro area recession, and around 2000 - 2001, soon after the introduction of the euro and corresponding to the early 2000s recession. We therefore create two dummy variables. The first, called $d_t^{EA\text{-}cri}$, has the value of 1 for the period 2007Q2 to 2013Q1, and 0 otherwise. The second, called d_t^{2000s}, has the value of 1 for the period 2000Q1 to 2001Q4, and 0 otherwise. We then re-estimate Model 2 by adding these two dummies. More precisely, Model 2.1 contains the independent variables in Model 2 plus the dummy for the Euro area crisis. Model 2.2 corresponds to Model 2 plus the dummy for the early 2000s recession.

Variable	Coefficient	Std. Error	t-Statistic	Prob.
C	0.375	0.040	9.271	0.000
IPR	0.301	0.025	11.812	0.000
SU	-0.021	0.013	-1.568	0.122
SR	0.006	0.005	1.196	0.236
Dea	-0.302	0.071	-4.278	0.000
R-squared	0.841	Mean dep var		0.350
Adjusted R-squared	0.831	S.D. dep var		0.629
S.E. of regression	0.259	Akaike IC		0.202
Sum squared resid	4.347	Schwarz IC		0.362
Log likelihood	-2.060	Hannan-Quinn		0.266
F-statistic	85.767	DW stat		1.792
Prob(F-statistic)	0.000			

Table 2.9.10: *Estimation output of Model 2.1*

The mathematical presentations of Models 2.1 and 2.2 are as follows:

$$Model\ 2.1:\ y_t = \alpha_0 + \beta_0 ipr_t + \gamma_0 su_t + \lambda_0 sr_t + \eta_0 d_t^{EA\_cri} + \varepsilon_t$$

$$Model\ 2.2:\ y_t = \alpha_0 + \beta_0 ipr_t + \gamma_0 su_t + \lambda_0 sr_t + \eta_1 d_t^{2000s} + \varepsilon_t$$

Our final forecasting specification, Model 2.3, is Model 2 with the dummies for both the financial crisis and the early 2000s recession:

$$Model\ 2.3:\ y_t = \alpha_0 + \beta_0 ipr_t + \gamma_0 su_t + \lambda_0 sr_t + \eta_0 d_t^{EA\_cri} + \eta_1 d_t^{2000s} + \varepsilon_t$$

The estimation outputs of these two models using the entire sample are presented in Tables 2.9.10, 2.9.11, and 2.9.12. It turns out that both dummies are significant at the 5% level in Models 1 and 2, but only the crisis dummy remains significant in Model 3. Interestingly, the inclusion of the dummies in Model 2.3 has brought down the significance of both the survey data and the stock returns compared to Model 2 (when no break dummies are included). Such findings could be seen as an indication that part of the significant explanatory power of the survey data and the stock returns are coming from the fact that they are useful in picking up some impact of the crisis on GDP growth.

Variable	Coefficient	Std. Error	t-Statistic	Prob.
C	0.247	0.037	6.705	0.000
IPR	0.314	0.028	11.302	0.000
SU	-0.022	0.015	-1.487	0.142
SR	0.009	0.005	1.906	0.061
D2000s	0.224	0.111	2.016	0.048
R-squared	0.808	Mean dep var		0.350
Adjusted R-squared	0.796	S.D. dep var		0.629
S.E. of regression	0.284	Akaike IC		0.389
Sum squared resid	5.243	Schwarz IC		0.550
Log likelihood	-8.619	Hannan-Quinn		0.453
F-statistic	68.334	DW stat		1.462
Prob(F-statistic)	0.000			

Table 2.9.11: *Estimation output of Model 2.2*

We could also add interaction dummies in Model 3, to allow for a change not only in the intercept but also in the coefficients of the other explanatory variables. However, when we do this, the interaction dummies are not significant, perhaps due to the rather short estimation sample. The results are not reported here, but we find that none of the intersections has coefficient significantly different from zero at the 5% confidence level.

We now move on to illustrate whether the inclusion of dummies can improve forecast accuracy. In Chapter 1, the estimation sample ended in 2006Q4 while the forecast evaluation period began in 2007Q1. To highlight the impact on forecast accuracy of the dummies we use here 1996Q1 to 2010Q4 as estimation sample, leaving the last 10 quarters between 2011Q1 and 2013Q2 as the new forecast evaluation period.

It turns out that the dummy $d_t^{EA\text{-}cri}$ is highly significant, the dummy d_t^{2000s} is not. Model 2.3 has a better in-sample fit than Model 2, and smaller values of all three reported information criteria, though the differences are not large.

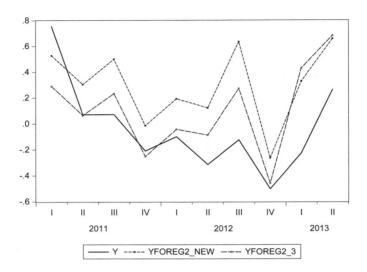

Figure 2.9.5: *Plot of forecasted GDP growth produced by Model 2 and by Model 2.3 alongside the actual GDP growth.*

Variable	Coefficient	Std. Error	t-Statistic	Prob.
C	0.381	0.043	8.883	0.000
IPR	0.302	0.027	11.156	0.000
SU	-0.023	0.015	-1.536	0.130
SR	0.006	0.005	1.349	0.183
Dea	-0.291	0.084	-3.473	0.001
D2000s	0.085	0.100	0.847	0.401
R-squared	0.868	Mean dep var		0.414
Adjusted R-squared	0.855	S.D. dep var		0.644
S.E. of regression	0.245	Akaike IC		0.119
Sum squared resid	3.238	Schwarz IC		0.328
Log likelihood	2.442	Hannan-Quinn		0.201
F-statistic	70.847	DW stat		1.965
Prob(F-statistic)	0.000			

Table 2.9.12: *Estimation output of Model 2.3*

Next, we perform a forecasting exercise using these two models for the newly defined forecast evaluation period, with results shown in Figure 2.9.5. It is clear from the graph that overall the forecasts from Model 2.3 track the outturn better than the forecasts from Model 2, particularly for the dips in 2011Q2 and 2012Q4. To further confirm this finding, we compute the RMSFE and the MAFE. Table 2.9.13 compares the forecast evaluation statistics, confirming the superiority of Model 2.3 and the importance of allowing for parameter change when forecasting.

	Model 2	Model 2 with dummies
RMSFE	0.412	0.326
MAFE	0.375	0.247

Table 2.9.13: *Forecast evaluation statistics: Model 2 without and with dummies (Model 2.3)*

2.9.2 Forecasting US GDP growth

In Chapter 1, we used the US GDP data to illustrate the estimation, parameter testing, model selection based on model fit, and variable selection procedures. We have also shown the impact of the choice of indicator variables on forecast accuracy. We now assess whether the assumptions underlying OLS estimation of the models in Chapter 1 are satisfied, following the same steps as in the previous examples and focusing on Model 2, which is:

$$y_t = \beta_0 + \beta_1 ipr_t + \beta_2 su_t + \beta_3 sr_t + \varepsilon_t.$$

The full sample covers the period from 1985Q1 to 2013Q4. The estimation results are shown in Table 2.9.14.

Variable	Coefficient	Std. Error	t-Statistic	Prob.
C	0.469	0.044	10.713	0.000
IPR	0.312	0.034	9.195	0.000
SU	0.007	0.007	0.979	0.330
SR	0.013	0.007	1.833	0.070
R-squared	0.523	Mean dep var		0.657
Adjusted R-squared	0.510	S.D. dep var		0.600
S.E. of regression	0.420	Akaike IC		1.137
Sum squared resid	19.763	Schwarz IC		1.232
Log likelihood	-61.951	Hannan-Quinn		1.176
F-statistic	40.919	DW stat		2.033
Prob(F-statistic)	0.000			

Table 2.9.14: *Estimation output for Model 2*

F-statistic	0.572	Prob. F(3,112)		0.635
Obs*R-squared	1.751	Prob. Chi-Sq(3)		0.626
Scaled explained SS	1.593	Prob. Chi-Sq(3)		0.661
Variable	Coefficient	Std.Error	t-Statistic	Prob.
C	0.176	0.025	7.023	0.000
IPR	0.003	0.019	0.158	0.875
SU	-0.001	0.004	-0.369	0.713
SR	-0.004	0.004	-0.931	0.354
R-squared	0.015	Mean dep var		0.170

Table 2.9.15: *Breusch-Pagan-Godfrey heteroskedasticity test*

F-statistic	0.697268	Prob. F(9,106)		0.7100
Obs*R-squared	6.484	Prob. Chi-Sq(9)		0.691
Scaled explained SS	5.901	Prob. Chi-Sq(9)		0.750
Variable	Coefficient	Std.Error	t-Statistic	Prob.
C	0.172	0.039	4.395	0.000
IPR^2	0.003	0.011	0.266	0.791
$IPR * SU$	0.004	0.003	1.200	0.233
$IPR * SR$	-0.003	0.003	-1.017	0.311
IPR	-0.009	0.024	-0.380	0.705
SU^2	-0.000	0.000	-1.044	0.299
$SU * SR$	0.001	0.001	0.889	0.376
SU	-0.005	0.005	-0.927	0.356
SR^2	0.000	0.000	0.262	0.793
SR	0.001	0.005	0.201	0.841
R-squared	0.056	Mean dep var		0.170

Table 2.9.16: *White heteroskedasticity test*

Chow Breakpoint Test: 2001Q1			
$CH(1)$	3.264	Prob. F(4,108)	0.014
$CH(2)$	0.999	Prob. F(47,61)	0.496
Chow Breakpoint Test: 2001Q2			
$CH(1)$	3.139	Prob. F(4,108)	0.017
$CH(2)$	0.977	Prob. F(46,62)	0.528
Chow Breakpoint Test: 2007Q3			
$CH(1)$	4.025	Prob .F(4,108)	0.004
$CH(2)$	1.055	Prob. F(21,87)	0.410
Chow Breakpoint Test: 2007Q4			
$CH(1)$	4.314	Prob. F(4,108)	0.003
$CH(2)$	1.120	Prob. F(20,88)	0.345

Table 2.9.17: *Chow breakpoint test*

Homoskedasticity   The Breusch-Pagan-Godfrey test output is shown in Table 2.9.15, while the output of the White test is presented in Table 2.9.16. It is clear that the null hypothesis of homoskedasticity cannot be rejected by both tests.

No Serial Correlation   We now investigate the absence of serial correlation in the residuals for Model 2. The diagnostic tests we consider here are the Durbin-Watson (DW) test and the Breusch-Godfrey LM test. The DW statistic is 2.033324, close to the theoretical value under the null of uncorrelated residuals. The LM tests confirm the same findings - we skip the details here.

Parameter stability   Continuing with Model 2, we now consider procedures to detect possible parameter instability. These include, as we have seen, the Chow breakpoint test, the Chow forecast test, and some recursive procedures that look into the recursive residuals, the one-step ahead forecast errors, and the recursively estimated coefficients.

As a first step, we implement the Chow breakpoint test to examine whether there was a breakpoint in, respectively, 2001Q1, 2001Q2, 2007Q3, and 2007Q4. Table 2.9.17 presents the results for the $CH(1)$ and $CH(2)$ statistics. At the 5% significance level, the null hypothesis of no break in the regression coefficients is rejected for each tested break date using the $CH(1)$ statistic, while according to the $CH(2)$ statistic there is no evidence of a break in the error variances.

To test for breaks without exogenously setting up the breakpoint data we use the Bai-Perron test. Results of the test are described in Table 2.9.18. The Bai-Perron test detects breaks at 5 dates: 1989Q4, 1996Q2, 2000Q3, 2004Q4, and 2009Q1. Breaks in the intercept term are detected for all of these dates. The hypothesis of no breaks in IPR can be rejected for observations 1996Q2, 2004Q4, 2009Q1. The Bai-Perron test also indicates a break for SR in 2004Q4.

In the above Chow breakpoint tests, the number of observations in the post-break subsample (T_2) is larger than the number of parameters k. However, when the latter is larger than the former, there are not enough degrees of freedom for estimation and we need to use the Chow forecast test, as discussed in Section 2.5.2.

Variable	Coefficient	Std. Error	t-Statistic	Prob.
1985Q1 - 1989Q3 − 19obs				
C	0.963	0.139	6.940	0.000
IPR	0.045	0.117	0.382	0.703
SU	-0.019	0.027	-0.677	0.500
SR	-0.017	0.015	-1.147	0.254
1989Q4 - 1996Q1 − 26obs				
C	0.328	0.122	2.680	0.009
IPR	0.416	0.094	4.441	0.000
SU	0.012	0.012	0.989	0.325
SR	0.002	0.022	0.072	0.943
1996Q2 - 2000Q2 − 17obs				
C	1.005	0.251	4.001	0.000
IPR	0.185	0.165	1.121	0.265
SU	-0.076	0.040	-1.881	0.063
SR	-0.007	0.026	-0.274	0.785
2000Q3 - 2004Q3 − 17obs				
C	0.604	0.088	6.832	0.000
IPR	0.248	0.100	2.487	0.015
SU	0.017	0.022	0.757	0.451
SR	0.023	0.019	1.180	0.241
2004Q4 - 2008Q4 − 17obs				
C	0.397	0.094	4.227	0.000
IPR	0.045	0.099	0.456	0.650
SU	0.001	0.012	0.053	0.958
SR	0.077	0.018	4.327	0.000
2009Q1 - 2013Q4 − 20obs				
C	0.286	0.092	3.118	0.002
IPR	0.251	0.057	4.430	0.000
SU	0.004	0.014	0.283	0.778
SR	0.008	0.019	0.403	0.688

Table 2.9.18: *Bai-Perron breakpoint test*

Suppose we are interested in whether there is a breakpoint in 2012Q3, close to the end of our full sample. The results for the Chow forecast tests,

$CH(3)$ and $CH(4)$ appearing in equations (2.5.11) and (2.5.12), are respectively 0.704589 (p-value 0.6465) and 4.536486 (p=value 0.6045). Both of them suggest no rejection of the null of no break in 2012Q3, at the 5% significance level.

We can also examine a recursive residual plot, as shown in the top left panel of Figure 2.9.6. The plus and minus 2 times standard error bands are also plotted in the figure. Evidence of parameter instability is found in the case when the recursive residuals are outside the stand error bands. From the plot, there is evidence for possible parameter instability in the beginning of the 1990s, 2000Q1, 2004Q1, 2007Q2, and 2010Q3.

Next we compute the one-step forecast test (top right graph in Figure 2.9.6). The points shown in the bottom part of the plots indicate rejection of the null hypothesis of parameter stability at the 15% significance level. Using instead a 5% significance level, evidence of parameter instability can be detected in the same quarters spotted above, i.e., in the beginning of the 1990s, 2000Q1, 2004Q1, 2007Q2, and 2010Q3.

The last set of plots produces recursive coefficients. For all four coefficients we observe significant variation before 1990, with a rather stable behavior afterwards.

Dummy variables As discussed in Section 2.5, one way to accommodate structural breaks (and/or correct for outliers) is to include dummies in the model. Here we first illustrate the use of these dummies, and then we examine their impact on the forecast accuracy . We introduce dummy variables corresponding to the recent financial crisis (2007Q4 - 2009Q2), as well the early 2000s recession (2000Q1 - 2001Q4). We re-estimate Model 2 by adding these two dummies separately. Model 2.1 contains the independent variables in Model 2 plus the dummy for the financial crisis. Similarly, Model 2.2 consists of Model 2 plus the dummy for the early 2000s recession. They are:

$$Model\ 2.1:\ y_t = \alpha_0 + \beta_0 ipr_t + \gamma_0 su_t + \lambda_0 sr_t + \eta_0 d_t^{fincris} + \varepsilon_t$$

$$Model\ 2.2:\ y_t = \alpha_0 + \beta_0 ipr_t + \gamma_0 su_t + \lambda_0 sr_t + \eta_1 d_t^{2000s} + \varepsilon_t$$

The estimation output of these two models is omitted. The dummy variables are insignificant in both models, implying that the other explanatory variables seem sufficient to capture the drop in GDP growth in the two recessions.

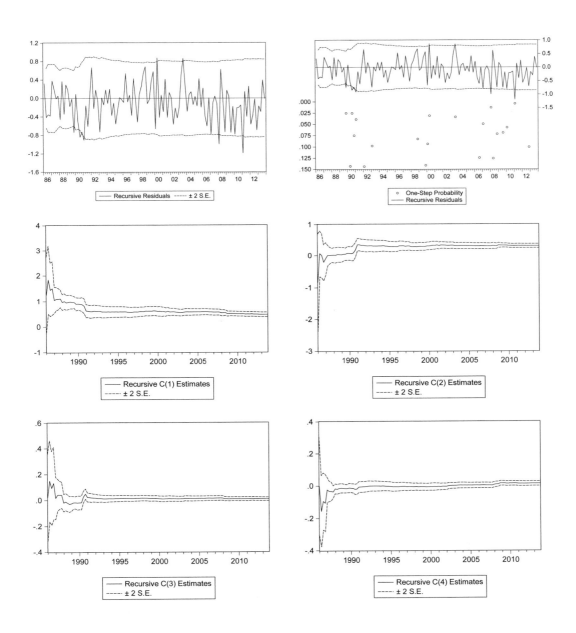

Figure 2.9.6: *Recursive estimation Model 2 for US GDP growth*

We now proceed and examine whether the inclusion of dummies can improve forecast accuracy. Note that our original estimation sample ends at 2006Q4, while the forecast evaluation period begins 2007Q1. In order to see the impact on forecast accuracy of the inclusion of the financial crisis dummy, we define the new estimation sample as 1985Q1 to 2010Q4, leaving the last 10 quarters between 2011Q1 and 2013Q2 as the new forecast evaluation period. Our forecasting model is simply Model 2 augmented with the dummies for the financial crisis, labeled as model 2.3 as in the previous example:

$$Model\ 2.3:\ y_t = \alpha_0 + \beta_0 ipr_t + \gamma_0 su_t + \lambda_0 sr_t + \eta_0 d_t^{EA\_cri} + \eta_1 d_t^{2000s} + \varepsilon_t$$

The estimation output (not reported) of Model 2.3 reveals that both dummy variables are insignificant. Yet, comparing Model 2 (cf. Table 2.9.14) with 2.3, it turns out that the latter has a better in-sample fit than Model 2, namely model 2.3 has larger values of R^2 and $\overline{R}^2$, and smaller values of AIC and HQ criteria.[9] Finally, also for this example we perform a one-step ahead recursive forecasting exercise, to see if there emerges any improvement in accuracy related to the use of the dummy variables. The evaluation statistics for the one-step ahead recursive forecasts and simple forecasts are presented in Table 2.9.19. Overall, there seems to be no major improvement in forecasting after the introduction of the dummy variables, although both RMSFE and MAFE decrease slightly

2.9.3   Default risk

We revisit the regression models estimated in the previous chapter using the sample from Jan. 1998 to Dec. 2015. In particular we estimate the following:

$$
\begin{aligned}
OAS_{t+1} &= \beta_0 + \beta_1 VIX_t + \varepsilon_{t+1}\\
OAS_{t+1} &= \beta_0 + \beta_1 SENT_t + \varepsilon_{t+1}\\
OAS_{t+1} &= \beta_0 + \beta_1 PMI_t + \varepsilon_{t+1}\\
OAS_{t+1} &= \beta_0 + \beta_1 sp500_t + \varepsilon_{t+1}\\
OAS_{t+1} &= \beta_0 + \beta_1 VIX_t + \beta_2 SENT_t + \beta_3 PMI_t + \beta_4 sp500_t + \varepsilon_{t+1}
\end{aligned}
$$

The Durbin-Watson statistics are respectively $DW_1 = 0.5660$, $DW_2 = 0.1219$, $DW_3 = 0.2390$, $DW_4 = 0.2634$, and $DW_5 = 0.7541$. Hence, in all cases

---

[9]The values for Model 2.3 are respectively: R^2 : 0.575632, Adjusted R^2 : 0.553980, Akaike IC: 1.118512 and Schwarz criterion: 1.271073.

	Model 2	Model 2.3
	Static Forecasts	
RMSFE	0.522	0.519
MAFE	0.422	0.419
	Recursive Forecasts	
RMSFE	0.531	0.528
MAFE	0.419	0.416

Table 2.9.19: *Forecast evaluation statistics from the simple forecast for Model 2 and for Model 2 with dummy variables and one-step ahead recursive forecasts of Model 2 and Model 2 with dummies*

the null of no autocorrelation is rejected. Similarly, when we look at the Breusch-Pagan-Godfrey test to check for the presence of heteroskedasticity we find: $BPG_1 = 58.60$, p-value ≈ 0, $BPG_2 = 17.90$, p-value $= 0.00002$, $BPG_3 = 24.76$, p-value ≈ 0, $BPG_4 = 7.65$, p-value $= 0.006$, $BPG_5 = 37.06$, p-value ≈ 0. This means that there is also evidence for the presence of heteroskedasticity.

Next, we construct a dummy variable D_t equal to one during the period Jan. 2008 until Dec. 2009 and estimate the regressions using the full sample of data ending in 2015:

$$OAS_{t+1} = \beta_0 + \beta_1 VIX_t + \beta_2 D_t + \varepsilon_{t+1}$$
$$OAS_{t+1} = \beta_0 + \beta_1 SENT_t + \beta_2 D_t + \varepsilon_{t+1}$$
$$OAS_{t+1} = \beta_0 + \beta_1 PMI_t + \beta_2 D_t + \varepsilon_{t+1}$$
$$OAS_{t+1} = \beta_0 + \beta_1 sp500_t + \beta_2 D_t + \varepsilon_{t+1}$$

and

$$OAS_{t+1} = \beta_0 + \beta_1 VIX_t + \beta_2 D_t + \beta_3 VIX_t \times D_t + \varepsilon_{t+1}$$
$$OAS_{t+1} = \beta_0 + \beta_1 SENT_t + \beta_2 D_t + \beta_3 SENT_t \times D_t + \varepsilon_{t+1}$$
$$OAS_{t+1} = \beta_0 + \beta_1 PMI_t + \beta_2 D_t + \beta_3 PMI_t \times D_t + \varepsilon_{t+1}$$
$$OAS_{t+1} = \beta_0 + \beta_1 sp500_t + \beta_2 D_t + \beta_3 sp500_t \times D_t + \varepsilon_{t+1}$$

The results appear in Tables 2.9.20 and 2.9.21. The results are easy to summarize, as the parameter estimates associated with the dummy variables

Models 1 - 4	Coefficient	t-Statistic	Prob.	R^2	Adjusted R^2
C	0.7544	2.586	0.01		
	(0.2918) [0.7355]	[1.026]	[0.31]		
VIX(-1)	0.233	17.082	0.00	0.73	0.73
	(0.0137) [0.0404]	[5.784]	[0.00]		
DUMMY	2.6355	7.493	0.00		
	(0.3517) [1.0737]	[2.455]	[0.01]		
C	8.2971	7.126	0.00		
	(1.1643) [2.0298]	[4.088]	[0.00]		
SENT(-1)	-0.0327	-2.505	0.01	0.39	0.38
	(0.0131) [0.0256]	[-1.281]	[0.20]		
DUMMY	4.6191	8.185	0.00		
	(0.5643) [2.9572]	[1.562]	[0.12]		
C	21.2224	15.121	0.00		
	(1.4035) [3.3970]	[6.247]	[0.00]		
PMI(-1)	-0.2991	-11.315	0.00	0.61	0.60
	(0.0264) [0.0639]	[-4.678]	[0.00]		
DUMMY	3.3139	7.846	0.00		
	(0.4223) [1.1226]	[2.952]	[0.00]		
C	5.5208	36.435	0.00		
	(0.1515) [0.4189]	[13.179]	[0.00]		
SP500(-1)	-0.1808	-5.568	0.00	0.45	0.45
	(0.0320) [0.0609]	[-2.966]	[0.00]		
DUMMY	5.1032	11.285	0.00		
	(0.4522) [2.7140]	[1.880]	[0.06]		

Table 2.9.20: *Default risk models augmented with dummies – Intercept. Square brackets are HAC estimator corrected standard errors and t-statistics using pre-whitening (1 lag) and Newey-West estimator (12 lags)*

are highly significant. Hence, the crisis period indicators are relevant in explaining the changes in OAS. Using the Chow test and January 2008 as a potential break point, the null hypothesis of no structural break is also rejected for all model specifications.

Facing the fact that the errors feature autocorrelation and heteroskedas-

Models 1 - 4	Coefficient	t-Statistic	Prob.	R^2	Adjusted R^2
C	1.6136	5.142	0.00		
	(0.3138) [0.6596]	[2.446]	[0.02]		
VIX(-1)	0.1904	12.725	0.00	0.77	0.77
	(0.0150) [0.0379]	[5.017]	[0.00]		
DUMMY	-1.9445	-2.192	0.03		
	(0.8870) [1.2098]	[-1.607]	[0.11]		
VIX(-1) × DUMMY	0.160	5.561	0.00		
	(0.0289) [0.0425]	[3.773]	[0.00]		
C	7.2609	6.497	0.00		
	(1.1175) [1.8078]	[4.017]	[0.00]		
SENT(-1)	-0.0210	-1.674	0.10	0.46	0.45
	(0.0125) [0.0213]	[-0.986]	[0.33]		
DUMMY	28.2095	6.144	0.00		
	(4.5911) [10.750]	[2.624]	[0.01]		
SENT(-1) × DUMMY	-0.3587	-5.173	0.00		
	(0.0693) [0.1468]	[-2.443]	[0.02]		
C	17.0234	11.028	0.00		
	(1.5436) [3.0382]	[5.603]	[0.00]		
PMI(-1)	-0.2197	-7.548	0	0.65	0.65
	(0.0291) [0.0549]	[-4.003]	[0.00]		
DUMMY	17.4956	6.435	0.00		
	(2.7187) [4.7411]	[3.690]	[0.00]		
PMI(-1) × DUMMY	-0.2966	-5.273	0.00		
	(0.0563) [0.0911]	[-3.255]	[0.00]		
C	5.4843	36.876	0.00		
	(0.1487) [0.5109]	[10.734]	[0.00]		
SP500(-1)	-0.1226	-3.393	0.00	0.48	0.47
	(0.0361) [0.0405]	[-3.024]	[0.00]		
DUMMY	4.9813	11.215	0.00		
	(0.4441) [1.8399]	[2.707]	[0.01]		
SP500(-1) × DUMMY	-0.2321	-3.218	0.00		
	(0.0721) [0.0927]	[-2.505]	[0.01]		

Table 2.9.21: *Default risk models augmented with dummies – Slope. Square brackets are HAC estimator corrected standard errors and t-statistics using pre-whitening (1 lag) and Newey-West estimator (12 lags).*

ticity, we should be worried about the standard errors – and therefore t-statistics reported in Tables 2.9.20 and 2.9.21. There are in fact two sets of standard errors and t-statistics reported in both tables, namely the OLS ones in curly brackets and those obtained with a HAC variance estimator (recall discussion in Section 2.3). Since the Durbin-Watson statistics suggest that the temporal dependence might be persistent (given the values close to zero for the statistic), it is often recommended to use a mixture of parametric models and HAC estimators to obtain better estimates of $\hat{V}_T$ (see Section 6.3 for further discussion). The standard errors and t-statistics reported in Tables 2.9.20 and 2.9.21 are based on pre-whitening (1 lag) and Newey-West estimator (12 lags). With the modified statistics, we do observe some differences in Table 2.9.20. It appears that the sentiment index is no longer significant, nor is the dummy in Model 2. The latter is also the case with the Model 4 dummy. Looking at the results in Table 2.9.21 we see that the sentiment index does become significant during the financial crisis, i.e., the interaction dummy with the sentiment index remains significant with the HAC corrected standard errors, although the index itself is insignificant.

2.10   Concluding remarks

Model mis-specification tests are a key ingredient in the formulation of forecasting models. In this chapter we reviewed a battery of tests that are commonly applied in a regression setting, together with possible remedies, such as the use of dummy variables. One has to keep in mind that many of the tests and remedies discussed in this chapter also apply to more complex models - such as those studied in later chapters of this book.

Chapter 3

The Dynamic Linear Regression Model

3.1 Introduction

In the previous chapters we have considered forecasting with the linear regression model, mostly assuming that past values of the endogenous and exogenous variables are not relevant regressors. However, due to the sluggish adjustment of most macroeconomic variables, often the past provides useful information about the future. Hence, we will now analyze forecasting with the dynamic linear regression model.

The chapter is structured as follows. In Section 3.2 we provide a classification of dynamic models and briefly describe their economic rationale. In Section 3.3 we discuss estimation and testing. Section 3.4 deals with specification issues. Section 3.5 presents forecasting in the context of the dynamic linear regression model. Section 3.6 illustrates the techniques using simulated data and Section 3.7 using actual data. Concluding remarks appear in Section 3.8.

Additional details on the topics covered in this chapter can be found, e.g., in Hendry (1995), Stock and Watson (2009), Wooldridge (2012), among others.

3.2   Types of dynamic linear regression models

Dynamic linear models are a particularly relevant class of econometric models, where the entire set of regressors is allowed to have a time dependent structure. Many economic phenomena can be described through a dynamic linear regression model. Notable examples are consumption patterns characterized by micro consumer behavior or staggered wage-setting from the macro side. Moreover, optimal monetary policy rules implemented by central banks imply that the target interest rate has to be adjusted gradually, resulting into a positive correlation between interest rates at different points in time. Similarly, aggregate macro variables like consumption and investment are generally quite persistent, and financial variables like share prices are generally best described by their past behavior. In what follows, we will try to provide a basic taxonomy of dynamic linear models, before dealing with estimation, inference, and diagnostics issues.

The most general specification for a dynamic linear model is the autoregressive distributed lags model (ARDL). In the ARDL(p,q) model the dependent variable, y, is allowed to depend on p lags of itself $(y_{t-1}, \dots, y_{t-p})$, the autoregressive component, and q lags of the regressors x_t $(x_{t-1}, \dots, x_{t-q})$, the distributed lag component. The simplest specification is the ARDL(1,1) model with a single explanatory variable:

$$y_t = \beta_0 + \beta_1 x_t + \beta_2 x_{t-1} + \alpha_1 y_{t-1} + \varepsilon_t, \qquad \varepsilon_t \overset{iid}{\sim} (0, \sigma_\varepsilon^2). \qquad (3.2.1)$$

Now we will consider a variety of commonly used models that originate from (3.2.1) once some restrictions are imposed on the model parameters. Generalizations to higher order dynamics and more explanatory variables are straightforward, see e.g., Hendry (1995) for more details.

$$\textit{Static regression: } \alpha_1 = \beta_2 = 0 \implies y_t = \beta_0 + \beta_1 x_t + \varepsilon_t \qquad (3.2.2)$$

This is the simplest type of interaction that we can see in economics, but clearly it can only be used when the relationship between the dependent and independent variable is static, as in most of the cases we saw in the previous chapters. There are many economic models formulated by means of static equations, such as the Keynesian consumption function or the entire structure of the IS-LM model. Additional examples are the Purchasing Power

Parity (PPP) relationship or some of the no arbitrage conditions for financial markets. Basically, the majority of static equations in economic theory are long-run relationships, while the short-run adjustment process towards these long-run equilibria is always more cumbersome to model and it generally requires the specification of a dynamic model.

It is important to note that if the restrictions in equation (3.2.2) are violated, and in particular if $\alpha_1 \neq 0$, then we are omitting a relevant lagged regressor, resulting into residual autocorrelation and possibly also heteroskedasticty and non-normality.

$$AR(1) \; model: \; \beta_1 = \beta_2 = 0 \Rightarrow y_t = \beta_0 + \alpha_1 y_{t-1} + \varepsilon_t \qquad (3.2.3)$$

In the autoregressive model of order one $(AR(1))$ the variability of the dependent variable y is explained by its lagged value only. This is the simplest example of a time series model, whose thorough study appears in the second part of the book. A notable example of an $AR(1)$ model is generated by some theories of efficient capital markets: if this assumption holds, then the price of a financial asset at time t must be equal to its price at time $t-1$ plus an error. This amounts to setting $\alpha = 1$ in equation (3.2.3), yielding what is typically called a random walk model:

$$Random \; walk \; model: \; \beta_i = 0, i = 0, 1, 2 \; \alpha_1 = 1 \Rightarrow y_t = y_{t-1} + \varepsilon_t \qquad (3.2.4)$$

We will see in the second part of the book that the restriction $\alpha_1 = 1$ plays a crucial role in time series models, as it completely changes the dynamic behavior of the dependent variable and the properties of standard estimation and testing methods.

$$Differenced \; model: \; \alpha_1 = 1, \; \beta_1 = -\beta_2 \Rightarrow \Delta y_t = \beta_0 + \beta_1 \Delta x_t + \varepsilon_t \qquad (3.2.5)$$

In the model in first differences, where $\Delta y_t = y_t - y_{t-1}$ and $\Delta x_t = x_t - x_{t-1}$, it is the change in y at time t to be explained by the change in x. This formulation has many applications in economics, as there are many variables displaying trending behavior and using model (3.2.5) allows to net out the effects of such trends. Furthermore, since for logarithmic variables the first difference in general approximates well the growth rate of the variable itself (when growth is small to modest), the model (3.2.5) is useful to explain relationships like the one linking the growth rate of consumption to the growth rate of disposable income.

Leading indicator model: $\alpha_1 = \beta_1 = 0 \Rightarrow y_t = \beta_0 + \beta_2 x_{t-1} + \varepsilon_t$ (3.2.6)

The leading indicator model is based on the assumption that the regressor x is a leading indicator for y, and that at time t it is more readily available than y itself. As an example, if our goal is to predict the GDP growth rate we could use an index of consumers confidence or an interest rate spread as leading indicators. Both of them generally fall during a recession and increase during an expansion, helping to predict the business cycle turning points and also GDP growth, and are more timely available than GDP itself. Another example of a leading indicator for GDP growth can be a commodity price index, which can signal in advance the arrival of supply shocks.

Distributed lag model: $\alpha_1 = 0 \Rightarrow y_t = \beta_0 + \beta_1 x_t + \beta_2 x_{t-1} + \varepsilon_t$ (3.2.7)

The distributed lag (DL) model has been widely used in the literature since it enables capturing the effect of adjustment costs and other types of frictions that typically also have a dynamic structure and do not impact only instantaneously on y.

A useful generalization of model (3.2.7) consists in introducing a (possibly) infinite number of lags for the independent variable. For example, the geometric distributed lags model (GDL) has the following specification:

$$
\begin{aligned}
y_t &= \alpha + \beta(x_t + \omega x_{t-1} + \omega^2 x_{t-2+\dots}) + \varepsilon_t \qquad 0 < \omega < 1, \quad (3.2.8) \\
&= \alpha + \beta \sum_{i=0}^{\infty} \omega^i x_{t-i} + \varepsilon_t.
\end{aligned}
$$

Here we have an exponential decay structure of the weights, and the long-run multiplier for the effect of a change in x on y amounts to $\beta \sum_0^{\infty} \omega^i = \beta/(1 - \omega)$. Consequently, the closer is ω to one, the greater the difference between the long-run multiplier and the impact multiplier β. The mean lag response instead is calculated as

$$
Mean\ lag = \frac{\sum_0^{\infty} i\beta\omega^i}{\sum_0^{\infty} \beta\omega^i} = \frac{\omega/(1 - \omega)^2}{1/1 - \omega} = \frac{\omega}{1 - \omega}.
$$

If, for example, $\omega = 0.5$ then mean lag equals one, implying that half of the total change induced in y by a change in x occurs in the first period after the change in x.

The GDL model (3.2.8) can also be rewritten as:

$$y_t - \omega y_{t-1} = \alpha(1 - \omega) + \beta x_t + \varepsilon_t \quad \varepsilon_t = \varepsilon_t - \omega \varepsilon_{t-1} \quad (3.2.9)$$

Hence, if we set $\beta = \beta_0$ and $\omega = \alpha_1$ then (3.2.9) becomes a special case of model ARDL(1,1) in equation (3.2.1). We will see in Chapter 12 that DL models play an important role for modeling mixed frequency data.

Partial adjustment model: $\beta_2 = 0 \Rightarrow y_t = \beta_0 + \beta_1 x_t + \alpha_1 y_{t-1} + \varepsilon_t$ (3.2.10)

The partial adjustment model takes its name from the procedure which enables to derive it. Let us suppose that y has a target level, indicated by y^* and given by

$$y_t^* = \alpha' + \beta' x_t + \varepsilon_t', \quad (3.2.11)$$

where y_t^* could be for example the baseline interest rate set by the central bank, or the profit maximizing level of production for a given firm. We assume that y cannot be instantaneously modified to reach the target y_t^* due to technical reasons or transaction costs. We then have

$$y_t - y_{t-1} = \gamma(y_t^* - y_{t-1}) \quad 0 < \gamma < 1. \quad (3.2.12)$$

The closer γ is to 1, the faster the adjustment of y_t to y_t^*. Moreover, if we substitute (3.2.11) in (3.2.12) we obtain

$$y_t = \underbrace{\gamma\alpha'}_{\beta_0} + \underbrace{\gamma\beta'}_{\beta_1} x_t + \underbrace{(1 - \gamma)}_{\alpha_1} y_{t-1} + \underbrace{\gamma\varepsilon'}_{\varepsilon_t}, \quad (3.2.13)$$

which is a specification similar to (3.2.9).

Error correction model $\beta_1 + \beta_2 + \alpha_1 = 1 \Rightarrow$
$$\Delta y_t = \beta_0 + \beta_1 \Delta x_t + (1 - \alpha_1)(y_{t-1} - x_{t-1}) + \varepsilon_t \quad (3.2.14)$$

The Error Correction Model (ECM) is a widely used specification in modern econometrics as it allows to describe the dynamic behavior of many economic relationships, and it will be described in greater details later on, in Chapter 7. The intuition behind it is that in the long-run y and x are moving together, so that deviations of y from x cannot persist over time and will gradually be evaporate. As a consequence, y, and possibly also x, change not only due to changes in the exogenous variable x but also as a consequence of changes in the deviations from the long-run equilibrium $y - x$. For example, if y represents a short term interest rate and x a long term one, in the long run the spread should be constant, but in the short run there can be deviations due to the shocks hitting the economy.

$$\text{Dead start model: } \beta_1 = 0 \Rightarrow y_t = \beta_0 + \beta_2 x_{t-1} + \alpha_1 y_{t-1} + \varepsilon_t \qquad (3.2.15)$$

In the dead start model the independent variable x has no contemporaneous effects on y. If we model the dynamics of x as

$$x_t = \gamma_0 + \gamma_1 x_{t-1} + \alpha_2 y_{t-1} + v_t, \qquad (3.2.16)$$

then the two equations (3.2.15) and (3.2.16) considered jointly give rise to the so called Vector Autoregressive (VAR) model, which is the multivariate equivalent of the autoregressive model (3.2.3), is well known in modern econometrics, and will be analyzed in details in Chapters 6 and 8.

$$\text{Autoregressive errors model:}$$
$$\alpha_1 \beta_1 + \beta_2 = 0 \Rightarrow y_t = \gamma_0 + \beta_1 x_t + u_t, u_t = \alpha_1 u_{t-1} + \varepsilon_t \qquad (3.2.17)$$

The autoregressive errors model is a special case of an AD(1,1) model with a non-linear restriction on the parameters, which is commonly know as a Common Factor Restriction (COMFAC), namely $\alpha_1 \beta_1 + \beta_2 = 0$. This is a model that we have considered in some details in Chapter 2, when discussing of serial correlation in the errors and possible remedies for it. If one estimates a static model and there is evidence of some error autocorrelation, it is advisable not to use a static model with correlated errors and instead to extend the model by means of a dynamic (ARDL-type) specification, unless the COMFAC restriction holds. In fact, if the COMFAC restriction does not hold, which is empirically often the case, the parameter estimators in the static model with AR errors are biased and inconsistent. Instead, the parameter estimators in the AD(1,1) model remain unbiased and consistent even though the COMFAC restriction holds, though they are less efficient than those resulting from estimating the, in this case, proper model in (3.2.17).

3.3   Estimation and testing

As a first step for the estimation of dynamic models, we need to discuss the conditions under which the OLS estimator remains valid. We already know from Chapter 1 that a requirement for the OLS estimator to be BLUE is that the independent variables and the errors are independent or at least uncorrelated: Will this assumption still hold in dynamic linear models? Intuitively, the answer seems to be negative, since lagged values of the dependent variable now appear among the regressors.

Let us analyze this issue in greater details. Consider the AR(1) model for simplicity:

$$y_t = \alpha_1 y_{t-1} + \varepsilon_t. \tag{3.3.1}$$

By substituting for y_{t-1} we obtain:

$$y_t = \alpha_1^2 y_{t-2} + \alpha_1 \varepsilon_{t-1} + \varepsilon_t.$$

By iterating this backward substitution we have:

$$y_t = \varepsilon_t + \alpha_1 \varepsilon_{t-1} + \alpha_1^2 \varepsilon_{t-2} + \alpha_1^3 \varepsilon_{t-3} + \dots$$

By defining $x_t = (y_{t-1}, y_{t-2}, y_{t-3}, \dots)'$ and $e_t = (\varepsilon_t, \varepsilon_{t-1}, \varepsilon_{t-2}, \dots)'$, it is evident that x_t and e_t are not independent. Hence, in general, the OLS estimator will be biased.

However, it is possible to show that if the errors of the dynamic model are uncorrelated, then the OLS estimator for the parameters of the dynamic model remains consistent and asymptotically normal. On the other hand, when the errors are correlated and the lagged dependent variable appears among the regressors, the conditions for consistency of the OLS estimator are violated.

For example, let us consider the AR(1) model (3.3.1) and assume that the errors evolve according to:

$$\varepsilon_t = e_t - \omega e_{t-1}. \tag{3.3.2}$$

where e_t is $\overset{iid}{\sim} (0, \sigma_e^2)$. In this case y_{t-1} is correlated with ε_{t-1}, hence we need to find some valid instruments for y_{t-1} and use an instrumental variable (IV) estimator (as introduced in Chapter 2), which will be consistent for the model parameters.

After proper parameter estimators are available, inference can be carried out by means of t or F statistics. Strictly speaking, these statistics only have an asymptotic justification, related to the limiting normal distribution of the OLS estimators. Hence, rather than using their finite sample $t-$ and $F-$distributions, it is better to rely on their asymptotic distribution. For example, for testing q hypotheses on the model parameters, instead of using an $F-$statistic we should use $qF \underset{H_0}{\overset{a}{\sim}} \chi^2(q)$.[1]

3.4 Model specification

Model specification is similar to the problem of variable selection in the context of the linear regression model, examined in Chapter 1.

Hypothesis testing can be applied for model specification in what is called a general to specific specification search. Hypothesis tests can be sequentially applied to verify whether subsequent lags are significant. For example, starting with an ARDL(p,p) model, it is possible to test whether y_{t-p} and x_{t-p} are both insignificant (their associated coefficients are not statistically different from zero). If the null is not rejected, then one considers an ARDL(p-1,p-1) model and tests the significance of y_{t-p+1} and x_{t-p+1}. The tests stop when one finally rejects the null.

In order to find the initial lag length p, a few considerations are useful. If p is too high with respect to the "true" data generating process, there will be multicollinearity problems among the regressors and loss of efficiency in the estimates. On the other hand, if p is lower than in the "true" data generating process, the estimates will be inconsistent. A criterion to select p could be based on the data frequency, e.g., $p = 4$ for quarterly data and $p = 12$ for monthly data, combined with a check for no mis-specification of the initial ARDL(p,p) model.

As discussed in Chapter 1, it is important to stress that the iterative procedures involved in sequential testing are statistically quite complex, since the statistics used in the different steps are correlated, which makes it difficult to evaluate their overall size and power. Hence, they need to be used with caution, being an empirical short-cut rather than a rigorously formalized procedure. An automated procedure based on shrinkage, such as LASSO or

---

[1]We refer the reader to standard econometric textbooks such as Hendry (1995), Stock and Watson (2009), Wooldridge (2012), for further discussion.

LARS, could also be applied in this context, in particular when the starting model has a large number of regressors, see again Chapter 1.

An alternative approach to model selection is based on information criteria (IC). Information criteria combine a measure of the model goodness of fit with a penalty accounting for the number of parameters. A general form for an information criterion is

$$\log(\sigma^2) + g(k, T), \tag{3.4.1}$$

where σ^2 is (an estimator of) the model error variance and $g(k, T)$ is a function of the number of parameters (k) and observations (T). Adding more parameters improves the model fit but is penalized because it decreases efficiency. Hence, in the case of the ARDL(p,p) model, one should compute an IC for any value $j = 1, \ldots, p$ and select the value j^* that minimizes the IC, so as to find a good compromise between goodness of fit and parsimony.

The most widely used information criteria are:

$$\begin{array}{ll} \text{Akaike information criterion (AIC):} & g(k, T) = 2k/T \\ \text{Schwarz information criterion (BIC):} & g(k, T) = k\log(T)/T \\ \text{Hannan-Quinn information criterion (HQ):} & g(k, T) = 2k\log\log(T)/T \end{array}$$

It can be shown that, under rather mild conditions, some of these criteria select the correct model with probability approaching one when T goes to infinity.[2] This is true for example for the BIC and HQ, but not for AIC. However, it is not possible to provide a uniformly valid ranking for the appropriateness of these criteria in finite samples, so that in applications a comparison of alternative IC can be useful. See Lütkepohl (2007) for additional details and derivations.

Finally, also within the dynamic linear regression modeling framework, it is crucial to verify that the hypotheses underlying the model hold. Diagnostic tests on the estimated errors, like those we have discussed in the context of the linear regression model for the hypotheses of no autocorrelation, homoskedasticity, linearity, and normality, are still applicable in this more general context, though they only have an asymptotic justification. However, the Durbin-Watson test should not be used, since it only applies to static specifications. Furthermore, parameter stability tests and the formulation of the dummy variables also need to be properly modified to account for

---

[2]The Schwarz information criterion is sometimes referred to as SC, or SIC. Most often it is called BIC because of its roots in Bayesian analysis.

the dynamic structure. For example, in an AR(1) model an impulse dummy that takes the value of 1 in period t and zero elsewhere will have an impact not only on y_t but also on y_{t+1} and all subsequent periods (though generally decreasing over time), contrary to the effects in a static model that are limited to period t.

3.5   Forecasting with dynamic models

Let us illustrate forecasting with dynamic models using the ARDL(1,1) specification:

$$y_t = \beta_0 x_t + \beta_1 x_{t-1} + \alpha_1 y_{t-1} + \varepsilon_t, \qquad \varepsilon_t \overset{iid}{\sim} (0, \sigma_\varepsilon^2).$$

To start with, we make the additional assumption that $\alpha_1 = 0$, so that the model simplifies to ARDL(0,1):

$$y_t = \beta_0 x_t + \beta_1 x_{t-1} + \varepsilon_t.$$

If we now group x_t and x_{t-1} into $z_t = (x_t, x_{t-1})$ and the parameters into $\beta = (\beta_0, \beta_1)'$, we can rewrite the model as

$$y_t = z_t \beta + \varepsilon_t.$$

At this point, we can use exactly the same reasoning as in the linear regression model of Chapter 1 to show that the optimal (in the MSFE sense) forecast for y_{T+h} is

$$\hat{y}_{T+h} = z_{T+h}\hat{\beta}, \tag{3.5.1}$$

where $\hat{\beta}$ is the OLS estimator of β. If the future values z_{T+h} are unknown, they too should be replaced by forecasts.

Let us now add y_{t-1} back, and write the ARDL(1,1) model as

$$y_t = z_t \beta + \alpha_1 y_{t-1} + \varepsilon_t.$$

The optimal one-step ahead forecast is simply

$$\hat{y}_{T+1} = z_{T+1}\hat{\beta} + \widehat{\alpha}_1 y_T.$$

For the two-steps ahead forecast, we would have

$$\hat{y}_{T+2} = z_{T+2}\hat{\beta} + \widehat{\alpha}_1 y_{T+1},$$

but y_{T+1} is unknown. Therefore, we replace it with its conditional expectation given all the available information up to period T, which coincides with $\hat{y}_{T+1}$. Hence, the optimal forecast for y_{T+2} is

$$\hat{y}_{T+2} = z_{T+2}\hat{\beta} + \hat{\alpha}_1\hat{y}_{T+1},$$

and the optimal h-steps ahead forecast is

$$\hat{y}_{T+h} = z_{T+h}\hat{\beta} + \hat{\alpha}_1\hat{y}_{T+h-1}. \tag{3.5.2}$$

The forecast error is

$$e_{T+h} = y_{T+h} - \hat{y}_{T+h}. \tag{3.5.3}$$

Assuming that both z_{T+h} and the parameters are known, so that there is not estimation uncertainty, we can write

$$e_{T+h} = \alpha_1(y_{T+h-1} - \hat{y}_{T+h-1}) + \varepsilon_{T+h} = \alpha_1 e_{T+h-1} + \varepsilon_{T+h}. \tag{3.5.4}$$

Therefore, the presence of an autoregressive component in the model creates correlation in the h-steps ahead forecast error. If in (3.5.4) we replace e_{T+h-1} with its expression we obtain

$$e_{T+h} = \alpha_1^2 e_{T+h-2} + \alpha_1 \varepsilon_{T+h-1} + \varepsilon_{T+h}.$$

Repeated substitution then yields

$$e_{T+h} = \alpha_1^{h-1}\varepsilon_{T+1} + ... + \alpha_1\varepsilon_{T+h-1} + \varepsilon_{T+h}, \tag{3.5.5}$$

since $e_{T+h} = 0$ for $h \leq 0$, which is an alternative representation for the dependence in e_{T+h}. We will see in Chapter 5 that the model in (3.5.5) is a moving average model of order $h - 1$, $MA(h - 1)$.

From (3.5.5) we can easily derive that

$$\begin{aligned} E(e_{T+h}) &= 0, \\ \text{Var}(e_{T+h}) &= (1 + \alpha_1^2 + ... + \alpha_1^{2(h-1)})\sigma_\varepsilon^2. \end{aligned}$$

If the parameters are unknown, as well as future values of the x, then the forecast error becomes

$$\begin{aligned} e_{T+h} &= (z_{T+h}\beta - \hat{z}_{T+h}\hat{\beta}) + (\alpha_1 y_{T+h-1} - \hat{\alpha}_1\hat{y}_{T+h-1}) + \varepsilon_{T+h} \\ &= z_{T+h}(\beta - \hat{\beta}) + (z_{T+h} - \hat{z}_{T+h})\hat{\beta} + (\alpha_1 - \hat{\alpha}_1)y_{T+h-1} \\ &\quad + \hat{\alpha}_1 e_{T+h-1} + \varepsilon_{T+h} \end{aligned} \tag{3.5.6}$$

The expression for the variance of the forecast error becomes more complex, see e.g., Lütkepohl (2007) for a precise derivation in a related context. Intuitively, the variance increases due to parameter estimation uncertainty, and uncertainty on the future values of the x. Note that there remains serial correlation in the forecast errors.

To conclude, if we make the additional assumption that the error terms ε_t are normally distributed, and the parameters and future values of x are known, then it follows that

$$\left(\frac{y_{T+h} - \hat{y}_{T+h}}{\sqrt{\mathrm{Var}(e_{T+h})}}\right) \sim N(0,1),$$

which implies

$$y_{T+h} \sim N(\hat{y}_{T+h}, \mathrm{Var}(e_{T+h})). \tag{3.5.7}$$

As in the context of the linear regression model, the latter expression can be used to compute density and interval forecasts of y_{T+h}. Parameter estimation and the use of forecasts for future unknown values of the x make the density more complex, but the formula above remains asymptotically valid, with a proper expression for $\mathrm{Var}(e_{T+h})$.

3.6   Examples with simulated data

The simulated data examples we considered in the first two chapters are based on the assumption that there are no lagged dependent variables, i.e., the model is static. But tests for no serial correlation rejected the null hypothesis, so that model re-specification is needed and the natural choice is to add lagged variables to the set of regressors. Hence, we now search for the best dynamic model specification, and build forecasts based on it, using the same dataset as in previous chapters.

We focus on the following set of equations:

$$\begin{aligned} y_t \quad &= \alpha_1 + \beta_1 D_t + \alpha_2 x_t + \beta_2 D_t x_t + \gamma_1^y y_{t-1} \\ &+ \ldots + \gamma_p^y y_{t-p} + \gamma_1^x x_{t-1} + \ldots + \gamma_m^x x_{t-m} + \varepsilon_t \end{aligned}$$

where $p = 0, 1, 2$ is the number of lags for y, and $m = 0, 1, 2$ is the number of lags of the independent variable x, so that the most general model for y is an ARDL(2,2). We also include the dummy variable, D_t, which is equal to 0 for observations from 101 to 201 and 1 otherwise. According to the analysis in Chapter 2 the dummy variable is significant. We estimate all the models and then select the specification with the lowest Akaike Information Criterion (AIC) and Schwarz Information Criterion (SC).

Table 3.6.1 sums up the information criteria for all the model specifications tested:

Model	AIC	Schwarz
DGP22	2.968	3.100
DGP12	2.959	3.075
DGP21	2.967	3.083
DGP11	2.958	3.057
DGP10	4.536	4.619
DGP01	5.906	5.989
DGP20	3.794	3.893
DGP02	4.950	5.049

Table 3.6.1: *Dynamic model: Model selection*

According to Table 3.6.1, the ARDL(1,1) is selected by both information criteria. This model actually coincides with our DGP:

$$y = \alpha_1 + \beta_1 D_t + \alpha_2 x_t + \beta_2 D_t x_t + \gamma_1^y y_{t-1} + \gamma_1^x x_{t-1} + \varepsilon_t$$

where $y = \ln(Y)$ from Chapter 1.

Table 3.6.2 presents the estimation output. All the coefficients are statistically significant (at the 1% confidence level). Also, we can not reject the hypothesis that each coefficient is equal to its actual value in the DGP, and the R^2, is equal to 99.9%, while the Durbin-Watson statistic indicates that there is no serial correlation in the residuals.

The final step of the analysis is forecasting, and as in the examples of the previous chapters we take 301 - 501 as the forecast sample. Since the model is dynamic, in this case static and dynamic forecasts will differ. The former are a set of one-step ahead forecasts, while the latter are forecasts for periods T+1 until T+h, where h =200. We also consider one-step ahead recursive forecasts, for the same forecast period. Table 3.6.3 compares the forecasting performance indicators for the two types of forecasts. In comparison to the forecast results in Chapter 2 we see a vast improvement. Also noteworthy is

	Coefficient	Std. Error	t-Statistic	Prob.
ALPHA(1)	1.030	0.109	9.408	0.000
BETA(1)	0.920	0.155	5.954	0.000
ALPHA(2)	0.969	0.018	54.381	0.000
BETA(2)	1.005	0.026	38.020	0.000
GAMMA-Y(1)	0.496	0.008	59.533	0.000
GAMMA-X(1)	0.494	0.018	27.499	0.000
R-squared	0.993	Mean dep var		6.695
Adjusted R-squared	0.993	S.D. dep var		12.560
S.E. of regression	1.046	Akaike IC		2.958
Sum squared resid	212.418	Schwarz IC		3.057
Log likelihood	-289.812	Hannan-Quinn		2.998
F-statistic	5695.113	DW stat		2.219
Prob(F-statistic)	0.000			

Table 3.6.2: *DGP model estimation*

	Forecasting Method	
	Static	*Recursive*
$RMSFE$	1.109	0.966
$MAFE$	0.865	0.761

Table 3.6.3: *One-step ahead ARDL(1,1) forecasting performance*

the fact that the S.E. of the regression reported in Table 3.6.2 is very close to the RMSFE reported in Table 3.6.3 – a consequence of the fact that the parameter estimates are extremely precise.

3.7   Empirical examples

Section 1.13 introduced a hint of dynamics by lagging the dependent variables. We now consider the rich class of dynamic regression models introduced in this chapter and re-examine the empirical examples studied in Chapter 1.

3.7.1 Forecasting Euro area GDP growth

The empirical examples using Euro-area GDP we considered in the previous chapters are based on simple linear regression without any lagged dependent or independent variables. If lagged variables have significant explanatory power but are excluded from the model, a likely impact will be that the omitted dynamics will appear in the errors that will be serially correlated as a result. Indeed, the tests we ran in the previous chapter rejected the null of serially uncorrelated errors. The inclusion of lagged variables helps capture the dynamics.

Variable	Coefficient	Std. Error	t-Statistic	Prob.
C	0.180	0.046	3.922	0.000
Y(-1)	0.287	0.116	2.473	0.016
IPR	0.261	0.034	7.696	0.000
IPR(-1)	-0.012	0.049	-0.250	0.803
SU	-0.009	0.017	-0.539	0.592
SU(-1)	-0.019	0.017	-1.115	0.269
SR	0.006	0.005	1.238	0.220
SR(-1)	0.007	0.005	1.384	0.171
R-squared	0.838	Mean dep var		0.350
Adjusted R-squared	0.820	S.D. dep var		0.629
S.E. of regression	0.267	Akaike IC		0.304
Sum squared resid	4.422	Schwarz IC		0.561
Log likelihood	-2.656	Hannan-Quinn		0.407
F-statistic	45.809	DW stat		2.138
Prob(F-statistic)	0.000			

Table 3.7.1: *ARDL Model 1*

We augment Model 2 presented in the previous empirical examples with lagged dependent and independent variables yielding ARDL-type models. We estimate two ARDL representations based on the indicator variables included in Model 2 using our full sample that covers 1996Q1 to 2013Q2. The first model, referred to as ARDL Model 1, includes the first lags of all variables, including the dependent variable. The results are presented in Table 3.7.1.

First of all, not all lagged terms included in the ARDL Model 1 are significant. Unlike its contemporaneous value, the lagged IP growth does not appear to have much explanatory power. The contemporaneous change of ESI also does not appear to be significant. We tried out a few alternative specifications based on reducing the ARDL Model 1, using information criteria to select the appropriate model. The outcome is ARDL Model 2, presented in Table 3.7.2, which includes the contemporaneous IP growth, the first lag of GDP growth, first lag of both the growth of ESI, and stock returns.

Variable	Coefficient	Std. Error	t-Statistic	Prob.
C	0.187	0.039	4.747	0.000
Y(-1)	0.273	0.065	4.174	0.000
IPR	0.262	0.027	9.827	0.000
SU(-1)	-0.025	0.012	-2.000	0.050
SR(-1)	0.008	0.005	1.673	0.099
R-squared	0.834	Mean dep var		0.350
Adjusted R-squared	0.823	S.D. dep var		0.629
S.E. of regression	0.264	Akaike IC		0.245
Sum squared resid	4.538	Schwarz IC		0.405
Log likelihood	-3.568	Hannan-Quinn		0.309
F-statistic	81.465	DW stat		2.099
Prob(F-statistic)	0.000			

Table 3.7.2: *ARDL Model 2*

The values of all information criteria reported in Table 3.7.2 are lower for the ARDL Model 2 compared to those for the ARDL Model 1 in Table 3.7.1. In addition, the $\overline{R}^2$ is slightly higher. This implies that the ARDL Model 2 has a better in-sample fit compared to the ARDL Model 1. This gain in a model fit is achieved by excluding from the model contemporaneous values of the change in ESI and the stock return, while still retaining the first lag of both variables. This, in turns, implies the lagged values of these two variables are more informative than their contemporaneous values. In fact, if we compare these results with those of Model 2 presented in Table 3.7.2, we can see the impact of the inclusion of dynamics into the model. There is not only an improvement of the model fit, but also an improvement in terms of capturing dynamics. The reported DW test statistics for testing first order serial correlation in both Tables 3.7.1 and 3.7.2 suggest that the null hypothesis of no serial correlation cannot be rejected. It means that inclusion of the lagged variables helps to capture dynamics that were present in the model errors without lagged terms, i.e., Model 2 in Chapter 2. Indeed, the Breusch-Godfrey serial correlation LM test results reported in Tables 3.7.3 and 3.7.4 show that the null hypothesis of no serial correlation up to order 2 cannot be rejected.

F-statistic	1.293	Prob. F(2,60)		0.282
Obs*R-squared	2.891	Prob. Chi-Square(2)		0.236
Variable	Coefficient	Std.Error	t-Statistic	Prob.
C	-0.103	0.093	-1.106	0.273
Y(-1)	0.384	0.325	1.184	0.241
IPR	-0.011	0.035	-0.325	0.747
IPR(-1)	-0.116	0.106	-1.094	0.279
SU	0.009	0.018	0.523	0.603
SU(-1)	0.007	0.018	0.389	0.699
SR	-0.001	0.005	-0.207	0.836
SR(-1)	-0.004	0.006	-0.650	0.518
RESID(-1)	-0.481	0.366	-1.315	0.193
RESID(-2)	0.004	0.164	0.022	0.982
R-squared	0.041	Mean dep var		0.000
Adjusted R-squared	-0.102	S.D. dep var		0.253
S.E. of regression	0.266	Akaike IC		0.319
Sum squared resid	4.239	Schwarz IC		0.641
Log likelihood	-1.180	Hannan-Quinn		0.447
F-statistic	0.287	DW stat		2.063
Prob(F-statistic)	0.976			

Table 3.7.3: *Breusch-Godfrey serial correlation LM test for ARDL Model 1*

Forecasting with dynamic models   To see whether accommodating dynamics in the model can improve predictive accuracy, we perform a forecasting exercise using the ARDL Model 2. In addition, we also include in the forecasting model the dummy variables we created for the example in Chapter 2, i.e., the dummies capturing the impact of the Euro area crisis and the early 2000s recession.

F-statistic	0.662	Prob. F(2,63)		0.519
Obs*R-squared	1.441	Prob. Chi-Square(2)		0.486
Variable	Coefficient	Std.Error	t-Statistic	Prob.
C	-0.005	0.042	-0.109	0.914
Y(-1)	0.012	0.075	0.154	0.878
IPR	-0.004	0.027	-0.155	0.877
SU(-1)	-0.002	0.013	-0.121	0.904
SR(-1)	0.000	0.005	0.036	0.971
RESID(-1)	-0.060	0.146	-0.409	0.684
RESID(-2)	0.135	0.134	1.002	0.320
R-squared	0.021	Mean dep var		0.000
AdjustedR-squared	-0.073	S.D. dep var		0.256
S.E. of regression	0.266	Akaike IC		0.281
Sum squared resid	4.445	Schwarz IC		0.506
Log likelihood	-2.840	Hannan-Quinn		0.370
F-statistic	0.221	DW stat		2.025
Prob(F-statistic)	0.969			

Table 3.7.4: *Breusch-Godfrey serial correlation LM test for ARDL Model 2*

We compare the forecast accuracy of this model against that of Model 2 and Model 2.3. The estimation sample we consider here is 1996Q1 to 2010Q4. The forecast evaluation period is therefore 2011Q1 to 2013Q2. We first re-estimate the ARDL Model 2 for this estimation period and in addition add the dummies as used in Model 2.3. Table 3.7.5 presents the estimation output for the ARDL Model 2 with those dummies, and note that there is evidence that the Euro crisis dummy matters again, judging by the *t* statistics.

Variable	Coefficient	Std. Error	t-Statistic	Prob.
C	0.333	0.055	6.049	0.000
Y(-1)	0.108	0.074	1.462	0.150
IPR	0.254	0.026	9.928	0.000
SU(-1)	-0.014	0.013	-1.062	0.293
SR(-1)	0.009	0.005	1.853	0.070
D_EA	-0.251	0.089	-2.828	0.007
D_2000S	0.101	0.096	1.046	0.300
R-squared	0.874	Mean dep var		0.414
Adjusted R-squared	0.860	S.D. dep var		0.644
S.E. of regression	0.241	Akaike IC		0.102
Sum squared resid	3.080	Schwarz IC		0.346
Log likelihood	3.942	Hannan-Quinn		0.198
F-statistic	61.369	DW stat		2.268
Prob(F-statistic)	0.000			

Table 3.7.5: *ARDL Model 2 with dummies*

	Model 2	Model 2 with dummies	ARDL Model 2 with dummies
		Static forecasts	
RMSFE	0.413	0.326	0.297
MAFE	0.376	0.248	0.236
		Recursive forecasts	
RMSFE	0.398	0.332	0.290
MAFE	0.363	0.256	0.236

Table 3.7.6: *Forecast evaluation statistics: 2011Q1 through 2013Q2*

	Model 2	Model 2 with dummies	ARDL Model 2 with dummies
		Static forecasts	
RMSFE	0.413	0.326	0.297
MAFE	0.376	0.248	0.236
		Recursive forecasts	
RMSFE	0.398	0.332	0.290
MAFE	0.363	0.256	0.236

Table 3.7.7: *Forecast evaluation statistics: 2011Q1 through 2013Q2*

Table 3.7.7 presents the forecast evaluation statistics of the three models. Comparing the ARDL Model 2 with dummies in Table 3.7.5 with Model 2 in Table 1.12.5, we note that the former has better in-sample fit as it has smaller values of information criteria, as well as (adjusted) R^2. The ARDL Model 2 is also preferred to Model 2.3 in Table 2.9.12 as two out of three reported information criteria of the former have smaller values, though the differences are small.

Table 3.7.7 shows the forecast evaluation statistics of these three models computed over the period 2011Q1 to 2013Q2, it is clear that the ARDL Model 2, having included the lagged terms, outperforms the other two models whether the forecasts are static or recursive. We also note that there is very little difference between static and recursive forecasts, at least for the ARDL Model 2 with dummies.

3.7.2   Forecasting US GDP growth

We estimate two alternative ARDL representations with dummy variables for Great Recession and the recession of the early 2000s based on the same indicator variables included in Model 1, using our full sample that covers 1985Q1 to 2013Q4. The first model, named ARDL Model 1, includes the first lags of all variables, including the dependent variable. The results are presented in Table 3.7.8. We can see that none of the lagged variables is significant, as well as dummy variables. However, as we will see the ARDL model will yield some gains in forecasting. Note also the considerable increase

Variable	Coefficient	Std.Error	t-Statistic	Prob.
C	0.498	0.074	6.694	0.000
Y(-1)	-0.033	0.098	-0.335	0.738
IPR	0.322	0.064	5.005	0.000
IPR(-1)	-0.020	0.057	-0.347	0.729
SU	0.006	0.007	0.832	0.407
SU(-1)	-0.010	0.007	-1.353	0.179
SR	0.010	0.008	1.217	0.226
SR(-1)	0.004	0.008	0.540	0.591
Dfincris	-0.309	0.276	-1.122	0.265
D2000s	0.069	0.170	0.408	0.684
R-squared	0.539	Mean dep var		0.657
Adjusted R-squared	0.500	S.D. dep var		0.600
S.E. of regression	0.424	Akaike IC		1.206
Sum squared resid	19.094	Schwarz IC		1.443
Log likelihood	-59.951	Hannan-Quinn		1.302
F-statistic	13.775	DW stat		1.943
Prob(F-statistic)	0.000			

Table 3.7.8: *Estimation output: ARDL Model 1 with dummy variables*

Variable	Coefficient	Std. Error	t-Statistic	Prob.
C	0.532	0.068	7.799	0.000
Y(-1)	-0.050	0.086	-0.577	0.565
IPR	0.308	0.054	5.668	0.000
SU(-1)	-0.011	0.007	-1.585	0.116
SR(-1)	0.007	0.008	0.848	0.399
Dfincris	-0.503	0.256	-1.967	0.052
D2000s	0.000	0.167	0.001	1.000
R-squared	0.521	Mean dep var		0.657
Adjusted R-squared	0.495	S.D. dep var		0.600
S.E. of regression	0.427	Akaike IC		1.192
Sum squared resid	19.833	Schwarz IC		1.359
Log likelihood	-62.156	Hannan-Quinn		1.260
F-statistic	19.777	DW stat		1.852
Prob(F-statistic)	0.000			

Table 3.7.9: *Estimation output: ARDL Model 2 with dummy variables*

in (adjusted) R^2 in comparison to Table 1.13.1, and the fact that the F-test for model non-significance strongly rejects the null hypothesis. This suggests that the outcome of the t-tests could be due to collinearity among the regressors.

The next step is to present a simplified version of Model 1, called ARDL Model 2 (see Table 3.7.9), which includes the contemporaneous IP growth, the first lag of GDP growth, the first lag of both the growth of CSI and stock returns. The estimation output shows that the dummy indicator for the Great Recession is significant while again none of the lagged variables are. Comparing the ARDL Models 1 and 2, the values of the AIC, SC, and HQ criteria are lower for the latter. At the same time the values of R^2 and $\overline{R}^2$ are modestly higher for Model 1. Hence, the ranking of the two models is not clear-cut. As an illustration, we will now continue our analysis with forecasting based on the ARDL Model 1, though the forecasts for the ARDL Model 2 are rather similar.

	Model 2 with dummies	Model 2 with dummies	ARDL Model 1
	Static Forecasts		
RMSFE	0.522	0.519	0.512
MAFE	0.422	0.419	0.397
	Recursive Forecasts		
RMSFE	0.531	0.528	0.520
MAFE	0.419	0.416	0.389

Table 3.7.10: *Forecast evaluations: 2011Q1 through 2013Q4*

Forecasting with dynamic models We compare the forecast accuracy of the ARDL Model 1 against Model 2 and Model 2.3 of Chapter 2. The estimation sample we consider here is 1985Q1 to 2010Q4, while the forecast evaluation period is 2011Q1 to 2013Q4. We first re-estimate ARDL Model 1 over this estimation period and then we compute the relevant forecast evaluation statistics. We consider forecasts generated by three different model specifications:

- ARDL Model 1 with dummies

- Model 2

- Model 2 with dummy variables

The forecasting evaluation results are reported in Table 3.7.10. In terms of RMSFE and MAFE, ARDL Model 1 with dummies shows the best forecasting performance, although the gains from adding lagged explanatory variables are minor. The upper panel covers static forecasts. We also investigate in the lower panel whether recursively updating the estimated parameters in the forecasting models can improve accuracy. The results show that ARDL Model 1 with dummies has better forecasting performance in the case of recursive forecasting as well. Yet, the gains are again rather modest compared to the models discussed in Chapter 2.

3.7.3   Default risk

In the third and final example we face a situation quite different from the previous case. The forecast gains resulting from including lagged dependent variables in forecasting models for US GDP growth were modest at best. With default risk the situation is quite different. Building further on the analysis in Chapter 1 we consider the following models:

- ARDL Model 1: $OAS_t = \alpha + \beta_1 \, OAS_{t-1} + \beta_2 \, VIX_{t-1} + \varepsilon_t$

- ARDL Model 2: $OAS_t = \alpha + \beta_1 \, OAS_{t-1} + \beta_2 \, SENT_{t-1} + \varepsilon_t$

- ARDL Model 3: $OAS_t = \alpha + \beta_1 \, OAS_{t-1} + \beta_2 \, PMI_{t-1} + \varepsilon_t$

- ARDL Model 4: $OAS_t = \alpha + \beta_1 \, OAS_{t-1} + \beta_2 \, SP500_{t-1} + \varepsilon_t$

We will call the models ARDL Models 1 – 4, by analogy with the labels used in Section 1.13. We re-estimate all the regressions again for the sample from Jan. 1998 to Dec. 2007 and produce forecasts out-of sample for the period Jan. 2008 until Dec. 2015. We then compute the in-sample regression statistics and the out-of-sample RMSFE for each of the regression models. The results are reported in Table 3.7.11. We observe vast improvements in model fit. For example, the R^2 more than quadruples in ARDL Models 2 and 4, involving respectively $SENT_t$ and $SP500_t$, in comparison to the findings reported in Tables 1.13.4 and 1.13.6. The other two models feature less dramatic, but nevertheless substantial improvements. Model 4 has the highest adjusted R^2, the lowest BIC, and the lowest Hannan-Quinn IC. Therefore, Model 4 presents the best in-sample fit. Yet, Model 3, based on PMI appears the have the best out-of-sample RMSFE. An important observation to make is that the parameter estimates for the lagged dependent regressors are quite close to one. A more subtle observation is that the Durbin-Watson statistics for the models reported in section 1.13 are all close to zero. All of this may lead us to think about using a differenced model appearing in equation (3.2.5) for the purpose of inference. This is a topic which will be addressed in Chapter 5.

3.8   Concluding remarks

The dynamic regression models discussed in this chapter lead naturally to time series models which will be discussed starting with Chapter 5. Many

ARDL Models 1-4	Coefficient	Std Error	t-Stat	R^2	RMSFE static	BIC	HQIC
C	-0.108	0.200	-0.540				
OAS(-1)	0.856	0.039	21.743	0.93	0.559	408.27	398.01
VIX(-1)	0.046	0.015	3.106				
C	0.179	0.647	0.782				
OAS(-1)	0.959	0.027	35.287	0.92	0.541	417.77	407.51
SENT(-1)	0.001	0.006	0.171				
C	0.970	1.142	0.850				
OAS(-1)	0.942	0.033	28.346	0.92	0.537	417.43	407.17
PMI(-1)	0.019	-0.002	-0.605				
C	0.517	0.148	3.499				
OAS(-1)	0.923	0.021	43.934	0.94	0.609	383.75	373.49
SP500(-1)	-0.085	0.014	-6.111				

Table 3.7.11: *Default risk models: In-sample and out-of-sample results*

econometric models involve lagged dependent variables, either because they appear to be better at forecasting or economic theory suggests a dynamic relationship. It is therefore a key topic of interest explored in this chapter.

Chapter 4

Forecast Evaluation and Combination

4.1 Introduction

In the previous three chapters we have discussed how to obtain forecasts from various types of linear regression models, possibly based on different information sets and different selections of indicators. In the next chapters we will consider forecasting using even more sophisticated models. And there are also a variety of alternative forecasts available, e.g., those produced by private banks, central banks, governments, and international organizations. Often all of these forecasts have the same target variable, e.g., GDP growth or inflation in a given country, or sales for a particular company.

Given this abundance of competing forecasts, in this chapter we try to answer the following questions:

(i) How "good," in some sense, is a particular set of forecasts?

(ii) Is one set of forecasts better than another one?

(iii) Is it possible to get a better forecast as a combination of various forecasts for the same variable?

To address (i) we define some key properties a good forecast should have and discuss how to test them. For (ii) we introduce some basic statistics to assess whether one forecast is equivalent or better than another with respect

145

to a given criterion (generally, the MSFE). For (iii) we discuss how to combine the forecasts and why the resulting pooled forecast can be expected to perform well.

These topics have been extensively studied in the econometrics literature. More details can be found, e.g., in Clements and Hendry (1998) about forecast evaluation, in Clark and McCracken (2013) about forecast comparison, and in Timmermann (2006) about forecast combination. Elliott and Timmermann (2016) provide a more rigorous and exhaustive treatment of these topics.

The chapter is structured as follows. In Section 4.2 we discuss forecast unbiasedness and efficiency, and the related testing procedures. In Section 4.3 we focus on fixed event forecasts. In Section 4.4 we introduce tests for predictive accuracy and in Section 4.5 forecast comparison tests. In Section 4.6 we consider forecast combination and in Section 4.7 forecast encompassing. Section 4.8 deals briefly with the evaluation, comparison and combination of density forecasts. Sections 4.9 and 4.10 present examples based on, respectively, simulated and actual data. Section 4.11 provides concluding remarks.

4.2   Unbiasedness and efficiency

Forecast unbiasedness and forecast efficiency are two basic properties a good prediction should have. The former is related to the fact that the optimal forecast under a MSFE loss function is the conditional expectation of the variable, so that it should be $E_t(y_{t+h}) = \hat{y}_{t+h|t}$, where $E_t(\cdot)$ is the conditional expectation given information at time t. A consequence of unbiasedness is that the expected value of the forecast error should be equal to zero, implying that on average the forecast should be correct.

Efficiency is instead related to the efficient use of the available information, in the sense that the optimal h-steps ahead forecast error should be at most correlated of order $h - 1$, and uncorrelated with available information at the time the forecast is made. When this is not the case, the forecast can be improved upon, typically by a more careful specification of the forecasting model.

Inefficient forecasts can still be unbiased, and biased forecasts can be efficient. For example, if y_t is a random walk, namely,

$$y_t = y_{t-1} + \varepsilon_t,$$

and we use as a forecast

$$\widetilde{y}_{t+h|t} = y_{t-g},$$

then $\widetilde{y}_{t+h|t}$ is unbiased but not efficient. Similarly, if y_t is a random walk with drift, namely,

$$y_t = a + y_{t-1} + \varepsilon_t,$$

and we use as a forecast

$$\widetilde{y}_{t+h|t} = y_t,$$

then $\widetilde{y}_{t+h|t}$ is biased but efficient.[1]

In order to test whether a forecast is unbiased, let us consider the regression

$$y_{i+h} = \alpha + \beta \hat{y}_{i+h|i} + \varepsilon_{i+h}, \quad i = T, ..., T + H - h, \qquad h < H \qquad (4.2.1a)$$

where h is the forecast horizon and $T + 1, ..., T + H$ the evaluation sample. The forecasts $\hat{y}_{i+h|i}$ are recursively updated in periods $i = T, \ldots, T + H$ - h. When ($\alpha = 0$, $\beta = 1$), $\hat{y}_{i+h|i}$ is an unbiased forecast of y_{i+h}, as can be observed by taking expectations in (4.2.1a). This condition is not necessary because unbiasedness only requires

$$\alpha = (1 - \beta)E(\hat{y}_{i+h|i}). \qquad (4.2.1b)$$

The sufficient condition ($\alpha = 0, \beta = 1$) can be tested by a "robust" F−test, where the fact that ε_{i+h} is in general autocorrelated (at least) of order $h - 1$ is taken into account in the derivation of the HAC variance covariance matrix of the estimators of the parameters, as we have seen in Chapter 2 for the case of a regression model with correlated errors. The necessary condition (4.2.1b) is equivalent to $\tau = 0$ in the regression:

$$e_{i+h} = y_{i+h} - \hat{y}_{i+h|i} = \tau + \varepsilon_{i+h},$$

which can be tested with a robust version of the t−test.

Note that ($\alpha = 0, \beta = 1$) also implies that the forecast and forecast errors are uncorrelated. Actually, (4.2.1a) can be rewritten as

$$e_{i+h} = \alpha + (\beta - 1)\hat{y}_{i+h|i} + \varepsilon_{i+h},$$

---

[1]In both cases, the target variable and the forecast are cointegrated. Hence, unbiasedness, efficiency, and cointegration (in the case of integrated target variable) are all necessary but not sufficient conditions for a good forecast. Integration and cointegration are discussed in more details in Chapters 5 and 7, respectively.

so that

$$E(\hat{y}_{i+h|i}e_{i+h}) = \alpha E(\hat{y}_{i+h|i}) + (\beta - 1)E(\hat{y}_{i+h|i}) + E(\underbrace{\hat{y}_{i+h|i}\varepsilon_{i+h}}_{=0}) = 0.$$

In this sense $(\alpha = 0, \beta = 1)$ also guarantees that the forecasts cannot be used to "reduce" the forecast error, and therefore it is also a condition that relates to efficiency of the forecasts, i.e., to full exploitation of the available information.

Moreover, when $(\alpha = 0, \beta = 1)$, we have that

$$var(y_{i+h}) = var(\hat{y}_{i+h|i}) + var(e_{i+h}),$$

implying that the volatility of the variable should be larger than that of the (optimal) forecast, the more so the larger the variance of the forecast error.

The coefficient of determination (R^2) from 4.2.1a can also be used as an indicator of the forecast quality, with good forecasts associated with high R^2. However, one should also consider that persistent variables are easier to forecast than volatile variables, given that their past is a useful leading indicator.

A second requirement for a good forecast (usually called weak efficiency) is that e_{i+h} is correlated, across time, at most of order h - 1, which implies that no lagged information beyond $h-1$ can explain the forecast errors. This property can be assessed by fitting a moving average model of order $h - 1$, $MA(h-1)$, to the h-steps ahead forecast error and testing that the resulting residuals are white noise.[2]

A third requirement for a good forecast (strong efficiency) is that $\gamma = 0$ in the regression

$$e_{i+h} = \gamma' z_i + \varepsilon_{i+h},$$

where z_i is a vector of potentially relevant variables for explaining the forecast errors. If the $h-$step ahead forecasts are strongly efficient, no indicators available when the forecasts were formulated can improve them and therefore explain the $h-$step ahead forecast error.[3] Note that in this case the observa-

---

[2]As an alternative, an $ARMA(p, q)$ model (presented in Chapter 5) can be fitted, and the non-significance of AR terms, and of MA terms higher than $h - 1$, tested.

[3]It is also worth noting parenthetically that if the target variable is non-stationary $I(1)$, a topic covered in Chapter 7, then a further natural requirement is that y_{i+h} and $\hat{y}_{i+h|i}$ are cointegrated, possibly with cointegrating vector equal to $(1, -1)$. Both features can be tested using standard procedures from the cointegration literature, see e.g., Johansen (1995) or Chapter 7.

tions on the dependent variable e_{i+h} are realizations of a set of h-steps ahead forecast errors, namely, $e_{i+h} = y_{i+h} - \hat{y}_{i+h|i}$.

To conclude, note that with a different loss function the conditions for a good forecast are different. For example, if underpredicting is more costly than overpredicting, then the expected value of the optimal forecast error will be negative. In particular, Granger (1999) has shown that the first derivative of the loss function (which is a linear function of the forecast error with MSFE loss) should have mean zero and be uncorrelated both over time and with variables available when making the forecast, see e.g., Artis and Marcellino (2001) for an application and Elliott and Timmermann (2016) for a detailed treatment.

4.3 Evaluation of fixed event forecasts

So far we have considered forecasts for period $T + h$ made in period T where T progressively increases, namely, $\{\hat{y}_{i+h|i}\}$ for $i = T, \ldots, T + H - h$. As an alternative, we can consider $\{\hat{y}_{\tau|\tau-h}\}$, $h = 1, 2, \ldots$ i.e., forecasts for a fixed target value (y_τ) made at different time periods that become closer and closer to τ. The $\{\hat{y}_{\tau|\tau-h}\}$ are known as fixed event forecasts. For example, for an AR(1) process, it is

$$\hat{y}_{\tau|\tau-h} = \rho^h y_{\tau-h}.$$

The properties of fixed events forecasts were studied by, e.g., Clements (1997). Let us decompose the forecast error as:

$$e_{\tau|\tau-h} = y_\tau - \hat{y}_{\tau|\tau-h} = v_{\tau|\tau-h+1} + v_{\tau|\tau-h+2} + \ldots + v_{\tau|\tau}, \qquad (4.3.1)$$

where

$$v_{\tau|J} = \hat{y}_{\tau|J} - \hat{y}_{\tau|J-1}, \quad \hat{y}_{\tau|\tau} = y_\tau, \quad J = \tau - h + 1, \ldots, \tau. \qquad (4.3.2)$$

For the AR(1) example, it is

$$v_{\tau|J} = \rho^{\tau-J} \varepsilon_J,$$

and

$$e_{\tau|\tau-h} = \rho^{h-1} \varepsilon_{\tau-h+1} + \ldots + \varepsilon_\tau.$$

In this context, unbiasedness requires that

$$E(e_{\tau|\tau-h}) = 0, \quad \forall \quad \tau - h.$$

For weak efficiency, the following should hold:

$$E(e_{\tau|\tau-h}|v_{\tau|\tau-h}, ..., v_{\tau|1}) = 0, \quad \forall \quad \tau - h,$$

i.e., the forecast error at $\tau - h$ is uncorrelated with all previous forecast revisions up to $\tau - h$. This condition is equivalent to

$$E(v_{\tau|\tau-h}|v_{\tau|\tau-h-1}, ..., v_{\tau|1}) = 0, \quad \forall \quad \tau - h$$

i.e., the forecast revision at time $\tau - h$ is independent of all previous revisions up to $\tau - h - 1$. These conditions also imply that

$$\hat{y}_{\tau|J} - \tilde{y}_{\tau|J-1} = \rho^{(\tau-J)}\varepsilon_J, \tag{4.3.3}$$

i.e., the evolution of the fixed event forecasts should follow a random walk, or the forecast revisions should be white noise, which are easily testable hypotheses.

Strong efficiency can be defined as the lack of explanatory power for $v_{\tau|J}$ of variables z included in the information set for period J. This property can be assessed as we have seen in the previous section, namely, by regressing $v_{\tau|J}$ on z_J and testing for the non-significance of z_J.

4.4   Tests of predictive accuracy

Tests of predictive accuracy compare an estimate of the forecast error variance obtained from the past residuals with the actual MSFE of the forecasts. Hence, they only provide a measure of how well the model performs in the future relative to the past. But they are often applied and reported in empirical analysis, so that it is worth analyzing them. They can be based on several testing principles, and we will focus on Wald-type tests.

As we will see in more detail in Chapter 5, if y_t admits the Wold MA(∞) representation:

$$y_t = \psi(L)\varepsilon_t,$$

then the $h - step$ ahead minimum MSFE predictor is

$$\hat{y}_{T+h|i} = \sum_{J=h}^{\infty} \psi_J \varepsilon_{T+h-J},$$

with associated forecast error

$$e_{T+h} = \sum_{J=0}^{h-1} \psi_J \varepsilon_{T+h-J},$$

where $\psi_0 = 1$.

We can group the errors in forecasting $(y_{T+1}, ..., y_{T+h})$ conditional on period T in

$$e_h = \psi \varepsilon_h, \tag{4.4.1}$$

where $e_h = (e_{T+1}, ..., e_{T+h})'$, $\varepsilon_h = (\varepsilon_{T+1}, ..., \varepsilon_{T+h})'$ and

$$\psi = \begin{pmatrix} 1 & 0 & \cdots & \cdots & 0 & 0 \\ \psi_1 & 1 & \cdots & \cdots & 0 & 0 \\ \psi_2 & \psi_1 & \cdots & \cdots & 0 & 0 \\ \vdots & \vdots & \ddots & & \vdots & \vdots \\ \vdots & \vdots & & \ddots & 1 & 0 \\ \psi_{h-1} & \psi_{h-2} & \cdots & \cdots & \psi_1 & 1 \end{pmatrix}.$$

If we define

$$\Phi_h = E(e_h e_h') = \psi E(\varepsilon_h \varepsilon_h') \psi' = \sigma_\varepsilon^2 \psi \psi',$$

and if the appropriate model over $[1, ..., T]$ remains valid over the forecast horizon and $\varepsilon \sim N$, then

$$Q = e_h' \Phi_h^{-1} e_h \sim \chi^2(h),$$

where $\Phi_h^{-1} = \sigma_\varepsilon^{-2} (\psi^{-1})' \psi^{-1}$.

Writing the autoregressive (AR) approximation of the Wold representation (see again the next chapter for details) as

$$\varphi(L) y_t = \varepsilon_t, \quad \varphi(L) = \psi(L)^{-1},$$

we also have

$$\varepsilon_h = \varphi e_h, \quad \varphi = \psi^{-1},$$
$$\Phi_h^{-1} = \sigma_\varepsilon^{-2} \varphi' \varphi.$$

We can therefore rewrite the statistic Q as

$$Q = \frac{e_h' \varphi' \varphi e_h}{\sigma_\varepsilon^2} = \frac{\varepsilon_h' \varepsilon_h}{\sigma_\varepsilon^2} = \frac{1}{\sigma_\varepsilon^2} \sum_{J=1}^{h} \varepsilon_{T+J}^2.$$

Given that ε_{T+J} is also the one-step ahead forecast error in forecasting y_{T+J}, we see that Q can be written as a sum of these errors.

An operational version of the test is therefore:

$$\hat{Q} = \frac{1}{\hat{\sigma}_\varepsilon^2} \sum_{J=1}^{h} e_{T+J|T+J-1}^2 \quad \sim \quad F(h, T-p),$$

where p is the number of parameters used in the model and $e_{T+J|T+J-1}$ indicates for clarity the one-step ahead forecast error.

4.5   Forecast comparison tests

After having discussed how to evaluate a given forecast, we now consider how to compare alternative predictions. The most common approach is to rank them according to the associated loss function, typically the MSFE or MAFE. However, these comparisons are deterministic, i.e., it is evaluated whether one MSFE is larger than the other but not whether their difference is statistically significant. We will now consider two tests for the hypothesis that two forecasts are equivalent, in the sense that the associated loss difference is not statistically different from zero. Additional and more advanced methods are surveyed, e.g, in West (2006) and Clark and McCracken (2013), including methods for the comparison of more than two models.

The first test we consider is due to Granger and Newbold (1986), and it is also known as the Morgan-Granger-Newbold test since it is related to earlier work by Morgan. It requires the forecast errors to be zero mean, normally distributed, and uncorrelated. If we indicate by e_1 and e_2 the forecast errors from the competing models, the test is based on the auxiliary variables:

$$u_{1,T+J} = e_{1,T+J} - e_{2,T+J}, \quad u_{2,T+J} = e_{1,T+J} + e_{2,T+J}. \tag{4.5.1}$$

It is

$$E(u_1 u_2) = MSFE_1 - MSFE_2,$$

so that the hypothesis of interest is whether u_1 and u_2 are correlated or not.

The proposed statistic is

$$\frac{r}{\sqrt{(H-1)^{-1}(1-r^2)}} \quad \sim \quad t_{H-1},$$

where (1) t_{H-1} a Student t distribution with $H-1$ degrees of freedom, (2) H is the length of the evaluation sample and

$$r = \frac{\sum_1^H u_{1,T+i}\, u_{2,T+i}}{\sqrt{\sum_1^H u_{1,T+i}^2 \sum_1^H u_{2,T+i}^2}}.$$

The second test is due to Diebold and Mariano (1995). It relaxes the requirements on the forecast errors and can deal with the comparison of general loss functions. Let us define the Diebold-Mariano test - statistic as

$$DM = H^{1/2}\frac{\sum_{j=1}^H d_j/H}{\sigma_d} = H^{1/2}\frac{\overline{d}}{\sigma_d}, \qquad (4.5.2)$$

where

$$d_j = g(e_{1j}) - g(e_{2j}),$$

g is the loss function of interest, e.g., the quadratic loss $g(e) = e^2$ or the absolute loss $g(e) = |e|$, e_1 and e_2 are the errors from the two competing forecasts, and σ_d^2 is the variance of $\overline{d}$. In order to take into account the serial correlation of the forecast errors, the latter can be estimated as

$$\widehat{\sigma}_d^2 = \left(\gamma_0 + 2\sum_{i=1}^{h-1}\gamma_i\right) \quad \text{with } \gamma_k = H^{-1}\sum_{t=k+1}^H (d_t - \overline{d})(d_{t-k} - \overline{d}),$$

where h is the forecast horizon, so that for $h = 1$ there is no correlation and the standard formula for variance estimation can be used. Diebold and Mariano (1995) suggested other alternative estimators for σ_d^2.

Under the null hypothesis that $E(d) = 0$, the statistic DM has an asymptotic standard normal distribution. Note that when DM is positive the loss associated with the first model is larger than that for the second one.

Harvey, Leybourne, and Newbold (1998) suggested a modified version of the DM statistic,

$$HLN = \left(\frac{H + 1 - 2h + H^{-1}h(h-1)}{HH}\right)^{1/2} DM,$$

to be compared with critical values from the Student t distribution with $H-1$ degrees of freedom, in order to improve the finite sample properties of the DM test.

When the models underlying the forecasts under comparison are nested, for example an AR(1) and an AR(2), then the asymptotic distribution of the DM test becomes non-standard and a functional of Brownian motions. A simple solution in this case is the use of rolling rather than recursive estimation, see Giacomini and White (2006) for details. More sophisticated methods are also available, see Clark and McCracken (2013). Finally, see also Diebold (2015) for some further insightful discussions of the DM test.

4.6   The combination of forecasts

When alternative models or forecasts are available, rather than selecting one of them we could combine them, constructing a pooled forecast. We will now discuss why pooling can work well and analyze some simple methods for forecast combination.

Let us assume that two forecasts $\hat{y}_1$ and $\hat{y}_2$ are available for the same target y, with associated forecast errors e_1 and e_2. We want to construct the combined (linear) forecast

$$\hat{y}_c = \alpha\hat{y}_1 + (1-\alpha)\hat{y}_2, \tag{4.6.1}$$

where the weights can be chosen in order to minimize the MSFE of $\hat{y}_c$, and we are assuming that $\hat{y}_1$ and $\hat{y}_2$ are unbiased and their relationship with y is constant over the forecast period. From 4.6.1 we have

$$e_c = y - \hat{y}_c = \alpha e_1 + (1-\alpha)e_2 \tag{4.6.2}$$

so that

$$\begin{aligned}
MSFE_c = {} &\alpha^2 MSFE_1 + (1-\alpha)^2 MSFE_2 \\
&+ 2\alpha(1-\alpha)\varphi(MSFE_1\, MSFE_2)^{1/2}
\end{aligned} \tag{4.6.3}$$

where φ is the correlation coefficient between e_1 and e_2.

The optimal pooling weights, the minimizers of 4.6.3, are (see e.g., Granger and Newbold (1986)):

$$\alpha^* = \frac{MSFE_2 - \varphi(MSFE_1 MSFE_2)^{1/2}}{MSFE_1 + MSFE_2 - 2\varphi(MSFE_1 MSFE_2)^{1/2}},$$

which yields

$$MSFE_c^* = \frac{MSFE_1\, MSFE_2\,(1-\varphi^2)}{MSFE_1 + MSFE_2 - 2\varphi(MSFE_1 MSFE_2)^{1/2}}$$

and

$$MSFE_c^* \le min(MSFE_1, MSFE_2),$$

where equality holds if either $\varphi^2 = MSFE_1/MSFE_2$ (i.e., $e_2 = e_1 + u$) or $\varphi^2 = MSFE_2/MSFE_1$ (i.e., $e_1 = e_2 + u$), which implies that $\hat{y}_1$ or $\hat{y}_2$ is the optimal forecasts.

If the forecast errors are uncorrelated ($\varphi = 0$), α^* only depends on the relative size of $MSFE_1$, and $MSFE_2$, which are commonly used weights in empirical applications even with correlated errors.

In practice α is not known and must be estimated. An easier way to obtain an estimate of α is to run, over the evaluation sample, the regression

$$y = \alpha\hat{y}_1 + (1 - \alpha)\hat{y}_2 + e, \qquad (4.6.4)$$

or

$$e_2 = \alpha(\hat{y}_1 - \hat{y}_2) + e. \qquad (4.6.5)$$

Actually, the estimated errors from 4.6.4 and 4.6.5 coincide asymptotically with e_c in 4.6.2 , so that the OLS estimator minimizes $MSFE_c(= \sum_1^H e_c^2/H)$.

In 4.6.5 we assume that the coefficients of $\hat{y}_1$ and $\hat{y}_2$ sum to one and that a constant is not significant in the regression, which are both reasonable restrictions given the maintained hypothesis of unbiasedness of $\hat{y}_1$ and $\hat{y}_2$. Yet, in general, a lower $MSFE_c$ can be obtained by running the unrestricted regression

$$y = \alpha_0 + \alpha_1\hat{y}_1 + \alpha_2\hat{y}_2 + u, \qquad (4.6.6)$$

with combined forecast

$$\tilde{y}_c = \alpha_0 + \hat{\alpha}_1\hat{y}_1 + \hat{\alpha}_2\hat{y}_2.$$

But the residuals from 4.6.6, i.e., $\hat{u} = y - \tilde{y}_c$, will be in general serially correlated. Indeed,

$$\hat{u} = -\hat{\alpha}_0 + (1 - \sum_{i=1}^2 \hat{\alpha}_i)y + \sum_{i=1}^2 \hat{\alpha}_i e_i.$$

While the e_is are in general uncorrelated (for one-step ahead forecasts), y is usually correlated and therefore $\hat{u}$ is also correlated when the restriction $\hat{\alpha}_1 + \hat{\alpha}_2 = 1$ is not imposed. Hence, a proper estimation method (such as GLS) should be adopted.

We also recall that the MSFE is not invariant to linear transformations so that, for example, optimal weights when combining forecasts of levels and differences of the same variable can be rather different (see for example Clements and Hendry (1998)). Also, the optimal weights can be time varying; this case and other generalizations are discussed, e.g., in Timmermann (2006).

To conclude, we should mention that in the presence of a rather large set of alternative forecasts, from a practical point view a combined forecast obtained by simply averaging all the alternative available forecasts (possibly after trimming some of the worst ones based on their past track record) tends to work well, in the sense of producing good and robust results in a variety of cases.

4.7   Forecast encompassing

One model encompasses another with respect to a certain property if from the first model it is possible to deduce the property of interest in the second model, see Mizon and Richard (1986). Forecast encompassing concerns whether the one-step forecast of one model can explain the forecast errors made by another (which is therefore not strongly efficient), see, e.g., Chong and Hendry (1986), Ericsson (1993).

From an operational point of view, we can use the regression 4.6.5 and test for $\alpha = 0$. If $\alpha \neq 0$ the difference between $\hat{y}_1$ and $\hat{y}_2$ can partly explain e_2, and therefore the second model cannot forecast encompass the first one. Similarly, if $\beta \neq 0$ in the regression

$$e_1 = \beta(\hat{y}_2 - \hat{y}_1) + v, \qquad (4.7.1)$$

the first model cannot forecast encompass the second one.

A more direct test can be based on the regression

$$e_1 = \delta \hat{y}_2 + \varphi, \qquad (4.7.2)$$

and it requires $\delta = 0$ for the second model not to forecast encompass the first one.

A third alternative is a test for $\alpha_1 = 1$, $\alpha_2 = 0$ in 4.6.6. With reference to equation 4.6.6, the first test that we considered requires $\alpha_2 = 0$ conditional on $\alpha_1 + \alpha_2 = 1$. The second test instead requires $\alpha_2 = 0$ conditional on $\alpha_1 = 1$.[4]

Even if the procedures for forecast combination and encompassing are similar, the suggestions from the two methods are different. The former simply indicates to combine the competing forecasts, the latter to respecify the models that produced the forecasts, because both of them are somewhat misspecified, see e.g., Diebold (1989) for further details.

4.8 Evaluation and combination of density forecasts

We have seen in Chapter 1 how to obtain (interval and) density forecasts from the linear regression model. Similar techniques can be used for the more complex models we study in subsequent chapters, though sometimes it will not be possible to obtain analytical formulae for the (interval and) density forecasts, but they have to be obtained using simulation methods (see Chapter 9).

In this section we briefly discuss how to evaluate, compare and combine density forecasts. Additional details and references can be found, e.g., in Mitchell and Wallis (2011), Geweke and Amisano (2010), and Geweke and Amisano (2011).

Let us indicate the density forecast by $f_{T+h|T}$, given information up to T (and X_{T+h}) with horizon h, and its cumulative distribution function (CDF) by $F_{T+h|T}$. Similarly, we indicate the true density of the target variable by $g_{T+h|T}$ and its CDF by $G_{T+h|T}$. For example, in the case of the linear regression model considered in Chapter 1, under the assumption of normal errors, we have seen that the (optimal) density forecast ($f_{T+h|T}$) is

$$y_{T+h} \sim N(\hat{y}_{T+h}, V(e_{T+h})),$$

---

[4]When the target variable is I(1) and cointegrated with both forecasts, it is important to choose a balanced regression (see Chapter 7 for more details). In the case of 4.7.2, e_1 is I(0) while $\hat{y}_2$ is I(1), so that δ would be forced to be equal to zero in large samples. In equation 4.7.1 there is a similar problem, unless $\hat{y}_2$ and $\hat{y}_1$ are such that $\hat{y}_2 - \hat{y}_1$ is stationary. In that case, standard inference can be applied, which makes this an attractive formulation. All the variables in equation 4.6.6 are instead I(1), so the equation is balanced but the distribution of the F-test is non-standard because of the non-stationarity of the variables.

where $\hat{y}_{T+h} = X_{T+h}\hat{\beta}_T$ and $V(e_{T+h})$ denotes the variance of the forecast error. The true density $(g_{T+h|T})$ is instead

$$y_{T+h} \sim N(X_{T+h}\beta, \sigma_\varepsilon^2).$$

4.8.1   Evaluation

For the evaluation of point forecasts we just compare the forecast and actual values, for the density forecasts we must instead compare the entire forecast and actual densities, or the corresponding CDFs, which makes the evaluation more complex.

It is convenient to introduce the Probability Integral Transformation (PIT), defined as

$$PIT_t(x) \equiv F_{t+h|t}(x), \tag{4.8.1}$$

for any forecast x. In practice, the PIT associates to each possible forecast value x its probability computed according to the density forecast $F_{t+h|t}$.

It can be shown that if $F_{t+h|t} = G_{t+h|t}$ for all t, then the PIT_ts are independent $U[0,1]$ variables, where U denotes the uniform distribution.[5] Therefore, to assess the quality of density forecasts we can check whether their associated $PITs$ are independent and uniformly distributed.

Uniformity (typically defined as probabilistic calibration) can be evaluated qualitatively, by plotting the histogram of the PIT_ts for the available evaluation sample. For a more formal assessment of probabilistic calibration, let us consider the inverse normal transformation:

$$z_t = \Phi^{-1}(PIT_t), \tag{4.8.2}$$

where Φ is the CDF of a standard normal variable. If PIT_t is $\overset{iid}{\sim} U(0,1)$ then z_t is $\overset{iid}{\sim} N(0,1)$.

It is more convenient to assess probabilistic calibration using z_ts rather than PIT_ts, since there are many more tests for normality than for uniformity.[6]

The combination of independent and uniform $PITs$ is typically defined complete calibration. Several procedures can be used to test for independence. For example, if the z_ts are indeed normally distributed and therefore

---

[5]See Diebold, Gunther, and Tay (1998) for further detail.
[6]See e.g., Mitchell and Wallis (2011) for a list of tests for uniformity and normality.

independence and lack of correlation are equivalent, we can use any of the tests for no correlation in the errors described in Chapter 2. See, e.g., Mitchell and Wallis (2011) for other procedures.

4.8.2 Comparison

As for point forecasts, a first method to compare alternative density forecasts is to consider whether each of them has a positive evaluation, in the sense of satisfying complete calibration. When that is the case, we may want to directly compare the two (or more) competing density forecasts. For this, it is convenient to introduce the logarithmic score, defined as

$$log\, S_j(x) \;=\; log\, f_{j,t+h|t}(x), \tag{4.8.3}$$

where j indicates the alternative densities.

If one of the densities under comparison coincides with $g_{t+h|t}$ (the true density), then the expected value of the differences in the logarithmic scores coincides with the Kullback-Leibler Information Criterion (KLIC):

$$KLIC_{j,t} = E_g[log\, g_{t+h|t}(x) \;-\; log\, f_{j,t+h|t}(x)] = E[d_{j,t}(x)].$$

We can interpret $d_{j,t}$ as a density forecast error, so that the $KLIC$ is a kind of "mean density error" (similar to the bias in the case of the point forecasts).

To compare two densities, f_j and f_k, we can then use:

$$\triangle L_t = log S_j(x_t) - log\, S_k(x_t). \tag{4.8.4}$$

To assess whether statistically the two densities are different (basically, to construct the counterpart of the Diebold-Mariano test in a density context), we can use:

$$\sqrt{T}(\frac{\sum \triangle L_t}{T}/std.dev.) \to N(0,1),$$

see Amisano and Giacomini (2007) for details, including the proper computation of the standard deviation in the denominator, and extensions.

4.8.3 Combination

We have seen in the previous sections that combining point forecasts can reduce the MSFE. Along the same lines, we may want to combine density forecasts, but this is more complex since we need to make sure that the resulting combination is still a density.

Following, e.g., Wallis (2005), to whom we refer for additional details and references, starting from n forecast densities f_j, $j = 1, ..., n$, the combined density forecast is

$$f_c = \sum_{j=1}^{n} w_j f_j,$$

where $w_j \geq 0$, $j = 1, ..., n$, and $\sum_{j=1}^{n} w_j = 1$. The combined density f_c is therefore a finite mixture distribution.

Defining values for the weights w_j, $j = 1, ..., n$, is not easy. A simple solution that often works well in practice (as in the case of the point forecasts), is to set $w_j = 1/n$, $j = 1, ..., n$. Alternatively, the weights could be set in order to improve the calibration properties of the combined densities with respect to those of its components. Finally, the weights could be chosen optimally, to maximize a certain objective function or minimize the KLIC with respect to the true unknown density, see e.g., Hall and Mitchell (2007).

4.9   Examples using simulated data

In the previous three chapters we have seen forecasts produced by linear regressions, the same models augmented with dummy variables and also models with lagged variables, which coincides with the following data generating process that we call the dynamic model:

$$
\begin{aligned}
y_t &= \alpha_1 + \alpha_2 x_t + \varepsilon_t \\
y_t &= \alpha_1 + \beta_1 D_t + \alpha_2 x_t + \beta_2 D_t x_t + \varepsilon_t \\
y_t &= \alpha_1 + \beta_1 D_t + \alpha_2 x_t + \beta_2 D_t x_t + \gamma_1^y y_{t-1} + \gamma_1^x x_{t-1} + \varepsilon_t
\end{aligned}
$$

Naturally, model (mis-)specification affects the forecast accuracy. In this chapter we will compare the performance of all three specifications. To do so, we will use simple forecast evaluation statistics, i.e., RMSFE and MAFE.

Table 4.9.1 represents indicators for all the models considered. The RMSFE and MAFE are the smallest for the dynamic regression model, where we were expecting this type of result as the dynamic model coincides with the DGP (ignoring parameter estimation error). The numbers reported in Table 4.9.1 clearly show us that mis-specification can be very severe and costly.

Forecasting Model	RMSFE	RMSFE recursive	MAFE	MAFE recursive
Linear Regression	9.536	9.490	7.995	7.950
Dummy variable model	10.130	9.642	8.314	7.938
Dynamic model	1.108	0.965	0.865	0.760

Table 4.9.1: *Forecasts evaluation: RMSFE and MAFE*

The next step is to compare individual forecasts. In section 4.5 we discussed two main tests: the Diebold-Mariano (DM) and Morgan-Granger-Newbold (MGN) tests. We start with the DM test. In this exercise we compare forecasts of three models:

Model 1 - linear regressions
Model 2 - model with dummy variable
Model 3 - dynamic model

The null hypothesis of the DM test is that the average loss differential between the forecasts of compared models is equal to zero. The DM test results for all three models are described in Table 4.9.2. If we consider a significance level of 5%, the null hypothesis that the loss differential between the forecasts from Model 1 and Model 2 being zero cannot be rejected. This result indicates that there is no difference between forecasts of Models 1 and 2. On the other hand, the results also indicate the dynamic model provides statistically significant better forecasts than Models 1 and 2.

Comparisons	$M1$ *vs* $M2$	$M1$ *vs* $M3$	$M2$ *vs* $M3$
DM test statistics	-1.113	8.582	11.445
P-value	0.132	0.000	0.000

Table 4.9.2: *Diebold-Mariano test for equality of MSFE*

The second test discussed in Section 4.5 is the Morgan-Granger-Newbold test. The null hypothesis of the MGN test is that the MSFEs associated with two forecasts are equal. The test results appear in Table 4.9.3 and are in line with the DM test findings.

Comparisons	M1 vs M2	M1 vs M3	M2 vs M3
MGN test statistics	-1.100	42.932	65.137
P-value	0.273	0.000	0.000

Table 4.9.3: *Morgan-Granger-Newbold test*

In exercises with simulated data that appeared in the previous chapters we generated recursive forecasts as well. We can compare those forecasts using DM and MGN tests. The results are omitted as they convey the same message.

	Coefficient	Std. Error		t-Statistic	Prob.
τ	-1.744	0.953		-1.830	0.069
R-squared	0.000	Mean dep var			-1.744
Adjusted R-squared	0.000	S.D.dependent var			9.609
S.E.of regression	9.609	Akaike IC			7.368
Sum squared resid	18375.640	Schwarz IC			7.385
Log likelihood	-735.834	Hannan-Quinn			7.375
DW stat	0.790				

Table 4.9.4: *Unbiasedness and weak efficiency (via DW) tests for Model 1*

Next, we turn our attention to unbiasedness and weak efficiency tests starting with the former which are performed using equation (4.2.1a), and can be implemented with a $t-$test (we do not need a robust one with $h = 1$) in the following regression:

$$e_{t+1} = y_{t+1} - \hat{y}_{t+1|t} = \tau + \varepsilon_{t+1}.$$

The results for Models 1 and 2 appear in respectively Tables 4.9.4 and 4.9.5. For M1 we accept the null $\tau = 0$ at the 5 % level, while for M2 we clearly reject the null. This means that forecasts for M1 appear to be unbiased, while the opposite is true for M2.

	Coefficient	Std. Error	t-Statistic	Prob.
τ	-3.223	0.810	-3.979	0.000
R-squared	0.000	Mean dep var		-3.223
Adjusted R-squared	0.000	S.D.dependent var		9.625
S.E.of regression	9.625	Akaike IC		7.372
Sum squared resid	18436.060	Schwarz IC		7.388
Log likelihood	-736.162	Hannan-Quinn		7.378
DW stat	1.369			

Table 4.9.5: *Unbiasedness and weak efficiency (via DW) tests for Model 2*

Variable	Coefficient	Std. Error	t-Statistic	Prob.
C	0.333	0.083	4.037	0.000
Y(-1)	0.197	0.139	1.413	0.166
IPR	0.201	0.069	2.907	0.006
SU(-1)	-0.002	0.018	-0.140	0.889
SR(-1)	0.009	0.006	1.435	0.159
R-squared	0.513	Mean dep var		0.564
Adjusted R-squared	0.463	S.D. dep var		0.355
S.E. of regression	0.260	Akaike IC		0.251
Sum squared resid	2.638	Schwarz IC		0.454
Log likelihood	-0.518	Hannan-Quinn		0.326
F-statistic	10.256	DW stat		2.220
Prob(F-statistic)	0.000			

Table 4.9.6: *Estimation output: ARDL Model 2*

To test for weak efficiency, we need to test whether e_t is correlated across time. In this case, we can look at the same regression output as the DW statistic tells us whether there is order-one autocorrelation in the ε_t, which amounts to testing the autocorrelation of e_t. Reading the output from both aforementioned tables, we find that there is evidence for serial correlation in the forecast errors for both models. In general, with $h > 1$ we need to fit a moving average model of order $h - 1$, $MA(h - 1)$, to the h-steps ahead forecast error and test that the resulting residuals are white noise. As an alternative, an $ARMA(p, q)$ model (presented in Chapter 5) can be fitted, and the non-significance of AR and MA terms higher than $h - 1$ tested.

4.10   Empirical examples

4.10.1   Forecasting Euro area GDP growth

In the last few chapters, we have seen some examples on producing forecasts using linear regressions with and without dynamics, and also the impact on forecast accuracy by including dummies to accommodate structural changes into forecasting models.

Simple forecast evaluation statistics, i.e., root MSFE and MAFE, were used for comparisons. In the example here, we illustrate the forecast comparison tests discussed in section 4.5. Using again the Euro area data series, we consider the Models 1 through 4, estimated over the period 1996Q1 to 2006Q4; and using 2007Q1 to 2013Q2 as the forecast evaluation period. Recall that Models 1 through 4 and the ARDL Model 2 contain different elements in their information sets:

$$y_t = \alpha + X_t \beta + \varepsilon_t$$

- Model 1: $X_t = (ipr_t, \ su_t, \ pr_t, \ sr_t)$

- Model 2: $X_t = (ipr_t, \ su_t, \ sr_t)$

- Model 3: $X_t = (ipr_t, \ su_t)$

- Model 4: $X_t = (ipr_t, \ pr_t, \ sr_t)$

- ARDL Model 2: : $X_t = (y_{t-1}, \ ipr_t, \ su_{t-1}, \ sr_{t-1})$

To proceed we need to re-estimate the ARDL Model 2, presented in Chapter 3, over the period 1996Q1 to 2006Q4 using this estimation sample, with the results appearing in Table 4.9.6. Comparing the in-sample fit of the ARDL Model 2 with those reported in Tables 1.12.1, 1.12.2 and 1.12.3, it appears that the ARDL Model 2 has a better fit in general than Models 1 - 3 in terms of AIC, and in most cases, R^2 and $\overline{R}^2$. By the same measures, it seems to be not as good as Model 4.

	M1	M2	M3	M4	ARDL M2
RMSFE	0.383	0.378	0.394	0.415	0.353
MAFE	0.327	0.331	0.344	0.364	0.310

Table 4.10.1: *Forecast evaluation measures*

We do know, however, that a good in-sample fit does not necessarily imply a good out-of-sample performance. To compare the forecasts produced by these models, we need to look at forecast sample evaluation statistics and also to perform forecast comparison tests.

We first produce one-step ahead static forecasts for the period 2007Q1 to 2013Q2 and compute the RMSFE and the MAFE of the forecasts produced by each of the models, as reported in Table 4.10.1. It is clear that one-step ahead forecasts produced by the ARDL Model 2 outperforms the other forecasts as indicated by both the values of RMSFE and MAFE. We assess forecast unbiasedness by regressing each forecast error on an intercept and then test its significance. It turns out that it is significant for all the models, indicating the presence of a bias (a systematic over-estimation of growth, which is not surprising as the evaluation sample contains the period of the Great Recession and of the sovereign debt crisis). Weak efficiency is not rejected for any of the models, however, as the one-step ahead forecasts errors are all serially uncorrelated.

We proceed now to illustrate how to compare alternative predictions, using again the Morgan-Granger-Newbold (MGN) and the Diebold-Mariano (DM) tests. Our interest here is to compare the one-step ahead static forecasts from the ARDL Model 2 with those of Models 1 through 4. Assuming the loss function is quadratic, we first illustrate the use of the Diebold-Mariano test. The test statistics are reported in Table 4.10.2. The null hypothesis of the Diebold-Mariano test is that the average loss differential, $\overline{d}$, is equal to zero, i.e., $H_0 : \overline{d} = 0$. The test statistic has an asymptotic standard normal distribution, i.e., $DM \overset{a}{\sim} N(0, 1)$. If we consider a significance level of 5%, the null hypothesis that the loss differential between the forecasts from ARDL Model 2 and those of the other models being zero cannot be rejected, indicating there is no significant difference between its forecasts and those of the other models. However, at 10% significance level, the test results suggest the loss differential between the forecasts from ARDL Model 2 and those of Model 3 and Model 4. Moreover, the reported test statistics here are all positive. This is an indication that the loss associated with Model

1, 2, 3, and 4 is larger than that of ARDL Model 2.

	vs M1	vs M2	vs M3	vs M4
Test Stat.	0.721	0.737	1.331	1.535
p-value	0.235	0.230	0.091	0.062

Table 4.10.2: *DM tests ARDL Model 2 against Models 1 through 4*

Now let us move next to the Morgan-Granger-Newbold (MGN) test. The computed test statistics and the corresponding p-values are reported in Table 4.10.3. The null hypothesis of the Morgan-Granger-Newbold test is that the mean of the loss differential is zero, meaning the variances of the two forecast errors are equal. Or in other words, the covariance of the auxiliary variables in equation 4.5.1 is equal to zero. The test statistic follows a Student t distribution with $H - 1$ degree of freedom (in this case $H = 26$). At 5% significance level, the null hypothesis cannot be rejected for all four cases. Note however, that the null hypothesis can be rejected for the first case at the 10% significance level.

	vs M1	vs M2	vs M3	vs M4
Test Stat.	1.756	0.735	0.900	1.651
p-value	0.090	0.468	0.375	0.110

Table 4.10.3: *MGN tests ARDL Model 2 against Models 1 through 4*

We now look into whether there is any change in the results if we consider recursive forecasts, i.e., the parameters in the models are re-estimated for each period in the forecast evaluation sample. We then re-compute the Diebold-Mariano and Morgan-Granger-Newbold test statistics for the same hypotheses of interest. Tables 4.10.4 and 4.10.5 present the test results. Looking at the Diebold-Mariano test statistics, the null hypothesis that the loss differential between the one-step ahead recursive forecasts from ARDL Model 2 and those from Models 2 through 4 being zero cannot be rejected at the 5% significance level. Whereas the null hypothesis that the one-step ahead recursive forecasts from ARDL Model 2 are no difference from those of Model 1 can be rejected at 5% significance level. The Morgan-Granger-Newbold test results confirm this finding at the 10 % level. At the 10 % level we can also reject the DM test null for the ARDL Model 2 against Models 3 and 4.

	vs M1	vs M2	vs M3	vs M4
Test stat.	1.716	0.737	1.331	1.535
p-value	0.043	0.230	0.091	0.062

Table 4.10.4: *DM tests recursive forecasts ARDL Model 2 vs Models 1 - 4*

	vs M1	vs M2	vs M3	vs M4
Test stat.	1.898	1.281	1.208	1.693
p-value	0.068	0.211	0.237	0.102

Table 4.10.5: *MGN tests recursive forecasts ARDL Model 2 vs Models 1 - 4*

To conclude, we have constructed pooled forecasts by combining the 5 available predictors, using equal weights for simplicity and as the sample size is rather short. It turns out that the MSFE of the combined forecasts is lower than that of the forecasts associated with Models 1 through 4, but larger than that of the ARDL Model 2. In this case forecast combination does not help because most of the forecasts we are combining are clearly dominated by one of the forecasts (from the ARDL type model).

4.10.2 Forecasting US GDP growth

Using again the US data series employed in the previous chapters, we consider Models 1 through 4, estimated over the period 1985Q1 to 2006Q4; and using 2007Q1 to 2013Q4 as the forecast evaluation period. Recall Models 1 through 4 and the ARDL Model 2 are the same as those in the previous subsection. In order to do so, we need to re-estimate the ARDL Model 2 over the shorter sample period 1985Q1 to 2006Q4 (detailed results are omitted).

We compute the RMSFE and the MAFE of the forecasts produced by these models, as reported in Table 4.10.6. It is clear that one-step ahead forecasts produced by the ARDL Model 2 is outperformed by the other forecasts as indicated by the values of RMSFE and the MAFE.

Now we proceed to illustrate how to compare alternative predictions, using the Morgan-Granger-Newbold (MGN) test and the Diebold-Mariano

	M1	M2	M3	M4	ARDL M2
RMSFE	0.537	0.531	0.539	0.537	0.567
MAFE	0.402	0.399	0.403	0.418	0.438

Table 4.10.6: *Simple forecast evaluation statistics*

(DM) test. Our interest here is to compare the one-step ahead static forecasts from ARDL Model 2 with those of Model 1, 2, 3, and 4. Assuming the loss function is quadratic, we first illustrate the use of the Diebold-Mariano test but consider the simple case when the forecast errors are assumed to be serially uncorrelated. Table 4.10.7 reports the test statistics and the corresponding p-values. If we consider a significance level of 5%, the null hypothesis that the loss differential between the forecasts from ARDL Model 2 and those of the other models being zero can be rejected for Models 2 and 4. Moreover, at 10% significance level, the test results suggest the loss differential between the forecasts from ARDL Model 2 and all models is non-zero. Note, however, that the reported test statistics here are all negative. This is an indication that the loss associated with Model 1, 2, 3 and 4 is smaller than that of ARDL Model 2.

	vs M1	vs M2	vs M3	vs M4
Test stat.	-1.516	-1.748	-1.375	-2.279
p-value	0.064	0.040	0.084	0.011

Table 4.10.7: *DM test on one-step ahead forecasts from ARDL model 2 against one-step ahead forecasts from Model 1 through 4.*

	vs M1	vs M2	vs M3	vs M4
Test stat.	-1.109	-1.308	-0.946	-2.007
p-value	0.276	0.201	0.352	0.054

Table 4.10.8: *MGN test on one-step ahead forecasts from ARDL model 2 against one-step ahead forecasts from Model 1 through 4*

Now let's move on to illustrate the Morgan-Granger-Newbold (MGN) test. The computed test statistics and the corresponding p-values are reported in Table 4.10.8. The null hypothesis of the MGN test is that the mean of the loss differential is zero, meaning the variances of the two forecast errors are equal. The null hypothesis cannot be rejected for first 3 cases, and can be rejected in the last case at the 10% significance level.

We now look into whether there is any change in inference of the two forecast comparison tests if the parameters in the forecasting models are re-estimated for each period in the forecast evaluation sample. We then recompute the Diebold-Mariano and the Morgan-Granger-Newbold test statistics to test the equality of the one-step ahead recursive forecast from the ARDL Model 2 against those from Model 1, 2, 3, and 4. Tables 4.10.9 and 4.10.10 present the test results. Looking at the Diebold-Mariano test statistics, the null hypothesis that the loss differential between the one-step ahead recursive forecasts from ARDL Model 2 and those from Model 2, 3, and 4 being zero can be rejected at 10% significance level. And the sign is again negative. However, the Morgan-Granger-Newbold test results show that the null hypothesis of the mean of the loss differential being zero cannot be rejected at 10% significance level for all 4 cases.

	vs M1	vs M2	vs M3	vs M4
Test stat.	-1.473	-1.748	-1.375	-2.279
p-value	0.070	0.040	0.084	0.011

Table 4.10.9: *DM test on one-step ahead recursive forecasts from ARDL Model 2 against those from Model 1 through 4*

	vs M1	vs M2	vs M3	vs M4
Test stat.	-1.258	-1.243	-0.735	-1.641
p-value	0.219	0.224	0.468	0.112

Table 4.10.10: *MGN test on one-step ahead recursive forecasts from ARDL Model 2 against those from Model 1 through 4*

4.10.3 Default risk

Let us now revisit the empirical default risk models reported in Table 3.7.11. We found that the in-sample Model 4 featured the best fit, whereas Model 3 had the best out-of-sample RMSFE. We use the Morgan-Granger-Newbold test for pairwise comparisons of the one-step ahead forecasts. The results appear in Table 4.10.11. The results indicate that the out-of-sample differences

across the different models is not statistically significant. The DM statistics
– not reported – also confirm the same finding.

Model 1	Model 2	t-stat	p-val	Superior
VIX	SENT	0.505	0.617	2
VIX	PMI	0.575	0.569	2
VIX	SP500	-1.042	0.305	1
SENT	PMI	0.662	0.513	2
SENT	SP500	-1.410	0.168	1
PMI	SP500	-1.463	0.153	1

Table 4.10.11: *MGN tests default risk models*

4.11   Concluding remarks

The main focus in this book is forecasting using econometric models. It
is important to stress, however, that the methods reviewed in this chapter
developed for the purpose of evaluating forecasts apply far beyond the realm
of econometric models. Indeed, the forecasts could simply be, say, analyst
forecasts at least not explicitly related to any specific model. Hence, the
reach of the methods discussed in this chapter is wide.

Part II

Forecasting with Time Series Models

Chapter 5

Univariate Time Series Models

5.1 Introduction

Box and Jenkins (1976) popularized the use of univariate time series models for forecasting. Since then they have become a workhorse for practitioners using economic and financial time series.

The key idea is to exploit the past behavior of a time series to forecast its future development. This requires the future to be rather similar to the past, which technically translates into an assumption of weak stationarity. In words, weak stationarity means that the variable under analysis has a stable mean and variance over time, and that the correlation of the variable with each of its own lags is also stable over time.

Previous results in the statistical literature showed that any weakly stationary stochastic process can always be represented as an (infinite) sum of the elements of a simpler, so-called white noise (WN) process, which has zero mean, is uncorrelated over time, and has a constant variance. In turn, this representation – known as the Wold decomposition – can be approximated by another one where the variable of interest depends on a finite number of its own lags, possibly combined with a finite number of lags of an uncorrelated and homoskedastic process. The latter is called an autoregressive moving average (ARMA) representation, where autoregressive means that the variable depends on its own past, and moving average means that it also depends on a weighted average of the present and past values of a WN process. An ARMA(p,q) is a model where the variable of interest depends on up to p of its own lags and on up to q lags of the white noise process.

In this chapter we will consider the specification, estimation, diagnostic checking, and use for forecasting of ARMA(p,q) models. We will also consider a particular case of non-stationarity, defined integration, where the variable of interest turns out to be driven by cumulated sums of the elements of a white noise process, so that it can be made stationary by differencing it a proper number of times, say d. The extended model is called ARIMA(p,d,q). As we will see, ARIMA models can be used not only for forecasting but also for permanent-transitory decompositions and, more generally, as a basis for filtering, where the variable of interest is decomposed into two or more components, each of which characterized by different time series properties.

The chapter is structured as follows. In Section 5.2 we introduce the representations of AR, MA, and ARMA processes. In Section 5.3 we deal with model specification and in Section 5.4 with parameter estimation. In Section 5.5 we discuss unit roots and tests for their presence. In Section 5.6 we consider diagnostic testing. In Sections 5.7 and 5.8 we derive optimal forecasts for the cases of known and unknown parameters, respectively. In Section 5.9 we introduce an alternative method for multi-steps ahead forecasting. In Section 5.10 we consider permanent-transitory decompositions. In Section 5.11 we describe exponential smoothing and discuss its relationship with ARIMA models. In Section 5.12 we briefly consider seasonality. In Sections 5.13 and 5.14 we present examples based on, respectively, simulated and actual data. Section 5.15 concludes the chapter.

A more detailed analysis of the topics considered in this chapter can be found in Box and Jenkins (1976), Hamilton (1994) or Lütkepohl (2007), among others.

5.2   Representation

A time series process is strictly stationary when

$$\mathcal{F}\{y_t, \ldots, y_{t+T}\} = \mathcal{F}\{y_{t+k}, \ldots, y_{t+T+k}\}, \qquad \forall\, t, T, k. \tag{5.2.1}$$

where $\mathcal{F}(\cdot)$ indicates the joint density for a segment of length T of the process y. A time series process is weakly stationary if

$$
\begin{aligned}
E\left(y_t\right) &= E\left(y_{t+k}\right), & \forall\, t, k, \\
Var\left(y_t\right) &= Var\left(y_{t+k}\right), & \forall\, t, k, \\
Cov\left(y_t, y_{t-m}\right) &= Cov\left(y_{t+k}, y_{t-m+k}\right), & \forall\, t, m, k.
\end{aligned}
\tag{5.2.2}
$$

Hence, a strictly stationary process is typically also weakly stationary but the reverse is not true in general, unless the joint density is Gaussian.[1] A weakly stationary process can be represented as:

$$
\begin{aligned}
y_t &= \varepsilon_t + c_1 \varepsilon_{t-1} + c_2 \varepsilon_{t-2} + \ldots \quad\quad (5.2.3) \\
&= \sum_{i=0}^{\infty} c_i \varepsilon_{t-i} = \sum_{i=0}^{\infty} c_i L^i \varepsilon_t \\
&= c(L) \varepsilon_t,
\end{aligned}
$$

where L is the lag operator: $L\varepsilon_t = \varepsilon_{t-1}$ and $L^i \varepsilon_t = \varepsilon_{t-i}$, $c_0 = 1$ and the error process ε_t is uncorrelated across time and has a constant variance, hence: $\varepsilon_t \sim \mathrm{WN}(0, \sigma^2)$, meaning white noise with mean zero and variance σ^2. The infinite moving average representation in (5.2.3) is known as the Wold decomposition.

Note that we assumed in equation (5.2.3) that the overall mean of the process y_t is zero. It will be convenient to abstract from the unconditional mean throughout the chapter, except for some special cases of interest. Therefore, if we denote the unconditional mean by μ, all the analysis in this chapter goes through with y_t replaced by $(y_t - \mu)$ whenever we have a non-zero mean process.

A problem with the model in (5.2.3) is that it has an infinite number of parameters. However, in general, we can approximate $c(L)$ via a ratio of two finite polynomials, namely:

$$
c(L) = \frac{\psi(L)}{\phi(L)},
$$

where $\psi(L) = 1 - \psi_1 L - \ldots - \psi_q L^q$ and $\phi(L) = 1 - \phi_1 L - \ldots - \phi_p L^p$. Furthermore, because of weak stationarity $\phi(L)$ is invertible, i.e., $\phi(z) = 0 = \sum_{j=0}^{p} \phi_j z^j$ has all the roots outside the unit circle, we can rewrite equation (5.2.3) as

$$
\phi(L) y_t = \psi(L) \varepsilon_t,
$$

or equivalently as

$$
y_t = \phi_1 y_{t-1} + \ldots + \phi_p y_{t-p} + \varepsilon_t - \psi_1 \varepsilon_{t-1} - \ldots - \psi_q \varepsilon_{t-q}.
$$

---

[1]A strictly stationary process which is not weakly stationary is one where the density $\mathcal{F}(\cdot)$ does not have first and/or second moments.

This is a moving average autoregressive process of order p and q, henceforth called $ARMA(p, q)$.

Two useful tools to study ARMA processes are respectively the autocorrelation (AC) and partial autocorrelation (PAC) functions. To define them, we first introduce the autocovariance function, which reports the covariance of y_t with its own lags:

$$
\begin{aligned}
Cov\left(y_t, y_{t-1}\right) &= \gamma\left(1\right), \\
Cov\left(y_t, y_{t-2}\right) &= \gamma\left(2\right), \\
\vdots \qquad &\qquad \vdots \\
Cov\left(y_t, y_{t-k}\right) &= \gamma\left(k\right).
\end{aligned}
\tag{5.2.4}
$$

Then, the AC is defined as:

$$
AC(k) = \frac{Cov\left(y_t, y_{t-k}\right)}{\sqrt{Var(y_t)}\sqrt{Var(y_{t-k})}} = \frac{\gamma\left(k\right)}{\gamma\left(0\right)}.
$$

The kth value of the PAC measures the correlation between y_t and y_{t-k}, conditional on $y_{t-1}, \dots, y_{t-k+1}$. Operationally, the elements of the PAC can be considered as specific coefficients in regression equations. In particular, they are

$PAC\left(1\right)$: coefficient of y_{t-1} in the regression of y_t on y_{t-1},

$PAC\left(2\right)$: coefficient of y_{t-2} in the regression of y_t on y_{t-1}, y_{t-2},

$\qquad \vdots \qquad\qquad\qquad \vdots \qquad\qquad\qquad \vdots$

$PAC\left(k\right)$: coefficient of y_{t-k} in the regression of y_t on $y_{t-1}, \dots, y_{t-k}$.

Note that inserting a deterministic component (like a constant) in the model changes the expected value of y_t, while both the AC and PAC remain the same.

Before studying the characteristics of the class of $ARMA$ processes, we analyze the pure AR and MA processes.

5.2.1   Autoregressive processes

We assume that $c\left(L\right)$ in (5.2.3) is invertible, i.e., $c(z) = 0 = \sum_{j=0}^{\infty} c_j z^j$ has all the roots outside the unit circle. Then we can rewrite (5.2.3) as

$$
y_t = \sum_{j=1}^{\infty} \phi_j y_{t-j} + \varepsilon_t, \qquad \varepsilon_t \sim \text{WN}(0, \sigma^2).
\tag{5.2.5}
$$

Weak stationarity implies that the effect of y_{t-j} onto y_t fades as j becomes large. Hence, in practice we can reasonably approximate (5.2.5) with a pth-order autoregressive process, defined as

$$y_t = \phi_1 y_{t-1} + \ldots + \phi_p y_{t-p} + \varepsilon_t. \tag{5.2.6}$$

If we view the $AR(p)$ process in (5.2.6) as an approximation of (5.2.3), then it is weakly stationary by definition. If instead (5.2.6) is the data generating process (DGP), then precise conditions on its parameters are needed to ensure that y_t is weakly stationary. Specifically, y_t is weakly stationary if the roots of $\phi(z) = 1 - \phi_1 z - \ldots - \phi_p z^p = 0$ are all larger than one in absolute value.

Weak stationarity also guarantees that $\phi(L)$ can be inverted, namely, y_t can be represented as

$$y_t = \frac{1}{\phi(L)} \varepsilon_t, \tag{5.2.7}$$

which is an MA(∞) representation. The latter will be convenient in certain situations, e.g., to compute impulse response functions, see Chapter 6. Weak stationarity also matters to determine the properties of the parameter estimators, as we will see later on. Finally, note also that adding a deterministic component in (5.2.6) does not create additional complications.

As an example, let us consider the $AR(1)$ process:

$$\begin{aligned} y_t &= \phi_1 y_{t-1} + \varepsilon_t. \\ \phi(L) &= 1 - \phi_1 L. \end{aligned} \tag{5.2.8}$$

Weak stationarity requires $|\phi_1| < 1$, since

$$\phi(z) = 1 - \phi_1 z = 0 \rightarrow z = \frac{1}{\phi_1}.$$

The $MA(\infty)$ representation is

$$\begin{aligned} y_t &= \varepsilon_t + \phi_1 \varepsilon_{t-1} + \phi_1^2 y_{t-2} = \\ &= \varepsilon_t + \phi_1 \varepsilon_{t-1} + \phi_1^2 \varepsilon_{t-2} + \phi_1^3 y_{t-3} \\ &\quad\quad \vdots \\ &= \sum_{i=0}^{\infty} \phi_1^i \varepsilon_{t-i} = \frac{1}{\phi(L)} \varepsilon_t. \end{aligned} \tag{5.2.9}$$

We can use the MA(∞) representation to compute the mean and variance of y_t, namely:

$$E\left(y_t\right) = 0$$

$$Var\left(y_t\right) = Var\left(\sum_{i=0}^{\infty}\phi_1^i\varepsilon_{t-i}\right) = \sum_{i=0}^{\infty}Var\left(\phi_1^i\varepsilon_{t-i}\right)$$

$$= \sum_{i=0}^{\infty}\phi_1^{2i}Var\left(\varepsilon_{t-i}\right) = \frac{\sigma^2}{1-\phi_1^2}.$$

Moreover, the autocovariance function appearing in (5.2.5) for the AR(1) is as follows:

$$\gamma\left(1\right) = Cov\left(\phi_1y_{t-1}+\varepsilon_t, y_{t-1}\right) = \phi_1Var\left(y_t\right) = \phi_1\gamma\left(0\right),$$
$$\gamma\left(2\right) = Cov\left(\phi_1y_{t-1}+\varepsilon_t, y_{t-2}\right) = \phi_1\gamma\left(1\right) = \phi_1^2\gamma\left(0\right),$$
$$\vdots$$
$$\gamma\left(k\right) = Cov\left(\phi_1y_{t-1}+\varepsilon_t, y_{t-k}\right) = \phi_1\gamma\left(k-1\right) = \phi_1^k\gamma\left(0\right).$$

Therefore, for $j = 1, 2, \ldots$, the AC is defined as:

$$AC(j) = \frac{Cov\left(y_t, y_{t-j}\right)}{\sigma_y\sigma_{y-j}} = \frac{\gamma\left(j\right)}{\gamma\left(0\right)} = \phi_1^j.$$

For the elements of the PAC we have:

$$PAC\left(1\right) = \phi_1,$$
$$PAC\left(j\right) = 0, \quad j > 1.$$

Let us consider now the case of an $AR(2)$ process:

$$y_t = \phi_1y_{t-1}+\phi_2y_{t-2}+\varepsilon_t. \tag{5.2.10}$$

To derive the weak stationarity conditions let us consider the solutions of

$$\phi\left(z\right) = 1-\phi_1z-\phi_2z^2 = 0,$$

which are

$$z_{1,2} = \frac{-\phi_1\pm\sqrt{\phi_1^2+4\phi_2}}{2\phi_2}.$$

Therefore, to have $|z_1| > 1$ and $|z_2| > 1$, we need:

$$\begin{aligned}
\phi_1 + \phi_2 &< 1, \\
\phi_2 - \phi_1 &< 1, \\
-\phi_2 &< 1,
\end{aligned}$$

see Harvey (1993) for further details. The autocovariance function for an AR(2) process is given by:

$$\begin{aligned}
\gamma(0) &= \phi_1 \gamma(1) + \phi_2 \gamma(2) + \sigma_\varepsilon^2, \\
\gamma(1) &= \phi_1 \gamma(0) + \phi_2 \gamma(1), \\
\gamma(2) &= \phi_1 \gamma(1) + \phi_2 \gamma(0), \\
&\vdots \\
\gamma(k) &= \phi_1 \gamma(k-1) + \phi_2 \gamma(k-2).
\end{aligned}$$

The general element j of the autocovariance function can be obtained as follows. First, one multiplies both sides of (5.2.10) with y_{t-j}. Second, one takes expectations on both sides and uses the fact that y_{t-j} and ε_t are uncorrelated and that $\gamma(i) = \gamma(-i)$.

Let us now form a system with the equations for the first three lags of the autocovariance function. Solving this system of three equations, expressing the γs as a function of the AR parameters, we obtain:

$$\begin{aligned}
\gamma(0) &= \frac{(1 - \phi_1)\sigma_\varepsilon^2}{(1 + \phi_2)\left[(1 - \phi_2)^2 - \phi_1^2\right]}, \\
\gamma(1) &= \frac{\phi_1 \gamma(0)}{1 - \phi_2}, \\
\gamma(2) &= \phi_1 \gamma(1) + \phi_2 \gamma(0),
\end{aligned}$$

The autocorrelation function for an AR(2) process therefore is:

$$\begin{aligned}
AC(1) &= \frac{\phi_1}{(1 - \phi_2)} \\
AC(2) &= \phi_2 + \frac{\phi_1^2}{(1 - \phi_2)}, \\
&\vdots \\
AC(k) &= \phi_1 AC(k-1) + \phi_2 AC(k-2).
\end{aligned}$$

These are known as the Yule-Walker equations, and they can be used to obtain estimators of ϕ_1 and ϕ_2. In fact, if we substitute $AC(1)$ and $AC(2)$ with their estimated counterparts, the first two equations can be solved for $\hat{\phi}_1$ and $\hat{\phi}_2$. Typically there are more efficient estimators than those based on the Yule-Walker equations, but the latter can provide a simple initial estimate.

For the partial autocorrelation function, it can be easily shown that its first two lags are different from zero, while $PAC(j) = 0$ for $j > 2$. Using methods similar to those seen in the examples considered so far, we can calculate the AC and PAC for any $AR\left(p\right)$ process. Moreover, the equations which define the first p lags of the AC function can also be used to obtain the initial (Yule-Walker) estimators of the parameters.

5.2.2   Moving average processes

The qth-order moving average process is defined as

$$y_t = \varepsilon_t - \psi_1 \varepsilon_{t-1} - \ldots - \psi_q \varepsilon_{t-q} = \psi\left(L\right)\varepsilon_t, \qquad \varepsilon_t \sim WN\left(0, \sigma_\varepsilon^2\right). \quad (5.2.11)$$

It can easily be shown that an MA(q) process is always weakly stationary. Its first two moments are

$$
\begin{aligned}
E\left(y_t\right) &= 0, \\
Var\left(y_t\right) &= \left(1 + \psi_1^2 + \ldots + \psi_q^2\right)\sigma_\varepsilon^2 = \gamma\left(0\right),
\end{aligned}
$$

whereas the autocovariance function is as follows:

$$
\begin{aligned}
\gamma(k) &= Cov\left(y_t, y_{t-k}\right) \\
&= Cov\left(\varepsilon_t - \psi_1 \varepsilon_{t-1} - \ldots - \psi_q \varepsilon_{t-q}, \varepsilon_{t-k} - \psi_1 \varepsilon_{t-k-1} - \ldots - \psi_q \varepsilon_{t-k-q}\right) \\
&= \begin{cases} \left(-\psi_k + \psi_{k+1}\psi_1 + \ldots + \psi_q \psi_{q-k}\right)\sigma_\varepsilon^2 & k = 1, \ldots, q \\ 0 & k > q \end{cases}.
\end{aligned}
$$

Dividing $\gamma(k)$ by $\gamma(0)$ yields the autocorrelation function.

Another relevant property for an MA process is invertibility, that is, the possibility to represent an MA process as an AR(∞). This requires that all the roots of $\psi\left(z\right) = 0$ are larger than one in absolute value. When the MA process is invertible, we can write:

$$\frac{1}{\psi\left(L\right)}y_t = \varepsilon_t.$$

The AR(∞) representation is useful to derive the PAC for an MA process, which will coincide with that of the AR(∞) process. Hence, the PAC elements decay (possibly non-monotonically) towards zero, but are always different from zero except in the limit.

As an example, let us consider the MA(1) process

$$y_t = \varepsilon_t - \psi_1 \varepsilon_{t-1}. \tag{5.2.12}$$

Its first two moments are

$$\begin{aligned} E\left(y_t\right) &= 0, \\ Var\left(y_t\right) &= \left(1 + \psi_1^2\right)\sigma_\varepsilon^2, \end{aligned}$$

while the autocovariance function is

$$\begin{aligned} \gamma(1) &= -\psi_1 \sigma_\epsilon^2 \\ \gamma(k) &= 0, \quad k > 1, \end{aligned}$$

and for the AC we have $AC(1) = -\psi_1/(1 + \psi_1^2)$ and $AC(k) = 0$, $k > 1$. The condition for invertibility is $|\psi_1| < 1$, with associated AR(∞) representation

$$\left(1 + \psi_1 L + \psi_1^2 L^2 + \psi_1^3 L^3 + \ldots\right) y_t = \varepsilon_t.$$

From the latter, we can see that the PAC of the $MA(1)$ process declines exponentially.

To conclude, let us note the different shapes of the AC and PAC for AR and MA processes. We have seen that the AC decays for an $AR(p)$ process but is always different from zero, except in the limit, while for an $MA(q)$ process the AC is only different from zero up to q lags. Conversely, the PAC of an $AR(p)$ process is only different from zero up to p lags, while that of an $MA(q)$ process decays but is always different from zero, except in the limit. These considerations suggest that the estimated AC and PAC could be used to determine whether the underlying process is of the AR or MA type, and what is the order of the lags. We will revisit this issue in Section 5.3.

5.2.3 ARMA processes

An $ARMA(p, q)$ process is defined as

$$\phi\left(L\right) y_t = \psi\left(L\right) \varepsilon_t. \tag{5.2.13}$$

The weak stationarity condition is, as for the AR processes,

$$\phi(z) = 0 \rightarrow |z_i| > 1, \qquad i = 1, \ldots, p,$$

where z_i are the roots of the AR polynomial. Likewise, the invertibility condition is, as for the MA processes,

$$\psi(z) = 0 \rightarrow |z_i| > 1, \qquad i = 1, \ldots, q.$$

where z_i are the roots of the MA polynomial. For a stationary $ARMA$, we can write the infinite MA representation as:

$$y_t = \phi^{-1}(L) \psi(L) \varepsilon_t = c(L) \varepsilon_t$$

Therefore, the expected value and variance are:

$$E(y_t) \quad = \quad 0 \tag{5.2.14}$$

$$Var(y_t) \quad = \quad \sigma_\varepsilon^2 \sum_{i=0}^{\infty} c_i^2. \tag{5.2.15}$$

The AC and the PAC are like those of an $MA(\infty)$ or $AR(\infty)$, so both decline exponentially.

As an example, let us derive the autocovariance structure for an ARMA(1,1) process:

$$y_t = \phi_1 y_{t-1} + \varepsilon_t - \psi_1 \varepsilon_{t-1}. \tag{5.2.16}$$

Moreover:

$$\begin{aligned} \gamma_0 \quad &= \quad Var(y_t) = E(\phi_1 y_{t-1} + \varepsilon_t - \psi_1 \varepsilon_{t-1})^2 = \\ &= \quad \phi_1^2 \gamma_0 + \sigma_\varepsilon^2 + \psi_1^2 \sigma_\varepsilon^2 - 2\phi_1 \psi_1 E(y_{t-1}\varepsilon_{t-1}) \\ &= \quad \phi_1^2 \gamma_0 + \sigma_\varepsilon^2 + \psi_1^2 \sigma_\varepsilon^2 - 2\phi_1 \psi_1 \sigma_\varepsilon^2, \end{aligned}$$

and:

$$\begin{aligned} \gamma_1 \quad &= \quad Cov(y_t, y_{t-1}) = E(y_{t-1}(\phi_1 y_{t-1} + \varepsilon_t - \psi_1 \varepsilon_{t-1})) \\ &= \quad \phi_1 \gamma_0 - \psi_1 \sigma_\varepsilon^2 = \frac{(1 - \phi_1 \psi_1)(\phi_1 - \psi_1)}{1 - \phi_1^2} \sigma_\varepsilon^2. \end{aligned}$$

Next,

$$\gamma_2 = Cov(y_t, y_{t-2}) = E(y_{t-2}(\phi_1 y_{t-1} + \varepsilon_t - \psi_1 \varepsilon_{t-1})) = \phi_1 \gamma_1.$$

Similarly, the generic element of the autocovariance function is

$$\gamma_k = Cov\left(y_t, y_{t-k}\right) = \phi_1 \gamma_{k-1},$$

while by definition: $AC(k) = \gamma_k/\gamma_0$. Therefore, for $k \ ¿ \ 2$ the shape of the AC is similar to that of an $AR(1)$ process. It can be easily shown that the MA component plays a similar role for the PAC, in the sense that for $k > 2$ the shape of the PAC is similar to that of an $MA(1)$ process.

Finally, to obtain a first estimate of the $ARMA(1,1)$ parameters ϕ_1, ψ_1, σ_ε^2 we can use the Yule-Walker approach. More specifically, one can form a system with the equations for γ_0, γ_1, γ_2. Then, using sample counterparts $\hat{\gamma}_0$, $\hat{\gamma}_1$, $\hat{\gamma}_2$, one obtains parameter estimates by solving the system for $\hat{\phi}_1, \hat{\psi}_1, \hat{\sigma}_\varepsilon^2$.

5.2.4   Integrated processes

An integrated process y_t is a non stationary process such that $(1 - L)^d y_t$ is stationary, where d is the order of integration and the process is typically labeled $I(d)$. These are also called unit root processes, since integration is associated with roots of the AR polynomial $\phi(L)$ exactly equal to one, namely, one or more values for z in $\phi(z) = 0$ are equal to one, while in the weakly stationary case we have seen that all the roots must be larger than one in absolute value.

The most common integrated process is the Random Walk (RW):

$$y_t = y_{t-1} + \varepsilon_t, \tag{5.2.17}$$

for which $d = 1$, since

$$(1 - L)y_t = \Delta y_t = \varepsilon_t.$$

A RW can also be written as

$$y_t = \varepsilon_t + \varepsilon_{t-1} + \varepsilon_{t-2} + \dots, \tag{5.2.18}$$

so that the effects of a shock do not decay over time, contrary to the case of a weakly stationary process (compare (5.2.18) with (5.2.9)).

From (5.2.18) we see that

$$E(y_t) = 0,$$

while the variance is not properly defined:

$$Var(y_t) = Var(\varepsilon_t + \varepsilon_{t-1} + \varepsilon_{t-2} + \dots) \to \infty.$$

The AC is also not properly defined, but the persistence of the effects of the shocks is such that if we computed empirically the AC, its elements would not decay as in the weakly stationary case but would remain close to one at all lags. For the PAC, we can easily see that $PAC(1) = 1$, while $PAC(j) = 0$ for $j > 1$.

Inserting a deterministic component into an integrated process can change its features substantially. As an example, let us consider the RW with drift:

$$y_t = \mu + y_{t-1} + \varepsilon_t. \tag{5.2.19}$$

Repeated substitution yields:

$$y_t = \mu + \varepsilon_t + \mu + \varepsilon_{t-1} + \mu + \varepsilon_{t-2} + \dots$$

so that

$$E\left(y_t\right) = E(\mu + \varepsilon_t + \mu + \varepsilon_{t-1} + \mu + \varepsilon_{t-2} + \dots) \quad \to \quad \infty,$$
$$Var\left(y_t\right) = Var(\mu + \varepsilon_t + \mu + \varepsilon_{t-1} + \mu + \varepsilon_{t-2} + \dots) \quad \to \quad \infty,$$

and the AC and PAC are as in the RW case. Also in this case first differencing eliminates the non-stationarity, since

$$\left(1 - L\right) y_t = \Delta y_t = \mu + \varepsilon_t.$$

Recall that throughout the chapter we assumed for convenience that the mean of y_t is zero. It is clear that from the above discussion that this assumption can be maintained for integrated processes once we subtract μ from $\left(1 - L\right) y_t$.

5.2.5   ARIMA processes

An $ARIMA(p, d, q)$ process is

$$\phi\left(L\right) \Delta^d y_t = \psi\left(L\right) \varepsilon_t. \tag{5.2.20}$$

with $\Delta^d \equiv \left(1 - L\right)^d$, whereas $\phi\left(L\right)$ and $\psi\left(L\right)$ are polynomials in the lag operator of order, respectively, p and q, while y_t is $I(d)$. If we define $x_t = \Delta^d y_t$, x_t is an $ARMA(p, q)$. Hence, the only additional complication with respect to the $ARMA$ case is the determination of the order of integration d.

5.3 Model specification

In order to specify an ARIMA model, we need to determine d, p and q, namely, the order of integration and the lag length of the AR and MA components. Three main approaches are available, based respectively on the AC/PAC, testing, and information criteria.

5.3.1 AC/PAC based specification

Using the available data on y_t, we can easily estimate the AC and PAC for different values of k. These values are typically graphed, with increasing values of k on the right axis, possibly together with their associated $(1-\alpha)\%$ confidence intervals, where typically $\alpha = 0.05$.

If the estimated values of both AC and PAC decay when k increases, there is evidence that y_t is weakly stationary and therefore we can set $d = 0$. If instead the AC declines very slowly and PAC(1) is close to one, then there is evidence for a unit root. Therefore, we difference y_t once, and repeat the analysis with Δy_t. If necessary, we further difference y_t, otherwise we set $d = 1$ and move to determine p and q.

If the estimated PAC presents some peaks and then it is close to zero, while the AC declines exponentially, there is evidence in favor of a pure AR(p), with p equal to the number of peaks (coefficients statistically different from zero) in the PAC.

If instead the AC has peaks and then it is close to zero, while the PAC declines exponentially, the evidence is in favor of a pure MA(q), with q equal to the number of peaks (coefficients statistically different from zero) in the AC.

Otherwise we have an ARMA process. The entity of the peaks of the AC and PAC can provide an idea on the order of the AR and MA components, but the identification of p and q from AC/PAC is clearly more complex in the ARMA case. One possibility is to make a guess on p and q, estimate the ARMA model, control whether the resulting residuals are WN, and if not go back and try with a higher value for p and/or q.

5.3.2   Testing based specification

A useful diagnostic tool to appraise the fit of a time series model pertains to testing whether a number of (residual) autocorrelations are equal to zero. Suppose we have selected the orders p and q of an ARMA model and estimated its parameters, then we should expect that the estimated errors, denoted by $\hat{\varepsilon}_t$, are temporally uncorrelated. A commonly used test is the Ljung-Box Q test (Ljung and Box (1978)), and an improved version known as the Box-Pierce test (Box and Pierce (1970)). Either test is often reported as *Portmanteau* test in standard software output. The null hypothesis is that the correlations in the population from which the sample is taken are zero. The Ljung-Box Q test is formally defined as:

$$Q_{LB} = T\,(T+2)\sum_{k=1}^{h}\frac{\hat{\rho}_k^2}{T-k}$$

where $\hat{\rho}_k$ is the sample autocorrelation at lag k, and h is the number of lags being tested. Under the null the statistic Q follows a $\chi^2_{(h)}$ distribution. When applied to the residuals of a fitted ARMA model, the degrees of freedom need to be adjusted however, to reflect the parameter estimation. For example, for an ARIMA(p,q) model, the degrees of freedom should be set to $h - p - q$ (see Davidson (2000, p. 162)). The Box-Pierce test, in the notation outlined above, is given by

$$Q_{BP} = T\sum_{k=1}^{h}\hat{\rho}_k^2,$$

and uses the same critical region as the Ljung-Box test.

Many regression-based model selection procedures exist for ARIMA(p,d,0) type models, i.e., models without MA terms, based on formal testing procedures, such as the Wald or LR statistics. The problem is similar to the regressor selection that we have discussed in Chapter 1 in the context of the linear model. This includes the vast array of unit root tests to determine d, which will be discussed in Section 5.5. Testing the lag length of the MA component is slightly more difficult, as we will see its presence prevents the use of OLS estimation, but can still be performed via ML or GMM procedures.

5.3.3 Testing for ARCH

While we will cover ARCH-type models in Chapter 14, it is worth mentioning a test for ARCH (autoregressive conditional heteroskedasticity) as it is closely related to the Box-Pierce and Ljung-Box tests. The test involves regressing ε_t^2 (note the square power transformation as we deal with time-varying variances) onto a constant and h lags $\varepsilon_{t-1}^2 \ldots, \varepsilon_{t-h}^2$. Using a straightforward derivation of the LM test leads to the TR^2 test statistic, where the R^2 pertains to the aforementioned regression. Under the null hypothesis that there is no ARCH, the test statistic is asymptotically distributed as chi-square distribution with h degrees of freedom.

5.3.4 Specification with information criteria

The third option for ARIMA model specification is the use of information criteria (IC), which were introduced in Chapter 1. IC combine model goodness of fit with a penalty function related to the number of model parameters, such that small models are preferred to large ones when they have similar fit.

Selecting the AR and MA orders p and q requires one to start with a general enough model, namely, an ARIMA(p_{MAX},d, q_{MAX}) where it is assumed that $p_{MAX} > p_0$ and $q_{MAX} > q_0$, where p_0 and q_0 are the true orders. A more technical condition is related to the penalty function and guarantees that the procedure provides consistent results asymptotically, in the sense of selecting the true orders p_0 and q_0 with probability approaching one when the sample size T diverges. This condition is satisfied by the BIC criterion

$$BIC = \log(\widehat{\sigma}_\varepsilon^2) + (p+q)\log(T)/T$$

but not by the AIC criterion

$$AIC = \log(\widehat{\sigma}_\varepsilon^2) + 2(p+q)/T$$

However, the relative performance of the AIC and BIC criteria in finite samples cannot be uniquely defined, even though generally the former leads to less parsimonious specifications than the latter since it penalizes less the number of model parameters. See Lütkepohl (2007) for additional details and derivations.

Empirically, we need to compute the IC for all combinations of p and q (and possibly d) and then select the one that minimizes the IC. Hence, this procedure requires to estimate a possibly large set of models, but estimation of ARIMA models, and particularly of AR models, is rather fast.

We conclude with a few general remarks. First, the three methods we have discussed for model specification can, of course, also be jointly applied, in order to assess whether they provide the same indications. In case of conflicting or uncertain results, which are possible also within the same method, we can proceed with a few alternative specifications, rather than selecting one, and compare their forecasting performance. Typically the latter will be fairly similar, suggesting that the data are not informative enough to discriminate across alternative specifications, but also that, at least from a forecasting point of view, this is not a relevant problem. If instead we wanted to associate a structural meaning to the parameters and/or to the alternative specifications, then the identification issue would be much more relevant.

Second, in general, the lower the p and q orders the better, as long as the model is correctly specified. Parsimonious specifications tend to forecast better and are less prone to overfitting problems, namely, tailoring the model to fit very well a specific sample, but not necessarily a longer sample and therefore with a deterioration in the out-of-sample (forecasting) performance.

Third, we have seen that, assuming invertibility, an MA process can be represented as an $AR(\infty)$ process. There are results showing that, under rather mild conditions, the latter can be approximated by a finite AR process. Intuitively, since most economic time series exhibit limited memory, very high AR lags can be omitted. Since, as we will see, estimation of an MA component can be complex, pure AR approximations are often used in forecasting exercises. However, the use of an MA component can yield a much more parsimonious specification, which can be helpful in a forecasting context.

Finally, the choice of the order of differencing d is in general not a major problem in a forecasting context. If we set $d = 0$ by mistake since y_t is I(1), then one of the AR roots will be anyway estimated to be close to one. If instead we set $d = 1$ by mistake since y_t is I(0), then one of the MA roots will be close to one, thus close to canceling the effects of the imposed unit AR root. The value of d, however, affects the properties of the forecasts, as we will see. It is also relevant in a structural context, where different economic theories can have alternative implications on whether a given variable is stationary or integrated.

5.4 Estimation

Once the order of the ARIMA(p,d,q) is specified, we need to estimate the parameters in $\phi(L)$ and $\psi(L)$, where

$$\phi(L) \Delta^d y_t = \psi(L) \varepsilon_t.$$

If we define $w_t = \Delta^d y_t$, then

$$\phi(L) w_t = \psi(L) \varepsilon_t$$

and again

$$\varepsilon_t = \psi(L)^{-1} \phi(L) w_t.$$

Suppose the objective function to be minimized is the usual sum of squared errors:

$$S_t = \sum \varepsilon_t^2.$$

Compared to the linear regression model considered in the previous chapters we face additional problems when $q > 0$. In fact, if there is an MA component, S_t is non-linear in the parameters. For example for an MA(1) process we have

$$y_t - \psi_1 y_{t-1} - \psi_1^2 y_{t-2} - \ldots = \varepsilon_t.$$

Therefore, we cannot find an analytical expression for the parameter estimators. Instead they will have to be determined using a numerical optimization method. The resulting estimators are labeled non-linear least squares (NLS) estimators.

The typical estimator used for ARMA models is not quite the resulting non-linear least squares, but rather the maximum likelihood estimator (MLE). To define this estimator, let us first recall that $\varepsilon_t \sim \text{WN}(0, \sigma^2)$, and add the distributional assumption that for all t ε_t is normally distributed, hence $\varepsilon_t \overset{iid}{\sim} N(0, \sigma^2)$. Furthermore, let us also collect all the parameters we need to estimate into a vector called θ. This will include the parameters determining $\phi(L)$ and $\psi(L)$, as well as σ^2. For ARMA time series models we also face the problem that, given a sample of size T, we need to think about how to deal with so-called starting values. Take, for example, the AR(1) model: How do we treat y_0 which enters in the specification of the first observation y_1? Likewise, how do we treat ε_0 in a MA(1) model? For the purpose of our analysis, we follow a recommendation of Box and Jenkins (1976, p. 211) and compute the likelihood of an ARMA(p,q) conditional on $y_1, \ldots, y_p$, equal to the first p observations and $\varepsilon_1 = \ldots = \varepsilon_{Max(p,q)} = 0$. Therefore, using the Gaussian density we have the sample log likelihood function of the ARMA(p,q) model equal to:

$$\mathcal{L}(y_{p+1}, \ldots, y_T; \theta) = -\frac{T-p}{2} \log(2\pi) - \frac{T}{2} \log(\sigma^2) \qquad (5.4.1)$$
$$-\sum_{t=p+1}^{T} \frac{\varepsilon_t^2}{2\sigma^2}$$

Under mild conditions, the MLE estimator is consistent and, when multiplied by $\sqrt{T}$, it has an asymptotically normal distribution, centered at the true parameter values denoted by θ_0. Note also that in the context of MLE there is no analytical expression for the estimator in the presence of an MA component.

In order to reach convergence of a numerical optimization method, it is important to start with reasonable initial values for the parameters. A possibility is to use the Yule-Walker estimators that we have discussed before, that is, estimate the AC and use the theoretic relations between its coefficients and the parameters of $\phi(L)$ and $\psi(L)$ to obtain an estimate of the latter. For a more detailed discussion of the MLE of ARMA models, see e.g., Hamilton (1994, Chapter 5).

When $q = 0$, i.e., in the absence of MA terms, we are back to the case of a linear dynamic model, discussed in Chapter 2, so that the parameters can be estimated by OLS.[2]

5.5   Unit root tests

To understand the econometric issues associated with unit root and stationarity tests, let us consider the following model:

$$\begin{aligned} y_t &= T_t + z_t \\ T_t &= \nu_0 + \nu_1 t \\ z_t &= \rho z_{t-1} + \varepsilon_t \end{aligned} \qquad (5.5.1)$$

---

[2]It is also possible to estimate MA models indirectly via AR approximate models using a technique known as indirect inference (see Gouriéroux, Monfort, and Renault (1993)). For further details see Ghysels, Khalaf, and Vodounou (2003).

with $\varepsilon_t \sim \text{WN}(0, \sigma^2)$, and T_t is a deterministic linear trend. If $\rho < 1$ then y_t is I(0) about the deterministic trend T_t, sometimes referred to as *trend-stationary*. If $\rho = 1$ and $\nu_1 = 0$, then z_t is a random walk and y_t is I(1) with drift.

Let us start with $\nu_0 = \nu_1 = 0$ and hence T_t is zero, yielding:

$$y_t = \rho y_{t-1} + \varepsilon_t, \tag{5.5.2}$$

or

$$\Delta y_t = (\rho - 1) y_{t-1} + \varepsilon_t. \tag{5.5.3}$$

We are interested in whether there is a unit root, $\rho = 1$, so that y_t is I(1) and we need to difference the process to achieve stationarity. Formally, we are interested in the hypothesis:

$$H_0: \quad \rho = 1 \quad \rightarrow y_t \quad \text{is I(1) without drift}$$
$$H_1: \quad |\rho| < 1 \quad \rightarrow y_t \quad \text{is I(0) with mean zero}$$

Note that the coefficient of y_{t-1} in equation (5.5.3) is equal to zero when $\rho = 1$. Hence, we might be tempted to use a $t-$test to verify the hypothesis of interest. Unfortunately, the problem is that under the unit root null, the usual sample moments of y_t used to compute the $t-$test do not converge to fixed constants. Instead, Dickey and Fuller (1979) and Phillips (1987) showed that the sample moments of y_t converge to random functions of Brownian motions on the unit interval.[3] In particular:

$$T^{-3/2} \sum_{t=1}^{T} y_{t-1} \quad \overset{d}{\rightarrow} \sigma \int_0^1 W(\tau) d\tau$$

$$T^{-2} \sum_{t=1}^{T} y_{t-1}^2 \quad \overset{d}{\rightarrow} \sigma^2 \int_0^1 W(\tau)^2 d\tau$$

$$T^{-1} \sum_{t=1}^{T} y_{t-1} \varepsilon_t \quad \overset{d}{\rightarrow} \sigma^2 \int_0^1 W(\tau) dW(\tau)$$

---

[3]A Brownian Motion – or also called a Wiener process – on the unit interval is a continuous-time stochastic process, associating with each $\tau \in [0, 1]$ a scalar random variable $W(\tau)$ that satisfies: (1) $W(0) = 0$; (2) for any dates $0 \leq \tau_1 \leq \ldots \leq \tau_k \leq 1$ the incremental changes $W(\tau_2) - W(\tau_1)$, $\ldots$, $W(\tau_k) - W(\tau_{k-1})$ are i.i.d. normal with $W(s) - W(t) \sim N(0, (s-t))$; (3) $W(s)$ is continuous in s.

Using the above results Phillips showed that under the unit root null:

$$T(\hat{\rho} - 1) \quad \xrightarrow{d} \quad \frac{\int_0^1 W(\tau)dW(\tau)}{\int_0^1 W(\tau)^2 d\tau}$$

$$t - test(\rho = 1) \quad \xrightarrow{d} \quad \frac{\int_0^1 W(\tau)dW(\tau)}{(\int_0^1 W(\tau)^2 d\tau)^{1/2}}$$

The above yields:

- The convergence rate of $\hat{\rho}$ is not the standard $\sqrt{T}$ but instead T, typically referred to as '*super-consistency*.

- Neither $\hat{\rho}$ nor $t - test(\rho = 1)$ are asymptotically normally distributed.

- The limiting distribution of $t - test(\rho = 1)$ is called the Dickey-Fuller (DF) (Dickey and Fuller (1979)) distribution, which does not have a closed form representation. Consequently, the p-values of the distribution must be computed by numerical approximation or by simulation. The critical values are available in tables, or they are automatically generated by econometric software packages.

- The $T(\hat{\rho} - 1)$ and $t - test(\rho = 1)$ statistics are called respectively Dickey-Fuller (DF) normalized bias test and DF t-test.

- The critical values of the DF distribution are generally larger than the standard t distribution ones, such that using the standard critical values will lead to rejecting the null hypothesis of a unit root too often.

The distribution of the test statistics is also different depending on the deterministic component since we have seen that the interaction of unit roots and deterministic components can change the model structure substantially. In practice, the trend properties of the data under the alternative hypothesis H_1 will determine the form of the test regression used. Furthermore, the type of deterministic terms in the test regression will influence the asymptotic distributions of the unit root test statistics. Hence, a careful choice of the deterministic component and associated critical value is required. The two most common trend cases can be summarized as follows:

Constant Only

The test regression is

$$\Delta y_t = \nu_0 + (\rho - 1) y_{t-1} + \varepsilon_t$$

and includes a constant to capture the nonzero mean under the alternative. More specifically:

$$H_0: \quad \rho = 1 \text{ and } \nu_0 = 0 \quad \to y_t \quad \text{is I(1) without drift}$$
$$H_1: \quad |\rho| < 1 \text{ and } \nu_0 \neq 0 \quad \to y_t \quad \text{is I(0) with non-zero mean}$$

Under H_0 the asymptotic distributions of the normalized biased and t test statistics are influenced by the presence but not the coefficient value of the intercept in the DF test regression.

Constant and Time Trend

The test regression is

$$\Delta y_t = \nu_0 + \nu_1 t + (\rho - 1) y_{t-1} + \varepsilon_t$$

and includes a constant and deterministic time trend to capture the deterministic trend under the alternative. The hypotheses to be tested are

$$H_0: \quad \rho = 1 \text{ and } \nu_1 = 0 \quad \to y_t \quad \text{is I(1) with drift}$$
$$H_1: \quad |\rho| < 1 \text{ and } \nu_1 \neq 0 \quad \to y_t \quad \text{is I(0) with deterministic trend}$$

Under H_0 the asymptotic distributions of the normalized biased and t test statistics are again influenced by the presence but not the parameter values of the intercept and trend slope coefficients in the DF test regression.

If the AR process is of order p, with $p > 1$, we can always rewrite the process as

$$\Delta y_t = \gamma y_{t-1} + \rho_1 \Delta y_{t-1} + \ldots + \rho_{p-1} \Delta y_{t-p+1} + \varepsilon_t, \tag{5.5.4}$$

where $\gamma = \phi(1)$, and the ρ coefficients are related to the original ϕ coefficients. If one of the roots of $\phi(z) = 0$ is $z = 1$, it follows that $\phi(1) = \gamma = 0$ and therefore the coefficient of y_{t-1} in (5.5.4) will be equal to zero. We can therefore apply the same test as before, namely a t-test for $\gamma = 0$, or normalized bias test, which are both known as Augmented Dickey Fuller (ADF) tests. Interestingly, the ADF test has the same distribution as the DF test, hence we can use the same critical values. To be more specific, we can run test regressions:

$$\Delta y_t = D_t \beta + \gamma y_{t-1} + \rho_1 \Delta y_{t-1} + \ldots + \rho_{p-1} \Delta y_{t-p+1} + \varepsilon_t$$

where D_t is a vector of deterministic terms (constant, trend). The specification of the deterministic terms depends on the assumed behavior under the alternative hypothesis of trend stationarity as noted before. The ADF t-statistic and normalized bias statistic (the latter being computed as $T(\hat{\gamma} - 1)/(1 - \hat{\rho}_1 \ldots - \hat{\rho}_{p-1})$) are based on the least squares estimates of the above regression and have the same limiting distribution as with $p = 1$. However, in finite samples, the size and power of the ADF test are affected by the number of lags included in (5.5.4), so that the determination of p is relevant and we can use any of the procedures discussed in Section 5.3.

Phillips and Perron (1988) developed a number of alternative unit root tests. The Phillips-Perron (PP) unit root tests differ from the ADF tests mainly in how they deal with serial correlation and heteroskedasticity in the errors. In particular, where the ADF tests use a parametric autoregression to approximate the (in general ARMA) structure of the errors in the test regression, the PP tests ignore any serial correlation in the test regression. The PP test regression essentially relies on HAC estimators (cfr. section 2.3) to account for the serial correlation and the heteroskedastcity.

Elliott, Rothenberg, and Stock (1996) proposed a modification of the DF test statistic based on the generalized least squares (GLS) principle. This modification, known as DF-GLS, can substantially improve the small-sample size and power of the test, in particular when an unknown mean or trend is present. The DF-GLS statistic, as well as the PP tests, are implemented in standard econometric software, such as *EViews* or *R*.

The size and power of unit root tests are also affected by the presence of deterministic breaks in the model parameters. Since the latter, when unaccounted, often spuriously increase the persistence of the series, it can happen that a unit root is not rejected even when the root is actually smaller than one (so the power of the test decreases). There exist more complex statistical procedures to allow for breaks when testing for unit roots, see, e.g., Perron (1989) and Stock (1994).

There are also procedures to test for the presence of more than one unit root, e.g., $d = 2$. The simplest approach is first to test whether Δy_t has a unit root (so that $d = 2$) and then, if the hypothesis is rejected, whether y_t has a unit root (so that $d = 1$). At each step we can use the DF or ADF tests that we have described above, though one should use proper critical values that control for the sequential applications of the procedure.

For forecasting, it is worth mentioning that if y_t is $I(d)$, so that

$$\Delta^d y_t = w_t, \tag{5.5.5}$$

then

$$y_t = \Sigma^d w_t, \tag{5.5.6}$$

where, as an example,

$$\Sigma w_t = \sum_{i=-\infty}^{t} w_i, \tag{5.5.7}$$

$$\Sigma^2 w_t = \sum_{i=-\infty}^{t} \sum_{i=-\infty}^{j} w_j. \tag{5.5.8}$$

To conclude, we mention that are many alternative procedures available for testing for unit roots (or for stationarity), notably where the null is trend-stationarity see e.g., Kwiatkowski, Phillips, Schmidt, and Shin (1992). However, it remains difficult in general to outperform the ADF procedure, which has the advantage of being easy to implement and understand. For further details, there are a number of excellent survey, one can read, including Campbell and Perron (1991), Stock (1994), and Phillips and Xiao (1998).

5.6 Diagnostic checking

We noted in Section 5.3 that the Ljung-Box and Box-Pierce statistics can be used to test whether estimated residuals are white noise.

More informally, we can verify whether the estimated values of the residual AC and PAC lie within the approximate asymptotic 95% confidence bands (around the null hypothesis of zero), which are $\pm 1.96/\sqrt{T}$. Graphical displays of the AC and PAC against two horizontal lines corresponding to respectively the negative and positive critical values is often standard output one examines.

We can use also the other tests for no correlation in the residuals that we have seen in the context of the linear regression model, as well as those for homoskedasticity and parameter stability, which all have an asymptotic justification.

If the model fails to pass the diagnostic checks, we need to re-specify it, for example by increasing the AR or MA orders. Empirically, if the diagnostic checks are passed but some of the model coefficients are not statistically significant, we could also assess whether the diagnostic checks remain satisfactory for a more parsimonious specification.

Having determined the ARIMA model order, estimated its parameters, and verified that the underlying assumptions are not rejected, we can use it for forecasting purposes, as discussed in the following sections.

5.7   Forecasting, known parameters

As we have seen in the case of the linear regression model, the optimal forecast of y_{T+h} in the MSFE sense is

$$\widehat{y}_{T+h} = E\left(y_{T+h} \,|\, y_T, y_{T-1}, \dots, y_1\right). \tag{5.7.1}$$

We consider optimal linear forecasts for $ARIMA(p, d, q)$ models, which certainly coincide with $E\left(y_{T+h} \,|\, y_T, y_{T-1}, \dots, y_1\right)$ if we assume that $\{\varepsilon_t\}$ is normal. We also assume for the moment that the ARIMA parameters are known. We discuss first the general case, then present some examples, and finally make a set of additional comments related to ARIMA forecasts.

5.7.1   General formula

To calculate the optimal linear forecast for an ARIMA(p,d,q), we can proceed as follows. We start by defining $\Delta^d y_t = w_t$, so that w_t is ARMA(p,q):

$$w_T = \phi_1 w_{T-1} + \dots + \phi_p w_{T-p} + \varepsilon_T - \psi_1 \varepsilon_{T-1} - \dots - \psi_q \varepsilon_{T-q}.$$

From

$$w_{T+1} = \phi_1 w_T + \dots + \phi_p w_{T-p+1} + \varepsilon_{T+1} - \psi_1 \varepsilon_T - \dots - \psi_q \varepsilon_{T-q+1},$$

it follows that

$$\widehat{w}_{T+1} = E\left(w_{T+1} \,|\, I_T\right) = \phi_1 w_T + \dots + \phi_p w_{T-p+1} - \psi_1 \varepsilon_T - \dots - \psi_q \varepsilon_{T-q+1}.$$

Similarly,

$$
\begin{aligned}
\widehat{w}_{T+2} &= E\left(w_{T+2}\,|I_T\right) = \phi_1\widehat{w}_{T+1} + \ldots \\
&\quad +\phi_p w_{T-p+2} - \psi_2\varepsilon_T - \ldots - \psi_q\varepsilon_{T-q+2} \\
&\qquad \ldots \\
\widehat{w}_{T+h} &= E\left(w_{T+h}\,|I_T\right) = \phi_1\widehat{w}_{T+h-1} + \ldots \\
&\quad +\phi_p\widehat{w}_{T-p+h} - \psi_h\varepsilon_T - \ldots - \psi_q\varepsilon_{T-q+h}
\end{aligned}
\tag{5.7.2}
$$

where $\widehat{w}_{T-j} = w_{T-j}$ if $j \leq 0$ and there is no MA component for $h > q$.

We obtain the forecast of y_{T+h} summing appropriately those for w_{T+j}, $j = 1, \ldots, h$. For example, for $d = 1$, we have

$$
\widehat{y}_{T+h} = y_T + \widehat{w}_{T+1} + \ldots + \widehat{w}_{T+h}.
\tag{5.7.3}
$$

To clarify the general derivation of the optimal ARIMA forecasts, we now discuss a few examples.

5.7.2 Some examples

We consider a number of specific examples which are relatively simple to work with.

AR(1) Model

Let us start with the AR(1) process:

$$
y_t = \phi y_{t-1} + \varepsilon_t.
\tag{5.7.4}
$$

The formula in (5.7.2) simplifies to:

$$
\begin{aligned}
\widehat{y}_{T+1} &= \phi y_T, \\
\widehat{y}_{T+2} &= \phi\widehat{y}_{T+1} = \phi^2 y_T, \\
&\qquad \ldots \\
\widehat{y}_{T+k} &= \phi^k y_T.
\end{aligned}
$$

Since

$$
\begin{aligned}
y_{T+1} &= \phi y_T + \varepsilon_{T+1}, \\
y_{T+2} &= \phi^2 y_T + \varepsilon_{T+2} + \phi\varepsilon_{T+1}, \\
&\qquad \ldots \\
y_{T+h} &= \phi^h y_T + \varepsilon_{T+h} + \phi\varepsilon_{T+h-1} + \ldots + \phi^{h-1}\varepsilon_{T+1},
\end{aligned}
$$

the forecast errors are

$$
\begin{aligned}
e_{T+1} &= \varepsilon_{T+1}, \\
e_{T+2} &= \varepsilon_{T+2} + \phi\varepsilon_{T+1},
\end{aligned}
$$

$$\ldots$$

$$
e_{T+h} = \varepsilon_{T+h} + \phi\varepsilon_{T+h-1} + \ldots + \phi^{h-1}\varepsilon_{T+1},
$$

and their variances

$$
\begin{aligned}
Var\left(e_{T+1}\right) &= \sigma_\varepsilon^2, \\
Var\left(e_{T+2}\right) &= \left(1+\phi^2\right)\sigma_\varepsilon^2,
\end{aligned}
$$

$$\ldots$$

$$
Var\left(e_{T+k}\right) = \left(1+\phi^2+\ldots+\phi^{2k-2}\right)\sigma_\varepsilon^2.
$$

Moreover, we have

$$
\begin{aligned}
\lim_{h\to\infty}\widehat{y}_{T+h} &= 0 = E\left(y_t\right) \\
\lim_{h\to\infty}Var\left(\widehat{y}_{T+h}\right) &= \frac{1}{1-\phi^2}\sigma_\varepsilon^2 = Var\left(y_t\right)
\end{aligned}
$$

MA(1) Model

Let us consider the case of an MA(1) process,

$$
y_t = \varepsilon_t - \psi_1\varepsilon_{t-1} \tag{5.7.5}
$$

From the general formula in (5.7.2), we have

$$
\begin{aligned}
\widehat{y}_{T+1} &= -\psi_1\varepsilon_T, \\
\widehat{y}_{T+2} &= 0,
\end{aligned}
$$

$$\ldots$$

$$
\widehat{y}_{T+h} = 0.
$$

Since

$$
\begin{aligned}
y_{T+1} &= \varepsilon_{T+1} - \psi_1\varepsilon_T, \\
y_{T+2} &= \varepsilon_{T+2} - \psi_1\varepsilon_{T+1},
\end{aligned}
$$

$$\ldots$$

$$
y_{T+h} = \varepsilon_{T+h} - \psi_1\varepsilon_{T+h-1},
$$

the forecast errors are

$$
\begin{aligned}
e_{T+1} &= \varepsilon_{T+1} \\
e_{T+2} &= \varepsilon_{T+2} - \psi_1 \varepsilon_{T+1} \\
&\cdots \\
e_{T+k} &= \varepsilon_{T+k} - \psi_1 \varepsilon_{T+k-1},
\end{aligned}
$$

with variances

$$
\begin{aligned}
Var\,(e_{T+1}) &= \sigma_\varepsilon^2 \\
Var\,(e_{T+2}) &= \left(1 + \psi_1^2\right) \sigma_\varepsilon^2 \\
&\cdots \\
Var\,(e_{T+h}) &= \left(1 + \psi_1^2\right) \sigma_\varepsilon^2
\end{aligned}
$$

Again, we have

$$
\begin{aligned}
\lim_{h\to\infty} \widehat{y}_{T+h} &= 0 = E\,(y_t) \\
\lim_{h\to\infty} Var\,(\widehat{e}_{T+h}) &= \left(1 + \psi_1^2\right) \sigma_\varepsilon^2 = Var\,(y_t).
\end{aligned}
$$

ARMA(p,q) Model

Let us now consider an alternative derivation of the optimal forecast for an ARMA(p,q), and show that it is equivalent to that in (5.7.2). We can write the model as

$$a(L)y_t = b(L)\varepsilon_t$$

$$a(L) = 1 - \sum_{j=1}^{p} a_j L^j, \quad b(L) = \sum_{j=0}^{q} b_j L^j, \quad b_0 = 1$$

or in $MA(\infty)$ representation

$$y_t = c(L)\varepsilon_t,$$

with $a(z)c(z) = b(z)$, namely,

$$c_k - \sum_{j=1}^{p} a_j c_{k-j} = b_k, \tag{5.7.6}$$

We have that

$$\hat{y}_{T+h} = \sum_{i=0}^{\infty} c_{i+h} \varepsilon_{T-i}.$$

The above equation implies that

$$\hat{y}_{T+h} - \sum_{j=1}^{p} a_j \hat{y}_{T+h-j} = \sum_{i=0}^{\infty} \left(c_{i+h} \varepsilon_{T-i} - \sum_{j=1}^{p} a_j c_{i+h-j} \varepsilon_{T-i} \right). \qquad (5.7.7)$$

If we now use (5.7.6) in (5.7.7), we have

$$\hat{y}_{T+h} - \sum_{j=1}^{p} a_j \hat{y}_{T+h-j} = \sum_{j=0}^{\infty} b_{j+h} \varepsilon_{T-j}, \qquad (5.7.8)$$

with $b_{j+h} \equiv 0$, $j+h > q$, which is indeed equivalent to what we would obtain with (5.7.2). With this formula we can generate optimal forecasts for all h, p and q.

Random Walk Model

For the random walk

$$y_t = y_{t-1} + \varepsilon_t, \qquad (5.7.9)$$

it is

$$\widehat{y}_{T+h} = y_T,$$

for any h, and

$$e_{T+h} = \varepsilon_{T+1} + \varepsilon_{T+2} + \ldots + \varepsilon_{T+h}..$$

Therefore, the variance of the forecast error is

$$Var\left(e_{T+h}\right) = h\sigma_\varepsilon^2.$$

From these expressions, it follows that

$$\lim_{k \to \infty} \widehat{y}_{T+k} = y_T,$$
$$\lim_{k \to \infty} Var\left(\widehat{y}_{T+k}\right) = \infty.$$

More generally, the presence of a unit root in the AR component implies that the variance of the forecast error grows linearly over time, while in the stationary it converges to the unconditional variance of the variable.

5.7.3 Some additional comments

The results on the optimal forecasts and associated forecast errors we have derived so far have a few other interesting implications, namely:

- Using the $MA(\infty)$ representation, it can be shown that the forecast error is:

$$e_{T+h} = y_{T+h} - \hat{y}_{T+h} = \sum_{j=0}^{h-1} c_j \varepsilon_{T+h-j}. \qquad (5.7.10)$$

  Therefore, even when using an optimal forecast, the h-steps ahead forecast error is serially correlated. In particular, it is an MA(h-1) process.

- Moreover

$$
\begin{aligned}
E(e_{T+h}) &= 0, \\
\text{Var}(e_{T+h}) &= \sigma_\varepsilon^2 \sum_{j=0}^{h-1} c_j^2, \\
\lim_{h \to \infty} \text{Var}(e_{T+h}) &= \text{Var}(y_t),
\end{aligned}
$$

  from which is also follows that

$$\text{Var}(e_{T+h+1}) - \text{Var}(e_{T+h}) = \sigma_\varepsilon^2 c_h^2 \geq 0,$$

  so that the forecast error variance increases monotonically with the forecast horizon. This result is no longer necessarily true if the parameters are estimated.

- If the error ε is Gaussian, so is the forecast error. In particular

$$\frac{y_{T+h} - \hat{y}_{T+h}}{\sqrt{\text{Var}(e_{T+h})}} \sim N(0, 1).$$

  We can use this result to construct $(1 - \alpha)\%$ interval forecasts as:

$$\left(\hat{y}_{T+h} - c_{\alpha/2} \sqrt{\text{Var}(e_{T+h})}; \hat{y}_{T+h} + c_{\alpha/2} \sqrt{\text{Var}(e_{T+h})} \right)$$

  where $c_{\alpha/2}$ are critical values from the standard normal distribution.

- From (5.7.10), for $h = 1$ we have

$$e_{T+1} = \varepsilon_{T+1}, \tag{5.7.11}$$

  which can also be read as

$$\varepsilon_{T+1} = y_{T+1} - \hat{y}_{T+1}, \tag{5.7.12}$$

  which provides an interpretation of the errors in the MA(∞) representation of a weakly stationary process.

- Consider $\hat{y}_{T+h}$ and $\hat{y}_{T+h+k}$, i.e., forecasts of y_{T+h} and y_{T+h+k} made in period T. From (5.7.10) it can be easily shown that:

$$E(e_{T+h} e_{T+h+k}) = \sigma_\varepsilon^2 \sum_{j=0}^{h-1} c_j c_{j+k},$$

  so that the forecast errors for different horizons are in general correlated.

- From (5.7.10) and the fact that ε_t is white noise, and considering the predictor $\hat{y}_{T+h}$ as an estimator (hence random), it follows that

$$Cov(\hat{y}_{T+h}, e_{T+h}) = 0.$$

  Therefore,
$$Var(y_{T+h}) = Var(\hat{y}_{T+h}) + Var(e_{T+h})$$
  and
$$Var(y_{T+h}) \geq Var(\hat{y}_{T+h}).$$
  Hence, the forecast is always less volatile than the actual realized value.

5.8   Forecasting, estimated parameters

So far we have assumed that the ARIMA parameters were known. However, in practice they are not, and the forecasts are based on estimated rather than true parameters. If we use consistent parameter estimators, the formulas we have derived for the optimal forecasts remain valid. The only additional complication is an increase in the variance of the forecast error due to the estimation uncertainty. Typically, the increase is minor when the estimation sample size is large enough. Therefore, we only focus on a few examples to illustrate this case, see, e.g., Clements and Hendry (1998) or Lütkepohl (2007) for a more general treatment.

The first case we assess is that of a stationary AR(1) with drift:

$$y_t = \mu + a y_{t-1} + \varepsilon_t. \tag{5.8.1}$$

If the parameters μ and a have to be estimated, by $\hat{\mu}$ and $\hat{a}$, the forecast error for $h = 1$ is:

$$e_{T+1} = \varepsilon_{T+1} + (\mu - \hat{\mu}) + (a - \hat{a})y_T = \varepsilon_{T+1} + (\Theta - \hat{\Theta})' x_T$$

$$x_T = \begin{pmatrix} 1 \\ y_T \end{pmatrix} \qquad \Theta - \hat{\Theta} = \begin{pmatrix} \mu - \hat{\mu} \\ a - \hat{a} \end{pmatrix}$$

and

$$\text{Var}(e_{T+1}) = \sigma_\varepsilon^2 + x_T' \text{Var}(\hat{\Theta}) x_T, \tag{5.8.2}$$

where

$$\text{Var}(\hat{\Theta}) = \text{Var}\begin{pmatrix} \hat{\mu} \\ \hat{a} \end{pmatrix} = \sigma_\varepsilon^2 E \left[\begin{array}{cc} T & \sum_{t=1}^{T} y_{t-1} \\ \sum_{t=1}^{T} y_{t-1} & \sum_{t=1}^{T} y_{t-1}^2 \end{array} \right]^{-1}$$

$$\cong T^{-1} \left[\begin{array}{cc} \sigma_\varepsilon^2 + \mu^2(1+a)(1-a)^{-1} & -\mu(1+a) \\ -\mu(1+a) & (1-a^2) \end{array} \right], \tag{5.8.3}$$

see Clements and Hendry (1998) for details. The expression in (5.8.2) is known as the approximate forecast error variance.

For the h-steps ahead prediction we have:

$$\hat{y}_{T+h} = \hat{\mu} \frac{(1 - \hat{a}^h)}{(1 - \hat{a})} + \hat{a}^h y_T.$$

Therefore,

$$\hat{e}_{T+h} = \sum_{i=0}^{h-1} (\mu a^i - \hat{\mu}\hat{a}^i) + (a^h - \hat{a}^h)y_T + \sum_{i=0}^{h-1} a^i \varepsilon_{T+h-i}$$

and

$$\text{Var}(\hat{e}_{T+h}) = \sigma_\varepsilon^2 \frac{(1-a^{2h})}{(1-a^2)} + E\left[\sum_{i=0}^{h-1} (\mu a^i - \hat{\mu}\hat{a}^i) \right]^2$$

$$+ \text{Var}\left[(a^h - \hat{a}^h) \right] y_T^2 + 2E\left[\sum_{i=0}^{h-1} (\mu a^i - \hat{\mu}\hat{a}^i)(a^h - \hat{a}^h) \right] y_T.$$

Details on this derivation can be found in Clements and Hendry (1998).

Let us evaluate now the effects of the presence of a unit root, by setting $a = 1$ in (5.8.1). We have seen that it is

$$\hat{y}_{T+h} = \mu h + y_T$$
$$e_{T+h} = \sum_{i=0}^{h-1} \varepsilon_{T+h-i}$$

and $\text{Var}(e_{T+h}) = h\sigma_\varepsilon^2$ increases with the forecast horizon h.

Using estimated parameters from an AR(1) with drift, without imposing the unit root, the forecast error becomes

$$e_{T+h} = (\mu - \hat{\mu})h + (1 - \hat{a}^h)y_T + \sum_{i=0}^{h-1} \varepsilon_{T+h-i}.$$

It can be shown that the OLS estimator of a converges at a rate of $T^{3/2}$, rather than $T^{1/2}$ as in the stationary case, so that its variance can be neglected. The variance of $\hat{\mu}$ decreases instead with T, so that the key determinant of the forecast uncertainty is the estimation of μ, the "local trend," combined with the cumulated future errors.

5.9   Multi-steps (or direct) estimation

When forecasting h-steps ahead with a quadratic loss function, we consider a loss function different from the one which is minimized in-sample for parameter estimation. The idea of multi-steps (or direct) estimation is to estimate the parameters that will be used in forecasting by minimizing the same loss function as in the forecast period.

As an example, let us consider the $AR(1)$:

$$y_t = ay_{t-1} + \varepsilon_t$$

so that

$$y_{T+h} = a^h y_T + \sum_{i=0}^{h-1} a^i \varepsilon_{T+h-i}$$

The standard forecast, as we have seen, is:

$$\widehat{y}_{T+h} = \widehat{a}^h y_T,$$

where

$$\widehat{a} = \operatorname*{argmin}_{a} \sum_{t=1}^{T}(y_t - a y_{t-1})^2 = \frac{\sum_{t=1}^{T} y_t y_{t-1}}{\sum_{t=1}^{T} y_{t-1}^2}$$

and

$$E(y_{T+h} - \widehat{y}_{T+h}) = (a^h - E(\widehat{a}^h))y_T.$$

The forecast $\widehat{y}_{T+h}$ is also called "iterated" since, as we have seen, it can be derived by replacing the unknown future values of y with their forecasts for $T+1, \ldots, T+h-1$.

The alternative forecast is

$$\widetilde{y}_{T+h} = \widetilde{a}_h y_T$$

where

$$\widetilde{a}_h = \operatorname*{argmin}_{a_h} \sum_{t=1}^{T}(y_t - a_h y_{t-h})^2 = \frac{\sum_{t=h}^{T} y_t y_{t-h}}{\sum_{t=h}^{T} y_{t-h}^2}$$

and

$$E(y_{T+h} - \widetilde{y}_{T+h}) = (a^h - E(\widetilde{a}_h))y_T.$$

The forecast $\widetilde{y}_{T+h}$ is labeled "direct" since it is derived from a model where the target variable y_{T+h} is directly related to the available information set in period T.

The relative performance of the two forecasts $\widehat{y}_{T+h}$ and $\widetilde{y}_{T+h}$ in terms of bias and efficiency depends on the bias and efficiency of the alternative estimators of a^h, $\widehat{a}^h$ and $\widetilde{a}_h$. In the presence of correct model specification, both estimators of a^h are consistent, but $\widehat{a}^h$ is more efficient than $\widetilde{a}_h$ since it coincides with the maximum likelihood estimator. Hence, at least in large samples, the standard iterated forecast $\widehat{y}_{T+h}$ can be expected to be better than $\widetilde{y}_{T+h}$. However, in the presence of model mis-specification the ranking can change.

Let us illustrate this statement with an example. Let us assume that the DGP is an MA(1):

$$y_t = \varepsilon_t + \psi \varepsilon_{t-1}, \tag{5.9.1}$$

with $\varepsilon_t \sim \mathrm{WN}(0, \sigma_\varepsilon^2)$, but the chosen model for y_t is the $AR(1)$:

$$y_t = \rho y_{t-1} + v_t, \tag{5.9.2}$$

where v_t is supposed to be $\mathrm{WN}(0, \sigma_v^2)$.

We wish to compare standard and direct estimation based forecasts, assuming $h = 2$ and using as usual the MSFE as a comparison criterion.

Standard estimation yields

$$\hat{\rho} = \sum_{t=1}^{T} y_t y_{t-1} \left(\sum_{t=1}^{T} y_{t-1}^2 \right)^{-1}$$

and to a first approximation

$$E(\hat{\rho}) \cong \frac{\psi}{(1 + \psi^2)} = \rho.$$

Then

$$\hat{y}_{T+2} = \hat{\rho}^2 y_T, \qquad E(\hat{y}_{T+2}) \cong \rho^2 y_T$$

and it can be shown that

$$\widehat{MSFE} = E\left[(y_{T+2} - \hat{\rho}^2 y_T)^2 | y_T\right]$$
$$\cong (1 + \psi^2)\sigma_\varepsilon^2 + \left(\text{Var}(\hat{\rho}^2) + \rho^4\right) y_T^2$$

In the case of direct estimation, it is

$$\tilde{\rho}_2 = \sum_{t=2}^{T} y_t y_{t-2} \left(\sum_{t=2}^{T} y_{t-2}^2 \right)^{-1} \cong 0$$

so that

$$\tilde{y}_{T+2} = \tilde{\rho}_2 y_T \cong 0$$

and

$$\widetilde{MSFE} = E\left[(y_{T+2} - \tilde{y}_{T+2}) | y_T\right]$$
$$\cong (1 + \psi^2)\sigma_\varepsilon^2 + \text{Var}(\tilde{\rho}_2) y_T^2.$$

It can be shown that for particular values of the parameters it is possible that

$$\widetilde{MSFE} \leq \widehat{MSFE}.$$

A necessary condition for this is that the AR(1) model is mis-specified otherwise, as said, $\hat{\rho}^2$ is the ML estimator of ρ^2 and the associated forecast cannot be beaten.

It is theoretically difficult to characterize in a general setting the trade-off between bias and estimation that exists in multi-period forecasts (see Findley (1983), Findley (1985), Lin and Granger (1994), Clements and Hendry (1996), Bhansali (1999), and Chevillon and Hendry (2005), among others). Marcellino, Stock, and Watson (2006) compare empirical iterated and direct forecasts from linear univariate and bivariate models by applying simulated out-of-sample methods to 170 US monthly macroeconomic time series spanning 1959 through 2002. The iterated forecasts typically outperform the direct forecasts, particularly if the models can select long lag specifications. The relative performance of the iterated forecasts improves with the forecast horizon.

5.10   Permanent-transitory decomposition

It is sometimes of interest to decompose a process y_t into two components, labeled as permanent and transitory, respectively. The former captures the long-run, trend-like behavior of y_t. The latter measures short term deviations from the trend.

There is no unique way to achieve a permanent-transitory decomposition. We will review two of the most common approaches. The first, often called the Beveridge and Nelson (1981) (BN) decomposition, features a permanent component which behaves as a random walk. The second, the Hodrick and Prescott (1997) (HP) decomposition, has potentially more complex dynamics for the permanent component.

5.10.1   The Beveridge Nelson decomposition

We saw in the previous section that a weakly stationary process can be written as an MA(∞), and that if $y_t \sim I(d)$, then $\Delta^d y_t$ is weakly stationary. Assuming $d = 1$, we have:

$$\Delta y_t = \mu + c(L)\varepsilon_t, \qquad \varepsilon_t \overset{iid}{\sim} \left(0, \sigma_\varepsilon^2\right). \tag{5.10.1}$$

Let us consider another polynomial in L, defined as

$$d(L) = c(L) - c(1). \tag{5.10.2}$$

Since $d(1) = 0$, 1 is a root of $d(L)$, which can therefore been rewritten as

$$d(L) = \tilde{c}(L)(1 - L). \tag{5.10.3}$$

Combining equations (5.10.2) and (5.10.3) we obtain

$$c(L) = \tilde{c}(L)(1 - L) + c(1)$$

and

$$\Delta y_t = \mu + \tilde{c}(L)\Delta\varepsilon_t + c(1)\varepsilon_t.$$

To obtain a representation for y_t, we need to integrate both sides:

$$y_t = \underbrace{\mu t + c(1)\sum_{j=1}^{t}\varepsilon_j}_{\substack{\text{trend}\\ \text{(permanent component)}\\ \text{(PC)}}} + \underbrace{\tilde{c}(L)\varepsilon_t}_{\substack{\text{cycle}\\ \text{(transitory component)}\\ \text{(CC)}}}.$$

It also follows that the permanent component is a random walk with drift:

$$PC_t = PC_{t-1} + \mu + c(1)\varepsilon_t. \qquad (5.10.4)$$

Moreover, the variance of the trend innovation is $c(1)^2\sigma_\varepsilon^2$, which is larger (smaller) than the innovation in y_t if $c(1)$ is larger (smaller) than one.

The innovation in the cyclical component is $\tilde{c}(0)\varepsilon_t$. Since $\tilde{c}(L) = \frac{c(L)-c(1)}{1-L}$, then $\tilde{c}(0) = c(0) - c(1) = 1 - c(1)$. Therefore, the innovation in the cyclical component is $(1 - c(1))\varepsilon_t$.

As an example, let us derive the BN decomposition for an ARIMA(1,1,1) model,

$$\Delta x_t = \phi\Delta x_{t-1} + \varepsilon_t + \psi\varepsilon_{t-1}.$$

From the MA representation for Δx_t, we have:

$$c(L) = \frac{1 + \psi L}{1 - \phi L}, \qquad c(1) = \frac{1 + \psi}{1 - \phi},$$

$$\tilde{c}(L) = \frac{c(L) - c(1)}{1 - L} = -\frac{\phi + \psi}{(1 - \psi)(1 - \psi L)};$$

It follows that the BN decomposition is

$$y_t = PC + CC = \frac{1 + \psi}{1 - \phi}\sum_{j=1}^{t}\varepsilon_j - \frac{\phi + \psi}{(1 - \psi)(1 - \psi L)}\varepsilon_t. \qquad (5.10.5)$$

Empirically, we need to specify the AR and MA orders of the ARIMA(p,1,q) model and estimate its parameters, obtaining $\widehat{c}(L)$ and $\widehat{\mu}$. Next, we can estimate the permanent component using the fact that $PC_t = PC_{t-1} + \mu + c(1)\varepsilon_t$. Starting with $PC_0 = \alpha$, with an arbitrary value for α, e.g., $\alpha = 0$, we then use $\widehat{\mu}$, $\widehat{c}(1)$, and $\widehat{\varepsilon}_1$ to construct PC_1. Then we use $\widehat{\mu}$, $\widehat{c}(1)$, PC_1 and $\widehat{\varepsilon}_2$ to construct PC_2, and so on. Finally, we obtain the cyclical component CC_t as $y_t - PC_t$. We can calculate the mean of CC, and recenter CC (so that it has zero mean) and use it as α to calculate the PC again, since it is reasonable that CC has zero mean.

5.10.2 The Hodrick-Prescott filter

The Hodrick-Prescott filter is an alternative way to compute the permanent component. Its use is widespread among macroeconomists, in particular in the United States. The permanent component is obtained as

$$\min_{PC} \underbrace{\sum_{t=1}^{T} (y_t - PC_t)^2}_{\text{Variance of CC}} + \lambda \sum_{t=2}^{T-1} \left[(PC_{t+1} - PC_t)^2 + (PC_t - PC_{t-1})^2 \right]. \quad (5.10.6)$$

The bigger is λ, the smoother is the trend. In practice, $\lambda = 100$ is used with annual data, $\lambda = 1600$ with quarterly data and $\lambda = 14400$ with monthly data. Note that if $\lambda = 0$, it is $PC_t = y_t$.

5.11 Exponential smoothing

Exponential smoothing (ES) is a method to produce short-term forecasts quickly and with sufficient accuracy, particularly suited when the estimation sample is short since, as we will see, the underlying model is tightly parameterized and corresponds to a specific ARIMA specification.

ES decomposes a time series into a "level" component and an unpredictable residual component. Once the level at the end of the estimation sample is obtained, say y_T^L, it is used as a forecast for y_{T+h}, $h > 1$.

If y_t is an i.i.d. process with a non-zero mean, we could estimate y_T^L as the sample mean of y. If instead y_t is persistent, then the more recent observations should receive a greater weight. Hence, we could use

$$y_T^L = \sum_{t=1}^{T-1} \alpha(1-\alpha)^t y_{T-t},$$

with $0 < \alpha < 1$ and

$$\widetilde{y}_{T+h} = y_T^L. \tag{5.11.1}$$

Since

$$(1-\alpha)y_T^L = \sum_{t=1}^{T-1} \alpha(1-\alpha)^{t+1} y_{T-t-1},$$

we have

$$y_T^L = \alpha y_T + (1-\alpha)y_{T-1}^L,$$

with the starting condition $y_1^L = y_1$. Hence, the larger α the larger the weight on the most recent observations. Note that in the limiting case where $\alpha = 1$, it is $y_T^L = y_T$ and the ES forecasts coincides with that from a RW model for y.

A more elaborate model underlies the Holt-Winters procedure

$$\begin{aligned} y_t^L &= a y_t + (1-a)(y_{t-1}^L + T_{t-1}), \\ T_t &= c(y_t^L - y_{t-1}^L) + (1-c)T_{t-1}, \end{aligned} \tag{5.11.2}$$

with $0 < a < 1$, and starting conditions $T_2 = y_2 - y_1$ and $y_2^L = y_2$. In this case, we have

$$\widetilde{y}_{T+h} = y_T^L + h T_T. \tag{5.11.3}$$

The coefficients α and a control the smoothness of y_t^L. The smaller they are the smoother y_T^L, since past observations of y_t receive a rather large weight. In practice, the smoothing coefficients, and c, are selected by minimizing the in-sample MSFE, namely,

$$\sum_{t=3}^{T-1} (y_t - \widetilde{y}_t)^2.$$

Let us now derive under what conditions the ES forecasts can be considered as optimal forecasts, focusing on the more general case in (5.11.3) for which we have:

$$e_t = y_t - \widetilde{y}_{t|t-1|} = y_t - y_{t-1}^L - T_{t-1}. \tag{5.11.4}$$

From (5.11.2) we have:

$$y_t^L - y_{t-1}^L = a(y_t - y_{t-1}^L) + (1-a)T_{t-1} = T_{t-1} + ae_t, \qquad (5.11.5)$$

due to the definition of e_t in (5.11.4). Again from (5.11.2) we have:

$$T_t - T_{t-1} = c(y_t^L - y_{t-1}^L) - cT_{t-1} = cae_t \qquad (5.11.6)$$

because of (5.11.5). Moreover, using again (5.11.5) we have

$$
\begin{aligned}
(y_t^L - y_{t-1}^L) - (y_{t-1}^L - y_{t-2}^L) &= T_{t-1} - T_{t-2} + ae_t - ae_{t-1} \\
&= cae_{t-1} + ae_t - ae_{t-1}
\end{aligned}
$$

so that

$$(1-L)^2 y_t^L = a\left[1 - (1-c)L\right]e_t.$$

From (5.11.6) we have

$$(1-L)^2 T_t = ca(1-L)e_t.$$

Putting together the expressions for $(1-L)^2 y_t^L$ and $(1-L)^2 T_t$ we obtain

$$(1-L)^2(y_t^L + T_t) = a(1+c)e_t - ae_{t-1}$$

and, since from (5.11.4) $e_t = y_t - y_{t-1}^L - T_{t-1}$, we can write

$$(1-L)^2 y_t = (1-L^2)e_t + a(1+c)e_{t-1} - ae_{t-2}.$$

Therefore, in conclusion, the Holt-Winter procedure forecast in (5.11.3) is optimal (in the MSFE sense) if y_t is an ARIMA(0,2,2). Similarly, it can be shown that the forecast in (5.11.1) is optimal when y_t is an ARIMA(0,1,1).

5.12 Seasonality

Seasonality is a systematic but possibly stochastic intra-year variation in the behavior of an economic variable, related, e.g., to the weather or the calendar and their impact on economic decisions. For example, sales are systematically higher in December due to Christmas, and electricity consumption can peak in the summer months due to the use of air conditioning.

A common approach in the analysis and forecasting of economic time series is to work with seasonally adjusted variables. The rationale is that the interesting movements in economic variables are typically not related to their seasonal component, which is therefore eliminated from the time series prior to modeling. However, seasonal adjustment procedures can spuriously alter the dynamic behavior of a variable, in particular when the seasonal pattern changes over time, see e.g., Canova and Ghysels (1994). It is also interesting to note that Ghysels, Granger, and Siklos (1996) show that seasonal adjusted white noise produces a series that has predictable patterns.

An alternative method is to work with not seasonally adjusted data and directly model the seasonal component. We will discuss two alternative approaches in this context, which treat seasonality as, respectively, deterministic or stochastic. We refer to, e.g., Ghysels and Osborn (2001) for further details.

5.12.1   Deterministic seasonality

Let us assume that the time series x_t can be decomposed into a deterministic seasonal component, s_t, and an ARMA component, y_t, so that we can write

$$x_t = s_t + y_t. \tag{5.12.1}$$

Under the additional assumption that t is measured in months and there is a deterministic monthly seasonality, we can write

$$s_t = \sum_{i=1}^{12} \gamma_i D_{it},$$

where D_{it} are seasonal dummy variables taking values 1 in each month i and 0 otherwise, $i = 1, \ldots, 12$.

The seasonal coefficients γ_i can be estimated in the ARMA model for x_t, which has only a more complex deterministic component than the one we have considered so far (e.g., the overall mean), so that estimation can be conducted as discussed above.

As an alternative, we could seasonally adjust the variable x_t by subtracting from each of its values $\widetilde{s}_t$, where

$$\widetilde{s}_t = \sum_{i=1}^{12} \widetilde{\gamma}_i D_{it}, \qquad \widetilde{\gamma}_i = \overline{x}_i,$$

and $\overline{x}_i$ is the sample mean of all month-i observations of x.

This approach can also easily handle a slow evolution in the shape or amplitude of the seasonal component, by using weighted averages of the month-i observations of x for the construction of $\widetilde{\gamma}_i$. For example, also based on the discussion of exponential smoothing in the previous section we could use

$$\widetilde{\gamma}_i(j) = \alpha\widetilde{\gamma}_i(j-1) + (1-\alpha)x_{j,i},$$

where $\alpha \in [0,1]$, j is measured in years, and $x_{j,i}$ indicates the value of x in month i of year j. The larger is α, the more stable the seasonal pattern.

Finally, a similar dummy variable approach can be used for different patterns of seasonality (e.g., quarterly), and also to handle other data irregularities such as working days effects and moving festivals.

5.12.2 Stochastic seasonality

The seasonal pattern could be stochastic rather than deterministic, and in this case the use of seasonal dummies would not be sufficient to take the seasonal time variation into account. In this case, we could extend the ARMA(p,q) specification to take into explicit account the possibility of seasonal dynamics. In particular, we could use a model such as

$$\phi_1\left(L\right)\phi_2\left(L^s\right)y_t = \psi_1\left(L\right)\psi_2\left(L^s\right)\varepsilon_t, \tag{5.12.2}$$

where L^s is the seasonal lag operator, e.g., $s = 12$ in the monthly case, so that

$$\begin{aligned} \phi_2\left(L^s\right) &= 1 - \phi_{21}L^s - \ldots - \phi_{2p_2}L^{sp_s}, \\ \psi_2\left(L^s\right) &= 1 + \psi_{21}L^s + \ldots + \psi_{2\psi_2}L^{sq_s}, \end{aligned}$$

where p_s and q_s are the orders of, respectively, the seasonal AR and MA polynomials. This model is typically known as a seasonal ARMA model and it can properly represent several seasonal time series.

A first example is the seasonal random walk model:

$$y_t = y_{t-s} + \varepsilon_t,$$

hence, year-to-year differences are white noise. Another example is the case where $p = p_s = q = q_s = 1$ and $s = 12$:

$$(1 - \phi_{11}L)(1 - \phi_{21}L^{12})y_t = (1 + \psi_{11}L)(1 + \psi_{21}L^{12})\varepsilon_t,$$

or

$$(1 - \phi_{11}L - \phi_{21}L^{12} + \phi_{11}\phi_{21}L^{13})y_t = (1 + \psi_{11}L + \psi_{21}L^{12} + \psi_{11}\psi_{21}L^{13})\varepsilon_t.$$

This can also be considered as an ARMA(13,13), though with a set of zero restrictions on the coefficients.

Since a seasonal ARMA is just a constrained version of a general ARMA model, the same tools for specification, estimation and diagnostic testing that we have seen for the ARMA case can be applied in this context, see, e.g., Granger and Newbold (1986, Section 3.7).

Finally, some of the roots of the seasonal AR polynomial $\phi_2\left(L^s\right)$ could be equal to one as in the seasonal random walk model. In the general case, these are known as seasonal unit roots. Tests for this case can be constructed along the lines of the ADF procedure discussed above, see Ghysels and Osborn (2001) for further details.

5.13   Examples with simulated data

We use standard Box–Jenkins procedure to specify and estimate several types of ARMA models. Once the appropriate ARMA specification is found, it is used for an out-of-sample forecasting exercise. The data set contains 600 simulated observations. In order to avoid dependence on the starting values, the first 100 observations are discarded.

5.13.1   Stationary ARMA processes

In this section three stationary ARMA processes will be taken into consideration: y_1, with an AR(2) data generating process; y_2, with an MA(2) DGP; and y_3, with an ARMA(2,2) DGP.

As we may note from Figure 5.13.1, the dynamic behavior of the variables looks similar although they have been generated from different DGPS: all of them display random fluctuations around their mean without an evident time trend.

This provides preliminary evidence on the weak stationarity of the processes, and justifies the Box-Jenkins approach that relies on the analysis of the complete and partial autocorrelation functions (respectively, AC and PAC) to select the most appropriate ARMA specification for each variable.

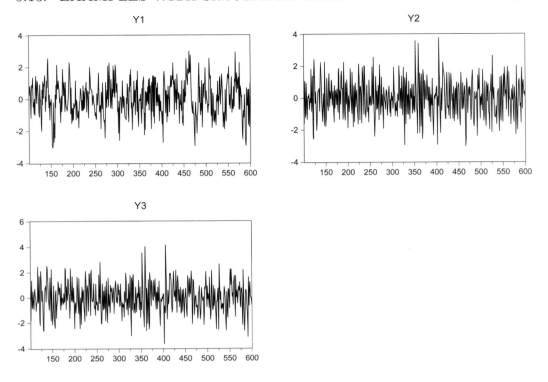

Figure 5.13.1: *Stationary ARMA process y_1 through y_3, sample 101 - 600*

Figures 5.13.2 - 5.13.4 show the (partial) correlograms of the three series for the entire sample under consideration. As we can see from Figure 5.13.2, y_1 has an exponentially decaying autocorrelation function and significant peaks at lags one and two in the PAC, hence strongly supporting an AR(2) specification. On the other hand, from Figure 5.13.3 we see an oscillating PAC function while the AC displays a significant peak at lag two, suggesting that y_2 could in fact follow a MA(2) process. Finally, from Figure 5.13.4 it is harder to make a proposal for a model for y_3 based on the reported AC and PAC functions. However, the presence of significant peaks in both of them suggests a combined ARMA specification.

We should mention that in small samples it can be more challenging to get a precise indication of the appropriate ARMA specification from the AC and PAC. In such situations, we can select the most likely specifications, use statistical testing, and compare their relative forecasting performance.

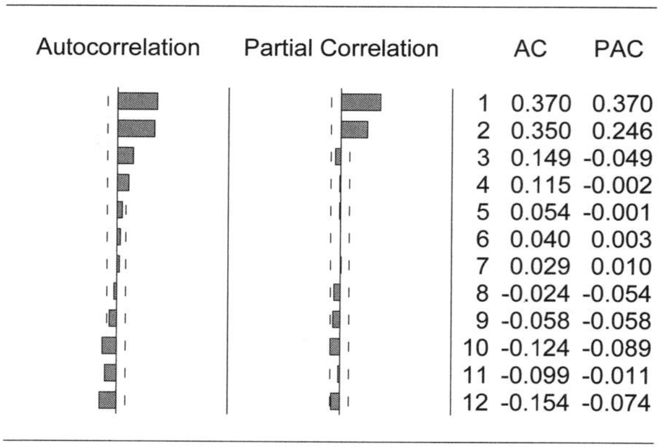

Autocorrelation	Partial Correlation		AC	PAC
		1	0.370	0.370
		2	0.350	0.246
		3	0.149	-0.049
		4	0.115	-0.002
		5	0.054	-0.001
		6	0.040	0.003
		7	0.029	0.010
		8	-0.024	-0.054
		9	-0.058	-0.058
		10	-0.124	-0.089
		11	-0.099	-0.011
		12	-0.154	-0.074

Figure 5.13.2: *AC and PAC functions for y_1 entire sample (101 -600)*

Let us now use the lag selection criteria, such as AIC and BIC, to select an appropriate ARMA specification for the three series, and compare the outcome with the suggestions that emerged from the AC and PAC analysis, (see Tables 5.13.1, 5.13.2 and 5.13.3).

AR / MA	0
0	3.042114
1	2.909087
2	**2.860312**
3	2.871777
4	2.885768
5	2.896720
6	2.910012

Table 5.13.1: *The ARIMA selection with BIC for y_1*

For y_1, for example, setting 10 as a sensible maximum number of AR lags, no differencing nor MA terms (as we inferred from the analysis of the AC and PAC), and the Schwarz as the relevant information criterion (i.e., the BIC), the procedure selects exactly an AR(2) specification. Specifically, it produces Table 5.13.1.

Autocorrelation	Partial Correlation		AC	PAC
		1	0.145	0.145
		2	-0.335	-0.364
		3	-0.022	0.114
		4	-0.014	-0.184
		5	-0.029	0.054
		6	0.009	-0.074
		7	0.055	0.089
		8	0.004	-0.060
		9	0.003	0.079
		10	-0.010	-0.067
		11	-0.056	-0.001
		12	0.005	-0.010

Figure 5.13.3: *AC and PAC functions for y_2 entire sample (101 - 600)*

AR / MA	0	1	2	3
0	3.038216	2.965412	**2.817112**	2.820006
1	3.024794	2.871028	2.819972	2.823934
2	2.886401	2.836022	2.823942	2.827933
3	2.877178	2.830599	2.827901	2.823809

Table 5.13.2: *The ARIMA selection with BIC for y_2*

Table 5.13.1 shows that the minimum BIC is achieved with two AR terms. Repeating the same exercise for both the BIC and the AIC and for the three series under examination we see that the procedure always selects the true DGPs when the entire sample is taken as a reference, as shown in Tables 5.13.2 and 5.13.3 for BIC.

AR / MA	0	1	2	3
0	3.187754	3.059214	2.981900	2.985839
1	3.142723	2.995391	2.985840	2.988778
2	3.051139	2.987988	**2.981839**	2.991453
3	3.028714	2.989539	2.993529	2.987754

Table 5.13.3: *The ARIMA selection with BIC for y_3*

In the next two subsections we will estimate the specifications selected

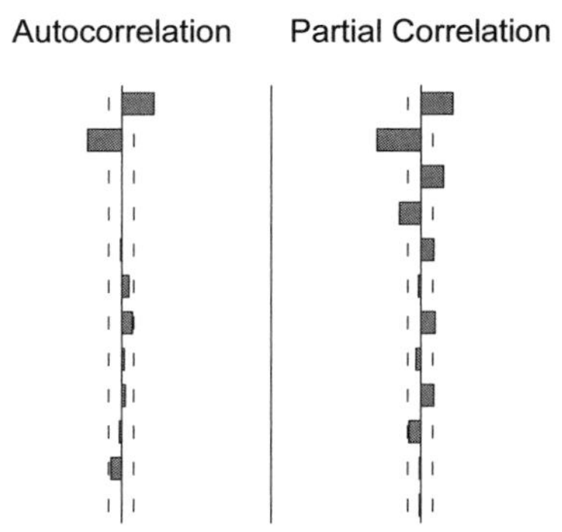

Autocorrelation	Partial Correlation		AC	PAC
		1	0.227	0.227
		2	-0.234	-0.301
		3	0.002	0.161
		4	0.001	-0.140
		5	-0.001	0.097
		6	0.052	-0.013
		7	0.079	0.105
		8	0.020	-0.029
		9	0.032	0.097
		10	-0.014	-0.082
		11	-0.072	-0.001
		12	0.008	-0.003

Figure 5.13.4: *AC and PAC functions for y_3 entire sample (101 - 600)*

by BIC. Finally, we will devote an entire subsection on illustrating the forecasting performance of the selected models.

5.13.2   Estimation: Full sample analysis

Tables 5.13.4 through 5.13.6 report the estimation results of the three models suggested by the ARIMA selection procedure; y_1 is modeled as an AR(2), y_2 as an MA(2), and y_3 as an ARMA(2,2). The results are quite satisfactory, with the selected AR and MA terms always significant and Durbin-Watson statistics always pretty close to the value of 2, signaling almost with noise residuals.

Let us have a closer look at the diagnostic tests for each of the estimated models. Diagnostics appear in Tables 5.13.7 though 5.13.9, showing some routine statistics for the residuals coming from the estimated models for y_1, y_2 and y_3, respectively. For all the three models, the actual vs fitted and residuals (see Figures 5.13.5 through 5.13.7) show a good fit for the selected models. The residuals display frequent sign changes, although there might be a few outliers; the Jarque-Bera statistics for the three residuals are still low, formally indicating no rejection of normality. Moreover, the no serial correlation LM test, and the White and ARCH heteroskedasticity tests never reject their respective null hypotheses, the only exception being

Dep Var: Y1				
Variable	Coefficient	Std. Error	t-Statistic	Prob.
C	0.042014	0.093569	0.449014	0.653
AR(1)	0.279133	0.043545	6.410269	0.000
AR(2)	0.245699	0.043530	5.644410	0.000
R-squared	0.189038	Mean dep var		0.03953
Adjusted R-squared	0.185774	S.D. dep var		1.10175
S.E. of regression	0.994163	Akaike IC		2.83215
Sum squared resid	491.2152	Schwarz IC		2.85743
Log likelihood	-705.0378	Hannan-Quinn		2.84207
F-statistic	57.92603	DW stat		1.96986
Prob(F-statistic)	0.000000			

Table 5.13.4: *Estimation results for y_1*

Dep Var: Y2 Variable	Coefficient	Std. Error	t-Statistic	Prob.
C	-0.009993	0.038195	-0.261621	0.793
MA(1)	0.281535	0.040840	6.893551	0.000
MA(2)	-0.414625	0.040851	-10.14959	0.000
R-squared	0.209487	Mean dep var		-0.01033
Adjusted R-squared	0.206306	S.D. dep var		1.10425
S.E. of regression	0.983775	Akaike IC		2.81114
Sum squared resid	481.0032	Schwarz IC		2.83643
Log likelihood	-699.7857	Hannan-Quinn		2.82106
F-statistic	65.85277	DW stat		1.96942
Prob(F-statistic)	0.000000			

Table 5.13.5: *Estimation results for y_2*

Dep Var: Y3 Variable	Coefficient	Std. Error	t-Statistic	Prob.
C	0.011417	0.054939	0.207816	0.835
AR(1)	-0.193760	0.283357	-0.683803	0.494
AR(2)	-0.076268	0.132683	-0.574815	0.565
MA(1)	0.594037	0.284018	2.091550	0.037
MA(2)	-0.135818	0.241172	-0.563158	0.573
R-squared	0.198335	Mean dep var		0.01040
Adjusted R-squared	0.191857	S.D. dep var		1.18998
S.E. of regression	1.069757	Akaike IC		2.98269
Sum squared resid	566.4681	Schwarz IC		3.02483
Log likelihood	-740.672	Hannan-Quinn		2.99922
F-statistic	30.61621	DW stat		1.99818
Prob(F-statistic)	0.000000			

Table 5.13.6: *Estimation results for y_3*

the residuals of the y_3 specification which seem to display some remaining serial correlation. These results on the lack of correlation of the residuals are also confirmed by the complete and partial correlograms, which present no significant spikes.

Having a simulated dataset allows us to answer also another interesting question: What if the researcher "gets it wrong" and estimates an AR(1), MA(1), ARMA(1,1) for, respectively, y_1, y_2 and y_3? Let us consider y_1 for instance. Estimating an AR(1) specification yields a reasonably good fit, with a slight decrease in the adjusted R^2 to 14% but no major signs of misspecification, see Table 5.13.10. Nevertheless, the correlogram of the residuals of the AR(1) question features a relevant peak exactly at lag 2, as the AR(2) term was omitted in the estimation. A similar feature emerges for the two other misspecified models, as indicated by Figure 5.13.8 that reports the empirical correlograms of the residuals.

5.13.3 Estimation: Subsample analysis

Table 5.13.11 illustrates in a synthetic way the results of applying the ARIMA selection procedure we employed in the previous section in two smaller sub-

Heteroskedasticity Test: ARCH			
F-statistic	0.009042	F(1,497)	0.924
Obs*R-squared	0.009078	Chi-Sq(1)	0.924
Breusch-Godfrey Serial Correlation LM Test:			
F-statistic	0.628107	F(2,495)	0.534
Obs*R-squared	1.265691	Chi-Sq(2)	0.531
Heteroskedasticity Test: White			
F-statistic	0.776695	F(5,494)	0.566
Obs*R-squared	3.899984	Chi-Sq(5)	0.563
Scaled explained SS	3.132991	Chi-Sq(5)	0.679
Jarque-Bera normality Test:	3.516553		0.172

Table 5.13.7: *Diagnostic tests on the AR(2) model for y_1*

Heteroskedasticity Test: ARCH			
F-statistic	0.169720	F(1,497)	0.680
Obs*R-squared	0.170345	Chi-Sq(1)	0.679
Breusch-Godfrey Serial Correlation LM Test:			
F-statistic	0.281619	F(2,495)	0.754
Obs*R-squared	0.568031	Chi-Sq(2)	0.752
Heteroskedasticity Test: White			
F-statistic	0.776314	F(9,490)	0.638
Obs*R-squared	7.029190	Chi-Sq(9)	0.634
Scaled explained SS	7.486218	Chi-Sq(9)	0.586
Jarque-Bera normality Test:	0.945034	Prob.	0.623

Table 5.13.8: *Diagnostic tests on the MA(2) model for y_2*

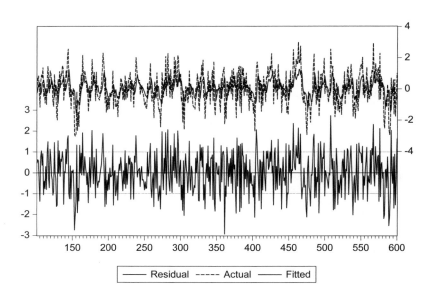

Figure 5.13.5: *Top panel: Actual vs fitted, and residuals; bottom panel: Correlogram of the residuals for the AR(2) model for y_1*

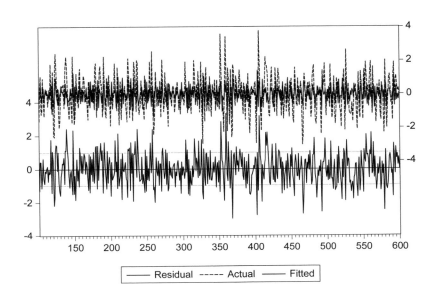

Figure 5.13.6: *Top panel: Actual vs fitted, and residuals; bottom panel: Correlogram of the residuals for the MA(2) model for y_2*

Heteroskedasticity Test: ARCH			
F-statistic	0.087968	F(1,497)	0.766
Obs*R-squared	0.088306	Chi-Sq.(1)	0.766
Breusch-Godfrey Serial Correlation LM Test:			
F-statistic	3.380311	F(2,495)	0.034
Obs*R-squared	6.736898	Chi-Sq.(2)	0.034
Heteroskedasticity Test: White			
F-statistic	1.475130	F(9,490)	0.154
Obs*R-squared	13.18975	Chi-Sq.(9)	0.154
Scaled explained SS	13.83836	Chi-Sq.(9)	0.128
Jarque-Bera normality Test:	0.504597	Prob.	0.777

Table 5.13.9: *Diagnostic tests on the ARMA(2,2) model for y_3*

Variable	Coefficient	Std. Error	t-Statistic	Prob.
C	0.025639	0.045844	0.559268	0.576
AR(1)	0.370487	0.041659	8.893349	0.000
R-squared	0.137052	Mean dep var		0.03953
Adjusted R-squared	0.135319	S.D. dep var		1.10175
S.E. of regression	1.024503	Akaike IC		2.89028
Sum squared resid	522.7037	Schwarz IC		2.90714
Log likelihood	-720.570	Hannan-Quinn		2.89689
F-statistic	79.09166	DW stat		2.17887
Prob(F-statistic)	0.000000			

Table 5.13.10: *Estimation results for the mis-specified model for y_1*

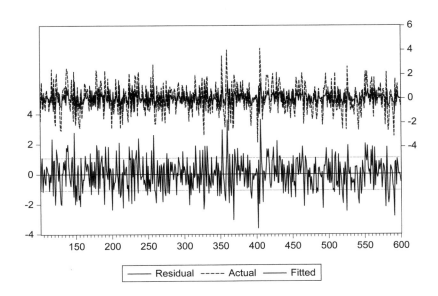

Figure 5.13.7: *Top panel: Actual vs fitted, and residuals; bottom panel: Correlogram of the residuals for the ARMA(2,2) model for y_3*

Autocorrelation	Partial Correlation		AC	PAC
		1	-0.091	-0.091
		2	0.238	0.231
		3	-0.004	0.036
		4	0.065	0.013
		5	0.003	0.002
		6	0.018	0.000
		7	0.031	0.031
		8	-0.020	-0.022
		9	-0.012	-0.031
		10	-0.096	-0.098
		11	-0.013	-0.021
		12	-0.140	-0.105

Autocorrelation	Partial Correlation		AC	PAC
		1	-0.179	-0.179
		2	-0.259	-0.300
		3	0.112	-0.003
		4	-0.062	-0.130
		5	0.011	0.003
		6	-0.025	-0.084
		7	0.067	0.071
		8	-0.027	-0.041
		9	0.006	0.051
		10	0.018	-0.006
		11	-0.071	-0.038
		12	0.038	0.005

Autocorrelation	Partial Correlation		AC	PAC
		1	-0.036	-0.036
		2	-0.101	-0.102
		3	-0.026	-0.034
		4	0.022	0.009
		5	-0.018	-0.023
		6	0.044	0.046
		7	0.061	0.063
		8	0.006	0.019
		9	0.025	0.043
		10	0.005	0.012
		11	-0.078	-0.072
		12	0.029	0.026

Figure 5.13.8: *Correlograms for mis-specified models; top to bottom, for y_1, y_2, y_3, respectively*

samples: the first goes from observation 101 to 200, the second from 201 to 300. As we can see, in shorter samples the criteria can select models rather different from the DGPs. This is not necessarily a bad outcome, as long as the residuals of the models satisfy the usual assumptions and the forecasting performance remains satisfactory.

	Subsample 101-200		Subsample 201-300	
	AIC	BIC	AIC	BIC
$y1$	AR(2)	AR(1)	AR(2)	AR(2)
$y2$	MA(2)	MA(2)	MA(2)	MA(10)
$y3$	ARMA(2,2)	ARMA(2,2)	ARMA(8,8)	ARMA(3,3)

Table 5.13.11: *Synthetic results of the ARIMA selection procedure for the two subsamples 101 - 200 and 201 - 300*

Several tests on the residuals are performed, and, as for the full sample analysis, there is evidence of good fit of these models where estimated using subsamples. As we can see, in the first subsample the AIC criterion seems to be slightly more accurate than the BIC, although they both yield quite satisfactory results in identifying the DGP. On the other hand, the second subsample results are much less accurate, signaling that the realizations in that portion of the sample are quite different from those of the first one and of the entire sample. Clearly, if the researcher's data availability is limited (around 100 observations is quite frequent in some macro applications) the results of the estimation procedure and inference may be very variable, hence the need of using robust methods in empirical practice.

5.13.4 Forecasting

We now use the three models to produce forecasts for the last 100 observations of the sample. Clearly, in ordinary forecasting practice, one tries to forecast closer future values of the variables under examination (for quarterly datasets, from 1 to 4 quarters ahead; from 1 to 12 months ahead in monthly datasets) as the forecast error grows larger with the forecast horizon. Nevertheless, for illustrative purposes here we chose to estimate the three models from observation 100 to 499 and to forecast the last 100 observations of the sample, although 100 periods ahead is quite a large forecast horizon. The static forecast is simply the one-step ahead forecast and the dynamic forecasting method calculates multi-steps ahead forecasts, from 1- up to 100-period ahead in our example.[4] In general, we expect static forecasts to be more accurate than dynamic ones, due to the shorter forecast horizon.

Figure 5.13.9 shows the results. The static forecasts track the actual values of the series, though not very closely, in line with the rather low values of the models' R^2. Instead, the dynamic forecasts quickly converge to the unconditional means of the variables. This result comes from the fact that the AR terms effect declines exponentially, while the MA effect is assumed to be zero for all the forecast periods beyond the MA order.

5.14   Empirical examples

5.14.1   Modeling and forecasting the US federal funds rate

The aim of this empirical application is to formulate an ARMA model suitable to describe the dynamics of the effective federal funds rate r in the United States. This is a key variable from a macroeconomic and financial point of view. Once such a specification is found, we will evaluate its forecasting performance through a simple out-of-sample forecasting exercise. We have a monthly dataset spanning from January 1985 until the end of 2012. The data are imported from the Federal Reserve Economic Data (FRED) website. The observations are averages of daily figures and have not been seasonally adjusted. We will first analyze the time frame going from 1985 to 2002, using the period from 2003 to 2006 for an out-of-sample forecasting exercise prior the global financial crisis. Then, we will enlarge the estimation sample to the start of the crisis, i.e., in August 2007, and we will see whether our model is able to forecast the steep fall that the federal funds rate displayed from 2008 until the end of the sample.

Figure 5.14.1 graphs the series, showing a major change when the global financial crisis happened and the federal funds rate was gradually taken to almost zero in order to ease the liquidity problems of the US economy and stimulate investment and consumption. Clearly, having this major regime change in our sample already tells us that structural instability might have occurred.

---

[4]More specifically, it uses the forecasted values in previous periods to construct forecasts in future periods, hence the starting point of the forecast sample has an important bearing on the forecasts using dynamic forecasting.

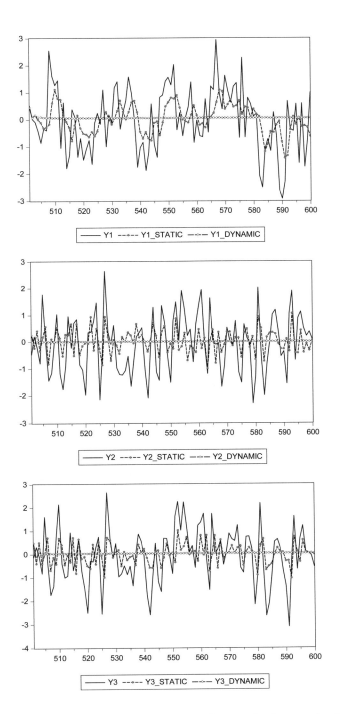

Figure 5.13.9: *Actual values and static vs dynamic forecasts for y_1, y_2, and y_3 in the sample 501 - 600*

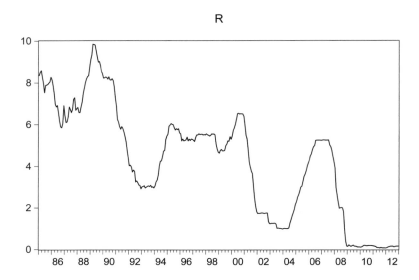

Figure 5.14.1: *The effective US federal funds rate 1985 - 2012*

The Augmented Dickey-Fuller test can help us investigate the dynamic properties of the series more thoroughly. Our conjecture regarding the non-stationarity of r is confirmed in Table 5.14.1, as the ADF test for the series in levels with the intercept (upper panel) cannot reject the null of a unit root at conventional significance levels. When we perform the same test on the differenced variable Dr instead (bottom panel) there is strong evidence in favor of stationarity, suggesting that a specification in differences for r is preferred.

Let us decide on the lag structure by looking at both the AIC and the BIC criteria with a maximum AR/MA order of 12. While the AIC favors an ARMA(5,2) specification, or equivalently an ARIMA(5,1,2) model for the series r, BIC picks an ARMA(10,1) specification (see Table 5.14.2). The long AR specification could capture either a mild seasonal component or possible breaks in the parameters.

ADF Test for r		t-Statistic	Prob.*
		-0.912779	0.782
Test critical values:	1% level	-3.460884	
	5% level	-2.874868	
	10% level	-2.573951	

ADF Test for Dr		t-Statistic	Prob.*
		-8.810261	0.000
Test critical values:	1% level	-2.575813	
	5% level	-1.942317	
	10% level	-1.615712	

Table 5.14.1: *The Augmented Dickey-Fuller test*

AR / MA	0	1	2
0	-0.276287	-0.514755	-0.544955
1	-0.596637	-0.611789	-0.627400
2	-0.600159	-0.622702	-0.622388
3	-0.615346	-0.621617	-0.616286
4	-0.611976	-0.615451	-0.610219
5	-0.619612	-0.615223	-0.621251
6	-0.616315	-0.612577	-0.621058
7	-0.613225	-0.607978	-0.621052
8	-0.611476	-0.607423	-0.611349
9	-0.614132	-0.610542	-0.609949
10	-0.615026	**-0.650287**	-0.644754
11	-0.615257	-0.645099	-0.641540
12	-0.609648	-0.640053	-0.638794

Table 5.14.2: *ARIMA selection with BIC for Dr*

We started specifying an ARMA(10,2) model for Dr, and then we noticed that some AR lags could be conveniently eliminated. At the end of this general-to-specific specification procedure we ended up with a parsimonious ARMA(5,2) model reported in Table 5.14.3.

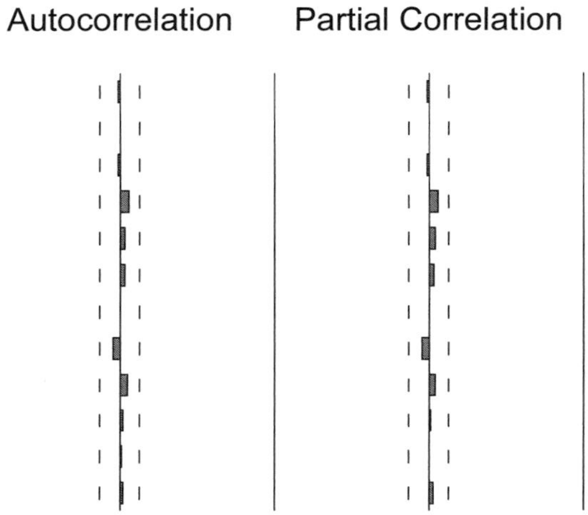

Autocorrelation	Partial Correlation		AC	PAC
		1	-0.016	-0.016
		2	0.005	0.005
		3	-0.014	-0.014
		4	0.064	0.064
		5	0.040	0.042
		6	0.035	0.036
		7	0.000	0.003
		8	-0.044	-0.047
		9	0.049	0.044
		10	0.020	0.016
		11	0.011	0.007
		12	0.021	0.027

Figure 5.14.2: *Correlogram of residuals from ARMA(5,2) for Dr*

The model results in a good statistical fit: the adjusted R^2 is about 26%, quite high for a specification in differences of a financial variable. The specification also passes most diagnostic tests, as shown in Figure 5.14.2 and Table 5.14.4. Although the residuals display some relevant outliers in the period around 1986, their correlogram looks clean, and the serial correlation LM test supports this intuition. Some signs of neglected heteroskedasticity emerge from both the White and the ARCH tests. A specification with dummy variables at the beginning of the sample does not improve the overall performance of the model though.

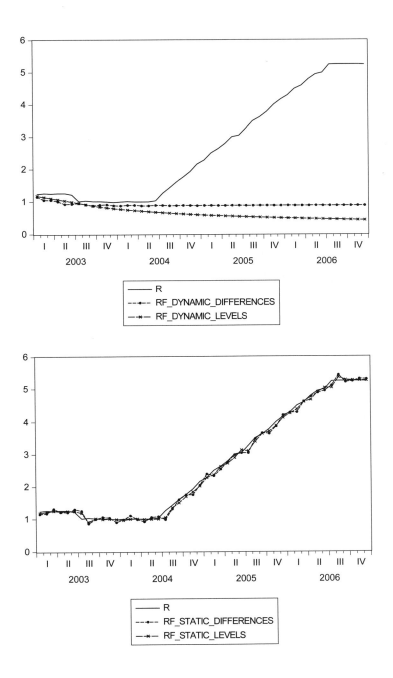

Figure 5.14.3: *The actual values of r against the forecasted series. The upper panel presents dynamic forecasts or multi-steps ahead, while the lower one presenets static or one-step ahead forecast, for the period 2003 - 2006*

Variable	Coefficient	Std. Error	t-Statistic	Prob.
AR(1)	0.169824	0.063523	2.673423	0.008
AR(2)	-0.799708	0.043098	-18.55554	0.000
AR(3)	0.515466	0.076887	6.704226	0.000
AR(5)	0.205128	0.066405	3.089048	0.002
MA(1)	0.262565	0.013437	19.54028	0.000
MA(2)	0.976636	0.009565	102.1080	0.000
R-squared	0.282454	Mean dep var		-0.02995
Adjusted R-squared	0.264867	S.D. dep var		0.22866
S.E. of regression	0.196060	Akaike IC		-0.39263
Sum squared resid	7.841698	Schwarz IC		-0.29700
Log likelihood	47.22639	Hannan-Quinn		-0.35397
DW stat	2.004751			

Table 5.14.3: *Paraneter estimates ARMA(5,2) model for Dr*

Breusch-Godfrey Serial Correlation LM Test:			
F-statistic	0.090390	F(2,202)	0.913
Obs*R-squared	0.187771	Chi-Sq(2)	0.910
Heteroskedasticity Test: ARCH			
F-statistic	35.80092	F(1,207)	0.000
Obs*R-squared	30.81699	Chi-Sq(1)	0.000
Heteroskedasticity Test: White			
F-statistic	4.645695	F(21,188)	0.000
Obs*R-squared	71.74515	Chi-Sq(21)	0.000

Table 5.14.4: *Diagnostic tests on the residuals of ARMA(5,2) model for Dr*

We now want to produce one-step ahead forecasts for r in the period 2003 - 2006. The first option is to construct forecasts for Dr and then cumulate them with the starting value for r, namely,

$$\widehat{r}_{T+1} = r_T + \widehat{Dr}_{T+1}.$$

When we use this method, we add to the forecast series the suffix "differences," in order to clarify that the forecast for r_{T+1} has been obtained indirectly from the model specified in differences.

As an alternative, we can specify a model for the level of the interest rate r and produce a forecast for r_{T+1} directly. Which model is suitable to represent r in levels? As we saw previously, the unit root test indicated that there was evidence for non-stationarity, and the correlogram showed a very persistent AR type of behavior. It turns out that an AR(11) specification, with many non-significant intermediate lags removed, is able to capture almost all the variability of the series. From the estimation output in Table 5.14.5, we note the very high R^2, which is not surprising for a specification for the levels of an I(1) variable, and a Durbin-Watson statistic close to 2. The latter statistic is not reliable in the case of dynamic models but the diagnostic tests on the residuals reported in Table 5.14.6 confirm the likely correctly specified dynamics, though there remain some problems of heteroskedasticity as in the case of the specification in differences.

Variable	Coefficient	Std. Error	t-Statistic	Prob.
AR(1)	1.410725	0.065970	21.38418	0.000
AR(2)	-0.385824	0.071123	-5.424708	0.000
AR(11)	-0.028306	0.011827	-2.393426	0.017
R-squared	0.989310	Mean dep var		5.51282
Adjusted R-squared	0.989204	S.D. dep var		1.92831
S.E. of regression	0.200362	Akaike IC		-0.36285
Sum squared resid	8.109257	Schwarz IC		-0.31422
Log likelihood	40.19299	Hannan-Quinn		-0.34318
DW stat	2.004220			

Table 5.14.5: *Parameter estimates restricted AR(11) model for r*

We can now compare the forecasting performance of the models specified in differences and in levels. Figure 5.14.3 shows the results of this forecasting exercise by graphing the actual values of r against the two forecasted series in the period 2003-2006: in the upper panel the forecasts are dynamic or multi-steps ahead, while in the lower panel they are static or one-step ahead. Table 5.14.7 complements the analysis by showing the standard forecast evaluation criteria, the RMSFE and the MAFE, for the one-step ahead forecasts.

As we can see, the forecasts from the two models are quite similar, even

Breusch-Godfrey			
Serial Correlation LM Test:			
F-statistic	0.660035	F(2,200)	0.518
Obs*R-squared	1.344200	Chi-Sq(2)	0.510
Heteroskedasticity Test: ARCH			
F-statistic	26.24542	F(1,202)	0.000
Obs*R-squared	23.45749	Chi-Sq(1)	0.000
Heteroskedasticity Test: White			
F-statistic	11.92362	F(6,198)	0.000
Obs*R-squared	54.41108	Chi-Sq(6)	0.000

Table 5.14.6: *Diagnostic tests on the residuals of AR(11) model for r*

	RMSFE	MAFE
Levels	0.0868	0.0637
Differences	0.1075	0.0834

Table 5.14.7: *Forecast evaluations for the one-step ahead forecasts*

if naturally in the dynamic case they are not capable at all of capturing the increase of the federal funds rate that started in 2004. More precisely, for the one-step ahead predictions, the forecasts from the model in levels yield a RMSFE of 0.09 while for the model in differences the value is 0.11. The MAFE is also slightly lower for the specification in levels.

The crisis period

The one-step predictive capacity of the above-selected models appear reasonable for the 2003 - 2006 period. Will it be any different if we enlarge our estimation sample and we forecast the financial crisis period?

Tables 5.14.8 and 5.14.9 clearly show that the models' fit remains quite similar also using the enlarged estimation sample. For the forecasting performance, Figure 5.14.4 and Table 5.14.10 report detailed forecast evaluation criteria. The quality of the dynamic predictions is lower now, but this was an expected result since from 2008 onward the US federal fund rate has reached the zero lower bound. Structural instability might have worsened also the short-term performance of our ARMA specifications. Nevertheless, both the specification in levels and that in difference yield similar results, with the one-step ahead forecasts remaining quite precise. The RMSFE is higher than that for the period 2003 - 2006, but the MAFE is comparable and the specification in levels remains slightly better.

Variable	Coefficient	Std. Error	t-Statistic	Prob.
AR(1)	0.309924	0.179822	1.723511	0.086
AR(2)	-0.529328	0.201804	-2.622974	0.009
AR(3)	0.385577	0.096964	3.976501	0.000
AR(5)	0.227198	0.056587	4.015022	0.000
MA(1)	0.099835	0.180357	0.553539	0.580
MA(2)	0.613386	0.175845	3.488216	0.000
R-squared	0.290327	Mean dep var		-0.00856
Adjusted R-squared	0.276627	S.D. dep var		0.21258
S.E. of regression	0.180808	Akaike IC		-0.56037
Sum squared resid	8.467142	Schwarz IC		-0.47932
Log likelihood	80.24991	Hannan-Quinn		-0.52781
DW stat	2.007645			

Table 5.14.8: *Parameter estimates ARMA(5,2) for Dr with enlarged sample*

Variable	Coefficient	Std. Error	t-Statistic	Prob.
AR(1)	1.417957	0.058500	24.23864	0.000
AR(2)	-0.388422	0.063316	-6.134685	0.000
AR(11)	-0.032273	0.010137	-3.183665	0.001
R-squared	0.992941	Mean dep var		4.97984
Adjusted R-squared	0.992886	S.D. dep var		2.15119
S.E. of regression	0.181445	Akaike IC		-0.56425
Sum squared resid	8.461069	Schwarz IC		-0.52316
Log likelihood	76.35278	Hannan-Quinn		-0.54773
DW stat	2.009223			

Table 5.14.9: *Parameter estimates AR(11) model for r with enlarged sample*

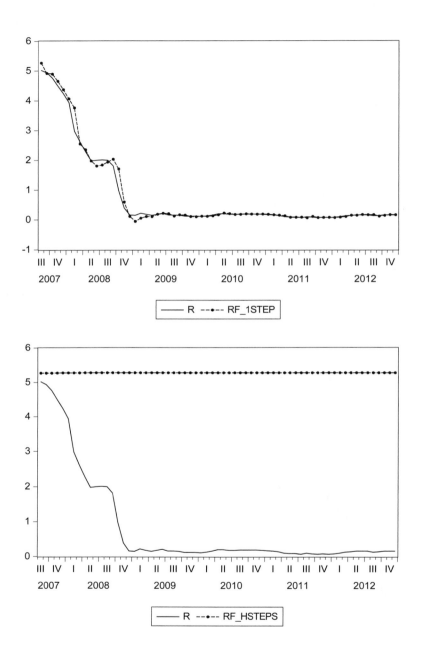

Figure 5.14.4: *Actual vs forecasted r series, period 2007 - 2012*
1-step forecasts (upper panel), h-step forecasts (lower panel)

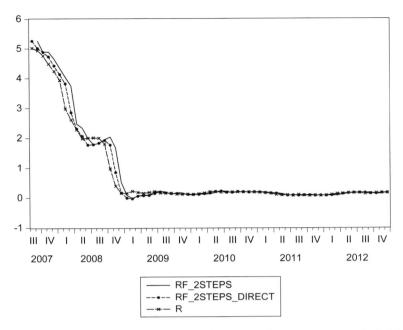

Figure 5.14.5: *Actual vs 2-step ahead forecasted r series, period 2007 - 2012*

	RMSFE	MAFE
Levels	0.1491	0.0694
Differences	0.1552	0.0703

Table 5.14.10: *Forecast evaluations for the one-step ahead forecasts*

Having evaluated already the one-step ahead and the multi-steps ahead forecasts from this model, let us conclude our exercise by producing also a sequence of two-steps ahead forecasts As we saw, there are two available methods: the iterated forecasts, where we analytically compute the expression for the two-steps ahead forecast from the chosen ARMA specification, and the direct forecast, where we lag our ARMA model one period backward and we produce static forecasts from this model.

Figure 5.14.5 displays the actual r series and these two types of two-steps ahead forecasts, showing that the direct method is slightly more precise in this example.

Table 5.14.11 complements the analysis by presenting the RMSFE and MAFE criteria of these methods, together with the previously computed one-step results. The RMSFE confirms the visual impression in favor of the direct method. However, the MAFE of the iterated forecasts is slightly lower than that of the direct forecasts.

	One-step ahead	Two-steps ahead iterated	ahead direct
RMSFE	0.1552	0.3160	0.1813
MAFE	0.0703	0.1461	0.1813

Table 5.14.11: *Forecast evaluation*

5.14.2   Modeling and forecasting US inventories

In this second empirical application, we focus on the quarterly time series of the change in real private inventories (*rcpi*), since this is a key driver of business cycles. We consider data for the United States, for the period 1985 - 2012, downloaded again from the FRED database. Note that since the series is given from the FRED database in percentage terms, for our calculations it is convenient to use the original series divided by 100.

The first step is identifying a suitable ARMA model for *rcpi*, graphed in Figure 5.14.6. We note that the series seems stationary around its mean while its variance seems to increase towards the end of the sample, consequently to the global financial crisis. We will start our exercise by simply postponing the analysis of this very complex period, ending the estimation sample in 2006.

Let us start by computing the empirical AC and PAC functions of the series, reported in Figure 5.14.7.

The AC shows a vaguely oscillatory pattern, and the PAC has a significant peak at lag 1, but also pronounced albeit non-significant peaks at lags 4 and 7. Hence, an AR component is needed, and an ARMA specification is also plausible.

The graph of the series and the value of the PAC are compatible with stationary of the series. In order to make sure there is no unit root, we also run the Augmented Dickey-Fuller test, shown in Figure 5.14.12.

The ADF test confirms that the series is stationary, hence we can model the variable in levels.

Let us check now what specification the ARIMA selection routine provides. The AIC- and BIC-based results this time are qualitatively the same,

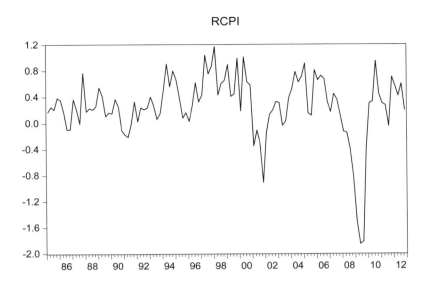

Figure 5.14.6: *The series of real changes in private inventories for the US for 2007 - 2012*

Autocorrelation	Partial Correlation		AC	PAC
		1	0.385	0.385
		2	-0.083	-0.272
		3	-0.087	0.075
		4	-0.320	-0.421
		5	-0.152	0.263
		6	-0.003	-0.303
		7	-0.002	0.290
		8	0.220	-0.093
		9	0.089	0.016
		10	-0.186	-0.272
		11	-0.206	-0.021
		12	-0.165	-0.009
		13	-0.048	-0.054
		14	0.039	-0.035
		15	0.020	-0.112

Figure 5.14.7: *Correlogram of rcpi*

		t-Statistic	Prob.*
Augmented Dickey-Fuller test statistic		-3.9513	0.002
Test critical values:	1% level	-3.4970	
	5% level	-2.8906	
	10% level	-2.5823	

Table 5.14.12: *Augmented Dickey-Fuller test for rcpi*

namely an ARMA(3,2) seems to be favored by both criteria.

We have estimated an ARMA(3,2) model and since all lags are significant in Table 5.14.13, we will continue our example with an ARMA(3,2) specification. Figure 5.14.13 shows that the overall goodness of fit seems satisfactory, and the diagnostic tests reported in Figures 5.14.8 and 5.14.9 and Table 5.14.14 indicate no remaining serial correlation or heteroskedasticity in the residuals.

Variable	Coefficient	Std. Error	t-Statistic	Prob.
C	0.311431	0.094479	3.296302	0.001
AR(1)	0.596686	0.113719	5.247034	0.000
AR(2)	-0.712288	0.098247	-7.249984	0.000
AR(3)	0.451393	0.106507	4.238135	0.000
MA(1)	-0.154118	0.034152	-4.512663	0.000
MA(2)	0.967220	0.020041	48.26132	0.000
R-squared	0.433316	Mean dep var		0.31330
Adjusted R-squared	0.388342	S.D. dep var		0.36738
S.E. of regression	0.287329	Akaike IC		0.42656
Sum squared resid	5.201136	Schwarz IC		0.62083
Log likelihood	-8.71634	Hannan-Quinn		0.50363
F-statistic	9.634632	DW stat		2.01732
Prob(F-statistic)	0.000001			

Table 5.14.13: *Parameter estimates ARMA(3,2) model for rcpi*

We will compare both one-step ahead/static and multi-steps ahead/dynamic

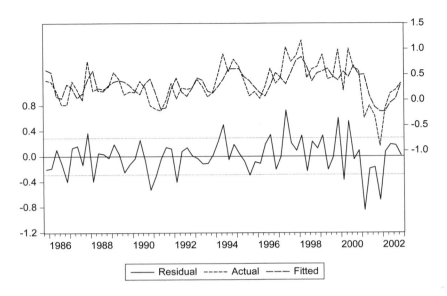

Figure 5.14.8: *Actual vs fitted and residuals from ARMA(3,2) for rcpi, 1986 - 2002*

Autocorrelation	Partial Correlation		AC	PAC
		1	-0.013	-0.013
		2	0.029	0.029
		3	0.054	0.055
		4	-0.017	-0.017
		5	0.015	0.012
		6	-0.071	-0.073
		7	0.054	0.053
		8	-0.215	-0.214
		9	0.064	0.073
		10	0.165	0.175
		11	0.005	0.031
		12	-0.031	-0.070

Figure 5.14.9: *Correlogram of the residuals from ARMA(3,2)*

Breusch-Godfrey Serial Correlation LM Test:			
F-statistic	0.054017	F(2,61)	0.947
Obs*R-squared	0.121987	Chi-Sq(2)	0.940

Heteroskedasticity Test: ARCH			
F-statistic	0.625783	F(1,66)	0.431
Obs*R-squared	0.638691	Chi-Sq(1)	0.424

Heteroskedasticity Test: White			
F-statistic	0.443385	F(27,41)	0.985
Obs*R-squared	15.59381	Chi-Sq(27)	0.960
Scaled explained SS	19.89035	Chi-Sq(27)	0.835

Table 5.14.14: *Diagnostic tests on the residuals from ARMA(3,2)*

forecasts.[5]

The results of the exercise are shown in Figure 5.14.10, where the one-step ahead and the h-steps ahead forecast series are graphed against the actual values of *rcpi*.

The quality of these forecasts is not very high, although predicting inventories is notoriously difficult. Let us also compute the two-steps ahead forecasts from the same model, both with the iterated and the direct method, as we did in the previous examples.

Figure 5.14.11 shows the two types of two-steps ahead forecasts against the actual values of *rcpi*.

To complement the analysis, Table 5.14.15 shows the standard evaluation criteria for the four types of forecasts we produced so far.

	1-step ahead	2-steps ahead, iterated	2-steps ahead, direct	1-to-x steps ahead
RMSFE	0.3110	0.5800	0.3152	0.3362
MAFE	0.2563	0.4393	0.2822	0.2961

Table 5.14.15: *Forecast evaluation*

---

[5]In the text we refer to these type of forecasts as both h-steps ahead and one-to-x steps ahead. Indeed, the two definitions can be used interchangeably although the latter is slightly more precise.

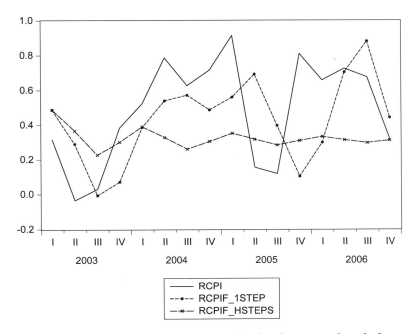

Figure 5.14.10: *The one-step ahead and the h-step ahead forecast series against the actual for rcpi, 1986 - 2002*

The iterated computation of the two-steps ahead forecasts yields slightly more precise results than the direct forecasts. One-step ahead forecasts, not surprisingly, are still the most accurate.

The crisis period

We now assess whether an ARMA model can produce reliable forecasts also during the global financial crisis period. We now include the crisis period in the estimation sample, which spans from 1985Q1 to 2009Q4, and we produce forecasts for 2010Q1 - 2012Q4. We use a simple tool to take into consideration the effects of the crisis on the previously specified ARMA model: a dummy variable equal to 1 in the period 2007Q4 - 2009Q4 and equal to 0 elsewhere.

The previously selected ARMA model requires some additional modifications in the presence of the dummy and the extended estimation sample. The selected most parsimonious specification is reported in Table 5.14.16. The dummy is inserted both for the autoregressive terms and for the constant. A seventh-order AR term had to be included, as otherwise the correlogram in-

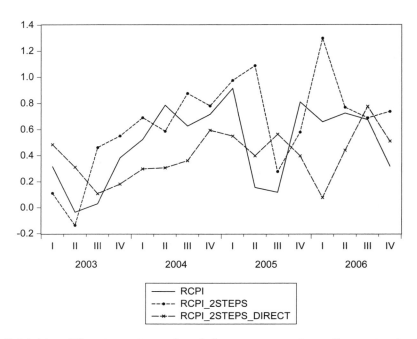

Figure 5.14.11: *The two-step ahead forecasts against the actuals for rcpi,*
1986 - 2002

dicated significant serial autocorrelation. The term is only mildly significant
if multiplied by the dummy, but it substantially improves the overall model
fit.

This specification yields an adjusted $R^2 = 0.67$, substantially higher than
the one for the pre-crisis period (which was 0.38), with a Durbin Watson
statistic of 2.12. Figures 5.14.12 and 5.14.13, and Table 5.14.17 report the
diagnostic tests on the residuals that overall support the model specification.

	1 step ahead	2-steps ahead, iterated	2-steps ahead, direct	1-to-x steps ahead
RMSFE	0.2896	0.3329	0.4305	0.3779
MAFE	0.2250	0.2751	0.3468	0.2997

Table 5.14.18: *Forecast evaluation*

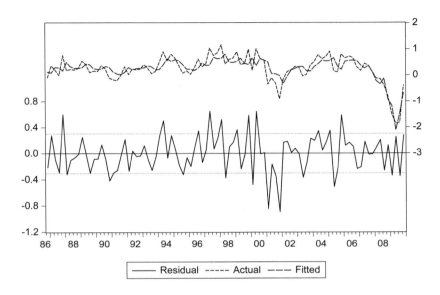

Figure 5.14.12: *The residuals of the estimated AR(7) model for rcpi in the extended sample*

Autocorrelation	Partial Correlation		AC	PAC
		1	-0.070	-0.070
		2	0.024	0.019
		3	0.112	0.115
		4	-0.089	-0.075
		5	-0.106	-0.126
		6	0.053	0.031
		7	0.134	0.174
		8	-0.138	-0.110
		9	0.066	0.004
		10	0.105	0.093
		11	-0.132	-0.064
		12	-0.130	-0.173

Figure 5.14.13: *Correlogram of the residuals of the AR(7) model for rcpi*

	Coefficient	Std. Error	t-Statistic	Prob.
C(1)	0.144059	0.048902	2.945845	0.004
C(2)	-0.567565	0.410887	-1.381317	0.170
C(3)	0.465738	0.109646	4.247637	0.000
C(4)	2.409279	0.546987	4.404637	0.000
C(5)	-2.893790	0.726124	-3.985256	0.000
C(6)	0.134667	0.109553	1.229241	0.222
C(7)	1.155596	0.855702	1.350465	0.180
R-squared	0.689825	Mean dep var		0.24323
Adjusted R-squared	0.668185	S.D. dep var		0.52727
S.E. of regression	0.303729	Akaike IC		0.52692
Sum squared resid	7.933607	Schwarz IC		0.71754
Log likelihood	-17.50192	Hannan-Quinn		0.60389
F-statistic	31.87716	DW stat		2.12359
Prob(F-statistic)	0.000000			

Table 5.14.16: *Estimation results for the AR(7) model for rcpi in the estimation period containing the global financial crisis.*

It is interesting to note how the dummy variable affects the estimated parameter values, since it is as if we had two separate equations

$$\text{Before the crisis:} \quad rcpi_t = 0.14 + 0.46 rcpi_{t-1} + 0.13 rcpi_{t-2} + \varepsilon_{1t} \tag{5.14.1a}$$

$$\text{During the crisis:} \quad rcpi_t = -0.43 + 2.88 rcpi_{t-1} - 2.76 rcpi_{t-2}$$
$$+ 1.15 rcpi_{t-7} + \varepsilon_{2t} \tag{5.14.1b}$$

In particular, the persistence (as measured by the sum of the AR coefficients) increases substantially during the crisis period.

Computing forecasts with this specification hence amounts to exploiting the information of both models (5.14.1a) and (5.14.1b) combined into a single specification.

Figure 5.14.14 reports the one-, h-, and two-steps ahead (dynamic) forecasts against the actual values of *rcpi*, while Table 5.14.18 presents the detailed forecast evaluation criteria.

Breusch-Godfrey			
Serial Correlation LM Test:			
F-statistic	3.429180	F(2,84)	0.037
Obs*R-squared	7.020020	Chi-Sq(2)	0.029

Heteroskedasticity Test: ARCH			
F-statistic	0.025863	F(1,90)	0.872
Obs*R-squared	0.026431	Chi-Sq(1)	0.870

Heteroskedasticity Test: White			
F-statistic	0.188135	F(14,78)	0.999
Obs*R-squared	3.037834	Chi-Sq(14)	0.999
Scaled explained SS	3.384554	Chi-Sq(14)	0.998

Table 5.14.17: *Diagnostic checks on the residuals from AR(7) model*

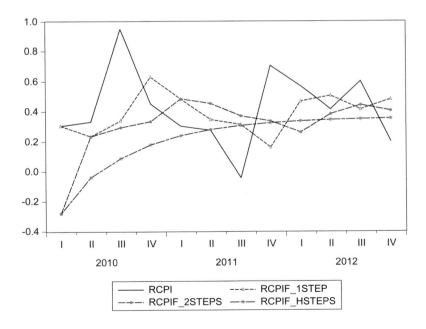

Figure 5.14.14: *Forecasts from AR(7) model for rcpi against the actual 2010 - 2012*

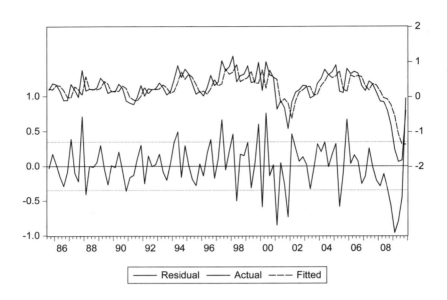

Figure 5.14.15: *Residuals of the mis-specified model which does not contain the dummy variable accounting for the crisis*

The overall impression from these results is that the forecast performance remains overall stable after the crisis, once the model is appropriately modified to allow for parameter changes during the crisis.

Related to the previous point, it is interesting to consider what would happen if we did not include the dummies for the financial crisis, and just produced forecasts with a simple AR(2) model (which is precisely the (5.14.1a) part of the model we have estimated). The estimation of the model without augmentation for the dummy produces the following equation:

$$rcpi_t = 0.048 + 0.7rcpi_{t-1} + 0.07rcpi_{t-2} + \varepsilon_{1t}. \qquad (5.14.2)$$

The associated residuals, graphed in Figure 5.14.15, are large and negative during the global financial crisis. Let us produce forecasts according to this model, which neglects the peculiar effects of the crisis, and compare them with the previously obtained results.

Figure 5.15.16 shows the forecasts obtained through model (5.14.2) against those we obtained through the richer specification (5.14.1a)-(5.14.1b), both at one-, two-, and one- to h-steps ahead. The two upper panels present, respectively, the static (right) and the dynamic (left) forecasts for the two models under examination, while the two lower panels are dedicated to the two-steps ahead forecasts both iterated (right) and direct (left). Generally, the forecasts from the specification without dummies underestimate *rcpi* more than the competing model with dummies. This is particularly evident in the case of the dynamic forecasts.

Hence, taking into explicit consideration parameter changes, when they occur, is relevant to improve the forecasting performance also when using ARMA models.

5.15 Concluding remarks

In this chapter we have discussed the specification, estimation, diagnostic checking of ARIMA models, and then shown how they can be used for forecasting and to obtain permanent-transitory decompositions.

The models are overall rather simple, since they basically explain the variable of interest using its past only. Hence, a natural question is whether these univariate time series methods are useful in practice. The answer is yes, for the following reasons.

First, from a theoretical perspective, any weakly stationary process (or integrated process after proper differencing) can be written as an $MA(\infty)$, and under mild conditions the latter can be approximated by an ARMA model.

Second, the high persistence of several economic variables suggests that forecasting methods that exploit the present and the past behavior of the variable to predict the future can perform well.

Third, the specification, estimation, and forecast construction for ARIMA models are quick and inexpensive.

Fourth, forecasts from these models can provide a benchmark for comparison of more elaborate forecasts or can be combined with forecasts from other models to assess whether a lower loss function can be obtained.

Fifth, forecast failure of these models can provide an indication of the type of information that is missing in more elaborate models, e.g., it can suggest that a substantial amount of dynamics should be included.

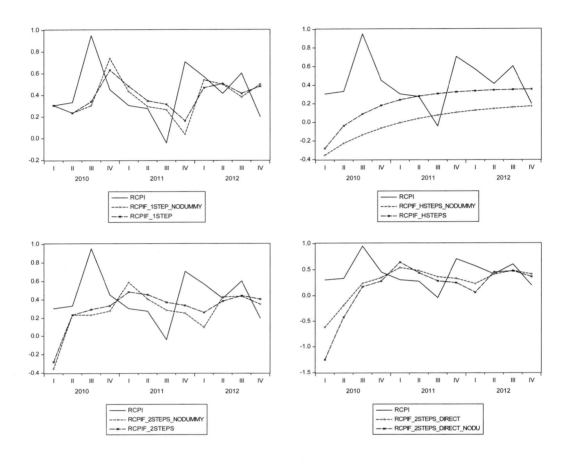

Figure 5.15.16: *Forecasts not accounting for the crisis (no dummy) against those obtained through the richer specification containing the dummy, against the actuals*

Finally, and more practically, empirically these forecasting methods tend to perform well for a variety of variables and across different evaluation samples, when used for short-term forecasting.

Chapter 6

VAR Models

A natural extension of the univariate time series models we have considered in the previous chapter is the vector (multivariate) ARMA class (VARMA). In these models, each variable depends on its own lags, on the lags of all the other variables, on its own current and lagged errors, and on the lagged errors for all the other variables. Hence, they provide a very general representation for the joint dynamics of the variables under analysis.

The main advantage of these models is their generality and that they do not impose any strong a priori restrictions on the cross-variable relationships. The cost is that they can be very heavily parameterized, which makes estimation challenging, in particular in short samples, and can reduce forecast efficiency. As usual, these pros and cons should be evaluated in the context of the specific application of interest. The seminal work by Sims (1980) led to the widespread use of VAR models, particularly for the purpose of macroeconomic modeling.

Since it is difficult to model and estimate a multivariate MA component, usually only Vector Autoregressive (VAR) models are used in the empirical literature. If the lag order of VAR models is large enough, they provide in general a good approximation for VARMA models. Hence, in this chapter we will focus on VAR models. We will consider the case of stationary variables, while the possibility of some unit roots (and cointegration) will be discussed in the next chapter.

After a succinct overview on representation, estimation and diagnostic checking, we will consider VAR-based forecasting and impulse response analysis. For more details on VAR models see, e.g., Lütkepohl (2007) or Hamilton (1994), and for a focus on forecasting Clements and Hendry (1998).

Section 6.1 considers representations of VAR models. Section 6.2 covers specification of VAR models, whereas estimation is discussed in section 6.3. Diagnostic checks appear in Section 6.4, and forecasting with VAR models is detailed in 6.5. Impulse response functions are the subject of Section 6.6 and forecast error variance decompositions the subject of 6.7. Structural VARs with long-run restrictions are illustrated in Section 6.8. Examples with simulated data appear in Section 6.9. Empirical examples are covered in Section 6.10. Concluding remarks appear in the final Section 6.11

6.1   Representation

A VAR(p) model for the set of m variables $y_{1t}, \ldots, y_{mt}$ grouped in the $m \times 1$ vector $y_t = (y_{1t}, \ldots, y_{mt})'$ is:

$$\underset{m\times 1}{y_t} = \underset{m\times 1}{\mu} + \underset{m\times m}{\Phi_1}\, y_{t-1} + \ldots + \Phi_p y_{t-p} + \underset{m\times 1}{\varepsilon_t}, \quad \varepsilon_t \sim \text{WN}\left(0, \underset{m\times m}{\Sigma}\right). \quad (6.1.1)$$

Hence, in a VAR(p) each variable depends on:

- Up to p of its own lags and up to p lags of each other variable, with coefficients grouped in the p matrices $\Phi_1, \ldots, \Phi_p$, each of dimension $m \times m$.

- Possibly an intercept, with all intercepts grouped in the $m \times 1$ vector $\mu = (\mu_1, \ldots, \mu_m)'$, or other deterministic components such as seasonal dummies or a time trend.

- An error term or residual, grouped into $\varepsilon_t = (\varepsilon_{1t}, \ldots, \varepsilon_{mt})'$, such that the error term of each equation has zero mean and is uncorrelated over time and homoskedastic, but it can be contemporaneously correlated with the errors in other equations; therefore, ε_t is a multivariate white noise process, $\varepsilon_t \sim \text{WN}(0, \Sigma)$, where Σ is an $m \times m$ variance covariance matrix. In expanded notation:

$$E(\varepsilon_{it}) = 0 \; i = 1, \ldots, m$$

$$E(\varepsilon_{it}\varepsilon_{jt-\tau}) = \begin{cases} 0 & \forall \tau, i \neq j \\ 0 & \tau \neq 0, i = j \end{cases}$$

$$E(\varepsilon_t \varepsilon_t') = \begin{bmatrix} \sigma_{11} & \sigma_{12} & \cdots & \sigma_{1m} \\ \sigma_{12} & \sigma_{22} & \cdots & \sigma_{2m} \\ \cdots & & & \cdots \\ \sigma_{1m} & \sigma_{2m} & \cdots & \sigma_{mm} \end{bmatrix}$$

Note that the total number of parameters in a VAR(p) is m (the intercepts) plus $m^2 p$ (the coefficients of the lagged variables) plus $m(m+1)/2$ (the variances and covariances of the errors). Hence, the total number of parameters grows very fast with the number of variables m, so that a careful choice of the variables to be considered in the analysis is needed, generally based on economic theory considerations.

As an example, let us consider the expanded form of a VAR(1) for three variables, with no intercept. We have:

$$\begin{aligned} y_{1t} &= \phi_{11}y_{1t-1} + \phi_{12}y_{2t-1} + \phi_{13}y_{3t-1} + \varepsilon_{1t}, \\ y_{2t} &= \phi_{21}y_{1t-1} + \phi_{22}y_{2t-1} + \phi_{23}y_{3t-1} + \varepsilon_{2t}, \\ y_{3t} &= \phi_{31}y_{1t-1} + \phi_{32}y_{2t-1} + \phi_{33}y_{3t-1} + \varepsilon_{3t}, \end{aligned}$$

with

$$\begin{bmatrix} \varepsilon_{1t} \\ \varepsilon_{2t} \\ \varepsilon_{3t} \end{bmatrix} \sim \text{WN} \left(\begin{bmatrix} 0 \\ 0 \\ 0 \end{bmatrix}, \begin{bmatrix} \sigma_{11} & \sigma_{12} & \sigma_{13} \\ \sigma_{12} & \sigma_{22} & \sigma_{23} \\ \sigma_{13} & \sigma_{23} & \sigma_{33} \end{bmatrix} \right).$$

As in the univariate case, weak stationarity is an important property for representation and estimation. In a multivariate context, it requires that

$$\begin{aligned} E(y_t) &= c, \\ Var(y_t) &= V_0 < \infty, \\ Cov(y_t, y_{t+k}) &= V_k \text{ depends on } k \text{ but not on } t, \end{aligned}$$

where c is now an $m \times 1$ vector and V_i an $m \times m$ matrix, $i = 0, 1, \ldots$. Hence, the unconditional first and second moments of the vector process y_t must exist and be stable across time.

For a VAR(p) process, weak stationarity is verified when all the roots z of $\det(I - \Phi_1 z - \ldots - \Phi_p z^p) = 0$ are larger than one in absolute value, an assumption we make in this chapter but will relax in the next.

To theoretically justify the use of VAR models, we should think of them as approximations to VMA(∞) models, along the lines of what we have seen in the univariate context. More precisely, if y_t is an m-dimensional weakly stationary process, from the Wold theorem it admits the representation

$$y_t = C(L)\varepsilon_t, \tag{6.1.2}$$

where $C(L)$ is an $m \times m$ matrix polynomial in L ($C(L) = I + C_1 L + C_2 L^2 + \ldots$), and ε_t is an $m \times 1$ vector white noise process, $\varepsilon_t \sim \mathrm{WN}(0, \Sigma)$.

Under mild conditions, $C(L)$ can be approximated by $A^{-1}(L)B(L)$, so that we can rewrite (6.1.2) as

$$A(L)y_t = B(L)\varepsilon_t \tag{6.1.3}$$

with $A(L) = I + A_1 L + \ldots + A_p L^p$, $B(L) = I + B_0 L + \ldots + B_q L^q$. Under slightly more stringent conditions, we can also assume that $q = 0$, such that (6.1.3) becomes a VAR(p) model.

6.2 Specification of the model

The specification of a VAR model requires selecting the variables under analysis, the deterministic component, and the number of lags, p.

As we mentioned, the choice of the variables under analysis should be driven by economic theory, related to the specific problem of interest, and kept as limited as possible in order to avoid the curse of dimensionality, i.e., an excessive number of parameters to be estimated. On the other hand, modeling too few variables can generate omitted variable problems, which are particularly relevant for structural analysis, e.g., for the consistent estimation of the dynamic reaction of the variables to structural shocks.

The deterministic component generally includes an intercept. Additional variables, such as seasonal dummies, other types of dummy variables to capture potential parameter breaks, and trends can also be inserted.

For the specification of the number of lagged variables, there are three main approaches, as we have seen in the ARIMA context. First, there exist multivariate versions of the AC and PAC, but they are rarely used. Second, we can start with a high number of lags, and then reduce it by sequential testing for their significance using the Wald or the LR tests. Third, we can use multivariate versions of the information criteria (IC) that, as we have seen in the univariate case, combine a measure of goodness of fit with a penalization related to the number of model parameters. In this case we compute the IC for a range of values, $j = 1, \ldots, p_{max}$, and select the number of lags that minimizes the IC. For consistency, i.e., for the criterion to pick-up the true lag order p_0 with probability one asymptotically, we need $p_{max} > p_0$ and some conditions on the penalty function $g(T)$. Specifically, when T diverges, it should be $g(T) \to \infty$ and $g(T)/T \to 0$. The most common multivariate IC are

$$
\begin{aligned}
AIC(j) &= \ln |\Sigma_j| + \frac{2}{T} jm^2, \\
BIC(j) &= \ln |\Sigma_j| + \frac{\ln T}{T} jm^2, \quad j = 1, \ldots, p_{\max},
\end{aligned}
$$

where AIC stands for Akaike's information criterion and BIC for Bayesian information criterion, also known as Schwarz information criterion, see Lütkepohl (2007) for more details. In the case of the AIC the penalty function is m^2, while it is $m^2 \ln T$ for the BIC. Hence, it can be easily seen that the BIC is consistent but the AIC is not. Moreover, since for $T \geq 8$ the penalty is larger for BIC than AIC, in general in empirical applications BIC will select a lower lag order than AIC, which can be convenient in forecasting applications, where often parsimony is convenient.

To conclude, one could use testing also to determine the deterministic component and reduce the dimensionality of the system. For example, if variable m is not of direct interest and its lags are not significant in any of the other $m - 1$ equations, it can be dropped from the system.

6.3 Estimation

The VAR is composed by m equations, one for each of the variables under joint analysis, linked by the correlation in the errors and the presence of the same explanatory variables into each equation. The former feature typically calls for a system estimation method, where all the system parameters are jointly estimated, taking into explicit account the error correlation structure. However, it can be shown that the latter feature justifies the use of equation by equation OLS parameter estimation. To be more precise, let us write the VAR(p) as follows:

$$
y_t = Bx_t + \varepsilon_t
$$

where

$$B = (\mu \quad \Phi_1 \ldots \Phi_p) \quad (m \times (mp + 1))$$

$$x_t = \begin{bmatrix} 1 \\ y_{t-1} \\ \vdots \\ y_{t-p} \end{bmatrix} \quad (mp + 1) \times 1.$$

Therefore:

$$y_t | y_{t-1}, \ldots, y_{t-p} \sim N(Bx_t, \Sigma)$$

and the log-likelihood function is:

$$\mathcal{L}(y_1, \ldots, y_T; B, \Sigma) = -\frac{Tm}{2} \log(2\pi) - \frac{T}{2} \log |\Sigma^{-1}|$$
$$-\frac{1}{2} \sum_{t=1}^{T} \left[(y_t - Bx_t)\Sigma^{-1}(y_t - Bx_t) \right]$$

The resulting ML estimator of the VAR model parameters is:

$$\widehat{B} = \left[\sum_{t=1}^{T} y_t x_t' \right] \left[\sum_{t=1}^{T} x_t x_t' \right]$$

This means that the ML estimator of the VAR parameters is equivalent to equation by equation OLS estimators. Consequently, OLS equation by equation is consistent and asymptotically efficient assuming that all the assumptions underlying the VAR are valid.

The OLS estimators are also asymptotically normal distributed (with the usual $\sqrt{T}$ rate of convergence), so that inference on the parameters can be conducted by standard Wald-type statistics, which will have χ^2 asymptotic distributions. Likelihood ratio testing procedures provide an alternative. The OLS estimator for each separate equation is also equivalent to the system (multivariate) estimator because a VAR is a Seemingly Unrelated Regression System (SUR) with the same regressors for each equation in the system, see Judge, Hill, Griffiths, Lütkepohl, and Lee (1988, pp. 450 - 451) for further details.

The ML estimator for the innovation variance is:

$$\widehat{\Sigma} = (1/T) \sum_{t=1}^{T} \hat{\varepsilon}_t \hat{\varepsilon}_t'$$

where $\hat{\varepsilon}_t = y_t - \widehat{B}x_t$. The ML estimator of the variance is consistent, but it is biased in small samples, so it is common to use the variance estimator adjusted by the number of degrees of freedom:

$$\widetilde{\Sigma} = \frac{T}{(T - mp - m)} \widehat{\Sigma}$$

There also happens to be a connection with HAC estimators (recall section 2.3) for the estimation of long-run variances worth discussing at this point. Andrews and Monahan (1992) suggest to remove *some* dependence via a finite order VAR to compute the long-run variance of a stationary process. Let us denote by V_y the long-run variance of y. We first fit a VAR(k) (often with $k = 1$), compute the residuals

$$\hat{\varepsilon}_t = y_t - \hat{\mu} + \sum_{i=1}^{k} \hat{\Phi}_i y_{t-i},$$

and compute $\widehat{\Gamma}_{j,T} = (1/(T-j)) \sum_{t=j+1}^{T} \hat{\varepsilon}_t \hat{\varepsilon}_{t-j}'$. Then we estimate $\widehat{V}_\varepsilon$ using the HAC estimator appearing in (2.3.2) to compute

$$\widehat{V}_y = \left[y_t - \hat{\mu} - \sum_{i=1}^{k} \hat{\Phi}_i y_{t-i} \right]^{-1} \widehat{V}_\varepsilon \left[y_t - \hat{\mu} - \sum_{i=1}^{k} \hat{\Phi}_i y_{t-i} \right]^{-1}$$

Hence, the Andrews and Monahan procedure relies on a VAR model to first pre-whiten a stationary series and compute a HAC estimator using the residuals (which are not necessarily white noise as typically a small number of lags is used – even only one lag). The above formula consists of so-called re-coloring the output of the HAC estimator $\widehat{V}_\varepsilon$ to obtain the desired estimator $\widehat{V}_y$.

Finally, it is worth making parenthetically some observations about estimating the VAR parameters of VARMA models, leaving the MA parameters unspecified, except for the order q. First, in a VARMA model, x_t is no longer a valid instrument for the estimation of the VAR parameters in B

since lagged, say y_{t-1} are correlated with the MA process determining ε_t. However, assuming q known, y_{t-q-k}, $k \geq 1$ are valid instruments, and therefore we can estimate via instrumental variables (cf. Section 2.7)

$$\widetilde{B} = \left[\sum_{t=1}^{T} y_t z_t' \right] \left[\sum_{t=1}^{T} x_t z_t' \right]$$

where the instrument set is

$$z_t = \begin{bmatrix} 1 \\ y_{t-q-1} \\ y_{t-q-2} \\ \vdots \\ y_{t-q-p} \end{bmatrix}.$$

See Stoica, Söderström, and Friedlander (1985) and Hansen, Heaton, and Ogaki (1988) for further details.

6.4   Diagnostic checks

As mentioned in the previous chapters, before using a model for forecasting or policy analysis, it is important to assess whether its underlying assumptions are supported by the data. In particular, we have assumed that the errors are (multivariate) white noise, namely, uncorrelated and homoskedastic. These properties can be tested equation by equation, using the testing procedures we have briefly discussed in the context of the linear dynamic model.

As an alternative, there exist multivariate versions of the statistics for no serial correlation and homoskedasticity (and possibly normality) in the residuals, which also consider the cross-linkages across the model errors. Specifically, there exist multivariate versions of the LM (Breusch-Godfrey) test for no correlation, of the White test for homoskedasticity, and of the Jarque-Bera test for normality. We refer again to Lütkepohl (2007) for derivations and formulas.

From a forecasting point of view, parameter stability is particularly important (both in- and out-of-sample). We can again use techniques considered in the context of the linear regression model to assess equation by equation whether the parameters are stable. For example, we can consider recursively estimated parameters and confidence intervals, or we can conduct

Chow tests in the case where the break dates are known (whose multivariate versions can also be derived).

Finally, and again as in the univariate case, if the assumptions are rejected we may want to reconsider the model specification, e.g., by increasing the lag length, including additional (possibly dummy) variables, changing the specification of the deterministic component, or modifying the estimation sample, in order to obtain a model whose underlying assumptions are more supported by the data.

6.5 Forecasting

The optimal forecast in the MSFE sense for a VAR(p) is obtained as a simple extension of the formula for the univariate case:

$$\widehat{y}_{T+h} = \Phi_1 \widehat{y}_{T+h-1} + \ldots \Phi_p \widehat{y}_{T+h-p} \qquad (6.5.1)$$

where $\widehat{y}_{T+h-j} = y_{T+h-j}$ for $h - j \leq 0$, possibly adding the intercept μ or any other proper deterministic component present in the model. Hence, to compute the forecast for $\widehat{y}_{T+h}$, we calculate $\widehat{y}_{T+1}$, use it to obtain $\widehat{y}_{T+2}$ and keep iterating until we obtain $\widehat{y}_{T+h}$. This approach is usually defined "iterated."

As an example, if y is VAR(1),

$$\begin{aligned}
\widehat{y}_{T+1} &= A y_T, \\
\widehat{y}_{T+2} &= A \widehat{y}_{T+1} = A^2 y_T, \\
&\ldots \\
\widehat{y}_{T+h} &= A \widehat{y}_{T+h-1} = A^h y_T.
\end{aligned}$$

The direct forecasting method presented in the previous chapter provides an alternative forecast for y_{T+h}. In the VAR(p) context, the direct model takes the form

$$y_t = A_1 y_{t-h} + \ldots + A_p y_{t-h-p} + u_t,$$

with forecast

$$\widetilde{y}_{T+h} = A_1 y_T + \ldots + A_p y_{T-p}. \qquad (6.5.2)$$

Under correct specification, $\widehat{y}_{T+h}$ is more efficient than $\widetilde{y}_{T+h}$. However, in the presence of model mis-specifications, $\widetilde{y}_{T+h}$ can be more robust than $\widehat{y}_{T+h}$.

In the context of forecasting, it is relevant to introduce the notion of Granger non-causality. Given a VAR written in the form:

$$\begin{bmatrix} a_{11}(L) & a_{12}(L) \\ a_{21}(L) & a_{22}(L) \end{bmatrix} \begin{bmatrix} y_t \\ x_t \end{bmatrix} = \begin{bmatrix} \varepsilon_{yt} \\ \varepsilon_{xt} \end{bmatrix}, \tag{6.5.3}$$

x_t does not Granger-cause y_t if $a_{12}(L) = 0$, that is y_t does not depend on the lags of x_t. Similarly, y_t does not Granger-cause x_t if $a_{21}(L) = 0$. Note that this notion of causality is only related to whether a given variable, or a set of them, improves the forecasts of another variable. Since the variables can be contemporaneously correlated through the errors, it is possible to have causality even in the presence of Granger non-causality.

From 6.1.2, the MA(∞) representation of y_t, we can also write the optimal forecast as

$$\widehat{y}_{T+h} = \sum_{j=0}^{\infty} C_{j+h}\varepsilon_{T-j}, \tag{6.5.4}$$

with associated forecast error

$$e_{T+h} = \sum_{j=0}^{h-1} C_j \varepsilon_{T+h-j}. \tag{6.5.5}$$

Hence, the variance covariance matrix of the forecast error is

$$V(e_{T+h}) = \Sigma + C_1 \Sigma C_1' + \ldots + C_{h-1} \Sigma C_{h-1}'.$$

The elements on the diagonal of $V(e_{T+h})$ contain the variances of the forecast errors for each specific variable, $V(e_{1T+h}),\ldots,V(e_{mT+h})$. These elements, under the additional assumption of normal errors, can be used to construct interval forecasts for each variable at a given level α. Specifically, the interval forecast for variable $\widehat{y}_{jT+h}$, $j = 1,\ldots,m$, takes the form

$$\left[\widehat{y}_{jT+h} - c_{\alpha/2}\sqrt{V(e_{jT+h})}, \widehat{y}_{jT+h} + c_{\alpha/2}\sqrt{V(e_{jT+h})} \right], \tag{6.5.6}$$

where $c_{\alpha/2}$ is the proper critical value from the standard normal distribution.

From equation (6.5.5), it also follows that for $h_2 > h_1$ one has $V(h_2) > V(h_1)$, in the sense that $V(h_2)$ - $V(h_1)$ is a positive definite matrix. As in the univariate case, it can be shown that this ranking is no longer necessarily true with estimated parameters.

The formula for the optimal forecast in (6.5.4) can be rearranged into

$$\widehat{y}_{T+h} = C_h \varepsilon_T + \sum_{j=0}^{\infty} C_{j+h+1} \varepsilon_{T-1-j} = \widehat{y}_{T+h|T-1} + C_h \varepsilon_T,$$

and using (6.5.5) gives

$$\widehat{y}_{T+h} = \widehat{y}_{T+h|T-1} + C_h \underbrace{(y_T - \widehat{y}_{T|T-1})}_{forecast\ error}. \tag{6.5.7}$$

In words, the updating formula in (6.5.7) indicates that the optimal forecast for period $T+h$ made in period T can be obtained by summing the optimal forecast for $T+h$ made in the previous period $(T-1)$ and the one-step ahead forecast error made in forecasting y_T in period $T-1$.

When the parameters are estimated, the expression for the forecast error variance must be modified to take into account parameter estimation uncertainty. Lütkepohl (2007, Chapter 3) presents a detailed derivation and the proper formulas which are very complex from a notational point of view.

To conclude, a usual problem with VAR models is overparameterization, which yields very good in-sample fit but bad out-sample forecasts. Several procedures have been proposed to alleviate this problem, based on – using the Bayesian paradigm – either a priori restrictions on the parameters or a different estimation method. We will revisit this issue in Chapter 8.

6.6 Impulse response functions

As we discussed, a stationary VAR for the m variables grouped in the vector y_t can be written in MA(∞) form as

$$y_t = \Phi^{-1}(L)\, \varepsilon_t = \Theta(L)\, \varepsilon_t, \quad \varepsilon_t \sim \text{WN}(0, \Sigma). \tag{6.6.1}$$

Since Σ is positive definite, there exists a non-singular matrix P such that

$$P\Sigma P' = I. \tag{6.6.2}$$

We can therefore rewrite equation (6.6.1) as

$$
\begin{aligned}
y_t &= \Theta(L)\, P^{-1} P \varepsilon_t = \Psi(L)\, v_t, \\
v_t &= P\varepsilon_t, \\
E(v_t) &= 0, \quad E(v_t v_t') = P\Sigma P' = I.
\end{aligned}
\tag{6.6.3}
$$

Equation (6.6.3) is the MA(∞) representation of the model

$$P\Phi\left(L\right)y_t = v_t, \tag{6.6.4}$$

which is typically known as a Structural VAR (SVAR), as there are contemporaneous relationships among the variables because of the P matrix. The orthogonal errors v_t are usually interpreted as structural (economic) shocks, e.g., demand or supply shocks.

It is interesting to compute how the variables under analysis react to the structural shocks. We can write

$$\begin{aligned} \Psi\left(L\right) &= P^{-1} - \Theta_1 P^{-1}L - \Theta_2 P^{-1}L^2 - \dots \\ &= \Psi_1 - \Psi_2 L - \Psi_3 L^2 - \dots \end{aligned} \tag{6.6.5}$$

A shock is a vector with one element equal to one and all the others equal to zero, e.g.,

$$v_{1,t+1} = \begin{bmatrix} 1 \\ 0 \\ 0 \\ \vdots \\ 0 \end{bmatrix}, v_{2,t+1} = \begin{bmatrix} 0 \\ 1 \\ 0 \\ \vdots \\ 0 \end{bmatrix}, \dots, v_{m,t+1} = \begin{bmatrix} 0 \\ 0 \\ 0 \\ \vdots \\ 1 \end{bmatrix}. \tag{6.6.6}$$

The non-zero elements can also be set to any other constant value, such as the standard deviation of the corresponding element of ε_t. In fact, since the system is linear, the size of the shock is irrelevant because the response of the variables is just proportional to the size of the shock.

The response in period $t + i$ of y to a shock in period $t + 1$ will be:

$$\frac{\partial y_{t+1}}{\partial v_{t+1}} = P^{-1} = \Psi_1, \tag{6.6.7}$$

$$\frac{\partial y_{t+2}}{\partial v_{t+1}} = -\Psi_2,$$

$$\frac{\partial y_{t+3}}{\partial v_{t+1}} = -\Psi_3,$$

$$\dots$$

where, for example,

$$\Psi_1 = \begin{bmatrix} \dfrac{\partial y_{1,t+1}}{\partial v_{1,t+1}} & \cdots & \dfrac{\partial y_{1,t+1}}{\partial v_{m,t+1}} \\ \vdots & \ddots & \vdots \\ \dfrac{\partial y_{m,t+1}}{\partial v_{1,t+1}} & \cdots & \dfrac{\partial y_{m,t+1}}{\partial v_{m,t+1}} \end{bmatrix}. \tag{6.6.8}$$

The term $\partial y_{k,t+i}/\partial v_{jt+1}$ is known as the impulse response in period $t+i$ of variable k to the shock j, with $k, j = 1, \ldots, m$ and $i = 1, 2, \ldots$. The collection of all impulse responses is knows as the impulse response function (IRF).

An important problem for the computation of the responses to structural shocks is that the choice of the matrix P, used to map the VAR residuals ε_t into the structural shocks v_t, is not unique. There are many invertible matrices P that satisfy $P\Sigma P' = I$. As a consequence, the IRF is also not unique.

Since Σ, the variance matrix of ε_t, has $m(m+1)/2$ distinct elements, this is the maximum number of unrestricted elements in P. Typically, P is chosen as a triangular matrix:

$$
P = \begin{bmatrix} p_{11} & 0 & \cdots & 0 \\ p_{12} & p_{22} & \cdots & 0 \\ \vdots & & \ddots & \\ p_{1m} & p_{2m} & \cdots & p_{mm} \end{bmatrix},
$$

where the elements p_{ij} are such that $P\Sigma P' = I$. In this context, different identification schemes are associated to a reshuffling of the rows of P, namely to different orderings of the m variables in y_t. Hence, we can consider different orderings of the variables to evaluate the sensitivity of the impulse response function. Of course, this does not exhaust the set of alternative identification schemes, since more general (non-triangular) forms for the P matrix are possible.

Empirically, the elements of P are unknown and, once its form is chosen, they must be estimated starting from those of $\widehat{\Sigma}$. Estimates of P are combined with those of the other VAR parameters $\Phi(L)$ in (6.6.4) to obtain estimates for $\Theta(L)$ and $\Psi(L)$ in (6.6.3). The estimates for $\Psi(L)$ correspond to the estimated IRF. Appropriate standard errors for the IRF can also be derived, either analytically or by means of Monte Carlo or Bootstrap methods, see e.g., Lütkepohl (2007) for details. As we will see in the empirical examples, typically, the elements of the estimated IRF and their associated confidence bands are reported in multi-panel graphs, showing the response over time of each variable to each structural shock.

An an illustration of the computation of IRF, let us assume that

$$
y_t = \begin{bmatrix} \text{output gap} \\ \text{inflation} \\ \text{short term interest rate} \end{bmatrix} = \begin{bmatrix} y_{1t} \\ y_{2t} \\ y_{3t} \end{bmatrix} .
$$

The interaction among these three key variables is of major interest for macroeconomists. In particular, they would like to know how these variables react to demand, supply and monetary policy shocks. Hence, we want to identify these three structural shocks starting from the VAR residuals, and then compute the reaction of the variables to the identified structural shocks.

Let us assume that y_t follows as VAR(1) process:

$$
y_t = A_1 y_{t-1} + \varepsilon_t, \quad \varepsilon_t \sim \text{WN}\,(0, \Sigma)
$$

In order to identify the structural shocks, as discussed above we assume that

$$
v_t = P\varepsilon_t, \quad P\Sigma P' = I = Var\,(v_t),
$$

with

$$
P = \begin{bmatrix} p_{11} & 0 & 0 \\ p_{21} & p_{22} & 0 \\ p_{31} & p_{32} & p_{33} \end{bmatrix} .
$$

It follows that

$$
P^{-1} = \begin{bmatrix} \alpha_{11} & 0 & 0 \\ \alpha_{21} & \alpha_{22} & 0 \\ \alpha_{31} & \alpha_{32} & \alpha_{33} \end{bmatrix} \tag{6.6.9}
$$

$$
= \begin{bmatrix} \frac{1}{p_{11}} & 0 & 0 \\ -\frac{1}{p_{11}}\frac{p_{21}}{p_{22}} & \frac{1}{p_{22}} & 0 \\ \frac{(p_{21}p_{32}-p_{22}p_{31})}{p_{11}p_{22}p_{33}} & -\frac{1}{p_{22}}\frac{p_{32}}{p_{33}} & \frac{1}{p_{33}} \end{bmatrix} ,
$$

$$
v_t = \begin{bmatrix} v_{1t} \\ v_{2t} \\ v_{3t} \end{bmatrix} = \begin{bmatrix} p_{11}\varepsilon_{1t} \\ p_{21}\varepsilon_{1t} + p_{22}\varepsilon_{2t} \\ p_{31}\varepsilon_{1t} + p_{32}\varepsilon_{2t} + p_{33}\varepsilon_{3t} \end{bmatrix} ,
$$

and the SVAR can be written as

$$
y_t = A_1 y_{t-1} + P^{-1}v_t. \tag{6.6.10}
$$

We interpret v_1 as a demand shock, v_2 as a supply shock, and v_3 as a monetary policy shock. Given the structure of the matrix P, and of P^{-1}, we assume that the demand shock influences all the three variables contemporaneously, the supply shock affects current inflation and interest rate but the output gap only with a delay, and the monetary shock has a delayed effect on both output gap and inflation, while the interest rate immediately reacts. This is a reasonable pattern from an economic point of view. Formula (6.6.10) implies that (1) y_{1t} is affected by $\alpha_{11}v_{1t}$, (2) y_{2t} is affected by $\alpha_{21}v_{1t} + \alpha_{22}v_{2t}$, (3) y_{3t} is affected by $\alpha_{31}v_{1t} + \alpha_{32}v_{2t} + \alpha_{33}v_{3t}$. The model in (6.6.10) can be rewritten as

$$Py_t = PA_1y_{t-1} + v_t, \tag{6.6.11}$$

where

$$Py_t = \begin{bmatrix} \alpha_{11}y_{1t} \\ \alpha_{21}y_{1t} + \alpha_{22}y_{2t} \\ \alpha_{31}y_{1t} + \alpha_{32}y_{2t} + \alpha_{33}y_{3t} \end{bmatrix}. \tag{6.6.12}$$

Hence, another way to interpret our identification scheme is that the output gap is only affected contemporaneously by its own shock, inflation by its own shock plus the output gap shock, interest rate by its own shock plus the output gap shock, and the inflation shock.

The MA(∞) representation of the model is

$$y_t = \varepsilon_t + A_1\varepsilon_{t-1} + A_1^2\varepsilon_{t-2} + A_1^3\varepsilon_{t-3} + \ldots = \Theta(L)\varepsilon_t$$

Hence, the impulse response functions are

$$\frac{\partial y_{t+i}}{v_t} = A^iP^{-1} = \Psi_i = \begin{bmatrix} \Psi_{11} & \Psi_{12} & \Psi_{13} \\ \Psi_{21} & \Psi_{22} & \Psi_{23} \\ \Psi_{31} & \Psi_{32} & \Psi_{33} \end{bmatrix},$$

where

$$\Psi_{qj,i} = \frac{\partial y_{qt+i}}{v_{jt}}, \quad q = 1,2,3 \quad j = 1,2,3, \quad i = 1,2,\ldots \tag{6.6.13}$$

and

$$v_{1t} = \begin{bmatrix} 1 \\ 0 \\ 0 \end{bmatrix}, v_{2t} = \begin{bmatrix} 0 \\ 1 \\ 0 \end{bmatrix}, v_{3t} = \begin{bmatrix} 0 \\ 0 \\ 1 \end{bmatrix}.$$

To conclude, we note that there exist more complex SVAR structures linking VAR residuals and structural shocks, typically expressed as

$$Bv_t = A\varepsilon_t. \tag{6.6.14}$$

It is again necessary to recover the parameters in the B and A matrices from those of the variance of the VAR residuals, Σ, with

$$A^{-1}BB'\left(A^{-1}\right)' = \Sigma.$$

Therefore, we need to impose a sufficient number of a priori restrictions on A and B to identify their remaining free parameters from those of Σ, see e.g., Amisano and Giannini (2012).

Both in the simple SVAR in (6.6.3) and in the more complex formulation in (6.6.14), it is also possible to impose more restrictions than those strictly needed to achieve identification. In these cases the SVAR is overidentified and the overidentification restrictions can be tested, with the required underlying estimation typically conducted with GMM methods.

6.7   Forecast error variance decomposition

We have seen before that the h-steps ahead forecast error can be written as

$$e_{T+h} = \varepsilon_{T+h} + \Theta_1 \varepsilon_{T+h-1} + \ldots + \Theta_{h-1} \varepsilon_{T+1},$$

so that

$$Var\left(e_{T+h}\right) = \Sigma + \Theta_1 \Sigma \Theta_1' + \ldots + \Theta_{h-1} \Sigma \Theta_{h-1}'.$$

Let us now write $Var\left(e_{T+h}\right)$ as

$$
\begin{aligned}
Var\left(e_{T+h}\right) &= P^{-1}P\Sigma P'(P^{-1})' + \Theta_1 P^{-1}P\Sigma P'(P^{-1})'\Theta_1' + \quad (6.7.1) \\
&\quad + \ldots + \Theta_{h-1}P^{-1}P\Sigma P'(P^{-1})'\Theta_{h-1}' \\
&= \Psi_1\Psi_1' + \Psi_2\Psi_2' \ldots + \Psi_h\Psi_h'
\end{aligned}
$$

since $P\Sigma P' = I$ and $\Theta_{i-1}P^{-1} = \Psi_i$.

It follows that

$$\Psi_{ij,1}^2 + \Psi_{ij,2}^2 + \ldots + \Psi_{ij,h}^2, \tag{6.7.2}$$

represents the contribution of the innovations in the jth variable in explaining the h-steps ahead forecast error variance for y_i, $i, j = 1, \ldots, m$. This is the so-called forecast error variance decomposition (FEVD). In practice, the FEVD tells us, for each forecast horizon, how relevant shocks to each variable are to explain the forecast error in any other variable.

Let us consider in more detail, as an example,

$$\begin{bmatrix} Var\,(e_{1,T+1}) & Cov\,(e_{1,T+1},e_{2,T+1}) & \cdots & Cov\,(e_{1,T+1},e_{m,T+1}) \\ Cov\,(e_{2,T+1},e_{1,T+1}) & Var\,(e_{2,T+1}) & \cdots & Cov\,(e_{2,T+1},e_{m,T+1}) \\ \vdots & \vdots & \ddots & \vdots \\ Cov\,(e_{m,T+1},e_{1,T+1}) & Cov\,(e_{m,T+1},e_{2,T+1}) & \cdots & Var\,(e_{m,T+1}) \end{bmatrix} = \Psi_1 \Psi_1',$$

where

$$\Psi_1 = \begin{bmatrix} \Psi_{11} & \cdots & \Psi_{1m} \\ \Psi_{21} & \cdots & \Psi_{2m} \\ \vdots & \ddots & \vdots \\ \Psi_{m1} & \cdots & \Psi_{mm} \end{bmatrix}$$

The one-step ahead forecast error variance for the first variable in the system can be decomposed

$$Var\,(e_{1,T+1}) = \Psi_{11}^2 + \Psi_{12}^2 + \ldots + \Psi_{1m}^2. \tag{6.7.3}$$

Similarly, for the second variable it is

$$Var\,(e_{2,T+1}) = \Psi_{21}^2 + \Psi_{22}^2 + \ldots + \Psi_{2m}^2.$$

And so on for the other variables.

Going back to the example where

$$y_t = \begin{bmatrix} \text{output gap} \\ \text{inflation} \\ \text{short term interest rate} \end{bmatrix},$$

we have that, e.g., Ψ_{21}^2 is the contribution of the "structural" shock 1 (demand shock) in explaining the variance of the one-step ahead forecast error of variable 2 (inflation), while Ψ_{22}^2 and Ψ_{23}^2 are the contributions of, respectively, the supply and monetary shocks.

6.8 Structural VARs with long-run restrictions

Identification of the structural shocks needed to compute IRF and FEVD can be achieved using more general techniques and restrictions than those considered in Section 6.6. In this section, we will consider the role of assumptions on the long-run behavior of some variables and/or effects of some shocks. We illustrate the method by means of an example, where we want to identify demand and supply shocks exploiting the generally accepted proposition that demand shocks do not have long-run effects, while supply shocks do. Blanchard and Quah (1989) explain how to identify VARs imposing these restrictions.

We consider a bivariate VAR(1) for GDP growth and unemployment, defined as

$$y_t = A y_{t-1} + B v_t, \qquad (6.8.1)$$

where v_t are the structural shocks, and $B = P^{-1}$ in the previous notation.

The MA representation is

$$y_t = (I - AL)^{-1} B v_t, \qquad (6.8.2)$$

from which the cumulative long-run response of y to the shocks in v is

$$(I - A)^{-1} B = \begin{bmatrix} \pi_{11} & \pi_{12} \\ \pi_{21} & \pi_{22} \end{bmatrix} \begin{bmatrix} b_{11} & b_{12} \\ b_{21} & b_{22} \end{bmatrix}. \qquad (6.8.3)$$

The ith, j^{th} element of this matrix captures the long-run effects of shock j on variable i. From the variance-covariance matrix Σ we obtain 3 parameters, so in order to identify B we need to impose one a priori restriction on its elements. As an example, the Cholesky decomposition imposes $b_{21} = 0$. If

$$y_t = \begin{bmatrix} \text{growth}_t \\ \text{unemployment}_t \end{bmatrix},$$

then the demand shock v_{1t} has no long-run effects on growth if

$$\pi_{11} b_{11} + \pi_{12} b_{21} = 0. \qquad (6.8.4)$$

In fact, with this restriction it is

$$(I - AL)^{-1} B v_t = \begin{bmatrix} 0 & * \\ * & * \end{bmatrix} \begin{bmatrix} v_1 \\ v_2 \end{bmatrix}. \qquad (6.8.5)$$

Hence, rather than imposing $b_{21} = 0$ as with the Cholesky approach, we can assume that b_{11} and b_{21} are linked by the linear relationship in (6.8.4).

6.9   VAR models with simulated data

We now illustrate the use of VAR models using simulated data. Specifically, we generate 600 observations using a bivariate VAR(1) DGP, and in order to avoid dependence on the starting values, we discard the first 100 observations. We will use the methods described in this chapter to specify and estimate an appropriate VAR model, and then to provide forecasts for the two series under analysis by using both deterministic and stochastic simulation. In the former, the iterated approach is applied to compute the forecasts (the model is solved forward deterministically). In the latter, bootstrapped errors are added to the forward solution in each of a set of simulations, and the average across all the simulations is treated as the forecast. As a final step, the computed forecasts will be evaluated in comparison with those obtained by an equivalent structural equation model.

The DGP is a simple bivariate model with the following specification:

$$
\begin{aligned}
y_t &= 1 + 0.8y_{t-1} + \varepsilon_{yt} \\
x_t &= 1 + 0.5x_{t-1} + 0.6y_{t-1} + \varepsilon_{xt}
\end{aligned}
\tag{6.9.1}
$$

with

$$
v_t = \begin{bmatrix} 1 & 0.5 \\ 0 & 1 \end{bmatrix} \varepsilon_t \quad \text{and} \quad v_t \overset{iid}{\sim} N(0.I).
\tag{6.9.2}
$$

The pattern of the simulated series is reported in Figure (6.9.1).

From the figure, the variables look stationary and tend to co-move. Of course, this is not surprising given the DGP. When using actual data, we should choose the variables under analysis based on the specific application we are interested in, with the help of economic theory. For example, y could be the growth rate of consumption and x of disposable income.

To specify a VAR model for y and x, we have to choose the deterministic component and the lag length, p. To keep things simple, here we only include the default deterministic variable, i.e., the intercept, and we focus on the selection of the appropriate lag length.

We can start with a sufficiently long lag length (a general model) and then we have two options to reduce it: either we use the multivariate version of the BIC and AIC information criteria or we perform a sequence of LR tests for the significance of the various lags, starting with testing the significance of p versus $p-1$ lags. In this example, all the information criteria and the

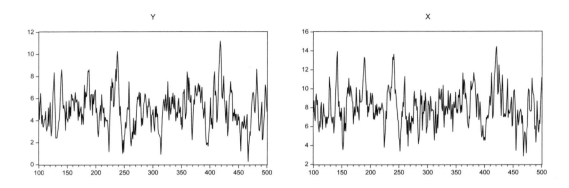

Figure 6.9.1: *Simulated series x and y*

LR test agree on selecting $p = 1$, as we can see from Table 6.9.1. Let us then try to estimate both a VAR(1) and a VAR(4) model, to assess the effects of over-parameterization.

Tables 6.9.2 and 6.9.3 report the estimation results for the two models. As we can see, the overall fit of the two models is quite similar, although the information criteria slightly favor the VAR(1) even when applied for each equation separately. Moreover, since we are in the privileged position of knowing the true values of the structural parameters, we can definitely say that the VAR(1) gets also closer to the actual DGP. Note also that the inverse roots of the characteristic polynomials of the two models in Figure 6.9.2 do not signal any problem of non-stationarity, as expected.

Let us consider diagnostic tests on the VAR(1) residuals in Tables 6.9.4 - 6.9.6. The pairwise cross-correlograms (sample autocorrelations) are not reported here. The estimated residuals in the two VAR models for the specified number of lags look quite "clean," never exceeding the interval of plus or minus two times the asymptotic standard errors of the lagged correlations. The same results are confirmed by the serial correlation LM test which in both cases cannot reject the null of no serial correlation up to lag 12. Moreover, the multivariate version of the White heteroskedasticity test does not find any sign of neglected residual heteroskedasticty. Finally, the multivariate version of the normality test does not reject the hypothesis that the residuals have a joint normal distribution (and the univariate tests are in agreement). Hence, both VARs provide a proper representation for the variables.

VAR Lag Order Selection Criteria

Lag	LogL	LR	FPE	AIC	SC	HQ
0	-1596.550	NA	9.945	7.973	7.993	7.981
1	-1120.800	944.396*	0.946*	5.620*	5.680*	5.644*
2	-1118.250	5.030	0.953	5.627	5.727	5.667
3	-1117.630	1.230	0.969	5.644	5.783	5.699
4	-1114.200	6.699	0.972	5.647	5.826	5.718
5	-1113.940	0.515	0.990	5.666	5.885	5.752
6	-1111.720	4.291	0.999	5.674	5.933	5.777
7	-1109.430	4.396	1.007	5.683	5.982	5.801
8	-1108.140	2.468	1.021	5.696	6.035	5.831
9	-1105.210	5.590	1.027	5.702	6.080	5.852
10	-1103.130	3.936	1.036	5.711	6.130	5.877
11	-1101.080	3.878	1.047	5.721	6.179	5.903
12	-1098.540	4.756	1.054	5.728	6.226	5.926

* Indicates lag order selected by the criterion. LR: sequential test (each at 5% level), FPE: final prediction error, AIC: Akaike information criterion, SC: Schwarz, HQ: Hannan-Quinn

Table 6.9.1: *Results of the lag length selection tests*

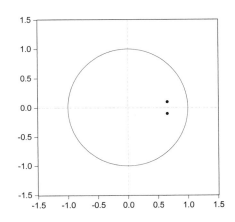 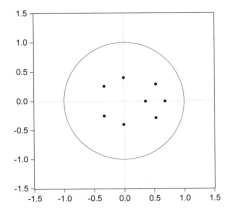

Figure 6.9.2: *Inverse roots of the AR characteristic polynomial for the VAR(1) (left panel) and the VAR(4) (right panel)*

Vector Autoregression Estimates

	Y	X
Y(-1)	0.790	0.597
	(0.035)	(0.031)
	[22.695]	[19.380]
X(-1)	-0.047	0.523
	(0.030)	(0.027)
	[-1.555]	[19.429]
C	1.421	0.862
	(0.242)	(0.214)
	[5.863]	[4.022]

Standard errors in() and t-statistics in []

	Y	X
R-squared	0.594	0.758
Adj. R-squared	0.591	0.757
Sum sq. resids	485.316	379.840
S.E. equation	1.104	0.977
F-statistic	290.570	624.674
Log likelihood	-607.258	-558.125
Akaike AIC	3.044	2.799
Schwarz BIC	3.074	2.829
Mean dep	4.972	8.014
S.D. dep	1.728	1.983

Determinant resid covariance (dof adj.)	0.932
Determinant resid covariance	0.918
Log likelihood	-1120.801
Akaike information criterion	5.620
Schwarz criterion	5.680

Table 6.9.2: *Estimation results of the VAR(1)*

We know that a usual problem with VAR models is overparameterization, which yields very good in-sample fit but bad out-sample forecasts: in our example both the VAR(1) and VAR(4) do very well in terms of in-sample fit, so we now try to assess comparatively their predictive capabilities. We use the observations 501-600 as the forecast sample, and construct both static (one-step ahead) and dynamic (one- to 100-steps ahead) forecasts for the two variables y and x.

In the deterministic setting, the inputs to the model are fixed at known values, and a single path is calculated for the output variables, using the the-

Vector Autoregression Estimates

	Y	X
Y(-1)	0.839	0.648
	(0.056)	(0.050)
	[14.936]	[13.080]
Y(-2)	-0.097	-0.105
	(0.094)	(0.083)
	[-1.027]	[-1.264]
Y(-3)	0.095	-0.061
	(0.094)	(0.083)
	[1.004]	[-0.733]
Y(-4)	-0.146	0.166
	(0.078)	(0.069)
	[-1.866]	[2.403]
X(-1)	0.011	0.577
	(0.064)	(0.056)
	[0.165]	[10.246]
X(-2)	-0.047	-0.049
	(0.074)	(0.065)
	[-0.633]	[-0.759]
X(-3)	0.112	-0.071
	(0.074)	(0.065)
	[1.524]	[-1.089]
X(-4)	-0.036	0.024
	(0.044)	(0.039)
	[-0.812]	[0.606]
C	1.215	0.943
	(0.309)	(0.272)
	[3.936]	[3.467]

Standard errors in() and t-statistics in []

	Y	X
R-squared	0.598	0.763
Adj. R-squared	0.590	0.759
Sum sq. resids	479.443	372.030
S.E. equation	1.106	0.974
F-statistic	73.024	158.072
Log likelihood	-604.816	-553.960
Akaike AIC	3.061	2.808
Schwarz BIC	3.151	2.897
Mean dep	4.972	8.014
S.D. dep	1.728	1.983

Determinant resid. covariance (dof adj.)	0.929
Determinant resid.covariance	0.888
Log likelihood	-1114.202
Akaike information criterion	5.647
Schwarz criterion	5.826

Standard errors in() and t-statistics in[]

Table 6.9.3: *Estimation results of the VAR(4)*

VAR residual normality tests

Component	Skewness	Chi-sq	df	Prob.
1	0.110	0.812	1	0.367
2	-0.260	4.501	1	0.034
Joint		5.313	2	0.070
Component	Kurtosis	Chi-sq	df	Prob.
1	2.911	0.133	1	0.715
2	2.806	0.631	1	0.427
Joint		0.764	2	0.682
Component	Jarque-Bera	df	Prob.	
1	0.945	2	0.623	
2	5.132	2	0.077	
Joint	6.077	4	0.193	

Table 6.9.4: *VAR(1) residual normality test*

VAR heteroskedasticity tests

Joint test:

Chi-sq	df	Prob.
11.059	12	0.524

Individual components:

Dependent	R-squared	F(4,396)	Prob.	Chi-sq(4)	Prob.
res1*res1	0.014	1.429	0.223	5.708	0.222
res2*res2	0.009	0.867	0.484	3.482	0.480
res2*res1	0.002	0.180	0.949	0.727	0.948

Table 6.9.5: *VAR(1) residual heteroskedasticity test*

oretical formula we have described in the previous sections. In the stochastic environment, uncertainty is incorporated into the model by adding a random element. To simulate the distributions of future values, the model object uses a Monte Carlo approach, where the model is solved many times with pseudo-random numbers substituted for the unknown errors at each repetition. As the number of repetitions increases, we expect the mean of the empirical distribution of future values to approach the conditional expectations of the

VAR residual serial correlation LM tests

Lags	LM-Stat	Prob
1	4.470	0.346
2	1.066	0.900
3	6.659	0.155
4	0.721	0.949
5	4.546	0.337
6	1.563	0.816
7	3.588	0.465
8	5.211	0.266
9	4.231	0.376
10	2.308	0.679
11	8.047	0.090
12	1.878	0.758

Table 6.9.6: *VAR(1) residual serial correlation LM tests*

variables. The default settings for these Monte Carlo experiments are 1000 simulations, with innovations generated from normal random numbers. The produced forecasts also have confidence intervals accounting for parameter estimation uncertainty, set by default at the 95% level.

The stochastic forecasts for both y and x (static and dynamic) generated from the VAR(1) specification are graphed in Figure 6.9.3 against the respective actual values. Table 6.9.7 provides the detailed forecast evaluation statistics for all the series.

If we consider first the one-step ahead forecasts, both the RMSFE and the MAFE are lower for the VAR(1) specification than for the VAR(4), both for the deterministic and the stochastic settings, though the differences are small. The pattern is reversed for the dynamic one- to 100-step(s) ahead forecasts (indicated by h-steps ahead in the table), but the differences remain small. Also graphically, the VAR(1) and VAR(4) forecasts are very similar.

Do we gain and how much in terms of forecast accuracy by using a bivariate model for x and y instead of two separate ARMA models for the two variables? Using the standard information criteria two parsimonious ARMA specifications to represent x and y are the following:

$$x_t = 7.97 + 0.73x_{t-1} + 0.15\varepsilon_{t-1} + 0.09\varepsilon_{t-2} + 0.16\varepsilon_{t-3} \quad (6.9.3)$$
$$R^2_{adj} = 0.71, \quad DW = 1.99$$

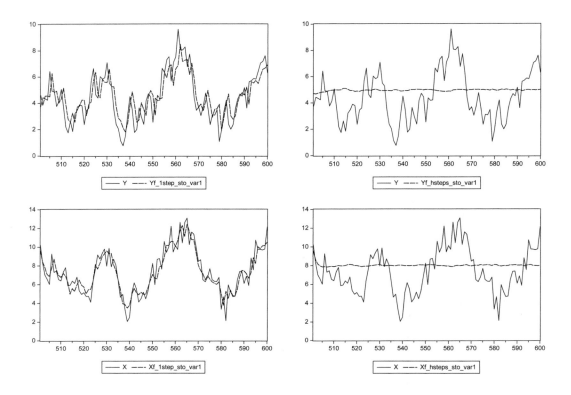

Figure 6.9.3: *Static one-step and dynamic h-step ahead stochastic forecasts against the actuals, VAR(1)*

$$y_t = 4.96 + 0.77y_{t-1} + u_t \qquad (6.9.4)$$
$$R^2_{adj} = 0.59, \quad DW = 1.98$$

We can now produce static and dynamic forecasts from the above models. The evaluation criteria reported in Table 6.9.8, show that the accuracy gain by using a bivariate instead of a univariate model is pretty modest, although it is more pronounced for x than y. Indeed, the actual DGP of x contains the interaction with y, hence we would expect that a VAR model is better in predicting it.

Another important application of VAR models concerns the evaluation of the impact of structural shocks, which can be done using the MA(∞)

VAR(1)

	x			y	
Stochastic setting					
	h-steps ahead	one-step ahead		h-steps ahead	one-step ahead
RMSFE	2.482	0.975	RMSFE	1.952	1.107
MAFE	2.071	0.788	MAFE	1.643	0.890
Deterministic setting					
	h-steps ahead	one-step ahead		h-steps ahead	one-step ahead
RMSFE	2.477	0.974	RMSFE	1.939	1.107
MAFE	2.063	0.788	MAFE	1.632	0.893

VAR(4)

	x			y	
Stochastic setting					
	h-steps ahead	one-step ahead		h-steps ahead	one-step ahead
RMSFE	2.473	1.003	RMSFE	1.917	1.105
MAFE	2.068	0.794	MAFE	1.617	0.896
Deterministic setting					
	h-steps ahead	one-step ahead		h-steps ahead	one-step ahead
RMSFE	2.479	0.998	RMSFE	1.939	1.100
MAFE	2.068	0.789	MAFE	1.633	0.894

Table 6.9.7: *Detailed forecast evaluation criteria for VAR(1) and VAR(4)*

	x ~ ARMA(1,3)		y ~ AR(1)
	h-steps ahead		h-steps ahead
RMSFE	2.505	RMSFE	1.942
MAFE	2.107	MAFE	1.641
	one-step ahead		one-step ahead
RMSFE	1.471	RMSFE	1.086
MAFE	1.180	MAFE	0.883

Table 6.9.8: *Forecast evaluation criteria for the ARMA models specified for x and y*

representation of the VAR, after proper identification of the structural shocks v_t starting from the VAR residuals ε_t, as discussed in the previous sections. In this example, we use the Cholesky decomposition of the variance matrix of the VAR residuals to identify the structural shocks and then study their dynamic transmission on the variables x and y.

Since the Cholesky decomposition is not unique, there is one for each possible ordering of the VAR variables, we have computed two sets of Impulse response functions (IRFs): the first is obtained by ordering x first and y second, and the other one is obtained with the inverse ordering of the variables. The results are visible respectively in Figures 6.9.4 and 6.9.5.

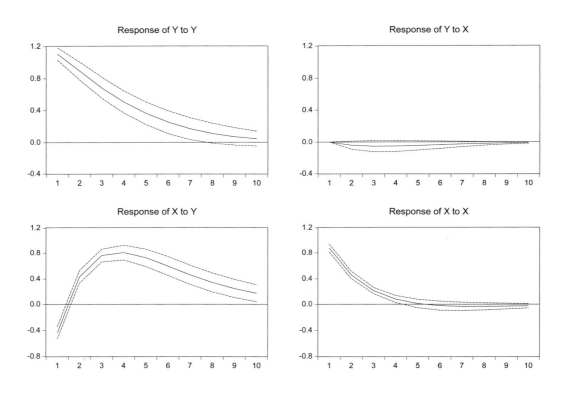

Figure 6.9.4: *Impulse response functions for the VAR(1) model. Response to Cholesky one s.d. innovations 2 s.e. The values are computed using a lower triangular mapping matrix P*

Looking at the IRFs for the VAR(1), the results are similar for both ordering of the variables: y does not seem to respond very much to structural

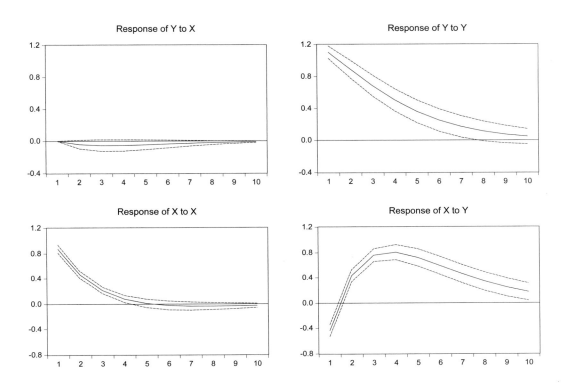

Figure 6.9.5: *Impulse response functions for the VAR(1) model. Response to Cholesky one s.d. innovations 2 s.e. The values are computed using an upper triangular mapping matrix P*

shocks coming from x, while x instead is very sensitive to shocks coming from y. The same is true for the IRFs for the $VAR(4)$. Furthermore, the figures provide additional evidence that both systems are stationary, as the IRFs tend to go to zero, as the impact of the shock vanishes after 10 periods.

Further, let us consider the variance decomposition of the two models, which is a different method of depicting the system dynamics. The variance decomposition splits the forecast error variance of each endogenous variable, at different forecast horizons, into the components due to each of the shocks, thereby providing information on their relative importance. Since the two types of Cholesky decompositions (where either y also depends on contemporaneous values of x, or vice versa x_t depends on y_t) generate similar IRFs, we only consider the (y, x) ordering.

For both models, the forecast error variance decomposition of y indicates that shocks to y itself dominate both in the short and in the long-run. According to the VAR(1), the effect grows in time from 83% to 85% of the forecast error variance, while with the VAR(4) the effect is more pronounced in the short term, 84%, and it decreases to 80% after 10 periods. The shocks to x contribute much less in explaining y, and they behave in a specular way with respect to the y shocks. Finally, the forecast error decomposition of x in both figures shows that also for x its own shock dominates in the short run, but the effects of the y shock increase over time while those of x decrease, so that the two shocks have comparable importance at longer horizons.

6.10 Empirical examples

6.10.1 GDP growth in the Euro area

In this example we apply the VAR estimation and forecasting techniques we saw in the theoretical sections of the chapter to study the relationship among the GDP growth rates of three major countries in the Euro area, namely, France, Germany and Italy, using the United States as an exogenous explanatory variable. The data set contains 108 quarterly observations from 1986Q1 to 2012Q4. The variables are the growth rates of real GDP expressed as percentage change from the previous year (%yoy), downloadable from DATASTREAM.[1] The series are all adjusted for seasonality and labeled as g_i where $i = fr, ger, it, us$; the dataset also contains some binary dummy variables labeled D_19XXqx accounting for exceptional episodes in the chosen temporal period.

As we can see from Figure 6.10.1, the three growth rates seem to be tightly linked, suggesting a synchronized business cycle through the entire Euro area, or at least its major economies. The gray shaded areas indicate the recessions occurring in the United States: the one that occurred in 1991 impacted our Euro area countries only in 1992 - 3, after the break-up of the European Monetary System (EMS), while the 2007 financial crisis arrived in Europe with only a few quarters delay, qualifying indeed as a "global" crisis.

---

[1]Note that the GDP growth rates can be manually calculated by using the log difference operator on the series of real GDP in levels. In this example we chose to use the (%yoy) growth rates calculated by Oxford Economics just because they are available from the 1980s on, while the real GDP series in levels are available only from the 1990s.

From the graph it also emerges that for the two main recessions of 1992 and 2008, Germany and Italy display more pronounced troughs than France, and this can be due to the tight commercial links existing between the German and Italian economies and their degree of openness.

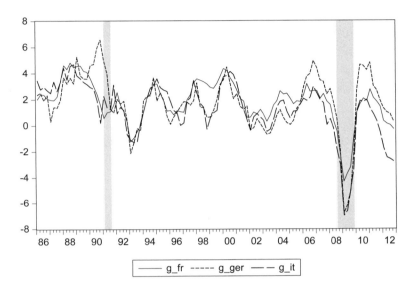

Figure 6.10.1: *Real GDP growth rates for France, Germany, and Italy during the period 1986Q1 - 2012Q4. The gray shaded areas indicate the NBER recessions for the United States*

Preliminary analysis on the series confirmed that g_fr, g_us, and g_ger can be considered as stationary at the 5% confidence level, while g_it cannot, and it is probably characterized by a unit root. However, from an economic point of view, it is surprising that the growth rate is integrated, and therefore we will treat it anyway as stationary.

The next step of our analysis is to see whether there are common intertemporal dependencies among the growth rates of the three Euro area countries, using g_us as an exogenous variable, due to the global importance of the United States and the limited effects of each of the Euro area countries on its large economy. First, we will specify suitable VAR models and estimate them over the period 1986 - 2003, next we will evaluate their forecasting performance from 2004 to 2006. Then, we will repeat the estimation until 2006Q4 and evaluate the forecasting performance of the model during 2007 - 2012, including the crisis period.

VAR Lag Order Selection Criteria

Lag	LogL	LR	FPE	AIC	SC	HQ
0	-324.200	NA	3.034	9.623	9.721	9.662
1	-217.244	201.331	0.170	6.742	7.134*	6.898
2	-198.730	33.217*	0.129*	6.463*	7.148	6.734*
3	-193.902	8.233	0.146	6.585	7.564	6.973
4	-183.820	16.310	0.143	6.553	7.827	7.058

* Indicates lag order selected by the criterion. LR: sequential test (each at 5% level), FPE: final prediction error, AIC: Akaike information criterion, SC: Schwarz, HQ: Hannan-Quinn

Table 6.10.1: *Choice of the appropriate lag length p through information criteria*

Let us start by selecting the appropriate lag length p for our VAR model. Table 6.10.1 reports the information criteria associated with the various lags of our VAR model. The AIC, the Hannan-Quinn criterion, the Final Prediction Error (FPE), and the LR criteria all suggest $p = 2$. while the more parsimonious BIC indicates $p = 1$. As a consequence, we will estimate two rival VAR models with, respectively, $p = 1$ and $p = 2$, and we will evaluate their relative performance.

Note that both models include the same set of exogenous variables, namely, the growth rate of US GDP and the dummy variables necessary to remove some outliers (in 1988Q1, 1993Q1, and 2000Q1). Table 6.10.2 reports the estimation results of the VAR(1) model. VAR(2) results are not reported. Both VARs display a good overall performance given the not so high number of observations in the sample, and in general the exogenous variables we chose are significant. On the other hand, while in the VAR(1) model the significance of some lagged variables is very low, the same is generally not true for the VAR(2) model, suggesting that the former is probably misspecified. The same impression emerges when we look at the residuals of the two models. Tables 6.10.3 - 6.10.5 report results from the diagnostic tests for the VAR(1); results for the VAR(2) are not reported since they are very similar. The residuals of both models look quite "clean," although from their correlograms (not shown here), it is even more evident that the VAR(2) captures some autocorrelation that the VAR(1) does not. On the other hand, there is no sign of heteroskedasticty or non-normality in any of the two models' residuals, and this is partly due to the dummies we have introduced. Finally, note that the inverse of the AR roots are all well within the unit circle, supporting our choice of treating the growth rate of Italy as stationary.

How are the variables dynamically related? We can answer this question through the Granger causality test, and to perform it we chose to use $p = 2$ lags.

From Table 6.10.6, it seems that the shocks are not significantly dynamically transmitted from Germany to France and Italy, while the reverse is not true and there are cross-linkages across France and Italy.

As the Granger causality test only considers lagged relationships, in order to better understand if there is correlation among contemporaneous shocks in our VAR(2) model, and hence contemporaneous correlation across the variables after conditioning on their lags, we can use an indirect method. In the absence of cross equation correlations, the ordering of the variables should not affect very much the behavior of the impulse response functions obtained with a Cholesky factorization of the variance covariance matrix of the VAR residuals. Hence, we can check whether this is the case.

We have tried two different orderings of variables to create the impulse response functions from the estimated VAR(2). The responses are rather similar for the two cases, here we present only results from the first order in Figure 6.10.2. Results suggest that indeed the contemporaneous correlation is limited, in line with economic reasoning that suggests that it takes some time for the shocks to be transmitted across countries. The response functions also indicate that there are positive spillovers across all countries, some of which become significant only 2 - 3 quarters after the shock.

Which of the two estimated models (VAR(1) or VAR(2)) will perform better from a forecasting point of view? We answer the question first for the forecast sample, 2004 - 2006. Then, we re-estimate the models until 2006 and use the second forecast sample, spanning from 2007 to 2012, to assess the robustness of the results and the performance of the models during problematic times.

The stochastic one-step ahead forecasts for the period immediately before the crisis are shown in Figure 6.10.3. The predicted series capture the overall behavior of the actual variables, though not their smaller shifts, and this is a common characteristic of both the deterministic and the stochastic forecasting methods. The detailed forecast metrics confirm the graphical impression that the VAR(2) is a little bit more precise in the prediction of the German

Vector Autoregression Estimates

	G_(FR)	G_(GER)	G_(IT)
G_FR(-1)	0.668	0.007	0.063
	(0.074)	(0.158)	(0.135)
	[9.064]	[0.047]	[0.470]
G_GER(-1)	0.009	0.745	0.122
	(0.042)	(0.089)	(0.076)
	[0.214]	[8.352]	[1.606]
G_IT(-1)	0.107	0.091	0.623
	(0.057)	(0.121)	(0.104)
	[1.893]	[0.751]	[6.008]
G_US	0.172	0.105	0.099
	(0.030)	(0.065)	(0.055)
	[5.695]	[1.632]	[1.794]
D_1988Q1	1.068	0.838	1.213
	(0.301)	(0.644)	(0.550)
	[3.551]	[1.301]	[2.206]
D_1993Q1	-1.624	-2.141	-1.604
	(0.310)	(0.663)	(0.566)
	[-5.247]	[-3.229]	[-2.834]
D_2000Q1	0.711	0.723	1.079
	(0.304)	(0.651)	(0.556)
	[2.339]	[1.110]	[1.942]
Standard errors in () and t-statistics in []			
R-squared	0.924	0.761	0.776
Adj. R-squared	0.917	0.739	0.755
Sum sq. resids	10.809	49.584	36.139
S.E.equation	0.411	0.880	0.751
F-statistic	129.747	33.982	37.044
Log likelihood	-33.923	-88.000	-76.771
Akaike AIC	1.153	2.676	2.360
Schwarz BIC	1.376	2.899	2.583
Mean dep	2.202	1.923	1.898
S.D.dependent	1.426	1.722	1.520
Determinant resid covariance (dof adj.)			0.066
Determinant resid covariance			0.048
Log likelihood			-194.456
Akaike information criterion			6.069
Schwarz criterion			6.738

Table 6.10.2: *Estimation results of the VAR(1) for the period 1986 - 2003*

Lags	LM-Stat	Prob
1	19.908	0.018
2	12.179	0.203
3	24.141	0.004
4	31.144	0.000
5	14.147	0.117
6	12.920	0.166
7	17.845	0.037
8	11.977	0.215
9	13.564	0.139
10	16.843	0.051
11	10.129	0.340
12	11.498	0.243

Table 6.10.3: *VAR(1) residuals serial correlation LM tests*

VAR Heteroskedasticity Tests:
Joint test:

Chi-sq	df	Prob.
72.340	66	0.277

Individual components:

Dependent	R-squared	F(11,59)	Prob.	Chi-sq(11)	Prob.
res1*res1	0.113	0.684	0.748	8.031	0.711
res2*res2	0.174	1.132	0.354	12.373	0.336
res3*res3	0.132	0.812	0.628	9.339	0.591
res2*res1	0.203	1.365	0.214	14.406	0.211
res3*res1	0.130	0.804	0.636	9.252	0.599
res3*res2	0.300	2.302	0.020	21.321	0.030

Table 6.10.4: *VAR(1) residuals heteroskedasticity test*

and French growth rates, but not of the Italian one.

As we expected, re-estimating the two VAR models in the longer sample 1986 - 2006 and producing forecasts for the period 2007 - 2012 proves more challenging. We present the forecasts in Figure 6.10.4.

For all the countries, both the RMSFE and the MAFE are much larger

VAR Residual normality Tests

Component	Skewness	Chi-sq	df	Prob.
1	-0.040	0.019	1	0.890
2	0.144	0.246	1	0.620
3	-0.333	1.311	1	0.252
Joint		1.576	3.000	0.665

Component	Kurtosis	Chi-sq	df	Prob.
1	2.541	0.623	1	0.430
2	3.543	0.873	1	0.350
3	4.112	3.661	1	0.056
Joint		5.157	3.000	0.161

Component	Jarque-Bera	df	Prob.
1	0.642	2	0.725
2	1.118	2	0.572
3	4.972	2	0.083
Joint	6.732	6	0.346

Table 6.10.5: *VAR(1) Residuals normality test*

Pairwise Granger Causality Tests

Null Hypothesis:	Obs	F-Statistic	Prob.
G_GER does not Granger cause G_FR	70	0.605	0.549
G_FR does not Granger cause G_GER		4.449	0.016
G_IT does not Granger cause G_FR	70	6.403	0.003
G_FR does not Granger cause G_IT		6.275	0.003
G_IT does not Granger cause G_GER	70	6.511	0.003
G_GER does not Granger cause G_IT		0.780	0.463

Table 6.10.6: *Granger causality test among the three variables using the lag length $p = 2$*

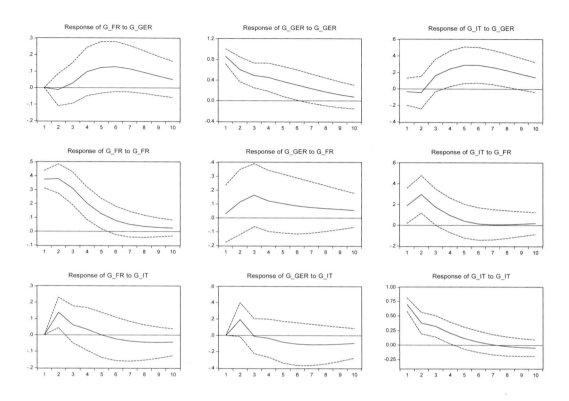

Figure 6.10.2: *Impulse response function from the VAR(1) model with the ordering (g_fr,g_ger,g_it)*

than during the first evaluation sample, often more than twice as large. Capturing the sharp decrease in the growth rates of the three countries' GDP growth is indeed quite complex, and even more sophisticated models could not achieve this goal at the time of the crisis. However, also in this sample the VAR(2) model yields more accurate predictions than the VAR(1) for all countries but Italy.

6.10.2 Monetary transmission mechanism

We can now analyze through a VAR model the transmission mechanism of monetary policy, describing how policy-induced changes in the nominal money stock or the short-term nominal interest rate impact real variables. In this example, we use US monthly data from 1986 until 2012. The dataset

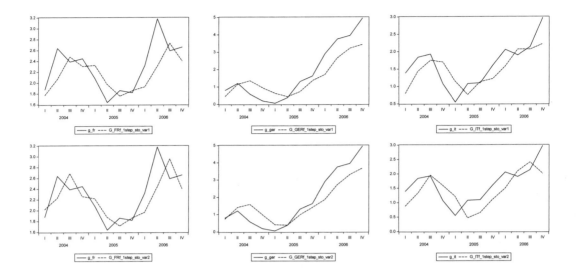

Figure 6.10.3: *One step ahead forecasts, stochastic method, from the VAR(1) model (upper panels) and the VAR(2) model (lower panels) in the period 2004 - 2006*

contains the following six variables:

- ly: the log of the index of industrial production, as an indicator of real activity.

- lp: the log of the index of personal consumption expenditures less food and energy, as an indicator of inflationary pressure.

- i: the federal funds rate, as an indicator of the monetary policy stance.

- $lpcm$: the log of the producer price index for all commodities.

- $lsmtr$: the log of reserve balances of depository institutions.

- $lsmnbr$: the log of non-borrowed reserves of depository institutions.

We conduct an analysis along the lines of Leeper, Sims, and Zha (1996). Hence, we consider as a starting point a VAR model with three endogenous variables (ly, lp, i), estimated over the period January 1986 to June 2007 in order to exclude the financial crisis period and the switch in monetary policy

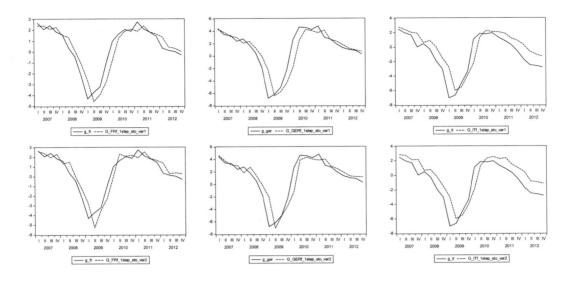

Figure 6.10.4: *One-step ahead forecasts, stochastic environment, from the VAR(1) model (lower panels) and the VAR(2) model (upper panels) in the period 2007 - 2012*

to quantitative easing, after the interest rate reached the zero lower bound. We start by estimating a VAR model with a long lag length $p = 12$, and then we use standard lag selection criteria and sequential LR tests to reduce the number of lags.

From Table 6.10.7, the most parsimonious specification is suggested by both the Hannan-Quinn and the BIC criterion, with $p = 2$. Table 6.10.8 shows the resulting estimated coefficients for the VAR(2).

The majority of the VAR(2) parameters are significant, and the overall model fit is extremely good, which is not surprising as the variables in levels are highly persistent. Indeed, preliminary analysis of the three time series suggests that both ly and i are non-stationary. Furthermore, a closer look at the model diagnostics in Figure 6.10.5 shows that the residuals display a few outliers and therefore some non-normality problems. More in depth tests on these residuals (not reported here) confirm the need to correct this non-normality problem through the use of dummy variables.

In particular, dummy variables need to be created for two months, September and October 2001, in correspondence of the terrorist attack at the World Trade Center in New York. Indeed the two dummy variables are signifi-

VAR Lag Order Selection Criteria

Lag	LogL	LR	FPE	AIC	SC	HQ
0	28.608	NA	0.000	-0.199	-0.157	-0.182
1	2431.464	4731.205	0.000	-18.756	-18.590	-18.689
2	2480.569	95.546	0.000	-19.066	-18.777*	-18.950*
3	2488.235	14.738	0.000	-19.056	-18.643	-18.890
4	2500.958	24.164	0.000	-19.085	-18.548	-18.869
5	2514.379	25.178	0.000*	-19.119*	-18.458	-18.853
6	2522.058	14.227	0.000	-19.109	-18.324	-18.793
7	2531.022	16.399	0.000	-19.109	-18.200	-18.743
8	2533.830	5.070	0.000	-19.061	-18.028	-18.645
9	2536.803	5.301	0.000	-19.014	-17.857	-18.549
10	2548.146	19.961*	0.000	-19.032	-17.751	-18.517
11	2550.463	4.023	0.000	-18.980	-17.576	-18.416
12	2555.384	8.432	0.000	-18.949	-17.420	-18.334

* Indicates lag order selected by the criterion. LR: sequential test (each at 5% level), FPE: final prediction error, AIC: Akaike information criterion, SC: Schwarz, HQ: Hannan-Quinn

Table 6.10.7: *Lag length criteria for VAR for (ly, lp, i)*

cant for lp and i, but not for ly, and the residuals' behavior is substantially improved.

The outliers related to the 9/11 period have been corrected but still the residuals show some other aberrant observations as well as some significant spikes in the correlogram. The normality test confirms that the null has to be rejected, and also the heteroskedasticity test signals some problems, see Tables 6.10.10 and 6.10.11. On top of that, some of the roots of the characteristic polynomial lie on the unit circle, and this is something that we expected given that we did not account for the non-stationarity of at least two of our indicators.

Despite the mentioned problems, the VAR(2) reproduces some common stylized facts related to the monetary transmission mechanism (MTM). However, it also gives rise to a puzzle. More specifically, let us have a look at the impulse response functions of the model up to 48 months (four years), obtained using the Cholesky structural factorization. The variables are ordered as lp, ly and i, so that price (demand) shocks can have a contemporaneous

Vector Autoregression Estimates

	LP	LY	I
LP(-1)	1.011	0.106	17.505
	(0.062)	(0.289)	(10.318)
	[16.387]	[0.369]	[1.697]
LP(-2)	-0.013	-0.100	-17.779
	(0.062)	(0.288)	(10.303)
	[-0.212]	[-0.348]	[-1.726]
LY(-1)	-0.018	0.962	8.604
	(0.013)	(0.062)	(2.217)
	[-1.322]	[15.514]	[3.880]
LY(-2)	0.016	0.029	-8.347
	(0.013)	(0.062)	(2.207)
	[1.223]	[0.478]	[-3.783]
I(-1)	0.000	0.006	1.413
	(0.000)	(0.002)	(0.054)
	[1.389]	[3.803]	[25.978]
I(-2)	-0.000	-0.006	-0.425
	(0.000)	(0.002)	(0.054)
	[-1.189]	[-4.039]	[-7.807]
C	0.016	0.013	0.103
	(0.003)	(0.016)	(0.572)
	[4.647]	[0.813]	[0.180]

Standard errors in () and t-statistics in []

	LP	LY	I
R-squared	1.000	0.999	0.993
Adj. R-squared	1.000	0.999	0.993
Sum sq. resids	0.000	0.007	8.679
S.E.equation	0.001	0.005	0.182
F-statistic	918307.100	65977.590	6367.156
Log likelihood	1451.289	1037.938	79.353
Akaike AIC	-10.778	-7.694	-0.540
Schwarz BIC	-10.684	-7.600	-0.446
Mean dep	4.412	4.312	5.081
S.D. dep	0.157	0.196	2.189

Determinant resid covariance(dof adj.)	0.000
Determinant resid covariance	0.000
Log likelihood	2573.232
Akaike information criterion	-19.047
Schwarz criterion	-18.765

Table 6.10.8: *VAR(2) model estimated for (ly, lp, i)*

Vector Autoregression Estimates

	LP	LY	I
LP(-1)	1.223	0.087	11.502
	(0.056)	(0.300)	(10.584)
	[21.665]	[0.289]	[1.087]
LP(-2)	-0.219	-0.076	-11.732
	(0.057)	(0.302)	(10.632)
	[-3.865]	[-0.250]	[-1.104]
LY(-1)	-0.016	0.960	8.246
	(0.012)	(0.062)	(2.188)
	[-1.404]	[15.455]	[3.769]
LY(-2)	0.013	0.029	-8.009
	(0.012)	(0.062)	(2.171)
	[1.091]	[0.471]	[-3.690]
I(-1)	0.001	0.006	1.400
	(0.000)	(0.002)	(0.054)
	[2.379]	[3.647]	[25.847]
I(-2)	-0.001	-0.006	-0.411
	(0.000)	(0.002)	(0.054)
	[-1.760]	[-3.809]	[-7.602]
D0109	-0.007	-0.005	-0.495
	(0.001)	(0.005)	(0.181)
	[-7.171]	[-0.936]	[-2.729]
D0110	0.007	-0.003	-0.236
	)0.001)	)0.006)	)0.199)
	[7.046]	[-0.612]	[-1.189]

Standard errors in () and t-statistics in []

	LP	LY	I
R-squared	1.000	0.999	0.993
Adj.R-squared	1.000	0.999	0.993
Sum sq. resids	0.000	0.007	8.402
S.E.equation	0.001	0.005	0.180
F-statistic	1018404.000	56453.350	5616.953
Log likelihood	1486.321	1038.217	83.696
Akaike AIC	-11.032	-7.688	-0.565
Schwarz BIC	-10.925	-7.581	-0.458
Mean dep	4.412	4.312	5.081
S.D. dep	0.157	0.196	2.189

Determinant resid covariance (dof adj.)	0.000
Determinant resid covariance	0.000
Log likelihood	2611.999
Akaike information criterion	-19.313
Schwarz criterion	-18.992

Table 6.10.9: *Estimated coefficient for the VAR(2) model for (ly,lp, i) including also dummy variables for 9/11 as exogenous*

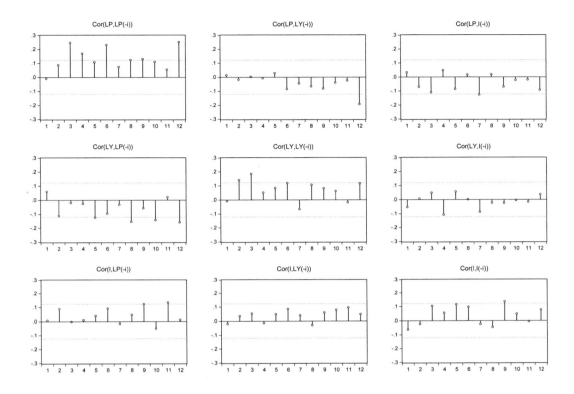

Figure 6.10.5: *Empirical correlograms of the residuals of the VAR(2) model*

effect on output and interest rate, output (supply) shocks can affect contemporaneously the interest rate (as indeed the Federal Reserve sets i by also looking at real and nominal indicators), and interest rate (monetary) shocks have only a delayed effect on output and prices, since it takes some time for both variables to adjust.

Figure 6.10.6 displays the responses of lp, ly, and i to a unitary shock to i at time 0 (first three panels) and the response of the policy variable i to a unitary shock to lp and ly (last two panels). Coherently with the major findings of the MTM literature, we see that i increases after demand and supply shocks, though the reaction to higher prices is lower than to higher output and not statistically significant.

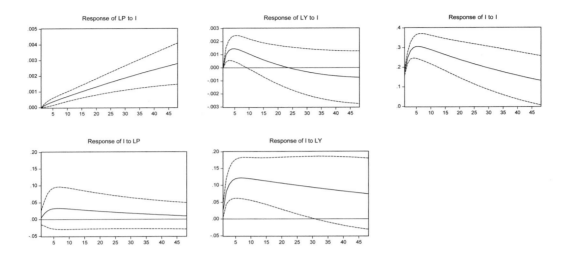

Figure 6.10.6: *MTM in the pre-crisis period: Impulse response function from the estimated VAR(2) model*

However, in the first panels we see a puzzling result: after an increase in the interest rate (contradictory monetary shock), both prices and output increase. These puzzling results still persist even when the number of lags is increased as suggested by other information criteria.

The MTM literature in general has tried to solve puzzles like the ones we obtained by including other indicators in the VAR model, so as to eliminate a possible omitted variable bias. For example, the price puzzle we obtained might be due to the fact that the model lacks a leading indicator for inflation: for this reason we can try and add the producer price index including commodities *lpcm*. On the other hand, the fact that *ly* was increasing with higher interest rates could be due to the fact the federal funds rate is not enough to capture the policy actions implemented by the Fed: the literature has then suggested to include in MTM models also some reserve aggregates, which the Fed can control directly.

Once again, we follow the approach of Leeper, Sims, and Zha (1996) and add to our indicators the borrowed (*lsmtr*) and non-borrowed reserves (*lsmnbr*).

Besides the dummies we previously employed, the analysis of the residuals underlined the need to add also a dummy for November 2001 and one for

VAR Residual normality Tests

Component	Skewness	Chi-sq	df	Prob.
1	0.259	2.985	1	0.084
2	-0.112	0.565	1	0.452
3	-0.176	1.389	1	0.239
Joint		4.939	3	0.176
Component	Kurtosis	Chi-sq	df	Prob.
1	3.121	0.165	1	0.685
2	4.660	30.764	1	0.000
3	7.078	185.688	1	0.000
Joint		216.618	3	0.000
Component	Jarque-Bera	df	Prob.	
1	3.150	2	0.207	
2	31.329	2	0.000	
3	187.077	2	0.000	
Joint	221.556	6	0.000	

Table 6.10.10: *Diagnostic test on residuals of the VAR(2) model with dummy variables*

January 1991. The chosen lag length this time is $p = 1$, and the results of the estimation are reported in Table 6.10.12.

Notwithstanding the dummies, the residuals still show some heteroskedasticity and non-normality problems. On the other hand, enlarging the set of indicators seems to at least partially solve the puzzles we previously discussed, as it emerges from Figure 6.10.7. In fact, now after a unitary increase in the federal funds rate at time 0, the reaction of both price measures is close to zero and not significant, while there is a negative and significant effect on output. Furthermore, both types of reserves decline as we expect. We also note that none of the responses eventually goes to zero, a further confirmation of the presence of stochastic trends in the system, which makes the effects of the shocks persistent. We will see in the next chapter how to properly handle this feature.

VAR Heteroskedasticity Tests:

Jointtest:

Chi-sq	df	Prob.
144.113	84	0.000

Individual components:

Dependent	R-squared	$F_{(14,253)}$	Prob.	Chi-sq(14)	Prob.
res1*res1	0.069	1.343	0.182	18.540	0.183
res2*res2	0.047	0.887	0.574	12.538	0.563
res3*res3	0.188	4.174	0.000	50.288	0.000
res2*res1	0.048	0.913	0.546	12.883	0.536
res3*res1	0.126	2.602	0.002	33.731	0.002
res3*res2	0.069	1.344	0.182	18.556	0.183

Table 6.10.11: *VAR(2) residuals heteroskedasticity tests*

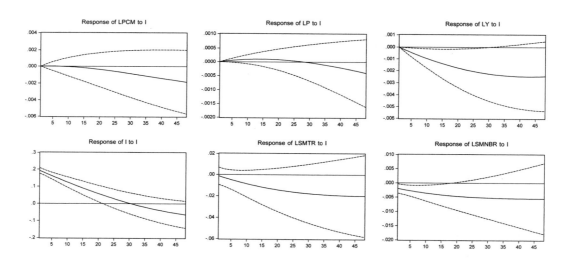

Figure 6.10.7: *Impulse response function on the VAR(1) model with the enlarged set of indicators (lpcm, lp, ly, i, lsmtr, lsmnbr)*

Vector Autoregression Estimates

	LPCM	LP	LY	I	LSMTR	LSMNBR
LPCM(-1)	0.969	0.001	0.004	0.523	0.188	0.033
	(0.014)	(0.002)	(0.009)	(0.371)	(0.123)	(0.025)
	[70.946]	[0.911]	[0.385]	[1.410]	[1.529]	[1.302]
LP(-1)	0.040	1.000	-0.033	-2.633	-0.325	0.021
	(0.026)	(0.003)	(0.018)	(0.719)	(0.239)	(0.050)
	[1.514]	[325.470]	[-1.829]	[-3.661]	[-1.362]	[0.421]
LY(-1)	0.013	0.000	1.009	1.380	0.050	-0.030
	(0.012)	(0.001)	(0.008)	(0.324)	(0.107)	(0.022)
	[1.114]	[0.201]	[123.070]	[4.265]	[0.469]	[-1.347]
I(-1)	-3.300	7.250	-0.001	0.964	-0.004	-0.001
	(0.000)	(3.900)	(0.000)	(0.009)	(0.003)	(0.001)
	[-0.098]	[1.849]	[-2.219]	[104.960]	[-1.440]	[-1.952]
LSMTR(-1)	0.007	0.001	-0.003	-0.026	0.985	0.010
	(0.002)	(0.000)	(0.001)	(0.057)	(0.019)	(0.004)
	[3.284]	[5.604]	[-1.994]	[-0.445]	[51.72]0	[2.501]
LSMNBR(-1)	-0.014	-0.002	0.012	0.334	0.044	0.980
	(0.005)	(0.001)	(0.004)	(0.141)	(0.047)	(0.010)
	[-2.666]	[-3.263]	[3.273]	[2.362]	[0.938]	[100.710]
D0109	-0.004	-0.007	-0.005	-0.566	1.227	0.318
	(0.007)	(0.001)	(0.005)	(0.202)	(0.067)	(0.014)
	[-0.519]	[-8.038]	[-1.023]	[-2.807]	[18.351]	[22.938]
D0110	-0.030	0.005	-0.007	-0.671	-0.745	-0.189
	(0.007)	(0.001)	(0.005)	(0.205)	(0.068)	(0.014)
	[-3.942]	[5.501]	[-1.444]	[-3.277]	[-10.959]	[-13.380]
D9101	0.001	0.003	-0.005	-0.263	-0.311	-0.000
	(0.007)	(0.001)	(0.005)	(0.203)	(0.067)	(0.014)
	[0.117]	[2.883]	[-0.958]	[-1.294]	[-4.604]	[-0.029]
D0111	-0.009	0.001	-0.008	-0.432	-0.305	-0.104
	(0.007)	(0.001)	(0.005)	(0.203)	(0.067)	(0.014)
	[-1.220]	[0.587]	[-1.548]	[-2.134]	[-4.542]	[-7.462]

Standard errors in () and t-statistics in []

R-squared	0.997	1.000	0.999	0.992	0.987	0.994
Adj.R-squared	0.997	1.000	0.999	0.992	0.987	0.994
Sum sq. resids	0.014	0.000	0.007	10.416	1.147	0.049
S.E.equation	0.007	0.001	0.005	0.201	0.067	0.014
F-statistic	9823.380	100859.000	44771.000	3537.160	2188.280	4706.770
Log likelihood	943.714	1523.120	1044.470	55.611	352.355	775.555
Akaike AIC	-6.942	-11.250	-7.691	-0.339	-2.545	-5.692
Schwarz BIC	-6.808	-11.116	-7.558	-0.205	-2.412	-5.558
Mean dep	4.828	4.410	4.311	5.093	9.709	10.679
S.D. dep	0.134	0.158	0.197	2.195	0.574	0.174

Determinant resid covariance	0.000
Determinant resid covariance	0.000
Log likelihood	4730.441
Akaike information criterion	-34.724
Schwarz criterion	-33.923

Table 6.10.12: *Estimated coefficients for the VAR(1) model for the enlarged set of indicators*

6.11   Concluding remarks

VAR models are a powerful tool for forecasting using time series methods. From a statistical theoretical point of view, they can be considered as approximations to the infinite order multivariate MA representation of weakly stationary processes implied by the Wold theorem. From an economic point of view, they can capture the dynamic inter-relationship across the variables, without imposing (too many) restrictions, as often done in more structural models. In addition, estimation, testing, and forecasting are rather easily considered theoretically and implemented empirically.

For these reasons, VARs have indeed been used extensively, and rather successfully. However, three main caveats should also be kept in mind, in addition to the usual warning that a careful specification and evaluation is required. First, typically there are many parameters in VARs, whose precise estimation in finite samples is problematic. Hence, just a few variables are typically modeled, which can create an omitted variable problem. This is more relevant for structural analysis than for forecasting, but also for forecasting relevant information can be missed. Two possible approaches can tackle this issue: either using Bayesian rather than classical estimation (that will be considered in Chapter 8) or using alternative specifications for large datasets such as factor models (considered in Chapters 11 and 13).

Second, the relationships across variables can be unstable, as well as the variance of the shocks hitting them. As we have discussed, parameter instability is indeed one of the main reasons for forecast failure. In this case, simpler univariate models can produce better forecasts, an issue to be considered in empirical applications. Pooling a set of small-scale VAR models can help (which also addresses the omitted variable problem mentioned above). A careful use of dummy variables can also be useful to try to model the breaks. As an alternative, models with time-varying parameters can be adopted, as we will discuss in Chapters 9 - 11, even though this complicates parameter estimation and forecasting.

Finally, in this chapter we have assumed that the variables are weakly stationary. However, as we have seen in the previous chapter, often this is not the case as stochastic trends are important drivers of several economic and financial variables. Hence, in the next chapter we will consider how to generalize the VAR analysis to handle stochastic trends and unit roots in a multivariate context.

Chapter 7

Error Correction Models

7.1 Introduction

Integrated variables can be made stationary by differencing, as we have discussed in the context of ARIMA models. However, in a multivariate context, there also exists the possibility that linear combinations of integrated variables are stationary, a case known as cointegration.

From an economic point of view, the presence of equilibrium relations among the variables, e.g., between consumption and income, interest rates at different maturities, or among money, interest rate, output and prices, justifies the presence of cointegration. In this sense, the stationary (cointegration) relationships of the integrated variable can be considered as long-run (equilibrium) relationships among the variables. Specifications of cointegrated processes were implicit in the so-called error correction models proposed by Davidson, Hendry, Srba, and Yeo (1978). Cointegration was introduced in a series of papers by Granger (1983) and Granger and Weiss (1983). Subsequently, Engle and Granger (1987) provided a formal development for cointegration and error-correction representations.

Since equilibrium relationships must be satisfied, at least in the long-run, the presence of cointegration implies that the changes in the variables should react to deviations from the equilibrium in such a way to bring them back towards the equilibrium. This type of adjustment is missing in a VAR in the first differences of the variables only, so that the latter is mis-specified in the presence of cointegration. As we will see, cointegration implies that a VAR in the levels of the variables remains correctly specified, but it can be conveniently reparameterized in the error correction form.

In the following sections, we consider the consequences of cointegration for modeling and forecasting. There are a number of excellent surveys on statistical issues in integrated and cointegrated systems, including Campbell and Perron (1991), Phillips (1988), and Watson (1994). Excellent textbook treatments can also be found in Banerjee, Dolado, Galbraith, and Hendry (1993) and Hamilton (1994).

The chapter starts out with Section 7.2 on spurious regressions. Cointegration and error correction models are covered in section 7.3, followed by Section 7.4 which introduces the Engle and Granger cointegration test and Section 7.5 the Johansen cointegration test. MA representations of cointegrated processes appear in Section 7.6, while forecasting in the presence of cointegration is discussed in Section 7.7. The effects of stochastic trends on forecasts is the subject of Section 7.8 An example using simulated series appears in Section 7.9, while two empirical applications are covered in section 7.10. Section 7.11 concludes the chapter.

7.2   Spurious regressions

The time series regression models discussed so far required all variables to be I(0), and therefore standard statistical results for the linear regression model hold. If some or all of the variables in the regression are I(1), then the usual statistical results may or may not hold. A case that illustrates this issue involves a simulation design considered by Granger and Newbold (1974). They considered two completely unrelated random walks y_{1t} and y_{2t} such that:

$$y_{it} = y_{it-1} + \varepsilon_{it} \quad \text{where} \quad \varepsilon_{it} \sim \text{WN}(0,1) \qquad i = 1, 2 \qquad (7.2.1)$$

and we regress y_{1t} onto y_{2t}, namely:

$$y_{1t} = \beta_0 + \beta_1 y_{2t} + u_t$$

Simulation evidence reported by Granger and Newbold featured properties that later were formalized by Phillips (1986). In particular:

- $\hat{\beta}_1$ does not converge in probability to zero but instead converges in distribution to a non-normal random variable not necessarily centered at zero.

- The usual t-statistic for testing $\beta_1 = 0$ diverges as $T \to \infty$

- The usual R^2 from the regression converges to unity as $T \to \infty$

The setting was dubbed "spurious regression" by Granger and Newbold. This is obviously problematic if we think of forecasting since we can mistakenly conclude that y_2 has high explanatory power for y_1, while in reality the relationship is spurious. The main signal of a spurious regression is high serial correlation in the residuals $\hat{u}_t$, which turn out to be I(1), typically associated with high R^2s and high t-statistics.

7.3 Cointegration and error correction models

Time series regressions that include integrated variables can behave very differently from standard regression models, as we saw in the previous section. Estimated coefficients in VARs with integrated components, can also behave differently than estimators in covariance stationary VARs. To discuss this, we can write a VAR(p) in the levels of y_t,

$$\Phi(L) y_t = \varepsilon_t, \tag{7.3.1}$$

as

$$\Delta y_t = -\underbrace{(I - \Phi_1 - \ldots - \Phi_p)}_{\Pi} y_{t-1} + \Gamma_1 \Delta y_{t-1} + \ldots + \Gamma_{p-1} \Delta y_{t-p+1} + \varepsilon_t, \tag{7.3.2}$$

where $\Gamma_i = -(\Phi_{i+1} + \ldots + \Phi_p)$. We know that y_t is weakly stationary if $|\Phi(z)| = 0$ has all the roots z outside the unit circle. In the presence of unit roots, it is instead $|\Phi(1)| = 0$, which also implies that $\Phi(1)$ has reduced rank, its rank is smaller than the number of variables m. Since $\Phi(1) = I - \Phi_1 - \ldots - \Phi_p$, we have that $\Phi(1) = \Pi$. Therefore, the rank of Π in (7.3.2) is associated with the presence of unit roots (and also of cointegration, as we will see).

If all the m variables are stationary, Π will have full rank m. In this case, the models in (7.3.1) and (7.3.2) are identical, and we can just use the specification in levels in (7.3.1).

If all the m variables are integrated and not cointegrated, we have $\Pi = 0$, and a VAR(p-1) in first differences, such as

$$\Delta y_t = \Gamma_1 \Delta y_{t-1} + \ldots + \Gamma_{p-1} \Delta y_{t-p+1} + \varepsilon_t, \qquad (7.3.3)$$

is the appropriate specification. In principle, we could still use the specification in levels in (7.3.1), since it can be shown that the OLS estimators remain consistent so that, in large samples, $\widehat{\Phi}_1 + \ldots + \widehat{\Phi}_p$ would converge to the identity matrix, making (7.3.1) equivalent to (7.3.3). However, the asymptotic distribution of the OLS estimators is non-standard, which complicates inference, and in finite samples there can be a loss of efficiency from not imposing the constraint $I = \Phi_1 + \ldots + \Phi_p$. Instead, the constraint is imposed in the VAR in differences in (7.3.3), and the OLS estimators of its parameters have standard properties.

If the variables are integrated and cointegrated, Π has rank r, with $0 < r < m$, where r represents the number of cointegration relations, namely, the number of independent stationary linear combinations of the m integrated variables. In this case, we can write

$$\Pi = \underset{m \times r}{\alpha} \cdot \underset{r \times m}{\beta'}, \qquad (7.3.4)$$

where the matrix β contains the coefficients of the r independent stationary combinations of the m integrated variables,

$$\beta' y_{t-1} \sim I(0).$$

The model (7.3.2) becomes

$$\Delta y_t = -\alpha \beta' y_{t-1} + \Gamma_1 \Delta y_{t-1} + \ldots + \Gamma_{p-1} \Delta y_{t-p+1} + \varepsilon_t, \qquad (7.3.5)$$

where the matrix α contains, for each equation, the loadings of the r cointegrating relationships $\beta' y_{t-1}$. The model in equation (7.3.5) is called (Vector) Error Correction Model (ECM). The term *error correction* is related to the fact that if $\beta' y_{t-1}$ is different from zero, namely the long-run equilibrium conditions are not satisfied, then Δy_t must adjust, by an extent measured by $-\alpha$, in order to reduce the disequilibrium.

Note that in the presence of cointegration, a VAR in differences, such as (7.3.3), is mis-specified, since it omits the information on the cointegration relationships. In other words, it assumes by mistake that $\Pi = 0$, which generates an omitted variable problem. A VAR in levels, such as (7.3.1), remains correctly specified but, at least in finite samples, it is not efficient, since it does not impose the reduced rank restriction on Π. Hence, it is important for modeling to understand whether the variables under analysis are integrated and cointegrated. Unfortunately, as in the case of the unit root tests we discussed in the previous chapter, testing for cointegration cannot be based on standard distribution theory.

7.4 Engle and Granger cointegration test

Engle and Granger (1987) suggest the following two-stage procedure to test for the presence of cointegration among a set of I(1) variables. First, estimate by OLS the regression:

$$y_{1t} = \beta_2 y_{2t} + \ldots + \beta_m y_{mt} + \varepsilon_t. \tag{7.4.1}$$

Second, test whether ε_t has a unit root. If it does, there is no cointegration. If it is does not, then the variables are cointegrated.

The critical values for the unit root test in the second step of the procedure, based on the Dickey Fuller (DF) or Augmented Dickey Fuller (ADF) procedures discussed in Chapter 5, are different from those of the standard DF (and ADF) tests. Intuitively, we have here the additional complication that the test is run not on ε_t but on the estimated residuals of the first step regression, $\widehat{\varepsilon}_t$. Since $\widehat{\varepsilon}_t$ are OLS residuals, their variance will be minimized, which could bias the test toward rejecting a unit root when using the DF critical values. Engle and Granger (1987) provided proper critical values, using simulation based methods since the asymptotic distribution of the test is not standard. The values are typically reported in standard econometric software.

We discussed in Section 7.2 what happens to the OLS estimators and standard regression statistics when the variables are not cointegrated, $\beta_2 = 0, \ldots, \beta_m = 0$, but we still run the model in (7.4.1). This is a case of spurious regression, since we can conclude by mistake that the variables $y_2, \ldots, y_m$ have high explanatory power for y_1, while what they are capturing is just spurious comovement due to the independent stochastic trends driving the variables. The main signal of a spurious regression is high serial correlation in the residuals $\widehat{\varepsilon}_t$, which remain I(1). Therefore, a test for cointegration can also be helpful to avoid the danger of a spurious regression.

The Engle and Granger (1987) test is intuitive and rather easy to apply. However, it is not efficient and it cannot be used to determine the number of cointegrating relationships, r. Moreover, even in the presence of cointegration, the distribution of the OLS estimator $\widehat{\beta}$ is not standard, which complicates inference on the cointegration parameters, i.e., on the long-run relationships across the variables. On the efficiency issue it is worth noting that several asymptotically efficient single equation methods have been proposed. Phillips (1991) suggests a regression in the spectral domain, Phillips and Loretan (1991) suggest a non-linear error-correction estimation procedure, Phillips and Hansen (1990) suggest an instrumental regression with a correction of the Phillips-Perron type (cf. Section 5.5), Saikkonen (1991) suggests including leads as well as lags in the polynomials of the error correction model in order to achieve asymptotic efficiency, and Engle and Yoo (1991) suggest a three-step estimator starting from the static Engle-Granger estimation. From all of those estimators it is possible to obtain simple t-values for the short-term adjustment parameters α.

7.5   Johansen cointegration test

Johansen (1995) developed a Maximum Likelihood (ML) procedure to test for the cointegration rank r, obtain ML estimators of α and β, and test specific hypotheses on their parameters. In order to apply it, we need the additional assumption that the VAR errors are normally distributed.

The procedure, implemented in several standard econometric packages, such as *EViews*, sequentially tests the following hypotheses:

$$
\begin{array}{lll}
 & H_0 & H_1 \\
(1) & r = 0 & r = 1 \\
(2) & r \leq 1 & r = 2 \\
(3) & r \leq 2 & r = 3 \\
 & \vdots & \\
(m-1) & r \leq m-1 & r = m
\end{array}
$$

If at step (1) the test does not reject H_0, we set $r = 0$. If at step (i) the test rejects H_0, we set $r = i$.

Johansen suggested two statistics to be used in each step of the above sequential procedure, the trace test and the maximum eigenvalue test. As their ranking is theoretically not clear-cut, it is common in practice to compute them both and compare their outcomes. It should also be considered that, as in the case of the ADF test, the asymptotic distribution of the test (and therefore the proper critical values) depend on the deterministic component included in the model. Also in this case, when economic theory does not suggest a specific choice, it is common to compute the cointegration statistics for different specifications of the deterministic component and compare the results. Moreover, other variables included, such as dummy variables or exogenous regressors, can also modify the limiting distribution, though in general this is not considered in the implementation of the Johansen's cointegration test in standard econometric packages. We refer to Johansen (1995) for additional details.

An alternative procedure to determine the cointegrating rank can be based on the use of information criteria, such as the multivariate AIC and BIC criteria that we discussed in Chapter 5. The criteria should be computed for all different values of r and possibly also for the different values of the lag order p. Then, the cointegrating rank (and possibly the lag order) are chosen as the minimizers of the selected information criterion, see e.g., Aznar and Salvador (2002) for more details.

Once r is determined, we need to identify the coefficients of the cointegration vectors. In fact, for any invertible $r \times r$ matrix Q, it is

$$\pi = \alpha\beta' = \alpha Q Q^{-1}\beta' = \gamma\delta'. \tag{7.5.1}$$

Therefore, the cointegration coefficients and the loadings are not uniquely identified. To obtain identification we have to impose a priori restrictions on the coefficients of α and/or β, similar to those used in simultaneous equation models or in the context of IRF analysis. For example, it can be shown that if

$$\underset{r \times m}{\beta'} = \left[\underset{r \times r}{I} : \widetilde{\beta} \right]', \tag{7.5.2}$$

then α and β' are exactly identified. This is a common choice but of course other identification schemes are possible.

Having determined r and identified α and β, estimation and inference for the VECM model parameters is standard. For example, we can conduct an LR test with an asymptotic χ^2 distribution for specific null hypotheses on the coefficients α and β.

7.6   MA representations of cointegrated processes

As in the univariate case, a stationary process admits an $MA(\infty)$ representation:

$$\Delta y_t = C\left(L\right)\varepsilon_t, \tag{7.6.1}$$

and using the same steps as in the univariate Beveridge and Nelson (1981) (BN) decomposition covered in Chapter 5, we have

$$y_t = \underbrace{C\left(1\right)\sum_{j=1}^{t}\varepsilon_t}_{PC_t} + \underbrace{C^*\left(L\right)\varepsilon_t}_{TC_t},$$

where PC_t and TC_t stand for, respectively, permanent and transitory components, and it is:

$$C\left(L\right) = C^*\left(L\right)\left(I - L\right) + C\left(1\right).$$

Looking closer at the permanent component, the presence of cointegration imposes constraints on $C\left(1\right)$. Given that $\beta'y_t \sim I\left(0\right)$, it must be that $\beta'C\left(1\right) = 0$, as stationary variables should not be influenced by stochastic trends. We can show, that

$$C\left(1\right) = I - \alpha\left(\beta'\alpha\right)^{-1}\beta', \tag{7.6.2}$$

and

$$I_n = \beta_\perp\left(\alpha'_\perp\beta_\perp\right)^{-1}\alpha'_\perp + \alpha\left(\beta'\alpha\right)^{-1}\beta', \tag{7.6.3}$$

where $\beta_\perp$ and $\alpha_\perp$ are $m \times (m-r)$ matrices of rank $m-r$, such that $\alpha'_\perp\alpha = 0$ and $\beta'_\perp\beta = 0$.

Therefore,

$$C\left(1\right) = \beta_\perp\left(\alpha'_\perp\beta_\perp\right)^{-1}\alpha'_\perp,$$

and

$$PC_t = \beta_\perp\left(\alpha'_\perp\beta_\perp\right)^{-1}\alpha'_\perp\sum_{j=1}^{t}\varepsilon_j. \tag{7.6.4}$$

Hence, the (m-dimensional) permanent component is driven by the $m - r$ stochastic trends

$$\alpha'_\perp\sum_{j=1}^{t}\varepsilon_j, \tag{7.6.5}$$

common to all the variables, where r is the cointegration rank. This result highlights the relationship between cointegration relationships and common stochastic trends: their number must sum up to m, the total number of variables under analysis. Therefore, if there are q cointegrating relationships there must be only $m - q$ common stochastic trends driving the m variables, and viceversa. In the absence of cointegration, $r = 0$, there are as many stochastic trends as variables. In the case of stationary variables, $r = m$, there are no stochastic trends.

Note that we can easily estimate both the PC in (7.6.4) and the stochastic trends in (7.6.5) from the estimated VECM parameters and residuals. In (7.6.4) the PC is a function of cumulative residuals. Other authors suggested permanent components that directly depend on y_t. Specifically, Gonzalo and Granger (1995) *GG* proposed:

$$PC_{GGt} = \alpha'_\perp y_t,$$

while Johansen (1995) *J* suggested:

$$PC_{Jt} = \beta'_\perp y_t.$$

In practice, the different measures of the common component are typically similar.

To illustrate the permanent-transitory decompositions in a multivariate context and the cointegration (common trends) relationship, let us discuss the following example. Following the theory of permanent income, the latter (y^p) rather than current income (y) should influence consumption (c). We can therefore write

$$
\begin{aligned}
y_t &= y_t^P + v_t, \\
y_t^P &= \mu + y_{t-1}^P + \varepsilon_t, \\
c_t &= y_t^P.
\end{aligned}
\tag{7.6.6}
$$

where v_t and ε_t are jointly white noise.

Note that y_t and c_t share the same stochastic trend, y_t^P, therefore they are cointegrated. In fact, $y_t - c_t = v_t \sim I(0)$.

We can rewrite the equations for y_t and c_t as the VAR:

$$
\begin{bmatrix} y_t \\ c_t \end{bmatrix} = \begin{bmatrix} \mu \\ \mu \end{bmatrix} + \begin{bmatrix} 0 & 1 \\ 0 & 1 \end{bmatrix} \begin{bmatrix} y_{t-1} \\ c_{t-1} \end{bmatrix} + \begin{bmatrix} w_t \\ \varepsilon_t \end{bmatrix},
$$

where $w_t = v_t + \varepsilon_t$, or as the Vector ECM:

$$\begin{bmatrix} \Delta y_t \\ \Delta c_t \end{bmatrix} = \begin{bmatrix} \mu \\ \mu \end{bmatrix} + \begin{bmatrix} -1 & 1 \\ 0 & 0 \end{bmatrix} \begin{bmatrix} y_{t-1} \\ c_{t-1} \end{bmatrix} + \begin{bmatrix} w_t \\ \varepsilon_t \end{bmatrix},$$

from which

$$\Pi = \begin{bmatrix} -1 & 1 \\ 0 & 0 \end{bmatrix} = \begin{bmatrix} -1 \\ 0 \end{bmatrix} \begin{bmatrix} 1 & -1 \end{bmatrix} = \alpha\beta'.$$

To obtain the MA representation, we recall that $y_t - c_t = v_t$, so that

$$\begin{bmatrix} \Delta y_t \\ \Delta c_t \end{bmatrix} = \begin{bmatrix} \mu \\ \mu \end{bmatrix} + \begin{bmatrix} 1 & 0 \\ 0 & 1 \end{bmatrix} \begin{bmatrix} w_t \\ \varepsilon_t \end{bmatrix} + \begin{bmatrix} -1 & 1 \\ 0 & 0 \end{bmatrix} \begin{bmatrix} w_{t-1} \\ \varepsilon_{t-1} \end{bmatrix},$$

from which

$$\begin{bmatrix} \Delta y_t \\ \Delta c_t \end{bmatrix} = \begin{bmatrix} \mu \\ \mu \end{bmatrix} + C\,(1) \begin{bmatrix} \sum_{j=1}^{t} w_j \\ \sum_{j=1}^{t} \varepsilon_j \end{bmatrix} + C^*\,(L) \begin{bmatrix} w_t \\ \varepsilon_t \end{bmatrix}$$

with $C\,(1) = \beta_{\perp} (\alpha'_{\perp}\beta_{\perp})^{-1} \alpha'_{\perp}$ and therefore

$$C\,(1) = \begin{bmatrix} 0 & 1 \\ 0 & 1 \end{bmatrix} = \begin{bmatrix} 1 \\ 1 \end{bmatrix} \left[\begin{bmatrix} 0 & 1 \end{bmatrix} \begin{bmatrix} 1 \\ 1 \end{bmatrix} \right]^{-1} \begin{bmatrix} 0 & 1 \end{bmatrix},$$

and

$$PC_t = \begin{bmatrix} \sum_{j=1}^{t} \varepsilon_j \\ \sum_{j=1}^{t} \varepsilon_j \end{bmatrix}.$$

The stochastic trend is $\sum_{j=1}^{t} \varepsilon_j$, which is coherent with equation (7.6.6). Using the Gonzalo - Granger definition, we have

$$PC_{GGt} = \alpha'_{\perp} y_t = c_t = y_t^P.$$

For the Johansen definition, it is

$$PC_{Jt} = \beta'_{\perp} y_t = y_t + c_t = 2y_t^P + v_t.$$

Since PC_t, PC_{GGt}, and PC_{Jt} are cointegrated (they are all driven by the same stochastic trend $\sum_{j=1}^{t} \varepsilon_j$) there can only be temporary deviations among them.

7.7 Forecasting in the presence of cointegration

For forecasting, we can use the Vector ECM representation in (7.3.5), where r and the unknown parameters are replaced by their ML estimates. Hence, it is

$$\Delta \widehat{y}_{T+h} = -\widehat{\alpha}\widehat{\beta}'\widehat{y}_{T+h-1} + \widehat{\Gamma}_1 \widehat{\Delta y}_{T+h-1} + \ldots + \widehat{\Gamma}_{p-1}\widehat{\Delta y}_{T+h-p+1}, \qquad (7.7.1)$$

for $h = 1, \ldots, H$, where as usual forecast values on the right hand side are replaced by actual realizations when available. Forecasts for the levels can be obtained as

$$\widehat{y}_{T+h} = y_T + \Delta \widehat{y}_{T+1} + \ldots + \Delta \widehat{y}_{T+h}. \qquad (7.7.2)$$

In practice, we iterate between (7.7.2) and (7.7.1) to obtain the desired h-steps ahead forecast for either differences or levels. From (7.7.1) we forecast $\Delta \widehat{y}_{T+1}$, from (7.7.2) we obtain $\widehat{y}_{T+1}$ using $\Delta \widehat{y}_{T+1}$, from (7.7.1) we forecast $\Delta \widehat{y}_{T+2}$ using $\widehat{y}_{T+1}$ and $\Delta \widehat{y}_{T+1}$, from (7.7.2) we obtain $\widehat{y}_{T+2}$ using $\widehat{y}_{T+1}$, $\Delta \widehat{y}_{T+1}$ and $\Delta \widehat{y}_{T+2}$, etc.

Alternative forecasts for Δy_{T+h} could be obtained from the VAR in differences in (7.3.3). As we have seen, in the presence of cointegration, the VAR in differences is mis-specified due to the omission of the cointegration relationships $\beta' y_{t-1}$. Hence, forecasts from (the estimated counterpart of) the model in (7.3.3) are suboptimal. However, in the presence of unaccounted changes in the cointegrating vectors β or in their loadings α, the forecasts from (7.3.3) could be more robust than those from (7.3.5). In particular, as we will see, the ECM model in (7.3.5) constraints the long-run forecasts to satisfy the relationship $\beta' \widehat{y}_{T+h} \sim I(0)$, which is good as long as the cointegrating relationship still holds in period $T + h$.

A third option is to forecast using the (estimated counterpart of) the VAR model in levels in (7.3.1). As we have discussed, this model is correctly specified but its parameters are not efficiently estimated, since the cointegration restrictions are not imposed. But if the sample is long enough, the OLS estimates, which remain consistent, will anyway reflect the cointegration restrictions. Moreover, the use of (7.3.1) does not require to test for the cointegration rank r, which can be an advantage when there is uncertainty on the choice of the proper r.

Clements and Hendry (1998) present detailed Monte Carlo experiments to rank the forecasts from ECMs and VARs in differences and levels, finding that in general the ECM forecasts should be preferred, as long as there is not substantial model mis-specification. Hence, a comparison of the three forecasts could be useful in a specific application, and rather simple.

7.8 The effects of stochastic trends on forecasts

To understand the effects of the stochastic trends on the forecasts, let us start from the MA(∞) representation in (7.6.1). Assuming $\varepsilon_j = 0$, $j \leq 0$ and $y_0 = 0$, we can rewrite (7.6.1) as

$$y_t = \sum_{i=1}^{t} \sum_{j=0}^{t-i} C_j \varepsilon_i$$

and

$$
\begin{aligned}
y_{T+h} &= \sum_{i=1}^{T+h} \sum_{j=0}^{T+h-i} C_j \varepsilon_i = \\
&= \sum_{i=1}^{T} \sum_{j=0}^{T+h-i} C_j \varepsilon_i + \sum_{i=T+1}^{T+h} \sum_{j=0}^{T+h-i} C_j \varepsilon_i.
\end{aligned}
\tag{7.8.1}
$$

Thus,

$$\widehat{y}_{T+h} = E(y_{T+h}|y_T) = \sum_{i=1}^{T} \sum_{j=0}^{T+h-i} C_j \varepsilon_i. \tag{7.8.2}$$

Given that

$$\lim_{h \to \infty} \sum_{j=0}^{T+h-i} C_j = C(1),$$

and the C_j decay rapidly, we can write

$$\sum_{j=0}^{T+h-i} C_j \approx C(1),$$

and

$$\widehat{y}_{T+h} \approx C(1) \sum_{i=1}^{T} \varepsilon_i,$$

so that, at least for long forecast horizons h, the forecasts are driven by the stochastic trends.

Note that

$$\beta' \widehat{y}_{T+h} \approx \beta' C(1) \sum_{i=1}^{T} \varepsilon_i = 0$$

so that the long horizon forecasts are tied together by the presence of cointegration among the variables under evaluation. This feature has also important implications for the construction of proper forecast accuracy measures, see Christoffersen and Diebold (1998) for more details.

From (7.8.1) and (7.8.2) we have

$$e_{T+h} = y_{T+h} - \widehat{y}_{T+h} = \sum_{i=T+1}^{T+h} \sum_{j=0}^{T+h-i} C_j \varepsilon_i = \sum_{i=1}^{h} \sum_{j=0}^{h-i} C_j \varepsilon_{T+i},$$

and

$$\text{Var}(e_{T+h}) = \sum_{i=1}^{h} \left[\left(\sum_{j=0}^{h-i} C_j \right) \Sigma \left(\sum_{j=0}^{h-i} C_j' \right) \right].$$

where $\Sigma = Var(\varepsilon_t)$. Hence, as in the case of a unit root in a univariate context, the variance of the forecasts for the levels grows with the forecast horizon, while $\lim_{h \to \infty} \text{Var}(e_{T+h})/h$ converges to a well defined matrix.

Finally, it can be shown that $\text{Var}(\beta' e_{T+h})$ converges to a proper matrix when h increases, which is not surprising since $\beta' y_t$ is stationary.

7.9 Example using simulated series

In this example we explain how to practically deal with cointegrated series using a dataset of simulated data generated by an ECM. More specifically, we generate 600 observations from the following bivariate DGP:

$$\begin{aligned} \Delta y_t &= \varepsilon_{1t}, & (7.9.1) \\ \Delta x_t &= 0.5(y_{t-1} + x_{t-1}) + \varepsilon_{2t}, \end{aligned}$$

$$\begin{bmatrix} \varepsilon_{1t} \\ \varepsilon_{2t} \end{bmatrix} = \begin{bmatrix} 1 & 0 \\ 1 & 1 \end{bmatrix} \begin{bmatrix} v_{1t} \\ v_{2t} \end{bmatrix}, \qquad \begin{bmatrix} v_{1t} \\ v_{2t} \end{bmatrix} \overset{iid}{\sim} N \left(\begin{bmatrix} 0 \\ 0 \end{bmatrix}, \begin{bmatrix} 1 & 0 \\ 0 & 1 \end{bmatrix} \right).$$

The dataset also contains two variables that follow two independent random walk DGPs:

$$\Delta z_t = v_{3t} \quad \text{with} \quad v_{3t} \overset{iid}{\sim} N(0,1), \tag{7.9.2}$$

$$\Delta w_t = v_{4t} \quad \text{with} \quad v_{4t} \overset{iid}{\sim} N(0,1). \tag{7.9.3}$$

Once again, in order to avoid dependence on the starting values, the first 100 observations are discarded and not included in the estimation sample. We will use the methods described in this chapter to specify and estimate an appropriate ECM model, and also to illustrate what are the dangers of ignoring common stochastic trends and estimating spurious regressions.

From Figure 7.9.1, all series show very persistent deviations from their average values, with even a trending behavior for w and z.

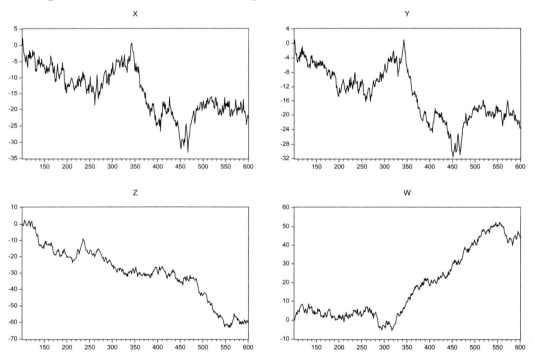

Figure 7.9.1: *The four generated series in the estimation time sample 101 - 600*

Let us have a look at the correlogram of these four series, and also run standard unit roots tests both on the variables in levels and in differences. All this information is reported in Figure 7.9.2 and Table 7.9.1 for series y;

the other three series deliver similar results. All the AC functions do not seem to die out even beyond lag 20, and the PAC shows a large spike at lag one. Parallel to this, the ADF tests performed on the variables in levels cannot reject the null of a unit root at the conventional significance levels, while the same test confirms that they are stationary in differences (rejects the null of a unit root in the differences).

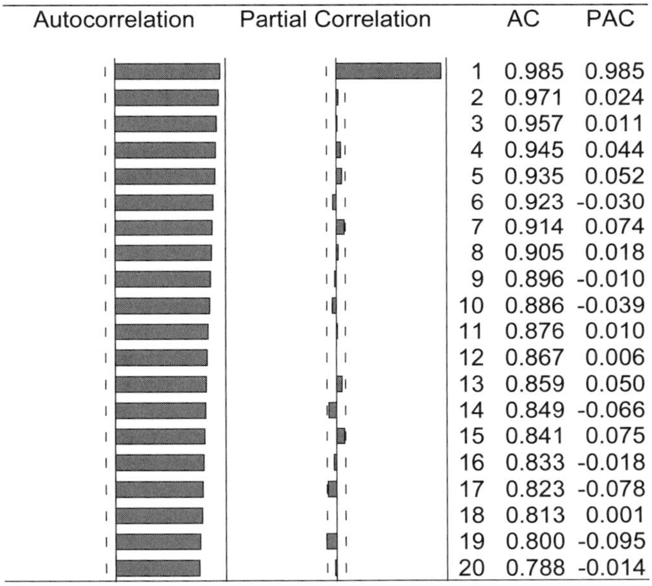

Autocorrelation	Partial Correlation		AC	PAC
		1	0.985	0.985
		2	0.971	0.024
		3	0.957	0.011
		4	0.945	0.044
		5	0.935	0.052
		6	0.923	-0.030
		7	0.914	0.074
		8	0.905	0.018
		9	0.896	-0.010
		10	0.886	-0.039
		11	0.876	0.010
		12	0.867	0.006
		13	0.859	0.050
		14	0.849	-0.066
		15	0.841	0.075
		16	0.833	-0.018
		17	0.823	-0.078
		18	0.813	0.001
		19	0.800	-0.095
		20	0.788	-0.014

Figure 7.9.2: *Correlogram of y*

We discussed the problems related to spurious regressions, the regression of unrelated variables driven by independent stochastic trends, and we now evaluate them empirically. Specifically, the z and w variables have been created as pure random walks with no connection between each other: what happens if we regress z onto w?

Table 7.9.2 shows that the signs of spuriousness are all present: very high R^2, extremely high t statistics, and a very low Durbin-Watson statistic.

ADF Unit Root Test on Y

		t-Stat	Prob.*
ADF test statistic		-1.895	0.335
Test critical values:	1% level	-3.443	
	5% level	-2.867	
	10% level	-2.570	

*MacKinnon (1996) one-sided p-values.

ADF Unit Root Test on D(Y)

		t-Stat	Prob.*
ADF test statistic		-23.999	0.000
Test critical values:	1% level	-2.570	
	5% level	-1.941	
	10% level	-1.616	

*MacKinnon (1996) one-sided p-values.

Table 7.9.1: *Results of the unit root tests for y and dy*

Variable	Coefficient	Std. Error	t-Stat	Prob.
C	-15.194	0.521	-29.154	0.000
W	-0.782	0.020	-38.360	0.000
R-squared	0.747	Mean dep var		-29.440
Adjusted R-squared	0.747	S.D. dep var		16.244
S.E. of regression	8.176	Akaike IC		7.044
Sum squared resid	33292.510	Schwarz IC		7.061
Log likelihood	-1759.089	Hannan-Quinn		7.051
F-statistic	1471.515	DW stat		0.026
Prob(F-statistic)	0.000			

Table 7.9.2: *Results of the spurious regression of z onto w*

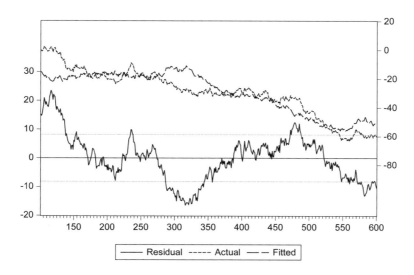

Figure 7.9.3: *Residuals of the spurious regression*

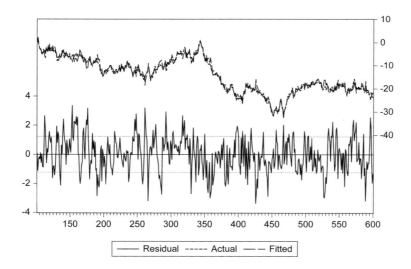

Figure 7.9.4: *First-step regression of the Engle-Granger procedure: Residuals of the regression*

The residuals are plotted in Figure 7.9.3. The residuals clearly show first order serial correlation, with a very persistent behavior. Indeed, in Table 7.9.3 we can see that we cannot reject the null hypothesis of no cointegration between z and w.

Null hypothesis: Series are not cointegrated				
Dependent	tau-statistic	Prob.*	z-statistic	Prob.*
Z	-2.067	0.493	-7.424	0.537
W	-1.923	0.569	-6.772	0.588

*MacKinnon (1996) p-values.

Table 7.9.3: *Engle-Granger test on the variables w and z*

Let us now analyze the other two series x and y, which have been generated according to a cointegrated DGP. First, we can investigate the properties of the residuals of an OLS regression of y onto x and a constant. According to the Engle and Granger (1987) approach to cointegration, finding evidence of their stationarity is an indication that x and y are linked by a cointegrating relationship. The residuals present some serial correlation, but to a limited extent.

Variable	Coefficient	Std. Error	t-Stat	Prob.
C	-0.073	0.119	-0.611	0.541
X	0.993	0.007	133.917	0.000
R-squared	0.973	Mean dep var		-14.238
Adjusted R-squared	0.973	S.D. dep var		7.442
S.E. of regression	1.225	Akaike IC		3.247
Sum squared resid	746.757	Schwarz IC		3.264
Log likelihood	-809.752	Hannan-Quinn		3.254
F-statistic	17933.640	DW stat		0.864
Prob(F-statistic)	0.000			

Table 7.9.4: *First-step regression of the Engle-Granger procedure: Estimated coefficients*

Looking at the ADF test on the residuals in Table 7.9.5, there is a clear rejection of the unit root, and hence evidence for cointegration, the existence of a stationary linear combination of x and y which qualifies as a long-run equilibrium relationship. The estimated coefficient on x, about 0.9, is close to the theoretical value of 1, see Table 7.9.4 (recall that the distribution of the parameter estimators is non-standard, so that we cannot use standard $t-$ and $F-$statistics to test hypotheses on the coefficients).

ADF Test

		t-Stat	Prob.*
ADF test statistic		-11.693	0.000
Test critical values:	1% level	-2.570	
	5% level	-1.941	
	10% level	-1.616	

*MacKinnon (1996) one-sided p-values.

Table 7.9.5: *ADF test on the residuals of the first-step regression of the Engle-Granger procedure.*

The Johansen (1995) cointegration test provides an alternative, more efficient procedure, to the two-step Engle-Granger method. It also allows to jointly examine more than two variables, determining the total number of cointegrating relationships. As we know from theory, the Johansen's approach differs from the one of Engle and Granger because it is not a residual-based test but a VAR-based one.

The results of the test are shown in Table 7.9.6, where we note that the results are compatible with what we found previously. Both the trace and the maximum eigenvalue tests confirm that at the 5% significance level there is evidence for one cointegrating relationship. The estimated parameter on x, -1.001, is also closer to the true value of -1 than what we found with the Engle and Granger method.

Coherently with what we expect, in the equation for Δy_t the adjustment coefficient (called cointEq1 by default) is not significant, while it has a significant estimated coefficient close to the true value, 0.5, in the equation for Δx_t, see Table 7.9.7. Hence, in this ECM model y is weakly exogenous and it is plausible to restrict the adjustment vector of the entire model to $\alpha' = (0, 0.5)$. Moreover, the coefficients of the long-run relationship could plausibly be restricted to $\beta = (1, -1)$.

The new VAR will now be estimated with the required restrictions on the adjustment coefficients and on the long-run equation, and a LR test can be computed to measure how binding is the restriction. All of this is reported in Table 7.9.8, and we note that in this case the restrictions are not rejected and, clearly, they yield to perfect identification of the cointegrating vector.

Let us now apply the different definitions of common trend we have seen in the chapter to our estimated VECM model to have an idea of what is the

Unrestricted Cointegration Rank Test (Trace)

Hypothesized No.of CE(s)	Eigen value	Trace Statistic	0.050 Critical Value	Prob.**
None*	0.200	111.058	12.321	0.000
Atmost 1	0.000	0.014	4.130	0.923

Trace test indicates 1 cointegrating eqn(s) at the 0.05 level

Unrestricted Cointegration Rank Test (Maximum Eigen value)

Hypothesized No.of CE(s)	Eigen value	Max-Eigen Statistic	0.050 Critical Value	Prob.**
None*	0.200	111.044	11.225	0.000
Atmost 1	0.000	0.014	4.130	0.923

Max-eigen value test indicates 1 cointegrating eqn(s) at the 0.05 level.
*denotes rejection of the hypothesis at the 0.05 level.
**MacKinnon-Haug-Michelis (1999) p-values.

Unrestricted Adjustment Coefficients (alpha)

D(Y)	-0.060	0.005
D(X)	-0.552	0.004

Cointegrating Equations(s) Log likelihood	-1432.409

Normalized cointegrating coefficients std.err.in ()

Y	X	
1.000	-1.001	(0.006)

Adjustment coefficients standard error in ()

D(Y)	0.056	(0.043)
D(X)	0.512	(0.057)

Table 7.9.6: *Johansen cointegration test on the variables y and x*

estimated permanent component. It is

1. Beveridge-Nelson's definition

$$PC_{BN=}\alpha'_{\perp} \sum_{j=1}^{t} \varepsilon_j = \begin{pmatrix} 0 & \alpha_{12} \end{pmatrix} \begin{bmatrix} \sum_{j=1}^{t} \varepsilon_{jx} \\ \sum_{j=1}^{t} \varepsilon_{jy} \end{bmatrix} = \alpha_{12} \cdot \sum_{j=1}^{t} \varepsilon_{jy} \qquad (7.9.4)$$

2. Gonzalo-Granger's definition

$$PC_{GG} = \alpha'_{\perp} \mathbf{y}_t = \begin{bmatrix} 0 & \alpha_{12} \end{bmatrix} \begin{bmatrix} x_t \\ y_t \end{bmatrix} = \alpha_{12} \cdot y_t \qquad (7.9.5)$$

Vector Error Correction Estimates

Cointegrating Eq:	Coint Eq1				
Y(-1)	1.000		Det resid cov (dof adj.)		1.093
			Det resid cov		1.080
X(-1)	-1.001		Log likelihood		-1432.409
	0.006		Akaike information criterion		5.785
	-165.677		Schwarz criterion		5.852

Error Correction:	D(Y)	D(X)		D(Y)	D(X)
Coint Eq 1	0.056	0.512	R-squared	0.007	0.166
	0.043	0.057	Adj.R-squared	0.003	0.163
	1.295	9.001	Sum sq.resids	534.512	925.880
			S.E.equation	1.039	1.368
D(Y(-1))	-0.087	-0.184	F-statistic	1.724	49.329
	0.064	0.084	Log likelihood	-724.249	-861.047
	-1.363	-2.185	Akaike AIC	2.921	3.470
D(X(-1))	0.007	0.038	Schwarz BIC	2.946	3.495
	0.046	0.061	Mean dep	-0.049	-0.049
	0.161	0.619	S.D. dep	1.041	1.495

Table 7.9.7: *Estimation results of the Vector ECM(1) model for y and x*

3. Johansen's definition

$$PC_J = \beta'_\perp \mathbf{y}_t = \begin{bmatrix} 1 & 1 \end{bmatrix} \begin{bmatrix} x_t \\ y_t \end{bmatrix} = x_t + y_t \qquad (7.9.6)$$

The common trend calculated according to the Beveridge-Nelson definition and the one of Gonzalo-Granger are quite similar in this example, as $\sum_{j=1}^{t} \varepsilon_{jy} \simeq y_t$.

From Figure 7.9.5, GG_trend and BN_trend are actually very close, while J_trend is much more volatile.

To evaluate the forecasting accuracy using simulated data, we perform a simple exercise. First, the estimation sample 101 - 500 is used to estimate a VAR(1) in levels, a VAR(1) in differences and the VECM. Then, one-step ahead forecasts (both stochastic and deterministic) are computed for the window 501 - 600.

Graphical results for the deterministic forecasts are reported in Figure 7.9.6 and the forecasting diagnostics are presented in Table 7.9.9. For the y variable, which is not affected by the cointegratiing relationship, all three

Vector Error Correction Estimates

Cointegration Restrictions:		
	B(1,1)=1,B(1,2)=-1,A(1,1)=0	
Chi-square(2)	1.703349	
Probability	0.427	

Cointegrating Eq:	Coint Eq1			
Y(-1)	1.000	Det resid cov(dof adj.)		1.093
		Det resid cov		1.080
X(-1)	-1.000	Log likelihood		-1433.261
		Akaike information criterion		5.788
		Schwarz criterion		5.856

Error Correction:	D(Y)	D(X)		D(Y)	D(X)
Coint Eq1	0.000	0.463	R-squared	0.007	0.166
	(0.000)	(0.042)	Adj.R-squared	0.003	0.166
	[NA]	[11.043]	Sum sq. resids	534.508	925.873
			S.E.equation	1.039	1.368
D(Y(-1))	-0.087	-0.184	F-statistic	1.726	49.331
	(0.064)	(0.084)	Log likelihood	-724.247	-861.045
	[-1.364]	[-2.189]	Akaike AIC	2.921	3.470
D(X(-1))	0.007	0.037	Schwarz BIC	2.946	3.495
	(0.046)	(0.061)	Mean dep	-0.049	-0.049
	[0.161]	[0.618]	S.D. dep	1.041	1.495
Standard errors in ()&t-statistics in []					

Table 7.9.8: *Results of the VECM model for y and x when the restriction $a_{11} = 0$ is imposed, together with the long-run restriction $\beta = (1, -1)$*

VAR (levels)	y		x	
	Deterministic	Stochastic	Deterministic	Stochastic
RMSFE	0.926	0.920	1.302	1.302
MAFE	0.758	0.754	1.004	1.006
VAR (differences)	y		x	
RMSFE	0.920	0.919	1.374	1.376
MAFE	0.750	0.751	1.095	1.095
VECM	y		x	
RMSFE	0.935	0.935	1.305	1.302
MAFE	0.767	0.767	1.002	0.998

Table 7.9.9: *One-step ahead forecast metrics (deterministic and stochastic) for the three models under examination*

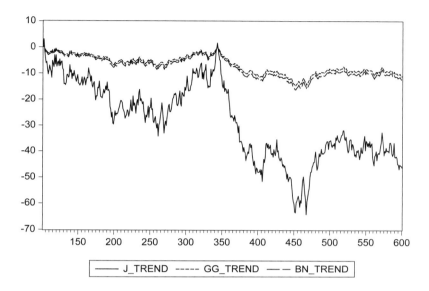

Figure 7.9.5: *Common trends embedded in the estimated VECM model*

models yield similar RMSFE and MAE. Instead, for the x variable, the performance of the VAR in differences is much worse than that of the other two models. The VAR in levels and the ECM are comparable, as the estimation sample is very long in this example.

7.10 Empirical examples

7.10.1 Term structure of UK interest rates

As an example of cointegrated stochastic processes, let us analyze the term structure of interest rates, i.e., the relationship linking interest rates at different maturities. If the efficient market hypothesis holds (together with the assumption of agents' perfect rationality), interest rates and bond yields at different maturities should all be connected by a relationship known as the yield curve. To be more precise, the so called Expectations Hypothesis (EH) relates the T-period interest rate, the yield to maturity on T-period bonds, R_t, to a weighted average of expected future one-period (short-term) interest rates $r_t, r_{t+1}, \ldots$ plus a constant term premium TP_T depending on

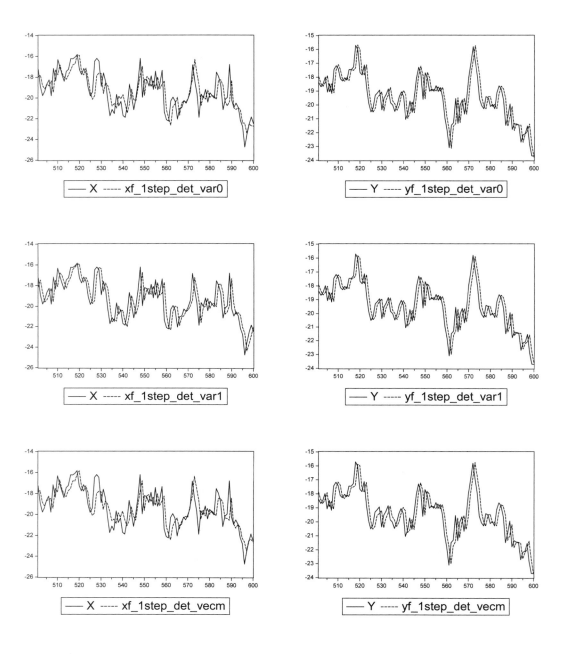

Figure 7.9.6: *Deterministic one-step ahead forecasts for the three models under examination: the VAR(1) in the upper row, the VAR(1) in differences in the middle, and the VECM in the lower row*

the maturity only:

$$R_t = \frac{1}{T} \sum_{i=0}^{T-1} E_t[r_{t+i}] + TP_T.$$

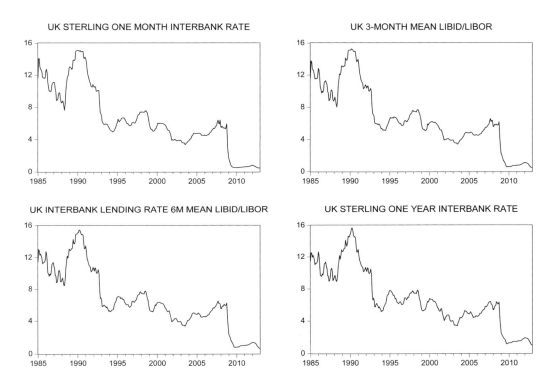

Figure 7.10.1: *The four interest rates under examination in the available sample 1985 - 2012*

Campbell and Shiller (1987) show that defining the spread $S_t = R_t - r_t$ and doing some algebra, S_t can be written as

$$S_t = \sum_{i=1}^{T-1}(1 - i/T)E_t(\Delta r_{t+i}) + TP_T \qquad (7.10.1)$$

Hence, if the short term rate r_t is I(1), then according to equation (7.10.1) the spread S_t has to be stationary. So in this case we have two I(1) variables, R_t and r_t, such that their combination $S_t = \beta \begin{bmatrix} r_t & R_t \end{bmatrix}'$ with

$$\beta = \begin{bmatrix} -1 & 1 \end{bmatrix}$$

is stationary. The vector β is the *cointegrating vector*.

In this example we will consider four UK interest rates, three of them have a short-term maturity and one has a longer maturity. More specifically we will use:

- r_{1t} the Libor interest rate with one month maturity.

- r_{3t} the Libor interest rate with three months maturity.

- r_{6t} the Libor interest rate with six months maturity.

- r_{24t} the Libor interest rate with two years (24 months) maturity.

The dataset contains monthly data on these variables from 1985 to 2012, all retrieved from DATASTREAM. It also contains the series of the real effective exchange rate of the British pound *real_ex* that will be used as an exogenous variable. From Figure 7.10.1, the interest rate series clearly show a similar pattern, characterized by persistent deviations from the mean, so that it is worth conducting an in depth analysis of their (possibly common) stochastic properties.

Table 7.10.1 confirms our conjecture that, for instance, the six-month Libor interest rate is I(1); a similar result holds for other maturities, thereby indicating that a cointegration approach should be used.

To do so, let us start by first estimating a simple VAR model with the lag length p chosen as to minimize one of the usual information criteria. This part of the analysis will be carried on in a reduced estimation sample 1985 - 2002, which will allow us to use the remaining data for an ex-post forecasting analysis.

Before actually selecting the lag length p and estimating the VAR, we create some exogenous variables which we will include in the estimation. Three simple 0-1 dummy variables D_1987M05, D_1988M07, and D_1992M10 account for particularly complicated periods of the English history. Another dummy variable is d_twopc assuming value 1 whenever the growth rate of $r1$ exceeds the threshold value of 2%. Finally, a group of variables called "exogenous" is created containing the mentioned dummy variables and also the growth rate of the real effective exchange rate g_re.[1]

---

[1]As mentioned, the proper critical values should be adjusted for the inclusion of the exogenous variables in the model. However, for the sake of simplicity, we will instead use the standard critical values.

ADF Unit Root Test on R6

		t-Stat	Prob.*
ADF test statistic		-1.522	0.521
Test critical values:	1% level	-3.461	
	5% level	-2.875	
	10% level	-2.574	

*MacKinnon (1996) one-sided p-values.

ADF Unit Root Test on D(R6)

		t-Stat	Prob.*
ADF test statistic		-10.404	0.000
Test critical values:	1% level	-2.576	
	5% level	-1.942	
	10% level	-1.616	

*MacKinnon (1996) one-sided p-values.

Table 7.10.1: *Unit root tests on one of the four interest rate (six months maturity) under examination*

As suggested by the AIC information criterion, a VAR(4) model is estimated, with details reported in Table 7.10.2 (we omitted lag 3 and lag 4 estimated coefficients for the sake of clearness). The in-sample performance of the model is quite good, although we know that the extremely high R^2 could be due to non-stationarity.

The roots of the characteristic polynomial and the residuals behavior in Figure 7.10.2 indicate that the specification could be further improved. However, for illustration, we consider it satisfactory as a starting point for the cointegration analysis, conducted using the Johansen's procedure.

Vector Autoregression Estimates

	R1	R3	R6	R24
R1(-1)	0.735	0.289	0.217	0.255
	(0.197)	(0.245)	(0.284)	(0.310)
	[3.740]	[1.179]	[0.765]	[0.821]
R1(-2)	-0.141	0.115	0.183	0.101
	(0.211)	(0.263)	(0.305)	(0.333)
	[-0.669]	[0.436]	[0.601]	[0.304]
R3(-1)	-0.027	-0.034	-0.698	-0.811
	(0.389)	(0.485)	(0.563)	(0.614)
	[-0.069]	[-0.071]	[-1.241]	[-1.320]
R3(-2)	-0.035	-0.198	-0.045	0.261
	(0.429)	(0.535)	(0.621)	(0.677)
	[-0.080]	[-0.371]	[-0.073]	[0.385]
R6(-1)	0.543	0.908	1.199	0.013
	(0.450)	(0.560)	(0.650)	(0.710)
	[1.210]	[1.621]	[1.843]	[0.018]
R6(-2)	0.722	0.634	0.637	0.621
	(0.529)	(0.659)	(0.766)	(0.836)
	[1.364]	[0.961]	[0.832]	[0.743]
R24(-1)	0.029	0.123	0.549	1.790
	(0.247)	(0.307)	(0.357)	(0.389)
	[0.116]	[0.400]	[1.540]	[4.600]
R24(-2)	-0.907	-0.909	-1.121	-1.344
	(0.343)	(0.427)	(0.496)	(0.541)
	[-2.646]	[-2.127]	[-2.261]	[-2.483]

Standard errors in ( ) & t-statistics in [ ]

	R1	R3	R6	R24
D.1987M05	-0.935	-0.916	-0.815	-0.706
	(0.207)	(0.258)	(0.300)	(0.327)
	[-4.500]	[-3.548]	[-2.717]	[-2.157]
D.1988M07	1.048	1.124	1.0238	0.865
	(0.219)	(0.273)	(0.317)	(0.345)
	[4.788]	[4.121]	[3.230]	[2.503]
D.1992M10	-1.126	-1.557	-1.760	-1.844
	(0.223)	(0.277)	(0.323)	(0.351)
	[-5.058]	[-5.616]	[-5.466]	[-5.248]
D.TWOPC	0.354	0.422	0.414	0.399
	(0.048)	(0.059)	(0.069)	(0.075)
	[7.457]	[7.132]	[6.028]	[5.325]
G_RE	-2.542	-2.858	-2.571	-2.189
	(0.923)	(1.150)	(1.336)	(1.457)
	[-2.753]	[-2.485]	[-1.925]	[-1.501]
R-squared	0.997	0.995	0.992	0.990
Adj. R-sq	0.996	0.994	0.992	0.989
Sum sq. resids	7.663	11.895	16.037	19.097
S.E. equation	0.200	0.250	0.290	0.316
F-statistic	2788.9	1755.6	1239.2	948.4471
Log likelihood	51.120	4.510	-27.154	-45.668
Akaike AIC	-0.284	0.156	0.454	0.629
Schwarz BIC	0.048	0.488	0.787	0.961
Mean dep	8.301	8.350	8.357	8.426
S.D. dep	3.262	3.228	3.152	3.013

Table 7.10.2: *Estimation results of the VAR(4) in the 1985 - 2002 estimation sample*

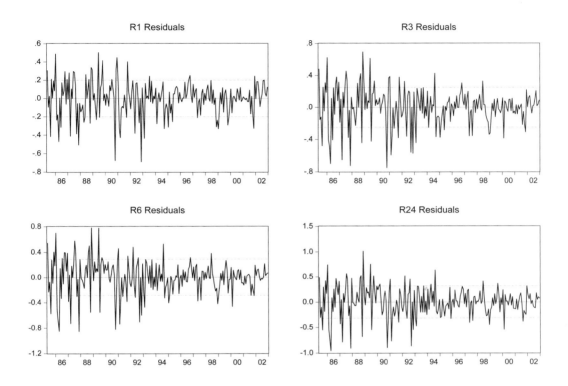

Figure 7.10.2: *Residuals' behavior from the estimated VAR(4)*

In line with economic theory, the cointegration test finds evidence for three cointegrating relationships (Table 7.10.3, top panel). Therefore, we proceed with three cointegrating vectors, and we also remove the constant in the short-run dynamics as it proves insignificant. The estimated coefficients are reported in the bottom panel of Table 7.10.3.

Estimation output for the resulting VECM model, whose lag length is simply set as $p_{vecm} = p_{var} - 1 = 3$, is shown in Table 7.10.4, where coefficients for lags bigger than one are again omitted for the sake of space.

The model displays a quite good in-sample fit (being a model in first differences), and we also note that, in line with theory, all the exogenous variables we have included are very significant. Moreover, the residuals behavior is similar to that of the VAR model, with not much autocorrelation left but some signs of heteroskedasticity and non-normality. The lower part of Table 7.10.3 reports the normalized cointegration coefficients and loadings.

Unrestricted Cointegration Rank Test (Maximum Eigen value)

Hypothesized No. of CE(s)	Eigenvalue	Max-Eigen Statistic	0.050 Crit Val	Prob.**
None*	0.162	37.319	27.584	0.002
Atmost 1*	0.155	35.498	21.132	0.000
Atmost 2*	0.091	20.049	14.265	0.005
Atmost 3	0.009	1.863	3.841	0.172

Max-eigen value test indicates 3 cointegrating eqn(s) at the 0.05 level
*denotes rejection of the hypothesis at the 0.05 level
**MacKinnon, Haug, and Michelis (1999) p-values.

3 Cointegrating Equation(s):	Log likelihood		805.339

Normalized cointegrating coefficients (st er in parentheses)

R1	R3	R6	R24
1.000	0.000	0.000	-1.088
			(0.027)
0.000	1.000	0.000	-1.077
			(0.021)
0.000	0.000	1.000	-1.050
			(0.013)

Adjustment coefficients (st er in parentheses)

D(R1)	-0.939	0.978	0.106
	(0.352)	(0.766)	(0.693)
D(R3)	-0.427	0.070	0.484
	(0.425)	(0.924)	(0.836)
D(R6)	-0.456	0.518	-0.171
	(0.468)	(1.018)	(0.922)
D(R24)	-0.403	0.558	-0.239
	(0.497)	(1.080)	(0.977)

Table 7.10.3: *Johansen cointegration test results on the four interest rates under examination*

Vector Autoregression Estimates

	D(R1)	D(R3)	D(R6)	D(R24)
D(R1(-1))	-0.018	-0.160	-0.212	-0.181
	(0.225)	(0.281)	(0.327)	(0.356)
	[-0.080]	[-0.571]	[-0.650]	[-0.510]
D(R3(-1))	0.243	0.493	0.436	0.172
	(0.487)	(0.608)	(0.707)	(0.769)
	[0.500]	[0.812]	[0.618]	[0.223]
D(R6(-1))	-0.432	-0.682	-0.821	-0.781
	(0.506)	(0.632)	(0.735)	(0.800)
	[-0.853]	[-1.079]	[-1.117]	[-0.976]
D(R24(-1))	0.496	0.641	0.874	1.047
	(0.253)	(0.315)	(0.367)	(0.399)
	[1.963]	[2.034]	[2.383]	[2.624]
Cointe1(-1)	-0.239	0.462	0.446	0.450
	(0.253)	(0.316)	(0.367)	(0.400)
	[-0.946]	[1.462]	[1.215]	[1.125]
Cointeq2(-1)	-0.317	-1.605	-1.238	-1.067
	(0.527)	(0.658)	(0.765)	(0.832)
	[-0.603]	[-2.441]	[-1.620]	[-1.282]
Cointeq3(-1)	1.055	1.720	1.195	0.937
	(0.412)	(0.515)	(0.598)	(0.651)
	[2.559]	[3.343]	[1.997]	[1.439]

	D(R1)	D(R3)	D(R6)	D(R24)
D.1987M05	-0.935	-0.919	-0.819	-0.709
	(0.207)	(0.259)	(0.300)	(0.327)
	[-4.510]	[-3.554]	[-2.722]	[-2.166]
D.1988M07	1.046	1.121	1.019	0.862
	(0.219)	(0.273)	(0.318)	(0.346)
	[4.781]	[4.104]	[3.209]	[2.492]
D.1992M10	-1.135	-1.572	-1.780	-1.860
	(0.222)	(0.278)	(0.323)	(0.351)
	[-5.104]	[-5.665]	[-5.516]	[-5.296]
D.twopc	0.362	0.435	0.432	0.414
	(0.047)	(0.058)	(0.068)	(0.074)
	[7.748]	[7.457]	[6.364]	[5.601]
G_RE	-2.482	-2.761	-2.440	-2.081
	(0.921)	(1.150)	(1.337)	(1.455)
	[-2.694]	[-2.401]	[-1.826]	[-1.430]
R-squared	0.701	0.591	0.501	0.447
Adj. R-sq	0.671	0.551	0.452	0.392
Sum sq. resids	7.70	12.00	16.22	19.22
S.E. equation	0.200	0.250	0.290	0.316
F-statistic	23.66	14.62	10.17	8.16
Log likelihood	50.59	3.61	-28.36	-46.35
Mean dep	-0.043	-0.042	-0.039	-0.037
S.D. dep	0.349	0.373	0.393	0.406

Standard errors in ( ) & t-statistics in [ ]

Table 7.10.4: *Estimation results of the VECM model*

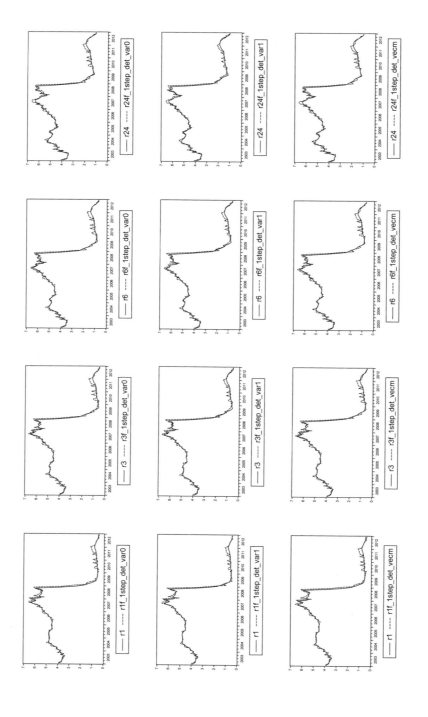

Figure 7.10.3: One-step ahead forecasts (deterministic environment) for the three models under examination: the VAR(4) in the upper row, the VAR(3) in differences in the middle, and the VECM in the lower row

As we did in other examples, we now estimate a rival model of the VECM, a simple VAR in first differences, where we ignore the possibility of a common stochastic trend and we eliminate the stationarity problem by simply differencing the variables. We can use the same lag length we used for the VECM. The estimated parameters are similar to those of the VECM, and so are the residuals. Which of these models, the VAR in levels, differences and VECM, will be more accurate in a forecasting exercise? To answer this question we have computed and assessed forecasts from 2003 to 2012.

Figure 7.10.3 shows the results of the deterministic one-step ahead forecasts. Table 7.10.5 reports more detailed forecast diagnostics.

VAR(lev.)	r1		r3		r6		r24	
	Det.	Sto.	Det.	Sto.	Det.	Sto.	Det.	Sto.
RMSFE	0.274	0.275	0.309	0.309	0.264	0.265	0.264	0.265
MAFE	0.160	0.160	0.153	0.154	0.161	0.162	0.168	0.169
VAR(diff.)	r1		r3		r6		r24	
RMSFE	0.276	0.276	0.289	0.289	0.265	0.266	0.265	0.266
MAFE	0.152	0.153	0.134	0.135	0.153	0.154	0.161	0.162
VECM	r1		r3		r6		r24	
RMSFE	0.272	0.272	0.308	0.308	0.262	0.262	0.263	0.263
MAFE	0.161	0.161	0.155	0.155	0.162	0.162	0.172	0.172

Table 7.10.5: *One-step ahead forecast metrics (deterministic and stochastic) for the three models under examination.*

All models yield quite precise results, with no significant differences of performance between the deterministic and stochastic environment (reminder: the former uses theoretical iterated formulas to compute the forecasts, while the latter draws from the residuals to also compute interval forecasts, and returns the average forecast, which is in general quite similar to the deterministic forecast). Despite all the three models being quite accurate, we note that for all indicators but r_{3t} the lowest RMSFEs are those pertaining to the VECM model, which indeed is the most appropriate instrument to handle cointegration.

A different loss function, the MAFE, provides a different ranking of models in this example, favoring the VAR in differences. As we have discussed, the MAFE assigns a smaller weight to large forecast errors than the RMSFE. Hence, the finding suggests that the VAR in differences sometimes produces rather large forecast errors, while it performs rather well in the remaining times.

Our conclusion from this example is that it is very important to acknowledge the role of modeling and cointegration in producing forecasts. In particular, in our case VAR models either in levels or in differences are generally worst forecasters than cointegrated VECM models according to the RMSFE. Including additional dummies, using more sophisticated estimation methods to capture structural breaks, adding other relevant exogenous variables, as well as imposing over-identifying theory consistent restrictions, could probably further improve the performance of the VECM model we used. We leave this as an interesting exercise for the reader.

7.10.2   Composite coincident and leading indexes

GDP is typically considered the best proxy of the overall economic situation. However, GDP is typically released only on a quarterly basis, often with substantial delays and major revisions in the subsequent periods. Hence, more timely indicators with a considerable coverage of the economy have been introduced, in the form of composite coincident indicators (CCIs) that combine in various ways information from a set of economic and/or financial time series. Similarly, composite leading indicators (CLIs) aim at anticipating the future economic conditions, see e.g., Marcellino (2006) for an overview of the construction and use of CCIs and CLIs.

In this example, we examine a simple way to use leading and coincident indicators for forecasting purposes. In particular, we use the Conference Board's Leading Economic Index (*cli*) and Coincident Economic Index (*cci*) for the United States. All through the exercise we will use two estimation and forecasting subsamples: first we isolate data from 1985 to 2003, and we predict from 2004 to 2006; then we extend the estimation sample from 1985 to 2006 and we try to forecast also the crisis period, using as a forecast sample the period 2007 - 2013.

7.10.3   Predicting coincident and leading indices in the period before the crisis

Let us start our analysis with the first sample called "pre-crisis," which ranges from 1985 to 2003. The two indicators under examination are plotted in Figure 7.10.4.

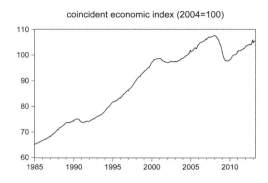
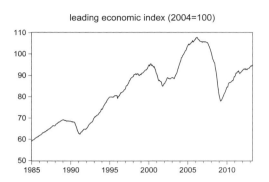

Figure 7.10.4: *The two composite indices cci and cli*

The two series display an upward trend, interrupted around the two recessions of the early 1990s and early 2000s. They might therefore be driven by a (possibly common) stochastic trend, hence the need to analyze them in more detail.

Augmented Dickey-Fuller Unit Root Test on CCI

		t-Statistic	Prob.*
Augmented Dickey-Fuller test statistic		-0.353	0.913
Test critical values:	1% level	-3.459	
	5% level	-2.874	
	10% level	-2.574	

*MacKinnon (1996) one-sided p-values.

Augmented Dickey-Fuller Unit Root Test on D(CCI)

		t-Statistic	Prob.*
Augmented Dickey-Fuller test statistic		-2.675	0.008
Test critical values:	1% level	-2.575	
	5% level	-1.942	
	10% level	-1.616	

*MacKinnon (1996) one-sided p-values.

Table 7.10.6: *Unit root test results for cci. The results for cli are similar*

The AC function shows marked persistence and for both series the Augmented Dickey-Fuller test cannot reject the null hypothesis of a unit root for the levels, while it strongly rejects it for the series in differences (see Table 7.10.6).

Let us then start formulating a VAR model for *cci* and *cli* in levels, which will also be the starting point for cointegration testing. Once again, we first specify a VAR model with $p = 12$, a suitable starting lag order for a monthly dataset as ours, and then reduce it to a more parsimonious model by using conventional lag length selection criteria.

As three criteria out of five, including the AIC, select the same value, $p = 4$, it is reasonable to specify a VAR(4) model. The standard diagnostic tests on the residuals of this model indicate that there is not much serial correlation left. Furthermore, the serial correlation LM test cannot reject the null of no serial correlation up to lag 12. Unfortunately, the multivariate version of the White heteroskedasticity test finds some signs of neglected heteroskedasticty in the residuals and the multivariate version of the normality test also indicates that the residuals do not have a joint normal distribution, with the univariate tests suggesting normality for the CCI residuals but not for the cli ones. Overall, it seems that the specification of the VAR in levels could be improved, likely with the inclusion of a proper set of dummy variables. However, this would complicate the cointegration analysis and therefore for the moment we just proceed with the VAR(4). Later on, we will use an alternative approach, the use of rolling estimation windows, to reduce the possible effects of unaccounted for parameter breaks on the forecasting performance of the model.

The Johansen cointegration test performed on the group containing the two series *cci* and *cli* shows that there is indeed evidence for one common stochastic trend for the more realistic choices of deterministic component given our variables (see Table 7.10.7).

Next, and according to the cointegration analysis, we specify a VECM model with intercept but no trend in the cointegrating relationship. As we see from the estimation results in Table 7.10.8, most of the parameters are significant, and the adjusted R^2 for both equations are quite high for a model in differences. The error correction coefficient is negative and significant, indicating that the error correction mechanism is operational, and the estimated long-run relationship is of the type $cci_t = 7.92 + 1.01cli_t$, suggesting that the

Selected (0.05 level*) Number of Cointegrating Relations by Model

Data Trend:	None	None	Linear	Linear	Quadratic
Test Type	No Intercept	Intercept	Intercept	Intercept	Intercept
	No Trend	No Trend	No Trend	Trend	Trend
Trace	2	1	1	1	2
Max-Eig	2	1	1	1	2

*Critical values based on MacKinnon, Haug, and Michelis (1999).

Table 7.10.7: *Johansen cointegration test on the two series cci and cli, based on the previously estimated VAR(4) model and different choices of deterministic component*

difference between the coincident and the leading index is stationary.[2]

A possible rival model to this VECM is a VAR model in differences, which attempts to remove the non stationarity of the two series not by exploiting their common stochastic trend, but simply by removing it with the first difference transformation. From a specification point of view, the VAR in differences is mis-specified, since it omits the error correction term. However, from a forecasting point of view, if either the error correction term is not strongly significant or the cointegration relationship changes over the forecast sample, then the VAR in differences could produce more accurate forecasts than the ECM.

This time only the BIC and the Hannan-Quinn criteria agree on the choice of a parsimonious $p = 3$. Nevertheless it is reasonable to follow this indication since the model in levels was specified with $p = 4$.

Also this VAR(3) model fits the data quite well for a model in differences, although again the tests performed on the residuals display almost the same problems that were already present for the other two specifications: uncorrelated residuals but with some remaining heteroskedasticity and non-normality. Again, these features are likely due to some parameter changes, but rather than modeling those explicitly we will later on evaluate whether the forecasting performance improves when using rolling estimation, which is more robust than recursive estimation in the presence of breaks, but less efficient in their absence.

We are now ready to evaluate the forecasting performance of the three rival models: the VAR(4) in levels, the VAR(3) in differences, and the VECM.

---

[2]For reasons of space we do not report here the residuals' diagnostic for the VECM model.

Vector Error Correction Estimates

Cointegrating Eq:	CointEq1		Error Correction:	D(CCI)	D(CLI)
CCI(-1)	1.000		D(CLI(-1))	0.082	0.327
				(0.029)	(0.076)
CLI(1)	-1.015			[2.827]	[4.307]
	(0.023)				
	[-44.58]		D(CLI(-2))	0.053	0.212
				(0.030)	(0.078)
C	-7.922			[1.782]	[2.704]
	(1.722)				
	[-4.600]		D(CLI(-3))	0.029	0.223
				(0.030)	(0.078)
Error Correction:	D(CCI)	D(CLI)		[0.966]	[2.835]
CointEq1	-0.035	-0.005	R-squared	0.404	0.300
	(0.005)	(0.014)	Adj. R-squared	0.388	0.281
	[-6.448]	[-0.338]	Sum sq. resids	5.014	34.21
			S.E. equation	0.151	0.393
D(CCI(-1))	-0.2953	-0.3590	F-statistic	24.936	15.777
	(0.077)	(0.200)	Log likelihood	111.63	-107.29
	[-3.852]	[-1.793]	Akaike AIC	-0.918	1.002
			Schwarz BIC	-0.812	1.108
D(CCI(-2))	0.005	0.084	Mean dep	0.148	0.160
	(0.078)	(0.205)	S.D. dep	0.192	0.464
	[0.059]	[0.411]			
			Det resid cov (dof adj.)		0.003
D(CCI(-3))	0.164	0.215	Det resid cov		0.002
	(0.077)	(0.201)	Log likelihood		41.27
	[2.135]	[1.070]	Akaike information criterion		-0.213
			Schwarz criterion		0.043
Standard errors in ( ) & t-statistics in [ ]					

Table 7.10.8: *VECM estimates for the series cci and cli in the 1985 - 2003 sample*

In this section the forecasting sample is 2004 - 2006, excluding the very complex period of the great financial crisis. For simplicity, we only focus on one-step ahead forecasts.

Figure 7.10.5 reports the results of the deterministic solution for the three models' forecasts. We note that all the forecast series track the actual values quite closely in this evaluation sample, although this is slightly more evident for *cci* than for *cli*. The upward trend of the series is captured by all the models, although not all the small fluctuations around it are predicted, and this is especially true for the VECM model (results of the stochastic approach

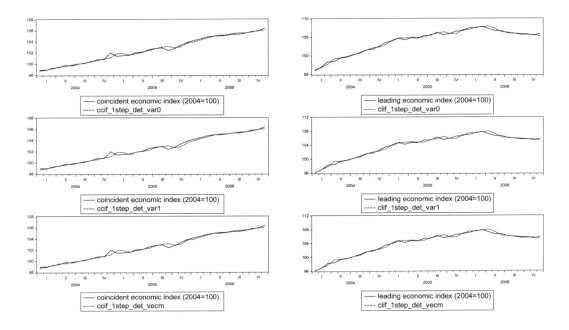

Figure 7.10.5: *Deterministic forecasts for cci (left side panels) and cli (right side panels) produced through a VAR(4) (upper panels), a VAR(3) in differences (middle panels) and a VECM (bottom panels)*

are similar).

It is now interesting to check whether using rolling rather than recursive estimation changes the accuracy of the predictions. Using rolling windows of 60 months each, we re-estimate each of the three models and in turn produce one-step ahead forecasts. The procedure is repeated until the whole forecast sample 2004-2006 is covered.

Figure 7.10.6 shows the results of using this procedure for the three models under examination.

In Table 7.10.9 we have calculated the standard forecast evaluation criteria for all the models and for the three types of forecasting procedures we have used so far. It seems that in this case using the rolling forecasts does not improve the accuracy of our predictions. On the other hand, we can see more clearly that in the prediction of *cci*, the VAR model in levels and the VECM both perform quite well and without significant performance differences (both between each other and between the stochastic and deterministic

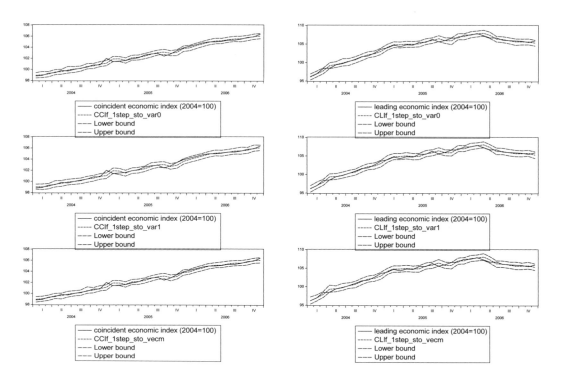

Figure 7.10.6: *Stochastic forecasts using rolling windows of 60 months for cci (left side panels) and cli (right side panels) produced through a VAR(4) (upper panels), a VAR(3) in differences (middle panels) and a VECM (bottom panels)*

environment), while the results of the VAR in differences are slightly less precise. Looking at the results for *cli* instead, reveals that the VAR model in levels is more precise than the other two approaches, with the deterministic and stochastic solution results again behaving equally well.

7.10.4   Predicting coincident and leading indices during the financial crisis

Our goal in this section is challenging: with the three types of models we previously specified, we want to predict the marked through that our indicators displayed during the financial crisis (see Figure 7.10.4).

The same steps we carried on in the previous section can be re-run using

	Det	Stoch	Rolling	Det	Stoch	Rolling
VAR (levels)		cci			cli	
RMSFE	0.265	0.264	0.348	0.382	0.379	0.604
MAFE	0.191	0.192	0.253	0.305	0.303	0.519
VAR (differences)		cci			cli	
RMSFE	0.281	0.281	0.362	0.403	0.401	0.523
MAFE	0.201	0.199	0.266	0.314	0.311	0.428
VECM		cci			cli	
RMSFE	0.268	0.271	0.346	0.409	0.411	0.537
MAFE	0.188	0.185	0.252	0.323	0.325	0.446

Table 7.10.9: *One-step ahead forecasts: Evaluation criteria for the three models under examination and for the three forecasting strategies used (deterministic, stochastic, and 60-month rolling windows)*

the extended estimation sample, as clearly the stochastic properties of the time-series do not change. Evidence for cointegration is again found, so two VAR models, one in levels and one in differences, and a VECM model can still be compared in terms of forecasting performance. This time, using the BIC lag-selection criterion, $p = 3$ is chosen for the VAR in levels, hence we set $p = 2$ for the VAR in differences and for the VECM.

The in-sample models' performance is less impressive over the shorter sample, but this is something we expected as adding the crisis period substantially increases the possibility of having structural instability.

Let us now consider how the models' forecasting performance changes when evaluated in the cumbersome period of the financial crisis. Specifically, we consider the period from January 2007 to April 2013. Table 7.10.10 presents the forecasting statistics.

Now rolling forecasts do slightly better, as they are able to gradually update and to predict the depth of the through occurred in 2009. On the other hand, simple one-step ahead forecasts, either with the deterministic or stochastic solution environment, are still quite precise even if *cli* seems always to be more complicated to predict than *cci*. Finally, in this case it seems that among the three models the VAR in differences displays the best forecasting performance with respect to both indicators, which is again likely due to the major instability related with the crisis.

In conclusion, we can be generally satisfied with the forecasting performance of our models, since on average they capture the direction of the changes happening to our composite indicators even during the crisis. Nev-

	Det	Stoch	Rolling	Det	Stoch	Rolling
VAR (levels)		cci			cli	
RMSFE	0.369	0.369	0.350	0.591	0.595	0.625
MAFE	0.263	0.262	0.249	0.476	0.478	0.492
VAR (differences)		cci			cli	
RMSFE	0.301	0.301	0.359	0.562	0.561	0.632
MAFE	0.215	0.214	0.249	0.433	0.432	0.494
VECM		cci			cli	
RMSFE	0.356	0.359	0.334	0.625	0.628	0.602
MAFE	0.258	0.260	0.235	0.495	0.495	0.477

Table 7.10.10: *One-step ahead forecasts, crisis period: Evaluation criteria for the three models under examination and for the three forecasting strategies used (deterministic, stochastic, and 60-month rolling windows)*

ertheless, for a complicated period like this one, it seems that using a more rapid updating procedure of estimation and forecast sample, like the one involved in rolling windows forecasts, improves the accuracy of the predictions.

7.11   Concluding remarks

In this chapter we studied the effects of cointegration for VAR models, where cointegration is a special feature of a set of I(1) variables that can be such that linear combinations of them are I(0). From a statistical point of view this is a rather particular feature, but from an economic point of view it is implied by several theories, and therefore it is a relevant property to be considered when modeling and forecasting sets of economic and/or financial variables.

We have seen that cointegration imposes particular restrictions on the coefficients of a VAR for I(1) variables in levels. In particular, the model can be written as a VAR in differences where the variables depend not only on their own lags but also on one lag of the cointegrating relationships. The latter are also called error correction terms, as they represent the deviations from the long-run or equilibrium values of the variables, and the resulting model is called Error Correction Model, or ECM.

The ECM encompasses both the VAR in levels, which is obtained when there are as many error correction terms as variables under analysis, and the VAR in differences, which is obtained when there are no error correction terms, meaning no cointegration among the I(1) variables under analysis.

Hence, the ECM also provides a general testing ground for the presence and extent of cointegration. Specifically, we have seen that the number of cointegration relationships (also called cointegration rank) can be tested by means of an iterative procedure based on a sequence of likelihood ratio tests. The tests have a non-standard asymptotic distribution, also dependent on the deterministic component and eventual exogenous variables, whose critical values are however available by means of proper simulation methods and typically included in standard econometrics software, such as *EViews*. This method for cointegration testing, usually labeled Johansen's procedure, extends a previous simpler single-equation approach, due to Engle and Granger, based on testing whether the residuals of a regression among I(1) variables are integrated or stationary with an ADF test, whose critical values are however slightly different from those of the original ADF test as the statistic is here computed based on a generated variable (the estimated residuals). More general testing procedures for cointegration are also available, and the cointegration rank can also be determined by means of information criteria, possibly jointly with the lag length.

We have also seen that the variables in differences, which are stationary, admit a particular Wold - $MA(\infty)$ representation. It is such that, if there are r cointegration relationships and N variables, then the variables in levels are driven by $N - r$ common stochastic (integrated) trends which are linear functions of the cumulated errors, plus stationary variable-specific components. The $MA(\infty)$ representation is convenient to compute both impulse response functions and optimal, in the MSFE sense, forecasts for all variables under evaluation. The latter are linked together in the long-run, in the sense that they will also have to satisfy the cointegration relationships.

For forecasting, we noted that, in the presence of cointegration, a VAR in levels is inefficient (as the cointegration relationships are not imposed, even though they will hold asymptotically) while a VAR in differences is mis-specified (as the error correction terms are omitted): the ECM (or its corresponding $MA(\infty)$ representation) is the proper model to obtain optimal forecasts. However, this is a theoretical result that empirically could be challenged by the presence of additional complications, such as changes in the number or composition of cointegrating vectors and/or of their loadings.

Finally, to illustrate the working of cointegration testing and ECM modelling and forecasting we have presented a set of examples based on either simulated or actual data, showing that, indeed, accounting for cointegration can improve the forecast precision.

Chapter 8

Bayesian VAR Models

8.1 Introduction

Recently there has been a resurgence of interest in applying Bayesian methods to forecasting, notably with Bayesian Vector Autoregressions (BVARs). BVARs have a long history in forecasting, stimulated by their effectiveness documented in the seminal studies of Doan, Litterman, and Sims (1984) and Litterman (1986). In recent years, the models appear to be used even more systematically for policy analysis and forecasting macroeconomic variables (e.g., Kadiyala and Karlsson (1997), Koop (2013)). At present, there is also considerable interest in using BVARs for these purposes in a large dataset context.[1]

With regards to model specification, besides the choice of the prior distribution for the parameters, the researcher needs to address issues such as (1) the choice of the tightness and of the lag length of the BVAR; (2) the treatment of the error variance and the imposition of cross-variable shrinkage; (3) whether to transform the variables to get stationarity, and whether to complement this choice with the imposition of priors favoring cointegration and unit roots. In this chapter we briefly consider model specification, estimation, and forecast construction, based on Carriero, Kapetanios, and Marcellino (2011) and Carriero, Clark, and Marcellino (2015), and for example Koop (2003) for an introduction to Bayesian econometrics. See also

---

[1]See e.g., Bańbura, Giannone, and Reichlin (2010), Carriero, Kapetanios, and Marcellino (2009), Carriero, Kapetanios, and Marcellino (2011), Koop (2013), Carriero, Clark, and Marcellino (2016) and Carriero, Clark, and Marcellino (2017).

Canova (2007, Chapter 10) and Karlsson (2012) for further discussions and references.

With regard to model estimation and forecast construction, under some approaches, estimating and forecasting with a BVAR can be technically and computationally demanding. For the homoskedastic BVAR with natural conjugate prior, the posterior and one-step ahead predictive densities have convenient analytical forms (Student t). However, even for this prior, multi-steps predictive densities do not have analytical forms and simulations methods are required. Under commonly used priors and posterior that treat each equation symmetrically, Monte Carlo methods can be used to efficiently simulate the multi-steps predictive densities, taking advantage of a Kronecker structure to the posterior variance of the model's coefficients.

To avoid costly simulation, Litterman's (1986) specification of the Minnesota prior treats the error variance matrix as fixed and diagonal. Litterman (1986) imposes such a strong assumption to allow for equation-by-equation ridge estimation of the system; treating the error variance matrix as random would have required MCMC simulations of the entire system of equations. In the empirical examples we will concentrate on this type of prior.

More generally, in the theory part we focus on approaches that make the computation of point and density forecasts from BVARs quick and easy, for example by making specific choices on the priors and by using direct rather than iterated forecasts (e.g., Marcellino, Stock, and Watson (2006)). In most cases, the resulting forecasts represent approximations of the posterior distribution. However, Carriero, Kapetanios, and Marcellino (2012), show that, for users focused on point forecasts, there is little cost to methods that do not involve simulation.

Section 8.2 contains a short introduction to Bayesian econometrics. Section 8.3 covers the baseline BVAR case. Next we discuss forecasting with the BVAR model in section 8.4. Examples using simulated and empirical data appear in Sections 8.5 and 8.6. Section 8.7 closes the chapter.

8.2   A primer on Bayesian econometrics

In this section we aim at providing a basic introduction to Bayesian econometrics, in order to make the Bayesian analysis of VAR models more accessible. As our treatment is introductory, interested readers should consult a book such as Koop (2003) or Zellner (1996) for additional details and a more comprehensive treatment.

8.2.1 Parameters as random variables

Let $\{y_t\} \overset{iid}{\sim} N(\mu, \sigma^2)$ be a sequence of random variables, sampled for $t = 1$, ..., T. We group the unknown parameters into the vector $\theta = [\mu, \sigma^2]$, and we would like to use the sample realizations $y_1, \ldots, y_T$ to estimate θ.

In the classical perspective we adopted so far, the vector θ is a set of unknown numbers. A (point) estimator for it is a vector of random variables that should be informative about θ and have some optimality properties (e.g., unbiasedness, consistency, efficiency). For example, the sample mean and variance together form an estimator denoted $\hat{\theta}$.

In a Bayesian perspective, the parameters in θ are instead viewed as random variables. We have some a priori (initial) beliefs about them, summarized by (prior) probability distributions. The sample $y_1, \ldots, y_T$ provides information about θ, summarized into the likelihood function associated with the econometric model that we have specified (in the example, the econometric model is the statement that $\{y_t\}$ is a set of i.i.d. random variables distributed $N(\mu, \sigma^2)$, so that the likelihood function would be a multivariate normal density, considered as a function of the parameters μ and σ^2). Our initial beliefs about θ, the prior distribution, should be combined with the information coming from the data and the chosen econometric model, the likelihood function, to obtain a posterior distribution for the parameters, which summarizes how our initial beliefs about θ have been updated given the information in the data $y_1, ..., y_T$.

The posterior distribution plays a key role in Bayesian econometrics, for example it is used in the computation of forecasts and impulse response functions. Hence, next we consider how to obtain the posterior distribution.

8.2.2 From prior to posterior distribution

Let us denote the prior distribution of the random parameters θ as $p(\theta)$, while the likelihood function for a given value θ is $f(y_1, ..., y_T | \theta)$. We can define the joint distribution of the unknown parameters and data as:

$$f(y_1, ..., y_T, \theta) = f(y_1, ..., y_T | \theta) \cdot p(\theta). \tag{8.2.1}$$

An additional object of interest is the marginal likelihood, which can be obtained by integrating θ out of the joint density $f(y_1, ..., y_T, \theta)$:

$$f(y_1, ..., y_T) = \int_{\theta \in \Theta} f(y_1, ..., y_T, \theta)d\theta \qquad (8.2.2)$$

$$= \int_{\theta \in \Theta} f(y_1, ..., y_T | \theta) \cdot p(\theta)d\theta.$$

At this point we have all the ingredients to derive the posterior distribution, which is obtained by applying the so-called Bayes rule:

$$p(\theta | y_1, ..., y_T) = \frac{f(y_1, ..., y_T, \theta)}{f(y_1, ..., y_T)} \qquad (8.2.3)$$

$$= \frac{f(y_1, ..., y_T | \theta) \cdot p(\theta)}{f(y_1, ..., y_T)}$$

As the marginal density in the denominator is independent of θ, the posterior distribution is proportional (denoted by $\propto$) to the product of the prior, $p(\theta)$, and of the likelihood, $f(y_1, ..., y_T | \theta)$:

$$p(\theta | y_1, ..., y_T) \propto f(y_1, ..., y_T | \theta) \cdot p(\theta).$$

The procedure outlined above to obtain the posterior distribution of the parameters can be always applied. Some prior distributions allow for an analytical derivation of the posterior distributions. When the latter are of the same type of the former (for example, normal), we are in the so-called conjugate case. Even if the posterior distribution cannot be obtained analytically, it can be approximated numerically by means of Monte Carlo simulation methods. We will not consider this case but we refer, for example, to Herbst and Schorfheide (2015) for a detailed treatment.

8.2.3   An example: The posterior of the mean when the variance is known

Let us consider again our example where $\{y_t\} \overset{iid}{\sim} N(\mu, \sigma^2)$, with $t = 1, ...,$ T. Let us assume, for simplicity, that the variance, σ^2, is known while the mean μ, is unknown.

We specify the prior distribution for μ as $\mu \sim N(m, \sigma^2/\nu)$ or, in expanded notation:

$$f(\mu; \sigma^2) = \frac{1}{(2\pi\sigma^2/\nu)^{1/2}} \exp\{-\frac{(\mu - m)^2}{2\sigma^2/\nu}\}.$$

The key parameters in the prior distribution are m and v. The former is the mean of the distribution that, due to the properties of the normal density, also indicates the value to which we assign highest probability. The latter controls the overall variance of the distribution. Hence, the larger v is, the more our prior beliefs about μ are concentrated around the value m.

The likelihood function is:

$$f(y_1, ..., y_T | \mu, \sigma^2) = \frac{1}{(2\pi\sigma^2)^{T/2}} \exp\{-\frac{1}{2\sigma^2} \sum_{t=1}^{T} (y_t - \mu)^2\}.$$

To obtain the posterior distribution, $f(\mu | y_1, ..., y_T; \sigma^2)$, we apply Bayes rule in (8.2.3). This gives:

$$f(\mu | y; \sigma^2) = \frac{1}{[2\pi\sigma^2/(\nu+T)]^{1/2}} \exp\{-\frac{(\mu - m^*)^2}{2\sigma^2/(\nu+T)}\},$$

where

$$m^* = \frac{\nu}{\nu+T} m + \frac{T}{\nu+T} \bar{y}, \quad \bar{y} = \frac{1}{T} \sum_{t=1}^{T} y_t.$$

Hence, we are in the conjugate case where the prior and posterior are within the same class of distribution, namely the posterior distribution is also normal, $N(m^*, \sigma^2/(\nu+T))$. Moreover, the posterior mean, m^*, is a linear combination of the prior mean, m, and of the sample mean, $\bar{y}$. The weights depend on the "tightness" parameter, v, and on the sample size, T. For fixed T, the larger is v the closer is m^* to m. In fact, when v is large, i.e., the prior distribution is highly concentrated around m, then the prior plays a relatively larger role than the likelihood in the determination of the posterior distribution. In other words, if we have strong beliefs that μ is close to m, it will be difficult to change those beliefs substantially based on the sample data $t = 1, \ldots, T$. On the other hand, if v is close to zero ("diffuse" prior), we are very uncertain about μ, and we are willing to put a lot of weight on the sample information. Moreover, note that when T grows, the weight on $\bar{y}$ increases and that on m decreases, for fixed v. Hence, as sample information accumulates, we are willing to give a larger weight to it in the determination of the posterior. Finally, both v and T have the same effect on the variance of the posterior distribution: it diminishes when the tightness is large and/or the sample size is large.

8.2.4   The Bayesian linear regression model

Let us now consider the Bayesian treatment of the linear regression model. This is particularly relevant because, as we have seen in Chapter 6, a VAR can be split into a set of linear regression models where each variable is regressed on its own lags and on the lags of all the other variables (plus possibly some deterministic components). Hence, the Bayesian analysis of the VAR model presented in the next section will rely heavily on the methods introduced for the linear regression model.

Recall from Chapter 1 that we can write a linear regression as:

$$y_t = X_{1t}\beta_1 + X_{2t}\beta_2 + \dots X_{kt}\beta_k + \varepsilon_t, \tag{8.2.4}$$

and we work under the strong OLS assumptions, so that ε_t is $\overset{iid}{\sim} N(0, \sigma^2)$. This specification also implies that y_t is $\overset{iid}{\sim} N(X_t\beta, \sigma^2)$, and the expected value of y_t is $X_t\beta$, while it was μ in the example in the previous subsection. Note also that normality of the errors was not required to derive most of the properties of the OLS estimator, while it is crucial in the Bayesian framework in order to characterize the likelihood function. Using again matrix notation, the likelihood function can then be written as:

$$f(y|\beta, \sigma^2, X) = \frac{1}{(2\pi\sigma^2)^{T/2}} \exp\{-\frac{(y - X\beta)'(y - X\beta)}{2\sigma^2}\}. \tag{8.2.5}$$

We will consider first the case where σ^2 is fixed and known, similar to the example in the previous subsection and to simplify the derivations. Next we will relax this assumption.

Known variance

We assume that the prior distribution of the vector β is multivariate normal, $N(m, \sigma^2 M)$, or in expanded form:

$$f(\beta; \sigma^2) = \frac{1}{(2\pi\sigma^2)^{k/2}} |M|^{-1/2} \exp\left\{-\frac{(\beta - m)' M^{-1}(\beta - m)}{2\sigma^2}\right\}. \tag{8.2.6}$$

The key parameters that control the first two moments of β are m and M. Applying Bayes rule in this model, we have:

$$f(\beta|y, X; \sigma^2) = \frac{f(y|\beta, \sigma^2, X) \cdot f(\beta; \sigma^2)}{f(y|\sigma^2, X)} \tag{8.2.7}$$

The expressions for the likelihood and the prior in the numerator are those in, respectively, (8.2.5) and (8.2.6). The marginal likelihood in the denominator can be obtained by integrating β out of $f(y, \beta | \sigma^2, X)$. Combining this yields the posterior distribution:

$$f(\beta | y, X; \sigma^2) = \frac{1}{(2\pi\sigma^2)^{k/2}} |M^{-1} + X'X|^{1/2} \cdot \tag{8.2.8}$$

$$\cdot \exp - \frac{(\beta - m^*)'(M^{-1} + X'X)(\beta - m^*)}{2\sigma^2}.$$

Not surprisingly, we are again in the conjugate case and the posterior distribution is $N(m^*, \sigma^2 M^*)$, with

$$m^* = (M^{-1} + X'X)^{-1}(M^{-1}m + X'y),$$
$$M^* = (M^{-1} + X'X)^{-1}.$$

Let us now briefly discuss how one obtains the above analytical expressions for m^* and M^*. The first possibility is to just do all the calculations by expanding on (8.2.7). The second option is to realize that the prior distribution is imposing a set of stochastic constraints on the β parameters of the linear regression model (see, e.g., Theil and Goldberger (1961)). Namely, the prior implies that

$$\beta = m + \varepsilon_\beta, \quad \varepsilon_\beta \sim N(0, \sigma^2 M),$$

which we can also write as

$$m = \beta + \varepsilon_\beta, \quad \varepsilon_\beta \sim N(0, \sigma^2 M), \tag{8.2.9}$$

since the sign of the error term does not really matter. We can then group these constraints with the linear regression model, and write

$$\begin{cases} m = \beta + \varepsilon_\beta, & E(\varepsilon_\beta \varepsilon_\beta') = \sigma^2 M \\ y = X\beta + \varepsilon, & E(\varepsilon \varepsilon') = \sigma^2 I_T \end{cases}$$

or

$$y^* = X^* \beta + \varepsilon^*, \tag{8.2.10}$$

where

$$y^* = \begin{bmatrix} m \\ y \end{bmatrix}, \quad X^* = \begin{bmatrix} I_k \\ X \end{bmatrix}$$

$$E[\varepsilon^* \varepsilon^{*\prime}] = \sigma^2 \begin{bmatrix} M & 0 \\ 0 & I_T \end{bmatrix}$$

The errors in the extended linear regression model appearing in (8.2.10) are heteroskedastic so that, in a classical context, we would estimate the β parameters by GLS, namely:

$$
\begin{aligned}
\widehat{\beta}^{GLS} &= \left[X^{*\prime} \left(\begin{array}{cc} \sigma^2 M & 0 \\ 0 & \sigma^2 I_T \end{array} \right)^{-1} X^* \right]^{-1} \left[X^{*\prime} \left(\begin{array}{cc} \sigma^2 M & 0 \\ 0 & \sigma^2 I_T \end{array} \right)^{-1} y^* \right] = \\
&= (M^{-1} + X'X)^{-1}(M^{-1}m + X'y) = m^*.
\end{aligned}
$$

Moreover,

$$
\begin{aligned}
Var[\widehat{\beta}^{GLS}] &= \left[X^{*\prime} \left(\begin{array}{cc} \sigma^2 M & 0 \\ 0 & \sigma^2 I_T \end{array} \right)^{-1} X^* \right]^{-1} = \\
&= \sigma^2 (M^{-1} + X'X)^{-1} = \sigma^2 M^*.
\end{aligned}
$$

Therefore, the Bayesian posterior distribution for the regression parameters β is centered on the classical GLS estimator of the regression parameters in the model where the prior is interpreted as a set of stochastic constraints. Moreover, the posterior variance coincides with the variance of the GLS estimator. A similar approach for the derivation of the posterior moments can be also applied in the VAR context.

Unknown variance

Let us now consider the more general case where the error variance is unknown and random. The posterior distribution becomes:

$$
f(\beta, \sigma^2 | y, X) = \frac{f(y|\beta, \sigma^2, X) \cdot f(\beta|\sigma^2) \cdot f(\sigma^2)}{f(y|X)}. \tag{8.2.11}
$$

The expression for the likelihood, $f(y|\beta, \sigma^2, X)$, remains as in (8.2.5). The prior distribution for β and σ^2 is written as the product of the conditional $f(\beta|\sigma^2)$ and the marginal $f(\sigma^2)$. The conditional distribution $f(\beta|\sigma^2)$ is the same as that in (8.2.6), so that we only need to specify the prior $f(\sigma^2)$.

We choose an inverse-gamma distribution, or inverted gamma, $\sigma^2 \sim IG(\lambda, v)$, which guarantees positivity of the variance and is in line with what is commonly done for the BVAR case. Equivalently, one could use a gamma distribution for σ^{-2}, $\sigma^{-2} \sim G(\lambda, v)$, which helps with the interpretation of the parameters, see for example Koop (2003). In particular, it is

$$G(\lambda, v) \propto (\sigma^{-2})^{\frac{v-2}{2}} \exp(-\frac{\sigma^{-2}v}{2\lambda}),$$

and $E(\sigma^{-2}) = \lambda$, $var(\sigma^{-2}) = 2\lambda^2/v$.

With the stated priors, the posterior distribution for $f(\beta|\sigma^2, y, X)$ remains the same as in (8.2.8). The posterior for σ^2, $f(\sigma^2|y, X)$, is instead $IG(\lambda^*, v^*)$, see for example Koop (2003) or Zellner (1996) for the details of the derivations. These references also show that the marginal posterior distribution for β, i.e., without conditioning on σ^2, $f(\beta|y, X)$ is a multivariate Student t distribution.

8.3 Baseline Bayesian VAR case

8.3.1 Baseline BVAR specification

Our baseline specification is a BVAR with a normal-inverted Wishart (N-IW) conjugate prior, as in the case of the linear regression model.[2] Given N different variables grouped in the vector $y_t = (y_{1t} \; y_{2t} \; ... \; y_{Nt})'$, we consider the following VAR

$$y_t = \Phi_c + \Phi_1 y_{t-1} + \Phi_2 y_{t-2} + ... + \Phi_p y_{t-p} + \varepsilon_t; \; \varepsilon_t \overset{iid}{\sim} N(0, \Sigma), \qquad (8.3.1)$$

where $t = 1, \ldots, T$. Each equation has $M = Np + 1$ regressors. By grouping the coefficient matrices in the $N \times M$ matrix $\Phi' = [\Phi_c \; \Phi_1 \; ... \; \Phi_p]$ and defining $x_t = (1 \; y'_{t-1} \; ... \; y'_{t-p})'$ as a vector containing an intercept and p lags of y_t, the VAR can be written as

$$y_t = \Phi' x_t + \varepsilon_t. \qquad (8.3.2)$$

An even more compact notation is

$$Y = X\Phi + E, \qquad (8.3.3)$$

where $Y = [y_1, .., y_T]'$, $X = [x_1, .., x_T]'$, and $E = [\varepsilon_1, .., \varepsilon_T]'$ are, respectively, $T \times N$, $T \times M$ and $T \times N$ matrices. If we apply the vec operator to both

---

[2]The inverted Wishart or inverse-Wishart distribution is the multivariate generalization of the inverse-gamma distribution discussed in the previous section.

sides of (8.3.3) we get $\text{vec}(Y) = (I \otimes X)\,\text{vec}(\Phi) + \text{vec}(E)$, which is a linear regression model similar to that analyzed in the previous section.

Finally, for representing multi-steps forecasts, another useful notation is the companion form

$$x_{t+1} = \Phi^+ x_t + \tilde{\varepsilon}_t, \tag{8.3.4}$$

where $\tilde{\varepsilon}_t$ is a $M \times 1$ vector containing ε_t and 0's elsewhere and Φ^+ is a $M \times M$ matrix defined as

$$\Phi^+ = \begin{bmatrix} 1 & \mathbf{0}_{1 \times N} & \mathbf{0}_{1 \times N} & \cdots & \mathbf{0}_{1 \times N} \\ \Phi_c & \Phi_1 & \Phi_2 & \cdots & \Phi_p \\ \mathbf{0}_{N \times 1} & I_N & \mathbf{0}_{N \times N} & \cdots & \mathbf{0}_{N \times N} \\ \vdots & \mathbf{0}_{N \times N} & \ddots & & \vdots \\ \mathbf{0}_{N \times 1} & \mathbf{0}_{N \times N} & & I_N & \mathbf{0}_{N \times N} \end{bmatrix}. \tag{8.3.5}$$

Note that in this notation y_t corresponds to rows $2, ..., N+1$ of x_{t+1}, so we can write $y_t = \mathbf{s} x_{t+1}$, defining $\mathbf{s}$ to be a selection matrix selecting the appropriate rows (i.e., row 2 to row $N+1$) of x_{t+1}. With this representation, multi-steps forecasts can be obtained as $\hat{x}_{t+h} = (\Phi^+)^h x_t$.

8.3.2   Prior parameterizations

As a prior density for the VAR parameters, we use the conjugate N-IW prior, that we introduced in the previous section in the context of the linear regression model:

$$vec\,(\Phi)\,|\Sigma \sim N(\Phi_0, \Sigma \otimes \Omega_0),\ \Sigma \sim IW(S_0, v_0). \tag{8.3.6}$$

As the N-IW prior is conjugate, the conditional posterior distribution of this model is also N-IW (Zellner (1996)):

$$vec\,(\Phi)\,|\Sigma, Y \sim N(\bar{\Phi}, \Sigma \otimes \bar{\Omega}),\ \Sigma|Y \sim IW(\bar{S}, \bar{v}). \tag{8.3.7}$$

Defining $\hat{\Phi}$ and $\hat{E}$ as the OLS estimates, then $\bar{\Phi} = (\Omega_0^{-1} + X'X)^{-1}(\Omega_0^{-1}\Phi_0 + X'Y)$, $\bar{\Omega} = (\Omega_0^{-1} + X'X)^{-1}$, $\bar{v} = v_0 + T$, and $\bar{S} = \Phi_0 + \hat{E}'\hat{E} + \hat{\Phi}'X'X\hat{\Phi} + \Phi_0'\Omega_0^{-1}\Phi_0 - \bar{\Phi}'\bar{\Omega}^{-1}\bar{\Phi}$. These formulas are the multivariate counterpart of those that we derived in the previous section for the univariate regression model. For example, the posterior mean of Φ is just a linear combination of the prior mean and of the OLS estimator, with weights depending on the tightness of the prior and on the sample size.

In the case of the natural conjugate N-IW prior, the marginal posterior distribution of Φ is matrix-variate-t with expected value $\bar{\bar{\Phi}}$.

We further assume the prior expectation and standard deviation of the coefficient matrices to be:

$$E[\Phi_k^{(ij)}] = \begin{cases} \Phi^* & \text{if } i = j, k = 1 \\ 0 & \text{otherwise} \end{cases} \quad , \quad \text{st.dev.}[\Phi_k^{(ij)}] = \begin{cases} \frac{\lambda_1 \lambda_2}{k} \frac{\sigma_i}{\sigma_j}, & k = 1, ..., p \\ \lambda_0 \sigma_i, & k = 0 \end{cases}$$
$$(8.3.8)$$

where $\Phi_k^{(ij)}$ denotes the element in position (i, j) in the matrix Φ_k. The prior mean Φ^* is set to 1 in the VAR in levels specifications and to 0 in the VAR in growth rates specification. For the intercept we assume an informative prior with mean 0 and standard deviation $\lambda_0 \sigma_i$. The shrinkage parameter λ_1 measures the overall tightness of the prior: when $\lambda_1 \to 0$ the prior is imposed exactly and the data do not influence the estimates, while as $\lambda_1 \to \infty$ the prior becomes loose and the prior information does not influence the estimates, which will approach the standard OLS estimates. The parameter λ_2 implements additional shrinkage on lags of other variables than for lags of the dependent variable. We refer to this as the cross-shrinkage parameter, and in our baseline specification we set it to $\lambda_2 = 1$, which implies that no cross-variable shrinkage takes place, as required for the normal-inverted Wishart case.

To set each scale parameter σ_i the common practice (see e.g., Litterman (1986) and Sims and Zha (1998)) is to set it equal to the standard deviation of the residuals from a univariate autoregressive model. Most of the studies cited above have considered the following parameterization for the prior:

$$\lambda_0 = 1; \ \lambda_1 = 0.2; \ \lambda_2 = 1, \tag{8.3.9}$$

and we will make similar choices in the empirical examples. Carriero et al. (2015), among others, discuss methods for the optimal choice of these parameters, as well as of the VAR lag length.

Note that the prior beliefs in (8.3.8), defining the traditional Minnesota prior, only include the prior mean and variances of the coefficients, and do not elicit any prior beliefs about the correlations among the coefficients. Doan, Litterman, and Sims (1984) and Sims (1993) have proposed to complement the prior beliefs in (8.3.6) with additional priors that favor unit roots and cointegration, and introduce correlations in prior beliefs about the coefficients in a given equation. Both these priors were motivated by the need to avoid having an unreasonably large share of the sample period variation in the data accounted for by deterministic components (Sims (1993)). These priors are also in line with the belief that macroeconomic data typically feature unit roots and cointegration. We refer to these papers for additional details.

8.4   Forecasting with the BVAR

In this section we discuss forecasting using the BVAR model. We first describe the proper method, which though can be computationally demanding in several cases for multi-steps forecasting. Hence, next we discuss two alternative approaches for multi-steps forecasting, that are less elegant but tend to perform well for point forecasts (not necessarily for density forecasts).

8.4.1   The proper method

Under the standard N-IW prior described above, the full distribution of the one-step ahead forecasts is given by:

$$y'_{T+1}|x'_{T+1} \sim MT(x'_{T+1}\bar{\Phi}, (x'_{T+1}\bar{\Omega}x_{T+1} + 1)^{-1}, \overline{S}, \overline{v}), \qquad (8.4.1)$$

where MT denotes the matrix-variate t-distribution.

Multi-steps ahead forecasts obtained by iteration are not available in closed form, but can be simulated using an MC algorithm that draws a sequence of Σ and parameters Φ from (8.3.7) and shocks and at each draw j computes the implied path of $\hat{y}_{t+h}^{(j)}$. Drawing a sequence of Φ can be in general rather demanding from a computational point of view, but in this specific case the matrix-variate structure of the N-IW prior ensures that there are efficient algorithms that considerably speed up the computations. An intuitive way to draw Φ, conditionally on a draw of the error variance Σ, is to vectorize it and draw from a multivariate normal. In this case a draw of Φ from (8.3.7) is obtained as follows:

$$vec(\Phi) = vec(\bar{\Phi}) + chol(\Sigma \otimes \bar{\Omega}) \times v \qquad (8.4.2)$$

where v is a $MN \times 1$ standard Gaussian vector process. The Cholesky decomposition above requires $(MN)^3$ elementary operations. The scheme outlined in (8.4.2) does not take advantage of the matrix-variate structure of the distribution of Φ. Indeed, by organizing the elements of v in a $M \times N$ matrix V such that $v =$vec(V), one could draw the matrix Φ as follows:

$$\Phi = \bar{\Phi} + chol(\bar{\Omega}) \times V \times chol(\Sigma)'. \qquad (8.4.3)$$

This can considerably speed up the computations, because the two Cholesky decompositions $chol(\bar{\Omega})$ and $chol(\Sigma)$ require only $M^3 + N^3$ operations, but can only be implemented when the variance matrix of the prior coefficients has a Kronecker structure.

8.4.2 The pseudo-iterated approach

As an alternative, one can choose to approximate the results by just integrating out the uncertainty in the coefficients and then using the posterior mean of the coefficients to produce posterior means of the multi-steps forecasts. In this case the multi-steps point forecast is computed as:

$$\hat{y}_{t+h} = \mathbf{s} \cdot (\bar{\Phi}^+)^h x_{t+1}. \tag{8.4.4}$$

This method has been used e.g., by Bańbura, Giannone, and Reichlin (2010), and we label it the "pseudo-iterated" approach. Of course, this approach has a clear computational benefit but it is, strictly speaking, inaccurate as it ignores the non-linearity inherent in multi-steps forecasting.

In some cases there can be little choice but to use the "pseudo-iterated" approach. If one departs from the N-IW conjugate prior, which ensures both a closed form solution for the joint posterior density of the parameters and a particularly convenient Kronecker structure of the posterior coefficient variance matrix, the computational costs involved in simulating the joint posterior distribution of the parameters increase rapidly with the dimension of the system, because to draw a sequence of Φ one must resort to manipulation of an $MN \times MN$ variance matrix without the efficient Kronecker structure of (8.3.7) and (8.4.3). The computational costs rise sharply with the number of lags and, in particular the number of variables, see e.g., Kadiyala and Karlsson (1997) and Karlsson (2012).

Moreover, the use of the pseudo-iterated approach may be necessary for some practitioners relying on common software packages, such as *EViews*, that do not provide simple, direct commands for simulating BVARs. These packages produce posterior moments, but do not permit direct simulation of the posterior distributions. Instead, users are required to write their own programs, as would also be the case for packages such as *Matlab*.

Finally, empirical results in Carriero, Kapetanios, and Marcellino (2009), indicate that the gains for point forecasts from the proper simulation-based approach with respect to the pseudo-iterated method are negligible. Therefore, if one is only interested in point forecasts, the loss from the quick and easy pseudo iterated approach is small. On the other hand, if the focus is on multi-steps density forecasts, the pseudo-iterated approach would not help from a computational point of view. Indeed, while one could compute a set of desired quantiles from an (approximate) predictive density based on an iteration of equation (8.4.1), the proper production of a whole density forecast would still require simulation methods.

8.4.3 The direct forecasting approach

Another way to overcome the problem of non-linearity in the multi-steps forecasts is to use the direct approach, which we have seen in previous chapters. Consider the following VAR:

$$y_t = \Phi_{c,h} + \Phi_{1,h} y_{t-(h-1)-1} + \Phi_{2,h} y_{t-(h-1)-2} + \dots + \Phi_{1,h} y_{t-(h-1)-p} + \varepsilon_t. \quad (8.4.5)$$

Note that in the above model the vector y_t is regressed directly onto y_{t-h} and $p-1$ additional lags, and that for each forecast horizon h a different model is employed. Such an approach has been implemented in a Bayesian framework by, e.g., Koop (2013).

As we discussed in previous chapters, generally, the iterated (or powering-up) approach is more efficient in a classical context, as the used estimators are equivalent to maximum likelihood, under correct model specification. It is, however, dangerous in the presence of mis-specification, because in general the mis-specification will inflate with the forecast horizon when the forecasts are computed recursively. In addition, the direct approach implies that the h-steps ahead forecast is still a linear function of the coefficients (because a different model is used for each forecast horizon), while in the traditional powering-up approach the multi-steps forecasts are highly non-linear functions of the estimated coefficients. As a result, there is an exact closed form solution for the distribution of the h-steps ahead forecasts computed using (8.4.5), while computing the forecasts resulting from the powering up strategy requires the use of simulation methods, as discussed above.[3]

Carriero, Clark, and Marcellino (2015) show that in their empirical examples and for horizons shorter than six-steps ahead, there is little loss in using the direct approach rather than the iterated one. However, as the forecast horizon increases, the direct method is outperformed.

---

[3]Admittedly, however, the closed form solution obtained with a direct forecasting approach assumes the error terms of the model are serially uncorrelated, which will not actually be the case with forecast horizons of more than one period.

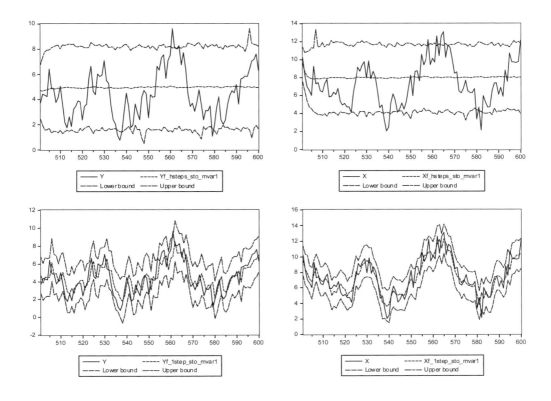

Figure 8.5.1: *Results of the forecasting exercise for the BVAR(1) model: the upper panels present the dynamic h-steps ahead forecasts and the lower panels the static one-step ahead forecasts*

8.5 Example with simulated data

In order to evaluate the benefits of a Bayesian approach when using VARs, a first example is conducted by means of simulated data. The same DGP of the example in Chapter 6 is applied: a VAR(1) bivariate stationary model. By choosing the same random seed, we can reproduce the same artificial series used previously. Also in this framework, a correct specification with one lag is compared to a mis-specified counterpart with four lags. But in this example, both correct and mis-specified specifications will be estimated with both frequentist (as in Chapter 6) and Bayesian techniques.

As in most Bayesian applications, setting the prior is important. For

MAFE	VAR(1)		VAR(4)		BVAR(1)		BVAR(4)	
				Stochastic				
	x	y	x	y	x	y	x	y
Static	0.788	0.890	0.785	0.894	0.793	0.895	0.783	0.886
Dynamic	2.069	1.634	2.068	1.617	2.051	1.629	2.062	1.632
				Deterministic				
	x	y	x	y	x	y	x	y
Static	0.788	0.893	0.789	0.893	0.789	0.892	0.786	0.888
Dynamic	2.063	1.632	2.068	1.633	2.066	1.634	2.069	1.634

RMSFE	VAR(1)		VAR(4)		BVAR(1)		BVAR(4)	
				Stochastic				
	x	y	x	y	x	y	x	y
Static	0.975	1.107	0.992	1.100	0.979	1.112	0.978	1.101
Dynamic	2.486	1.942	2.473	1.917	2.458	1.929	2.475	1.936
				Deterministic				
	x	y	x	y	x	y	x	y
Static	0.974	1.107	0.998	1.101	0.976	1.105	0.979	1.100
Dynamic	2.477	1.939	2.479	1.939	2.478	1.939	2.479	1.940

Table 8.5.1: *Mean absolute error and root mean squared error for each model and type of forecast*

example, consider the Litterman/Minnesota prior. Recalling the following structure for the moments of the prior:

$$E[\Phi_k^{(ij)}] = \left\{ \begin{array}{ll} \Phi^* & \text{if } i = j, k = 1 \\ 0 & \text{otherwise} \end{array} \right. , \quad \text{st.dev.}[\Phi_k^{(ij)}] = \left\{ \begin{array}{ll} \frac{\lambda_1 \lambda_2}{k} \frac{\sigma_i}{\sigma_j}, & k = 1, ..., p \\ \lambda_3 \sigma_i, & k = 0 \end{array} \right. ,$$

the tightness parameter λ_1 is set to 0.2, the relative cross-variable weight λ_2 to 0.99, the decay hyper-parameter λ_3 to 1, and, given the stationarity of both artificial series, the VAR(1) diagonal coefficients mean Φ^* is set to 0. This allows the researcher to incorporate some pre-existing information within the estimation phase.

In the VAR(1) case, the estimation results are not much different between the Bayesian and the classical approaches, while a more pronounced differ-

ence can be noticed in the mis-specified VAR(4) case, probably because of
the decay pattern for lags higher than 1 prescribed by the prior. In order
to assess any forecasting benefits for the Bayesian technique, it is important
to show and compare forecasts between the different estimation approaches
across models. In particular, as in Chapter 6, both stochastic and deterministic VAR forecasts are computed for each model (1 lag and 4 lags) and with
each estimation approach (Bayesian with Minnesota Prior and classical).

Figure 8.5.1 reports the static (one-step) and dynamic (h-step) forecasts
for the BVAR(1) model in both the deterministic and stochastic cases. By
comparing this picture with its classical approach counterpart (in Chapter
6 section 6.9), no relevant differences can be noticed. Similar conclusions
can be made for the VAR(4)/BVAR(4) graphical comparison. The RMSFE
and MAFE for each set of specifications are reported in Table 8.5.1. From
the table it emerges that the BVAR performs better in many instances, even
though the differences in many cases are minor in size as the number of
variables is small and the sample size large.

As for the structural analysis, both the impulse responses and the variance decompositions are very similar in shape, and present very small numerical differences with respect to the classical VAR for this small dimensional
example. When dealing with larger models, the differences can be more
pronounced.

8.6 Empirical examples

8.6.1 GDP growth in the Euro area

The same example with real data reported in Chapter 6 is now analyzed
using Bayesian VARs, while keeping the same specifications, i.e., a VAR(1)
and a VAR(2). As in Chapter 6, the data used are GDP growth rates of three
major countries in the Euro area, namely, France, Germany, and Italy, along
with the US GDP growth as an exogenous reference point outside the EU. For
each country there are 108 quarterly observations from 1986Q1 to 2012Q4
of the growth rates of real GDP expressed as percentage change from the
previous year, downloadable from DATASTREAM. The Bayesian VAR is
implemented adopting a Minnesota prior, with decay hyper-parameter equal
to 1, tightness parameter to 0.2 and, because of stationarity of growth rates,
AR(1) prior mean equal to zero (basically the same prior used in the example

BVAR(1)	G_FR		G_GER		G_IT	
	det	stoch	det	stoch	det	stoch
RMSFE	0.875	0.866	0.349	0.346	0.427	0.432
MAFE	0.727	0.735	0.263	0.263	0.355	0.361

BVAR(2)	G_FR		G_GER		G_IT	
	det	stoch	det	stoch	det	stoch
RMSFE	0.853	0.860	0.328	0.339	0.460	0.469
MAFE	0.708	0.709	0.250	0.244	0.400	0.395

Table 8.6.1: *One-step ahead forecast evaluation statistics 2003 - 2006*

BVAR(1)	G_FR		G_GER		G_IT	
	det	stoch	det	stoch	det	stoch
RMSFE	1.565	1.575	0.799	0.803	1.623	1.629
MAFE	0.978	0.981	0.615	0.616	1.264	1.268

BVAR(2)	G_FR		G_GER		G_IT	
	det	stoch	det	stoch	det	stoch
RMSFE	1.546	1.542	0.765	0.760	1.647	1.650
MAFE	0.974	0.974	0.592	0.598	1.333	1.327

Table 8.6.2: *One-step ahead forecast evaluation statistics 2007-2012*

with simulated data). The forecasts and the structural analysis give very similar results to the classical ones. It is then useful to look at the forecast evaluation statistics, in order to measure the tiny differences (Tables 8.6.1 and 8.6.2). However, also looking at diagnostics, there does not seem to be a clear ranking of the alternative estimation approaches. Bayesian models may offer advantages when forecasting with larger models, an issue we consider in the next example.

8.6.2   Multi-country inflation rates

In this example, we consider inflation rate forecasting, exploiting the cross-country linkages in inflation rates. A larger VAR example is implemented using the log-differences of the monthly HICP index for 6 large Western coun-

BVAR(4)			dp_fra	VAR(4)		
	det	stoch			det	stoch
RMSFE	0.144	0.144		RMSFE	0.160	0.159
MAFE	0.114	0.114		MAFE	0.129	0.129
			dp_ger			
	det	stoch			det	stoch
RMSFE	0.182	0.181		RMSFE	0.172	0.172
MAFE	0.137	0.137		MAFE	0.137	0.137
			dp_ita			
	det	stoch			det	stoch
RMSFE	0.157	0.156		RMSFE	0.165	0.165
MAFE	0.125	0.125		MAFE	0.135	0.135
			dp_spa			
	det	stoch			det	stoch
RMSFE	0.248	0.248		RMSFE	0.257	0.256
MAFE	0.192	0.193		MAFE	0.203	0.203
			dp_uk			
	det	stoch			det	stoch
RMSFE	0.163	0.164		RMSFE	0.178	0.178
MAFE	0.121	0.122		MAFE	0.139	0.139
			dp_usa			
	det	stoch			det	stoch
RMSFE	0.306	0.305		RMSFE	0.305	0.306
MAFE	0.203	0.203		MAFE	0.222	0.222

Table 8.6.3: *One-step ahead forecast evaluation statistics July 2008 - October 2014 for HICP inflation*

tries: France, Germany, Italy, Spain, the United Kingdom and the United States. A total of 191 observations for the period 1998M12-2014M10 were downloaded from the EUROSTAT database.

A VAR model with 4 lags is estimated both with a classical and with a Bayesian approach with Minnesota prior. As in previous examples, dealing with stationary variables, a zero AR(1) prior mean is used for the Minnesota prior implementation. Given the larger number of coefficients to be estimated (more than 100), a higher benefit is expected from adopting a Bayesian strategy.

Recursive forecasting is implemented for the forecasting window 2008M7 - 2014M10, which includes the recent financial crisis. Figures 8.6.1 and 8.6.2 report the static stochastic forecasts for each variable for both BVAR(4) and VAR(4) models. From the picture it emerges a more stable pattern for the forecasts when using the Bayesian approach.

Table 8.6.3 contains the forecast measures for each variable and each model. The figures confirm the suggestions of the graphical inspection: the BVAR(4) has a clearly better performance than the VAR(4) in almost all instances, though the differences are small.

8.7   Concluding remarks

In this chapter we have presented the Bayesian version of VARs, known as BVARs. They combine the flexibility of classical VAR models with the shrinkage that characterizes Bayesian estimation, reducing the curse of dimensionality. As classical VARs, they can be used both for forecasting and for more structural analysis. We have briefly discussed model specification and estimation, and introduced alternative methods for computing forecasts, based either on analytical or simulation methods and either on proper models or on approximations.

The applications confirmed that BVARs tend to forecast in general at least as well as classical VARs.

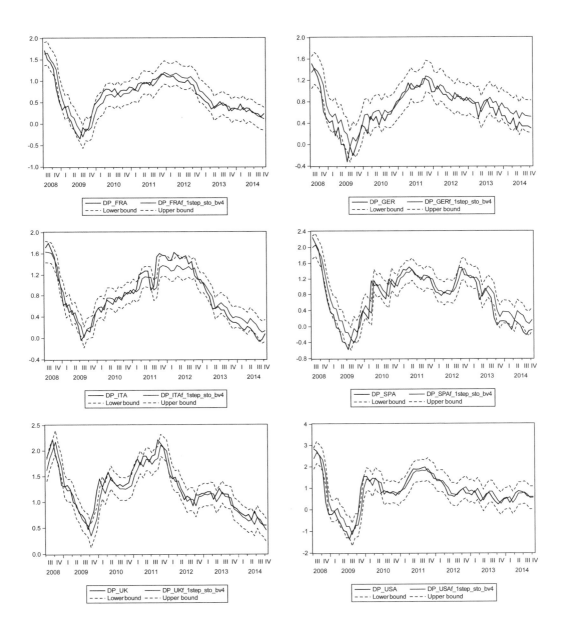

Figure 8.6.1: *Stochastic forecasts 2006M7 - 2014M10 for HICP log-differences using a BVAR(4) specification*

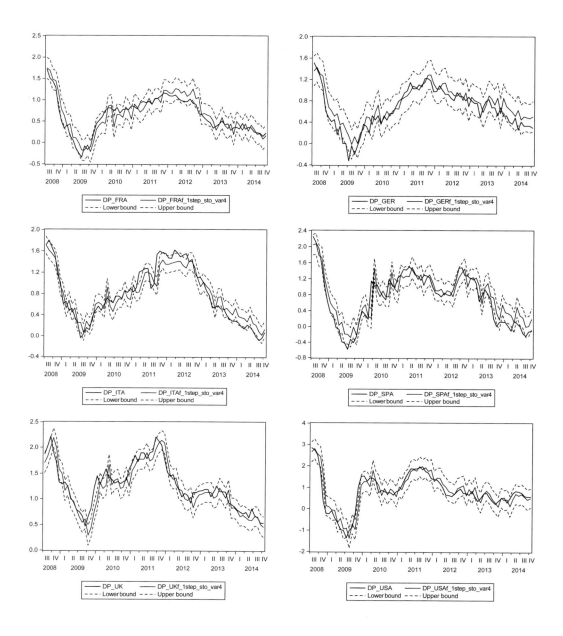

Figure 8.6.2: *Stochastic forecasts 2006M7 - 20141M10 for HICP log-differences using a VAR(4) specification*

Part III

TAR, Markov Switching, and State Space Models

Chapter 9

TAR and STAR Models

9.1 Introduction

All the models we have considered so far are linear and feature stable parameters. These are convenient assumptions since they simplify parameter estimation and forecast construction. However, there can be cases where they are invalid, based on either theory or empirical evidence.

For example, in the case of a Cobb Douglas production function, output (Y) is related to capital (K) and labor (L) according to the relationship

$$Y_t = A_t K_t^\alpha L_t^\beta, \tag{9.1.1}$$

where A_t measures technological progress and has both a deterministic and a random component, $A_t = C\varepsilon_t$, while parameters α and β are related to the returns to scale.

The model in (9.1.1) is clearly non-linear in the parameters α and β, and in addition the error term ε_t enters in a multiplicative form. However, if we apply the logarithmic transformation to both sides of (9.1.1) and denote the log of a variable with a lower case letter, we obtain

$$y_t = c + \alpha k_t + \beta l_t + \log \varepsilon_t, \tag{9.1.2}$$

which is again a linear model, though likely with non-normal errors. Similarly, if the parameters α, β, or c in (9.1.2) are not constant but switch to new values at a known date T^*, the model has time-varying parameters. However, we can transform it in a constant parameter model by the proper use of dummy variables, as we have seen in Chapter 2.

Unfortunately, it is not always possible to transform a non-linear or time-varying parameter model into a linear constant parameter specification. For example, the model could be

$$y_t = f(x_t, z_t; \theta_t) + \varepsilon_t, \qquad (9.1.3)$$

where f is a generic known function linking the explanatory variables x and z to the dependent variable y, according to the time-varying parameters θ_t.

Abandoning the linear constant parameter modeling framework creates a set of additional problems. First, model specification is more complex. For example, in (9.1.3) we need to define the functional relationship (f) that links x and z to y, and specify the process governing the evolution of the parameters θ_t. Second, parameter estimation is much more complex, and typically analytical solutions for the parameter estimators are not available. Finally, the derivation of optimal forecasts can be cumbersome, and again analytical expressions for them are generally not available.

In this third part of the book we introduce a set of specific non-linear and/or time-varying parameter models, focusing on those most commonly used in empirical applications and that proved useful in a forecasting context. We start in this chapter with the Threshold Autoregressive (TAR) and Smooth Transition Autoregressive (STAR) models. In Section 9.2 we discuss model specification and parameter estimation in Section 9.3, while testing for non-linearity is covered in Section 9.4. Diagnostic checking and forecasting are the topics of the next two sections. We also devote a section (namely 9.7) to artificial neural networks and related literature.

A set of examples using simulated and actual data are presented in Sections 9.8 and 9.9. Section 9.10 concludes the chapter. Additional details on TAR and STAR models can be found, e.g., in Granger and Teräsvirta (1993), Franses and Van Dijk (2000), Teräsvirta, Tjøstheim, and Granger (2010), Teräsvirta (2006) and Van Dijk, Teräsvirta, and Franses (2002).

Note that we have focused on univariate models for simplicity, but multivariate versions are also feasible, see for example Artis, Galvão, and Marcellino (2007), as well as structural applications, even though computation of the impulse response functions to structural shocks is more complex, see e.g., Koop, Pesaran, and Potter (1996).

9.2 Specification

Let us consider the model:

$$y_t = \begin{cases} \phi_{0,1} + \phi_{1,1} y_{t-1} + \varepsilon_t & \text{if } q_t \le c \\ \phi_{0,2} + \phi_{1,2} y_{t-1} + \varepsilon_t & \text{if } q_t > c \end{cases}$$

This is an AR(1), but its parameters change depending on whether the variable q_t is above or below the threshold value c. It is therefore called Threshold AR (TAR). If $q_t = y_{t-d}$, e.g., y_{t-1}, then the model is called Self Exciting TAR (SETAR). More lags or a more general deterministic component can be inserted in the model.

From an economic point of view, the rationale of TAR and SETAR models is that when q_t exceeds a certain value the dynamics of y_t changes. For example, if inflation goes beyond a certain level, then hyperinflation can emerge, changing the dynamics of inflation itself. Or when the budget deficit goes beyond a threshold value, the dynamics of GDP growth can change since consumers and firms can expect massive future increases in taxation or cuts in public transfers.

Note that we can rewrite a SETAR (or TAR) as a single equation, such as:

$$\begin{aligned} y_t &= (\phi_{0,1} + \phi_{1,1} y_{t-1})(1 - I(y_{t-1} > c)) \\ &\quad + (\phi_{0,2} + \phi_{1,2} y_{t-1}) I(y_{t-1} > c) + \varepsilon_t \end{aligned} \qquad (9.2.1)$$

where I is the indicator function. This form will be more convenient for estimation. It also highlights that the resulting model is non-linear in the parameters.

In the SETAR model the transition between sets of parameter values is abrupt and discontinuous. As an alternative, we can consider a smoother transition between the two regimes, by using a different transition function. In particular, instead of the indicator function I in (9.2.1), we could use the logistic function G, with

$$G(q_t; \gamma, c) = \frac{1}{1 + exp(-\gamma[q_t - c])}. \qquad (9.2.2)$$

The resulting model is called Logistic Smooth Transition AR (LSTAR or simply STAR). The parameter γ determines the smoothness: when γ is very large the model becomes similar to the TAR model, while for $\gamma = 0$ the model becomes linear.   There can be a more complex deterministic component, additional lags, and possibly exogenous explanatory variables and their lags.

A few further comments are worth making.   First, in general the auto-correlation and partial autocorrelation functions (AC and PAC) also change over time when y_t follows a TAR or STAR model. Second, it is possible to use information criteria (IC) to determine the lag length, even if computational costs are higher than in the standard ARMA case due to additional estimation complexity and larger number of models to evaluate. For example, with maximum lag length of p_1 and p_2 in the two regimes, $p_1 \times p_2$ models have to be estimated and IC computed and compared. Note that IC can also be used to select the transition variables. Third, it is possible to allow for more than two regimes. Given that the STAR model with two regimes can be rewritten as

$$y_t = \phi_1' x_t + (\phi_2 - \phi_1)' x_t G(q_t; \gamma, c) + \varepsilon_t, \qquad (9.2.3)$$

where $x_t = (1, y_{t-1})$ and $\phi_j = (\phi_{0,j}, \phi_{1,j})'$, $j = 1, 2$, for 3 regimes we have

$$y_t = \phi_1' x_t + (\phi_2 - \phi_1)' x_t G_1(q_{1t}; \gamma_1, c_1) + (\phi_3 - \phi_2)' x_t G_2(q_{2t}; \gamma_2, c_2) + \varepsilon_t. \quad (9.2.4)$$

It is also possible that the regimes are determined by more than one variable, see, e.g., Van Dijk and Franses (1999).

Contrary to the linear case, in the non-linear world it can be better to start with a specific model and then generalize it if necessary. In particular, Granger (1993) suggested the following procedure:

1. specify a linear model (e.g., an AR(p));

2. test the null hypothesis of linearity against a specific form of non-linearity (e.g., SETAR or STAR);

3. if linearity is rejected, estimate the specific non-linear model;

4. run diagnostics on the model and modify it if necessary;

5. use the model for the required application, e.g., forecasting or computation of impulse response functions.

Let us now consider these steps in some detail, starting with estimation, which is also required for testing linearity against STAR type non-linearity.

9.3 Estimation

If we denote the conditional mean of y_t by $F(x_t; \theta)$, for example $F = \phi_1' x_t + (\phi_2 - \phi_1)' x_t G(y_{t-1}; \gamma, c))$ and $\theta = (\phi_1, \phi_2, \gamma, c)$ in the case of the STAR model in (9.2.3), then we can derive the parameter estimators $\hat{\theta}$ as the minimizers of the objective function:

$$\sum_{t=1}^{T}(y_t - F(x_t; \theta))^2 = \sum_{t=1}^{T} \varepsilon_t^2. \qquad (9.3.1)$$

This is the same objective function as the one we used in Chapter 1 to derive the OLS estimators for the linear regression model parameters. However, now an analytical solution is in general no longer available, so that the minimizers of (9.3.1) must be determined numerically.

The resulting estimators are called NLS, $\hat{\theta}_{NLS}$. Under mild conditions on the functional form F, which are satisfied for the case of STAR and TAR models, $\hat{\theta}_{NLS}$ is consistent and $\sqrt{T}\hat{\theta}_{NLS}$ has an asymptotically normal distribution, see, e.g., Gallant and White (1988) and White (2014).

In the case of TAR (or SETAR) models, a simpler estimation procedure is provided by conditional least squares. Indeed, conditioning on a given threshold variable and threshold value c, these models are linear, since for example $I(y_{t-1} > c)$ in (9.2.1) is just a dummy variable. Hence, we can obtain OLS estimators for $\phi = (\phi_{0,1}, \phi_{0,2}, \phi_{1,1}, \phi_{1,2})$. To highlight the dependence of ϕ on c let us use the notation $\hat{\phi}(c)$. For each choice of c and associated OLS estimators $\hat{\phi}(c)$, we can then estimate the variance of the error term, $\hat{\sigma}^2(c)$, using the standard formula. Finally, among a set of preselected values for c, we choose the one that minimizes $\hat{\sigma}^2(c)$, say $\hat{c}$, with associated estimators $\hat{\phi}(\hat{c})$ and $\hat{\sigma}^2(\hat{c})$.

Two issues that deserve attention in the case of STAR models are the choice of the starting values for the numerical optimization procedure underlying NLS, and the estimation of γ, the smoothing parameter.

To select proper starting values we can follow a grid search procedure similar to the one for the TAR model. First, we decide a set of values for γ and c, which form the grid. Then, we fix a value for γ and c, say $\bar{\gamma}$ and $\bar{c}$. Conditional on these values, the model becomes linear in ϕ_1 and ϕ_2, since $G(y_{t-1}; \gamma, c)$ is just a dummy variable, though with a logistic pattern. Hence, we can estimate ϕ_1 and ϕ_2 by OLS as

$$\hat{\phi}(\gamma, c) = (X_t' X_t)^{-1} X_t y_t, \qquad (9.3.2)$$

with $X_t = (x_t'(1 - G(y_{t-1}; \bar{\gamma}, \bar{c})),\ x_t' G(y_{t-1}; \bar{\gamma}, \bar{c}))$. Using the resulting residuals, we can calculate $\hat{\sigma}_\varepsilon^2(\bar{\gamma}, \bar{c})$. Next, we repeat the estimation for all the other values of γ and c in the grid. Finally, we select the values of γ and c as those with the minimum associated $\hat{\sigma}_\varepsilon^2(\gamma, c)$. The resulting values, say γ^*, c^*, $\hat{\phi}_1^*$, and $\hat{\phi}_2^*$ are used as starting values for the numerical optimization procedure that will deliver the NLS estimators of all the parameters.

About the estimation of the γ parameter, when γ is large the G function changes only a bit for changes in γ. More generally, a precise estimate of γ requires many observations around the threshold value c, which often are not available. Hence, in general, the standard errors of $\hat{\gamma}_{NLS}$ are very large, and the parameter is not statistically different from zero according to a $t-$test. Therefore, we could wrongly conclude that $\gamma = 0$ and the model is linear. Hence, it is better not to use a $t-$statistic for $\gamma = 0$ when interested in testing for linearity against STAR. The proper procedure will be described in the next section.

9.4   Testing for STAR and TAR

The problem of testing for a linear versus a STAR model is that under the null hypothesis, that can be written as $(\phi_2 - \phi_1)' = 0$ in (9.2.3), the parameters c and γ are unidentified, they can take any value. The null can also be written as $\gamma = 0$, but then c, ϕ_1 and ϕ_2 are unidentified. This problem – the presence of nuisance parameters under the null hypothesis – is well known in the literature and substantially complicates the derivation of the test statistics limiting distribution. Yet, it is possible to apply an alternative testing procedure with an asymptotic χ^2 distribution. To derive the test, let us rewrite the model in (9.2.3) as

$$y_t = \frac{1}{2}(\phi_1 + \phi_2)' x_t + (\phi_2 - \phi_1)' x_t G^*(q_t; \gamma, c) + \varepsilon_t, \qquad (9.4.1)$$

where $G^*(q_t; \gamma, c) = G(q_t; \gamma, c) - \frac{1}{2}$. Note that when $\gamma = 0$, $G^* = 0$. Then, let us approximate $G^*(q_t; \gamma, c)$ with a first order Taylor expansion around zero:

$$T_1(q_t; \gamma, c) \approx G^*(q_t; 0, c) + \gamma \left. \frac{\partial G^*(q_t; \gamma, c)}{\partial \gamma} \right|_{\gamma=0}$$

$$= \frac{\gamma}{4}(q_t - c),$$

since $G^*(q_t; 0, c) = 0$. Now, we substitute T_1 for G^* in (9.4.1) and reparamaterize the model as:

$$y_t = \alpha' + \beta' \tilde{x}_t + \delta' \tilde{x}_t q_t + u_t, \tag{9.4.2}$$

where $\tilde{x}_t = y_{t-1}$ ($\tilde{x}_t = y_{t-1}, ..., y_{t-p}$ if in the original model there were more lags), and the exact relationship between the parameters in (9.4.1) and (9.4.2) can be found in Franses and Van Dijk (2000) or Luukkonen, Saikkonen, and Teräsvirta (1988) who introduced this testing procedure.

Then, it can be shown that $\gamma = 0$ if and only if $\delta' = 0$. Therefore, we can use a standard F–statistic for $\delta' = 0$ to test linearity versus STAR, and the asymptotic distribution is χ_p^2, where p is the number of restrictions we are testing ($p = 1$ in the STAR(1) model considered).

The above test has no power when only the intercept changes across regimes. Luukkonen, Saikkonen, and Teräsvirta (1988) suggest this problem can be resolved by taking a third order instead of a first order expansion of G^*, which implies more variables in the "instrumental" regression (9.4.2).

Teräsvirta (1996) suggests using this test to also choose the transition variable from a pre-specified list. The idea is to select the variable minimizing the p-value when testing linearity versus STAR.

Finally, when the alternative hypothesis is TAR or SETAR, we can use an F–statistic to test for linearity, and we can write it as

$$F(c) = \frac{RSS_1 - RSS_2}{\hat{\sigma}_2^2(c)}, \tag{9.4.3}$$

where RSS_1 and RSS_2 are the residual sum of squares from, respectively, the linear and TAR models, and $\hat{\sigma}_2^2(c)$ is the residual variance from the TAR model for the threshold c.

Since the threshold is unknown, Hansen (1997) suggested to use the supremum among the F-statistics computed for all possible thresholds, i.e.,

$$F_s = \sup_{c_i \in C} F(c_i),$$

where C is the set of all possible values of the threshold. The distribution of F_s is not known analytically, but it can be computed using numerical techniques, see e.g., Hansen (2000) for details.

9.5   Diagnostic tests

Since the error terms in the TAR and STAR models still enter additively, the tests for homoskedasticity, no correlation, and normality that we discussed in Chapter 2 in the context of the linear regression model are in general still applicable. Note, however, that they only have an asymptotic justification, see Eitrheim and Teräsvirta (1996) for details and Franses and Van Dijk (2000) for some applications and a discussion of the additional complications arising from testing in the TAR case.

One test of interest is whether there exists an additional regime. The approach is similar to the one introduced above for linearity testing. Let us start from the model in (9.2.4). Then, we take a first-order expansion of G_2 around $\gamma_2 = 0$ and substitute it into the model to get:

$$y_t = \beta_0' x_t + (\phi_2 - \phi_1)' x_t G_1(q_{1t}; \gamma, c) + \beta_1' \tilde{x}_t q_{2t} + u_t, \qquad (9.5.1)$$

and we test for $\beta_1' = 0$. Again, Eitrheim and Teräsvirta (1996) provide additional details.

9.6   Forecasting

9.6.1   Point forecasts

Computing point forecasts and standard errors is much more involved with non-linear models. Let us assume for simplicity that y_t only depends on y_{t-1}, (more complex models can be treated along the same lines) and write the model in general form as

$$y_t = F(y_{t-1}; \theta) + \varepsilon_t,$$

where $\varepsilon_t \overset{iid}{\sim} (0, \sigma_\varepsilon^2)$ and $t = 1, \ldots, T$. Then, the optimal (in the MSFE sense) h-steps ahead forecast is

$$\hat{y}_{T+h} = E(y_{T+h} | I_T),$$

with $I_T = y_T$ in this case. For $h = 1$, the computation of $\hat{y}_{T+1}$ is simple since

$$\hat{y}_{T+1} = F(y_T; \theta),$$

or

$$\hat{y}_{T+1} = F(y_T; \hat{\theta}),$$

if the parameters θ are unknown. For $h = 2$, additional issues to consider arise. Even assuming that θ is known, we have:

$$\hat{y}_{T+2} = E[F(y_{T+1}; \theta)] \neq F(E[y_{T+1}]; \theta) = F(\hat{y}_{T+1}; \theta).$$

In other words, we can no longer use the simple iterative procedure for h-steps forecasting that we adopted in the context of linear models, where unknown future values were simply replaced by their forecasts. Of course we could use $\widetilde{y}_{T+2} = F(\hat{y}_{T+1}; \theta)$ as a two-steps ahead forecast, but in general it would be biased and certainly not optimal. The optimal two-steps ahead forecast is

$$
\begin{aligned}
\hat{y}_{T+2} &= E[F(F(y_T; \theta) + \varepsilon_{T+1}; \theta)|I_T] & (9.6.1)\\
&= E[F(\hat{y}_{T+1} + \varepsilon_{T+1}; \theta)|I_T]\\
&= \int F(\hat{y}_{T+1} + \varepsilon_{T+1}; \theta) f(\varepsilon) d\varepsilon.
\end{aligned}
$$

The main problem with the expression for $\hat{y}_{T+2}$ in (9.6.1) is that it is quite difficult to compute the integral analytically. As an alternative, we can use Monte Carlo or bootstrapping to approximate numerically the integral, obtaining:

$$\hat{y}_{T+2}^{(mc)} = \frac{1}{R} \sum_{i=1}^{R} F(\hat{y}_{T+1} + \varepsilon_i; \theta), \qquad (9.6.2)$$

where $\varepsilon_{i=1}^{R}$. We draw the entire distribution, not the individual ε_i. We can either drawn from a pre-specified distribution (Monte Carlo) or re-sampled from the in-sample estimated errors (bootstrap). In general, both approaches work rather well in empirical applications.

The computational problems increase with the forecast horizon. For example, to compute analytically $\hat{y}_{T+h}$ we should solve an $h - 1$ dimensional integral. In this case, even Monte Carlo or bootstrap methods become cumbersome, in particular when the forecast has to be computed recursively over many periods and/or for many variables. A further option to compute h-steps ahead forecasts from non-linear models is direct estimation. As we saw

in Chapter 5, direct estimation is based on a specification that directly relates y_t to the information available in period $t - h$, so that a one-step ahead
forecast from the direct model produces the required h-steps ahead forecast
for y. In the linear context, the direct model remains linear. Instead, in the
non-linear context in general the direct model should have a different functional form with respect to the starting model. However, in practice, when
constructing direct forecasts the same functional form is assumed, perhaps
allowing for a richer dynamic specification, so that the forecast error also
includes a component related to the functional form mis-specification. We
would therefore consider the specification

$$y_t = F(y_{t-h}; \eta) + u_t,$$

and construct the direct h-steps ahead forecast as $\tilde{y}_{T+h}^{(dir)} = F(y_T; \eta)$.

9.6.2   Interval forecasts

We have seen in Chapter 1 in the case of linear models with normal errors we can construct (symmetric) forecast intervals knowing that $y_{T+h} \sim$
$N(\hat{y}_{T+h}, \text{Var}(e_{T+h}))$. Specifically, we represented a $[1 - \alpha]\%$ forecast interval
as

$$\hat{y}_{T+h} - c_{\alpha/2}\sqrt{\text{Var}(e_{T+h})}; \hat{y}_{T+h} + c_{\alpha/2}\sqrt{\text{Var}(e_{T+h})}, \qquad (9.6.3)$$

where $c_{\alpha/2}$ is the $(\alpha/2)\%$ critical value for the standard normal density. A
similar procedure can be used in the context of non-linear models, with the
additional complication that the density function of y_{T+h} can be asymmetric
and even bimodal. Let us consider, for example, Figure 9.6.1, where a dot
indicates the point forecast and PF the corresponding value of the density.
There are now three alternative methods to construct an interval forecast.
First, we can use a symmetric interval (S) around the point forecast, containing y_{T+h} with a $(1 - \alpha)\%$ probability. Second, we can construct the interval
(Q) between the $\alpha/2$ and $(1 - \alpha)/2$ density quantiles. Finally, we can choose
the highest density region (HDR), namely, the smallest region containing
y_{T+h} with a $(1 - \alpha)\%$ probability. In practice, in Figure 9.6.1 we can draw
the horizontal line g_σ and move it downward until the integral of the density
over the intervals identified by the intersection of the horizontal line and the
density equals $(1 - \alpha)$. As the figure indicates, the HDR can be disjoint.

   The three intervals (S), (Q) and (HDR), which coincide in the normal
density case, can in general be rather different. Without specifying a loss

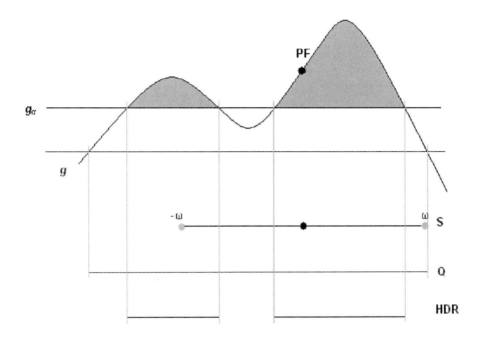

Figure 9.6.1: *Types of interval forecasts with a bimodal density for y_{T+h} : (S) is symmetric, (Q) is quantile based, (HDR) is highest density region*

function, there is no generally optimal choice of an interval forecasting strategy.

9.7 Artificial neural networks

Artificial neural network (ANN) models can provide a valid approximation for the generating mechanism of a vast class of non-linear processes, see e.g., Hornik, Stinchcombe, and White (1989) and Swanson and White (1997) for their use as forecasting devices. On the negative side, they are a kind of "black-box," whose parameters, and therefore forecasts, are hardly interpretable. To alleviate these issues, it is possible to add an ANN component to an otherwise linear model, so that the latter has the usual interpretation while the former captures possible non-linearities in the relationship between the dependent and independent variables.

A univariate single layer feed-forward neural network model with n_1 hidden units (and a linear component) is specified as

$$y_t = \zeta_{t-h}\beta_0 + \sum_{i=1}^{n_1} \gamma_{1i} G(\zeta_{t-h}\beta_{1i}) + \varepsilon_t, \qquad (9.7.1)$$

where y_t is the target variable, G is an activation function (typically the logistic function, $G(x) = 1/(1 + \exp(x))$), and $\zeta_t = (1, y_t, y_{t-1}, y_{t-p+1})$. In the ANN terminology, the variables in ζ_t are the inputs that enter the hidden layer represented by the activation functions $g(\zeta_{t-h}\beta_i)$ with connection strengths β_{1i} $i = 1, \ldots, n_1$, and through the weights γ_{1i} determine the output layer y.

The non-linear component of (9.7.1), namely $\sum_{i=1}^{n_1} \gamma_{1i} G(\zeta_{t-h}\beta_{1i})$ can be interpreted as a set of time-varying intercepts, whose time-variation is driven by the evolution of the logistic functions $G(\zeta_{t-h}\beta_{1i})$ $i = 1, \ldots, n_1$. For this reason, when n is large enough, the model can basically fit very well any type of temporal evolution.

Even more flexibility can be obtained with a double layer feed-forward neural network with n_1 and n_2 hidden units:

$$y_t = \zeta_{t-h}\beta_0 + \sum_{i=1}^{n_1} \gamma_{2i} G\left(\sum_{j=1}^{n_2} \beta_{2ji} G(\zeta_{t-h}\beta_{1i})\right) + \varepsilon_t,$$

Due to their high non-linearity, ANN models are estimated by non-linear least squares, but particular attention should be paid to the existence of multiple local minima.[1] While the parameters γ_{1i} and β_{1i}, $i = 1, \ldots, n_1$, generally do not have an economic meaning, a plot of the estimated non-linear component, $G(\zeta_{t-h}\beta_{1i})$ or $\sum_{i=1}^{n_1} \gamma_{2i} G\left(\sum_{j=1}^{n_2} \beta_{2ji} G(\zeta_{t-h}\beta_{1i})\right)$, can provide information on the type/shape of detected non-linearity. For example, it could indicate whether the ANN is capturing true non-linearities, such as changes in regimes, or just outliers or other anomalous effects. Standard diagnostic tests, with an asymptotic justification, can be applied to the residuals.

---

[1] An efficient estimation algorithm for macroeconomic forecasting applications was developed by Stock and Watson (1999). It also carefully considers the specification of starting values.

Note that the ANN models above are based on direct estimation (or direct forecasting). Iterative estimation is also feasible and can improve forecast accuracy, at the cost of increased computational complexity as multi-steps ahead forecasts require simulation methods, as discussed in Section 9.6.

Typically, various choices for n_1, n_2, and p are considered, with either information criteria used to select the preferred specification, or combination of the resulting forecasts. For example, Marcellino (2004a) and Marcellino (2004b) evaluate recursively the forecasting performance of a variety of non-linear and time-varying models for Euro area macroeconomic time series, and of combinations of them. For ANN, he reports results for the following specifications: $n_1 = 2$, $n_2 = 0$, $p = 3$; $n_1 = 2$, $n_2 = 1$, $p = 3$; $n_1 = 2$, $n_2 = 2$, $p = 3$; AIC or BIC selection with $n_1 = (1, 2, 3)$, $n_2 = (1, 2)$, $p = (1, 3)$. Recursive evaluation is relevant because, due to their flexibility, ANN are prone to overfitting. In practice, the dataset can be split into three subsets for, respectively, training/estimation, validation, and testing. The training set is used to adjust/estimate the weights of the network; the validation set is used to minimize the overfitting through proper choice of the specification. Finally, the testing set is used to assess the actual out-of-sample predictive power of the model.

In terms of empirical applications, the performance of ANN models is mixed for macroeconomic variables. For example, ANN models produce the best forecasts for about 20% of the many euro area variables considered by Marcellino (2004a) and Marcellino (2004b), with an even larger fraction for US variables in the analysis of Stock and Watson (1999), whose time series are much longer than those for the Euro area. However, sometimes the ANN can produce large forecast errors, typically due to estimation problems, in particular in short samples. Hence, their automated implementation requires the introduction of some "insanity filters," which trim forecasts that are too different from previously observed values, see e.g., Stock and Watson (1999) for an example.

It is worth mentioning that ANN models are also extensively used in the context of machine learning, for example in the context of deep learning, see e.g., Hinton and Salakhutdinov (2006). Deep learning has been mostly applied in the economic context for financial applications based on big data. For example, Giesecke, Sirignano, and Sadhwani (2016) use it to analyze mortgage risk using a dataset of over 120 million prime and subprime US mortgages between 1995 and 2014. Heaton, Polson, and Witte (2016) and Heaton, Polson, and Witte (2017) also employ neural networks in the context of portfolio theory.

The capacity of handling big datasets in a nearly fully automated way makes neural network-based methods, and more generally machine learning, appealing for specific applications, in particular in finance. Yet, a comparison with more traditional and user-driven approaches is generally suggested, to have a better understanding of the actual forecasting ability of ANN methods in a specific application. Finally, the interpretation of ANN-based forecasts and the analysis of the sources of forecast errors is generally difficult, due to the highly non-linear specification.

9.8   Example: Simulated data

For this example, simulated series are generated with either discontinuous or smooth transition between two states, i.e., adopting a TAR and STAR models respectively as DGP. Artificial series will be generated for both TAR and STAR models, separately. A unit threshold and only one lag are used for simplicity. In both cases, normally distributed homoskedastic errors are assumed. The TAR DGP is

$$y_t = (\theta_{0,1} + \theta_{1,1}y_{t-1})(1 - D_t) + (\theta_{0,2} + \theta_{1,2}y_{t-1})D_t + \varepsilon_t, \quad \varepsilon_t \overset{iid}{\sim} N(0, \sigma_\varepsilon)$$
$$D_t = I(y_{t-1} > 1)$$

with additional details about the parameters reported in Table 9.8.2. The STAR DGP is:

$$y_t = \theta_{0,1} + \theta_{1,1}y_{t-1} + (\theta_{0,2} + \theta_{1,2}y_{t-1})G(y_{t-1}; \gamma, c) + \varepsilon_t,$$
$$G(y_{t-1}; \gamma, c) = \frac{1}{1 + \exp\left(-\gamma\left(y_{t-1} - 1\right)\right)} \qquad \varepsilon_t \overset{iid}{\sim} N(0, \sigma_\varepsilon).$$

A sample of 600 observations is generated, the first 100 observations are discarded, and the last 100 observations are used to test the predictive power of the estimated models. The sample containing observations from 100 to 500 is called "estimation" sample, while the last 100 observations "forecasting" sample. The estimation models will resemble the DGP to avoid additional issues related to mis-specification.

9.8.1   Testing for linearity versus non-linearity

As working with non-linear models is rather complex as we have seen, it is important to test whether any non-linear model fits the data statistically

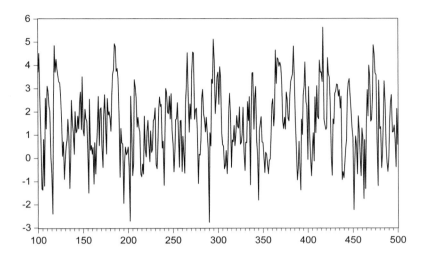

Figure 9.8.1: *Simulated series for TAR model*

better than a linear specification. To discriminate between a linear and a TAR model, we apply to the data simulated according to the TAR DGP the Hansen (1997) procedure described in Section 9.4. In this example we use the bootstrap method to simulate the distribution of the F_s statistic and to determine the acceptance (or rejection) region. For the simulated data, a 95% acceptance region of F_s for the null hypothesis of linearity is: [1.897751, 10.50999]. Since the outcome of the test is 54.92206, the linear specification is rejected in favor of the non-linear (TAR model).

In order to test for linearity versus the STAR model on the simulated STAR data, the procedure discussed in Section 9.4 is implemented, see Luukkonen, Saikkonen, and Teräsvirta (1988) or Van Dijk and Franses (1999) for more details. Specifically, we use an F-statistic to test for $\delta' = 0$ in the augmented model:

$$y_t = \alpha' + \beta'\widetilde{x}_t + \delta'\widetilde{x}_t q_t + u_t, \tag{9.8.1}$$

where $q_t = \frac{\gamma}{4}(y_{t-1} - c)$, $\widetilde{x}_t = y_{t-1}$, and for simplicity we us the true values of γ and c. Given that δ' is a scalar coefficient, a simple significance t test can be considered. The test outcome is presented in Table 9.8.1.

	Coefficient	Std. Error	t-Statistic	Prob.
ETA(1)	2.810	1.171	2.399	0.017
ETA(2)	0.586	0.201	2.916	0.004
DELTA(1)	-0.055	0.014	-3.834	0.000
R-squared	0.061	Mean dep var		6.151
Adjusted R-squared	0.056	S.D. dep var		1.149
S.E. of regression	1.116	Akaike IC		3.065
Sum squared resid	495.899	Schwarz IC		3.095
Log likelihood	-611.582	Hannan-Quinn		3.077
F-statistic	12.871	DW stat		1.962
Prob(F-statistic)	0.000			

Table 9.8.1: *Outcome of the augmented regression required for the linearity test on the simulated STAR data*

At the 1% confidence level the null hypothesis $\delta' = 0$ is rejected, i.e., there is significant evidence against the linear model and in favor of a STAR specification.

9.8.2   Estimation

Since analytical formulas for the parameter estimators of TAR and STAR models are not available, we need to apply numerical solution techniques to solve the NLS problem as discussed in section 9.3. For the TAR model, we proceed as follows:

- Step 1: Prepare a grid of M values for the threshold parameter, c in our notation.

- Step 2: In the loop for each iteration i, where $i = 1, .., M$, for each value c_i create a dummy variable D_i such that

$$D_i = I(y_{t-1} > c_i) \ for \ i = 1, .., M.$$

- Step 3: Using OLS, estimate the following model for each $i = 1, .., M$:

$$y_t = (\phi_{0,1} + \phi_{1,1}y_{t-1})(1 - D_i) + (\phi_{0,2} + \phi_{1,2}y_{t-1})D_i + \varepsilon_t, \ \varepsilon_t \overset{iid}{\sim} N(0, \sigma_\varepsilon).$$

- Step 4: For each i and resulting estimates of $\phi^i = (\phi_{0,1}, \phi_{0,2}, \phi_{1,1}, \phi_{1,2})$ find the variance of the error term, $\hat{\sigma}_\varepsilon^2(c_i)$.

- Step 5: Search for $c^* = \underset{\{c_i\}_{i=1}^M}{\arg\min}[\hat{\sigma}_\varepsilon^2(c_i)]$, namely, among the set of preselected values for c, we choose the one that minimizes $\hat{\sigma}_\varepsilon^2(c_i)$ as the estimator for c. The other estimated parameters ϕ^* are those associated with the value c^*.

The series is generated using an actual threshold parameter $c_{true} = c^* = 1$. Figure 9.8.1 depicts the simulated series. Following the steps of the algorithm described above, we create a grid of 200 values for the threshold parameter c in the interval $[-.05; 1.5]$. After going through Steps 2 to 5, we get the function of the estimated variance, $\hat{\sigma}_\varepsilon^2(c_i)$, in Figure 9.8.2. As a result of estimation, we then get the parameter values reported in Table 9.8.2. The resulting estimators are rather precise perhaps with the exception of $\phi_{0,2}$.

Parameter	True value (simulation)	Estimate
c	1	1
$\phi_{0,1}$	0.5	0.441
$\phi_{1,1}$	-0.3	-0.288
$\phi_{0,2}$	0.1	0.466
$\phi_{1,2}$	0.8	0.669

Table 9.8.2: *Results from estimates: estimated against true values (TAR)*

The numerical algorithm for the estimation of the STAR model is similar to the TAR counterpart, except that the additional smoothing parameter γ needs to be estimated. Therefore, the algorithm has the following steps:

- Step 1: Choose the appropriate grid for c, the threshold parameter, and γ, the smoothing parameter (of size M and K respectively);

- Step 2: For each combination of γ_i and c_j, where $i = 1, \ldots, K$ and $j = 1, \ldots, M$, calculate the function:

$$G^{i,j}(y_{t-1}; \gamma_i, c_j) = \frac{1}{1 + \exp(-\gamma_i(y_{t-1} - c_j))}.$$

- Step 3: Using OLS, estimate the following linear model:

$$y_t = \phi_{0,1} + \phi_{1,1}y_{t-1} + (\phi_{0,2} + \phi_{1,2}y_{t-1})G^{ij}(y_{t-1}; \gamma_i, c_j) + \varepsilon_t, \ \varepsilon_t \overset{iid}{\sim} N(0, \sigma_\varepsilon).$$

- Step 4: For each pair of γ_i and c_j and resulting estimates of the parameters ϕ, calculate the variance of the error term, $\hat{\sigma}^2(\gamma_i, c_j)$;

- Step 5: Among all pairs of γ_i and c_j choose the one that minimizes $\hat{\sigma}^2(\gamma_i, c_j)$, i.e., find $(\gamma^*, c^*) = \arg\min_{\{\gamma_i, c_j\}_{i.j}}[\hat{\sigma}^2(\gamma_i, c_j)]$. The ϕ^* parameters are those associated with γ^*, c^*.

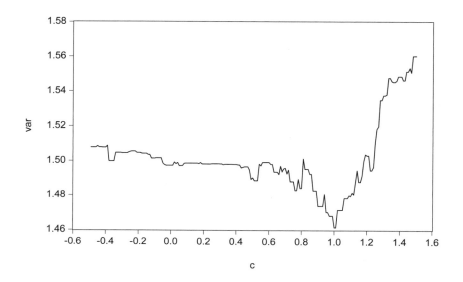

Figure 9.8.2: *Variance of residuals for different values of* c_i

The simulated series using the STAR model as DGP is represented in Figure 9.8.3. As for the estimation, we obtain the parameter values reported in Table 9.8.3.

From Table 9.8.3, it turns out that the estimated values are rather close to the true ones, except for the smoothing parameter γ. This is unfortunately a common result in practice as already noted in section 9.3, as precise estimation of γ requires a very long sample and a finer grid for c and γ.

9.8.3   Forecasting

For the forecasting exercise, the "forecasting" sample containing the last 100 observations (of the simulated 600 observations) is considered. The optimal

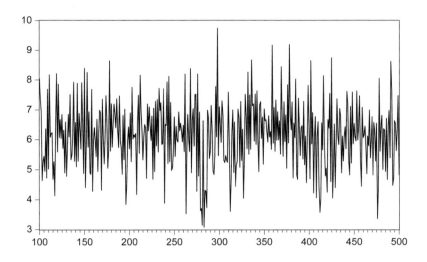

Figure 9.8.3: *Simulated series for STAR*

(in the MSFE terms) h-steps ahead forecast for the non-linear model is:

$$\hat{y}_{T+h} = E\left(y_{T+h}|I_T\right),$$

where $y_t = F(y_{t-1}; \theta) + \varepsilon_t$. In the special case $h = 1$, we then get:

$$\hat{y}_{T+1} = F(y_t; \hat{\theta}),$$

which can be computed analytically.

For the TAR model, the vector of parameters is $\theta = (c; \phi_{0,1}, \phi_{0,2}, \phi_{1,1}, \phi_{1,2})$. Then, the one-step ahead forecast can be computed as:

$$\hat{y}_{T+1} = (\phi_{0,1}^* + \phi_{1,1}^* y_T)(1 - I(y_T > c^*)) + (\phi_{0,2}^* + \phi_{1,2}^* y_T)I(y_T > c^*).$$

For the STAR model, the vector of parameters is $\theta = (c, y; \phi_{0,1}, \phi_{0,2}, \phi_{1,1}, \phi_{1,2})$. Then, the one-step ahead STAR forecast is:

$$y_{t+1} = \phi_{0,1}^* + \phi_{1,1}^* y_t + (\phi_{0,2}^* + \phi_{1,2}^* y_t)G(y_t; \gamma^*, c^*).$$

The one-step ahead (recursive) forecasts for the TAR model are presented in Figure 9.8.4, in comparison with a linear AR(1) specification as benchmark.

Parameter	True value (simulation)	Estimate
c	6	6
γ	5	8.6
$\phi_{0,1}$	2	1.97
$\phi_{1,1}$	0.9	0.9103
$\phi_{0,2}$	3	3.7815
$\phi_{1,2}$	-0.8	-0.9099

Table 9.8.3: *Results from estimates: estimated against true values (STAR)*

The one-step ahead (recursive) STAR forecasts are presented in Figure 9.8.5, including the corresponding AR(1) benchmark forecasts. In both cases, from a graphical inspection, the non-linear forecasts track the actual values more closely than the linear counterparts. However, to have a precise grasp of the forecasting performance of these non-linear models, some diagnostics have been computed: the TAR forecasts obtained a RMSFE of 1.08525 against a RMSFE of 1.2266 of the linear AR(1) benchmark; the STAR forecasts obtained a RMSFE of 0.9596 against 1.04395 of the linear benchmark. In both cases the non-linear models prove themselves to better perform with respect to a linear model, when tested on simulated data with non-linear DGP.

9.8.4   Two-steps ahead forecasting

Performing non-linear forecasting for $h > 1$ is more complex than in the linear case. Indeed, as discussed in Section 9.6, the linear properties of the expectation operator no longer apply. For this reason, the computation of the correct conditional expectation requires some integration. Specifically, the following procedure generates a simulation based two-steps ahead forecast for the TAR and STAR models.

Let us assume that we are in observation T, and estimate the model parameters $\hat{\theta}$ using the sample $1, \ldots, T$ (where the model is either TAR or STAR). Next, we compute the one-step ahead forecast as discussed above, namely,

$$E[y_{T+1}|I_T] = E[F(y_T; \hat{\theta}) + \varepsilon_{T+1}|I_T] = F(y_T; \hat{\theta}).$$

Then, we have

$$E[y_{T+2}|I_T] = E[F(y_{T+1}; \hat{\theta}) + \varepsilon_{T+2}|I_T] = E[F(F(y_T; \hat{\theta}) + \varepsilon_{T+1}; \hat{\theta})|I_T].$$

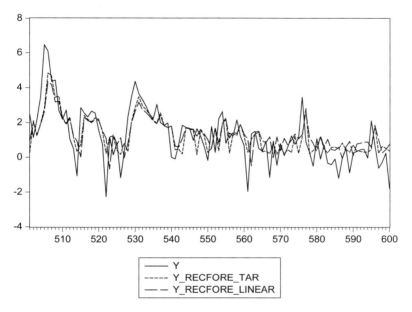

Figure 9.8.4: *One-step ahead forecast comparison: TAR model against AR(1)*

Given a distributional assumption on ε_{T+1}, such as $\varepsilon_{T+1} \sim N\left(0, \sigma_\varepsilon^2\right)$, it is possible to simulate the distribution for y_{T+1} by generating random errors from $N\left(0, \hat{\sigma}_\varepsilon^2\right)$, where $\hat{\sigma}_\varepsilon^2$ is the in-sample estimate, obtaining an empirical distribution of $y_{T+1} = F(y_T; \hat{\theta}) + \varepsilon_{T+1}$. Hence, for a given value y_{T+1}^i of the empirical distribution of y_{T+1}, the non-linear two-steps ahead forecast is $\hat{y}_{T+2}^i = F(y_{T+1}^i; \hat{\theta})$. Repeating this procedure for all the values y_{T+1}^i, $i = 1, \ldots,$ B, generates an empirical distribution for the two-steps forecast, $\left(\hat{y}_{T+2}^i\right)_{i=1}^B$. Finally, the sample average of $\left(\hat{y}_{T+2}^i\right)_{i=1}^B$ can be used to approximate the optimal two-steps forecast $E[y_{T+2}|I_T]$:

$$\hat{y}_{T+2}^{sim} \approx E[y_{T+2}|I_T] = \frac{1}{B}\sum_{i=0}^{B}\hat{y}_{T+2}^i.$$

A simpler possibility is to compute the two-steps forecast by simply iterating the non-linear operator without any integration, that is,

$$\hat{y}_{T+2}^{plain} = F\left(F(y_T; \hat{\theta}); \hat{\theta}\right).$$

As we have discussed in the theory part, $\hat{y}_{T+2}^{plain}$ is generally biased due to the

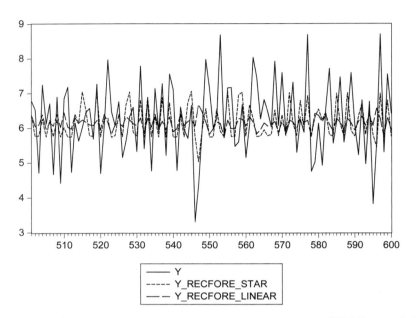

Figure 9.8.5: *One-step ahead forecast comparison: STAR model against AR(1)*

non-linearity of the F function.

A third alternative is to use the direct forecasting technique, again described in Section 9.5. This implies estimating the non-linear model using only the second lag both in the switching function and in the equation, so that the non-linear operator depends already on the twice lagged variable, and the forecast is simply

$$\hat{y}_{T+2}^{dir} = F_2(y_T; \hat{\theta}),$$

where $F_2(\cdot)$ is the non-linear operator that depends directly on the two-steps lagged information. Unfortunately, $\hat{y}_{T+2}^{dir}$ is also generally biased, as the direct model assumes the same functional relationship F as in the original model, but this is in general incorrect as in this case the original model is not linear.

The three types of two-steps ahead forecasts (optimal, plain, and direct) are computed and compared using the last 100 simulated data. Using the artificial series generated by the TAR DGP, we get the outcome reported in Figure 9.8.6 and Table 9.8.4. According to the RMSFE and in line with theory, the simulation based two-steps forecast is the best performing, followed by the direct forecast, and then the plain forecast and that resulting from the linear benchmark.

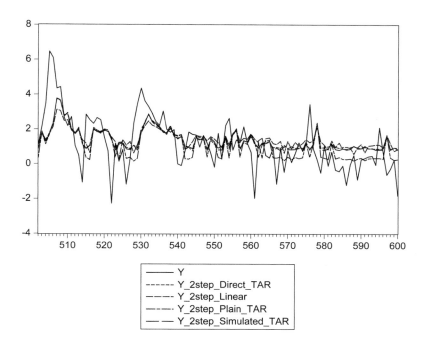

Figure 9.8.6: *Two-steps ahead forecasts from TAR versus actual data*

Model	RMSFE
Linear	1.393
TAR, simulated	1.344
TAR, direct	1.354
TAR, plain	1.371

Table 9.8.4: *Root mean square errors of two-steps ahead forecasts (TAR vs. Linear)*

The same exercise performed for the STAR DGP data gives the results presented in Figure 9.8.7 and Table 9.8.5.

As in the TAR case, the simulation based forecast is the best performer, but now the linear forecast wins over the direct method.

Model	RMSFE
Linear	1.072
STAR, simulated	1.060
STAR, direct	1.084
STAR, plain	1.183

Table 9.8.5: *Root mean square errors of two-steps ahead forecasts (STAR vs. Linear)*

9.9   Example: Forecasting industrial production growth

To perform a real data exercise, we consider the growth rate for the United States industrial production index downloaded from the FRED database. The full quarterly sample available in the database covers more than eight decades, from 1930Q1 to 2014Q4. A longer sample is useful to detect non-linearities in the data. Therefore, the estimation sample is set to start in 1930Q1 and end in 2000Q1, while the forecasting sample covers the period from 2000Q2 to 2014Q4. Figure 9.9.1 presents the data in both estimation and forecasting samples. The first step of the analysis is to determine whether a TAR model is more appropriate than a linear model. To do so we use the Hansen's sup-LR test.

The benchmark linear specification for the growth rate of US industrial production is set to be an AR(2) specification. Therefore the TAR/STAR specification is adapted to have two lags and two regimes, the regime depending only on the first lag as for the simulated data. The estimated AR(2) appears in Table 9.9.1.

To test the linear specification versus the TAR model, we need to determine the grid for the threshold parameter. Since using real data the true threshold parameter is unknown, in general the range of possible values should be wide enough to cover reasonable values. Moreover, economic considerations could help. For example, as we could imagine the dynamics of industrial production growth differs in expansions and recessions, we use the interval $[-1.00; 4.00]$, and construct a grid of 200 points.

The Hansen's sup-LR test produces an F sup equal to 56.9106. Using the bootstrap procedure described above, it is possible to build the distribution of the F sup statistic under the hypothesis of linearity. According

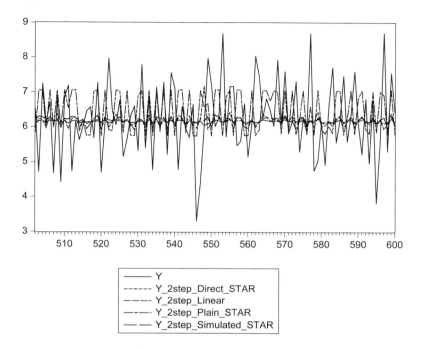

Figure 9.8.7: *Two-steps ahead forecasts from STAR versus actual data*

Variable	Coefficient	Std. Error	t-Statistic	Prob.
C	0.703	0.239	2.939	0.004
Y(-1)	0.400	0.060	6.667	0.000
Y(-2)	-0.079	0.060	-1.316	0.189
R-squared	0.143	Mean dep var		1.030
Adjusted R-squared	0.137	S.D. dep var		4.128
S.E. of regression	3.836	Akaike IC		5.537
Sum squared resid	4060.311	Schwarz IC		5.576
Log likelihood	-769.437	Hannan-Quinn		5.553
F-statistic	23.039	DW stat		1.957
Prob(F-statistic)	0.000			

Table 9.9.1: *Estimation output for an AR(2) model*

to the simulated distribution, a 95% confidence interval for the F sup is [4.106512, 17.88015]. Therefore, it is possible to reject linearity; the test pro-

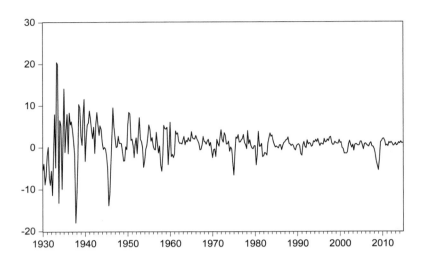

Figure 9.9.1: *Series for industrial production*

vides enough evidence that the TAR model better describes the data when compared with the linear AR(2) model.

Performing the estimation of the TAR model, the variance of the residuals is minimized among the grid of possible threshold values. These variances are plotted in Figure 9.9.2 as a function of the threshold, while the full estimation results for the model

$$y_t = (\phi_{0,1} + \phi_{1,1}y_{t-1} + \phi_{2,1}y_{t-2})(1 - D_i) + (\phi_{0,2} + \phi_{1,2}y_{t-1} + \phi_{2,2}y_{t-2})D_i + \varepsilon_t$$

are presented in Table 9.9.2. The variance is minimized at the threshold $c = 2.375$ (which is larger than zero as on average over the sample average industrial production growth was indeed around 1). We also note that there is a substantial increase in the adjusted R^2 with respect to the linear case, from about 0.14 to about 0.25.

As for the STAR model, estimation is conducted as illustrated with the simulated data. The model with two lags and two regimes is given by

$$
\begin{aligned}
y_t \;=\; & \phi_{0,1} + \phi_{1,1}y_{t-1} + \phi_{2,1}y_{t-2} + \\
& (\phi_{0,2} + \phi_{1,2}y_{t-1} + \phi_{2,2}y_{t-2})G^{ij}(y_{t-1}; \gamma_i, c_j) + \varepsilon_t, \ \varepsilon_t \overset{iid}{\sim} N(0, \sigma_\varepsilon).
\end{aligned}
$$

Variable	Coefficient	Std. Error	t-Statistic	Prob.
C	0.450	0.254	1.773	0.077
DUMMY_C_EST(-1)	2.912	0.835	3.489	0.001
Y(-1)*DUMMY_C_EST(-1)	0.200	0.125	1.601	0.111
Y(-1)*(1-DUMMY_C_EST(-1))	0.367	0.084	4.355	0.000
Y(-2)*DUMMY_C_EST(-1)	-0.532	0.093	-5.711	0.000
Y(-2)*(1-DUMMY_C_EST(-1))	0.165	0.069	2.385	0.018
R-squared	0.267	Mean dep var		1.030
Adjusted R-squared	0.253	S.D. dep var		4.128
S.E. of regression	3.567	Akaike infocriterion		5.403
Sum squared resid	3474.043	Schwarz IC		5.481
Log likelihood	-747.684	Hannan-Quinn		5.434
F-statistic	19.868	DW stat		1.847
Prob(F-statistic)	0.000			

Table 9.9.2: *Estimation output for a TAR model*

Differently from the TAR model, the variance is minimized for boundary grid values of the γ and c parameters, reaching $\gamma = 0.2$ and $c = 4$. This is probably due to the fact that the estimation is trying to smooth further between the two regimes and simultaneously to polarize the regimes, implying that probably a higher number of regimes would be needed. The results of the estimation is contained in Table 9.9.3. There is a further increase in the adjusted R^2, to about 0.28, and the information criteria are generally lower than for the TAR model (and for the linear specification).

Having estimated the two models, a recursive forecasting exercise is performed using the TAR, the STAR, and the linear AR(2) specifications. Graphical results are displayed in figure 9.9.3 for the case $h = 1$.

From a graphical inspection it seems that the linear model has a poorer forecasting performance during the crisis, when compared with the non-linear models. Table 9.9.4 compares the RMSFEs for the different models and shows the p-values resulting from a Diebold-Mariano test. It turns out the RMSFE of the TAR and STAR models are lower than the AR(2) specification. However, we never reject the null hypothesis of same forecasting accuracy for each pair of models.

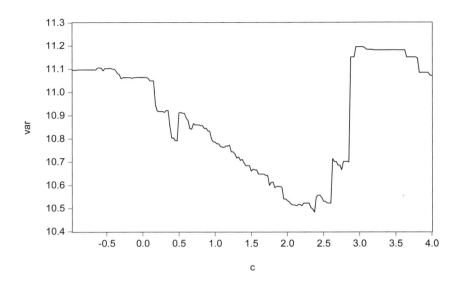

Figure 9.9.2: *Variance of residuals for different threshold values in the grid*

Variable	Coefficient	Std. Error	t-Statistic	Prob.
C	-1.962	2.046	-0.959	0.338
G_EST	8.913	6.235	1.430	0.154
(1-G_EST)*Y(-1)	0.189	0.196	0.962	0.337
G_EST*Y(-1)	0.153	0.287	0.534	0.594
(1-G_EST)*Y(-2)	0.382	0.086	4.426	0.000
G_EST*Y(-2)	-1.004	0.141	-7.141	0.000
R-squared	0.294	Mean dep var		1.030
Adjusted R-squared	0.281	S.D. dep var		4.128
S.E. of regression	3.502	Akaike IC		5.366
Sum squared resid	3347.206	Schwarz IC		5.444
Log likelihood	-742.495	Hannan-Quinn		5.397
F-statistic	22.690	DW stat		1.817
Prob(F-statistic)	0.000			

Table 9.9.3: *Estimation output for STAR model*

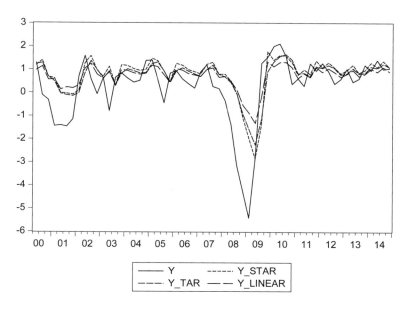

Figure 9.9.3: *One-step ahead forecast comparison: AR(2), TAR, and STAR versus actual data*

	RMSFE	p- value	
		AR	TAR
AR	1.167	-	0.18
TAR	1.112	0.18	-
STAR	1.113	0.26	0.48

Table 9.9.4: *Root mean square errors and Diebold-Mariano tests for AR, TAR, and STAR.*

9.10 Concluding remarks

In this chapter we have discussed forecasting with non-linear models, focusing on two interesting types of specifications characterized by time-varying parameters. In TAR models, the parameters change abruptly over time when a threshold variable reaches a threshold value. In STAR models the same happens, but the transition from the old to the new parameter values is smoother. Estimation of TAR and STAR models requires the use of non-linear least squares, with starting values generally obtained from a proper grid search. Testing for linearity versus TAR or STAR is complicated by the presence of nuisance parameters, but simple procedures to address this problem can be designed. Finally, multi-steps point forecasting with non-linear models is complicated, as well as the derivation of interval forecasts, but simulation based methods can be applied. Empirically, they seem to work fairly well, according to the results we obtained with both simulated and actual data.

Chapter 10

Markov Switching Models

10.1 Introduction

Econometric models in a time series context are subject to parameters instability, for a variety of reasons. Therefore, a constant parameter model, which does not allow for any change of parameters across time, can lead to substantial estimation bias and a poor forecasting performance.

Let us consider as an example the model

$$y_t = (\phi_{01} + \phi_{11} y_{t-1}) S_t + (\phi_{02} + \phi_{12} y_{t-1})(1 - S_t) + \varepsilon_t, \qquad (10.1.1)$$

where $\varepsilon_t \sim iid\ N(0, \sigma^2)$ and $S_t \in \{0, 1\}$. This is an AR(1) whose coefficients are either ϕ_{01} and ϕ_{11} or ϕ_{02} and ϕ_{12}, depending on the value (also called regime) of the binary variable S_t.

If the values of S_t are known, we can just use S_t as a dummy variable, as we have seen in Chapter 2. However, often the values of S_t are not known, either in sample or, more importantly from a forecasting perspective, out of sample.

If S_t is not known but depends on observable variables, we can use a specification similar to that used in the previous chapter for the TAR model, e.g., $S_t = I(y_{t-1} > c)$, where c is an unknown threshold value. We can also allow for a more general form of parameter transition, as e.g., in the STAR model, where $S_t = G(y_{t-1}; \gamma, c)$.

If S_t is not observable, we need to make assumptions about its generating mechanism. If S_t is a continuous variable, we could for example assume that it follows an AR model, as will be further discussed in the next chapter. If instead, as in (10.1.1), S_t is a discrete binary variable, the simplest hypothesis is to assume that S_t is a Markov chain. This is the case we will consider in this chapter, as it underlies an important class of time varying parameter models, known as Markov Switching (MS) models.

The chapter is structured as follows. In Section 10.2, we review some basic notions about Markov chains. In Section 10.3 we consider the case where $\phi_{11} = \phi_{12} = 0$ (i.e., y_t is a mixture of i.i.d. distributions with different means, ϕ_{01} and ϕ_{02}). In Section 10.4 we discuss the more general dynamic case, with a focus on forecasting. In Sections 10.5 and 10.6 we present examples using, respectively simulated and actual data. Conclusions appear in Section 10.7. For additional details and generalizations, see Hamilton (1994, Chapter 22), which is the main reference for the theoretical framework adopted in this chapter.

10.2   Markov chains

Let us consider the random variable S_t that takes integer values $\{1, 2, \ldots, N\}$. From an economic point of view, the states of S_t (or regimes) could describe for example the unobservable conditions of the economy, e.g., expansion ($S_t = 1$) or recession ($S_t = 0$), or whether the central bank is credible or not, or a high-, medium-, or low-risk level in the financial sector.

Let us assume that

$$P\{S_t = j | S_{t-1} = i, S_{t-2} = k, \ldots\} = P\{S_t = j | S_{t-1} = i\} = p_{ij}, \quad (10.2.1)$$

so that only the previous state influences the probability of the following state. S_t is then called an N-state Markov chain, with transition probabilities $\{p_{ij}\}_{i,j=1,\ldots,N}$, where p_{ij} is the probability that state i will be followed by state j. Note that

$$p_{i1} + p_{i2} + \ldots + p_{iN} = 1.$$

Let us group the transition probabilities into the transition matrix P :

$$P = \begin{bmatrix} p_{11} & p_{21} & \cdots & p_{N1} \\ p_{12} & p_{22} & \cdots & p_{N2} \\ \cdots & & & \\ p_{1N} & p_{2N} & \cdots & p_{NN} \end{bmatrix} \quad (10.2.2)$$

Let us now define the vector ξ_t as

$$\underset{N\times 1}{\xi_t} = \begin{cases} (1,0,\ldots,0)' & \text{if } S_t = 1 \\ (0,1,\ldots,0)' & \text{if } S_t = 2 \\ \vdots \\ (0,0,\ldots,1)' & \text{if } S_t = N \end{cases} \tag{10.2.3}$$

Note that

$$E(\xi_t) = \begin{pmatrix} 1*P\{S_t = 1\} + 0*P\{S_t = 2\} + \ldots + 0*P\{S_t = N\} \\ 0*P\{S_t = 1\} + 1*P\{S_t = 2\} + \ldots + 0*P\{S_t = N\} \\ \vdots \\ 0*P\{S_t = 1\} + 0*P\{S_t = 2\} + \ldots + 1*P\{S_t = N\} \end{pmatrix}$$

$$= \begin{pmatrix} P\{S_t = 1\} \\ P\{S_t = 2\} \\ \vdots \\ P\{S_t = N\} \end{pmatrix} = \begin{pmatrix} \pi_1 \\ \pi_2 \\ \vdots \\ \pi_N \end{pmatrix} \tag{10.2.4}$$

where the vector $\pi = (\pi_1, \ldots, \pi_N)'$ contains the unconditional probabilities of the states. Similarly,

$$E(\xi_{t+1}|S_t = i) = \begin{pmatrix} p_{i1} \\ p_{i2} \\ \ldots \\ p_{iN} \end{pmatrix},$$

so that $E(\xi_{t+1}|S_t = i)$ is equal to the ith column of the transition matrix P.

Moreover, when $S_t = i$, $\xi_t = (0,0,\ldots,1,0,\ldots,0)'$, which is the ith column of I_N. Therefore, we can write

$$E(\xi_{t+1}|\xi_t) = P\xi_t.$$

For example,

$$\begin{aligned} E(\xi_{t+1}|S_t &= 1) = E(\xi_{t+1}|(1,0,\ldots,0)') \\ &= \begin{bmatrix} P_{11} & P_{21} & \ldots & P_{N1} \\ P_{12} & P_{22} & \ldots & P_{N2} \\ \ldots & & & \\ P_{1N} & P_{2N} & \ldots & P_{NN} \end{bmatrix} \begin{bmatrix} 1 \\ 0 \\ \ldots \\ 0 \end{bmatrix} = \begin{bmatrix} P_{11} \\ P_{12} \\ \ldots \\ P_{1N} \end{bmatrix}. \end{aligned}$$

From the Markov property,

$$P(S_{t+1} = i | S_t = j, S_{t-1} = k, \ldots) = P(S_{t+1} | S_t = j),$$

it follows that

$$E(\xi_{t+1} | \xi_t, \xi_{t-1}, \ldots) = P\xi_t.$$

As a consequence, we can write

$$
\begin{aligned}
\xi_{t+1} &= P\xi_t + \upsilon_{t+1}, \\
\upsilon_{t+1} &= \xi_{t+1} - E(\xi_{t+1} | \xi_t, \xi_{t-1}, \ldots).
\end{aligned}
\tag{10.2.5}
$$

In other words, ξ_{t+1} follows a VAR(1) process, and υ_{t+1} is a (zero mean) one-step ahead forecast error. Using the standard formula for VARs, it follows that

$$E(\xi_{t+m} | \xi_t, \xi_{t-1}, \ldots) = P^m \xi_t, \tag{10.2.6}$$

and since the jth element of $\xi_{t+m} = 1$ only if $S_{t+m} = j \ (= 0$ otherwise), the jth element of $E(\xi_{t+m} | \xi_t, \xi_{t-1}, \ldots)$ indicates the probability that the system will be in state j in period $t + m$ conditional on the state in period t.

An implication of this result is that the $m-$period ahead transition matrix is given by P^m. For example, $P(S_{t+m} = 2 | S_t = 1)$ is the $(2, 1)$ element of P^m.

Finally, we derive a formula that links the conditional and unconditional transition probabilities. Taking unconditional expectations of the VAR representation for ξ_{t+1} yields

$$E(\xi_{t+1}) = PE(\xi_t) + E(\upsilon_{t+1}),$$

and, using (10.2.4) and (10.2.5), we have

$$\pi = P\pi.$$

Moreover, defining $i' = (1, 1, \ldots, 1)$, it holds that

$$i'\pi = 1.$$

Therefore, we can write

$$\underset{N+1 \times N}{\begin{bmatrix} I_N - P \\ i' \end{bmatrix}} \underset{N \times 1}{\pi} = \begin{bmatrix} 0_N \\ 1 \end{bmatrix}$$

or

$$A\pi_{N+1\times N} = \begin{bmatrix} 0_N \\ 1 \end{bmatrix},$$

and hence

$$Pr\begin{pmatrix} S_t = 1 \\ S_t = 2 \\ \ldots \\ S_t = N \end{pmatrix} = \pi = (A'A)^{-1}A'\begin{bmatrix} 0_N \\ 1 \end{bmatrix}, \tag{10.2.7}$$

which is a convenient formula to compute the unconditional probabilities of each state from the conditional probabilities in P (which is contained in A).

10.3 Mixture of i.i.d. distributions

Before discussing the general dynamic case, let us consider in details the simplest model whose parameters change with the unobservable discrete random variable S_t, which in turn follows a Markov chain. Let us assume that

$$y_t = \mu_{S_t} + \varepsilon_t, \tag{10.3.1}$$

with $\varepsilon_t \sim N(0, \sigma_{S_t}^2)$ and $S_t = \{1, 2, \ldots, N\}$. In this case

$$f(y_t | S_t = j; \theta) = \frac{1}{\sqrt{2\pi\sigma_j^2}} exp\left\{-\frac{(y_t - \mu_j)^2}{2\sigma_j^2}\right\}, \tag{10.3.2}$$

for $j = 1, \ldots, N$, with $\theta = \{\mu_1, \ldots, \mu_N, \sigma_1^2, \ldots, \sigma_N^2\}$. Let us also assume that

$$P\{S_t = j; \theta\} = \pi_j$$

$j = 1, \ldots, N$, so that now $\theta = \{\mu_1, \ldots, \mu_N, \sigma_1^2, \ldots, \sigma_N^2, \pi_1, \ldots, \pi_N\}$.

Since $f(x, y) = f(x|y)f(y)$, we have that the joint density of y_t and S_t is

$$\begin{aligned} P(y_t, S_t = j; \theta) &= f(y_t | S_t = j; \theta)P(S_t = j; \theta) \tag{10.3.3} \\ &= \frac{\pi_j}{\sqrt{2\pi\sigma_j^2}} exp\left\{-\frac{(y_t - \mu_j)^2}{2\sigma_j^2}\right\}. \end{aligned}$$

To obtain the marginal density of y_t, we integrate out S_t,

$$f(y_t; \theta) = \sum_{j=1}^{N} P(y_t, S_t = j; \theta). \tag{10.3.4}$$

This is the relevant density to describe the actual data, since the regime S_t is unobserved. It can also be used to construct the likelihood function, as we will see later on.

Another quantity of interest is the probability that a given regime was responsible for producing the observation y_t (e.g., expansion or recession). Again using the formula for conditional probabilities, we have

$$P(S_t = j|y_t; \theta) \;=\; \frac{P(y_t, S_t = j; \theta)}{f(y_t; \theta)} \qquad (10.3.5)$$
$$=\; \frac{\pi_j f(y_t|S_t = j; \theta)}{f(y_t; \theta)}.$$

With this formula we can make (probabilistic) statements about the unobservable variable S_t given the observable variable y_t. For example, we could say what is the probability of being in a recession given an observed level of GDP growth, or what is the probability that the central bank is credible given a certain discrepancy between long-term inflation expectations and the inflation target.

All the distributions we have considered so far are known, assuming that θ is known. Since in practice θ is not known, we now consider how it can be estimated. Applying the chain rule, the log likelihood function for the observed data is

$$\mathcal{L}(\theta) = \sum_{t=1}^{T} log(f(y_t; \theta)). \qquad (10.3.6)$$

Therefore, the maximum likelihood estimator (MLE) for θ solves

$$\hat{\theta} \;\equiv\; \underset{\theta}{\mathrm{argmax}} \mathcal{L}(\theta)$$
$$s.t. \; \sum_{j=1}^{N} \pi_j = 1, \; \pi_j \geq 0, \quad j = 1, \ldots, N.$$

The first order conditions (F.O.C.) are (see e.g., Hamilton (1994, Appendix to Chapter 22)) for $j = 1, \ldots, N$:

$$(F1): \quad \hat{\mu}_j = \sum_{t=1}^{T} y_t \frac{P(S_t = j | y_t; \hat{\theta})}{\sum_{t=1}^{T} P(S_t = j | y_t; \hat{\theta})}, \qquad (10.3.7)$$

$$(F2): \quad \hat{\sigma}_j^2 = \sum_{t=1}^{T} (y_t - \hat{\mu}_j)^2 \frac{P(S_t = j | y_t; \hat{\theta})}{\sum_{t=1}^{T} P(S_t = j | y_t; \hat{\theta})}, \qquad (10.3.8)$$

$$(F3): \quad \hat{\pi}_j = T^{-1} \sum_{t=1}^{T} P(S_t = j | y_t; \hat{\theta}). \qquad (10.3.9)$$

These F.O.C. have an intuitive interpretation. Consider the expression for $\hat{\mu}_j$. With one regime only, we would estimate μ as $\hat{\mu} = \sum_{t=1}^{T} y_t / T$. If $\mu = \mu_1$ for $t = 1, \ldots, T_1$ and $\mu = \mu_2$ for $t = T_1 + 1, \ldots, T$, we would use $\hat{\mu}_1 = \sum_{t=1}^{T_1} y_t / T_1$ and $\hat{\mu}_2 = \sum_{t=T_1+1}^{T} y_t / (T - T_1)$. Here, in $(F1)$, we take the weighted average of the observed y_t, where the weights are proportional to the probability that regime j is responsible for observation y_t, $t = 1, \ldots, T$.

A similar interpretation holds for $\hat{\sigma}_j^2$ in $(F2)$, while $\hat{\pi}_j$ in $(F3)$, the unconditional probability $P(S_t = j | \theta)$, is obtained by averaging the probabilities conditional on y_t.

The F.O.C. are a system of $3N$ non-linear equations in $3N$ unknowns, $\hat{\theta} = (\hat{\mu}_j, \hat{\sigma}_j^2, \hat{\pi}_j, j = 1, \ldots, N)$. To solve them, one could use either a numerical method, or the following iterative algorithm.

- First, start with a guess for $\hat{\theta}$, say $\theta^{(1)}$. With $\theta^{(1)}$, calculate $P(S_t = j | y_t; \theta^{(1)})$ from (11.2.1). Using these quantities and $\theta^{(1)}$, get $\theta^{(2)} = (\hat{\mu}_j, \hat{\sigma}_j^2, \hat{\pi}_j)_{j=1}^{N}$ from the F.O.C.

- Second, use $\theta^{(2)}$ to compute $P(S_t = j | y_t; \theta^{(2)})$ and $\theta^{(3)} = (\hat{\mu}_j, \hat{\sigma}_j^2, \hat{\pi}_j)_{j=1}^{N}$ from the F.O.C.

- Next, keep iterating until the difference between $\theta^{(m+1)}$ and $\theta^{(m)}$ is smaller than some specified value.

This algorithm is a special case of the Expectation Maximization (EM) algorithm of Dempster, Laird, and Rubin (1977).

10.4 Markov switching dynamic models

Let us now consider the general case where y_t depends on its own lags, on a set of exogenous variables x and their lags, and the dependence varies in different regimes. Let us group all the observations on y and x up to period t into

$$Y_t = (y_t, y_{t-1}, \ldots, x'_t, x'_{t-1}, \ldots)'.$$

If at date t the system is in regime j, the conditional density of y_t is

$$f(y_t | S_t = j, x_t, Y_{t-1}; \alpha), \quad j = 1, \ldots, N. \tag{10.4.1}$$

Let us group the N densities for different values of j into the vector η_t, such that

$$\eta_t = \begin{bmatrix} f(y_t | S_t = 1, x_t, Y_{t-1}; \alpha) \\ \ldots \\ f(y_t | S_t = N, x_t, Y_{t-1}; \alpha) \end{bmatrix}. \tag{10.4.2}$$

For example, if the model is the Markov switching AR(1)

$$
\begin{aligned}
y_t &= \phi_{0,S_t} + \phi_{1,S_t} y_{t-1} + \varepsilon_t, \\
\varepsilon_t &\overset{iid}{\sim} N(0, \sigma^2), \qquad S_t = \{1, 2\},
\end{aligned}
$$

then $x_t = 1$, $\alpha = (\phi_{0,1}, \phi_{0,2}, \phi_{1,1}, \phi_{1,2}, \sigma^2)$ and

$$\eta_t = \begin{bmatrix} f(y_t | S_t = 1, Y_{t-1}; \alpha) \\ f(y_t | S_t = 2, Y_{t-1}; \alpha) \end{bmatrix} = \begin{bmatrix} \frac{1}{\sqrt{2\pi\sigma^2}} exp\left\{ -\frac{(y_t - \phi_{0,1} - \phi_{1,1} y_{t-1})^2}{2\sigma^2} \right\} \\ \frac{1}{\sqrt{2\pi\sigma^2}} exp\left\{ -\frac{(y_t - \phi_{0,2} - \phi_{1,2} y_{t-1})^2}{2\sigma^2} \right\} \end{bmatrix}.$$

Back to the general case, let us also assume that

$$P(S_t = j | S_{t-1} = i, S_{t-2} = k, \ldots, x_t, Y_{t-1}) = P(S_t = j | S_{t-1} = i) = p_{ij}.$$

To start with, we are interested in the probability that a given regime is responsible for the observation y_t. In the i.i.d. case we saw that this probability depends on y_t only. Now, because of the dynamics, it will in general depend on the whole history of y, and possibly of x. Therefore, we want to evaluate

$$P(S_t = j | Y_t; \theta), \quad j = 1, \ldots, N, \tag{10.4.3}$$

where θ groups α and the p_{ij}s. We have:

$$P(S_t = j | Y_t; \theta) = P(S_t = j | y_t, x_t, Y_{t-1}; \theta) = \frac{P(y_t, S_t = j | x_t, Y_{t-1}; \theta)}{f(y_t | x_t, Y_{t-1}; \theta)}.$$

Now:

$$P(y_t, S_t = j|x_t, Y_{t-1}; \theta) = P(S_t = j|x_t, Y_{t-1}; \theta)f(y_t|S_t = j, x_t, Y_{t-1}; \alpha)$$

$$= P(S_t = j|Y_{t-1}; \theta)f(y_t|S_t = j, x_t, Y_{t-1}; \alpha),$$

assuming that x_t does not influence S_t. Then,

$$
\begin{aligned}
f(y_t|x_t, Y_{t-1}; \theta) &= \sum_{j=1}^{N} P(y_t, S_t = j|x_t, Y_{t-1}; \theta) \\
&= \sum_{j=1}^{N} f(y_t|S_t = j, x_t, Y_{t-1}; \alpha)P(S_t = j|x_t, Y_{t-1}; \theta) \\
&= \sum_{j=1}^{N} f(y_t|S_t = j, x_t, Y_{t-1}; \alpha)P(S_t = j|Y_{t-1}; \theta).
\end{aligned}
$$

Therefore,

$$P(S_t = j|Y_t; \theta) = \frac{P(S_t = j|Y_{t-1}; \theta)f(y_t|S_t = j, x_t, Y_{t-1}; \alpha)}{\sum_{j=1}^{N} P(S_t = j|Y_{t-1}; \theta)f(y_t|S_t = j, x_t, Y_{t-1}; \alpha)}, \quad (10.4.4)$$

with $j = 1, \ldots, N$. In order to find a more compact notation for (10.4.4), we define

$$
\xi_{t|t} \atop N \times 1 = \begin{pmatrix} P(S_t = 1|Y_t; \theta) \\ P(S_t = 2|Y_t; \theta) \\ \cdot \\ \cdot \\ \cdot \\ P(S_t = N|Y_t; \theta) \end{pmatrix}, \quad \xi_{t|t-1} \atop N \times 1 = \begin{pmatrix} P(S_t = 1|Y_{t-1}; \theta) \\ P(S_t = 2|Y_{t-1}; \theta) \\ \cdot \\ \cdot \\ \cdot \\ P(S_t = N|Y_{t-1}; \theta) \end{pmatrix}.
$$

Then, we can write (10.4.4) as

$$\xi_{t|t} = \frac{\xi_{t|t-1} \odot \eta_t}{i'(\xi_{t|t-1} \odot \eta_t)}, \quad (10.4.5)$$

where $\odot$ indicates element-by-element multiplication and $i' = (1, 1, \ldots, 1)$ is of dimension $1 \times N$.

We saw before that for a Markov chain:

$$\xi_{t+1} = P\xi_t + \upsilon_{t+1}, \quad (10.4.6)$$

where P is the matrix of transition probabilities with generic element p_{ij}. Taking expectations conditional on Y_t yields

$$E(\xi_{t+1}|Y_t) = PE(\xi_t|Y_t) + E(v_{t+1}|Y_t)$$

or

$$\xi_{t+1|t} = P\xi_{t|t}, \qquad\qquad (10.4.7)$$

which is the formula to forecast future states (or more precisely the probability of each future state).

Given (10.4.4), (10.4.7) and a starting value $\xi_{1|0}$, we can calculate $\xi_{t|t}$ (and $\xi_{t+1|t}$) for any t. A possible starting value is the vector of unconditional probabilities (π) which we derived in the section on Markov chains (see equation (10.2.7)).

Let us now consider forecasting future values of y. The starting point is the conditional density

$$f(y_t|S_t = j, x_t, Y_{t-1}; \alpha). \qquad\qquad (10.4.8)$$

If Y_t, x_{t+1} and S_{t+1} are known in period t, the optimal (in the MSFE sense) forecast is

$$E(y_{t+1}|S_{t+1} = j, x_{t+1}, Y_t; \alpha) = \int y_{t+1} f(y_{t+1}|S_{t+1} = j, x_{t+1}, Y_t; \alpha)dy_{t+1},$$
$$(10.4.9)$$

with $j = 1, \ldots N$. Yet, typically, the future regime S_{t+1} is not known. Therefore, the forecast must be

$$E(y_{t+1}|x_{t+1}, Y_t; \alpha) = \sum_{j=1}^{N} P(S_{t+1} = j|Y_t; \theta) E(y_{t+1}|S_{t+1} = j, x_{t+1}, Y_t; \alpha).$$
$$(10.4.10)$$

If we group the state dependent forecasts $E(y_{t+1}|S_{t+1} = j, x_{t+1}, Y_t; \alpha)$ into the $N \times 1$ vector h_t, then we can write $E(y_{t+1}|x_{t+1}, Y_t; \alpha) = h_t'\xi_{t+1|t}$.

Similar techniques can be used to forecast y_{t+m}. Note also that the covariance matrix of the errors will, in general, change across time.

A third object of interest from a forecasting point of view is the duration of a regime, i.e., if today we are in regime j, how long will we remain in this regime? To answer this question, let us assume for simplicity that the model is such that

$$P(S_t = j|S_{t-1} = i, S_{t-2} = k, \ldots, Y_t) = P(S_t = j|S_{t-1} = i) = p_{ij}.$$

Let us consider the following events and associated probabilities:

$$
\begin{aligned}
D &= 1, \ if \ S_t = j \ and \ S_{t+1} \neq j; \ Pr(D = 1) = (1 - p_{jj}), \\
D &= 2, \ if \ S_t = j, S_{t+1} = j \ and \ S_{t+2} \neq j; \ Pr(D = 2) = p_{jj}(1 - p_{jj}), \\
D &= 3, \ if \ S_t = j, S_{t+1} = j, S_{t+2} = j \ and \ S_{t+3} \neq j; \ Pr(D = 3) = p_{jj}^2(1 - p_{jj}), \\
&\quad \dots
\end{aligned}
$$

Then, the expected duration of regime j is

$$
E(D) = \sum_{i=1}^{\infty} i Pr(D = i) = \frac{1}{1 - p_{jj}}.
$$

So far we have assumed that θ (which includes α and the p_{ij}s) are known. Let us now see how to get MLEs for θ. The log-likelihood function is given by

$$
\mathcal{L}(\theta) = \sum_{t=1}^{T} \log f(y_t | x_t, Y_{t-1}; \theta). \tag{10.4.11}
$$

We have

$$
\begin{aligned}
f(y_t, S_t &= j | x_t, Y_{t-1}; \theta) = P(S_t = j | x_t, Y_{t-1}; \theta) f(y_t | S_t = j, x_t, Y_{t-1}; \alpha) \\
&= P(S_t = j | Y_{t-1}; \theta) f(y_t | S_t = j, x_t, Y_{t-1}; \alpha). \tag{10.4.12}
\end{aligned}
$$

Therefore, the elements to be inserted into (10.4.11) are

$$
\begin{aligned}
f(y_t | x_t, Y_{t-1}; \theta) &= \sum_{j=1}^{N} P(S_t = j | Y_{t-1}; \theta) f(y_t | S_t = j, x_t, Y_{t-1}; \alpha) \\
&= i'(\xi_{t|t-1} \odot \eta_t) \tag{10.4.13}
\end{aligned}
$$

where $i' = (1, 1, \dots 1)$. The maximizer of (10.4.11), $\hat{\theta}$, can be found either numerically or using a modified version of the EM algorithm we have seen for the i.i.d. case, see, e.g., Hamilton (1994, Chapter 22) for details.

We also assumed that the number of regimes, N, is known. In practice this is not the case, and testing for the proper value of N is not easy. Empirically, as in the STAR model case, it is easier to start with two regimes and check whether there is evidence of model misspecification. The opposite strategy, i.e., starting with three regimes and testing two versus three creates complications since parameters of the third regime are not identified under the null hypothesis of two regimes.

Psaradakis and Spagnolo (2006) studied the performance of information criteria, finding that the AIC, BIC, and HQ criteria perform well for selecting the correct number of regimes and lags as long as the sample size and the parameter changes are large enough. Smith, Naik, and Tsai (2006) proposed a new information criterion for selecting simultaneously the number of variables and the lag length of the Markov switching model.

10.5   Empirical example: Simulated data

In the first part of the example we illustrate estimation and forecasting a Hamilton-type Markov switching regression model with intercept and some autoregressive terms that vary across regimes, using simulated data. The DGP is the following:

$$
y_t = \begin{cases} \alpha_{1,1} + \alpha_{2,1} \cdot y_{t-1} + \alpha_{3,1} \cdot y_{t-2} + \varepsilon_t, & if \ state = 1 \\ \alpha_{1,2} + \alpha_{2,2} \cdot y_{t-1} + \alpha_{3,2} \cdot y_{t-2} + \varepsilon_t, & if \ state = 2 \end{cases}
$$

The data was simulated using the following parameters:

	State 1	*State 2*
α_1	-0.2	0.2
α_2	1.2	0.4
α_3	-0.3	-0.3

To generate the series we use the following procedure:

1. Generate the Markov chain state variable. In this exercise we use a two-state Markov chain with the following transition matrix P,

$$
P = \begin{bmatrix} 0.83 & 0.17 \\ 0.25 & 0.75 \end{bmatrix}
$$

2. Conditional on the generated state variable, we simulate the series with AR(2) dynamics and state-dependent intercept.

The simulated series contains 600 observations. In order to avoid dependence on the starting values, the first 100 observations will be discarded. The data is represented in Figure 10.5.1. The available sample is divided into two parts: estimation sample, from the 101st observation to the 500th observation, and forecasting sample, from the 501st to the 600th observation.

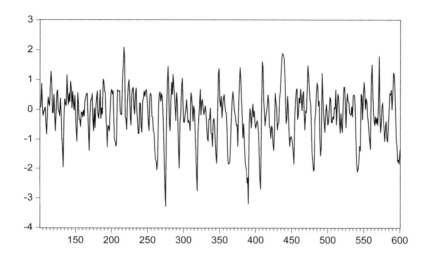

Figure 10.5.1: *Series for simulated MS-AR(2)*

The Markov switching AR specification will be compared with a linear model specification, i.e., an AR(2) model

$$y_t = \alpha_1 + \alpha_2 y_{t-1} + \alpha_3 y_{t-2} + \varepsilon_t, \quad \varepsilon_t \overset{iid}{\sim} N\left(0, \sigma^2\right).$$

As we can see from the results reported in Table 10.5.1, the estimated coefficients are significantly different from zero, but also different from those of the DGP (except for the AR(2) coefficient, α_3).

We estimate a MS model with the first lag and intercept coefficients changing between two regimes and the coefficient of the second lag remaining constant, i.e., the following model

$$\begin{aligned} y_t &= (\alpha_{1,1} + \alpha_{2,1} \cdot y_{t-1}) \cdot I\left(s_t = 1\right) + (\alpha_{1,2} + \alpha_{2,2} \cdot y_{t-1}) I\left(s_t = 2\right) \\ &\quad + \alpha_3 \cdot y_{t-2} + \varepsilon_t, \qquad \varepsilon_t \overset{iid}{\sim} N\left(0, \sigma^2\right) \end{aligned}$$

	Coefficient	Std. Error	t-Statistic	Prob.
ALPHA(1)	-0.056	0.029	-1.938	0.053
ALPHA(2)	0.956	0.047	20.267	0.000
ALPHA(3)	-0.342	0.047	-7.259	0.000
R-squared	0.565	Mean dep var		-0.142
Adjusted R-squared	0.563	S.D. dep var		0.856
S.E. of regression	0.566	Akaike IC		1.708
Sum squared resid	127.325	Schwarz IC		1.738
Log likelihood	-338.631	Hannan-Quinn		1.720
F-statistic	257.576	DW stat		2.025
Prob(F-statistic)	0.000			

Table 10.5.1: *Estimation output for AR(2) model*

where s_t is a Markov process with two states. The estimation results are shown in Table 10.5.2. The estimated value of the intercept term for the first regime is equal to -0.1268 (s.e.=0.06743), while that for the second regime is equal to 0.1676 (s.e.=0.0493). Both estimated intercepts are reasonably close to the actual DGP parameters, and significant at 10% confidence level. All the autoregressive terms estimates are significant and close to the DGP counterparts. The estimated transition matrix using the simulated data is reported in Table 10.5.3.

Forecasting

In this part of the example we assess the forecasting performance of the following two types of models for the simulated data: the AR(2) model and the Markov switching model with intercept and first lag changing between regimes (while the second lag and the error variance remain constant across regimes). We consider one-step ahead recursive forecasts for the last 100 observations in the sample. The results are presented in Figure 10.5.2.

From a graphical inspection, the AR(2) and MSAR forecasts seem very close. Table 10.5.4 presents the associated RMSFE of both models, from which the forecasting performance of the MSAR model comes out to be slightly better than that of the AR(2) model even if a Diebold-Mariano test fails to reject the null hypothesis of equal forecasting accuracy.

Variable	Coefficient	Std. Error	z-Statistic	Prob.
Regime 1				
C	-0.127	0.067	-1.881	0.060
AR(1)	1.391	0.049	28.256	0.000
Regime 2				
C	0.168	0.049	3.403	0.001
AR(1)	0.536	0.060	8.957	0.000
Common				
AR(2)	-0.404	0.045	-9.067	0.000
Log(Sigma)	-0.956	0.048	-19.899	0.000
Transition Matrix Para.				
P11-C	0.604	0.255	2.371	0.018
P21-C	-0.408	0.454	-0.900	0.368
Mean dep var	-0.142	S.D. dep var		0.856
S.E. of regression	0.570	Sum squared resid		128.137
DW stat	2.028	Log likelihood		-282.828
Akaike IC	1.454	Schwarz IC		1.534
Hannan-Quinn	1.486			

Table 10.5.2: *Estimation output for Markov switching AR(2)*

10.6 Empirical example: Industrial production

To illustrate the estimation of a Markov switching model with real economic data, the growth rate of the United States industrial production index from the FRED database is used, as in Chapter 9. Also in this case, the sample used runs from 1930Q1 to 2014Q4. The estimation sample is set to start in 1930Q1 and end in 2000Q1, while the forecasting sample covers the period from 2000Q2 to 2014Q4.

We estimate a Hamilton-type Markov switching regression model with intercept and first AR lag changing between regimes.

p_{ij}	$j = 1$	$j = 2$
$i = 1$	0.601	0.399
$i = 2$	0.354	0.647

Table 10.5.3: *Estimated transition probabilities*

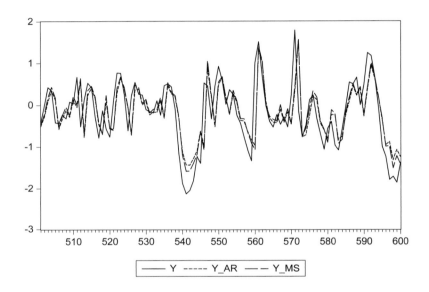

Figure 10.5.2: *One-step ahead forecast comparison: AR(2) vs Markov switching AR(2)*

The estimation results are represented in Table 10.6.1. Both the intercept and the coefficient of the first autoregressive lag turn out to be quite different in the two regimes. The smoothed probabilities for the regimes are displayed in Figure 10.6.1. It can be seen that the first regime is estimated mainly in the first part of the sample, associated with the Great Depression and a few instance in the 1950s and 1960s.

For comparison, Table 10.6.2 provides results from estimation of a simple AR(2) specification. It runs out that there is a slight deterioration both in the explanatory power and in the information criteria.

Model	RMSFE	DM pval
AR(2)	0.555	-
MSAR	0.550	0.248

Table 10.5.4: *Forecast evaluation comparison between AR model and MSAR model: Root mean squared errors and p-value for a Diebold-Mariano test (H_0: same forecasting accuracy)*

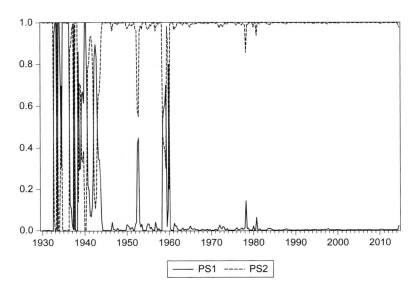

Figure 10.6.1: *Smoothed probabilities for the two regimes*

Forecasting

In this part of the example we compare the forecasting performance of the AR(2) against the Markov switching models. Recursive one-step ahead forecasts are computed using both models over the sample 2000Q2 - 2014Q4, which contains 59 observations.

The forecasts are plotted in Figure 10.6.2, together with actual values.

Already from a graphical inspection, the MSAR forecasts show a better performance than their AR(2) counterpart. To have a more accurate measure of performance, Table 10.6.3 reports the RMSFE for both models' forecasts.

The Markov switching model forecasting performance is much better than that of the AR(2) model, and the difference is statistically significant according to a Diebold-Mariano test. We can also compare these results with the

Variable	Coefficient	Std. Error	z-Statistic	Prob.
Regime 1				
C	4.563	0.411	11.105	0.000
AR(1)	-0.591	0.076	-7.745	0.000
Regime 2				
C	-0.021	0.174	-0.119	0.905
AR(1)	0.926	0.052	17.827	0.000
Common				
AR(2)	-0.339	0.044	-7.725	0.000
Log(Sigma)	0.886	0.044	20.086	0.000
Transition Matrix Para.				
P11-C	0.792	0.540	1.465	0.143
P21-C	-3.452	0.398	-8.671	0.000
Mean dep var	0.863	S.D. dep var		3.820
S.E. of regression	3.438	Sum squared resid		3946.807
DW stat	2.341	Log likelihood		-829.383
Akaike IC	4.926	Schwarz IC		5.016
Hannan-Quinn	4.962			

Table 10.6.1: *Estimation output for a Markov switching AR model*

	Coefficient	Std. Error	t-Statistic	Prob.
ALPHA(1)	0.572	0.197	2.906	0.004
ALPHA(2)	0.420	0.054	7.797	0.000
ALPHA(3)	-0.074	0.054	-1.372	0.171
R-squared	0.160	Mean dep var		0.863
Adjusted R-squared	0.155	S.D. dep var		3.820
S.E. of regression	3.512	Akaike IC		5.359
Sum squared resid	4156.312	Schwarz IC		5.393
Log likelihood	-908.024	Hannan-Quinn		5.372
F-statistic	32.042	DW stat		1.975
Prob(F-statistic)	0.000			

Table 10.6.2: *Estimation output for AR model*

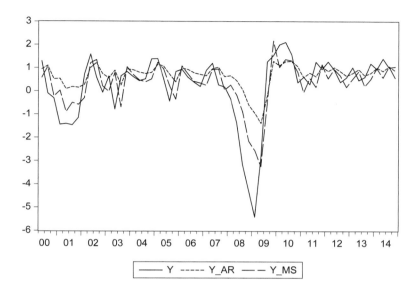

Figure 10.6.2: *One-step ahead forecast comparison: AR vs. MS vs. actual data*

Model	RMSFE	DM pval
AR(2)	1.149	-
MSAR	0.881	0.023

Table 10.6.3: *Forecast evaluation comparison between AR model and MSAR model: Root mean squared errors and p-value for a Diebold-Mariano test (H_0 : same forecasting accuracy)*

ones obtained with the threshold models (TAR and STAR) in Chapter 9. The forecasting performance of the MS model is statistically better than the one of a TAR or STAR model in Chapter 9.

10.7 Concluding remarks

Markov switching models represent an interesting specification choice for economic variables, whose behavior could change during different phases of the business cycle or different policy stances. In this chapter we have considered specification, estimation and forecasting with Markov switching models, illustrating their practical use with simulated and actual data. In both cases, the MS model turned out to be better than a linear specification, highlighting the importance of taking parameter change into proper account.

Chapter 11

State Space Models

11.1 Introduction

A large set of econometric models can be cast into a so-called state space form, where observable variables are related to a set of unobservable (state) variables, and the law of motion of the latter is specified. We will consider the case where all the aforementioned relationships are linear and with normally distributed errors, though more general specifications are possible.

Once a model is written in state space form, the Kalman filter provides a procedure forecasts of both the observable and unobservable variables. The filter also yields the likelihood function for the model, which can be used to derive maximum likelihood estimators of the parameters. The procedure is named after Rudolf E. Kalman, who wrote a seminal paper on the topic (see Kalman (1960)).

The Kalman filter has numerous applications in technology. A common application is for guidance, navigation, and control of vehicles, particularly aircraft and spacecraft. Furthermore, the Kalman filter is a widely applied concept in time series analysis, especially in fields such as signal processing, linear systems control theory, robotic motion control, central nervous system's control of movement, trajectory optimization and last but not least econometrics.

The algorithm works in a two-step process. In the prediction step, the Kalman filter produces estimates of current state variables, along with their uncertainties. Once the outcome of the next measurement (affected by some type of error, such as random noise) is observed, these estimates are updated using a weighted average, where more weight is attributed to estimates with higher certainty. The algorithm is recursive. It can run in real time, using only the current input measurements, the previously calculated state and its uncertainty matrix; no additional past information is required.

In general, the Kalman filter does not require any assumption that the errors are Gaussian. However, the filter yields an exact conditional probability estimate in the special case that all errors are normally distributed.

Extensions and generalizations to the method have also been developed, such as the extended Kalman filter and the unscented Kalman filter that work on non-linear systems. The underlying model is a Bayesian model similar to a hidden Markov model but where the state space of latent processes is continuous and all variables, hidden or observed, have Gaussian distributions.

In this chapter, we will show how to cast a model in state space form, illustrating the procedure with a number of examples. Then we will derive the main components of the Kalman filter. Finally, we will discuss some examples using both simulated and actual data. In particular, we will consider models with continuous parameter evolution and dynamic factor models. Additional details, examples and a more complete treatment can be found, e.g., in Hamilton (1994, Chapter 14) and Harvey (1993, Chapter 4).

Section 11.2 covers state models, while the Kalman filter is discussed in section 11.3. Examples involving simulated and empirical data are in respectively Sections 11.4 and 11.5. Concluding remarks appear in Section 11.6.

11.2   Models in state space form

A general formulation of a (linear) state space form is

$$\alpha_t \;=\; T\alpha_{t-1} + R\eta_t, \tag{11.2.1}$$

$$y_t \;=\; Z\alpha_t + S\xi_t, \tag{11.2.2}$$

$$\begin{bmatrix} \eta_t \\ \xi_t \end{bmatrix} \;\overset{iid}{\sim}\; N\left(\begin{bmatrix} 0 \\ 0 \end{bmatrix}, \begin{bmatrix} Q & 0 \\ 0 & H \end{bmatrix} \right), \tag{11.2.3}$$

where α_t is a vector containing the unobservable state variables, y_t is a vector of observable variables, the state equation (11.2.1) describes the evolution of the state variables, the transition or measurement equation (11.2.2) models observable processes as a linear function of state variables and noise. The error terms η_t and ξ_t are zero mean, jointly normally distributed and uncorrelated random variables, as in (11.2.3). A word of caution before proceeding further. There is no unique way of formulating state space models. Equations (11.2.1) through (11.2.3) reveal this already. Indeed, we will not be able to separately identify the matrices R and Q, nor the matrices S and H. Yet, we will keep the representation as it appears in the above equations because it will be convenient in the context of the various examples that follow.

In some cases there can be no state variables in the model we are interested in, but we just introduce some ad hoc state variables in order to rewrite the model of interest in state space form. While in other cases the model includes already unobservable variables, that can be treated as state variables. Let us discuss a few examples to illustrate these points.

11.2.1 An ARMA(2,2) model

The model is

$$y_t = a_1 y_{t-1} + a_2 y_{t-2} + \varepsilon_t + b_1 \varepsilon_{t-1} + b_2 \varepsilon_{t-2}, \tag{11.2.4}$$

with $\varepsilon_t \overset{iid}{\sim} N(0, \sigma^2)$. Let us introduce four state variables, labeled α_{1t}, α_{2t}, α_{3t}, α_{4t}. The state equations are

$$\begin{bmatrix} \alpha_{1t} \\ \alpha_{2t} \\ \alpha_{3t} \\ \alpha_{4t} \end{bmatrix} = \begin{bmatrix} a_1 & a_2 & 1 & 0 \\ 1 & 0 & 0 & 0 \\ 0 & 0 & 0 & 1 \\ 0 & 0 & 0 & 0 \end{bmatrix} \begin{bmatrix} \alpha_{1t-1} \\ \alpha_{2t-1} \\ \alpha_{3t-1} \\ \alpha_{4t-1} \end{bmatrix} + \begin{bmatrix} 1 \\ 0 \\ b_1 \\ b_2 \end{bmatrix} \eta_t \tag{11.2.5}$$

or, in compact notation

$$\alpha_t = T\alpha_{t-1} + R\eta_t.$$

As transition equation (a single one in this example), we have

$$y_t = \begin{bmatrix} 1 & 0 & 0 & 0 \end{bmatrix} \alpha_t, \tag{11.2.6}$$

so that $Z = \begin{bmatrix} 1 & 0 & 0 & 0 \end{bmatrix}$ and $S = 0$ in (11.2.2). To make sure that the state space form in (11.2.5) - (11.2.6) is equivalent to the ARMA model in (11.2.4), let us proceed as follows. From the first state equation in (11.2.5) we obtain

$$\alpha_{1t} = a_1 \alpha_{1t-1} + a_2 \alpha_{2t-1} + \alpha_{3t-1} + \eta_t.$$

We can then replace α_{2t-1} and α_{3t-1} with their expressions from the second and third state equations, obtaining

$$\alpha_{1t} = a_1\alpha_{1t-1} + a_2\alpha_{1t-2} + \alpha_{4t-2} + b_1\eta_{t-1} + \eta_t.$$

From the fourth state equation, it is $\alpha_{4t-2} = b_2\eta_{t-2}$, and the previous equation becomes

$$\alpha_{1t} = a_1\alpha_{1t-1} + a_2\alpha_{1t-2} + b_2\eta_{t-2} + b_1\eta_{t-1} + \eta_t.$$

From the transition equation in (11.2.6), it is $y_t = \alpha_{1t}$, so that we can rewrite the equation above as

$$y_t = a_1y_{t-1} + a_2y_{t-2} + b_2\eta_{t-2} + b_1\eta_{t-1} + \eta_t,$$

which is indeed an ARMA(2,2) model. To conclude, we noted earlier that state space model representations are not unique. Indeed, the same model can be cast in different state space forms, see, e.g., Hamilton (1994, Chapter 14) for an alternative representation of the ARMA(2,2) model.

11.2.2   A time-varying parameters (TVP) regression model

In the previous chapters we have considered models whose parameters where changing either deterministically (based on dummy variables) or stochastically, depending on either some observable continuous variables (as in TAR and STAR models) or some discrete unobservable variable (as in MS models). Another option is to consider models with continuous and unobserved time variation in the parameters. In particular, let us consider the specification

$$y_t \quad = \quad X_t\beta_t + \varepsilon_t, \tag{11.2.7}$$

$$\beta_t \quad = \quad \beta_{t-1} + \eta_t,$$

$$\begin{bmatrix} \varepsilon_t \\ \eta_t \end{bmatrix} \overset{iid}{\sim} N\left(\begin{bmatrix} 0 \\ 0 \end{bmatrix}, \begin{bmatrix} \sigma_\varepsilon^2 & 0 \\ 0 & \lambda Q \end{bmatrix} \right).$$

In (11.2.7) X_t is a $1 \times k$ vector of explanatory variables, β_t is a $k \times 1$ vector of time-varying regression coefficients, each of which evolves as a random walk, with the random walk models possibly correlated among themselves but uncorrelated with ε_t. The scalar parameter λ controls the overall amount of parameter time variation, with stable parameters when $\lambda = 0$.

The model in (11.2.7) is already in state space form. With respect to the general formulation in (11.2.1)-(11.2.2) it is $\beta_t = \alpha_t$, $T = R = I$, $S = 1$, $H = \sigma_\varepsilon^2$, and $Z = Z_t = X_t$. The fact that Z is time varying can be easily accommodated.

11.2.3 A model with stochastic volatility

Most of the models we have considered so far have homoskedastic residuals, possibly after variable transformation and model re-specifications. However, in certain cases, and in particular for financial variables, the errors can be truly heteroskedastic (see Chapter 14). While in general neglecting this feature does not affect sensibly the computation of point forecasts, it is quite important for interval and density forecasts.

More generally, the estimation of models with heteroskedastic errors can be of interest by itself. A general form of heteroskedasticity is known as stochastic volatility (SV). Hence, we now consider a simple model with SV and show how to cast it in state space form, following the discussion in Harvey (1993, Chapter 8).

We have

$$
\begin{aligned}
y_t &= \sigma_t \varepsilon_t, & (11.2.8)\\
\sigma_t^2 &= \exp(h_t),\\
h_t &= \gamma + \phi h_{t-1} + \eta_t,\\
\begin{bmatrix} \varepsilon_t \\ \eta_t \end{bmatrix} &\overset{iid}{\sim} N\left(\begin{bmatrix} 0 \\ 0 \end{bmatrix}, \begin{bmatrix} 1 & 0 \\ 0 & \sigma_\eta^2 \end{bmatrix} \right).
\end{aligned}
$$

We can transform the model in (11.2.8) as

$$
\log y_t^2 = h_t + \log \varepsilon_t^2,
$$

where $E(\log \varepsilon_t^2) = -1.27$ and $var(\log \varepsilon_t^2) = 4.93$, see Harvey (1993, Chapter 8). Let us define $\varepsilon_t^* = \log \varepsilon_t^2 + 1.27$, so that $E(\varepsilon_t^*) = 0$, and $q_t = \log y_t^2 + 1.27$. Then we have

$$
\begin{aligned}
q_t &= h_t + \varepsilon_t^*, & (11.2.9)\\
h_t &= \gamma + \phi h_{t-1} + \eta_t,
\end{aligned}
$$

which is a state space form similar to that in (11.2.1)-(11.2.2), with q_t being the observable variable and h_t the state.

The main difference with respect to (11.2.1)-(11.2.2) is that ε_t^* in (11.2.9) is not normally distributed. Hence, the resulting parameter estimators will only be quasi-maximum likelihood estimators. Since estimation of SV models is quite complex and requires simulation methods, this approximation can be useful.[1]

11.2.4 A dynamic factor model

Factor models decompose each variable into a common and an idiosyncratic component. The latter is variable specific while the former is driven by a limited number of forces, the factors, which are common across all variables. This feature makes factor models particularly suited to represent economic variables, which theoretically are driven by a limited number of key shocks, e.g., demand, supply, or monetary conditions, tend to co-move and share not only trends but also cyclical fluctuations.

Estimation of factor models is complicated by the fact that factors are unobservable. However, we can now treat them as state variables in a state space representation. In particular, let us assume that n stationary variables grouped in the vector y_t share a single common factor and that the effects of this factor on variables are dynamic (in the sense that variables are affected by current and past values of the factor), and that both factor and idiosyncratic components evolve as AR processes. Specifically, let us consider the model

$$y_t \;=\; \gamma(L)\Delta f_t + u_t, \tag{11.2.10}$$

$$
\begin{aligned}
\phi(L)\Delta f_t &= v_t, \\
D(L)u_t &= \varepsilon_t, \\
\begin{bmatrix} v_t \\ \varepsilon_t \end{bmatrix} &\overset{iid}{\sim} N\left(\begin{bmatrix} 0 \\ 0 \end{bmatrix}, \begin{bmatrix} \sigma_v^2 & 0 \\ 0 & \Sigma_\varepsilon \end{bmatrix} \right)
\end{aligned}
$$

where $D(L)$ and Σ_ε are diagonal matrices, and all the lag polynomials are of order 2. To make the state space as similar as possible to the general formulation in (11.2.1)-(11.2.2), we write the dynamic factor model in (11.2.10)

---

[1] See however Jacquier, Polson, and Rossi (1994) for an elaborate discussion of situations where the state space Kalman filter performs poorly.

as:

$$
\begin{bmatrix} \Delta f_t \\ \Delta f_{t-1} \\ u_t \\ u_{t-1} \\ f_{t-1} \end{bmatrix} = \begin{bmatrix} \phi_1 & \phi_2 & 0 & 0 & 0 \\ 1 & 0 & 0 & 0 & 0 \\ 0 & 0 & D_1 & D_2 & 0 \\ 0 & 0 & I & 0 & 0 \\ 1 & 0 & 0 & 0 & 1 \end{bmatrix} \begin{bmatrix} \Delta f_{t-1} \\ \Delta f_{t-2} \\ u_{t-1} \\ u_{t-2} \\ f_{t-2} \end{bmatrix} + \begin{bmatrix} 1 & 0 \\ 0 & 0 \\ 0 & I \\ 0 & 0 \\ 0 & 0 \end{bmatrix} \begin{bmatrix} v_t \\ \varepsilon_t \end{bmatrix}, \qquad (11.2.11)
$$

which is of the form

$$
\alpha_t = T\alpha_{t-1} + R\eta_t,
$$

and

$$
y_t = \begin{bmatrix} \gamma_1 & \gamma_2 & I & 0 & 0 \end{bmatrix} \alpha_t, \qquad (11.2.12)
$$

which in turn is of the form

$$
y_t = Z\alpha_t + S\xi_t,
$$

with $S = 0$. If there is interest in the factor, f_t, this can be easily recovered from

$$
f_t = \begin{bmatrix} 1 & 0 & 0 & 0 & 1 \end{bmatrix} \alpha_t.
$$

Additional details on this model can be found, e.g., in Stock and Watson (1989) who used it to construct a coincident indicator of economic conditions in the United States.

11.2.5 Unobserved component models

Unobserved Component Models (UCM) decompose a variable into a trend, cyclical, seasonal, and irregular components, each of which follows a given model. Therefore, an UCM is directly cast in state space form and can be analyzed with the Kalman filter, see, e.g., Harvey (1993). As an example, let us consider the simplest UCM, which is

$$
\begin{aligned}
y_t &= \mu_t + \xi_t, & (11.2.13) \\
\mu_t &= \mu_{t-1} + \eta_t,
\end{aligned}
$$

where the errors are zero mean, uncorrelated among themselves and over time, and jointly normally distributed. In this model, y_t is decomposed into a trend component, which is modeled as a pure random walk, and an idiosyncratic component. The model is just a special case of the general state space specification in (11.2.1)-(11.2.3). If we difference both sides of (11.2.13) we obtain

$$\Delta y_t = \eta_t + \Delta \xi_t. \tag{11.2.14}$$

It can be easily shown that the autocorrelation function (AC) of Δy_t is

$$
\begin{aligned}
AC(1) &= -\sigma_\xi^2/(\sigma_\eta^2 + 2\sigma_\xi^2), \\
AC(j) &= 0, \quad j > 1.
\end{aligned}
\tag{11.2.15}
$$

From Chapter 5, we know that this pattern of AC is equal to that of an MA(1) model. Indeed, we can rewrite the model in (11.2.14) as

$$\Delta y_t = \varepsilon_t + \theta \varepsilon_{t-1}, \tag{11.2.16}$$

where ε_t is white noise $N(0, \sigma_\varepsilon^2)$. The parameter θ can be determined by equating the $AC(1)$ of (11.2.16) with (11.2.15). It turns out that

$$\theta = \left[(q^2 + 4q)^{0.5} - 2 - q \right] /2,$$

where $q = \sigma_\eta^2/\sigma_\xi^2$ is the signal to noise ratio, while $\sigma_\varepsilon^2 = -\sigma_\xi^2/\theta$, see Harvey (1993, Chapter 5) for details. The only invertible root of the above equation is such that $-1 \leq \theta \leq 0$, so that MA parameter is forced to be negative, with exact value depending on q.

In conclusion, the equations in (11.2.13) are equivalent to a constrained $ARIMA(0, 1, 1)$ model, which is often known as the reduced form of the UCM. This is a more general result, in the sense that typically UCMs can be represented as constrained ARIMA models.

11.3   The Kalman filter

The Kalman filter is a recursive method that permits to derive optimal (linear) forecasts for the state and observable variables in a state space model, and the model likelihood itself. In this section we present the filter main equations, discuss the recursion, and then derive the main formula.

11.3.1 The key equations of the Kalman filter

Let us rewrite for convenience the general state space representation in (11.2.1) - (11.2.3) as

$$
\begin{aligned}
\alpha_t &= T\alpha_{t-1} + R\eta_t, \\
y_t &= Z\alpha_t + S\xi_t, \\
\begin{bmatrix} \eta_t \\ \xi_t \end{bmatrix} &\overset{iid}{\sim} N\left(\begin{bmatrix} 0 \\ 0 \end{bmatrix}, \begin{bmatrix} Q & 0 \\ 0 & H \end{bmatrix} \right).
\end{aligned}
$$

Due to the normality assumption, we can also represent the state and measurement equations in terms of normal densities as

$$
\begin{aligned}
f(\alpha_t | \alpha_{t-1}, Y_{t-1}) &= N(T\alpha_{t-1}, RQR'), \\
f(y_t | \alpha_t, Y_{t-1}) &= N(Z\alpha_t, SHS'),
\end{aligned}
$$

where $Y_{t-1} = (y_{t-1}, y_{t-2}, \ldots)$.

The first object of interest is

$$
f(\alpha_t | Y_{t-1}) = N(\alpha_{t|t-1}, P_{t|t-1}), \tag{11.3.1}
$$

$t = 1, \ldots, T$, namely, the state variable's density conditional on all the past observable information. From (11.3.1) we can construct optimal (one-step ahead point and density) forecasts for α_t. Hence, (11.3.1) is known as prediction equations. As we will show later on, it is

$$
\begin{aligned}
\alpha_{t|t-1} &= T\alpha_{t-1|t-1}, \\
P_{t|t-1} &= TP_{t-1|t-1}T' + RQR'.
\end{aligned} \tag{11.3.2}
$$

The second object of interest is

$$
f(\alpha_t | Y_t) = N(\alpha_{t|t}, P_{t|t}), \tag{11.3.3}
$$

$t = 1, \ldots, T$, that is, state variable's density conditional on current and past observable information. We will show later on that

$$
\begin{aligned}
\alpha_{t|t} &= \alpha_{t|t-1} + P_{t|t-1}Z'F_t^{-1}v_t, \\
P_{t|t} &= P_{t|t-1} - P_{t|t-1}Z'F_t^{-1}ZP_{t|t-1},
\end{aligned} \tag{11.3.4}
$$

where

$$
\begin{aligned}
v_t &= y_t - y_{t|t-1}, \\
F_t &= E(v_t v_t').
\end{aligned}
\tag{11.3.5}
$$

Equation (11.3.4) indicates how to optimally update our forecasts for α_t made in period $t - 1$ when new information on y_t becomes available. It shows how to construct a "nowcast" for α_t. Therefore, (11.3.3) is known as updating equation.

Note that the prediction equation depends on the elements of the updating equations, $\alpha_{t-1|t-1}$ and $P_{t-1|t-1}$. In turn, the updating equations depend on the updating's elements of the previous step, $\alpha_{t|t-1}$ and $P_{t|t-1}$, and also on v_t and F_t.

The third object of interest is

$$
f(y_t|Y_{t-1}) = N(y_{t|t-1}, F_t),
\tag{11.3.6}
$$

$t = 1, \ldots, T$, which is the conditional likelihood of y_t given the past. Since the joint likelihood can be written as:

$$
f(y_1, \ldots y_t) = \Pi_{t=1}^{T} f(y_t|Y_{t-1}),
\tag{11.3.7}
$$

from (11.3.6), given $f(y_1)$, we can obtain the joint likelihood. Hence, (11.3.6) is known as likelihood equations, or simply likelihood. Note that from (11.3.6) we can also obtain optimal (one-step ahead point and density) forecasts for y_t. We will show later on that this is

$$
\begin{aligned}
y_{t|t-1} &= Z\alpha_{t|t-1}, \\
F_t &= ZP_{t|t-1}Z' + SHS'.
\end{aligned}
\tag{11.3.8}
$$

Hence, the likelihood equation depends on $\alpha_{t|t-1}$ and $P_{t|t-1}$.

To conclude, we need to discuss initial conditions for α_t. The common choice is to pick the unconditional mean and variance of α_t. From (11.2.1) we have

$$
\alpha_t = (I - TL)^{-1} R\eta_t.
$$

From this it follows that

$$
\alpha_{1|0} = E(\alpha_t) = 0.
\tag{11.3.9}
$$

Moreover, if we define

$$P_{1|0} = E(\alpha_t \alpha_t'),$$

the law of motion for α_t in (11.2.1) implies that

$$P_{1|0} = TP_{1|0}T' + RQR'.$$

It can be shown (e.g., Hamilton (1994, p. 265)) that by solving this set of equations it is possible to obtain:

$$vec(P_{1|0}) = [I - (T \otimes T)]^{-1} vec(RQR'), \qquad (11.3.10)$$

where $vec(P_{1|0})$ is the column vector coming from vertical stacking obtained of $P_{1|0}$ columns and $\otimes$ indicates the Kronecker product.

Finally, from the initial conditions for α we obtain those for y, using (11.3.8).

11.3.2 The iterative procedure

We have seen that the prediction, updating, and likelihood equations are closely inter-related. In order to derive all the required forecasts and likelihoods, we can adopt the following iterative procedure:

1. obtain $\alpha_{2|1}$ and $P_{2|1}$ from the initial conditions in (11.3.9)-(11.3.10)

2. use $\alpha_{2|1}$ and $P_{2|1}$, to obtain $y_{2|1}$ and F_2 by way of the likelihood equations (11.3.8)

3. use $\alpha_{2|1}$, $P_{2|1}$, $y_{2|1}$ and F_2, to obtain $\alpha_{2|2}$ and $P_{2|2}$ via the updating equations (11.3.4),

4. use $\alpha_{2|2}$ and $P_{2|2}$, to obtain $\alpha_{3|2}$ and $P_{3|2}$ from the prediction equations (11.3.2),

5. use $\alpha_{3|2}$ and $P_{3|2}$, to obtain $y_{3|2}$ and F_3 via the likelihood equations (11.3.8),

6. use $\alpha_{3|2}$, $P_{3|2}$, $y_{3|2}$ and F_3, to obtain $\alpha_{3|3}$ and $P_{3|3}$ via the updating equations (11.3.4),

7. keep iterating steps 4 - 6 until one reaches the final period, $t = T$. At this
point, with all the required forecast and likelihoods, we can construct
the full likelihood using either (11.3.7) or directly the expression

$$\log L\left(\theta\right) = -\frac{NT}{2}\log 2\pi - \frac{1}{2}\sum_{t=1}^{T}\log |F_t| - \frac{1}{2}\sum_{t=1}^{T}v_t'F_t v_t,$$

where v_t are the one-step ahead forecast errors defined in (11.3.5) -
(11.3.8) and F_t is the covariance matrix in (11.3.8).

11.3.3   Some derivations and additional results

We now derive in more detail the conditional means and variances appearing
in the Kalman filter equations. Let us start with (11.3.2), namely:

$$\alpha_{t|t-1} = E(\alpha_t|Y_{t-1}) = E(T\alpha_{t-1} + R\eta_t|Y_{t-1}) = T\alpha_{t-1|t-1}.$$

and

$$\alpha_t - \alpha_{t|t-1} = T(\alpha_{t-1} - \alpha_{t-1|t-1}) + R\eta_t,$$

so that

$$P_{t|t-1} = \mathrm{Var}(\alpha_t - \alpha_{t|t-1}) = TP_{t-1|t-1}T' + RQR'.$$

Let us consider next, for convenience, the likelihood equations (11.3.8). For
(11.3.8) we have

$$y_{t|t-1} = E(Z\alpha_t + S\xi_t|Y_{t-1}) = Z\alpha_{t|t-1},$$

which also implies that

$$v_t = y_t - y_{t|t-1} = Z(\alpha_t - \alpha_{t|t-1}) + S\xi_t.$$

and

$$F_t = E(v_t v_t') = ZP_{t|t-1}Z' + SHS'.$$

The derivation of the updating equations (11.3.4) is slightly more complex. Let us start with the following decomposition

$$\begin{bmatrix} v_t \\ \alpha_t \end{bmatrix} = \begin{bmatrix} 0 \\ \alpha_{t|t-1} \end{bmatrix} + \begin{bmatrix} Z(\alpha_t - \alpha_{t|t-1}) + S\xi_t \\ \alpha_t - \alpha_{t|t-1} \end{bmatrix}.$$

The last term on the right-hand side contains the one-step ahead forecast errors for, respectively, y_t and α_t. Hence, both terms are unpredictable using information up to and including period $t-1$. Therefore, it is

$$\begin{bmatrix} v_t \\ \alpha_t \end{bmatrix} | Y_{t-1} \sim N \left(\begin{bmatrix} 0 \\ \alpha_{t|t-1} \end{bmatrix}, \begin{bmatrix} F_t & P_{t|t-1}Z' \\ ZP_{t|t-1} & P_{t|t-1} \end{bmatrix} \right). \tag{11.3.11}$$

From (11.3.3), we are interested in

$$f(\alpha_t|Y_t) = N(\alpha_{t|t}, P_{t|t}). \tag{11.3.12}$$

However, it is

$$f(\alpha_t|Y_t) = f(\alpha_t|v_t, Y_{t-1}),$$

and we can use (11.3.11), together with standard results for conditional normal densities, to derive $f(\alpha_t|Y_t)$. Specifically, we have

$$\begin{aligned} \alpha_{t|t} &= \alpha_{t|t-1} + P_{t|t-1}Z'F_t^{-1}v_t, \\ P_{t|t} &= P_{t|t-1} - P_{t|t-1}Z'F_t^{-1}ZP_{t|t-1}, \end{aligned}$$

which coincides with (11.3.4). This concludes our derivation of Kalman filter equations.

We have seen that Kalman filter produces optimal (recursive) one-step ahead forecasts for α and y. However, we can be interested in h-steps ahead forecasts. They can be derived as follows. From (11.2.1) we have

$$\alpha_{t+h} = T^h\alpha_t + R\eta_{t+h} + TR\eta_{t+h-1} + \ldots + T^{h-1}R\eta_{t+1}.$$

Therefore, the optimal h-steps ahead forecast for α is

$$E(\alpha_{t+h}|Y_t) = \alpha_{t+h|t} = T^h\alpha_{t|t}, \tag{11.3.13}$$

with associated forecast error

$$\begin{aligned} u_{t+h} &= \alpha_{t+h} - \alpha_{t+h|t} = \\ &= T^h(\alpha_t - \alpha_{t|t}) + R\eta_{t+h} + TR\eta_{t+h-1} + \ldots + T^{h-1}R\eta_{t+1}, \end{aligned}$$

whose variance is

$$\text{Var}(u_{t+h}) = T^h P_{t|t} T^{h\prime} + RQR' + \ldots + T^{h-1}RQR'T^{h-1\prime}. \tag{11.3.14}$$

For y, from (11.2.5) it is

$$y_{t+h} = Z\alpha_{t+h} + S\xi_{t+h},$$

from which it follows that the optimal h-steps ahead forecast for y is

$$E(y_{t+h}|Y_t) = y_{t+h|t} = Z\alpha_{t+h|t}. \qquad (11.3.15)$$

The forecast error is then

$$
\begin{aligned}
e_{t+h} &= y_{t+h} - y_{t+h|t} = \\
&= Z(\alpha_{t+h} - \alpha_{t+h|t}) + S\xi_{t+h} = Zu_{t+h} + S\xi_{t+h},
\end{aligned}
$$

with

$$\mathrm{Var}(e_{t+h}) = Z\mathrm{Var}(u_{t+h})Z' + SHS'. \qquad (11.3.16)$$

To conclude, in all Kalman filter equations we condition on information up to the previous period. This is particularly convenient in a forecasting context. However, in a more structural context, we may be interested in conditioning inference on all the available information, namely, we would like to condition on Y_T. For example, if α_t is an unobservable economic variable of interest, such as the output gap or a business cycle indicator, we may want to assess ex-post, at the end of the sample, what were its most likely values over the sample. All the equations we have seen can be modified to condition on the full sample information Y_T rather than on Y_{t-1}, and the resulting procedure is known as the Kalman smoother, see, e.g., Harvey (1993) for details.

11.4 Example with simulated data: The TVP regression model

We now illustrate the TVP regression model using simulated data. Specifically, we generate simulated observations using an appropriate DGP. We then specify and estimate an appropriate state space form, and compare this model with some benchmark models using several diagnostics.

Simulation

We want to generate data from the following DGP:

$$
\begin{aligned}
y_t &= X_t \beta_t + \varepsilon_t \\
\beta_t &= \beta_{t-1} + \eta_t
\end{aligned}
$$

$$
\begin{bmatrix} \varepsilon_t \\ \eta_t \end{bmatrix} \overset{iid}{\sim} N\left(\begin{bmatrix} 0 \\ 0 \end{bmatrix}, \begin{bmatrix} \sigma_\varepsilon^2 & 0 \\ 0 & \lambda Q \end{bmatrix} \right)
$$

Since this is a bit different from the DGPs we have seen so far, we start by explaining how to generate data from this DGP.

The sample size is T = 356, and we assume the data covers the period 1925Q1 to 2013Q4, on a quarterly basis. Data are actually generated for a larger sample, but the first observations are discarded, in order to avoid dependence on the starting values. As first, we generate the k regressors of the vector X_t using a VAR structure

$$
X_t = \begin{bmatrix} a_1 & 0 & \cdots & 0 \\ 0 & a_2 & \ddots & \vdots \\ \vdots & \ddots & \ddots & 0 \\ 0 & \cdots & 0 & a_k \end{bmatrix} X_{t-1} + e_t \qquad e_t \overset{iid}{\sim} N\left(0_{k \times 1}, \Xi \right)
$$

where Ξ is a full (non-diagonal) matrix. The produced regressors are reported in Figure 11.4.1.

Subsequently, we can simulate the time varying coefficients, modeled as a random walk. The DGP for the β is

$$
\beta_t = \beta_{t-1} + \eta_t \qquad \eta_t \overset{iid}{\sim} N\left(0, \lambda Q \right)
$$

where Q is a full non diagonal matrix. Figure 11.4.2 reports the simulated random walk coefficients.

Finally, we can use the DGP for the dependent variable, which lays upon the regressors and the time varying coefficients:

$$
y_t = \underbrace{X_t}_{1xk} \underbrace{\beta_t}_{kx1} + \varepsilon_t \qquad \varepsilon_t \overset{iid}{\sim} N\left(0, \sigma_\varepsilon^2 \right)
$$

Now, we simulate the dependent variable y_t, reported in Figure 11.4.3.

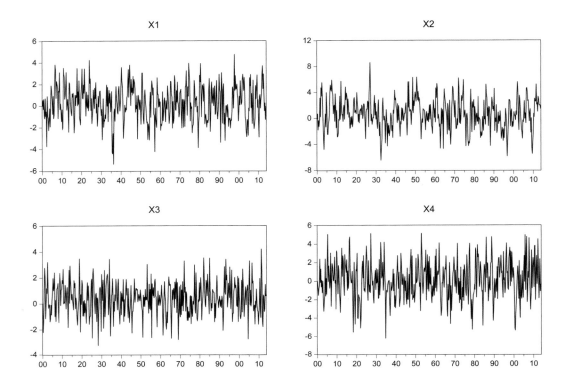

Figure 11.4.1: *Regressors X_t, 1925Q1 to 2013Q4*

Specification and estimation

Consider the following state space form:

$$
\begin{aligned}
y_t &= c_t + Z_t \alpha_t + \varepsilon_t \\
\alpha_{t+1} &= d_t + T_t \alpha_t + v_t \\
\begin{bmatrix} \varepsilon_t \\ v_t \end{bmatrix} &= N\left(\mathbf{0}, \Omega_t\right) \\
\Omega_t &= \begin{bmatrix} H_t & G_t \\ G'_t & Q_t \end{bmatrix}
\end{aligned}
$$

In our example, we have just one signal equation for y_t, where we used the k observable regressors stacked in Z_t

$$
Z_t = X_t = \begin{bmatrix} x_{1,t} & x_{2,t} & \cdots & x_{k,t} \end{bmatrix}
$$

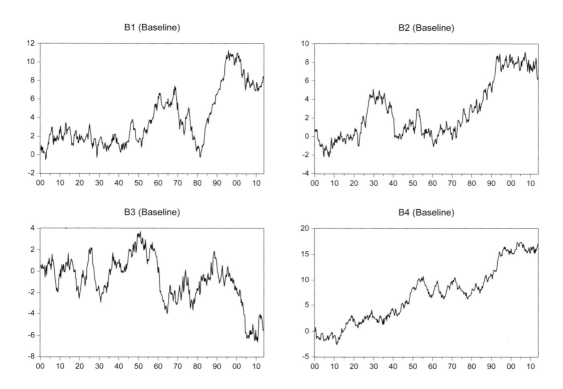

Figure 11.4.2: *Simulated random walk coefficients β_t, 1925Q1 to 2013Q4*

The time varying coefficients are estimated as state variables α_t

$$\alpha_t = \beta_t = \begin{bmatrix} \beta_{1,t} \\ \beta_{2,t} \\ \vdots \\ \beta_{k,t} \end{bmatrix}$$

Note that in our case the signal equation has only one random innovation ε_t. Since we assume independence between respectively observable process and state innovations, one can write

$$\forall t, \quad H_t = \sigma_\varepsilon^2, \quad G_t = \mathbf{0}$$

As for the state equation, being β_t a vector of random walks with no drift, we have:

$$T_t = I_k, \quad d_t = 0_{k \times 1}$$

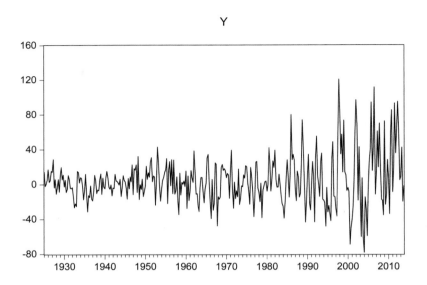

Figure 11.4.3: *Simulated dependent variable y_t, 1925Q1 to 2013Q4*

Finally, our specification assumes time invariant variance matrix for the coefficients' innovations, scaled by parameter λ:

$$Q_t = \lambda Q$$

Note that now we can estimate the model and initialize the states with their actual values coming from simulation.

Evaluation

After having estimated the model, we can graph the series of smoothed states and their standard errors, as in Figure 11.4.4. Comparing these results with Figure 11.4.2, we find good estimates for β_t.

We can then compare actual and estimated states using the pairwise correlation matrix, or regress the actual β_t on the estimated counterpart $\hat{\beta}_t$. Table 11.4.1 reports results for the first coefficient $\hat{\beta}_{1,t}$, while Figure 11.4.5 shows its residuals.

From the test-statistics and residuals plot we observe that our state space is producing a reliable estimate for the time-varying coefficients. As a further check, performing some cointegration tests between the actual TV coefficients and the estimated counterpart, we find that for almost all specifications we

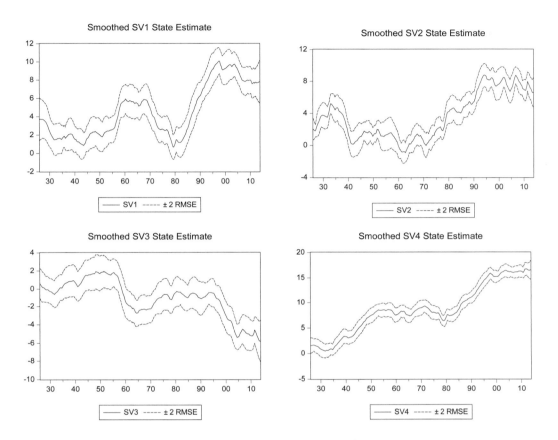

Figure 11.4.4: *Estimated states variables $\hat{\beta}_t$, 1925Q1 to 2013Q4*

do not reject the presence of one cointegrating relation. The tests for $\hat{\beta}_{1,t}$ are reported in Table 11.4.2.

Let's now try to compare the forecasting power of our state space TVP estimation with a benchmark OLS equation model with fixed coefficients, whose specification is simply:

$$y_t = \underbrace{X_t}_{1xk} \underbrace{\beta}_{kx1} + \varepsilon_t, \qquad \varepsilon_t \overset{iid}{\sim} N\left(0, \sigma^2\right)$$

Figure 11.4.6 reports the residuals of this regression, which seem to present evidence of serial correlation and heteroskedasticity.

Having estimated both models, we perform an out-of-sample one-step ahead static forecasting exercise, in which for all observations in the forecasting period we adapt the estimation period recursively. We construct

	Coefficient	Std. Error	t-Statistic	Prob.
C	-0.266	0.089	-2.988	0.003
F_SV1	1.048	0.017	63.197	0.000
R-squared	0.919	Mean dep var		4.493
Adjusted R-squared	0.919	S.D. dep var		3.126
S.E. of regression	0.892	Akaike IC		2.615
Sum squared resid	280.935	Schwarz IC		2.637
Log likelihood	-462.189	Hannan-Quinn		2.624
F-statistic	3993.852	DW stat		0.209
Prob(F-statistic)	0.000			

Table 11.4.1: *OLS regression of the actual $\beta_{1,t}$ over the estimated $\hat{\beta}_{1,t}$*

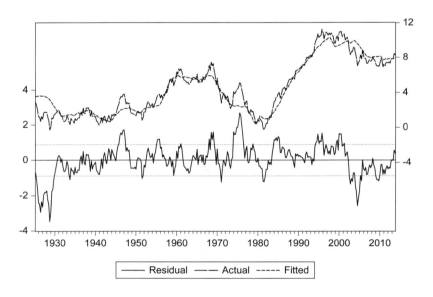

Figure 11.4.5: *Residuals from the OLS regression of $\beta_{1,t}$ over $\hat{\beta}_{1,t}$, 1925Q2 to 2013Q4*

then out of sample forecasts from 2006Q4 to 2013Q4, using each period the recursive estimates of both models. Having actual observations, we can compute the RMSFE for both the constant and time varying parameters model.

Data Trend:	None	None	Linear	Linear	Quadratic
Test Type	No Intercept	Intercept	Intercept	Intercept	Intercept
	No Trend	No Trend	No Trend	Trend	Trend
Trace	1	1	1	1	2
Max-Eig	1	1	1	1	2

*Critical values based on MacKinnon, Haug, and Michelis (1999).

Table 11.4.2: *Cointegration tests for actual $\beta_{1,t}$ and estimated states $\hat{\beta}_{1,t}$*

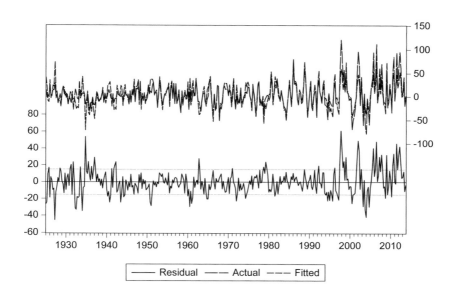

Figure 11.4.6: *Residuals from the OLS regression of y_t over x_t, 1925Q1 to 2013Q4*

As we can see from Figure 11.4.7 and from the RMSFE, the TVP model provides better forecasting performance than its OLS counterpart.

The computed RMSFE of the TVP regression is roughly 7, while the RMSFE is of about 22 for the fixed-parameter benchmark model. Nevertheless, the recursive estimation of OLS coefficients takes somehow into account structural instability of the parameters, since for each augmented observation estimates are updated. For this reason, overall it also provides reasonable forecasts over the period 2006Q4 - 2013Q4.

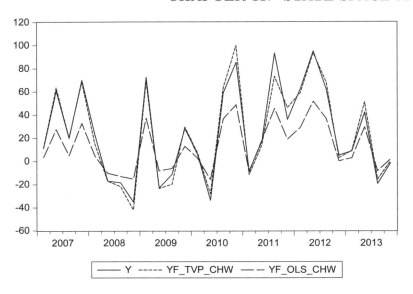

Figure 11.4.7: *Actual data y_{T+h} and one-step forecast $\hat{y}_{t+h}$ for OLS and TVP, 2006Q4 to 2013Q4*

11.5   Empirical examples

11.5.1   Forecasting US GDP growth with a TVP model

We now use the TVP regression model on GDP growth rates data, for the period 1986Q1 - 2012Q4. We will apply an AR(2) estimation with time varying autoregressive coefficients that follow a random walk

$$y_t = c_t + \rho_{1t}y_{t-1} + \rho_{2t}y_{t-2} + \varepsilon_t$$

$$\begin{bmatrix} c_t \\ \rho_{1t} \\ \rho_{2t} \end{bmatrix} = \begin{bmatrix} 1 & 0 & 0 \\ 0 & 1 & 0 \\ 0 & 0 & 1 \end{bmatrix} \begin{bmatrix} c_{t-1} \\ \rho_{1t-1} \\ \rho_{2t-1} \end{bmatrix} + \begin{bmatrix} \eta_{1t} \\ \eta_{2t} \\ \eta_{3t} \end{bmatrix}$$

$$\begin{bmatrix} \varepsilon_t \\ \eta_{1t} \\ \eta_{2t} \\ \eta_{3t} \end{bmatrix} \overset{iid}{\sim} N \left(\begin{bmatrix} 0 \\ 0 \\ 0 \\ 0 \end{bmatrix}, \begin{bmatrix} \sigma_\varepsilon^2 & 0 & 0 & 0 \\ 0 & \sigma_{\eta_1}^2 & 0 & 0 \\ 0 & 0 & \sigma_{\eta_2}^2 & 0 \\ 0 & 0 & 0 & \sigma_{\eta_3}^2 \end{bmatrix} \right).$$

As an alternative, we also specify a simpler version of the model when only the drift is time varying:

$$
\begin{aligned}
y_t &= c_t + \rho_1 y_{t-1} + \rho_2 y_{t-2} + \varepsilon_t \\
c_t &= c_{t-1} + \eta_t
\end{aligned}
$$

$$
\begin{bmatrix} \varepsilon_t \\ \eta_t \end{bmatrix} \overset{iid}{\sim} N\left(\begin{bmatrix} 0 \\ 0 \end{bmatrix}, \begin{bmatrix} \sigma_\varepsilon^2 & 0 \\ 0 & \sigma_{\eta_1}^2 \end{bmatrix} \right).
$$

Estimation

Consider the following state space form:

$$
\begin{aligned}
y_t &= c_t + Z_t \alpha_t + \varepsilon_t \\
\alpha_{t+1} &= d_t + T_t \alpha_t + v_t \\
\begin{bmatrix} \varepsilon_t \\ v_t \end{bmatrix} &= N\left(\mathbf{0}, \Omega_t \right) \\
\Omega_t &= \begin{bmatrix} H_t & G_t \\ G_t' & Q_t \end{bmatrix}.
\end{aligned}
$$

In our example, we have just one signal equation for y_t, the US GDP growth rate. The regressors are just the first two lags of y_t:

$$
Z_t = X_t = \begin{bmatrix} y_{t-1} & y_{t-2} \end{bmatrix}.
$$

The time-varying coefficients are estimated as state variables α_t:

$$
\alpha_t = \varrho_t = \begin{bmatrix} \rho_{1,t} \\ \rho_{2,t} \end{bmatrix}.
$$

Note that in our case the signal equation has only one random innovation ε_t. We assume independence between innovations of the coefficients and of the dependent variable. As in the simulation example, we set

$$
\begin{aligned}
\forall t, \quad H_t &= \sigma_\varepsilon^2, \quad G_t = \mathbf{0} \\
T_t &= I_2, \quad d_t = 0_{2\times 1}
\end{aligned}
$$

Finally, our specification assumes time invariant variance matrix for the coefficients' innovations

$$
Q_t = Q
$$

where Q is a diagonal matrix.

Evaluation

After having estimated the TVP regression model, it is possible to compare the forecasting power of our state space TVP estimation with a benchmark OLS equation model with fixed coefficients, whose specification is simply

$$y_t = c + \rho_1 y_{t-1} + \rho_2 y_{t-2} + \varepsilon_t, \quad \varepsilon_t \sim N\left(0, \sigma^2\right).$$

OLS estimation results are reported in Table 11.5.1. Having these models

	Coefficient	Std. Error	t-Statistic	Prob.
C	2.594	0.488	5.316	0.000
AR(1)	1.320	0.089	14.916	0.000
AR(2)	-0.464	0.088	-5.265	0.000
SIGMASQ	0.487	0.067	7.309	0.000
R-squared	0.855	Mean dep var		2.591
Adjusted R-squared	0.851	S.D. dep var		1.842
S.E. of regression	0.711	Akaike IC		2.213
Sum squared resid	52.644	Schwarz IC		2.313
Log likelihood	-115.525	Hannan-Quinn		2.254
F-statistic	204.285	DW stat		2.139
Prob(F-statistic)	0.000			

Table 11.5.1: *Output of the OLS estimation with fixed AR coefficient*

estimated, we perform two out-of-sample one-step ahead static forecasting exercises for all the models. In the first exercise the start of the forecast period is set at 2001Q1, the starting date for estimation sample remains fixed while the ending date shifts with the forecasting horizon, as in the regression with simulated data. In the second exercise, we implement a forecasting procedure using a rolling window of 60 observations. Rolling forecasting is typically a well-suited approach in order to tackle instability of parameters. In this case, also the starting date of the estimation sample moves with the forecasting dates, while the size remains fixed.

Using the actual observations, we can compute the RMSFE for both the OLS estimation and the TVP in both exercises. Table 11.5.2 shows the results for the three models under analysis: the OLS, the TVP with all time-varying coefficients, and the TVP with only time-varying drift. Then for both exercises, we can compare the forecasts to the actual data (Figure 11.5.1). Since the differences are not so dramatic, we better analyze the RMSFE for

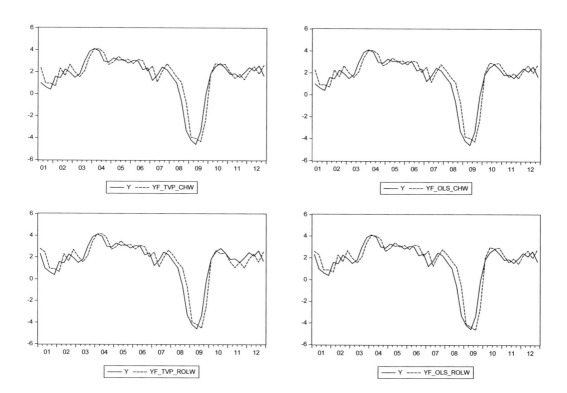

Figure 11.5.1: *Out-of-sample forecasts for TVP-all coefficients, OLS AR specification, and actual data, from 2001Q1 to 2012Q4. Upper panels show the out-of-sample one-step ahead recursive forecasts, while lower panels report the out-of-sample one-step ahead rolling window forecasts*

the alternative models and forecasting techniques (Table 11.5.2).

RMSFE	OLS	TVP-all	TVP-drift
one-step ahead recursive	0.802	0.886	0.799
one-step ahead rolling window	0.823	0.933	0.814

Table 11.5.2: *RMSFE for all models and forecasting techniques, from 2001Q1 to 2012Q4*

Both TVP and OLS forecasts are perform better with the largest sample possible, and somehow suffer from sample reduction due to the rolling forecasting. However, the classical OLS and the TV-only-drift models experience a much smaller deterioration of the forecasting performance than the TVP-all analogue, probably because of the relatively higher number of coefficients to estimate.

In general, in this exercise we find evidence of instability of model coefficients, and both the non-rolling TVP forecasts and the rolling OLS forecasts display satisfactory performance. It was noted that rolling or recursive estimation of a constant parameter model takes at least partially into account possible time variation of the parameters.

11.5.2   Forecasting GDP growth with dynamic factor models

We now estimate a dynamic factor model using GDP growth. Data consists of quarterly real GDP growth rates of three EMU countries (Italy, Germany, and France) and the United States, spanning from 1986Q1 to 2012Q4 (108 observations). We compare two specifications, one having just one common factor as common component of the four GDP growth rates, and the other less parsimonious with two factors and a richer autoregressive structure of the factors.

Estimation

Consider the following state space form:

$$
\begin{aligned}
y_t &= c_t + Z_t \alpha_t + \varepsilon_t \\
\alpha_{t+1} &= d_t + T_t \alpha_t + v_t \\
\begin{bmatrix} \varepsilon_t \\ v_t \end{bmatrix} &= N\left(\mathbf{0}, \Omega_t\right) \\
\Omega_t &= \begin{bmatrix} H_t & G_t \\ G_t' & Q_t \end{bmatrix}
\end{aligned}
$$

In our example, we have four observables contained in the vector y_t, the growth rates of the United States, Germany, Italy, and France.

First, we consider a specification having only one factor and four idiosyncratic components. The state variables vector for this specification is

$$\alpha_t = \begin{bmatrix} f_t \\ u_{US,t} \\ u_{FR,t} \\ u_{GER,t} \\ u_{IT,t} \end{bmatrix}.$$

If we model the factor and the idiosyncratic components as uncorrelated AR(1) processes, the state equations are

$$\alpha_t = \begin{bmatrix} \phi & 0 & 0 & 0 & 0 \\ 0 & t_{us} & 0 & 0 & 0 \\ 0 & 0 & t_{FR} & 0 & 0 \\ 0 & 0 & 0 & t_{GER} & 0 \\ 0 & 0 & 0 & 0 & t_{IT} \end{bmatrix} \alpha_{t-1} + \begin{bmatrix} v_t \\ \varepsilon_{US,t} \\ \varepsilon_{FR,t} \\ \varepsilon_{GER,t} \\ \varepsilon_{IT,t} \end{bmatrix}$$

and the state innovations are modeled as

$$\begin{bmatrix} v_t \\ \varepsilon_{US,t} \\ \varepsilon_{FR,t} \\ \varepsilon_{GER,t} \\ \varepsilon_{IT,t} \end{bmatrix} \sim N\left(\mathbf{0}, \underbrace{\begin{bmatrix} \sigma_v^2 & \mathbf{0} \\ \mathbf{0} & \Sigma_\varepsilon \end{bmatrix}}_{5\times 5} \right).$$

The signal equations are then contained in the following matrix form

$$\begin{bmatrix} y_{US,t} \\ y_{FR,t} \\ y_{GER,t} \\ y_{IT,t} \end{bmatrix} = \begin{bmatrix} \gamma_{US} & 1 & 0 & 0 & 0 \\ \gamma_{FR} & 0 & 1 & 0 & 0 \\ \gamma_{GER} & 0 & 0 & 1 & 0 \\ \gamma_{IT} & 0 & 0 & 0 & 1 \end{bmatrix} \alpha_t.$$

Note that in this case the measurement equation has no random innovations.

The alternative specification to model our GDP data would has two factors and four idiosyncratic components, for example because we may think that the United States and Euro area business cycles are driven by different factors. Moreover, the factors are modeled as orthogonal AR(2) processes,

while the idiosyncratic components are kept as AR(1) processes. The vector
of state variables in this case is

$$\alpha_t = \begin{bmatrix} f_{1,t} \\ f_{1,t-1} \\ f_{2,t} \\ f_{2,t-1} \\ u_{US,t} \\ u_{FR,t} \\ u_{GER,t} \\ u_{IT,t} \end{bmatrix}.$$

Given our assumptions on the state variables motion, the state equations
are

$$\alpha_t = \begin{bmatrix} \phi_{1,1} & \phi_{1,2} & 0 & 0 & 0 & 0 & 0 & 0 \\ 1 & 0 & 0 & 0 & 0 & 0 & 0 & 0 \\ 0 & 0 & \phi_{2,1} & \phi_{2,2} & 0 & 0 & 0 & 0 \\ 0 & 0 & 1 & 0 & 0 & 0 & 0 & 0 \\ 0 & 0 & 0 & 0 & t_{us} & 0 & 0 & 0 \\ 0 & 0 & 0 & 0 & 0 & t_{FR} & 0 & 0 \\ 0 & 0 & 0 & 0 & 0 & 0 & t_{GER} & 0 \\ 0 & 0 & 0 & 0 & 0 & 0 & 0 & t_{IT} \end{bmatrix} \alpha_{t-1} + \begin{bmatrix} v_{1,t} \\ 0 \\ v_{2,t} \\ 0 \\ \varepsilon_{US,t} \\ \varepsilon_{FR,t} \\ \varepsilon_{GER,t} \\ \varepsilon_{IT,t} \end{bmatrix}$$

and the state innovations are modeled as

$$\begin{bmatrix} v_{1,t} \\ v_{2,t} \\ \varepsilon_{US,t} \\ \varepsilon_{FR,t} \\ \varepsilon_{GER,t} \\ \varepsilon_{IT,t} \end{bmatrix} \sim N \left(\mathbf{0}, \begin{bmatrix} \Sigma_v & \mathbf{0} \\ \mathbf{0} & \Sigma_\varepsilon \end{bmatrix} \right).$$

The measurement equations are contained in the following matrix form

$$\begin{bmatrix} y_{US,t} \\ y_{FR,t} \\ y_{GER,t} \\ y_{IT,t} \end{bmatrix} = \begin{bmatrix} \gamma_{1,US} & 0 & \gamma_{2,US} & 0 & 1 & 0 & 0 & 0 \\ \gamma_{1,FR} & 0 & \gamma_{2,FR} & 0 & 0 & 1 & 0 & 0 \\ \gamma_{1,GER} & 0 & \gamma_{2,GER} & 0 & 0 & 0 & 1 & 0 \\ \gamma_{1,IT} & 0 & \gamma_{2,IT} & 0 & 0 & 0 & 0 & 1 \end{bmatrix} \alpha_t.$$

Evaluation

In this section, we compare the state space (Kalman filter) estimation of the factor model with a benchmark principal component/OLS equation model in which the common factors are estimated as PC scores of the observables y_t, and each $y_{j,t}$ is then regressed on the scores; see Chapter 13 for additional details on the use of principal components as estimators for the unobservable factors.

For the two-factor model, the scores $f_{1,t}^{PC}$ and $f_{2,t}^{PC}$ are estimated and the following regression is run separately for each country $j = \text{US, GER, FR, IT}$:

$$y_{j,t} = \beta_{1,j} f_{1,t-1}^{PC} + \beta_{2,j} f_{2,t-1}^{PC} + e_{j,t}, \qquad e_{j,t} \sim N\left(0, \sigma_j^2\right)$$

where $e_{j,t}$ represent the idiosyncratic components. Note that we used the first lag of the PC scores in order to avoid excessive multicollinearity between dependent variables and factors. We can then plot the PC estimated factors along with the KF state space estimated factors, as shown in Figure 11.5.2.

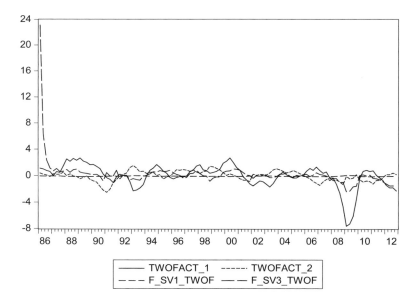

Figure 11.5.2: *PC and KF state space estimated factors for the two-factor model, 1986Q1 - 2012Q4*

To further check the closeness between factors estimated via different techniques, we can run regressions of PC factors projected onto the KF estimated counterparts and see how much variation we are able to explain. Table 11.5.3 reports such regression for the first factor.

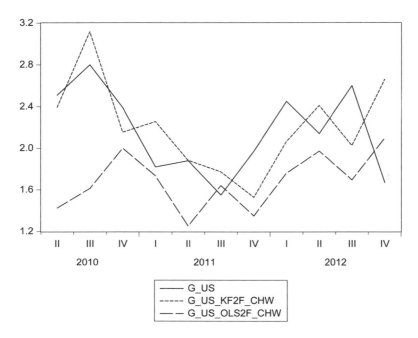

Figure 11.5.3: *Out-of-sample forecasts of both KF and PC/OLS models, and actual data $y_{US,T+h}$ for the US, 1986Q1 - 2012Q4*

Finally, to compare the two-factor estimation methods, we can perform an out-of-sample one-step ahead recursive forecasting exercise for both the KF estimation and the PC/OLS counterpart, setting the start of the forecast period in the second half of the entire sample available. We then plot forecasts from the PC/OLS and the KF, with two factors, for the US growth rate (Figure 11.5.3).

In this case, the RMSFE analysis can be of help to evaluate the forecasts obtained with the two-factor estimation methods (see Table 11.5.4). Overall, the KF estimation displays a better performance, except for the French GDP growth rate.

	Coefficient	Std.Error	t-Statistic	Prob.
C	-2.217	0.099	-22.414	0.000
F_SV1_TWOF	-36.789	1.357	-27.113	0.000
F_SV3_TWOF	0.068	0.018	3.767	0.000
R-squared	0.884	Mean dep var		0.000
Adjusted R-squared	0.882	S.D. dep var		1.770
S.E. of regression	0.607	Akaike IC		1.868
Sum squared resid	38.731	Schwarz IC		1.942
Log likelihood	-97.869	Hannan-Quinn		1.898
F-statistic	401.649	DW stat		0.211
Prob(F-statistic)	0.000			

Table 11.5.3: *OLS regression of the first PC score $f_{1,t}^{PC}$ over the KF factors*

RMSFE	g_fr	g_ger	g_it	g_us
KF_two_factors	0.517	0.846	0.889	0.441
OLS/PC	0.475	1.280	1.569	0.677

Table 11.5.4: *RMSFE for the KF state space and the OLS/PC forecasts, from 2010Q1 to 2012Q4.*

11.6 Concluding remarks

In this chapter, we first showed how to cast a model in state space form, using a number of examples, and then we derived the main components of the Kalman filter. We showed indeed that a large set of econometric models can be cast into a state space form, where observable variables are related to a set of unobservables, and the law of motion of the latter is specified. Once a model is written in state space form, the Kalman filter provides a procedure to compute both forecasts of the observable and unobservable variables and the model likelihood, and to derive maximum likelihood estimators of the model parameters.

We discussed some examples using both simulated and actual data of US and Euro area GDP growth. The first two examples allowed us to estimate

TVP models and compare them to standard OLS models with constant parameters. Finally, in the last example, we also defined a dynamic factor model to forecast national GDP growth rates and compared a PC/OLS estimation model to the KF approach.

Part IV

Mixed Frequency, Large Datasets, and Volatility

Chapter 12

Models for Mixed-Frequency Data

12.1 Introduction

When faced with data sampled at different frequencies, the simplest approach is to aggregate the high-frequency data to obtain a balanced dataset at the same low-frequency. For example, if a researcher combines quarterly data on GDP growth with monthly data on industrial production (IP), and wants to study their relationship. The researcher might consider aggregating the IP data to the quarterly frequency – either taking an average of the monthly data or using the last month of each quarter. While simple, in general, temporal aggregation entails a loss of information. Moreover, it also modifies the generating mechanism of the data, so that the dynamics of the aggregate model can be rather different from that in high or mixed frequency. This implies that key econometric features, such as Granger causality or exogeneity, can be spuriously modified when working with aggregated data.[1]

In recent times, econometric models that take into account the information in unbalanced datasets have attracted substantial attention. Policymakers, in particular, need to assess in real-time the current state of the economy and its expected developments, when only incomplete information is available. As noted, one of the key indicators of macroeconomic activity, namely GDP, is released quarterly (and with a substantial temporal

---

[1]See, e.g., Granger (1980), Marcellino (1999), Ghysels, Hill, and Motegi (2016), Ghysels, Hill, and Motegi (2015) for details.

delay), while a range of leading and coincident indicators is timely available at a monthly or even higher frequency. Hence, we may want to construct a forecast of the current quarter GDP growth based on the available higher frequency information. Mixed-frequency data in a forecasting setting invariably relate to the notion of nowcasting. Let us consider GDP forecasting as an example. In this context, nowcasting means that in a particular calendar month, GDP for the current quarter is not observed. It can even be the case that GDP is only available with considerable publication delay beyond the end of the quarter. The question then arises whether we can make a prediction about the *current* quarter GDP using monthly, weekly, daily economic time series.

In this chapter we review some of the methods proposed so far in the literature to deal with mixed-frequency data.[2]

In what follows, we will consider three alternative approaches to directly model the mixed-frequency data, avoiding the mentioned problems related to temporal aggregation. First, the bridge models, which linearly relate (bridge) the low- and high-frequency indicators. This approach is often employed in central banks and other policy-making institutions, especially for nowcasting and short-term forecasting, see, e.g., Baffigi, Golinelli, and Parigi (2004), Diron (2008), Schumacher (2016), among others.

Second, the mixed-data sampling (MIDAS) models, parsimonious specifications based on distributed lag polynomials, which flexibly deal with data sampled at different frequencies and provide a direct forecast of the low-frequency variable (see, e.g., Ghysels, Santa-Clara, and Valkanov (2004), Ghysels, Santa-Clara, and Valkanov (2006) and Clements and Galvão (2009)).

Third, a particular class of mixed-frequency VAR (MF-VAR) models. While bridge and MIDAS are univariate methods, the MF-VAR is a system approach that jointly describes the dynamics of the high and low-frequency variables. Certain MF-VAR models are estimated by means of Kalman filter

---

[2]The material presented in this chapter is in part based on recent surveys by Andreou, Ghysels, and Kourtellos (2011), Foroni, Ghysels, and Marcellino (2013) and Foroni and Marcellino (2013). See also Bańbura, Giannone, and Reichlin (2011) and Bańbura, Giannone, Modugno, and Reichlin (2013) for complementary overviews with a stronger focus on more complex Kalman filter-based factor modeling techniques. These papers also discuss how to handle the "ragged edge" of the data (cf. Wallis (1986)), namely, that since the release date of the indicators is typically different, at any given point in time there is asynchronous information, i.e., some of the latest observations for some of the indicators are missing. For simplicity, we will not consider this additional issue and just focus on modeling using the mixed-frequency data.

(see Chapter 11), which provides not only predictions of the future observations but also estimates of the current latent state.

For each of the alternative approaches to mixed-frequency modeling listed above, we will first describe their key theoretical features and then summarize empirical applications.

We will focus on the methods but we wish to stress that the choice of the indicators is particularly relevant in the context of nowcasting. Specifically, different indicators may have to be used over time, depending on the specific information set available at the time of nowcasting, on the business cycle phase, and on the largest shocks hitting the system. Moreover, some indicators can shift the point forecasts, while others can have a stronger effect on the density forecasts, improving forecast precision. Data revisions and data pre-treatment, such as seasonal adjustment and outlier removal also play an important role for the final outcome. Finally, the use of real-time data is particularly relevant for a proper evaluation of the relative performance and reliability of a nowcasting model. All these issues have been discussed in other parts of the book and are considered in more details in the papers covering the empirical applications surveyed in this chapter.

The chapter is organized as follows. In Section 12.2, we deal with bridge models, while in Sections 12.3 and 12.4 we consider, respectively, MIDAS, MF-VAR, and MIDAS-VAR models. In Section 12.5 we assess the relative performance of the alternative mixed-frequency model using simulated data, while in Section 12.6 we do that in the context of an empirical application on nowcasting US GDP growth using a set of timely monthly indicators. Finally, in Section 12.7 we summarize and conclude.

12.2 Bridge equations

Bridge equations are linear regressions that link (bridge) high-frequency variables, such as industrial production or retail sales, to low-frequency ones, e.g., the quarterly real GDP growth, providing some estimates of current and short-term developments in advance of the release. The bridge model technique allows computing early estimates of the low-frequency variables by using high-frequency indicators. They are not standard macroeconometric models, since the inclusion of specific indicators is not mainly based on causal relations, but more on the statistical fact that they contain timely updated information.

In principle, bridge equation models require that the whole set of regressors should be known over the projection period, but this is rarely the case. Taking forecasting GDP as an example, since the monthly indicators are usually only partially available over the projection period, the predictions of quarterly GDP growth are obtained in two steps. First, monthly indicators are predicted over the remainder of the quarter, usually on the basis of univariate time series models (in some cases VAR have been implemented in order to obtain better forecasts of the monthly indicators), and then aggregated to obtain their quarterly correspondent values. Second, the aggregated values are used as regressors in the bridge equation to obtain forecasts of GDP growth.

It will be convenient to focus on a mixture of two frequencies, respectively high and low. In terms of notation, $t = 1, \ldots, T$ indices the low-frequency time unit, and m is the number of times the higher sampling frequency appears in the same basic time unit (assumed fixed for simplicity). For example, for quarterly GDP growth and monthly indicators as explanatory variables, $m = 3$. The low-frequency variable will be denoted by y_t^L, whereas a generic high-frequency series will be denoted by $x_{t-j/m}^H$ where $t - j/m$ is the jth (past) high-frequency period with $j = 0, \ldots m - 1$. For a quarter/month mixture one has x_t^H, $x_{t-1/3}^H$, $x_{t-2/3}^H$ as the last, second to last, and first months of quarter t. Obviously, through some aggregation scheme, such as flow or stock sampling, we can always construct a low-frequency series x_t^L. We will simply assume that $x_t^L = \sum_{i=0}^{m-1} a_i x_{t-i/m}^H$.[3]

Bridge models involving a single regressor typically start with a distributed lag model (cf. equation 3.2.7). For pedagogical reasons and notational convenience, we will work with a static regression model instead, namely:

$$y_t^L = a + b x_t^L + u_t^L \qquad (12.2.1)$$

where u_t^L is an error term assumed to be i.i.d. We know from Chapter 1 that the parameters can be estimated via OLS, and let us call the estimated parameters $\hat{a}_T$ and $\hat{b}_T$. Suppose now we want to predict the first out-of-sample (low-frequency) observation, namely:

$$\hat{y}_{T+1}^L = \hat{a}_T + \hat{b}_T x_{T+1}^L$$

---

[3]For further discussion of aggregation schemes see for example or Lütkepohl (2012) or Stock and Watson (2002b, Appendix).

Unfortunately, we do not have x^L_{T+1}, but recall that we do have high-frequency observations $x^H_{T+1-i/m}$ available. For example, if we have values for x^H for the first two months of quarter $T+1$ ($x^H_{T+1-2/m}$ and $x^H_{T+1-1/m}$), then only x^H_{T+1} is missing to complete the quarterly value x^L_{T+1}. Using an empirically suitable univariate time series model, as we studied in Chapter 5, applied to the *high-frequency* observations, we can obtain prediction formulas:

$$\hat{x}^H_{T+1|T+1-1/m} = \hat{\phi}(L^{1/m})x^H_{T+1-1/m}$$

where $\hat{\phi}(\cdot)$ is a polynomial lag operator for one high-frequency horizon prediction with parameter estimates obtained over a sample of size $T_H = T \times m + 2$ (as we also have two months for quarter $T+1$) and $L^{1/m}x^H_{T+1-i/m} = x^H_{T+1(i+1)/m}$.

We can index $\hat{\phi}_h(\cdot)$ with h the forecast horizon in high-frequency, to emphasize that it does depend on the forecast horizon (the index was dropped when $h = 1$ in the above formula). Then, in general for consecutive high-frequency observations we can replace the unknown regressor x^L_{T+1} with partial realizations of the high-frequency observations and complemented with estimates of the missing ones, namely the missing ones with high-frequency-based predictions, namely:

$$
\begin{aligned}
\hat{y}^L_{T+1|T+1-(m-i)/m} =\ & \hat{a}_T + \hat{b}_T[\textstyle\sum_{j=1}^i a_{m-j}x^H_{T+1-(m-j)/m}] \\
& +\hat{b}_T[\textstyle\sum_{h=1}^{i-m} a_{m-(i-h)}\hat{\phi}_h(L^{1/m})x^H_{T+1-(m-1)/m}]
\end{aligned}
\tag{12.2.2}
$$

for $i = 1, \ldots, m - 1$. These are a collection of nowcasts (or flash estimates in statistical terminology), using bridge equations.[4]

Note that in the above equation we froze the parameter estimates $\hat{a}_T$ and $\hat{b}_T$ while updating the regressors. We used a static regression and a single regressor for illustrative purposes. In practice, the bridge equations can involve multiple regressors or (low-frequency) distributed lag type of models – often also involving lagged dependent variables, i.e. low-frequency ARDL models are the starting point with regressors that are available at higher frequencies.

The usual setting is one involving a combination of quarterly and monthly data series. The selection of the monthly indicators included in the bridge

---

[4]A flash estimate or nowcast is defined exactly as a preliminary estimate produced/published as soon as possible after the end of the reference period, using a more incomplete set of information than the one used for the final estimates.

model is typically based on a general-to-specific methodology and relies on different in-sample or out-of-sample criteria, like information criteria or RMSFE performance.

Bridge equations have been one of the first methods employed in nowcasting the current state of the economy, making use of the available monthly information. A common finding is that the exploitation of intra-period information reduces the forecasting error in the majority of cases. Looking, for example, at US data, Ingenito and Trehan (1996) constructed a model that predicts current quarter real GDP using nonfarm payrolls, industrial production, and real retail sales, which have the advantage of being released at a monthly frequency by the middle of the subsequent month. In order to produce a model that predicts real GDP, the authors rely on auxiliary models that generate forecasts of the indicator variables themselves. Their evidence shows that consumption data provide key information about current output, and that retail sales yield a good forecast of contemporaneous consumption.

A study by Barhoumi, Darné, Ferrara, and Pluyaud (2012) presents a model to predict French GDP quarterly growth rate. The authors employ the bridge equations to forecast each component of GDP, and select the monthly explanatory variables among a large set of hard and soft data. They find that changing the set of equations over the quarter is superior to keeping the same equations.

Studies involving bridge equations can be found for many other countries. In particular, bridge models have been used for nowcasting Euro area GDP growth. As an example, we consider Baffigi, Golinelli, and Parigi (2004). In their paper, bridge models are estimated for aggregate GDP and its components, both area-wide and for the main countries of the Euro area. Their short-term performance is assessed with respect to benchmark univariate and multivariate standard models, and a small structural model. The results shown in the paper are clear-cut: bridge models performance is always better than benchmark models, provided that at least some indicators are available over the forecasting horizon. As far as the type of aggregation is concerned, the supply-side approach (modeling aggregate GDP) performs better than the demand-side approach (aggregation of forecasts by national account components). The supply-side models highlight the role of industrial production and manufacturing surveys as the best monthly indicators. Looking at the demand-side models, it appears that private consumption is well tracked by retail sales, while the consumer confidence index plays a minor role; in the case of investment a major role seems to be played by survey variables.

Diron (2008) also makes use of bridge equations with Euro area data to provide an assessment of forecast errors, which takes into account data-revisions. Using four years of data vintages, the paper provides estimates of forecast errors for Euro area real GDP growth in genuine real-time conditions and assesses the impact of data revisions on short-term forecasts of real GDP growth. Given the size of revision to indicators of activity, the assessment of reliability of short-term forecasts based on revised series could potentially give a misleading picture (see also Ghysels, Horan, and Moench (2017)). Nevertheless, averaging across all bridge equations, forecasts of individual quarters tend to be similar whether they are based on preliminary or revised data. More specifically, the RMSFEs based on real-time and pseudo real-time exercises are quite similar and both smaller compared with AR forecasts of GDP, considered the benchmark. The difference in forecast accuracy is significant according to Diebold and Mariano (1995) tests, highlighting the that short-term forecasts based on bridge equations are informative.

12.3   MIDAS Regressions

In order to take into account mixed-frequency data, Ghysels, Santa-Clara, and Valkanov (2004), introduced the MIxed-DAta Sampling (MIDAS) approach, which is closely related to the distributed lag (DL) model (cf. equation (3.2.7)), but in this case the dependent variable y_t^L, sampled at a lower-frequency, is regressed on a distributed lag of x_t^H, which is sampled at a higher-frequency. It is why the simplest specification is called a DL-MIDAS regression.

One way to think about MIDAS regressions – although that was not the original motivation – is to note that the bridge equations studied in the previous subsection have a rather unusual estimation structure, namely on the one hand we estimate $\hat{a}_T$ and $\hat{b}_T$ only with low-frequency data, and we estimate separately $\hat{\phi}_h(\cdot)$ only with high-frequency data. In a MIDAS regression, the estimation involves standard one-step estimators.

In what follows, we first present the basic features of the model as presented by Ghysels, Santa-Clara, and Valkanov (2004), the corresponding unrestricted version as in Foroni, Marcellino, and Schumacher (2015), and then some extensions that have been introduced in the literature.

12.3.1   The basic MIDAS regression model

MIDAS regressions are essentially tightly parameterized, reduced form regressions that involve processes sampled at different frequencies. The response to the higher-frequency explanatory variable is modeled using highly parsimonious distributed lag polynomials, to prevent the proliferation of parameters that might otherwise result, as well as the issues related to lag-order selection.

The basic single high-frequency regressor MIDAS model for h-steps ahead (low-frequency) forecasting, with high-frequency data available up to x_t^H is given by

$$y_{t+h}^L = a_h + b_h C(L^{1/m}; \theta_h) x_t^H + \varepsilon_{t+h}^L \qquad (12.3.1)$$

where $C(L^{1/m}; \theta) = \sum_{j=0}^{j_{max}-1} c(j; \theta) L^{j/m}$, and $C(1; \theta) = \sum_{j=0}^{j_{max}-1} c(j; \theta) = 1$.

The parameterization of the lagged coefficients of $c(k; \theta)$ in a parsimonious way is one of the key MIDAS features. Various other parsimonious polynomial specifications have been considered, including (1) beta polynomial, (2) Almon lag polynomial specifications, and (3) step functions, among others. Ghysels, Sinko, and Valkanov (2006) provide a detailed discussion.[5] One of the most used parameterizations is the one known as exponential Almon lag, since it is closely related to the smooth polynomial Almon lag functions that are used to reduce multicollinearity in the distributed lag literature. It is often expressed as

$$c(k; \theta) = \frac{\exp(\theta_1 k + \ldots + \theta_Q k^Q)}{\sum_{k=0}^{K} \exp(\theta_1 k + \ldots + \theta_Q k^Q)} \qquad (12.3.2)$$

This function is known to be quite flexible and can take various shapes with only a few parameters. These include decreasing, increasing or hump-shaped patterns. Ghysels, Santa-Clara, and Valkanov (2006) use the functional form with two parameters, which allows a great flexibility and determines how many lags are included in the regression.

Another possible parameterization, also with only two parameters, is the

---

[5]Various software packages including the MIDAS *Matlab* Toolbox (Ghysels (2013)), the R Package *midasr* (Ghysels, Kvedaras, and Zemlys (2016)), *EViews* and *Gretl* cover a variety of polynomial specifications.

so-called beta lag, because it is based on the beta function:

$$
\begin{aligned}
c(k; \theta_1, \theta_2) &= \frac{f(\frac{k}{K}, \theta_1; \theta_2)}{\sum_{k=0}^{K} f(\frac{k}{K}, \theta_1; \theta_2)} \\
f(x, a, b) &= \frac{x^{a-1}(1-x)^{b-1}\Gamma(a+b)}{\Gamma(a)\Gamma(b)}
\end{aligned}
\tag{12.3.3}
$$

and $\Gamma(a) = \int_0^\infty e^{-x} x^{a-1} dx$. One attractive specific case of the MIDAS beta polynomial involves only one parameter, namely setting $\theta_1 = 1$ and estimating the single parameter θ_2 with the restriction that it be larger than one. Such a specification yields single-parameter downward sloping weights more flexible than exponential or geometric decay patterns.

Ghysels, Rubia, and Valkanov (2009) propose also three other different parameterizations of the lag coefficients:

- a linear scheme, with $c(k; \theta) = \frac{1}{K}$, where there are no parameters to estimate in the lagged weight function;

- a hyperbolic scheme, with

$$
c(k; \theta) = \frac{g(\frac{k}{K}, \theta)}{\sum_{k=0}^{K} g(\frac{k}{K}, \theta)}, \qquad g(k, \theta) = \frac{\Gamma(k + \theta)}{\Gamma(k + 1)\Gamma(\theta)}
$$

  where the gamma function has only one parameter to estimate. In general this specification is not as flexible as the Beta specification;

- a geometric scheme, where $|\theta| \leq 1$ and

$$
c(k; \theta) = \frac{\theta^k}{\sum_{k=0}^{K} \theta^k}.
$$

These are among the most popular parameterizations besides U-MIDAS and MIDAS with step functions that will be discussed in a later subsection. The parameterizations described above are all quite flexible. For different values of the parameters, they can take various shapes: weights attached to the different lags can decline slowly or quickly, or even have a hump shape. Therefore, estimating the parameters from the data automatically determines the shape of the weights and, accordingly, the number of lags to be included in the regression.

A few words about model selection are in order. First, how do we decide on K, the maximal lag in the MIDAS polynomial? It might be tempting to use an information criterion as typically is done for ARMA or ARDL models. However, the number of lags in the high-frequency polynomial is not affecting the number of parameters. Hence, the usual penalty functions such as those in the Akaike (AIC), Schwarz (BIC) or Hannan-Quinn (HQ) criteria will not apply. The only penalty of picking K too large is that we require more (high-frequency) data at the beginning of the sample as the weights typically vanish to zero with K too large. Picking K too small is more problematic. This issue has been discussed extensively in the standard literature on distributed lag models, see, e.g., Judge, Hill, Griffiths, Lütkepohl, and Lee (1988, Chapters 8 and 9). Nevertheless, using information criteria will be useful once we introduce lagged dependent variables, see the next subsection, as the selection of AR augmentations falls within the realm of IC-based model selection. For this reason Andreou, Ghysels, and Kourtellos (2013) recommend using AIC or BIC for example. Finally, Kvedaras and Zemlys (2012) present model specification tests for the polynomial choices in MIDAS regressions.

Suppose now, we want to predict the first out-of-sample (low-frequency) observation, namely considering equation (12.3.1) with $h = 1$:

$$\hat{y}^L_{T+1|T} = \hat{a}_{1,T} + \hat{b}_{1,T} C(L^{1/m}; \hat{\theta}_{1,T}) x^H_T \qquad (12.3.4)$$

where the MIDAS regression model can be estimated using non-linear least squares (NLS), see Ghysels, Santa-Clara, and Valkanov (2004) and Andreou, Ghysels, and Kourtellos (2010) for more details. Nowcasting, or MIDAS with leads as coined by Andreou, Ghysels, and Kourtellos (2013), involving equation (12.3.4) can also be obtained. For example, with i/m additional observations the horizon h shrinks to $h - i/m$, and the above equation becomes:

$$\hat{y}^L_{T+h|T+i/m} = \hat{a}_{h-i/m,T} + b_{h-i/m,T} C(L^{1/m}; \theta_{h-i/m,T}) x^H_{t+i/m}$$

where we note that all the parameters are horizon specific. Therefore, the MIDAS regression needs to be re-estimated specifically for each forecast horizon. In other words, for a given choice of h, we will obtain different estimates of the model parameters, since we are projecting on a different information set (as usual in direct forecasting). Therefore MIDAS regressions always yield direct forecasts (cf. section 5.9). This is even more so with lagged dependent variables – a topic we turn to next.

12.3.2 The AR-MIDAS and ADL-MIDAS models

Since autoregressive models often provide competitive forecasts compared to those obtained with static models that include explanatory variables, the introduction of an autoregressive term in the MIDAS model is a desirable extension.

Clements and Galvão (2008) suggest the introduction of the AR dynamics as a common factor, namely letting $h = 1$ in equation (12.3.1) we have

$$y_{t+1}^L = a_1 + \lambda y_t^L + b_1 C(L^{1/m}; \theta_1)(1 - \lambda L)x_t^H + \varepsilon_{t+1}^L \qquad (12.3.5)$$

that they call the AR-MIDAS regression model. If we write ε_{t+1}^L as $(1 - \lambda L)\tilde{\varepsilon}_{t+1}^L$ then the above equation can be written as a DL-MIDAS in terms of $\tilde{y}_{t+1}^L \equiv (1 - \lambda L)y_{t+1}^L$ and $\tilde{x}_t^H \equiv (1 - \lambda L)x_t^H$.[6]

Note that the right-hand side of the equation contains a product of a polynomial in $L^{1/m}$ and a polynomial in L. This product generates a periodic response of y^L to x^H, irrespective of whether the latter displays a seasonal pattern. To avoid this inconvenience, Andreou, Ghysels, and Kourtellos (2013) introduce the class of ADL-MIDAS regressions, extending the structure of ARDL models to a mixed-frequency setting. Assuming an autoregressive augmentation of order one, the model can be written as

$$y_{t+h}^L = a_h + \lambda_h y_t^L + b_h C(L^{1/m}; \theta_h)x_t^H + \varepsilon_{t+h}^L \qquad (12.3.6)$$

Hence, an ADL-MIDAS regression is a direct forecasting tool projecting a low-frequency series, at some horizon h, namely y_{t+h}^L onto y_t^L (or more lags if we consider higher order AR augmentations) and high-frequency data x_t^H. Nowcasting, or MIDAS with leads, can again be obtained via shifting forward the high-frequency data with $1/m$ increments. The parameters are horizon specific and the forecast is one that is direct (instead of iterated).[7]

12.3.3 Slope or no slope?

So far we wrote all the MIDAS regressions with a product of a slope coefficient, i.e., like b_h in equation (12.3.6), and a weighting scheme, i.e., $C(L^{1/m}; \theta_h)$

---

[6]This is also the rationale for the iterative estimation procedure suggested by Cochrane and Orcutt (1949).

[7]Bridge equations can also feature autoregressive augmentations. Their relationship with ADL-MIDAS is studied by Schumacher (2016).

in the same equation. Identification requires that the sum of the weights adds up to one, see for example equations (12.3.2) and (12.3.3). Do we need to estimate the parameters b and θ separately? The answer depends on the context. If we want to test hypotheses whether the high-frequency series are significant regressors, e.g., Granger non-causality tests, then we clearly need to identify the slope parameter and impose the unit sum restriction on the polynomial weights. Before we discuss the details of such tests, it is worth noting that in many situations there is no need to separately estimate the slope and weighting scheme parameters. Indeed, if we only care about a forecasting equation, then equation (12.3.6) can be rewritten as

$$y_{t+h}^L = a_h + \lambda_h y_t^L + C(L^{1/m}; \tilde{\theta}_h) x_t^H + \varepsilon_{t+h}^L \tag{12.3.7}$$

where the MIDAS polynomials are used without normalization. In some cases this requires some adjustments. Recall that $C(L^{1/m}; \theta) = \sum_{k=0}^{K} c(k; \theta) L^{k/m}$ and, $C(1; \theta) = \sum_{k=0}^{K} c(k; \theta) = 1$. With the exponential Almon, starting from $k = 0$, the non-normalized polynomial always yields a weight equal to one for the zero lag. Therefore, for the exponential Almon it is better to write

$$C(L^{1/m}; \tilde{\theta}_h) = \sum_{k=1}^{K} \exp(\tilde{\theta}_{h1} k + \ldots + \tilde{\theta}_Q k^{hQ}) L^{(k-1)/m}$$

such that the zero lag becomes $\exp(\tilde{\theta}_{h1} + \ldots + \tilde{\theta}_{hQ})$.

What if we do want to test say the hypothesis $b_h = 0$ in equation (12.3.6)? Technically speaking, this is a non-standard test as under the null hypothesis the parameters θ_h are unidentified and standard testing procedures, like t-statistics, do not provide the correct inference. Following Davies (1987), a t-statistic can still be used to evaluate statistical significance if the impact of nuisance parameters is properly accounted for. This is done by computing $\hat{b}_h$ over a grid of θ_h^i for $i = 1, \ldots, G$ (works well with beta-polynomial MIDAS specification – putting the first parameter equal to one, and looking at downward sloping weights only). Hence, one has: $t_{b_h}(\theta_h^i)$ for $i = 1, \ldots, G$. Davies suggests to compute

$$t_{max} \equiv \sup_i t_b(\theta_i).$$

One can compute t_{max} for the grid and typically simulate its distribution under the null, see Hansen (1996) for details.

12.3.4 U-MIDAS and MIDAS with step functions

Foroni, Marcellino, and Schumacher (2015) study the performance of a variant of MIDAS which does not resort to functional distributed lag polynomials. In the paper, the authors discuss how unrestricted MIDAS (U-MIDAS) regressions can be derived in a general linear dynamic framework, and under which conditions the parameters of the underlying high-frequency model can be identified, see also Koenig, Dolmas, and Piger (2003).

Suppose m is small, like equal to three – as in quarterly/monthly data mixtures. Instead of estimating $b_h C(L^{1/m}; \theta_h)$ in equation (12.3.6) or $C(L^{1/m}; \tilde{\theta}_h)$ in (12.3.7), let us estimate the individual lags separately – hence the term unrestricted – yielding the following U-MIDAS regression:

$$
\begin{aligned}
y_{t+h}^L &= a_h + \lambda_h y_t^L + c_h^0 x_t^H + c_h^1 x_{t-1/m}^H + c_h^2 x_{t-2/m}^H \\
&\quad + \ldots + c_h^{m\tilde{K}} x_{t-\tilde{K}}^H + \varepsilon_{t+h}^L,
\end{aligned}
\tag{12.3.8}
$$

which implies that in addition to the parameters a_h and λ_h we estimate $1 + m\tilde{K}$ additional parameters. With $m = 3$ and $\tilde{K}$ small, like say up to four (annual lags) and large enough to make the error term ε_{t+h}^L uncorrelated, it is reasonable to estimate all the U-MIDAS regression parameters via OLS. From a practical point of view, the lag order could differ across variables, and selected by an information criterion such as AIC, BIC, or Hannan-Quinn criteria.

The U-MIDAS regression has all parameters unconstrained and therefore runs against the idea that high-frequency data parameter proliferation has to be avoided. That is why U-MIDAS only works for small values of m. Is there an intermediate solution where we keep the appeal of simple OLS estimation, avoiding the non-linear estimation setting of typical MIDAS regressions, and still keep the number of parameters small? The solution to this is called MIDAS with step functions, as introduced by Ghysels, Sinko, and Valkanov (2006) and Forsberg and Ghysels (2006). A MIDAS regression with S steps and K lags can be written as:

$$
y_{t+h}^L = a_h + \lambda_h y_t^L + \sum_{k=0}^{K} \left(\sum_{s=0}^{S-1} c_s I_{k \in (a_{s-1}, a_s]} \right) x_{t-k/m}^H + \varepsilon_{t+h}^L
$$

$$
\tag{12.3.9}
$$

$$
I_{k \in (a_{s-1}, a_s]} = \begin{cases} 1, & a_{s-1} < k \leq a_s \\ 0, & otherwise \end{cases}
$$

where $a_0 = 0 < a_1 < \ldots < a_{S-1} = K$. Hence, we only estimate S parameters for the high-frequency data projection with $S \ll K$. The indicator function $I_{k \in (a_{s-1}, a_s]}$ applies parameters c_s to segments of high-frequency data lags past a_{s-1} and prior or equal to a_s. The appeal is obvious, as we approximate the smooth polynomial lags via discrete step functions. Model selection amounts to selecting the appropriate set of steps, which can be again guided via information criteria. A popular application of MIDAS with step functions is the so called HAR model of Corsi (2009) involving daily, weekly, and monthly realized volatility, see Chapter 14.

12.3.5   Extensions of the MIDAS regression model

Different extensions of the MIDAS models have been analyzed in the literature, to introduce the use of mixed-frequency data in specific applications or studies, in which there is a need to capture particular features. For example, some studies incorporate regime changes in the parameters or asymmetric reactions to negative or positive values of the explanatory variables. In what follows, we provide a brief overview of some extensions of the MIDAS regression models discussed so far.

Multiple explanatory variables   To allow for the inclusion of several additional explanatory variables into the MIDAS framework, it is necessary to extend the basic model above as follows:

$$y_{t+h}^L = a_h + b_h^1 C(L^{1/m}; \theta_h^1) x_{1,t}^H + \ldots + b_h^I C(L^{1/m}; \theta_h^I) x_{I,t}^H + \varepsilon_{t+h}^L$$

where I is the number of high-frequency series. Within the more general framework, it is also possible to include explanatory variables at different frequencies, since each indicator is modeled with its own polynomial parameterization. As an example, quarterly GDP growth can be explained not only by monthly indicators but also by weekly financial variables, with the explanatory variables, therefore, sampled at two different frequencies. Generically, this includes regression models with different high frequencies, say m_1, $\ldots, m_p$:

$$y_{t+h}^L = a_h + b_h^1 C(L^{1/m}; \theta_h^1) x_{1,t}^H + \ldots + b_h^I C(L^{1/m}; \theta_h^I) x_{I,t}^H + \varepsilon_{t+h}^L$$

Obviously, the above specification may be extended to allow for the presence of an autoregressive structure.

In practice, adding explanatory variables substantially complicates estimation. An alternative, easier procedure, is to work with single indicator MIDAS models and then pool the resulting forecasts. This approach works well, e.g., in an empirical application on nowcasting US GDP growth, see Kuzin, Marcellino, and Schumacher (2013). Alternatively, Andreou, Ghysels, and Kourtellos (2013) use time-varying forecast combination rules to handle large data of daily financial market time series.

Nonparametric MIDAS regression models Breitung and Roling (2015) introduce a nonparametric MIDAS regression, which they use to forecast inflation with daily data. The model can be written as:

$$y_{t+h}^L = a_h + c_h^0 x_t^H + c_h^1 x_{t-1/m}^H + c_h^2 x_{t-2/m}^H + \ldots + c_h^K x_{t-K/m}^H + \varepsilon_{t+h}^L$$

where instead of imposing a polynomial specification, Breitung and Roling propose an alternative nonparametric approach that does not impose a particular functional form but merely assumes that the coefficient c_h^j is a smooth function of j in the sense that the absolute values of the second differences:

$$\nabla^2 c_h^j = c_h^j - 2c_h^{j-1} + c_h^{j-2} \qquad j = 2, \ldots, K$$

are small. Specifically, the coefficients $c_h \equiv c_h^0, \ldots, c_h^K$ are obtained by minimizing the penalized least-squares objective function

$$S(\lambda_h, c_h) = \sum_{t=1}^T (y_{t+h}^L - a_h - c_h^0 x_t^H - \ldots - c_h^K x_{t-K/m}^H)^2 + \gamma \sum_{j=2}^K \nabla^2 c_h^j$$

where γ is a pre-specified smoothing parameter. This objective function provides a trade-off between the traditional goodness-of-fit and an additional term that penalizes large fluctuations of the high-frequency regression parameters. To implement the estimator one has to select the smoothing parameter γ. Breitung and Roling (2015) suggest using a cross-validation method or an information criterion. Monte Carlo experiments suggest that the nonparametric estimator may provide more reliable and flexible approximations to the actual lag distribution than the conventional parametric MIDAS approach based on exponential lag polynomials. Parametric and nonparametric methods are applied to assess the predictive power of various daily indicators for forecasting monthly inflation. Breitung and Roling (2015) find that a commodity price index is a useful predictor for inflation 20 to 30 days ahead with a hump-shaped lag structure.

Asymmetric, non-linear and semi-parametric MIDAS models   Various MIDAS regression models involving asymmetries or other non-linearities have been proposed in the context of volatility forecasting and will be covered in Chapter 14. Also originated in the volatility literature, but of general interest, is the semi-parametric MIDAS regression model of Chen and Ghysels (2011):

$$y_{t+h}^L = a_h + b_h C(L^{1/m}; \theta_h) g(x_t^H) + \varepsilon_{t+h}^L$$

where $g(\cdot)$ is a function estimated via kernel-based non-parametric methods. Hence, the time series dependence is a standard MIDAS polynomial and therefore parametric in combination with the estimation of a generic function. The asymptotic distribution of the estimation procedure has a parametric and nonparametric part. The latter is kernel based, involves solving a so called inverse problem and is inspired by Linton and Mammen (2005). The mixed-frequency data sampling scheme in semi-parametric MIDAS regressions adds an extra term to the asymptotic variance compared to the result obtained by Linton and Mammen.

Smooth Transition MIDAS models   Galvão (2013) proposes a new regression model that combines a smooth transition regression with a mixed-frequency data sampling approach, which she calls STMIDAS. In particular, let us write equation (12.3.1) as follows:

$$y_{t+h}^L = a_h + b_h x(\theta)_t^H + \varepsilon_{t+h}^L$$

where $x(\theta)_t^H = C(L^{1/m}; \theta_h) x_t^H = \sum_{k=0}^{K} c(k; \theta) L^{k/m} x_t^H$. Then the smooth transition MIDAS regression can be written as:

$$y_{t+h}^L = a_h + b_{1h} x(\theta)_t^H \left[1 - G(x(\theta)_t^H; \gamma, c)\right] + b_{2h} x(\theta)_t^H G(x(\theta)_t^H; \gamma, c) + \varepsilon_{t+h}^L$$

where

$$G(x(\theta)_t^H; \gamma, c) = \frac{1}{1 + \exp(-\gamma/\hat{\sigma}_x(x(\theta)_t^H; \gamma, c))}$$

The transition function is a logistic function that depends on the weighted sum of the explanatory variable in the current quarter. The time-varying structure allows for changes in the predictive power of the indicators. When forecasting output growth with financial variables in real time, statistically significant improvements over a linear regression are more likely to arise from forecasting with STMIDAS than with MIDAS regressions, since changes in the predictive power of asset returns on economic activity may be related to business cycle regimes.

Markov Switching MIDAS models Guérin and Marcellino (2013) incorporate regime changes in the parameters of the MIDAS models. The basic version of the Markov Switching MIDAS (MS-MIDAS) regression model they propose is:

$$y_{t+h}^L = a_h(S_t) + b_h(S_t)C(L^{1/m}; \theta_h)x_t^H + \varepsilon_{t+h}^L$$

where $\varepsilon_{t+h}^L|S_t \sim N(0, \sigma^2(S_t))$. The regime-generating process is an ergodic Markov-chain with a finite number of states S_t. These models allow also mixed-sample estimation of the probabilities of being in a given regime, which is relevant, for example, to predict business cycle regimes.

Quantile regressions Ghysels, Plazzi, and Valkanov (2016) propose conditional MIDAS quantile regression models. While such regression models are of general interest, the specific application involves estimating conditional skewness of the h-period-horizon returns of interest to portfolio allocation, say for example monthly/quarterly returns, while using high-frequency (i.e., daily) returns as the information set. The mixed-sampling approach allows one to use all the richness of the high-frequency (daily) data while the objective remains a longer horizon returns. Ghysels, Plazzi, and Valkanov (2016) use MIDAS quantile model to measure conditional skewness used in portfolio allocation rules. There are a several conditional quantile models such as the CAViaR of Engle and Manganelli (2004). These conditional quantile models work exclusively with low-frequency data, which means that monthly and quarterly portfolio allocations would be confined to information sets that ignore the wealth of daily data.

Let $q_{a,t}(r_{t+h}; \kappa_{a,h})$ be the ath quantile (with $a \in (0,1)$) for return over horizon h (say $h = 22$ days) conditional on information at time t parameterized by parameter θ depends on the horizon and a.

Ghysels, Plazzi, and Valkanov (2016) model $q_{a,t}(r_{t+h}; \kappa_{a,h})$ as an affine function of $x_t^d(\theta_{a,h}) = C(L_d; \theta_{a,h})x_t = \sum_{k=0}^K c(k; \theta_{a,h})L_d^k x_t$ where L_d is a daily (high-frequency) lag operator and x_t is a daily (high-frequency) series – typically absolute or squared daily returns as in Engle and Manganelli (2004). Hence,

$$q_{a,t}(r_{t+h}; \kappa_{a,h}) = b_{a,h}^0 + b_{a,h}^1 x_t^d(\theta_{a,h})$$

where $\kappa_{a,h} = \left(b_{a,h}^0, b_{a,h}^1, \theta_{a,h}\right)$ are unknown parameters to estimate. The conditional quantiles are an affine function of linearly filtered x_t representing daily conditioning information with lag of K days. The weights are parameterized as a standard MIDAS regression. For example, Ghysels, Plazzi, and Valkanov (2016) use a beta polynomial. To estimate the parameters, one uses the usual "check" function as is common in the quantile regressions literature – see Koenker and Bassett (1978), Engle and Manganelli (2004), among others.

It was noted that one area of application of MIDAS quantile regressions is modeling conditional skewness. Sensitivity to outliers is the main reason why Ghysels, Plazzi, and Valkanov (2016) consider measures of asymmetry that are not based on sample estimates of the third moment. A conditional version of the Hinkley (1975) robust coefficient of asymmetry (skewness) is defined as (where we drop the $\kappa_{a,h}$ argument):

$$RA_{a,t}\left(r_{t+h}\right) = \frac{[q_{a,t}(r_{t+h}) - q_{.50,t}(r_{t+h})] - [q_{.50,t}(r_{t+h}) - q_{1-a,t}(r_{t+h})]}{q_{a,t}(r_{t+h}) - q_{1-a,t}(r_{t+h})},$$

where a common choice for $a = .75$ corresponding to using the quartiles of the conditional return distribution. Substituting the estimated MIDAS quantile regressions yields an empirical measure of conditional skewness.

12.4   Mixed-frequency VAR

So far, we have seen models that take into account mixed-frequency data in a univariate approach. Now we focus on multivariate methods and in particular VAR models. Broadly speaking, there are two approaches dealing with mixed-frequency data, which can be classified as either parameter-driven or observation-driven using the terminology of Cox (1981). Parameter-driven approaches rely on state space model representations involving latent processes, treating high-frequency observations of low-frequency series as missing data and therefore relying on filtering to extract hidden states. Contributions to this literature include Harvey and Pierse (1984), Bernanke, Gertler, and Watson (1997), Zadrozny (1990), Mariano and Murasawa (2003), Mittnik and Zadrozny (2004), and more recently Nunes (2005), Giannone, Reichlin, and Small (2008), Aruoba, Diebold, and Scotti (2009), Ghysels and Wright (2009), Kuzin, Marcellino, and Schumacher (2011), Marcellino and Schumacher (2010), Foroni and Marcellino (2014), Schorfheide and Song (2015), Eraker, Chiu, Foerster, Kim, and Seoane (2015), among others. The observation-driven mixed-frequency VAR models are formulated exclusively in terms of observable data and therefore closely related to the standard VAR models discussed in Chapter 6. Contributions to this literature include

Anderson, Deistler, Felsenstein, Funovits, Koelbl, and Zamani (2015) and
Ghysels (2016). In either case, both classical and Bayesian estimation has
been considered. A subsection is devoted to each approach.

12.4.1 Parameter-driven approach

The approach treats all the series as generated at the highest frequency, but
some of them are unobserved. Those variables that are observed only at
the low-frequency are therefore considered as periodically missing. Slightly
changing the notation of Mariano and Murasawa (2003), we consider the
state space representation of a VAR model in a classical framework, treating
quarterly series as monthly series with missing observations and taking GDP
growth as an example.

The disaggregation of the quarterly GDP growth, y_t^L, observed every t
$= 1, \dots, T$, into the month-on-month GDP growth, y_t^*, never observed, is
obtained as follows. Let us assume that the quarterly GDP series (in logs),
Y_t^L, is the geometric mean of the latent monthly random sequence Y_t^*, $Y_{t-1/3}^*$
and $Y_{t-2/3}^*$. Taking the three-period differences and defining $y_t^L = \Delta_3 Y_t^L$ and
$y_t^* = \Delta Y_t^*$, we obtain the following equation:

$$
\begin{aligned}
y_t^L &= \frac{1}{3}(y_t^* + y_{t-1/3}^* + y_{t-2/3}^*) + \frac{1}{3}(y_{t-1}^* + y_{t-2/3}^* + y_{t-1}^*) + \\
&\quad + \frac{1}{3}(y_{t-2/3}^* + y_{t-1}^* + y_{t-4/3}^*) \\
&= \frac{1}{3}y_t^* + \frac{2}{3}y_{t-1/3}^* + y_{t-2/3}^* + \frac{2}{3}y_{t-1}^* + \frac{1}{3}y_{t-4/3}^*. \quad (12.4.1)
\end{aligned}
$$

Let us now also assume we have a high-frequency series x^H such that
the combination of the latent month-on-month GDP growth y_t^* and the corresponding monthly indicator x_t^H follow a bivariate high-frequency VAR(p)
process

$$
\phi(L^{1/m}) \begin{bmatrix} y_t^* - \mu_y^* \\ x_t^H - \mu_x^H \end{bmatrix} = u_t^H \quad (12.4.2)
$$

where $u_t^H \sim N(0, \Sigma)$. The VAR(p) process in equation (12.4.2) together
with the aggregation equation (12.4.1) are then cast in a state space model

representation assuming $p \le 4$.[8] In particular, let us define

$$s_t = \begin{bmatrix} z_t \\ \vdots \\ z_{t-4/3} \end{bmatrix}, \qquad z_t = \begin{bmatrix} y_t^* - \mu_y^* \\ x_t^H - \mu_x^H \end{bmatrix},$$

yielding a state space model representation of the MF-VAR as

$$
\begin{aligned}
s_t &= F s_{t-1/3} + G v_t & (12.4.3) \\
\begin{bmatrix} y_t - \mu_y \\ x_t^H - \mu_x^H \end{bmatrix} &= H(L^{1/m}) s_t
\end{aligned}
$$

with $\mu_y = 3\mu_y^*$, and $v_t \sim N(0, I_2)$ and where the matrices are defined as

$$
\begin{aligned}
F &= \begin{bmatrix} F_1 \\ F_2 \end{bmatrix}; & F_1 &= \begin{bmatrix} \phi_1 & \cdots & \phi_p & 0_{2\times 2(5-p)} \end{bmatrix}; & F_2 &= \begin{bmatrix} I_8 & 0_{8\times 2} \end{bmatrix}, \\
G &= \begin{bmatrix} \Sigma^{1/2} \\ 0_{8\times 2} \end{bmatrix}
\end{aligned}
$$

and:

$$
\begin{aligned}
H(L^{1/m}) &= \begin{bmatrix} 1/3 & 0 \\ 0 & 1 \end{bmatrix} + \begin{bmatrix} 2/3 & 0 \\ 0 & 0 \end{bmatrix} L^{1/m} + \begin{bmatrix} 1 & 0 \\ 0 & 0 \end{bmatrix} L^{2/m} \\
&\quad + \begin{bmatrix} 2/3 & 0 \\ 0 & 0 \end{bmatrix} + \begin{bmatrix} 1/3 & 0 \\ 0 & 0 \end{bmatrix} L^{4/3}
\end{aligned}
$$

that also implicitly defines the matrix $H = [H_0 \ldots H_4]$. Equation (12.4.3) is observed at $t = 1, \ldots$ For any high-frequency intervening observations $t + i/m$ we treat y_t as missing.

The state space model consisting of the equations in (12.4.3) can be estimated via maximum-likelihood techniques using the Kalman Filter, where we have to take into account missing values due to the low-frequency nature of the GDP.[9]

---

[8]For the sake of conciseness, we do not report the state space model representation for $p > 4$. Details for this case can be found in Mariano and Murasawa (2003).

[9]This setup can also handle missing values due to publication lags. A topic we do not cover here, see, however, for further details Mariano and Murasawa (2003), Zadrozny (1990) and Ghysels, Horan, and Moench (2017), among others.

As Mariano and Murasawa (2003) note in their paper, when the number of parameters is large, the ML estimation procedure can fail to converge. In these cases, it is useful to implement the EM algorithm of Dempster, Laird, and Rubin (1977) modified to allow for missing observations.[10] Mariano and Murasawa (2003) consider the missing values as realizations of some i.i.d. standard normal random variables, i.e.

$$y_t^+ = \left\{ \begin{array}{ll} y_t^L & \text{if } y_t \text{ is observable} \\ \zeta_t & \text{otherwise} \end{array} \right.$$

where ζ_t is a draw from a standard normal distribution independent of the model parameters.

The measurement equation is modified accordingly in the first two months of each quarter, where the upper row of H is set to zero and a standard normal error term is added, so that the Kalman filter skips the random numbers. Since the realizations of the random numbers do not matter in practice, the authors suggest to replace the missing values with zeros. Then, the EM algorithm is used to obtain estimates of the parameters.

Mittnik and Zadrozny (2004) forecast German real GDP at monthly intervals based on a VAR(2) model of quarterly GDP and up to three monthly indicator variables (industrial production, current and expected business conditions). They find that in general monthly models produce better short-term GDP forecasts, while quarterly models produce better long-term GDP forecasts.

Kuzin, Marcellino, and Schumacher (2011) compare the MF-VAR and the MIDAS approaches, in the presence of monthly and quarterly series. MIDAS leads to parsimonious models, while MF-VAR does not restrict the dynamics but suffers from the curse of dimensionality. The two approaches tend to be more complementary than substitutive, since the MF-VAR performs better for longer horizons, whereas MIDAS for shorter horizons. Looking at the relative MSFE of the different models with respect to an AR low-frequency benchmark, the mixed-frequency models perform relatively well, especially when forecast combinations are adopted. Similar evidence is provided by Foroni and Marcellino (2012), who also provide results for the Euro area GDP components and assess the relative performance of a very large set of monthly indicators.

---

[10]Stock and Watson (2002b, Appendix A) propose a modification of the EM algorithm to estimate high-frequency factors from potentially large unbalanced panels, with mixed-frequency being a special case. See section 13.4.1 for further discussion.

12.4.2   Observation-driven approach

Ghysels (2016) introduces a different mixed-frequency VAR representation, in which he constructs the mixed-frequency VAR process as stacked skip-sampled processes. We will call the approach MIDAS-VAR to distinguish it from the parameter-driven approach. An example of an order one stacked VAR involving two series x_t^H and y_t^L with $m = 3$ would be as follows (ignoring intercept terms):

$$
\begin{bmatrix} x_{t+1-2/3}^H \\ x_{t+1-1/3}^H \\ x_{t+1}^H \\ y_{t+1}^L \end{bmatrix} = \begin{bmatrix} \phi_{11} & \phi_{12} & \phi_{13} & \phi_{14} \\ \phi_{21} & \phi_{22} & \phi_{23} & \phi_{24} \\ \phi_{31} & \phi_{32} & \phi_{33} & \phi_{34} \\ \phi_{41} & \phi_{42} & \phi_{43} & \phi_{44} \end{bmatrix} \begin{bmatrix} x_{t-2/3}^H \\ x_{t-1/3}^H \\ x_t^H \\ y_t^L \end{bmatrix} + \varepsilon_{t+1} \quad (12.4.4)
$$

Note that a bivariate system turns into a four-dimensional VAR due to the stacking. Moreover, the approach does not involve latent shocks/states or latent factors. This means there is no need for (Kalman) filtering. Technically speaking the approach adapts techniques typically used to study seasonal time series with periodic structures (see, e.g., Gladyshev (1961)). The innovation vector is obviously also of dimension 4×1. This means that each entry to the VAR has its own shock. Note that there are no latent high-frequency shocks to the low-frequency series. One implication is that we can apply standard VAR model techniques such as impulse response functions and variance decompositions (see sections 6.6 and 6.7).

When we examine the last equation in the system (12.4.4) we recognize a U-MIDAS regression model:

$$
y_{t+1}^L = \phi_{41} x_{t-2/3}^H + \phi_{42} x_{t-1/3}^H + \phi_{43} x_t^H + \phi_{44} y_t^L + \varepsilon_{4,t+1}
$$

In contrast, the first equation (as well as the second and third) measures the impact of low-frequency on series, namely:

$$
x_{t+1-2/3}^H = \phi_{11} x_{t-2/3}^H + \phi_{12} x_{t-1/3}^H + \phi_{13} x_t^H + \phi_{14} y_t^L + \varepsilon_{1,t+1}
$$

What about nowcasting? For this we need a structural VAR extension. Building on the analysis in Section 6.8 we can pre-multiply equation (12.4.4) with a lower triangular matrix and obtain the following system:

$$
\begin{bmatrix}
1 & 0 & 0 & 0 \\
a_{21} & 1 & 0 & 0 \\
a_{31} & a_{32} & 1 & 0 \\
a_{41} & a_{42} & a_{43} & 1
\end{bmatrix}
\begin{bmatrix}
x^H_{t+1-2/3} \\
x^H_{t+1-1/3} \\
x^H_{t+1} \\
y^L_{t+1}
\end{bmatrix}
=
\begin{bmatrix}
1 & 0 & 0 & 0 \\
a_{21} & 1 & 0 & 0 \\
a_{31} & a_{32} & 1 & 0 \\
a_{41} & a_{42} & a_{43} & 1
\end{bmatrix}
\times
$$

$$
\begin{bmatrix}
\phi_{11} & \phi_{12} & \phi_{13} & \phi_{14} \\
\phi_{21} & \phi_{22} & \phi_{23} & \phi_{24} \\
\phi_{31} & \phi_{32} & \phi_{33} & \phi_{34} \\
\phi_{41} & \phi_{42} & \phi_{43} & \phi_{44}
\end{bmatrix}
\begin{bmatrix}
x^H_{t-2/3} \\
x^H_{t-1/3} \\
x^H_t \\
y^L_t
\end{bmatrix}
+ \tilde{\varepsilon}_{t+1}
$$

Reading from the above system for the second equation, we have:

$$
x^H_{t+1-1/3} = -a_{21}x^H_{t+1-2/3} + \tilde{\phi}_{21}x^H_{t-2/3} + \tilde{\phi}_{12}x^H_{t-1/3} + \tilde{\phi}_{13}x^H_t + \tilde{\phi}_{14}y^L_t + \tilde{\varepsilon}_{2,t+1}
$$

and for the last equation:

$$
y^L_{t+1} = -\sum_{j=1}^{3} a_{4j}x^H_{t+1-(3-j)/3} + \tilde{\phi}_{41}x^H_{t-2/3} + \tilde{\phi}_{42}x^H_{t-1/3} + \tilde{\phi}_{43}x^H_t + \tilde{\phi}_{44}y^L_t + \tilde{\varepsilon}_{4,t+1}
$$

The latter is a MIDAS with leads equation we encountered in the discussions on nowcasting, whereas the former is a regression predicting high-frequency data in real time.

It should be clear by now that the MIDAS-VAR approach discussed in this subsection only relies on standard VAR techniques. Note that this also applies to estimation, which can be either classical or Bayesian, where the latter is appealing when the dimension of the VAR is large, which is easily the case with MIDAS-VAR systems due to the stacking of low and high-frequency series.

McCracken, Owyang, and Sekhposyan (2015) assess point and density forecasts from an observation-driven MIDAS-VAR to obtain intra-quarter forecasts of output growth as new information becomes available, imposing restrictions on the MIDAS-VAR to account explicitly for the temporal ordering of the data releases. They show that the MIDAS-VAR, estimated via Bayesian shrinkage, performs well for GDP nowcasting: it outperforms the considered time series models and does comparably well relative to the Survey of Professional Forecasters. Bacchiocchi, Bastianin, Missale, and Rossi

(2016) study how monetary policy, economic uncertainty and economic policy uncertainty impact on the dynamics of gross capital inflows in the United States using a MIDAS-VAR. While no relation is found when using standard quarterly data, exploiting the variability present in the series within the quarter shows that the effect of a monetary policy shock is greater the longer the time lag between the month of the shock and the end of the quarter. In general, the effect of economic and policy uncertainty on US capital inflows are negative and significant. Finally, the effect of the three shocks is different when distinguishing between financial and bank capital inflows from one side, and FDI from the other.

12.5   Example: Nowcasting with simulated data

This empirical application shows how to produce nowcasts with bridge and MIDAS models, using simulated data for clarity of exposition. The DGP is a simple bivariate model at high-frequency with the following specification:

$$
\begin{aligned}
y_t^H &= 1 + 0.25(x_t^H + x_{t-1/4}^H + x_{t-1/2}^H + x_{t-3/4}^H) + \varepsilon_{yt}^H \qquad (12.5.1)\\
x_t^H &= 1 + 0.4x_{t-1/4}^H + 0.4x_{t-1/2}^H + \varepsilon_{xt}^H
\end{aligned}
$$

We generate data on a quarterly variable $x_{t+k/4}^H$, spanning from 1949Q1 to 2012Q4, and observations for the same time period but at an annual frequency on the variables x_t^L and y_t^L. The data for x_t^L and y_t^L are obtained as the sum of the quarterly high-frequency variables (other aggregation schemes would work as well). Hence, $x_t^L \equiv \sum_{k=0}^{3} x_{t-k/4}^H$. We will use the observations for 1949 as starting values and focus our analysis on the period 1950-2012.

Our goal is to construct a model for y_t^L and $x_{t+k/4}^H$ that can be used to produce nowcasts of the yearly value of y^L based on the quarterly observations of x^H. For example, if we are in the first quarter of 2012, we observe x^H up to 2012Q1, y^L up to 2011, and we want to obtain an estimate of the value for y^L in 2012.

In economic terms, y^L could represent for example a fiscal variable, which is typically only released on an annual basis, and x^H GDP. In some countries GDP is only released at an annual basis. In these cases, y^L could be GDP and x^H industrial production, or an interest rate spread or a survey indicator.

	$\hat{x}^H_{k|2012Q1}$	$\hat{x}^H_{k|2012Q2}$	$\hat{x}^H_{k|2012Q3}$	$\hat{x}^H_{k|2012Q4}$
k = 2012Q1	3.192	3.192	3.192	3.192
k = 2012Q2	4.635	3.496	3.496	3.496
k = 2012Q3	3.975	3.570	2.297	2.297
k = 2012Q4	4.444	3.742	3.265	3.005

Table 12.5.1: *Forecasts from the AR(2) model for x^H*

12.5.1 The bridge equation approach

To facilitate the presentation we will use two types of notation for high and low-frequency data that differ from the notation used so far. Namely y^L_t for the year 2011 will also be denoted y^L_{2011} and $x^H_{t+1/4}$ for t corresponding to 2011 will be denoted x^H_{2012Q1}, since it is the first quarterly observation after the end of 2011. Our starting point is the high-frequency data. Clearly, the information we have on x^H depends on the quarter of 2012 we are in. More specifically, we look at four scenarios:

- In 2012Q1 we only have information up to the first quarter of the year, so that values for 2012Q2 ($k = 2$), Q3 and Q4 are obtained as the best forecasts from a model for x^H, estimated over the 1950Q1-2012Q1 sample. As a consequence, we will create forecasts $\hat{x}^H_{2012Q2|2012Q1}$, $\hat{x}^H_{2012Q3|2012Q1}$ and $\hat{x}^H_{2012Q4|2012Q1}$

- In 2012Q2 only the first two quarters of 2012 are available, so Q3 and Q4 are replaced by the best forecasts from a model for x^H, estimated over the 1950Q1-2012Q2 time span, resulting in $\hat{x}^H_{2012Q3|2012Q2}$ and $\hat{x}^H_{2012Q4|2012Q2}$

- In 2012Q3 the first three quarters of 2012 are available, so the information for Q4 must be replaced by the best forecast $\hat{x}^H_{2012Q4|2012Q3}$

- In 2012Q4 all the four quarters of 2012 are available and we can exploit a complete information set of within-year data.

We need first to find a good quarterly ARMA specification to represent x^H and to produce reliable forecasts. In a second step, we will need a yearly model that links y^L to x^H. We will call the different flash estimates for y^L as $\hat{y}^L_{2012|2012k}$, $k = 'Q1', \ldots, 'Q4'$ depending on which quarter of 2012 we are in.

	Coefficient	Std.Error	t-Statistic	Prob.
BETA(1)	1.010	0.063	16.008	0.000
BETA(2)	0.249	0.003	81.241	0.000
R-squared	0.991	Mean dep var		6.000
Adjusted R-squared	0.991	S.D. dep var		1.184
S.E. of regression	0.113	Akaike IC		-1.485
Sum squared resid	0.771	Schwarz IC		-1.416
Log likelihood	48.032	Hannan-Quinn		-1.458
F-statistic	6600.148	DW stat		2.284
Prob(F-statistic)	0.000			

Table 12.5.2: *Bridge equation (12.5.2) estimates 1950 - 2011*

Not surprisingly given the DGP, an AR(2) model provides a good representation for x^H. Having estimated the AR(2) model up to 2012Q1, we can now use it to produce forecasts for x^H in 2012Q2, Q3 and Q4. In Table 12.5.1, we compare $\hat{x}^H_{k|2012j}$ for k '2012Q1' through '2012Q4' and $j = $ 'Q1' through 'Q4'.

The yearly database now contains 63 observations (1949 - 2012) on y^L and x^L. We will focus on the sample 1950 - 2011, assuming that the value for y^L_{2012} is not available and needs to be estimated based on within-year information on x^H. More precisely, we will produce flash estimates $\hat{y}^L_{2012|2012k}$, $k = $ 'Q1' through 'Q4.'

We model the relationship between y^L and the quarterly (aggregated to yearly) variables x^L estimated over the sample 1950-2011 as a simple linear model:

$$y^L_t = b_1 + b_2 x^L_t + \varepsilon^L_t \qquad t = 1950, \dots, 2011. \qquad (12.5.2)$$

works well, not surprisingly given the DGP. We call this a bridge equation and the results of its estimation are displayed in Table 12.5.2. We will call these estimated parameters $\hat{b}^{2011}_1$ and $\hat{b}^{2011}_2$ as they use data up to 2011.

As a final step, the estimated coefficients in Table 12.5.2 can be combined with information we have in each quarter of 2012 to obtain a flash estimate for y^L in 2012. More formally, we construct the flash estimates as:

$$\hat{y}^L_{2012|2012Q1} = \hat{b}^{2011}_1 + \hat{b}^{2011}_2 (x^H_{2012Q1} + \sum_{k=2012Q2}^{2012Q4} \hat{x}^H_{k|2012Q1})$$

$$\hat{y}^L_{2012|2012Q2} = \hat{b}^{2011}_1 + \hat{b}^{2011}_2 (\sum_{k=2012Q1}^{2012Q2} x^H_k + \sum_{k=2012Q3}^{2012Q4} \hat{x}^H_{k|2012Q2})$$

$$\hat{y}^L_{2012|2012Q3} = \hat{b}^{2011}_1 + \hat{b}^{2011}_2 (\sum_{k=2012Q1}^{2012Q3} x^H_k + \hat{x}^H_{2012Q4|2012Q3})$$

$$\hat{y}^L_{2012|2012Q4} = \hat{b}^{2011}_1 + \hat{b}^{2011}_2 x^L_{2012}$$

although for the latter we could possibly update the parameter estimates as well. Table 12.5.3 compares the actual value for y^L in 2012 and the four flash estimates of y^L, each of them employing an increasingly more complete information set. Clearly, the more information we use, the closer the estimate gets to the actual value.

Nevertheless, the estimation error can still be sizable, and it is related to six main sources of uncertainty:

1. Mis-specification errors in the model selected for the high-frequency series.

2. Bias in the estimation of the model parameters for x^H.

3. Uncertainty on future values for x^H implied by its possibly substantial forecast error component.

4. Mis-specification errors in the model for the low-frequency variable, y^L.

5. Bias in the estimation of the model parameters for y^L.

6. Uncertainty about future values for y^L implied by its model residual component.

While the researcher has is general no power to reduce the noise components of the actual time-series (points 3 and 6), she should, of course, do her best when dealing with model specification, estimation, and forecasting issues.

12.5.2   The MIDAS regression approach

In the bridge equation approach we used as explanatory variable for y^L an average of the quarterly x^H variables, and used univariate model forecasts for the missing observations to produce flash estimates. In this section instead we will employ an alternative approach based on MIDAS regression models. We will work with both restricted and unrestricted MIDAS models.

Suppose again we are in the first quarter of 2012 and we want to produce a flash estimate for y^L exploiting all the available information. The estimation sample is again 1950 - 2011 as in equation (12.5.2), since we assume that y^L is not available in 2012, and the information set is $I_{2012Q1} = [x^H_{2012Q1}, (x^H_{t-k/4}, y^L_t), k = 0, \ldots, 3; t = 1950, \ldots, 2011]$. We can estimate respectively equations (12.3.6) and (12.3.8). For the latter – i.e., the U-MIDAS specification – we will use up to one lag of the variables, for the sake of simplicity.

At this point we can regress y^L on the x^H variables, using the U-MIDAS specifications, and provide flash estimates/nowcasts with the estimated regressions for the value of $y^L_{2012|k}$ for $k = 2012Q1, \ldots, 2012Q4$. Similarly, we will estimate the MIDAS specifications and provide flash estimates/nowcasts for the value of $y^L_{2012|k}$ using the estimated parameters.

A U-MIDAS model for $y^L_{2012|2012Q1}$ is simply given by an OLS regression of y^L on a constant and all the variables in the information set I_{2012Q1} as in equation (12.3.8). Additionally, a restricted MIDAS model for y^L in the same quarter requires to use an Almon lag polynomial (or any other polynomial specification) instead of a linear structure on the same set of regressors in equation (12.3.6). The estimate for $y^L_{2012|2012Q1}$ according to these two models can now be easily computed by simply producing the static forecasts of these two equations through the whole sample.

The last observations of the series y^L are our nowcasts for $y^L_{2012|2012Q1}$ according to the two models and are obtained using only the information available until the first quarter of 2012.

The same procedure can be carried on also in the other quarters of 2012, only keeping in mind that the information sets have to be modified in the following way:

- In 2012Q2 the information set is $I_{2012Q2} = [x^H_{2012Q1}, x^H_{2012Q2}] \cup I_{2011Q4}$

- In 2012Q3 the information set is $I_{2012Q3} = [x^H_{2012Q1}, x^H_{2012Q2}, x^H_{2012Q3}] \cup I_{2011Q4}$

	y^L	$\hat{y}^L_{2012|2012Q1}$	$\hat{y}^L_{2012|2012Q2}$	$\hat{y}^L_{2012|2012Q3}$	$\hat{y}^L_{2012|2012Q4}$
BRIDGE	4.016	5.056	4.497	4.061	3.996
MIDAS	4.016	6.347	5.157	4.509	4.017
U − MIDAS	4.016	5.122	4.514	4.127	3.989

Table 12.5.3: *Comparison of the actual value for y^L in 2012 and its flash estimates using subsequent quarters for the bridge, U-MIDAS and MIDAS models in subsequent quarters of 2012*

- In 2012Q4 we have the richest information set, I_{2012Q4}.

where $I_{20xxQ4} = [(x^H_{t-k/4}, y^L_t), k = 0, \ldots, 3; t = 1950, \ldots, 20xx]$.

As a final step, we can compare the actual value of y^L_{2012} with its nowcasts produced by the U-MIDAS and MIDAS models in each quarter, as shown in Table 12.5.3. Also in this case we observe that the more information we use, the closer the flash estimates are to the actual value of y^L in 2012. In this specific example, U-MIDAS performs better than MIDAS at each horizon, except for the last quarter.

A comparison of the flash estimates across the three methods indicates that the bridge models perform slightly better than U-MIDAS and MIDAS, except for the last quarter when MIDAS performs better than both bridge equations and U-MIDAS. This is again an application-specific result since in this example the data were generated with a bridge model, so that the finding is not surprising. Perhaps the more important lesson to learn is that despite the DGP being generated by a bridge equation, it is worth noting that MIDAS specifications yield comparable nowcasts.

In conclusion, this simple example allowed us to underline the main differences between the bridge equation approach and the mixed-data sampling regression approach, and to illustrate their practical implementation. Here, we focused on producing flash estimates for a low-frequency variable y^L by means of a high-frequency explanatory variable x^H. In the bridge approach equation we used as explanatory variable for y^L a sum of the quarterly x^H variables, after completing the missing observations at the end of x^H with their best forecasts. The U-MIDAS approach instead is more general. It still uses the different quarters of x^H, but it does not impose a fixed weight on each quarter. This has the advantage of being able to capture a more general dynamic relationship between y^L and x^H but, on the other hand, it requires to estimate more parameters, resulting in a loss of precision. The MIDAS approach can be a convenient compromise, since it substantially restricts the number of parameters to be estimated but still allows for sufficient flexibility in the parameterization.

12.6   Example: Nowcasting US GDP growth

This example complements the previous one based on simulated data. We now propose an application of the nowcasting procedures to a dataset containing indicators of real economic activity for the United States.

The database contains the monthly series, for the period 1985 - 2012, of the Index of Coincident Indicators and its four main components, namely non-farm payroll employees, personal income less transfer payments, the index of industrial production, and manufacturing and trade sales.[11] In addition, it also contains the series of the US real GDP at a quarterly frequency, again from 1985 to 2012. All the variables are transformed into growth rates through the log-difference operator. As a consequence of this transformation, we have also the new five growth rates variables called ci (for the Index of Coincident Indicators), e (for employees on non-farm payrolls), ip (for the index of industrial production), inc (for personal income), and sa (for manufacturing and trade sales); plus the quarterly growth rate of GDP indicated as y^L. It is important to note that all the monthly variables are released with a one-month publication delay, except sa which has a two-month publication delay, while y^L has a three-month publication delay.

Our aim is to build a separate model for y^L as a function of each of the possible explanatory variables in $x^H = (ci, e, ip, inc, sa)$ so that these can be used to produce nowcasts of the quarterly value of y^L based on the monthly observations in x^H. We consider three separate cases. In the first one, we do as if we were in 2008M10 and tried to forecast the deepest trough that US GDP growth has experienced during the global financial crisis, namely 2008Q4 with $y^L = -2.237$. In the second example, we try to assess more generally the ability of our models to predict y^L in expansionary and re-

---

[11]The Index of Coincident Indicators is published monthly by the Conference Board along with the Index of Leading Indicators and the Index of Lagging Indicators to give the public a reading on whether the economy is expanding or contracting and at what pace.

cessionary periods, by nowcasting first 2011Q4 ($y^L = 1.0029\%$) and then 2012Q4 ($y^L = -0.0362\%$). Then, in the last section, we forecast the US GDP growth rate over a longer period 2007Q1 - 2012Q2.

As before, the complexity of producing these nowcasts lies in the fact that we want to update our information sets as the different sources of monthly information become available in each month of the quarter we are in. To clarify, suppose we are in October of year 20xx, we observe ci, e, ip, inc up to 20xxM9 and sa up to 20xxM8, plus we only have a final estimate for y^L for 20xxq2.[12] Our aim is to produce an estimate of the 20xxQ4 value for y^L. In this application, we will use both the bridge and the other mixed-frequency approaches, as in the simulated data example. Let us first have a look at how our real-time models forecast the worst trough of the crisis.

12.6.1 Predicting the worst trough of the crisis

Modeling the monthly variables

In this first scenario we get rid of the information we do not use by resizing the sample to end in 2008Q4. We use the notation y^L for, say quarter i in 2008 as y^L_{2008Qi}, $i = 1, 2, 3, 4$ and monthly data x^H_{2008Mj}, $j = 1, \ldots, 12$.

The bridge approach requires us to find the appropriate ARMA specifications for each of the x^H variables, so that we can use these selected models to produce the forecasts we are interested in. To do so, let us first have a look at how the variables behave in the estimation sample we have chosen, which is from January 1985 to September 2008. As we can see from Figure 12.6.1, they do not show any trend and look quite stationary around their means.

ADF tests performed on these variables confirm their stationarity. A closer look at their correlograms can be useful to detect a possible ARMA structure. The analysis of the correlograms suggests an ARMA structure for each of the high-frequency variables, but the proper orders are unclear. Using an information criteria-based selection procedure provides additional information. The ARIMA selection procedure used in this example allows

---

[12]More specifically, the release schedule for y^L is the following: "Advance" estimates are released near the end of the first month after the end of the quarter; as more detailed and more comprehensive data become available, "preliminary," and "final" estimates are released near the end of the second and third months, respectively – see, A Guide to the National Income and Product Accounts of the United States, p. 21.

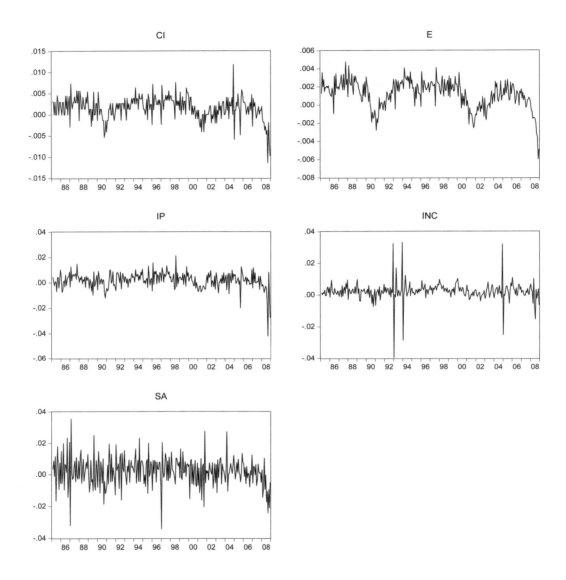

Figure 12.6.1: *Monthly variables in the estimation sample 1985 - 2008*

us to choose either the AIC or BIC criterion. The reader can check that the most parsimonious specifications according to the BIC criterion are: *ci* - ARMA(1,2), *e* - ARMA(1,1), *inc* ARMA(0,1), *ip* - ARMA(1,2), *sa* ARMA(3,0).

Diagnostic tests confirm that we can rely on these specifications to model the five high-frequency variables within the bridge approach, although there are some signs of neglected heteroskedasticity probably due to some outliers.

Clearly, the information the forecaster has on the variables in x^H depends on the month she is in, as publication delays render different information available in different points in time.

To be more precise, let us illustrate how the procedure works in this example. Starting from 2008M10 the forecaster has to prepare the nowcast of quarterly GDP growth for 2008Q4:

- In 2008M10 she only has information up to 2008M9, at best, so that values for x^H from 2008M10 onwards will be obtained as the best forecasts from an appropriate model for the various $x^H = (ci, e, ip, inc)$, estimated over the 1985 - 2008M9 sample. Similarly, for $x^H = sa$ she has information up to 2008M8, so that values for sa from 2008M9 onwards will be forecast according to the appropriate model. As a consequence, we will create five variables $x1$ that are exactly equal to x for the period 1985 - 2008, but the observations from 2008M10 (2008M9 for $x = sa$) to 2008M12 are replaced by the forecasts produced by the above selected ARMA models.

- In 2008M11 only info up to 2008M10 is available, so the remaining observations of the quarter are replaced by the best forecasts from the selected ARMA models for x, estimated over the 1985 - 2008M10 time span, resulting in the variables $x2$ with $x = (ci, e, ip, inc)$. Once again for $x = sa$ only info up to 2008M9 is available and the remaining observations will be replaced by the forecasts.

- In 2008M12 information up to 2008M11 is available and so we proceed in a similar manner as in the previous points, generating suitable $x3$ variables with $x = (ci, e, ip, inc)$. Similarly, for $x = sa$ information up to 2008M10 is available and the remaining observations are replaced by the forecasts.

If we want a flash estimate of y for 2008Q4, in 2008M10 we can rely on the information in $x1 = (ci1, e1, ip1, inc1, sa1)$, in 2008M11 we can do the same with $x2 = (ci2, e2, ip2, inc2, sa2)$, and similarly for 2008M12. A comparison of the various $x1$, $x2$, and $x3$ with the actual data can give us a first intuition on how good the forecasts are as a replacement of the missing observations.

	Coefficient	Std. Error	t-Statistic	Prob.
Independent Variable: ci				
C	0.004	0.001	7.533	0.000
BETA	0.604	0.072	8.389	0.000
Independent Variable: e				
C	0.004	0.001	6.494	0.000
BETA	0.848	0.120	7.079	0.000
Independent Variable: ip				
C	0.006	0.000	11.998	0.000
BETA	0.259	0.034	7.619	0.000
Independent Variable: inc				
C	0.006	0.001	9.474	0.000
BETA	0.161	0.049	3.302	0.001
Independent Variable: sa				
C	0.006	0.000	11.527	0.000
BETA	0.239	0.034	6.968	0.000

Table 12.6.4: *Estimated bridge equations for each of the explanatory variables*

For the bridge approach, the final step only consists in aggregating these variables for all the months in one quarter.

The database now contains our quarterly GDP growth rate variable y^L and a set of quarterly variables imported from the monthly series, each of them indicating which information is available when we are respectively in month 1, 2, or 3 of the fourth quarter of 2008, the period we are interested in forecasting. These information sets can be denoted by $I_{2008M10}$, $I_{2008M11}$ and $I_{2008M12}$, respectively. Therefore, as in equation (12.2.2), we can construct $x^L_{2008Q4|2008M10}$, $x^L_{2008Q4|2008M11}$ and $x^L_{2008Q4|2008M12}$.

Nowcasting through bridge equations

As we previously saw, using the bridge approach entails first estimating five quarterly bridge equations of the type

$$y^L_t = b_1 + b_2 x^L_t + \varepsilon^L_t, \qquad t = 1985, \dots, 2008Q3.$$

one for each of the explanatory variables, and then using the estimated coefficients to produce flash estimates for y^L in each month of 2008Q4, using $x^L_{2008Q4|2008M10}$, $x^L_{2008Q4|2008M11}$ and $x^L_{2008Q4|2008M12}$. Table 12.6.4 shows the estimated coefficients for the five models based on the largest information set available, each of which passes common diagnostic tests.

To obtain the nowcasts of y^L in 2008Q4 according to the bridge approach, the coefficients in Table 12.6.4 are used to construct the flash estimates as:

$$y^L_{2008Q4|2008Mj} = \hat{b}_1 + \hat{b}_{i2} x^L_{2008Q4|2008Mj}$$
$$\text{for} \quad j = 10, 11, 12 \quad \text{and} \quad x = (ci, e, ip, inc, sa)$$

After obtaining five bridge nowcasts of y^L with each of the x^L variables, with the information available in October, November and December of 2008, we can also pool them to obtain a combined forecast of y^L exploiting all the available information.

Table 12.6.5 reports the results of the pooled forecasts and those based on each single indicator. For the pooled forecasts we can say that, although they are not precise, the more monthly information we include the closer they get to the actual value of y^L_{2008Q4}. The single best predictors are ci and e, and their usefulness increases with the arrival of additional intra quarter information.

Pooled forecasts

BRIDGE	y^L	$\hat{y}^L_{2008Q4|2008M10}$	$\hat{y}^L_{2008Q4|2008M11}$	$\hat{y}^L_{2008Q4|2008M12}$
2008Q4	-0.0233	0.0015	0.0007	0.0004

Forecasts based on each single indicator

2008Q4	y^L	$\hat{y}^L_{2008Q4|2008M10}$	$\hat{y}^L_{2008Q4|2008M11}$	$\hat{y}^L_{2008Q4|2008M12}$
ci	-0.0233	-0.0028	-0.0034	-0.0037
e	-0.0233	0.0003	-0.0059	-0.0071
inc	-0.0233	0.0075	0.0072	0.0070
ip	-0.0233	-0.0037	0.0025	0.0027
sa	-0.0233	0.0064	0.0033	0.0031

Table 12.6.5: *Forecasts for y^L in 2008Q4 obtained by means of the bridge approach: in the first row pooled results are presented, while in the other rows the results are based on each single indicator in x^H*

Pooled forecasts

$MIDAS$	y^L	$\hat{y}^L_{2008Q4|2008M10}$	$\hat{y}^L_{2008Q4|2008M11}$	$\hat{y}^L_{2008Q4|2008M12}$
2008Q4	-0.0233	-0.0041	-0.0032	-0.0075

Forecasts based on each single indicator

2008Q4	y^L	$\hat{y}^L_{2008Q4|2008M10}$	$\hat{y}^L_{2008Q4|2008M11}$	$\hat{y}^L_{2008Q4|2008M12}$
ci	-0.0233	-0.0072	-0.0087	-0.0119
e	-0.0233	-0.0046	-0.0064	-0.0114
inc	-0.0233	0.0029	0.0008	0.0006
ip	-0.0233	-0.0089	0.0043	-0.0046
sa	-0.0233	-0.0026	-0.0061	-0.0100

Table 12.6.6: *Nowcasts for y^L in 2008Q4 obtained through the MIDAS approach: in the first row pooled results are presented, while in the other rows the results are based on each single indicator in x^H*

Nowcasting by MIDAS and U-MIDAS models

Let us start by assuming that we are in the first month of 2008Q4, i.e., in October, and we want to produce a flash estimate for y in 2008Q4 exploiting all the available information. The associated estimation sample is 1985 - 2008M9. Note also that in October 2008 we only have a final estimate for y^L in 2008Q2, hence the need to adjust the estimation sample accordingly.

We can estimate a U-MIDAS model and a MIDAS model for y^L for each of the five explanatory variables, taking into account the relevant information sets. We can also pool the forecasts obtained from all explanatory variables to obtain a sort of average forecast for y in each of the three months of 2008Q4.

As previously, pooling is simply executed by grouping the nowcast series and then computing their average. Note that indeed more sophisticated methods of aggregation would be available but here we consider mean-pooling for sake of simplicity.[13]

The results we obtain in terms of forecasts, both pooled and based on the single indicators, are reported in Tables 12.6.6 and 12.6.7.

From a first look at the tables, we note that the forecasts produced with the MIDAS approach track the actual values of y^L_{2008Q4} more closely than their comparable estimates obtained through the bridge equation approach. In particular, in this case the MIDAS model performs better than both the U-MIDAS and the BRIDGE approaches in each quarter. Once again, the single best predictors are ci and e, and their usefulness increases with additional intra-quarter information. On the other hand, inc seems to be unable to predict the recession as it predicts positive GDP growth in each quarter. Further, it seems that none of these models was able to capture the depth of the financial crisis in 2008, as both of them predict a much milder recession than the one that actually occurred. Note that this is in general true for a large class of econometric models; for a discussion about central bank forecasts during the crisis, see Alessi, Ghysels, Onorante, Peach, and Potter (2014). They show that MIDAS regression models should incorporate financial market signals typically not taken into account in more traditional macro forecasting models.

---

[13]Andreou, Ghysels, and Kourtellos (2013) consider time-varying forecast combinations using various weighting schemes. Focusing of forecasting and nowcasting US GDP growth, they find that the discounted mean squared forecasting error yields the best results in an exercise involving a large cross-section of daily financial time series.

Pooled forecasts

$U - MIDAS$	y^L	$\hat{y}^L_{2008Q4|2008M10}$	$\hat{y}^L_{2008Q4|2008M11}$	$\hat{y}^L_{2008Q4|2008M12}$
2008Q4	-0.0233	0.0017	0.0001	-0.0039

Forecasts based on each single indicator

2008Q4	y^L	$\hat{y}^L_{2008Q4|2008M10}$	$\hat{y}^L_{2008Q4|2008M11}$	$\hat{y}^L_{2008Q4|2008M12}$
ci	-0.0233	-0.0025	-0.0045	-0.0082
e	-0.0233	0.0005	-0.0016	-0.0071
inc	-0.0233	0.0098	0.0068	0.0053
ip	-0.0233	0.0005	0.0025	0.0008
sa	-0.0233	0.0002	-0.0030	-0.0105

Table 12.6.7: *Nowcasts for y^L in 2008Q4 obtained through the U-MIDAS approach: in the first row pooled results are presented, while in the other rows the results are based on each single indicator in x^H*

Pooled forecasts

$BRIDGE$	y^L	$\hat{y}^L_{2011Q4|2011M10}$	$\hat{y}^L_{2011Q4|2011M11}$	$\hat{y}^L_{2011Q4|2011M12}$
2011Q4	0.0100	0.0065	0.0066	0.0065

Forecasts based on each single indicator

2011Q4	y^L	$\hat{y}^L_{2011Q4|2011M10}$	$\hat{y}^L_{2011Q4|2011M11}$	$\hat{y}^L_{2011Q4|2011M12}$
ci	0.0100	0.0059	0.0063	0.0062
e	0.0100	0.0071	0.0070	0.0070
inc	0.0100	0.0044	0.0043	0.0043
ip	0.0100	0.0078	0.0080	0.0080
sa	0.0100	0.0073	0.0073	0.0072

Table 12.6.8: *Forecasts for y^L in 2011Q4 according to the bridge: in the first row pooled results are presented, while in the other rows the results are based on each single indicator in x^H*

12.6.2 Predicting mild positive and negative growth rates

One could argue that the worst trough of the 2008 financial crisis is too hard of an example to asses the predictive capabilities of our models. In the second part of our empirical application we will test our models first in a period of mild expansion, 2011Q4, and then in a period of mild negative growth, 2012Q4, see Figure 12.6.2.

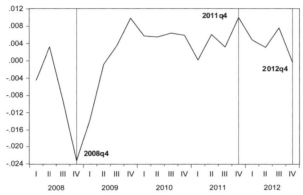

Figure 12.6.2: *US GDP growth from 2008 to 2012: the graph highlights the three different quarters we produce nowcasts for*

We can use the same approach as we did in the previous example for predicting 2011Q4 and 2012Q4: by simply changing the end of the sample to respectively 2011M9 and 2012M9 we will be able to automatically update the estimation sample to the one we need. Also, the bridge equation can be entirely reused here by simply changing the sample to respectively 2011M9 or 2012M9.

We are now able to produce nowcasts for the low-frequency variable y by means of both the bridge and the mixed data sampling approach.

Tables 12.6.8 - 12.6.10 report the nowcasts for the 2011Q4 obtained both when all the indicators are pooled together, and when we consider each of them separately.

For the mildly expansionary period of 2011Q4, the pooled forecasts from the bridge and the MIDAS approaches show the desired temporal pattern: the more monthly information becomes available, the closer the nowcasts get to the true value of y. In particular, this time the U-MIDAS forecasts do not improve in the last month of the quarter, but overall these achieve much

Pooled forecasts

$MIDAS$	y^L	$\hat{y}^L_{2011Q4|2011M10}$	$\hat{y}^L_{2011Q4|2011M11}$	$\hat{y}^L_{2011Q4|2011M12}$
2011Q4	0.0100	0.0016	0.0018	0.0022

Forecasts based on each single indicator

	y^L	$\hat{y}^L_{2011Q4|2011M10}$	$\hat{y}^L_{2011Q4|2011M11}$	$\hat{y}^L_{2011Q4|2011M12}$
ci	0.0100	0.0007	0.0026	0.0025
e	0.0100	0.0025	0.0022	0.0027
inc	0.0100	-0.0013	-0.0004	-0.0003
ip	0.0100	0.0020	0.0034	0.0034
sa	0.0100	0.0042	0.0013	0.0025

Table 12.6.9: *Forecasts for y^L in 2011Q4 according to both the MIDAS: in the first row pooled results are presented, while in the other rows the results are based on each single indicator in x^H*

Pooled forecasts

$U - MIDAS$	y^L	$\hat{y}^L_{2011Q4|2011M10}$	$\hat{y}^L_{2011Q4|2011M11}$	$\hat{y}^L_{2011Q4|2011M12}$
20011Q4	0.0100	0.0057	0.0065	0.0064

Forecasts based on each single indicator

2011Q4	y^L	$\hat{y}^L_{2011Q4|2011M10}$	$\hat{y}^L_{2011Q4|2011M11}$	$\hat{y}^L_{2011Q4|2011M12}$
ci	0.0100	0.0048	0.0066	0.0062
e	0.0100	0.0071	0.0064	0.0065
inc	0.0100	0.0035	0.0035	0.0040
ip	0.0100	0.0070	0.0083	0.0082
sa	0.0100	0.0062	0.0075	0.0072

Table 12.6.10: *Forecasts for y^L in 2011Q4 according to both the U-MIDAS approach: in the first row pooled results are presented, while in the other rows the results are based on each single indicator in x^H*

better results than the MIDAS approach in terms of accuracy, predicting roughly 0.64% instead of 1%. This has probably to do with the fact that the single indicator-based nowcasts are much more precise. In particular, the U-MIDAS nowcasts based on industrial production ip (or manufacturing and trade sales sa) and on the information available in $M3$ go close to the target value of y, and this reflects into the overall performance of the pooled nowcasts, although the latter also combines the other less precise nowcasts.

Unfortunately, the same does not hold for the nowcasts for 2012Q4, which is again a period of negative growth, though much less dramatic than 2008Q4.

Tables 12.6.11 - 12.6.13 report the nowcasts for the 2012Q4 under examination obtained both when all the indicators are pooled together and when we consider each of them separately.

Our overall conclusion for this specific empirical application is that the MIDAS model might be slightly better in predicting recessionary periods and the U-MIDAS model performs slightly better in predicting expansions. Further, pooling (averaging) single indicators' nowcasts is not the most efficient aggregation method, as "good" nowcasts get mixed up with "bad" ones. More refined aggregation methods would probably improve our results. On the other hand, these results are based on specific quarters (which is often of interest for policy-making), and so they could be not generally valid. For this reason we now repeat the evaluation exercise for a longer evaluation period.

12.6.3   Predicting GDP growth rates, 2007-2012

As a final application of the nowcasting procedure, we forecast the quarterly growth rate of GDP over the period 2007Q1 and 2012Q4. Once again, we can use the same approach as we did in the previous examples.

To be more precise, let us illustrate how the procedure works in this example.

1. Let us assume that we want to forecast quarterly GDP growth in the first month of each quarter. Hence, starting from 2007M1 the forecaster has to prepare the nowcast of quarterly GDP growth for 2007Q1, then in 2007M4, she prepares the nowcast of y for 2007Q2 and so on. In 2007M1, she only has information up to 2006M12, at best, so that values for x^H from 2007M1 to 2007M3 will be obtained as the best forecasts from an appropriate ARMA model for the various $x^H = (ci, e, ip, inc, sa)$, estimated over the 1985 - 2006M12 sample. Then in 2007M4, she only has information up to 2007M3;

Pooled forecasts

$BRIDGE$	y^L	$\hat{y}^L_{2012Q4|2012M10}$	$\hat{y}^L_{2012Q4|2012M11}$	$\hat{y}^L_{2012Q4|2012M12}$
2012Q4	-0.0004	0.0057	0.0065	0.0065

Forecasts based on each single indicator

2012Q4	y^L	$\hat{y}^L_{2012Q4|2012M10}$	$\hat{y}^L_{2012Q4|2012M11}$	$\hat{y}^L_{2012Q4|2012M12}$
ci	-0.0004	0.0048	0.0073	0.0073
e	-0.0004	0.0068	0.0068	0.0068
inc	-0.0004	0.0058	0.0066	0.0067
ip	-0.0004	0.0049	0.0068	0.0068
sa	-0.0004	0.0064	0.0048	0.0048

Table 12.6.11: *Forecasts for y^L in 2012Q4 according to both the Bridge: in the first row pooled results are presented, while in the other rows the results are based on each single indicator in x^H*

Pooled forecasts

$MIDAS$	y^L	$\hat{y}^L_{2012Q4|2012M10}$	$\hat{y}^L_{2012Q4|2012M11}$	$\hat{y}^L_{2012Q4|2012M12}$
2012Q4	-0.0004	-0.0006	-0.0004	0.0021

Forecasts based on each single indicator

2012Q4	y^L	$\hat{y}^L_{2012Q4|2012M10}$	$\hat{y}^L_{2012Q4|2012M11}$	$\hat{y}^L_{2012Q4|2012M12}$
ci	-0.0004	-0.0009	-0.0003	0.0040
e	-0.0004	0.0024	0.0024	0.0029
inc	-0.0004	-0.0009	-0.0011	0.0024
ip	-0.0004	-0.0031	-0.0034	0.0025
sa	-0.0004	-0.0004	0.0002	-0.0014

Table 12.6.12: *Forecasts for y^L in 2012Q4 according to both the MIDAS: in the first row pooled results are presented, while in the other rows the results are based on each single indicator in x^H*

Pooled forecasts

$U - MIDAS$	y^L	$\hat{y}^L_{2012Q4|2012M10}$	$\hat{y}^L_{2012Q4|2012M11}$	$\hat{y}^L_{2012Q4|2012M12}$
2012Q4	-0.0004	0.0042	0.0036	0.0063

Forecasts based on each single indicator

2012Q4	y^L	$\hat{y}^L_{2012Q4|2012M10}$	$\hat{y}^L_{2012Q4|2012M11}$	$\hat{y}^L_{2012Q4|2012M12}$
ci	-0.0004	0.0032	0.0036	0.0077
e	-0.0004	0.0068	0.0065	0.0069
inc	-0.0004	0.0041	0.0029	0.0069
ip	-0.0004	0.0019	0.0015	0.0072
sa	-0.0004	0.0051	0.0035	0.0028

Table 12.6.13: *Forecasts for y^L in 2012Q4 according to both the U-MIDAS approach: in the first row pooled results are presented, while in the other rows the results are based on each single indicator in x^H*

thus values for x from 2007M4 to 2007M7 will be replaced with the forecasts estimated over the 1985 - 2007M3 sample. This process is repeated for each quarter always assuming that we are in the first month of the quarter.

2. Now let's assume that we want to forecast quarterly GDP growth every second month of the quarter. Starting from 2007M2, the forecaster has to prepare the nowcast of quarterly GDP growth for 2007Q1. In 2007M2, she only has information up to 2007M1, at best, so that values for x from 2007M2 to 2007M3 will be obtained as the best forecasts from the ARMA model for each variable in x^H, estimated over the 1985 - 2007M1 sample.

3. Finally, let's assume we want to forecast quarterly GDP growth in each last month of the quarter. Starting from 2007M3, the forecaster only has information up to 2007M2, so that values for x^H from 2007M3 will be replaced by the best forecasts for each variable in x^H, estimated over the 1985 - 2007M2 sample.

	$\hat{y}^L_{20xxQk\|20xxM10}$	$\hat{y}^L_{20xxQk\|20xxM11}$	$\hat{y}^L_{20xxQk\|20xxM12}$
BRIDGE			
RMSFE	0.0079	0.0069	0.0069
MAFE	0.0051	0.0046	0.0046
MIDAS			
RMSFE	0.0068	0.0064	0.0058
MAFE	0.0055	0.0048	0.0046
U-MIDAS			
RMFSE	0.0075	0.0067	0.0060
MAFE	0.0048	0.0045	0.0042

Table 12.6.14: *Forecast evaluation criteria for bridge, MIDAS, and U-MIDAS and each month of the quarter, evaluation period 2007Q1 - 2012Q4*

Table 12.6.14 provides the detailed forecast evaluation statistics for the pooled series. For all models, both the RMSFE and the MAFE decline when we increase the information available at each quarter. Therefore, as expected, in the last month of the quarter we get better forecasts compared to those obtained in the first month of the quarter (i.e., M1). Overall, it seems that the MIDAS model produces the best nowcasts over the 2007M1 - 2012M12 period, although the ranking can change depending on the year and the monthly variable considered. Once again, pooling the forecasts by averaging the individual series might not be the best approach; indeed, we observe that some monthly variables, such as ci, individually perform much better than others.

12.7 Concluding remarks

In this chapter we have seen that several methods have been proposed in the literature to deal with mixed-frequency data. In general, there is agreement that exploiting data at different frequencies matters for nowcasting and short-term forecasting, but there is disagreement on what is the preferred approach for modeling using mixed-frequency data. Hence, we now try to summarize the advantages and disadvantages of the different methods, comparing their most important features.

Bridge equations are still one of the most used techniques, especially in short-run forecasting, because they are pretty easy to estimate and interpret, and allow computing early estimates of the low-frequency variable. The drawback is that they are purely statistical models, where the regressors are included only because they contain timely updated information. Therefore, if the model that exploits the high-frequency information is mis-specified, the error transmits to the bridge equation and to the forecasts that are obtained recursively.

An alternative way to deal with mixed-frequency data is the MIDAS approach. With respect to the bridge model, the use of lag polynomials based on a very small number of parameters, allows the MIDAS models to be parsimonious and permits the use of very high-frequency information. However, it is not clear which is the best polynomial specification, and if the imposed constraints on the parameters are invalid the resulting model is also suboptimal. An unrestricted MIDAS (U-MIDAS) specification alleviates both problems, but can be only used when the frequency mismatch is limited, e.g., quarterly and monthly. MIDAS models can be easily estimated by NLS, U-MIDAS models even by OLS.

Both bridge and MIDAS are univariate models, relying on a direct approach in the case of multi-steps ahead forecasting. With them it is only possible to obtain a high-frequency update of the expected low-frequency realization (e.g., an intra-quarter forecast of GDP growth based on timely information), not an estimate of the missing values in the low-frequency variable (e.g., not an estimate of unobservable monthly GDP growth). A MF-VAR has the advantage of jointly specifying the dynamics of the indicators and of the variable to be explained, without imposing any a priori restriction. Moreover, since the low-frequency series is seen as a high-frequency series with missing values, the use of the Kalman filter permits the estimation of these missing data and forecasting can be based on an iterative procedure, which is more efficient that the direct method in the case of correct model specification. On the other side, estimation of the MF-VAR is computationally complex, and the complexity increases with the number of variables involved, so that most of the time only small-scale models can be estimated. Moreover, the state space approach requires the correct specification of the model in high frequency, which is even more complex than usual given the missing observations in the dependent variable.

In conclusion, it is difficult to provide a unique ranking of the alternative mixed-frequency models, the choice should be based on the specific empirical application. However, any of the three methods we have considered is in general better than the use of temporally aggregated data, since it permits to exploit all the available information in a timely way.

Chapter 13

Models for Large Datasets

13.1   Introduction

The use of large sets of economic variables for the purpose of forecasting has received increased attention in the recent literature. Various econometric methods have been suggested, based on variable selection, or on variable combination, or on shrinkage.

Variable selection methods are similar to those discussed in Chapter 1, though proper modifications are required to handle the large number of possible subsets of regressors to be compared when their number is large, see, e.g., Kapetanios, Marcellino, and Papailias (2016) for a review and forecasting applications.

Variable combination is mainly implemented via factor models, starting with the seminal papers of Stock and Watson (2002a), Stock and Watson (2002b) and Forni, Hallin, Lippi, and Reichlin (2000). As we have seen in Chapter 10, the idea of factor models is that many economic variables are driven by few unobservable forces, the factors, plus idiosyncratic components. Hence, we can summarize the information contained in the many variables using estimated factors, and use them for forecasting the specific variable(s) of interest. Different types of large factor models have been developed, see for example the comparisons and surveys by Boivin and Ng (2005), Stock and Watson (2006), Eickmeier and Ziegler (2008) and Schumacher (2007).

Shrinkage is the third approach to handle models with a large number of regressors, possibly larger than the number of temporal observations. This approach has been mainly implemented in the context of large BVARs, and it basically requires the use of priors that introduce a large amount of shrinkage, increasing with the number of variables under analysis, see De Mol, Giannone, and Reichlin (2008), Carriero, Clark, and Marcellino (2016), and Carriero, Clark, and Marcellino (2017).

As selection methods for large sets of regressors can be rather complex, while the treatment of large BVARs is theoretically and empirically similar to that of smaller models (considered in Chapter 8), in this chapter we focus on large factor models and related techniques.

In Section 13.2 we introduce large factor models and discuss estimation and forecasting. In Section 13.3 we consider the three pass regression filter, which extends the method of partial least squares that can be considered as a way of targeting the factors to the specific variables of interest. In section 13.4 we extend the analysis to handle large unbalanced datasets. In section 13.5 we present an empirical example using simulated data. In Section 13.6 we discuss forecasting US and Euro area GDP growth using large information sets. Finally, in Section 13.7 we summarize and conclude.

13.2　Factor models

Let us consider the following model:

$$y_{t+1} = \beta_0 + \beta' F_t + \eta_{t+1}, \tag{13.2.1}$$
$$x_t = \Phi F_t + \varepsilon_t, \tag{13.2.2}$$

where y is the target variable of interest, for example GDP growth or inflation; F_t are r common driving forces of all variables under analysis, and β' is the vector of loadings, measuring the effects of the factors on the target variable y; x_t is a set of N weakly stationary variables, standardized for convenience, also driven by F_t via the loading matrix Φ; and $t = 1, \ldots, T$. We refer to Stock and Watson (2002a), Stock and Watson (2002b) (henceforth SW) for precise conditions on the factors, loadings, residuals, allowed temporal and cross-sectional dependence, and existence of proper central limit theorems.

If we augment the observation equations (13.2.1)-(13.2.2) with a set of transition equations for the factors F_t, we obtain a state space form whose parameters and unobservable state variables (the factors) can be estimated by the Kalman filter, as we saw in Chapter 10. However, when the number of variables N is large, the computational complexity and required time increase substantially. Hence, SW suggested an alternative (non-parametric) estimation method for the unobservable factors, which has the additional benefit of not requiring a specific model for the factor structure.

To get an intuition of how the SW estimation method works, and under which conditions, let us suppose at first that the $N \times r$ matrix Φ in (13.2.2) is known. Then, for each t, we could estimate the $r \times 1$ factors F_t using

$$\widehat{F_t} = (\Phi'\Phi)^{-1}\Phi'x_t. \tag{13.2.3}$$

If we now replace x_t by its expression in (13.2.2), and after a few simple computations, we obtain:

$$\widehat{F_t} = F_t + \left(\frac{\Phi'\Phi}{N}\right)^{-1}\left(\frac{\Phi'\varepsilon_t}{N}\right).$$

If (a) the minimum eigenvalue of $\Phi'\Phi/N$ is bounded away from zero (so that the matrix is invertible) and (b) $\Phi'\varepsilon_t/N$ converges in probability to zero, then when N diverges and for each t, the estimator $\widehat{F_t}$ converges in probability to F_t. Condition (a) basically requires the factors F_t to have non-zero loadings for all the variables in x_t, and hence to really be their common drivers. Condition (b) limits the extent of correlation among the idiosyncratic components ε_t, and it is clearly satisfied if each element of ε_t is uncorrelated with the others, as in the case of the strict factor models. Note that if N is finite, as in the case of Chapter 10, we can never get a consistent estimator for F_t, as F_t is random. What gives consistency in this case is the fact that N goes to infinity.

Let us now consider what happens when Φ is also unknown. The model in (13.2.2) becomes non-linear, as the product ΦF_t appears on the right-hand side, so that we need to use a form of non-linear least squares estimation for Φ and F_t. Specifically, writing the model in the more compact notation

$$x = \Phi F + \varepsilon, \tag{13.2.4}$$

where x, F, and ε are of dimensions $N \times T$, $r \times T$ and $N \times T$, respectively, we want:

$$\min_{\Phi, F} (x - \Phi F)' (x - \Phi F). \tag{13.2.5}$$

We also need to impose an identification condition, as $\Phi F = \Phi PP^{-1}F$ for an invertible $r \times r$ matrix P. Hence, we require $\Phi'\Phi = I_r$.

In order to solve (13.2.5), we use the envelope theorem. Hence, first we derive the loss function with respect to F and equate the first order conditions to zero, obtaining

$$\Phi' x = (\Phi'\Phi)^{-1}\widehat{F},$$

or

$$\widehat{F} = (\Phi'\Phi)^{-1}\Phi' x,$$

as in (13.2.3). The loss function therefore becomes

$$\left(x - \Phi(\Phi'\Phi)^{-1}\Phi' x\right)' \left(x - \Phi(\Phi'\Phi)^{-1}\Phi' x\right)$$

or

$$x'x - x'\Phi(\Phi'\Phi)^{-1}\Phi' x.$$

Minimization of this quantity with respect to Φ is then equivalent to

$$\max_{\Phi} \, tr\left(x'\Phi(\Phi'\Phi)^{-1}\Phi' x\right).$$

Because of the properties of the trace, we can also write the problem as

$$\max_{\Phi} \, tr\left((\Phi'\Phi)^{-1/2}\Phi'(xx')\Phi(\Phi'\Phi)^{-1/2}\right),$$

or, as for identification we have imposed $\Phi'\Phi = I_r$,

$$\max_{\Phi} tr\left(\Phi'(xx')\Phi\right).$$

Therefore, the optimal solution $\tilde{\Phi}$ is given by the r eigenvectors associated with the r largest eigenvalues of the $N \times N$ matrix xx'. Substituting $\tilde{\Phi}$ in (13.2.3), we obtain the estimator for the factors

$$\tilde{F} = (\tilde{\Phi}'\tilde{\Phi})^{-1}\tilde{\Phi}' x. \tag{13.2.6}$$

As an alternative, we could write the model as

$$x = F\Phi + \varepsilon, \tag{13.2.7}$$

where now x, F and ε are of dimensions $T \times N$, $T \times r$ and $T \times N$, respectively, and we do not change the notation for simplicity. The optimization problem becomes

$$\min_{\Phi, F} (x F\Phi)' (x F\Phi), \tag{13.2.8}$$

with the identification condition $F'F = I_r$. Proceeding as above, but now solving first for Φ as a function of F (which yields, $\hat{\Phi} = (F'F)^{-1}F'x$), and then for F, yields the alternative factor estimator $\hat{F}$ given by the r eigenvectors associated with the r largest eigenvalues of the $T \times T$ matrix xx'. These eigenvectors are also known as the principal components of x, and hence $\hat{F}$ is known as the principal components based factor estimator, or estimator based on principal component analysis (PCA).

The estimators $\tilde{F}$ and $\hat{F}$ are equivalent, in the sense that they span the same space. Using one or the other is just a matter of computational convenience, generally we want to take eigenvectors of smaller matrices and therefore the choice depends on whether empirically N or T is larger.

SW show that, under proper conditions, $\tilde{F}$ and $\hat{F}$ are consistent for the space spanned by the true factors F, though not necessarily for the true factors F themselves, due to the mentioned identification problem. Space consistency is however sufficient to use the estimated factors for forecasting purposes.

An additional issue is whether we can use $\hat{F}$ instead of F in the forecasting equation (13.2.1). Normally, we would have generated regressor problems. However, SW also show that in general this is not the case, and we indeed just replace F with $\hat{F}$, see Bai and Ng (2006) for more details and formal proofs. Therefore, using (13.2.1) and estimating β_0 and β' by OLS, the optimal one-step ahead forecast for y is

$$\hat{y}_{t+1} = \hat{\beta}_0 + \hat{\beta}'\hat{F}_t. \tag{13.2.9}$$

Let us consider now the case where

$$x_t = \Phi_1 F_t + \Phi_2 F_{t-1} + \ldots + \Phi_g F_{t-g+1} + \varepsilon_t, \tag{13.2.10}$$

so that the variables are driven by the factors and their lags. We can rewrite (13.2.10) as

$$x_t = \Psi G_t + \varepsilon_t, \tag{13.2.11}$$

where $\Psi = (\Phi_1, \ldots, \Phi_g)$ is $N \times rg$ and $G_t = (F'_t, F'_{t-1}, \ldots, F'_{t-g+1})'$ is $rg \times 1$. As (13.2.11) is of the same form as (13.2.2), with just rg instead of r factors, we can still use the first rg eigenvectors of $\mathbf{xx}'$ as factor estimators ($\hat{G}$).

More efficient factor estimators exist, which can take explicitly into account the dynamic characteristics of (13.2.10). Among them, we mention, the factor estimator by Altissimo, Cristadoro, Forni, Lippi, and Veronese (2010), which builds upon the one-sided non-parametric dynamic principal component analysis (DPCA) factor estimator of Forni, Hallin, Lippi, and Reichlin (2005), and the two-steps parametric state-space factor estimator based on the Kalman smoother of Doz, Giannone, and Reichlin (2011).[1] Which estimator performs best empirically is a priori unclear. There is a large literature on comparing factor estimation methods based on large datasets , see, e.g., Boivin and Ng (2005), Stock and Watson (2006), Schumacher (2007). We will focus on PCA based factor estimators, mostly for their computational simplicity combined with good empirical performance, and ease of implementation.

We can also extend the forecasting equation (13.2.1), e.g., to allow for AR terms, lags of the factors, or dummy variables. The resulting more general dynamic model can be treated in the same way as we have seen in the previous chapters.

So far we have considered the number of factors as known, r or rg. In practice, it is instead unknown and either economic considerations or proper information criteria can be used to determine it. In particular, Bai and Ng (2002) suggest the following three criteria:

$$
\begin{aligned}
IC_{p1}(k) &= \ln(V(k, \hat{F}_k) + k\left(\frac{N+T}{NT}\right)\ln\left(\frac{NT}{N+T}\right), \\
IC_{p2}(k) &= \ln(V(k, \hat{F}_k) + k\left(\frac{N+T}{NT}\right)\ln C_{NT}^2, \\
IC_{p3}(k) &= \ln(V(k, \hat{F}_k) + k\left(\frac{\ln C_{NT}^2}{C_{NT}^2}\right),
\end{aligned}
$$

where $C_{NT} = \min(\sqrt{N}, \sqrt{T})$ and $V(k, \hat{F}_k)$ is the average residual variance when k factors are assumed, namely:

$$
V(k, \hat{F}_k) = \frac{1}{N}\sum_{i=1}^{N}\hat{\sigma}_i^2, \quad \hat{\sigma}_i^2 = \frac{\hat{\varepsilon}_i'\hat{\varepsilon}_i}{T}.
$$

These criteria are similar to the AIC and BIC, but they also take the cross-sectional dimension N into account. Under proper assumptions, Bai and Ng (2002) show that they are consistent, i.e., they select the true number

---

[1]Using the Kalman filter it is also possible to allow for parameter time-variation, see Eickmeier, Lemke, and Marcellino (2015).

of factors with probability approaching one when both N and T diverge. Empirically, the performance of the criteria will depend on various characteristics, mainly the amount of cross-correlation among the idiosyncratic components and the relative size of the loadings (the signal-to-noise ratio), with substantial cross-correlation and small loadings making it difficult to disentangle what is common from what is not.

A more heuristic approach to the determination of the number of factors is based on the fraction of variance of x explained by the principal components (estimated factors). Under the assumption of r factors, the first r principal components should explain a large fraction of the variance of x (though each of them a progressively smaller fraction), while the components from $r + 1$ onwards should give a negligible contribution.

Factor models can also be used for structural analysis. Specifically, VARs for selected variables can be augmented with factors, which in turn evolve according to a VAR. The resulting model, known as factor augmented VAR (FAVAR), can be used to compute the responses of the variables of interest to specific structural shocks, identified in the VAR for the factors and therefore based on a large information set. This generally helps identification and reduces omitted variable problems. See Bernanke, Boivin, and Eliasz (2005) and Stock and Watson (2005) for interesting applications.

Finally, so far we have assumed that the variables under analysis are weakly stationary. However, factor models for I(1) variables can also be developed, and possible cointegration taken into account, see, e.g., Bai (2004), Bai and Ng (2004), Banerjee and Marcellino (2009), Banerjee, Marcellino, and Masten (2014) and Banerjee, Marcellino, and Masten (2017).

13.3 The three pass regression filter

A drawback of principal component analysis is that the target variable is not taken into consideration when summarizing the information in the large set of explanatory variables. The three pass regression filter (3PRF), developed by Kelly and Pruitt (2013) and Kelly and Pruitt (2015) (henceforth KP), addresses this issue. In particular, the 3PRF, which is an extension of Partial Least Squares (PLS), permits to obtain targeted factors for forecasting a specific variable of interest in a simple and intuitive manner. Moreover, it has a number of (asymptotic) optimality properties, performs well in finite samples compared to more complex alternatives, and produces good nowcasts and short-term forecasts for a variety of macroeconomic and financial variables; see KP for further details.

In this section, we provide an overview of the 3PRF, closely following the notation of KP, to whom we refer for additional details. In the next section, we will extend the 3PRF to handle mixed-frequency data, possibly with ragged edges, and discuss a number of possible extensions of the basic set-up.

Let us consider the following model:

$$
\begin{aligned}
y_{t+1} &= \beta_0 + \beta' F_t + \eta_{t+1}, & (13.3.1) \\
z_t &= \lambda_0 + \Lambda F_t + \omega_t, \\
x_t &= \Phi_0 + \Phi F_t + \varepsilon_t,
\end{aligned}
$$

where y is again the target variable of interest; $F_t = (f_t', g_t')'$ are the $K = K_f + K_g$ common unobservable factors driving all variables; $\beta = (\beta_f', 0')'$, so that y only depends on F; z is a small set of L proxies that are driven by the same underlying forces as y, so that $\Lambda = (\Lambda_f, 0)$ and Λ_f is nonsingular; x_t is a large set of N variables, driven by both f and g; and $t = 1, \ldots, T$. To achieve identification, the covariance of the loadings is assumed to be the identity matrix, and the factors are orthogonal to one another. We refer to KP for precise conditions on the factors, loadings, residuals, allowed temporal and cross-sectional dependence, and existence of proper central limit theorems.

With respect to the factor model analyzed in the previous section, here the large dataset x_t is possibly driven by more factors than the target variable y. Asymptotically and with a strong factor structure, this should not matter for forecasting, as if we include more factors than those strictly needed in (13.3.1), then their estimated coefficients will converge to zero. However, in finite samples, or if the f_t are weak while g_t are strong factors, estimating and using only the required factors f_t in (13.3.1) would be very convenient. This is a well-known problem, see, e.g., Boivin and Ng (2006) who suggested some form of variable pre-selection prior to factor extraction.

KP provide a general, elegant, and simple solution to the problem of estimating in the model (13.3.1) F_t only, which can be represented by the three following steps (that give the name to the procedure):

- Pass 1: run a (time series) regression of each element of x, x_i, on z:

$$
x_{i,t} = \phi_{0,i} + z_t' \phi_i + \varepsilon_{i,t},
$$

where $i = 1, \ldots, N$, and keep the OLS estimates $\hat{\phi}_i$.

- Pass 2: run a (cross section) regression of x_t on $\hat{\phi}_i$:

$$x_{i,t} = \phi_{0,t} + \hat{\phi}_i' F_t + \varepsilon_{i,t},$$

where $t = 1, \ldots, T$, and keep the OLS estimates $\hat{F}_t$.

- Pass 3: run a (time series) regression of y_{t+1} on $\hat{F}_t$:

$$y_{t+1} = \beta_0 + \beta' \hat{F}_t + \eta_{t+1},$$

keep the OLS estimators $\hat{\beta}_0$ and $\hat{\beta}'$, and use them in combination with $\hat{F}_t$ to construct the forecast $\hat{y}_{t+1} = \hat{\beta}_0 + \hat{\beta}' \hat{F}_t$.

KP show that the 3PRF factor estimator, $\hat{F}_t$, is consistent for the space spanned by the true factors. Moreover, they demonstrate that the 3PRF based forecast, $\hat{y}_{t+1} = \hat{\beta}_0 + \hat{\beta}' \hat{F}_t$, converges to the unfeasible forecast $\beta_0 + \beta' F_t$ when N and T diverge. In addition,

$$\frac{\sqrt{T}(\hat{y}_{t+1} - \beta_0 + \beta' F_t)}{Q_t} \xrightarrow{d} N(0, 1),$$

where Q_t is defined in KP.

For the case with just one f_t factor, KP suggest to use directly the target variable y as proxy z. They refer to this case as target-proxy 3PRF. In the case of more factors, they propose to either use theory suggested proxies, or a simple automated procedure, which can be implemented with the following steps, indicating a proxy by r_j and assuming that $j = 1, \ldots, L$.

- Pass 1: set $r_1 = y$, get the 3PRF forecast $\hat{y}_t^1$, and the associated residuals $e_t^1 = y_t - \hat{y}_t^1$.

- Pass 2: set $r_2 = e^1$, get the 3PRF forecast $\hat{y}_t^2$ using r_1 and r_2 as proxies, and the associated residuals $e_t^2 = y_t - \hat{y}_t^2$.

- Pass 2 $<$j$<$ L: set $r_j = e^{j-1}$, get the 3PRF forecast $\hat{y}_t^j$ using r_1 through r_j as proxies, and the associated residuals $e_t^j = y_t - \hat{y}_t^j$.

- Pass L: set $r_L = e^{L-1}$, get the 3PRF forecast $\hat{y}_t^L$ using $r_1, r_2, \ldots, r_L$ as proxies.

Finally, KP study the relationship between 3PRF and PLS, see Wold (1966) and Helland (1990) for theoretical results on PLS and, e.g., Kapetanios, Marcellino, and Papailias (2016) for an application to GDP forecasting. Specifically, KP show that PLS is a special case of 3PRF obtained when the predictors are standardized, the first two regression passes of 3PRF are run without intercept, and the proxies are automatically selected.

13.4   Large unbalanced datasets

As we saw in the previous chapter, mixed-frequency information can be quite useful for modeling and predicting economic and financial variables. In order to handle large unbalanced dataset, we need to combine the MIDAS, UMIDAS, or Kalman filter-based techniques for mixed-frequency data analyzed in the previous chapter with the methods for large datasets considered in this chapter.

13.4.1   Mixed-frequency factor models

Relevant papers dealing with large mixed-frequency factor models with small N (cross-sections) are, e.g., Bańbura and Rünstler (2011), who further extend the model of Giannone, Reichlin, and Small (2008) and Bańbura and Modugno (2014), who discuss maximum likelihood estimation of factor models on datasets with arbitrary patterns of missing data. These papers use the Kalman filter, which is more efficient but requires the specification of a parametric model in high-frequency and can be computationally very demanding for large datasets and high/low-frequency mismatch. For large cross-sections, there are a number of alternatives. For example, Marcellino and Schumacher (2010) propose a simpler alternative, which combines the Stock and Watson (2002b) EM algorithm for factor estimation from irregular datasets with the MIDAS regression technique or its unrestricted counterpart (U-MIDAS) (cf. Chapter 12). Let us first summarize the Stock and Watson (2002b) EM algorithm for factor estimation from irregular datasets, and then present the main proposals in Marcellino and Schumacher (2010) (henceforth MS).

Let us assume for simplicity that the x variables are standardized. Focusing on a variable i, let the vector x_i^{obs} contain the available observations and formulate the relationship between observed and not fully observed data by

$$x_i^{\text{obs}} = A_i x_i, \qquad (13.4.1)$$

where A_i is a $Tk \times Tk$ matrix that tackles the mixed frequencies (or missing values). In case no observations are missing, A_i is the identity matrix. In case of an observable value every k (point in time or stock sampling), A_i is the identity matrix where the ones in the diagonal corresponding to the missing observations are replaced by zeros. In case of average or flow sampling, again with frequency k and assuming for example that $k = 3$, the A_i matrix takes the form

$$A_i = \begin{bmatrix} 0 & 0 & 0 & \dots & 0 & 0 & 0 \\ 0 & 0 & 0 & \dots & 0 & 0 & 0 \\ 1 & 1 & 1 & \dots & 0 & 0 & 0 \\ \vdots & \vdots & \vdots & \dots & \vdots & \vdots & \vdots \\ 0 & 0 & 0 & \dots & 0 & 0 & 0 \\ 0 & 0 & 0 & \dots & 0 & 0 & 0 \\ 0 & 0 & 0 & \dots & 1 & 1 & 1 \end{bmatrix}.$$

The EM algorithm proceeds as follows:

1. Provide an initial (naive) guess of observations $\hat{x}_i^{(0)}$ $\forall i$. These guesses, together with the fully observable monthly time series, yield a balanced dataset $\hat{x}^{(0)}$. Standard principal component analysis (PCA) provides initial monthly factor estimates $\hat{F}^{(0)}$ and loadings $\hat{\Phi}^{(0)}$.

2. E-step: an update estimate of the missing observations for variable i is provided by the expectation of x_i conditional on observations x_i^{obs}, factors $\hat{F}^{(j-1)}$ and loadings $\hat{\Phi}_i^{(j-1)}$ from the previous iteration

$$\hat{x}_i^{(j)} = \hat{F}^{(j-1)}\hat{\Phi}_i^{(j-1)} + A_i'(A_i'A_i)^{-1}\left(x_i^{\text{obs}} - A_i\hat{F}^{(j-1)}\hat{\Phi}_i^{(j-1)}\right). \quad (13.4.2)$$

The update consists of two components: the common component from the previous iteration $\hat{F}^{(j-1)}\hat{\Phi}_i^{(j-1)}$, plus the low-frequency idiosyncratic component $x_i^{\text{obs}} - A_i\hat{F}^{(j-1)}\hat{\Phi}_i^{(j-1)}$, distributed by the projection coefficient $A_i'(A_i'A_i)^{-1}$ on the high-frequency periods.

3. M-step: repeat the E-step for all i yielding again a balanced dataset. Re-estimate the factors and loadings, $\hat{F}^{(j)}$ and $\hat{\Phi}^{(j)}$ by PCA, and go to step 2 until convergence.

After convergence, the EM algorithm provides high-frequency factor estimates and estimates of the missing values of the time series, $\hat{x}_i$ for each i.[2]

Andreou, Gagliardini, Ghysels, and Rubin (2016) consider mixed-frequency factor models of a different nature and that involve PCA applicable to mixed-frequency data. Using the terminology of the approximate factor model literature, they consider a panel consisting of N_H series sampled across MT time periods, where $M = 4$ for quarterly data and $M = 12$ for monthly data, with T the number of years. Moreover, they assume one also has a panel of N_L series that is only observed over T periods. Hence, generically speaking we have a high-frequency panel data set of size $N_H \times MT$ and a corresponding low-frequency panel data set of size $N_L \times T$.

To be more specific, we have a latent factor structure in mind to explain the panel data variation for both the low and high-frequency observations. To that end, we assume that there are three types of factors, which we denote respectively $g_{m,t}^C$, $g_{m,t}^H$ and $g_{m,t}^L$ for $m = 1, \ldots, M$. The former represents factors that affect both high- and low-frequency data (throughout we use superscript C for common), whereas the other two types of factors affect exclusively high- (superscript H) and low- (marked by L) frequency data. We denote by k^C, k^H, and k^L, the dimensions of these factors. The latent factor model with high-frequency data sampling is

$$\begin{aligned}
x_{m,t}^H &= \Lambda_{HC} g_{m,t}^C + \Lambda_H g_{m,t}^H + e_{m,t}^H, \\
x_{m,t}^{L*} &= \Lambda_{LC} g_{m,t}^C + \Lambda_L g_{m,t}^L + e_{m,t}^L,
\end{aligned} \tag{13.4.3}$$

where $m = 1, \ldots, M$ and $t = 1, \ldots, T$, and Λ_{HC}, Λ_H, Λ_{LC} and Λ_L are matrices of factor loadings. The vector $x_{m,t}^{L*}$ is unobserved for each high-frequency subperiod and the measurements, denoted by x_t^L, depend on the observation scheme, which can be either flow sampling or stock sampling (or some general linear scheme).

In the case of flow sampling, the low-frequency observations are the sum (or average) of all $x_{m,t}^{L*}$ across all m, that is: $x_t^L = \sum_{m=1}^M x_{m,t}^{L*}$. Then, model (13.4.3) implies

$$\begin{aligned}
x_{m,t}^H &= \Lambda_{HC} g_{m,t}^C + \Lambda_H g_{m,t}^H + e_{m,t}^H, \quad m = 1, \ldots, M, \\
x_t^L &= \Lambda_{LC} \sum_{m=1}^M g_{m,t}^C + \Lambda_L \sum_{m=1}^M g_{m,t}^L + \sum_{m=1}^M e_{m,t}^L.
\end{aligned} \tag{13.4.4}$$

---

[2]For recent further extensions see also Jungbacker, Koopman, and Van der Wel (2011) and Gagliardini, Ghysels, and Rubin (2016).

Let us first assume that k^C, k^H, k^L, i.e., the number of respectively common, high- and low-frequency factors in equation (13.4.3), are known and are all strictly larger than zero. A simple estimation procedure for the factor values and the factor loadings, consists of the following three steps:

1. *PCA performed on the HF and LF panels separately*
   Define the (T, N_H) matrix of temporally aggregated (in our application flow-sampled) HF observables as $X^H = [x_1^H, \ldots, x_T^H]'$, and the (T, N_L) matrix of LF observables as $X^L = [x_1^L, \ldots, x_T^L]'$. The estimated pervasive factors of the HF data, which are collected in $(T, k^C + k^H)$ matrix $\hat{h}_H = [\hat{h}_{H,1}, \ldots, \hat{h}_{H,T}]'$, are obtained performing PCA on the HF data:

$$\left(\frac{1}{TN_H}X^H X^{H\prime}\right)\hat{h}_H = \hat{h}_H \hat{V}_H,$$

   where $\hat{V}_H$ is the diagonal matrix of the eigenvalues of $(TN_H)^{-1}X^H X^{H\prime}$. Analogously, the estimated pervasive factors of the LF data, which are collected in the $(T, k^C + k^L)$ matrix $\hat{h}_L = [\hat{h}_{L,1}, \ldots, \hat{h}_{L,T}]'$, are obtained performing PCA on the LF data:

$$\left(\frac{1}{TN_L}X^L X^{L\prime}\right)\hat{h}_L = \hat{h}_L \hat{V}_L,$$

   where $\hat{V}_L$ is the diagonal matrix of the eigenvalues of $(TN_L)^{-1}X^L X^{L\prime}$.

2. *Canonical correlation analysis performed on estimated principal components*
   Let $\hat{W}_H^C$ be the $(k^C + k^H, k^C)$ matrix whose columns are the canonical directions for $\hat{h}_{H,t}$ associated with the k^C largest canonical correlations between $\hat{h}_H$ and $\hat{h}_L$. Then, the estimator of the (in our application flow sampled) common factor is $\hat{\bar{g}}_t^C = \hat{W}_H^C{}'\hat{h}_{H,t}$, for $t = 1, \ldots, T$, and the estimated loadings matrices $\hat{\Lambda}_{HC}$ and $\hat{\Lambda}_{LC}$ are obtained from the least squares regressions of x_t^H and x_t^L on estimated factor $\hat{\bar{g}}_t^C$. Collect the residuals of these regressions:

$$\begin{aligned}
\hat{\bar{\xi}}_t^H &= x_t^H - \hat{\Lambda}_{HC}\hat{\bar{g}}_t^C, \\
\hat{\bar{\xi}}_t^L &= x_t^L - \hat{\Lambda}_{LC}\hat{\bar{g}}_t^C,
\end{aligned}$$

in the following (T, N_U), with $U = H, L$, matrices:

$$\hat{\Xi}^U \;=\; \left[\hat{\xi}_1^U, \dots, \hat{\xi}_T^U\right]', \qquad U = H, L.$$

Then, the estimators of the HF and LF factors, collected in the (T, k^U), $U = H, L$, matrices:

$$\hat{G}^U \;=\; \left[\hat{g}_1^U, \dots, \hat{g}_T^U\right]', \qquad U = H, L,$$

are obtained extracting the first k^H and k^L PCs from the matrices of residuals:

$$\left(\frac{1}{TN_U}\hat{\Xi}^U\hat{\Xi}^{U\,'}\right)\hat{G}^U \;=\; \hat{G}^U\hat{V}_S^U, \qquad U = H, L,$$

where $\hat{V}_S^U$, with $U = H, L$, are the diagonal matrices of the associated eigenvalues. Next, the estimated loadings matrices $\hat{\Lambda}_H$ and $\hat{\Lambda}_C$ are obtained from the least squares regression of $\hat{\xi}_t^H$ and $\hat{\xi}_t^L$ on, respectively, the estimated factors $\hat{g}_t^H$ and $\hat{g}_t^L$.

3. *Reconstruction of the common and high-frequency specific factors*
   The estimates of the common and HF factors for each HF subperiod, denoted by $\hat{g}_{m,t}^C$ and $\hat{g}_{m,t}^H$, for any $m = 1, \dots, M$ and $t = 1, \dots, T$, are obtained by cross-sectional regression of $x_{m,t}$ on the estimated loadings $[\hat{\Lambda}_{HC} \vdots \hat{\Lambda}_H]$ obtained from the second step.

Since the factors dimensions are unknown, the aforementioned procedure is implemented with estimated factors dimensions $\hat{k}^C$, $\hat{k}^H$, and $\hat{k}^L$. Inference on the number of common, low and high-frequency specific factors is described in detail in Andreou, Gagliardini, Ghysels, and Rubin (2016).

13.4.2 Mixed-frequency three pass regression filter

As discussed in the previous section, principal component based factor estimators are not targeted to the variable of interest, while 3PRF tilts the summary information in the right direction. We now consider the extension of the 3PRF to the case where the target variable y (or the proxies z) are sampled at lower frequency than the indicators x. Next, we allow for some of the components of x to be also only available in low-frequency. Both cases are considered in details in Hepenstrick and Marcellino (2016) (henceforth HM), to whom we refer for further details and examples.

Low-frequency target or proxy variables and high-frequency indicators

This is an empirically frequent situation. It happens, for example, when the target variable is GDP growth or GDP deflator inflation, which are available on a quarterly basis, while the indicators are available on a monthly basis, e.g., industrial production and its components, labor market variables, financial indicators, and survey variables.

To handle the frequency mismatch, HM propose to modify the steps in 3PRF as follows.

- Pass 1: as in 3PRF and run at quarterly frequency.

- Pass 2: as in 3PRF and run at monthly frequency to get monthly predictive factor(s).

- Pass 3: use the U-MIDAS approach to construct a nowcasting or forecasting model that links the quarterly target variable to the monthly factors.

HM label the resulting procedure the mixed-frequency three pass regression filter, MF-3PRF. A few comments on each step are in order. First, as the regression in Pass 1 of 3PRF is static, running it in MF-3PRF with quarterly rather than monthly indicators leads to consistent parameter estimators, which have the same properties as in 3PRF.

Second, step 2 of MF-3PRF uses monthly rather than quarterly indicators, but the properties of the resulting factor estimators are the same as in 3PRF, as the cross-sectional dimension is only exploited in this step.

Third, in step 3 HM suggest the use of the U-MIDAS method, as the frequency mismatch (monthly/quarterly) is small. As we have seen, this requires to split the estimated monthly factors $\hat{F}_t$ into J quarterly factors $(\hat{F}_t^1, \hat{F}_t^2, \ldots, \hat{F}_t^J)$. The first (second/third) new quarterly series contains the values of $\hat{F}_t$ in, respectively, the first (second/third) month of each quarter. The fourth (fifth/sixth) series are first lags of $\hat{F}_t^1$ ($\hat{F}_t^2/\hat{F}_t^3$) etc. Next, $\hat{F}_t^1$, $\hat{F}_t^2, \ldots, \hat{F}_t^J$ are used as explanatory variables for y_t in the third step of 3PRF, thus balancing the frequency of the left- and right-hand side variables while maintaining linearity of the equation and still using all the available information.[3] The number of new variables J can be estimated using various information criteria or simply be fixed.

The third step of MF-3PRF, the forecasting step, can be implemented based on the direct method, as in KP. As an alternative, a VAR model for F_t can be added to the system in (13.3.1):

$$F_t = \sum_{k=1}^{K} \Theta_k F_{t-k} + \mathbf{v}_t, \qquad (13.4.5)$$

and used, in combination with the estimated factors $\hat{F}$, to generate forecasts for $\hat{F}_{t+h}$, to be inserted in an iterated procedure to predict y_{t+h}. See, e.g., Marcellino, Stock, and Watson (2006) for a comparison of the properties of direct and iterated forecasts.

Note that the MF-3PRF inherits all the theoretical properties of 3PRF, under the same assumptions, as it is based on the same three steps and an efficient use of all the available information. Its finite sample properties are evaluated by HM by means of Monte Carlo experiments and found to be satisfactory, clearly better than 3PRF run on aggregated quarterly data.

Finally, Kapetanios, Marcellino, and Papailias (2016) apply U-MIDAS to obtain a mixed-frequency version of PLS (MF-PLS). Since we noted in the previous section that PLS is a special case of 3PRF, also MF-PLS can be considered as a special case of MF-3PRF.

Low-frequency indicators

Not only the target or proxy variables in (13.3.1) but also some of the indicators in x_t can be only available in low-frequency. This situation can be handled either by using the Kalman filter, as in the case of ragged edges described in the next subsection, which requires the specification of a model for the unobservable factors (e.g., as in (13.4.5)), or by applying the EM algorithm of Stock and Watson (2002b), described above, and without specifying a model for the factors. In both cases, the systematically missing observations in the low-frequency variables are replaced by their best estimates, and then the analysis proceeds as in the previous subsection.

---

[3]In case of larger frequency mismatch, e.g., for quarterly and daily data, U-MIDAS can be replaced by MIDAS, which, however, requires the use of non-linear least squares for parameter estimation.

13.4.3 Missing observations and ragged edges

Mixed-frequency sampling generates systematic patterns of missing observations in x, but other types of missing observations are also frequent in empirical analysis, due to the different start and/or end dates of some indicators. The case of missing observations at the end of the sample, due to different release timing, was labeled "ragged edge" by Wallis (1986). We focus on this situation, as it is more relevant for forecasting, but missing observations at the start of the sample can be handled in a similar manner (as well as scattered missing observations).

In addition to the EM algorithm that can also be applied in this context with a proper choice of the A_i matrix, we propose to apply two approaches that can also be used in the factor MIDAS case, as suggested by MS. Marcellino and Schumacher (2010) consider various ways of combining factor methods to handle large datasets with approaches to allow for mixed-frequency data, finding that in general they outperform single (low) frequency methods.

First, they use the Kalman filter, where the VAR for the factors in (13.4.5) contains the state equations to be used in combination with the observation equations. Note that this approach can also be used to handle mixed-frequencies in x, see, e.g., Mariano and Murasawa (2003) and Mariano and Murasawa (2010).

The second method simply requires to fit time series models to the variables with ragged edge (AR(2), for example), and then replace the missing observations at the end of each time series with their forecast values using the same approach as in bridge equations (see Chapter 12).

The use of the Kalman filter to handle ragged edges is optimal, in the sense of producing the best linear estimates of the missing observations conditional on the correct specification of the state space form. However, it can be computationally demanding in the presence of several series with ragged edge, and requires to specify a model for the unobservable factors. The second method is much faster, but can be suboptimal.

MS also consider a third method, based on a simple vertical re-alignment of the data, as suggested by Altissimo, Cristadoro, Forni, Lippi, and Veronese (2010) for estimating the New Eurocoin indicator. The problem of this procedure is that it changes the correlation structure of the data. Hence, factors should be estimated by dynamic principal components, see, e.g., Forni, Hallin, Lippi, and Reichlin (2005).

MS and HM experiment empirically with the various procedures, finding no clear-cut rankings in terms of forecasting performance.

13.5 Example with simulated data

We now illustrate the use of the mixed-frequency three pass regression filter and other econometric methods for large datasets using simulated data. Specifically, we generate 480 monthly observations for 70 variables that are going to be the large dataset and 160 quarterly observation for one variable. We assume to be in a situation where we are interested in nowcasting, i.e., we observe some variables at high frequency, but not the low-frequency variable we want indeed to nowcast. The DGP has the following specification:

$$\begin{aligned} y_{t+1} &= \beta_0 + \beta_1 F_t + \eta_{t+1} \qquad\qquad (13.5.1) \\ x_t &= \Phi F_t + \varepsilon_t \\ F_t &= \rho F_{t-1} + \upsilon_t, \end{aligned}$$

where υ and η are i.i.d. normal variables and $\varepsilon_t \overset{iid}{\sim} N(0, I_{70})$, with I_{70} being the 70×70 identity matrix.

We will use the mixed-frequency three pass regression filter described in this chapter to extract the factors driving x_t for providing forecasts for the target variable y_t and compare the forecasts to two benchmarks. As a first benchmark we use principal component analysis (PCA) to extract the factor(s) and use them for predicting y_t (SW approach). As a second benchmark we just estimate an AR(1) to forecast y_t. To simplify the interpretation of the results, let us assume that the 480 monthly observations span the time range Jan. 1975 - Dec. 2014. The pattern of the variable we want to nowcast is shown in Figure 13.5.1.

Let's first compare the in-sample fit of the three different models. Tables 13.5.1, 13.5.2, and 13.5.3 refer to the 3PRF, the SW approach, and the AR respectively. We note that the 3PRF has the best fit, and all the three quarterly factors we extracted through the algorithm are significant, while for the SW approach only the first principal component turns out to be significant.

The out-of-sample analysis is performed starting from Dec. 1999 so that the first estimation sample has 100 (quarterly) observations. We assume that

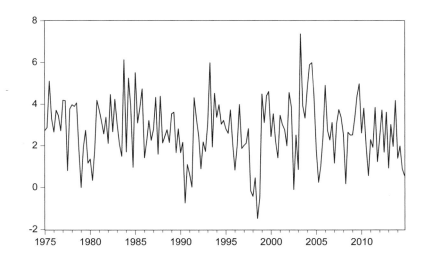

Figure 13.5.1: *Series for the simulated data*

in Dec. 1999 we observe all the monthly variables until that date, but not the target variable at 1999Q4. In every iteration of the out-of-sample exercise we add one new quarterly observation, we run the 3PRF with the three new monthly observations for x_t, we estimate the new PCs for the SW approach and we estimate an AR(1). For each of the three models we compute the nowcasts.

Figure 13.5.2 compares the forecasts from the different models. Already from this visual inspection we can see that the 3PRF is outperforming with respect to the other models. We can run a forecast comparison test to assess whether the RMSFEs are statistically different. Table 13.5.4 shows the RMSFE of the three models and the p-values of a Diebold-Mariano test on each pair: the 3PRF has the lowest RMSFE and we reject the null hypothesis of same forecasting accuracy with respect to the other two models at 1%.

13.6 Empirical example: Forecasting GDP growth

In this section we apply factor model techniques to three large datasets for US, Euro area, and Poland and we compare in-sample estimation and out-

Variable	Coefficient	Std. Error	t-Statistic	Prob.
C	2.980	0.081	36.684	0.000
FS1	-0.301	0.056	-5.407	0.000
FS2	0.177	0.053	3.369	0.001
FS3	0.549	0.048	11.398	0.000
R-squared	0.569	Mean dep var		2.715
Adjusted R-squared	0.561	S.D. dep var		1.502
S.E. of regression	0.995	Akaike IC		2.853
Sum squared resid	154.530	Schwarz IC		2.930
Log likelihood	-224.247	Hannan-Quinn		2.884
F-statistic	68.689	DW stat		2.135
Prob(F-statistic)	0.000			

Table 13.5.1: *Results from the 3PRF*

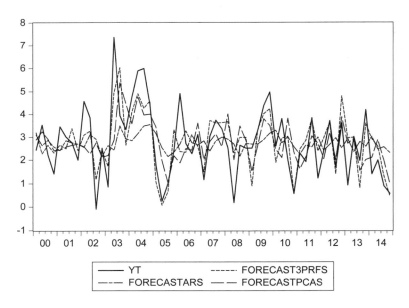

Figure 13.5.2: *Comparison of the forecasts from the different models*

of-sample forecasting GDP growth for different modeling techniques. In particular, we compare the Stock and Watson (SW) and its targeted factor (SWTF) version, described below, with the 3PRF, a small scale VAR and

Variable	Coefficient	Std. Error	t-Statistic	Prob.
C	2.715	0.099	27.335	0.000
PC1	0.200	0.024	8.171	0.000
PC2	-0.053	0.068	-0.782	0.435
PC3	0.137	0.070	1.964	0.051
R-squared	0.313	Mean dep var		2.715
Adjusted R-squared	0.300	S.D. dep var		1.502
S.E. of regression	1.256	Akaike IC		3.319
Sum squared resid	246.228	Schwarz IC		3.396
Log likelihood	-261.517	Hannan-Quinn		3.350
F-statistic	23.743	DW stat		2.135
Prob(F-statistic)	0.000			

Table 13.5.2: *Results from the SW approach*

a Factor Augmented VAR (FAVAR). The large datasets are composed of monthly variables (70 for the US, 34 for the EA and 32 for Poland) of several kinds: hard indicators (e.g., industrial production), survey data (e.g., sentiment index), financial indicators (e.g., financial condition index), interest rates and price indicators.

Data are from 1985 to 2013 for the United States and from 1995 to 2013 for Euro area and Poland. All the variables are aggregated to quarterly frequency, standardized and transformed in growth rate if non-stationary.

For what concerns the SW approach the first thing we need to decide is the number r of principal components. The most common criterion for choosing the number of principal components (PCs) is based on the fraction of the variance of data explained: if we order the PCs from the one explaining most of the variance to the one explaining the least, we set r so that the additional fraction of explained variance by the last included PC is large enough with respect to that of the first excluded one.

A good choice for r based on the criterion described above is 4, as we can see in Figure 13.6.1; with $r = 4$ we explain 52% of the total variance. For comparability with United States we set $r = 4$ also for Euro area (67% of explained variance) and Poland (63% of explained variance).

Once having estimated the PCs we can regress GDP growth at time

Variable	Coefficient	Std. Error	t-Statistic	Prob.
C	2.125	0.244	8.708	0.000
YT(-1)	0.216	0.078	2.758	0.006
R-squared	0.046	Mean dep var		2.715
Adjusted R-squared	0.040	S.D. dep var		1.507
S.E. of regression	1.476	Akaike IC		3.629
Sum squared resid	342.085	Schwarz IC		3.668
Log likelihood	-286.521	Hannan-Quinn		3.645
F-statistic	7.604	DW stat		2.046
Prob(F-statistic)	0.007			

Table 13.5.3: *Results from the AR(1)*

	RMSFE	DM pval vs 3PRF	DM pval vs SW
3PRF	0.984	-	-
SW	1.302	0.006	-
AR	1.461	0.001	0.017

Table 13.5.4: *RMSFE and p-values for Diebold-Mariano test*

$t + h$ on the PCs, where in this example $h = 1$. Tables 13.6.1 and 13.6.2 compare the fit of such estimated model with a small-scale VAR including GDP growth, inflation and central bank policy rate where the number of lags is selected according to the Schwarz criterion. The tables refer to US data.

From comparing the two tables we see that the two models have a similar fit, with the SW having a lower SC being less parameterized. Also, note that only two of the four PCs turn out to be significant in explaining GDP growth for the United States.

The second method we perform and evaluate is the SW approach using targeted factors (SWTF) (cf. Boivin and Ng (2006)). This method consists in removing all the variables whose correlation with the target variable is less than a generic threshold value which we set in this example equal to 0.4. Hence, we compute PCs on a smaller dataset than the original one; the smaller dataset is obtained by removing from the original dataset all the variables featuring a correlation with GDP growth less than 0.4 in absolute value. Figure 13.6.2 plots GDP growth with the first principal component and the first targeted principal component, with the two being sometimes

	GDP_US	INFL_US	IRATE_US
GDP_US(-1)	0.262	0.029	0.048
	(0.097)	(0.030)	(0.015)
	[2.696]	[0.954]	[3.163]
GDP_US(-2)	0.264	0.007	-0.010
	(0.09)8	(0.030)	(0.015)
	[2.700]	[0.228]	[-0.632]
INFL_US(-1)	-0.611	0.971	-0.111
	(0.309)	(0.096)	(0.048)
	[-1.976]	[10.146]	[-2.294]
INFL_US(-2)	0.049	-0.278	0.093
	(0.320)	(0.099)	(0.050)
	[0.152]	[-2.807]	[1.865]
IRATE_US(-1)	0.267	0.123	1.607
	(0.521)	(0.161)	(0.081)
	[0.512]	[0.760]	[19.747]
IRATE_US(-2)	-0.136	-0.051	-0.632
	(0.512)	(0.159)	(0.080)
	[-0.266]	[-0.322]	[-7.901]
C	2.318	0.471	0.023
	(0.615)	(0.190)	(0.096)
	[3.770]	[2.476]	[0.243]
R-squared	0.282	0.738	0.985
Adj. R-squared	0.241	0.723	0.984
Sum sq. resids	479.882	45.978	11.702
S.E. equation	2.138	0.662	0.334
F-statistic	6.887	49.378	1172.741
Log likelihood	-240.403	-109.063	-32.431
Akaike AIC	4.418	2.073	0.704
Schwarz BIC	4.588	2.242	0.874
Mean dep	2.664	2.825	4.063
S.D. dep	2.455	1.258	2.678
Determinant resid covariance (dof adj.)		0.189	
Determinant resid covariance		0.156	
Log likelihood		-372.749	
Akaike information criterion		7.031	
Schwarz IC		7.541	

Table 13.6.1: *Results from small-scale VAR*

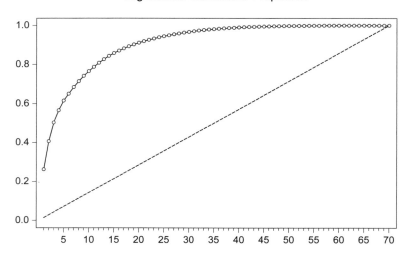

Figure 13.6.1: *Cumulative proportion of explained variances by each principal component, from the one explaining the most to the one explaining the least*

different, in particular during the crisis.

From Table 13.6.3 we see that using targeted principal components we actually slightly worsen the fit. This probably means that discarding data based only on bivariate correlations with GDP growth is not ideal, as it leads to discarding useful information.

The third method we compare is the 3PRF with 4 factors. We use the automated procedure described previously in this chapter to generate proxies for the factors. Table 13.6.4 shows the fit of the 3PRF for US data and we note that the adjusted R^2 of the 3PRF is much higher than the one of the SWTF and of the SW approach (compare with Tables 13.6.2 and 13.6.3).

We now evaluate and compare the out-of-sample performance of all these models for the three different datasets. In addition to the models described before we also estimate and compute forecasts from a small scale VAR augmented with the first three principal components (FAVAR). The out-of-sample exercise is performed starting from 2001 for the United States and from 2005 for the Euro area and Poland: at each iteration we add one observation to the dataset, estimate all the models, and save the one-step-ahead forecast for each model. Once the out-of-sample iteration is concluded we compute the RMSFE for each model and perform Diebold-Mariano tests for

Variable	Coefficient	Std. Error	t-Statistic	Prob.
C	2.701	0.203	13.308	0.000
PC1	0.272	0.050	5.407	0.000
PC2	0.049	0.065	0.751	0.454
PC3	0.233	0.079	2.950	0.004
PC4	-0.033	0.100	-0.335	0.739
R-squared	0.263	Mean dep var		2.697
Adjusted R-squared	0.236	S.D. dep var		2.468
S.E. of regression	2.157	Akaike IC		4.419
Sum squared resid	502.594	Schwarz IC		4.539
Log likelihood	-244.660	Hannan-Quinn		4.468
F-statistic	9.655	DW stat		2.019
Prob(F-statistic)	0.000			

Table 13.6.2: *Results from SW approach*

each pair of models.

Table 13.6.5 summarizes the results for each country. The 3PRF has always the lowest RMSFE, with p-values that indicate almost always a rejection of the null hypothesis of similar forecasting accuracy compared with any other model. The only model that seems to have a similar forecasting performance is SW (both plain and targeted), but only when we use Euro area data.

13.7 Concluding remarks

In this chapter we have focused on factor models and related methods for modeling and forecasting in the presence of a large, possibly unbalanced, dataset.

The derivation of the theoretical properties of the econometric methods is rather complex, but their empirical implementation is instead relatively easy and, as we have seen, the gains from the use of a large information set can be substantial.

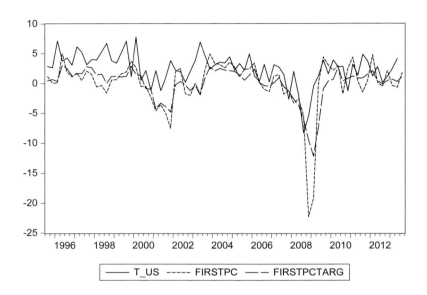

Figure 13.6.2: *Comparison of the first principal component against the first targeted principal component computed on US data*

Variable	Coefficient	Std. Error	t-Statistic	Prob.
C	2.702	0.204	13.224	0.000
TPC1	0.443	0.075	5.939	0.000
TPC2	0.147	0.167	0.881	0.381
TPC3	-0.174	0.237	-0.736	0.463
TPC4	-0.090	0.266	-0.338	0.736
R-squared	0.254	Mean dep var		2.697
Adjusted R-squared	0.226	S.D. dep var		2.468
S.E. of regression	2.172	Akaike IC		4.432
Sum squared resid	509.318	Schwarz IC		4.553
Log likelihood	-245.411	Hannan-Quinn		4.481
F-statistic	9.171	DW stat		2.035
Prob(F-statistic)	0.000			

Table 13.6.3: *Results from targeted PCs*

Variable	Coefficient	Std. Error	t-Statistic	Prob.
C	1.658	0.295	5.620	0.000
F1	0.401	0.053	7.559	0.000
F2	0.764	0.190	4.017	0.000
F3	0.135	0.280	0.481	0.631
F4	-0.738	0.210	-3.519	0.001
R-squared	0.530	Mean dep var		2.697
Adjusted R-squared	0.513	S.D. dep var		2.468
S.E. of regression	1.723	Akaike IC		3.969
Sum squared resid	320.474	Schwarz IC		4.089
Log likelihood	-219.236	Hannan-Quinn		4.018
F-statistic	30.486	DW stat		2.395
Prob(F-statistic)	0.000			

Table 13.6.4: *Results from three pass regression filter*

	RMSFE	pval. vs			
		VAR	SW	SWTF	FAVAR
U.S.					
VAR	2.62	-	-	-	-
SW	2.69	0.35	-	-	-
SWTF	2.58	0.43	0.30	-	-
FAVAR	2.58	0.11	0.09	0.27	-
3PRF	**2.08**	0.03	0.01	0.02	0.02
Euro Area					
VAR	2.47	-	-	-	-
SW	2.00	0.08	-	-	-
SWTF	2.04	0.11	0.43	-	-
FAVAR	2.27	0.16	0.15	0.11	-
3PRF	**1.93**	0.06	0.19	0.21	0.09
POL					
VAR	5.03	-	-	-	-
SW	4.56	0.29	-	-	-
SWTF	5.32	0.28	0.06	-	-
FAVAR	5.42	0.30	0.02	0.34	-
3PRF	**3.20**	0.05	0.03	0.02	0.02

Table 13.6.5: *RMSFE and p-values for Diebold-Mariano test*

Chapter 14

Forecasting Volatility

14.1 Introduction

The models considered so far focused on conditional mean forecasts. In this chapter we consider conditional variance. Time-variation in the conditional variance of financial time-series is important when pricing derivatives, calculating measures of risk, portfolio risk management, and dynamic hedging. Not surprisingly, there has been an enormous interest amongst researchers and practitioners to forecast conditional variances. As a result, a large number of volatility forecasting models have been developed, starting with the ARCH model of Engle (1982).[1]

Another major source of interest in volatility stems from modern option pricing theory, beginning with Black and Scholes (1973). Their famous model accords volatility a central role in determining the fair value for an option, or any derivative instrument with option features. The basic Black-Scholes (BS) option pricing formula involves a number of inputs – and the most prominent is volatility as it happens also to be the only one that is not directly observable.[2] Option pricing theory is typically rooted in a continuous time stochastic setting – either diffusion or jump-diffusion in nature. Thinking about volatility in such a context is a bit more challenging, both from an asset pricing theory and econometric analysis perspective (see, e.g., Garcia, Ghysels, and Renault (2010)). Continuous time diffusions with stochastic

---

[1]We will use the terms conditional variance and volatility interchangeably – although the latter is sometimes associated with conditional standard deviations.

[2]The other determinants, stock price, strike price, time to option expiration, and the interest rate are all known or can be easily obtained.

volatility are not that easy to handle and beyond the scope of this book. However, the framework has over the last two decades resulted in models of volatility forecasting based on the notion of realized volatility – typically measured as the sum of intra-daily squared returns to obtain a daily realized measure. The availability of high-frequency data has made realized volatility easy to compute and the models using such measures have been shown to feature appealing forecasting performance.

This chapter will therefore focus on two types of volatility forecasting models: (1) ARCH-type models and (2) models based on realized volatility. Excellent surveys of the ARCH literature appear in Bollerslev, Engle, and Nelson (1994) (univariate models) and Bauwens, Laurent, and Rombouts (2006) (multivariate models). Surveys of stochastic volatility models appear in Ghysels, Harvey, and Renault (1996) and Shephard (2005). Realized volatility and its use for the purpose of forecasting is reviewed by Andersen, Bollerslev, Christoffersen, and Diebold (2006). Some excellent textbooks related to the topics covered in this chapter include Brooks (2014), Gouriéroux and Jasiak (2001), Taylor (2007), Tsay (2005), among others.

Section 14.2 covers ARCH-type models, followed by Section 14.3 dealing with MIDAS regressions for volatility forecasting. Section 14.4 revisits GARCH models, in light of the MIDAS regression results. Volatility forecasting evaluation is discussed in Section 14.5. Empirical examples appear in Section 14.6 and concluding remarks in Section 14.7.

14.2   ARCH-type models

We will illustrate the use of ARCH-type models in the context of forecasting conditional variances (viewed as a measure of risk) – not conditional returns – which has attracted a lot of interest in the academic literature and among practitioners. We start, however, with the return process. A time series of continuously compounded returns (including dividends) is denoted by $\{r_t\}_{t=1}^T$ and I_{t-1} denotes the information set available at $t-1$. The unobserved variance of returns over some horizon $t-1+h$ conditional on I_{t-1} is $V_{t+h|t-1} = Var(r_{t+h}|I_{t-1})$. Typical applications of ARCH-type models involve daily returns. It will therefore be convenient to think of t as a daily time index. If we focus on one-day horizon for the moment ($h = 1$), and simplify notation to $\sigma_t^2 = Var(r_t|I_{t-1})$, then the class of ARCH-type models can be written as

$$r_t = \sqrt{\sigma_t^2} u_t \qquad (14.2.1)$$

where σ_t^2 is a measurable function of I_{t-1} and u_t is an i.i.d. zero mean/unit variance innovation, denoted by $u_t \sim D(0, 1)$, which is not necessarily Gaussian.[3] This definition basically implies that the conditional distribution of tomorrow's return r_{t+1} has conditional mean zero and conditional variance equal to σ_{t+1}^2. Note that the returns process is uncorrelated. The dependence appears in the conditional variance, not the conditional mean. In the remainder of this section we will review some of the most popular models for the latter.

14.2.1 Model specifications

Engle's original ARCH(q) model assumes that:

$$\sigma_t^2 = \omega + \sum_{i=1}^{q} \alpha_i r_{t-i}^2, \qquad (14.2.2)$$

where $\alpha_i \geq 0$, $\omega > 0$ are imposed to ensure that the conditional variance is strictly positive. The conditional variance can be expressed as

$$\sigma_t^2 = \omega + \alpha(L) r_t^2 \qquad (14.2.3)$$

where $\alpha(L) = \alpha_1 L + \ldots + \alpha_q L^q$. Let us consider conditional variance innovations: $v_t = u_t^2 - \sigma_t^2$, with $E[v_t | I_{t-1}] = 0$. Replacing σ_t^2 by $r_t^2 - v_t$ in the ARCH representation yields

$$r_t^2 = \omega + \sum_{i=1}^{q} \alpha_i r_{t-i}^2 + v_t, \qquad (14.2.4)$$

which corresponds to an AR(q) model for squared returns. The process is covariance stationary if and only if the sum of the positive autoregressive parameters is less than one, in which case the unconditional variance of

---

[3]A conditional mean is sometimes added to equation (14.2.1), such that the equation becomes: $r_t = \mu_t + \sqrt{\sigma_t^2} u_t$. This yields a regression model with ARCH-type errors. To simplify the analysis we do not include conditional means, particularly since we focus on daily financial returns where the conditional mean is typically negligible – especially for daily return series.

returns equals $Var(r_t) = \sigma^2 = \omega/(1 - \alpha_1 - \ldots - \alpha_q L^q)$. Hence, while the returns r_t are serially uncorrelated, they feature serial dependence via the conditional variance dynamics parameterized via the ARCH model. To put it differently, returns are not predictable, but their volatility risk is. Given the autoregressive nature, we capture the phenomenon known as volatility clustering – large (small) asset price changes tend to be followed by large (small) ones. This volatility clustering phenomenon is immediately apparent when asset returns are plotted through time.[4]

The ARCH model also captures the fact that returns tend to have fat-tailed distributions. In order to clarify this, let us assume that u_t defined in equation (14.2.1) is Gaussian. For instance, if $q = 1$, i.e., we have an ARCH(1) then $E[r_t^4]/(E[r_t^2])^2 = 3(1 - \alpha_1^2)/(1 - 3\alpha_1^2)$ is larger than the normal value of three and finite if $3\alpha^2 < 1$ and infinite otherwise: both implying excess kurtosis or fat tails.

We introduced ARMA models in Chapter 5 which had the appealing property to capture temporal dependence via a parsimonious scheme involving a ratio of two finite lag polynomials. The same idea is used for ARCH-type models. In particular, the GARCH(p,q) model, due to Bollerslev (1986) assumes the following form of variance

$$\sigma_t^2 = \omega + \sum_{i=1}^{q} \alpha_i u_{t-i}^2 + \sum_{j=1}^{p} \beta_j \sigma_{t-j}^2, \qquad (14.2.5)$$

where $\alpha_i \geq 0$, $\beta_i \geq 0$, $\omega > 0$ are imposed to ensure that the conditional variance is strictly positive. The conditional variance can be expressed as

$$\sigma_t^2 = \omega + \alpha(L)u_t^2 + \beta(L)\sigma_t^2 \qquad (14.2.6)$$

where $\alpha(L) = \alpha_1 L + \ldots + \alpha_q L^q$ and $\beta(L) = \beta_1 L + \ldots + \beta_p L^p$. If the roots of $1 - \beta(Z)$ lie outside the unit circle, we can rewrite the conditional variance as

$$\sigma_t^2 = \frac{\omega}{1 - \beta(1)} + \frac{\alpha(L)}{1 - \beta(L)}u_t^2.$$

Hence, this expression reveals that a GARCH(p,q) process can be viewed as an ARCH(∞) with a rational lag structure imposed on the coefficients, which may be rewritten in an alternative form, as an ARMA model on squared

---

[4]This is notably displayed in Figure 14.6.1, discussed later, where we plot the time series of daily returns on the S&P 500 index.

perturbations. Indeed, let us consider conditional variance innovations: $v_t = u_t^2 - \sigma_t^2$. Replacing σ_t^2 by $u_t^2 - v_t$ in the GARCH representation yields

$$u_t^2 - v_t = \omega + \sum_{i=1}^{q} \alpha_i u_{t-i}^2 + \sum_{j=1}^{p} \beta_j (u_{t-j}^2 - v_{t-j}) \tag{14.2.7}$$

and therefore

$$u_t^2 = \omega + \sum_{i=1}^{\max(p,q)} (\alpha_i + \beta_i) u_{t-i}^2 + v_t - \sum_{j=1}^{p} \beta_j v_{t-j} \tag{14.2.8}$$

with $\alpha_i = 0$ for $i > q$ and $\beta_i = 0$ for $i > p$. It is therefore an ARMA$(\max(p,q),p)$ representation for the process u_t^2 but with an error term, which is a white noise process that does not necessarily have a constant variance.

The most used heteroscedastic model is the GARCH(1,1):

$$\sigma_t^2 = \omega + \alpha_1 u_{t-1}^2 + \beta_1 \sigma_{t-1}^2 \tag{14.2.9}$$

Using the law of iterated expectations

$$\begin{aligned}
\mathrm{E}(u_t^2) = \mathrm{E}(\mathrm{E}(u_t^2 | I_{t-1})) &= \mathrm{E}(\sigma_t^2) = \omega + \alpha_1 \mathrm{E}(u_{t-1}^2) + \beta_1 \mathrm{E}(\sigma_{t-1}^2) \\
&= \omega + (\alpha_1 + \beta_1)\mathrm{E}(u_{t-1}^2) \tag{14.2.10}
\end{aligned}$$

Assuming the process began infinitely far in the past with a finite initial variance, the sequence of the variances converge to a constant

$$\sigma^2 = \frac{\omega}{1 - \alpha_1 - \beta_1}, \quad \text{if } \alpha_1 + \beta_1 < 1 \tag{14.2.11}$$

therefore, the GARCH process is unconditionally homoscedastic. The α_1 parameter indicates the contributions to conditional variance of the most recent news, and the β_1 parameter corresponds to the moving average part in the conditional variance, that is to say, the recent level of volatility. In this model, it could be convenient to define a measure, in the forecasting context, about the impact of present news on future volatility. To carry out a study of this impact, we calculate the expected volatility k-steps ahead can be characterized recursively as

$$\mathrm{E}(\sigma_{t+k}^2 | \sigma_{t+k-1}^2) = \omega + (\alpha_1 + \beta_1)\sigma_{t+k-1}^2. \tag{14.2.12}$$

Therefore, the persistence depends on the $\alpha_1 + \beta_1$ sum. By implication, if $\alpha_1 + \beta_1 < 1$, the shocks u_t have a decaying impact on future volatility.

The Integrated GARCH, or IGARCH, is a restricted version of the GARCH model, where the persistent parameters sum up to one, or $\sum_{i=1}^{p} \beta_i + \sum_{i=1}^{q} \alpha_i = 1$, which amounts to a unit root in the GARCH process. The presence of unit roots in ARCH-type models is neither as razor edge nor as consequential as in ARIMA models discussed in Section 5.5, including the fact that we can continue to use standard ML estimation and inference methods.[5]

Note that in a GARCH model the impact of "news" u_t is symmetric, positive and negative have the same impact as u_t^2 only matters. Many empirical studies have found evidence that bad news (negative returns) and good news (positive ones) have different impacts on volatility. For this reason Nelson (1991) proposes a new model, called EGARCH as it requires an exponential transformation. For the commonly used EGARCH(1,1) the natural log of the conditional variance is specified as

$$\ln \sigma_t^2 = \omega + \alpha(|u_{t-1}| - E|u_{t-1}|) + \gamma u_{t-1} + \beta \ln \sigma_{t-1}^2$$

where the formulation allows the sign and the magnitude of u_t to have separate effects on the volatility. The expression $\alpha(|u_{t-1}| - E|u_{t-1}|) + \gamma u_{t-1}$ is sometimes called the News Impact Curve (NIC), which relates the impact of innovations u on future volatility. Finally, since $\ln \sigma_t^2$ may be negative there are no positivity restrictions on the parameters. The expected volatility k-steps ahead for the EGARCH(1,1) is:

$$\sigma_{t+k}^2 = \sigma_{t+k-1}^{2\beta} \exp\left[\omega + \sqrt{\frac{2}{\pi}}\right] \times \qquad (14.2.13)$$
$$\left(\exp\left[\frac{(\gamma+\alpha)^2}{2}\right] \Phi(\gamma+\alpha) + \exp\left[\frac{(\gamma-\alpha)^2}{2}\right] \Phi(\gamma-\alpha) \right)$$

where $\Phi(\cdot)$ is the cumulative density of the standard normal. It is important to note, however, that the above formula assumes that u_t is Gaussian (see Tsay (2005, pp. 128–129))

Two other popular models which feature asymmetry are the Quadratic GARCH (QGARCH) model of Sentana (1995) and the so-called GJR-GARCH

---

[5]See Francq and Zakoian (2011) for an excellent textbook treatment of the asymptotic estimation theory of GARCH for further details.

proposed by Glosten, Jagannathan, and Runkle (1993). Regarding the former, a QGARCH(1,1) model is characterized as

$$\sigma_t^2 = \omega + \alpha\ u_{t-1}^2 + \beta\ \sigma_{t-1}^2 + \phi\ u_{t-1}$$

while the GJR-GARCH(1,1) model is written as

$$\sigma_t^2 = \omega + \beta\sigma_{t-1}^2 + \alpha u_{t-1}^2 + \phi u_{t-1}^2 I_{t-1}$$

where $I_{t-1} = 0$ if $u_{t-1} \geq \mu$, and $I_{t-1} = 1$ if $u_{t-1} < \mu$ (with μ often set to zero). The expected volatility k-steps ahead for the GJR-GARCH(1,1) closely resembles that of the GARCH(1,1), although we need to make a specific distributional assumption about u_t to achieve that. When the latter is standard normal, we can characterize recursively the conditional volatility as

$$\mathrm{E}(\sigma_{t+k}^2|\sigma_{t+k-1}^2) = \omega + (\alpha + \beta + \frac{\gamma}{2})\sigma_{t+k-1}^2.$$

where the multiplication of γ by $1/2$ comes from the normality assumption.

There are many other ARCH-type model specifications, capturing various stylized facts of financial return series, such as non-trading day effects, non-synchronous trading, announcement effects, etc. The references mentioned in the introductory section provide further elaborations on the rich class of ARCH-type models with various specifications designed to match empirical stylized facts of asset returns data. Of course, how the various models fair in terms of out-of-sample forecasting is a topic we will discuss later.

14.2.2 Estimation

We cover the ARCH(1) case explicitly, as it is the simplest to discuss and provides the essential insights for all other ARCH-type models that are both computationally and notational more involved. Recall from equation (14.2.1) that

$$r_t = \sqrt{\sigma_t^2} u_t$$

where $u_t \sim N(0, 1)$, i.e., we assume that the innovations are standard normal to proceed with estimation. We use the Gaussian distribution for convenience – other mean zero and unit variance distributions are suitable too, but they complicate the derivation of the likelihood. For that reason, one usually uses the normal density although it may not be the "correct" distribution. In such circumstances, we deal with a Quasi-Maximum Likelihood estimator instead of MLE. Let the process $\{u_t\}_{t=1}^{T}$ be generated by an ARCH(1) process and T is the sample size. Conditioned on an initial observation, the joint density function can be written as

$$f(u) = \prod_{t=1}^{T} f(u_t|I_{t-1}). \tag{14.2.14}$$

Using this result, and ignoring a constant factor, the log-likelihood function $L(\omega, \alpha_1)$ for a sample of size T sample is

$$L(\omega, \alpha_1) = \sum_{t=1}^{T} l_t$$

where the conditional log-likelihood of the tth observation for (ω, α_1) is,

$$l_t = -\frac{1}{2}\log(\sigma_t^2) - \frac{1}{2}\frac{u_t^2}{\sigma_t^2} \tag{14.2.15}$$

$$= -\frac{1}{2}\log(\omega + \alpha_1 u_{t-1}^2) - \frac{1}{2}\frac{u_t^2}{\omega + \alpha_1 u_{t-1}^2} \tag{14.2.16}$$

The first order conditions to obtain the maximum likelihood estimator are:

$$\frac{\partial l_t}{\partial \omega} = \frac{1}{2(\omega + \alpha_1 u_{t-1}^2)}\left(\frac{u_t^2}{\omega + \alpha_1 u_{t-1}^2} - 1\right)$$

$$\frac{\partial l_t}{\partial \alpha_1} = \frac{1}{2(\omega + \alpha_1 u_{t-1}^2)}u_{t-1}^2\left(\frac{u_t^2}{\omega + \alpha_1 u_{t-1}^2} - 1\right) \tag{14.2.17}$$

More generally, the partial derivation of L is:

$$\frac{\partial L}{\partial \alpha} = \sum_t \frac{1}{2\sigma_t^2}\frac{\partial \sigma_t^2}{\partial \alpha}\left(\frac{u_t^2}{\sigma_t^2} - 1\right) = \sum_t \frac{1}{2\sigma_t^2}z_t\left(\frac{u_t^2}{\sigma_t^2} - 1\right) \tag{14.2.18}$$

where $z_t' = (1, u_{t-1}^2)$. Note that the log-likelihood function depends on $\alpha = (\omega, \alpha_1)$. However, we have simplified it by imposing the restriction $\hat{\omega} = \hat{\sigma}^2(1 - \hat{\alpha}_1)$ where $\hat{\sigma}^2$ is an unconditional variance estimate.

The ML estimator, $\hat{\alpha} = (\hat{\omega}, \hat{\alpha}_1)'$, is asymptotically normal under assumptions discussed notably by Francq and Zakoian (2011),

$$\sqrt{T}(\hat{\alpha} - \alpha) \to N(0, I_{\alpha\alpha}^{-1})$$

where

$$I_{\alpha\alpha} = -E\left[\frac{\partial^2 l_t}{\partial\alpha\partial\alpha'}\right] = \begin{pmatrix} I_{\omega\omega} & I_{\omega\alpha_1} \\ I_{\alpha_1\omega} & I_{\alpha_1\alpha_1} \end{pmatrix}$$

where $I_{\alpha\alpha}$ must be approximated. The information matrix is simply the negative expectation of the Hessian averaged across all observations

$$I_{\alpha\alpha} = -\frac{1}{T}\sum_{t=1}^{T}\mathrm{E}\left[\frac{\partial^2 l_t}{\partial\alpha\partial\alpha'}|I_{t-1}\right]. \tag{14.2.19}$$

and $I_{\alpha\alpha}$ is consistently estimated by

$$\hat{I}_{\alpha\alpha} = \frac{1}{2T}\sum_{t=1}^{T}\frac{z_t z_t'}{\hat{\sigma}_t^4}. \tag{14.2.20}$$

In practice, the maximum likelihood estimator is computed via numerical methods, typically iterative in nature, computing the $k+1$ step $\alpha^{(k+1)}$ by

$$\alpha^{(k+1)} = \alpha^{(k)} + \lambda^{(k)}\left(\hat{I}_{\alpha\alpha}^{(k)}\right)^{-1}\left(\frac{\partial L}{\partial\alpha}\right)^{(k)} \tag{14.2.21}$$

where the step length $\lambda^{(k)}$ is usually obtained by a one-dimensional search. For further details, see for instance Berndt, Hall, Hall, and Hausman (1974).

14.3 MIDAS regressions and volatility forecasting

The wide availability of intra-daily – even transaction-based tick-by-tick data – has generated interest in a different class of volatility forecasting models. In this section we discuss the high-frequency data measures emerged from the recent surge in the technology of financial markets data recording. This led to a new class of volatility models. As we typically are interested in forecasting volatility at longer horizons, while maintaining high-frequency data as inputs, we are faced with a mixed-frequency data setting. Not surprisingly we will find that MIDAS regressions are a useful tool for the purpose of volatility forecasting.

In the first subsection we cover the high-frequency data-driven volatility measures, followed by a subsection elaborating on direct versus iterated

volatility forecasting. The next subsection discusses variations on the theme
of MIDAS regressions, and a final subsection deals with microstructure noise
and MIDAS regressions.

14.3.1   Realized volatility

The foundations of the new measures are rooted in continuous time finance
models. For simplicity, assume that the logarithmic price of an asset evolves
according to the continuous time random walk process,

$$d \log P_t = \mu_t dt + \sigma_t dW_t \qquad (14.3.1)$$

where μ_t and σ_t denote respectively the drift and instantaneous volatility
and W_t is a standard Brownian motion.[6]

We are interested in a daily measure of volatility. It follows from standard
arguments (see, e.g., Jacod and Shiryaev (2013)) that conditional on the
sample path realization of the instantaneous volatilities σ_t from time $t-1$ to
t, the variance of $r_t \equiv \log (P_t/P_{t-1})$ equals the so-called Integrated Variation,
which we shall denote by $IV_t \equiv \int_{t-1}^{t} \sigma_s^2 ds$. Unfortunately, neither σ_s^2 nor the
its integral IV_t are observable and have to be "estimated." The estimate
is so-called Realized Variation, or RV, defined by the summation of high-
frequency intraday squared returns,

$$RV_t = \sum_{i=1}^{1/\Delta} \left[\log \left(P_{t-1+i\Delta} \right) - \log \left(P_{t-1+(i-1)\Delta} \right) \right]^2 . \qquad (14.3.2)$$

It can be shown that RV_t consistently estimates IV_t as the number of intra-
daily observations increases, i.e., $\Delta \to 0$ where Δ is the (equal) spacing
between the recorded high-frequency asset prices. It is common in the literature to use two terms for RV_t interchangeably, namely daily realized variation
or daily realized volatility.[7]

Finally, we are often interested in multi-horizon volatility forecasts, i.e.,
$IV_{t+h,t} \equiv \int_{t}^{t+h} \sigma_s^2 ds$, which is measured via the discretely sampled estimate
$RV_{t+h,t}$, defined similarly to the above single-day realized variation. When
a single index is used, we refer to a single-day measure, with the subscript
$(t+h,t)$ we refer to a multi-day horizon measure.

---

[6]Brownian motions are defined in footnote 3 in Chapter 5 – although with a slightly
different notation, $W(\tau)$ instead of W_t used here for convenience.

[7]Sometimes realized volatility refers to $\sqrt{RV_t}$. It will be straightforward from the context, which one is used.

14.3.2   Realized volatility and MIDAS regressions

Ghysels, Santa-Clara, and Valkanov (2006) consider MIDAS type regressions to predict realized volatility over some future horizon h. In particular, considering the DL-MIDAS specification (recall Section 12.3.1) we have

$$RV_{t+h,t} = a_h + b_h C(L^{1/m}; \theta_h) x_t^H + \varepsilon_{t+h}^L \qquad (14.3.3)$$

where the polynomial choices are those discussed in Chapter 12. While the object of interest is $RV_{t+h,t}$, we can think of many possible high-frequency predictors x^H. For example, we could think of functions of intra-daily high-frequency returns $(\log(P_{t-1+i\Delta}) - \log(P_{t-1+(i-1)\Delta}))$, such as squared or absolute returns (see in particular Forsberg and Ghysels (2006) for the latter). In this case $m = 78$ (typical 5-min equity market trading) or $m = 288$ in a 24-hour trading setting. Alternatively, we could formulate the prediction model in terms of daily realized measures, such as daily RV, i.e.,

$$RV_{t+h,t} = a_h + b_h C(L^{1/m}; \theta_h) RV_t + \varepsilon_{t+h}^L \qquad (14.3.4)$$

and set $m = 1$ to obtain daily lags of past realized volatilities. Using S&P 500 data, Ghysels, Santa-Clara, and Valkanov (2006) find that models involving daily measures, as in equation (14.3.4), appear to be as successful if not better at prediction as models involving directly intra-daily returns, as in equation (14.3.3). This is convenient, as we are not required to handle the intra-daily high-frequency data directly, but rather compute daily summary statistics, i.e., RV_t. For future reference, we will refer to equations of the type appearing in (14.3.4) as MIDAS-RV regressions.

14.3.3   HAR models

The discussion at the end of the previous subsection highlights an interesting feature about MIDAS regressions alluded to before, namely that the sampling frequency of the regressors is part of the model specification. Choosing between using directly intra-daily high-frequency returns is at one end of the spectrum of possible choices. Picking daily RV's is one of many other possible aggregation schemes. This brings us to the Heterogeneous Autoregressive Realized Volatility (HAR-RV) regressions proposed by Corsi (2009) that are specified as

$$RV_{t+1,t} = \mu + \beta^D RV_t^D + \beta^W RV_t^W + \beta^M RV_t^M + \varepsilon_{t+1}, \qquad (14.3.5)$$

which has a simple linear prediction regression using RV over heterogeneous interval sizes, daily (D), weekly (W) and monthly (M). In other words, RV_t^D = $RV_{t,t-1}$, $RV_t^W = RV_{t,t-5}$ and $RV_t^M = RV_{t,t-22}$, assuming t is a daily timer and there are 22 trading days in a month. The above equation is a MIDAS regression with step functions (see Section 12.3.4) of Ghysels, Sinko, and Valkanov (2006) and Forsberg and Ghysels (2006). Indeed, the weight for $RV_{t,t-1}$ equals $\beta^D + \beta^W + \beta^M$, that of $RV_{t-1,t-2}$ equals $\beta^W + \beta^M$, etc. In this regard the HAR-RV can be related to the MIDAS-RV in (14.3.4), using different weight functions, namely step functions versus beta, exponential Almon, etc. The HAR models have been proven useful in forecasting future volatility, see for instance Andersen, Bollerslev, and Diebold (2007).

14.3.4   Direct versus iterated volatility forecasting

For ARCH-type models we typically think of daily data, so that σ_{t+1}^2 amounts to predicting tomorrow's volatility with daily information available on day t. The equivalent with the regression models, is running regressions with $RV_{t+1,t}$ like in the HAR model. The existent literature, particularly of ARCH-type models, has placed most of the emphasis on the accuracy of one-period-ahead forecasts (see Engle (1982), Bollerslev (1986), Hansen and Lunde (2005), among many others). Long-horizon volatility forecasts have received significantly less attention. Yet, financial decisions related to risk management, portfolio choice, and regulatory supervision, are often based on multi-period-ahead volatility forecasts.

The preeminent long-horizon volatility forecasting approach is to scale the one-period-ahead forecasts by $\sqrt{h}$ so that the h-period conditional standard deviation equals $\sqrt{h}\sigma_{t+1}$. Christoffersen and Diebold (2000), and others have shown that this "scaling" approach leads to poor volatility forecasts at horizons as short as ten days.

The volatility measure appearing on the left-hand side of equation (14.3.3) and the predictors on the right-hand side are sampled at different frequencies. As a result MIDAS-type volatility predictions can be formulated at different horizons (e.g., daily, weekly, and monthly frequencies), whereas the forecasting variables x_t^H are available at daily or higher frequencies. Therefore, the specification allows us not only to forecast volatility with data sampled at different frequencies, but also forecast at various horizons h.

In Section 5.9 we discussed the topic of direct versus iterated forecasting. This issue is obviously also relevant for volatility forecasting. When considering ARCH-type models, then formulas (14.2.12) and (14.2.13) are examples of iterated forecasts commonly used in the literature. What about direct forecasting? The regression-based volatility models discussed in this section are better suited to address the differences between direct, iterated, and mixed-frequency settings.

Ghysels, Rubia, and Valkanov (2009) undertake a comprehensive empirical examination of multi-period volatility forecasting approaches, beyond the simple $\sqrt{h}$-scaling rule. They consider three alternative approaches – direct and iterative – of forming long-horizon forecasts and a MIDAS regression approach. The direct forecasting method consists of estimating a horizon-specific model of the volatility at, say, monthly or quarterly frequency, which can then be used to form direct predictions of volatility over the next month or quarter. Note that this is a same-frequency model specification. Hence, say monthly horizon forecasts involve past monthly data. An iterative forecast obtains by estimating a daily autoregressive volatility forecasting model and then iterate over the daily forecasts for the necessary number of periods to obtain monthly, or quarterly predictions of the volatility. A MIDAS method uses daily data to produce directly multi-period volatility forecasts and can thus be viewed as a middle ground between the direct and the iterated approaches. The results of their study suggest that long-horizon volatility is much more predictable than previously suggested at horizons as long as 60 trading days (about three months). The direct and iterated methods Ghysels, Rubia, and Valkanov (2009) use are based on two volatility models: GARCH and autoregressive models of realized volatility, see, e.g., Andersen, Bollerslev, Diebold, and Labys (2003).

To establish the accuracy of the long-term forecasts, Ghysels, Rubia, and Valkanov (2009) use a loss function that penalizes deviations of predictions from the ex-post realizations of the volatility and a test for predictive accuracy that allows them to compare the statistical significance of competing forecasts. They use (1) the mean square forecasting error (MSFE) as one loss function, because of its consistency property, i.e., it delivers the same forecast ranking with the proxy as it would with the true volatility (see subsection 14.5 and Hansen and Lunde (2006) and Patton and Timmermann (2007)) and (2) a Value-at-Risk as an alternative metric of forecast accuracy.

Ghysels, Rubia, and Valkanov (2009) find that for the volatility of the market portfolio, iterated and MIDAS forecasts perform significantly better than the scaling and the direct approaches. At relatively short horizons of 5- to 10-days ahead, the iterated forecasts are quite accurate. However, at horizons of 10-days ahead and higher, MIDAS forecasts have a significantly lower MSFE relative to the other forecasts. At horizons of 30- and 60-days ahead, the MSFE of MIDAS is more than 20% lower than that of the next best forecast. These differences are statistically significant at the 1% level according to the West (1996) and Giacomini and White (2006) tests. Hence, they find that suitable MIDAS models produce multi-period volatility forecasts that are significantly better than other widely used methods.

14.3.5   Variations on the theme of MIDAS regressions

The MIDAS approach can also be used to study various other interesting aspects of forecasting volatility. In Chapter 12 we noted that semi-parametric MIDAS regression models were introduced by Chen and Ghysels (2011) in the context of volatility models. In particular, they provide a novel method to analyze the impact of news on forecasting volatility. The following semi-parametric regression model is proposed to predict future realized volatility (RV) with past high-frequency returns

$$RV_{t+h,t} = a_h + b_h C(L^{1/m}; \theta_h) NIC(r_t) + \varepsilon_{t+1}, \qquad (14.3.6)$$

where $NIC(.)$ is the news impact curve and r_t is the intra-daily log asset price difference (return) series. Hence, the regression model in (14.3.6) shows that each intra-daily return has an impact on future volatility measured by NIC and fading away through time with weights characterized by $C(L^{1/m}; \theta_h)$. One can consider (14.3.6) as the semi-parametric (SP) model that nests a number of volatility forecasting models with $NIC(r) \equiv r^2$ and the polynomial weights are such that equal weights apply intra-daily (this is achieved via a product polynomial specification – sometimes called a multiplicative MIDAS – see Chen and Ghysels (2011) and Bai, Ghysels, and Wright (2013)). This nesting emphasizes the role played by both the news impact curve NIC and the lag polynomial structure. Finally, the MIDAS-NIC model can also nest existing parametric specifications of news impact curves adopted in the ARCH literature, namely, the daily symmetric one when $NIC(r) = br^2$, the asymmetric GJR model when $NIC(r) = br^2 + (cr^2)\mathbf{1}_{r<0}$ (see Glosten, Jagannathan, and Runkle (1993)) and the asymmetric GARCH model when $NIC(r) = (b(r - c)^2)$ (see Engle and Ng (1993)).

14.4 GARCH models again

The approach in the previous is regression-based, whereas ARCH-type models appearing in Section 14.2 were likelihood-based. Is there a way to combine the insights from both approaches?

We start with a version of the Realized GARCH model proposed by Hansen, Huang, and Shek (2012), namely in the GARCH(1,1) we have:

$$\sigma_t^2 = \omega + \alpha_1 RV_{t-1} + \beta_1 \sigma_{t-1}^2 \qquad (14.4.1)$$

so that daily squared returns are replaced by realized volatilities. If volatility is a persistent process, it would be natural to weight intra-daily data differently, as pointed out recently by Malliavin and Mancino (2005). This is one example of the class of models Chen, Ghysels, and Wang (2011) and Chen, Ghysels, and Wang (2015) called HYBRID GARCH models. They are a unifying framework, based on a generic GARCH-type model, that addresses the issue of volatility forecasting involving forecast horizons of a different frequency than the information set. Hence, Chen, Ghysels, and Wang (2015) propose a class of GARCH models that can handle volatility forecasts over the next five business days and use past daily data, or tomorrow's expected volatility while using intra-daily returns.[8]

A generic HYBRID GARCH model has the following dynamics for volatility:

$$\sigma_t^2 = \omega + \alpha_1 H_{t-1} + \beta_1 \sigma_{t-1}^2 \qquad (14.4.2)$$

where $H_t \equiv C(L^{1/m}; \theta) r_t^2 = \sum_{j=0}^{m-1} c(j; \theta) L^{j/m} r_t^2$, is called a HYBRID process, wit $C(1; \theta) = 1$. When H_t is simply a daily squared return we have the volatility dynamics of a standard daily GARCH(1,1). However, what would happen if we want to attribute an individual weight to each of the intra-period returns? This is an example of a parameter-driven HYBRID process where we estimate an additional MIDAS-type weighting scheme. Is it worth estimating these extra parameters θ, compared to the Realized GARCH for example? Chen, Ghysels, and Wang (2011) show that is indeed the case, when judged in terms of out-of-sample forecast performance.

So far we did not cover component models of volatility. Empirical evidence suggests that volatility dynamics is better described by component

---

[8]The models are called HYBRID GARCH, which stands for **H**igh Frequenc**Y** Data-**B**ased P**R**oject**I**on-**D**riven GARCH models as the GARCH dynamics are driven by what Chen, Ghysels, and Wang (2015) call HYBRID processes.

models. Engle and Lee (1999) introduced a GARCH model with a long- and short-run component. The volatility component model of Engle and Lee decomposes the equity conditional variance as the sum of the short-run (transitory) and long-run (trend) components. So far we considered MIDAS filters that applied to high-frequency data. Here we use the same type of filters to extract low-frequency components. Hence, it is again a MIDAS setting, using different frequencies, but this time we use the polynomial specifications to extract low-frequency movements in volatility.

Engle, Ghysels, and Sohn (2013) propose a class of models called GARCH-MIDAS, since it uses a mean reverting unit *daily* GARCH process, similar to Engle and Rangel (2008), and a MIDAS polynomial that applies to monthly, quarterly, or bi-annual macroeconomic or financial variables. They study long historical data series of aggregate stock market volatility, starting in the 19th century, as in Schwert (1989). Their empirical findings show that for the full sample the long-run component accounts for roughly 50% of predicted volatility. During the Great Depression era even 60% of expected volatility is due to the long-run component. For the most recent period the results show roughly a 40% contribution. Finally, they also introduce refinements of the GARCH-MIDAS model where the long-run component is driven by macroeconomic series.

14.5   Volatility forecasting evaluation

Suppose we want to appraise forecasts for the HAR model of Corsi (2009). Having a sample of size T, which yields parameter estimates $\hat{\mu}_T$, $\hat{\beta}_T^D$, $\hat{\beta}_T^W$ and $\hat{\beta}_T^M$ and forecast:

$$\widehat{RV}_{T+1,T} = \hat{\mu}_T + \hat{\beta}_T^D RV_T^D + \hat{\beta}_T^W RV_T^W + \beta^M RV_T^M \qquad (14.5.1)$$

How good is this forecast? It would be natural to measure the performance by comparing $\widehat{RV}_{T+1,T}$ with $\int_T^{T+1} \sigma_s^2 ds$. Unfortunately, we only have $RV_{T+1,T}$, which is a noisy proxy for integrated volatility, i.e., the integral IV is approximated by a discrete sum which is RV.

How do we evaluate volatility forecasts when we recognize the fact that the "true" volatility process is never observed and only proxies are available? Hansen and Lunde (2006) studied the problems introduced by the presence of noise in the volatility proxy. They provide a sufficient condition on the loss function to ensure that the ranking of various forecasts is preserved when a noisy but conditionally unbiased proxy for the conditional variance is employed rather than the conditional variance itself. Patton (2011) builds further on the original work of Hansen and Lunde and derive explicitly the undesirable outcomes that may arise when some common loss functions are employed, considering the most commonly used volatility proxies, such as the daily squared return (in the case of ARCH-type models) and realized variance estimator. Moreover, he provides necessary and sufficient conditions on the loss function to ensure that the ranking of various forecasts is preserved when using a noisy volatility proxy. These conditions are related to those of Gouriéroux, Monfort, and Trognon (1984) for quasi-maximum likelihood estimation.

Patton (2011) considers the following loss functions $L(\widehat{RV}_{T+1,T}, RV_{T+1,T})$:

$$
\begin{aligned}
MSE: \quad & (\widehat{RV}_{T+1,T} - RV_{T+1,T})^2 \\
QLIKE: \quad & \log \widehat{RV}_{T+1,T} + RV_{T+1,T}/\widehat{RV}_{T+1,T} \\
MSE-LOG: \quad & (\log \widehat{RV}_{T+1,T} - \log RV_{T+1,T})^2 \\
MSE-SD: \quad & ((\widehat{RV}_{T+1,T})^{1/2} - (RV_{T+1,T})^{1/2})^2 \\
MSE-prop: \quad & (RV_{T+1,T}/\widehat{RV}_{T+1,T} - 1)^2 \\
MAE: \quad & |RV_{T+1,T} - \widehat{RV}_{T+1,T}| \\
MAE-SD: \quad & |(\widehat{RV}_{T+1,T})^{1/2} - (RV_{T+1,T})^{1/2}| \\
MAE-prop: \quad & |RV_{T+1,T}/\widehat{RV}_{T+1,T} - 1|
\end{aligned}
\tag{14.5.2}
$$

and provides both sufficient and necessary conditions on loss functions for the consistent ranking of volatility forecasts. It turns out that the loss functions MSE and QLIKE are shown to be appropriate loss functions when using a conditionally unbiased volatility proxy.

Note that the same analysis applies to ARCH-type model predictions. Take a GARCH(1,1) as example. With a sample of size T returns and parameter estimates $\hat{\omega}_T$, $\hat{\alpha}_T$ and $\hat{\beta}_T$, we can produce the forecast:

$$
\hat{\sigma}_{T+1}^2 = \hat{\omega}_T + \hat{\alpha}_T u_T^2 + \hat{\beta}_T \sigma_T^2
\tag{14.5.3}
$$

where, by analogy, we can for example consider the loss functions $L(\hat{\sigma}_{T+1}^2, r_{T+1}^2)$: $MSE : (\hat{\sigma}_{T+1}^2 - r_{T+1}^2)^2$, and $QLIKE : \log \hat{\sigma}_{T+1}^2 + r_{T+1}^2/\hat{\sigma}_{T+1}^2$.

14.6   Forecasting S&P 500 index volatility

In this example we apply the volatility forecasting techniques we saw in the theoretical sections of the chapter to study the time-variation in the conditional variance of a financial time series, namely, the S&P 500 index. We have a daily dataset spanning from January 2000 until the end of August 2016. The data have been imported from the website Oxford-Man Institute's realized library.[9] We will first analyze the time frame going from 2000 to 2006, using the period from 2006 to 2016 for an out-of-sample forecasting exercise. Then, we will enlarge the estimation sample until the onset of the financial crisis, i.e., in August 2008, and we will see whether our model is able to forecast the steep peak that the S&P 500 volatility displayed in late 2008, see Figures 14.6.1 and 14.6.2.

For this exercise the rolling estimation windows approach, which is more robust than recursive estimation in the presence of breaks, is utilized by rolling each estimation window by one-week and re-estimating each model and in turn producing h-steps ahead forecasts. The procedure is repeated until the end of the forecast sample 2006-2016.

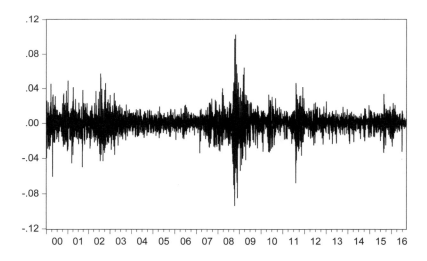

Figure 14.6.1: *Time series of daily returns on the S&P 500 index*

---

[9]See http://realized.oxford-man.ox.ac.uk/.

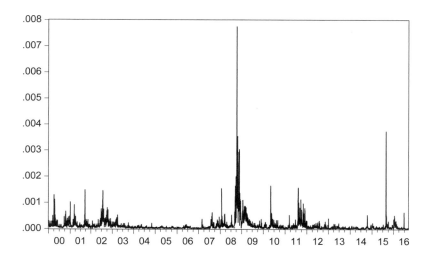

Figure 14.6.2: *S&P 500 Index 5-minute realized volatility*

14.6.1 ARCH-type models

Table 14.6.1 reports the estimation output of the most used heteroscedastic model in financial time series, GARCH(1,1), model 14.2.9 for the S&P 500 index. As the persistence depends on the condition that $\alpha_1 + \beta_1 = 0.955 < 1$, the shocks u_t have a decaying impact on future volatility of S&P 500.

To account for the evidence that negative returns and positive ones have different impacts on volatility, the commonly used EGARCH(1,1) the natural log of the conditional variance is estimated. The estimation results for the pre-crisis period are presented in Table 14.6.2.

Another popular model featuring asymmetry, GJR-GARCH(1,1), is also estimated and the results for the pre-crisis period are presented in Table 14.6.3.

To compare forecast performance of GARCH, EGARCH, and GJR-GARCH models, Diebold-Mariano test statistics are calculated with the loss functions MSE and QLIKE. Tables 14.6.4, 14.6.5, and 14.6.6 present DM test statistics and corresponding p-values for the pre-crisis, crisis and, post-crisis samples, respectively.

For the pre-crisis models, looking at the DM test statistics with MSE, the null hypothesis of same forecasting performance at different horizons for

Variable	Coefficient	Std.Error	z-Statistic	Prob.
Variance Equation				
C	0.000	0.000	2.491	0.013
RESID(-1)^2	0.063	0.009	7.368	0.000
GARCH(-1)	0.932	0.008	110.352	0.000
R-squared	-0.000	Mean dep var		-0.000
Adjusted R-squared	0.001	S.D. dep var		0.011
S.E. of regression	0.011	Akaike IC		-6.454
Sum squared resid	0.217	Schwarz IC		-6.445
Log likelihood	5608.576	Hannan-Quinn		-6.451
DW stat	2.065			

Table 14.6.1: *GARCH(1,1) estimation output, Jan. 2000 - Dec. 2006*

Variable	Coefficient	Std.Error	z-Statistic	Prob.
Variance Equation				
C(1)(ω)	-0.128	0.019	-6.800	0.000
C(2)(α)	0.044	0.012	3.599	0.000
C(3)(γ)	-0.100	0.009	-11.115	0.000
C(4)(β)	0.990	0.001	693.075	0.000
R-squared	-0.000	Mean dep var		-0.000
Adjusted R-squared	0.001	S.D. dep var		0.011
S.E. of regression	0.011	Akaike IC		-6.508
Sum squared resid	0.217	Schwarz IC		-6.495
Log likelihood	5656.202	Hannan-Quinn		-6.503
DW stat	2.065			

Table 14.6.2: *EGARCH(1,1) estimation output, Jan. 2000 - Dec. 2006*

GARCH and EGARCH cannot be rejected at 5% significance level. Whereas with QLIKE, they are rejected in favor of the GARCH model. Except six-month forecasts, GJR-GARCH performs as good as GARCH for both MLE

Variable	Coefficient	Std.Error	z-Statistic	Prob.
Variance Equation				
C(ω)	0.000	0.000	5.186	0.000
RESID(-1)^2(α)	-0.022	0.008	-2.972	0.003
RESID(-1)^2*(RESID(-1)¡0)(ϕ)	0.134	0.015	8.867	0.000
GARCH(-1)(β)	0.946	0.009	106.776	0.000
R-squared	0.001	Mean dep var		-0.000
Adjusted R-squared	0.001	S.D. dep var		0.011
S.E. of regression	0.011	Akaike IC		-6.500
Sum squared resid	0.217	Schwarz IC		-6.488
Log likelihood	5649.427	Hannan-Quinn		-6.496
DW stat	2.065			

Table 14.6.3: *GJR-GARCH(1,1) estimation output, Jan. 2000 - Dec. 2006*

and QLIKE loss functions, while it performs better than the EGARCH model at all horizons. DM tests with QLIKE tend to be rejected at lower significance levels. On the other hand, during crisis, almost all DM tests are strongly rejected favoring GARCH over both EGARCH and GJR-GARCH, while DM tests with QLIKE favors EGARCH over GARCH and GJR-GARCH at all horizons. For the post-crisis forecast performance comparison, DM tests with MSE indicate that GARCH outperforms both EGARCH and GJR-GARCH, whereas QLIKE version chooses EGARCH over GJR-GARCH, and GJR-GARCH over GARCH, and these results are more significant at longer horizons.

14.6.2 Realized volatility

Compared to the models in the previous subsection, there are two main differences with what we are about to discuss next. First, we formulate the prediction models in terms of daily realized measures, daily RV of S&P 500, not daily squared returns as was the case with ARCH-type models. Second, we consider direct forecasting as opposed to the iterated forecasting used in ARCH-type models. We consider again one-day, one-week, one-month and

	GARCH vs EGARCH	GARCH vs GJR-GARCH	EGARCH vs GJR-GARCH
One-day ahead			
MSE			
DM test stat	-1.097	-0.718	1.304
p-value	0.136	0.236	0.096
QLIKE			
DM test stat	-1.624	-1.322	1.666
p-value	0.052	0.093	0.048
One-week ahead			
MSE			
DM test stat	-1.658	-0.717	1.506
p-value	0.049	0.237	0.066
QLIKE			
DM test stat	-1.918	-0.582	2.081
p-value	0.028	0.280	0.019
One-month ahead			
MSE			
DM test stat	-1.172	-0.541	1.109
p-value	0.121	0.294	0.134
QLIKE			
DM test stat	-2.197	1.454	2.286
p-value	0.014	0.073	0.011
Six-months ahead			
MSE			
DM test stat	0.527	1.267	0.914
p-value	0.299	0.103	0.180
QLIKE			
DM test stat	-1.537	1.828	1.582
p-value	0.062	0.034	0.057

Table 14.6.4: *Pre-crisis, forecast comparison, forecast sample Jan. 2007 - Aug. 2016*

six-months forecast horizons, which means that for each horizon we formulate a different regression prediction model.

Two types of regression models are considered: (1) MIDAS-RV as in equation 14.3.4, setting $m = 1$ to obtain daily lags of past realized volatilities and (2) HAR models as in equation (14.3.5). We estimate the MIDAS-RV regression with a quadratic Almon polynomial and do not separately identify a slope parameter. As a consequence, both HAR and MIDAS-RV have three parameters and are therefore at par in terms of the dimension

	GARCH vs EGARCH	GARCH vs GJR-GARCH	EGARCH vs GJR-GARCH
One-day ahead			
MSE			
DM test stat	-2.081	-1.535	1.797
p-value	0.019	0.062	0.036
QLIKE			
DM test stat	2.357	2.000	-2.080
p-value	0.009	0.023	0.019
One-week ahead			
MSE			
DM test stat	-2.522	-1.761	2.643
p-value	0.006	0.039	0.004
QLIKE			
DM test stat	2.389	2.241	-1.775
p-value	0.008	0.013	0.038
One-month ahead			
MSE			
DM test stat	-2.804	-1.294	3.240
p-value	0.003	0.098	0.001
QLIKE			
DM test stat	3.701	3.385	-2.683
p-value	0.000	0.000	0.004
Six-months ahead			
MSE			
DM test stat	-1.674	-1.852	-0.927
p-value	0.047	0.032	0.177
QLIKE			
DM test stat	2.074	0.987	-2.315
p-value	0.019	0.162	0.010

Table 14.6.5: *During crisis, forecast comparison, forecast sampleNov. 2008 - Aug. 2016*

of the parameter space. For the pre-crisis sample, the estimation output for the HAR in Table 14.6.7 and for the MIDAS-RV model in Table 14.6.8. It is useful perhaps to compute the implied lags of the MIDAS-RV and compare them to the HAR model estimates. Namely the MIDAS-RV implies a lag one RV parameter equal to 0.466314, whereas for the HAR model we have an estimate of 0.525832. for the next lag in the MIDAS-RV we have an estimate of 0.157171, and the next one equal to 0.161642, whereas both have weight equal to 0.204848 in the HAR model. Hence, the weighting schemes

	GARCH vs EGARCH	GARCH vs GJR-GARCH	EGARCH vs GJR-GARCH
One-day ahead			
MSE			
DM test stat	-1.689	-2.158	-1.884
p-value	0.046	0.015	0.030
QLIKE			
DM test stat	1.782	0.218	-3.062
p-value	0.037	0.414	0.001
One-week ahead			
MSE			
DM test stat	-0.231	-1.544	-1.677
p-value	0.409	0.061	0.047
QLIKE			
DM test stat	2.473	0.949	-2.740
p-value	0.007	0.171	0.003
One-month ahead			
MSE			
DM test stat	-2.646	-1.367	2.324
p-value	0.004	0.086	0.010
QLIKE			
DM test stat	1.768	0.665	-2.113
p-value	0.039	0.253	0.017
Six-months ahead			
MSE			
DM test stat	-0.810	-1.084	-0.937
p-value	0.209	0.139	0.174
QLIKE			
DM test stat	3.467	3.179	-2.725
p-value	0.000	0.001	0.003

Table 14.6.6: *Post-crisis, forecast comparison, forecast sample Jan. 2010 - Aug. 2016*

differ quite a bit. Does it matter in terms of forecast performance?

Table 14.6.9 compares forecasts performances of the RV-MIDAS model versus the HAR model, presenting DM test statistics and corresponding p-values for the pre-crisis, crisis and, post-crisis samples. It contains not only the one-day ahead forecast, but also the other horizons. We do not report all the HAR and MIDAS-RV regression output for the sake of brevity. That also applies to the estimates during and post-crisis. Some interesting conclusions emerge from Table 14.6.9. During the crisis we see that the MIDAS-RV

Variable	Coefficient	Std.Error	t-Statistic	Prob.
C	0.000	0.000	4.961	0.000
$REVOL^D$	0.526	0.045	11.743	0.000
$REVOL^W$	0.205	0.041	4.962	0.000
$REVOL^M$	0.089	0.031	2.882	0.004
R-squared	0.486	Mean dep var		0.000
Adjusted R-squared	0.485	S.D. dep var		0.000
S.E. of regression	0.000	Akaike IC		-15.671
Sum squared resid	0.000	Schwarz IC		-15.658
Log likelihood	13441.680	Hannan-Quinn		-15.666
F-statistic	539.272	DW		2.209
Prob(F-statistic)	0.000	Wald F-stat		118.543
Prob(Wald F-statistic)	0.000			

Table 14.6.7: *HAR one-day ahead estimation results for the pre-crisis estimation period*

is superior at all horizons, both in terms of MSE and QLIKE (only one insignificant – the one-week MSE case). The pre-crisis results are not so clear cut at least at the 5% level. For the one-day horizon we see that MIDAS-RV is better, but not so at the one-week horizon. At longer horizons, MIDAS-RV does again better, in terms of both forecast evaluation criteria. Finally, post-crisis the results are similar to those during the crisis, although without the same overwhelming statistical significance.

14.7 Concluding remarks

We did not cover multivariate models of volatility and therefore refer to Bauwens, Laurent, and Rombouts (2006) for an excellent survey. It is worth noting that the estimation of multivariate volatility models with mixed sampling frequencies is a relatively unexplored area. One approach that appears promising was proposed by Colacito, Engle, and Ghysels (2011) and also applied by Baele, Bekaert, and Inghelbrecht (2010) to the determinants of stock and bond return co-movements. In particular, Colacito, Engle, and Ghysels (2011) address the specification, estimation, and interpretation of correlation models that distinguish short and long-run components driven

	Coefficient	Std.Error	t-Statistic	Prob.
C	0.000	0.000	7.143	0.000
Almon polynomial				
PDL01	1.089	0.133	8.184	0.000
PDL02	-0.780	0.154	-5.069	0.000
PDL03	0.157	0.038	4.109	0.000
R-squared	0.488	Mean dep var		0.000
Adjusted R-squared	0.487	S.D. dep var		0.000
S.E. of regression	0.000	Akaike IC		-15.681
Sum squared resid	0.000	Schwarz IC		-15.668
Log likelihood	13599.330	Hannan-Quinn		-15.676

Table 14.6.8: *RV-MIDAS one-day ahead estimation results for the pre-crisis estimation period*

by mixed-frequency data. They show that the changes in correlations are indeed very different. The model is called DCC-MIDAS, where DCC stands for dynamic conditional correlation following Engle (2002) and MIDAS refers to the mixed-frequency specification for the long-run component. In terms of empirical implementation, Colacito, Engle, and Ghysels (2011) and Baele, Bekaert, and Inghelbrecht (2010) consider examples involving stocks and bonds. Both papers show the usefulness of the component specification in correlations and in particular the appeal of using MIDAS filters to specify long-run component of correlations. Formal testing reported in both papers show that the DCC-MIDAS models outperform standard DCC models. Colacito, Engle, and Ghysels (2011) also study asset allocation with multiple international equities (five international stock markets) and a single MIDAS filter. Using the methodology proposed by Engle and Colacito (2012) pertaining to minimum variance portfolio management, they document the economic significance of using the DCC-MIDAS specification as well. Other applications include Asgharian, Christiansen, and Hou (2016), Baele and Londono (2013), Boffelli, Skintzi, and Urga (2015), Conrad, Loch, and Rittler (2014), Perego and Vermeulen (2016), among others.

	RV-MIDAS vs HAR Pre-crisis	RV-MIDAS vs HAR During crisis	RV-MIDAS vs HAR Post-crisis
One-day ahead			
MSE			
DM test stat	-1.351	-2.175	-2.416
p-value	0.088	0.015	0.008
QLIKE			
DM test stat	-2.103	-1.738	-1.818
p-value	0.018	0.041	0.035
One-week ahead			
MSE			
DM test stat	-0.216	-0.903	-1.409
p-value	0.414	0.183	0.079
QLIKE			
DM test stat	5.833	-1.881	-1.263
p-value	0.000	0.030	0.103
One-month ahead			
MSE			
DM test stat	-1.715	-3.661	-1.507
p-value	0.043	0.000	0.066
QLIKE			
DM test stat	-2.320	-2.093	-1.700
p-value	0.010	0.018	0.045
Six-months ahead			
MSE			
DM test stat	-1.651	-2.419	-2.001
p-value	0.049	0.008	0.023
QLIKE			
DM test stat	-2.467	-2.029	-1.609
p-value	0.007	0.021	0.054

Table 14.6.9: *Forecast comparison; RV-MIDAS vs. HAR models*

Bibliography

Alessi, Lucia, Eric Ghysels, Luca Onorante, Richard Peach, and Simon Potter, 2014, Central bank macroeconomic forecasting during the global financial crisis: The European Central Bank and Federal Reserve Bank of New York experiences, *Journal of Business and Economic Statistics* 32, 483–500.

Altissimo, Filippo, Riccardo Cristadoro, Mario Forni, Marco Lippi, and Giovanni Veronese, 2010, New eurocoin: Tracking economic growth in real time, *Review of Economics and Statistics* 92, 1024–1034.

Amisano, Gianni, and Raffaella Giacomini, 2007, Comparing density forecasts via weighted likelihood ratio tests, *Journal of Business and Economic Statistics* 25, 177–190.

Amisano, Gianni, and Carlo Giannini, 2012, *Topics in Structural VAR Econometrics* (Springer, Berlin).

Andersen, Torben G., Tim Bollerslev, Peter F. Christoffersen, and Francis X. Diebold, 2006, Volatility and correlation forecasting, in G. Elliott, C. Granger, and A. Timmermann, ed.: *Handbook of Economic Forecasting, Volume 1* . pp. 777–878 (Elsevier).

Andersen, Torben G., Tim Bollerslev, and Francis X. Diebold, 2007, Roughing it up: Including jump components in the measurement, modeling, and forecasting of return volatility, *Review of Economics and Statistics* 89, 701–720.

——— , and Paul Labys, 2003, Modeling and forecasting realized volatility, *Econometrica* 71, 579–625.

Anderson, Brian D.O., Manfred Deistler, Elisabeth Felsenstein, Bernd Funovits, Lukas Koelbl, and Mohsen Zamani, 2015, Multivariate AR systems and mixed frequency data: G-identifiability and estimation, *Econometric Theory* 31, 1–34.

Andreou, Elena, Patrick Gagliardini, Eric Ghysels, and Mirco Rubin, 2016, Is industrial production still the dominant factor for the US Economy?, Swiss Finance Institute Research Paper.

Andreou, Elena, Eric Ghysels, and Andros Kourtellos, 2010, Regression models with mixed sampling frequencies, *Journal of Econometrics* 158, 246–261.

———— , 2011, Forecasting with mixed-frequency data, in Clements. Michael P., and David F. Hendry, ed.: *Oxford Handbook of Economic Forecasting* pp. 225–245. Oxford University Press.

———— , 2013, Should macroeconomic forecasters use daily financial data and how?, *Journal of Business and Economic Statistics* 31, 240–251.

Andrews, Donald W.K., 1991, Heteroskedasticity and autocorrelation consistent covariance matrix estimation, *Econometrica* 59, 817–858.

———— , 1993, Tests for parameter instability and structural change with unknown change point, *Econometrica* 61, 821–856.

———— , and J. Christopher Monahan, 1992, An improved heteroskedasticity and autocorrelation consistent covariance matrix estimator, *Econometrica* 60, 953–966.

Andrews, Donald W.K., and Werner Ploberger, 1994, Optimal tests when a nuisance parameter is present only under the alternative, *Econometrica* 62, 1383–1414.

Artis, Michael, Ana B. Galvão, and Massimiliano G. Marcellino, 2007, The transmission mechanism in a changing world, *Journal of Applied Econometrics* 22, 39–61.

Artis, Michael, and Massimiliano G. Marcellino, 2001, Fiscal forecasting: The track record of the IMF, OECD and EC, *The Econometrics Journal* 4, 20–36.

Aruoba, S. Boragan, Frank X. Diebold, and Chiara Scotti, 2009, Real-time measurement of business conditions, *Journal of Business and Economic Statistics* 27, 417–427.

Asgharian, Hossein, Charlotte Christiansen, and Ai Jun Hou, 2016, Macro-finance determinants of the long-run stock–bond correlation: The dcc-midas specification, *Journal of Financial Econometrics* 14, 617–642.

Aznar, Antonio, and Manuel Salvador, 2002, Selecting the rank of the cointegration space and the form of the intercept using an information criterion, *Econometric Theory* 18, 926–947.

Bacchiocchi, E., A. Bastianin, A. Missale, and E. Rossi, 2016, Monetary policy, uncertainty and gross capital flows: A mixed frequency approach, Discussion Paper University of Milan and University of Pavia.

Baele, Lieven, Geert Bekaert, and Koen Inghelbrecht, 2010, The determinants of stock and bond return comovements, *Review of Financial Studies* 23, 2374–2428.

Baele, Lieven, and Juan M. Londono, 2013, Understanding industry betas, *Journal of Empirical Finance* 22, 30–51.

Baffigi, Alberto, Roberto Golinelli, and Giuseppe Parigi, 2004, Bridge models to forecast the Euro area GDP, *International Journal of Forecasting* 20, 447–460.

Bai, Jushan, 2004, Estimating cross-section common stochastic trends in nonstationary panel data, *Journal of Econometrics* 122, 137–183.

Bai, Jennie, Eric Ghysels, and Jonathan H. Wright, 2013, State space models and MIDAS regressions, *Econometric Reviews* 32, 779–813.

Bai, Jushan, and Serena Ng, 2002, Determining the number of factors in approximate factor models, *Econometrica* 70, 191–221.

———, 2004, A PANIC attack on unit roots and cointegration, *Econometrica* 72, 1127–1177.

———, 2006, Confidence intervals for diffusion index forecasts and inference for factor-augmented regressions, *Econometrica* 74, 1133–1150.

———— , 2008, Forecasting economic time series using targeted predictors, *Journal of Econometrics* 146, 304–317.

Bai, Jushan, and Pierre Perron, 1998, Estimating and testing linear models with multiple structural changes, *Econometrica* 66, 47–78.

———— , 2003a, Computation and analysis of multiple structural change models, *Journal of Applied Econometrics* 18, 1–22.

———— , 2003b, Critical values for multiple structural change tests, *The Econometrics Journal* 6, 72–78.

Bańbura, Marta, Domenico Giannone, Michele Modugno, and Lucrezia Reichlin, 2013, Now-casting and the real-time data flow, in Graham Elliott, and Allan Timmermann, ed.: *Handbook of Economic Forecasting, Volume 2 Part A* pp. 195–233. Elsevier.

Bańbura, Marta, Domenico Giannone, and Lucrezia Reichlin, 2010, Large Bayesian vector auto regressions, *Journal of Applied Econometrics* 25, 71–92.

———— , 2011, Nowcasting, in Michael P. Clements, and David F. Hendry, ed.: *Oxford Handbook of Economic Forecasting* pp. 193–224. Oxford University Press.

Bańbura, Marta, and Michele Modugno, 2014, Maximum likelihood estimation of factor models on datasets with arbitrary pattern of missing data, *Journal of Applied Econometrics* 29, 133–160.

Bańbura, Marta, and Gerhard Rünstler, 2011, A look into the factor model black box: Publication lags and the role of hard and soft data in forecasting GDP, *International Journal of Forecasting* 27, 333–346.

Banerjee, Anindya, Juan J. Dolado, John W. Galbraith, and David F. Hendry, 1993, *Co-integration, Error Correction, and the Econometric Analysis of Non-stationary Data* (Oxford University Press).

Banerjee, Anindya, and Massimiliano G. Marcellino, 2009, Forecasting with factor-augmented error correction models, in Jennifer Castle, and Neil Shephard, ed.: *The Methodology and Practice of Econometrics: A Festschrift in Honour of David F. Hendry* pp. 227–254. Oxford University Press.

———— , and Igor Masten, 2014, Forecasting with factor-augmented error correction models, *International Journal of Forecasting* 30, 589–612.

———— , 2017, Structural FECM: Cointegration in large-scale structural FAVAR models, *Journal of Applied Econometrics* (forthcoming).

Barhoumi, Karim, Olivier Darné, Laurent Ferrara, and Bertrand Pluyaud, 2012, Monthly gdp forecasting using bridge models: Application for the french economy, *Bulletin of Economic Research* 64, s53–s70.

Bartlett, Maurice Stevenson, 1955, *An Introduction to Stochastic Processes* (Cambridge University Press).

Bauwens, Luc, Sébastien Laurent, and Jeroen V.K. Rombouts, 2006, Multivariate garch models: A survey, *Journal of Applied Econometrics* 21, 79–109.

Bernanke, Ben, Jean Boivin, and Piotr Eliasz, 2005, Factor augmented vector autoregressions (FVARs) and the analysis of monetary policy, *Quarterly Journal of Economics* 120, 387–422.

Bernanke, Ben, Mark Gertler, and Mark Watson, 1997, Systematic monetary policy and the effects of oil price shocks, *Brookings Papers on Economic Activity* 1, 91–157.

Berndt, Ernst R., Bronwyn H. Hall, Robert E. Hall, and Jerry A. Hausman, 1974, Estimation and inference in nonlinear structural models, *Annals of Economic and Social Measurement* 3, 653–665.

Beveridge, Stephen, and Charles R. Nelson, 1981, A new approach to decomposition of economic time series into permanent and transitory components with particular attention to measurement of the business cycle, *Journal of Monetary Economics* 7, 151–174.

Bhansali, Rajendra J., 1999, Parameter estimation and model selection for multistep prediction of a time series: A review, in S. Ghosh, ed.: *Asymptotics, Nonparametrics and Time Series* pp. 201–225. Marcel Dekker.

Black, Fischer, and Myron Scholes, 1973, The pricing of options and corporate liabilities, *Journal of Political Economy* 81, 637–654.

Blanchard, Olivier Jean, and Danny Quah, 1989, The dynamic effects of aggregate demand and supply disturbances, *American Economic Review* 79, 655–673.

Boffelli, Simona, Vasiliki D Skintzi, and Giovanni Urga, 2015, High-and low-frequency correlations in european government bond spreads and their macroeconomic drivers, *Journal of Financial Econometrics* 15, 62–105.

Boivin, Jean, and Serena Ng, 2005, Understanding and comparing factor-based forecasts, *International Journal of Central Banking* 1, 117–151.

——— , 2006, Are more data always better for factor analysis?, *Journal of Econometrics* 132, 169–194.

Bollerslev, Tim, 1986, Generalized autoregressive conditional heteroskedasticity, *Journal of Econometrics* 31, 307–327.

——— , Robert F. Engle, and Daniel B. Nelson, 1994, Arch models, in Daniel McFadden, and Robert F. Engle, ed.: *Handbook of Econometrics, Volume 4* pp. 2959–3038. Elsevier.

Box, George E.P., and Gwilym M. Jenkins, 1976, *Time Series Analysis: Forecasting and Control, Revised edition* (Holden-Day).

Box, George E. P., and David A. Pierce, 1970, Distribution of residual autocorrelations in autoregressive-integrated moving average time series models, *Journal of the American Statistical Association* 65, 1509–1526.

Breitung, Jörg, and Christoph Roling, 2015, Forecasting inflation rates using daily data: A nonparametric MIDAS approach, *Journal of Forecasting* 34, 588–603.

Brooks, Chris, 2014, *Introductory Econometrics for Finance* (Cambridge University Press).

Brown, Robert L., James Durbin, and John M. Evans, 1975, Techniques for testing the constancy of regression relationships over time, *Journal of the Royal Statistical Society. Series B (Methodological)* 37, 149–192.

Bulligan, Guido, Massimiliano Marcellino, and Fabrizio Venditti, 2015, Forecasting economic activity with targeted predictors, *International Journal of Forecasting* 31, 188–206.

Campbell, John Y., and Pierre Perron, 1991, Pitfalls and opportunities: What macroeconomists should know about unit roots, in *NBER Macroeconomics Annual, Volume 6* . pp. 141–220 (MIT Press).

Campbell, John Y, and Robert J Shiller, 1987, Cointegration and tests of present value models, *Journal of Political Economy* 95, 1062–1088.

Canova, Fabio, 2007, *Methods for Applied Macroeconomic Research* (Princeton University Press).

——— , and Eric Ghysels, 1994, Changes in seasonal patterns: Are they cyclical?, *Journal of Economic Dynamics and Control* 18, 1143–1171.

Carriero, Andrea, Todd E. Clark, and Massimiliano G. Marcellino, 2015, Bayesian vars: Specification choices and forecast accuracy, *Journal of Applied Econometrics* 30, 46–73.

——— , 2016, Large vector autoregressions with stochastic volatility and flexible priors, Working Paper 1617, Federal Reserve Bank of Cleveland.

——— , 2017, Measuring uncertainty and its impact on the economy, *Review of Economics and Statistics* (forthcoming).

Carriero, Andrea, George Kapetanios, and Massimiliano Marcellino, 2009, Forecasting exchange rates with a large Bayesian VAR, *International Journal of Forecasting* 25, 400–417.

——— , 2011, Forecasting large datasets with Bayesian reduced rank multivariate models, *Journal of Applied Econometrics* 26, 735–761.

——— , 2012, Forecasting government bond yields with large Bayesian vector autoregressions, *Journal of Banking and Finance* 36, 2026–2047.

Castle, Jennifer L., Jurgen A. Doornik, and David F. Hendry, 2011, Evaluating automatic model selection, *Journal of Time Series Econometrics* 3.

Chen, Xilong, and Eric Ghysels, 2011, News – good or bad – and its impact on volatility predictions over multiple horizons, *Review of Financial Studies* 24–81, 46.

————, and Fangfang Wang, 2011, On the role of Intra-Daily seasonality in HYBRID GARCH Models, *Journal of Time Series Econometrics* 3.

————, 2015, The HYBRID GARCH class of models, *Statistica Sinica* 25, 759–786.

Chevillon, Guillaume, and David F. Hendry, 2005, Non-parametric direct multi-step estimation for forecasting economic processes, *International Journal of Forecasting* 21, 201–218.

Chong, Yock Y., and David F. Hendry, 1986, Econometric evaluation of linear macro-economic models, *Review of Economic Studies* 53, 671–690.

Christoffersen, Peter F., and Francis X. Diebold, 1998, Cointegration and long-horizon forecasting, *Journal of Business and Economic Statistics* 16, 450–456.

————, 2000, How relevant is volatility forecasting for financial risk management?, *Review of Economics and Statistics* 82, 12–22.

Clark, Todd E., and Michael W. McCracken, 2013, Advances in forecast evaluation, in Graham Elliott, and Allan Timmermann, ed.: *Handbook of Economic Forecasting, Volume 2 part B* pp. 1107–1197. Elsevier.

Clements, Michael P., 1997, Evaluating the rationality of fixed-event forecasts, *Journal of Forecasting* 16, 225–239.

————, and Ana B. Galvão, 2008, Macroeconomic forecasting with mixed frequency data: Forecasting US output growth, *Journal of Business and Economic Statistics* 26, 546–554.

————, 2009, Forecasting US output growth using leading indicators: An appraisal using MIDAS models, *Journal of Applied Econometrics* 24, 1187–1206.

Clements, Michael P, and David F Hendry, 1996, Multi-step estimation for forecasting, *Oxford Bulletin of Economics and Statistics* 58, 657–684.

Clements, Michael P., and David F. Hendry, 1998, *Forecasting Economic Time Series* (Cambridge University Press).

Cochrane, Donald, and Guy H. Orcutt, 1949, Application of least squares regression to relationships containing auto-correlated error terms, *Journal of the American Statistical Association* 44, 32–61.

Colacito, Riccardo, Robert F. Engle, and Eric Ghysels, 2011, A component model for dynamic correlations, *Journal of Econometrics* 164, 45–59.

Conrad, Christian, Karin Loch, and Daniel Rittler, 2014, On the macroeconomic determinants of long-term volatilities and correlations in US stock and crude oil markets, *Journal of Empirical Finance* 29, 26–40.

Corsi, F., 2009, A simple approximate long-memory model of realized volatility, *Journal of Financial Econometrics* 7, 174–196.

Cox, D.R., 1981, Statistical analysis of time series: Some recent developments [with discussion and reply], *Scandinavian Journal of Statistics* 8, 93–115.

Davidson, James, 2000, *Econometric Theory* (Basil Blackwell, Oxford).

Davidson, James E.H., David F. Hendry, Frank Srba, and Stephen Yeo, 1978, Econometric modelling of the aggregate time-series relationship between consumers' expenditure and income in the united kingdom, *Economic Journal* 88, 661–692.

Davies, Robert B., 1987, Hypothesis testing when a nuisance parameter is present only under the alternative, *Biometrika* 74, 33–43.

De Mol, Christine, Domenico Giannone, and Lucrezia Reichlin, 2008, Forecasting using a large number of predictors: Is Bayesian shrinkage a valid alternative to principal components?, *Journal of Econometrics* 146, 318–328.

Del Negro, Marco, and Frank Schorfheide, 2013, DSGE model-based forecasting, in Graham Elliott, and Allan Timmermann, ed.: *Handbook of Economic Forecasting, Volume 2 Part A* pp. 57–140. Elsevier.

Dempster, Arthur P., Nan M. Laird, and Donald B. Rubin, 1977, Maximum likelihood from incomplete data via the EM algorithm, *Journal of the Royal Statistical Society. Series B* 39, 1–38.

Den Haan, Wouter J., and Andrew T. Levin, 2000, Robust covariance matrix estimation with data-dependent var prewhitening order, NBER Working Paper, T0255.

Dickey, David A., and Wayne A. Fuller, 1979, Distribution of the estimators for autoregressive time series with a unit root, *Journal of the American Statistical Association* 74, 427–431.

Diebold, Francis X., 1989, Forecast combination and encompassing: Reconciling two divergent literatures, *International Journal of Forecasting* 5, 589–592.

——— , 2008, *Elements of Forecasting, Fourth Edition* (South-Western).

——— , 2015, Comparing predictive accuracy, twenty years later: A personal perspective on the use and abuse of diebold–mariano tests, *Journal of Business and Economic Statistics* 33, 1–24.

——— , Todd A. Gunther, and Anthony S. Tay, 1998, Evaluating density forecasts with applications to financial risk management, *International Economic Review* 39, 863–83.

Diebold, Francis X., and Robert S. Mariano, 1995, Comparing predictive accuracy, *Journal of Business and Economic Statistics* 13, 253–263.

Diron, Marie, 2008, Short-term forecasts of euro area real GDP growth: An assessment of real-time performance based on vintage data, *Journal of Forecasting* 27, 371–390.

Doan, Thomas, Robert Litterman, and Christopher Sims, 1984, Forecasting and conditional projection using realistic prior distributions, *Econometric Reviews* 3, 1–100.

Doornik, Jurgen A., 2009, *An Object-Oriented Matrix Programming Language Ox 6* (Timberlake Consultants).

Doz, Catherine, Domenico Giannone, and Lucrezia Reichlin, 2011, A two-step estimator for large approximate dynamic factor models based on Kalman filtering, *Journal of Econometrics* 164, 188–205.

Efron, Bradley, Trevor Hastie, Iain Johnstone, and Robert Tibshirani, 2004, Least angle regression, *Annals of Statistics* 32, 407–499.

Eickmeier, Sandra, Wolfgang Lemke, and Massimiliano Marcellino, 2015, Classical time varying factor-augmented vector autoregressive models - estimation, forecasting and structural analysis, *Journal of the Royal Statistical Society: Series A (Statistics in Society)* 178, 493–533.

Eickmeier, Sandra, and Christina Ziegler, 2008, How successful are dynamic factor models at forecasting output and inflation? A meta-analytic approach, *Journal of Forecasting* 27, 237–265.

Eitrheim, Øyvind, and Timo Teräsvirta, 1996, Testing the adequacy of smooth transition autoregressive models, *Journal of Econometrics* 74, 59–75.

Elliott, Graham, Ivana Komunjer, and Allan Timmermann, 2008, Biases in macroeconomic forecasts: Irrationality or asymmetric loss?, *Journal of the European Economic Association* 6, 122–157.

Elliott, Graham, Thomas J Rothenberg, and James H. Stock, 1996, Efficient tests for an autoregressive unit root, *Econometrica* 64, 813–836.

Elliott, Graham, and Allan Timmermann, 2016, *Economic Forecasting* (Princeton University Press).

Engle, Robert F, 1982, Autoregressive conditional heteroscedasticity with estimates of the variance of united kingdom inflation, *Econometrica* 50, 987–1007.

Engle, Robert F., 2002, Dynamic conditional correlation: A simple class of multivariate generalized autoregressive conditional heteroskedasticity models, *Journal of Business and Economic Statistics* 20, 339–350.

———, and Riccardo Colacito, 2012, Testing and valuing dynamic correlations for asset allocation, *Journal of Business and Economic Statistics* 24, 238–253.

Engle, Robert F., Eric Ghysels, and Bumjean Sohn, 2013, Stock market volatility and macroeconomic fundamentals, *Review of Economics and Statistics* 95, 776–797.

Engle, Robert F., and Clive W. J. Granger, 1987, Co-integration and error correction: Representation, estimation, and testing, *Econometrica* 55, 251–276.

Engle, Robert F., and Gary Lee, 1999, A long-run and short-run component model of stock return volatility, in Robert F. Engle, and Halbert White, ed.: *Cointegration, Causality, and Forecasting: A Festschrift in Honour of Clive W.J. Granger* pp. 475–497. Oxford University Press.

Engle, Robert F., and Simone Manganelli, 2004, Caviar: Conditional autoregressive value at risk by regression quantiles, *Journal of Business and Economic Statistics* 22, 367–381.

Engle, Robert F., and Victor K. Ng, 1993, Measuring and testing the impact of news on volatility, *Journal of Finance* 48, 1749–1778.

Engle, Robert F., and J. Gonzalo Rangel, 2008, The Spline-GARCH model for low-frequency volatility and its global macroeconomic causes, *Review of Financial Studies* 21, 1187–1222.

Engle, Robert F., and B.S. Yoo, 1991, Cointegrating times series: A survey with new results, in Robert F. Engle, and Clive W.J. Granger, ed.: *Long-Run Economic Relationships: Readings in Cointegration*. Oxford University Press.

Epanechnikov, Vassiliy A., 1969, Non-parametric estimation of a multivariate probability density, *SIAM - Theory of Probability and Its Applications* 14, 153–158.

Eraker, Bjørn, Ching Wai Jeremy Chiu, Andrew T. Foerster, Tae Bong Kim, and Hernán D. Seoane, 2015, Bayesian mixed frequency VARs, *Journal of Financial Econometrics* 13, 698–721.

Ericsson, N. R., 1993, Comment on – On the limitations of comparing mean squared forecast errors by M.P. Clements and D.F. Hendry, *Journal of Forecasting* 12, 644–651.

Findley, David F., 1983, On the use of multiple models for multi-period forecasting, in *Proceedings of Business and Economic Statistics, American Statistical Association* pp. 528–531.

———— , 1985, Model selection for multi-step-ahead forecasting, in H. A. (Baker, and P. C. Young, ed.: *Proceedings of the 7th Symposium on Identification and System Parameter* pp. 1039–1044.

Forni, Mario, Marc Hallin, Marco Lippi, and Lucrezia Reichlin, 2000, The generalized dynamic-factor model: Identification and estimation, *Review of Economics and Statistics* 82, 540–554.

———— , 2005, The generalized dynamic factor model, *Journal of the American Statistical Association* 100, 830–840.

Foroni, Claudia, Eric Ghysels, and Massimiliano Marcellino, 2013, Mixed-frequency vector autoregressive models, in Thomas B. Fomby, Lutz Kilian, and Anthony Murphy, ed.: *VAR Models in Macroeconomics–New Developments and Applications: Essays in Honor of Christopher A. Sims* . pp. 247–272 (Emerald Group Publishing).

Foroni, Claudia, and Massimiliano G. Marcellino, 2012, A comparison of mixed frequency approaches for modelling euro area macroeconomic variables, EUI ECO Working Papers, 2012/07.

———— , 2013, A survey of econometric methods for mixed-frequency data, Available at SSRN 2268912.

———— , 2014, Mixed-frequency structural models: Identification, estimation, and policy analysis, *Journal of Applied Econometrics* 29, 1118–1144.

———— , and Christian Schumacher, 2015, Unrestricted mixed data sampling (MIDAS): MIDAS regressions with unrestricted lag polynomials, *Journal of the Royal Statistical Society: Series A* 178, 57–82.

Forsberg, Lars, and Eric Ghysels, 2006, Why do absolute returns predict volatility so well?, *Journal of Financial Econometrics* 6, 31–67.

Francq, Christian, and Jean-Michel Zakoian, 2011, *GARCH models: Structure, Statistical Inference and Financial Applications* (Wiley).

Franses, Philip Hans, and Dick Van Dijk, 2000, *Non-linear Time Series Models in Empirical Finance* (Cambridge University Press).

Gagliardini, Patrick, Eric Ghysels, and Mirco Rubin, 2016, Indirect inference estimation of mixed frequency stochastic volatility state space models using MIDAS regressions and ARCH models, Swiss Finance Institute Research Paper.

Gallant, A. Ronald, and Halbert White, 1988, *A Unified Theory of Estimation and Inference for Nonlinear Dynamic Models* (Blackwell).

Galvão, Ana B., 2013, Changes in predictive ability with mixed frequency data, *International Journal of Forecasting* 29, 395–410.

Garcia, René, Eric Ghysels, and Eric Renault, 2010, The econometrics of option pricing, in Yacine Aït-Sahalia, and Lars Peter Hansen, ed.: *Handbook of Financial Econometrics: Volume 1 - Tools and Techniques* . pp. 479–552 (Elsevier).

Geweke, John, and Gianni Amisano, 2010, Comparing and evaluating bayesian predictive distributions of asset returns, *International Journal of Forecasting* 26, 216–230.

———, 2011, Optimal prediction pools, *Journal of Econometrics* 164, 130–141.

Ghysels, Eric, 2013, Matlab Toolbox for mixed sampling frequency data analysis using MIDAS regression models, Available http://www.mathworks.com/matlabcentral/fileexchange/45150-midas-matlab-toolbox.

———, 2016, Macroeconomics and the reality of mixed frequency data, *Journal of Econometrics* 193, 294–314.

———, Clive W.J. Granger, and Pierre L. Siklos, 1996, Is seasonal adjustment a linear or nonlinear data-filtering process?, *Journal of Business and Economic Statistics* 14, 374–386.

Ghysels, Eric, Andrew C. Harvey, and Eric Renault, 1996, Stochastic volatility, in G. S. Maddala, and C. R. Rao, ed.: *Handbook of Statistics - Statistical Methods in Finance, Volume 14* pp. 119–191. Elsevier.

Ghysels, Eric, Jonathan B. Hill, and Kaiji Motegi, 2015, Simple Granger Causality Tests for Mixed Frequency Data, Available at SSRN 2616736.

———, 2016, Testing for Granger causality with mixed frequency data, *Journal of Econometrics* 192, 207–230.

Ghysels, Eric, Casidhe Horan, and Emanuel Moench, 2017, Forecasting through the rear-view mirror: Data revisions and bond return predictability, *Review of Financial Studies* (forthcoming).

Ghysels, Eric, Lynda Khalaf, and Cosmé Vodounou, 2003, Simulation based inference in moving average models, *Annales d'économie et de statistique* 69, 85–99.

Ghysels, Eric, Virmantas Kvedaras, and Vaidotas Zemlys, 2016, Mixed frequency data sampling regression models: The R package midasr, *Journal of Statistical Software* 72, 1–35.

Ghysels, Eric, and Denise Osborn, 2001, *The Econometric Analysis of Seasonal Time Series* (Cambridge University Press).

Ghysels, Eric, Alberto Plazzi, and Rossen Valkanov, 2016, Why invest in emerging markets? the role of conditional return asymmetry, *Journal of Finance* 71, 2145–2194.

Ghysels, Eric, Antonio Rubia, and Rossen Valkanov, 2009, Multi-period forecasts of volatility: Direct, iterated, and mixed-data approaches, Discussion Paper UNC/UCSD.

Ghysels, Eric, Pedro Santa-Clara, and Rossen Valkanov, 2004, The MIDAS touch: Mixed Data Sampling Regressions, Discussion paper UNC and UCLA.

———— , 2006, Predicting volatility: Getting the most out of return data sampled at different frequencies, *Journal of Econometrics* 131, 59–95.

Ghysels, Eric, Arthur Sinko, and Rossen Valkanov, 2006, MIDAS regressions: Further results and new directions, *Econometric Reviews* 26, 53–90.

Ghysels, Eric, and Jonathan Wright, 2009, Forecasting professional forecasters, *Journal of Business and Economic Statistics* 27, 504–516.

Giacomini, Raffaella, and Halbert White, 2006, Tests of conditional predictive ability, *Econometrica* 74, 1545–1578.

Giannone, Domenico, Lucrezia Reichlin, and David Small, 2008, Nowcasting: The real-time informational content of macroeconomic data, *Journal of Monetary Economics* 55, 665–676.

Giesecke, Kay, Justin Sirignano, and Apaar Sadhwani, 2016, Deep learning for mortgage risk, Working paper, Stanford University.

Gladyshev, E. G., 1961, Periodically correlated random sequences, *Soviet Mathematics* 2, 385–388.

Glosten, Lawrence R., Ravi Jagannathan, and David E. Runkle, 1993, On the relation between the expected value and the volatility of the nominal excess return on stocks, *Journal of Finance* 48, 1779–1801.

Gonzalo, Jesus, and Clive W. J. Granger, 1995, Estimation of common long-memory components in cointegrated systems, *Journal of Business and Economic Statistics* 13, 27–35.

Gouriéroux, Christian, and Joann Jasiak, 2001, *Financial Econometrics: Problems, Models, and methods* (Princeton University Press).

Gouriéroux, Christian, Alain Monfort, and Eric Renault, 1993, Indirect inference, *Journal of applied econometrics* 8, S85–S118.

Gouriéroux, Christian, Alain Monfort, and Alain Trognon, 1984, Pseudo maximum likelihood methods: Theory, *Econometrica* 52, 681–700.

Granger, Clive W.J., 1980, Testing for causality: A personal viewpoint, *Journal of Economic Dynamics and control* pp. 329–352.

———— , 1993, Strategies for modelling nonlinear time-series relationships, *Economic Record* 69, 233–238.

———— , and Paul Newbold, 1974, Spurious regressions in econometrics, *Journal of Econometrics* 2, 111–120.

Granger, Clive W. J., 1983, Co-Integrated variables and Error-Correcting Models, UCSD Discussion Paper 93-13.

———— , 1999, Outline of forecast theory using generalized cost functions, *Spanish Economic Review* 1, 161–173.

———— , and Paul Newbold, 1986, *Forecasting Economic Time Series, Second Edition* (Academic Press).

Granger, Clive W. J., and Timo Teräsvirta, 1993, *Modelling Non-linear Economic Relationships* (Oxford University Press).

Granger, Clive W. J., and Andrew A. Weiss, 1983, Time series analysis of error-correction models, in *Studies in Econometrics, Time Series, and Multivariate Statistics* pp. 255–278. Academic Press.

Guérin, Pierre, and Massimiliano G. Marcellino, 2013, Markov-switching midas models, *Journal of Business and Economic Statistics* 31, 45–56.

Hall, Alastair R., 2005, *Generalized Method of Moments* (Oxford University Press).

Hall, Stephen G, and James Mitchell, 2007, Combining density forecasts, *International Journal of Forecasting* 23, 1–13.

Hamilton, James D., 1994, *Time Series Analysis* (Princeton University Press).

Hannan, Edward J., 1970, *Multiple Time Series* (Wiley).

Hansen, Bruce E., 1996, Inference when a nuisance parameter is not identified under the null hypothesis, *Econometrica* 64, 413–430.

———, 1997, Inference in TAR models, *Studies in Nonlinear Dynamics and Econometrics* 2, 1–14.

———, 2000, Sample splitting and threshold estimation, *Econometrica* 68, 575–603.

Hansen, Lars Peter, 1982, Large sample properties of generalized method of moments estimators, *Econometrica* 50, 1029–1054.

———, John C. Heaton, and Masao Ogaki, 1988, Efficiency bounds implied by multiperiod conditional moment restrictions, *Journal of the American Statistical Association* 83, 863–871.

Hansen, Peter R., Zhuo Huang, and Howard H. Shek, 2012, Realized garch: a joint model for returns and realized measures of volatility, *Journal of Applied Econometrics* 27, 877–906.

Hansen, Peter R., and Asger Lunde, 2005, A forecast comparison of volatility models: Does anything beat a GARCH (1,1)?, *Journal of Applied Econometrics* 20, 873–889.

———— , 2006, Consistent ranking of volatility models, *Journal of Econometrics* 131, 97–121.

Harvey, Andrew C., 1993, *Time Series Models* (Harvester).

———— , and Richard G. Pierse, 1984, Estimating missing observations in economic time series, *Journal of the American Statistical Association* 79, 125–131.

Harvey, David S., Stephen J. Leybourne, and Paul Newbold, 1998, Tests for forecast encompassing, *Journal of Business and Economic Statistics* 16, 254–259.

Hastie, T., R. Tibshirani, and J. H. Friedman, 2008, *The Elements of Statistical Learning: Data Mining, Inference, and Prediction* (Springer Series in Statistics).

Hausman, Jerry A., 1978, Specification tests in econometrics, *Econometrica* 46, 1251–1271.

Heaton, Jeff B., Nicholas G. Polson, and Jan Hendrik Witte, 2016, Deep learning in finance, arXiv preprint arXiv:1602.06561.

———— , 2017, Deep learning for finance: Deep portfolios, *Applied Stochastic Models in Business and Industry* 33, 3–12.

Helland, Inge S., 1990, Partial least squares regression and statistical models, *Scandinavian Journal of Statistics* 17, 97–114.

Hendry, David F., 1995, *Dynamic Econometrics* (Oxford University Press).

———— , and Hans-Martin Krolzig, 2005, The properties of automatic GETS modelling, *The Economic Journal* 115, C32–C61.

Hepenstrick, Christian, and Massimiliano G. Marcellino, 2016, Forecasting with large unbalanced datasets: The mixed frequency three-pass regression filter, Discussion Paper, Bocconi University.

Herbst, Edward P., and Frank Schorfheide, 2015, *Bayesian Estimation of DSGE Models* (Princeton University Press).

Hinkley, David V, 1975, On power transformations to symmetry, *Biometrika* 62, 101–111.

Hinton, Geoffrey E., and Ruslan R. Salakhutdinov, 2006, Reducing the dimensionality of data with neural networks, *Science* 313, 504–507.

Hodrick, Robert J., and Edward C. Prescott, 1997, Postwar US business cycles: An empirical investigation, *Journal of Money, Credit, and Banking* 29, 1–16.

Hoover, Kevin D., and Stephen J. Perez, 1999, Data mining reconsidered: Encompassing and the general-to-specific approach to specification search, *The Econometrics Journal* 2, 167–191.

Hornik, Kurt, Maxwell Stinchcombe, and Halbert White, 1989, Multilayer feedforward networks are universal approximators, *Neural Networks* 2, 359–366.

Ingenito, Robert, and Bharat Trehan, 1996, Using monthly data to predict quarterly output, *Economic Review - Federal Reserve Bank of San Francisco* pp. 3–11.

Jacod, Jean, and Albert Shiryaev, 2013, *Limit Theorems for Stochastic Processes* (Springer).

Jacquier, Eric, Nicholas G. Polson, and Peter E. Rossi, 1994, Bayesian analysis of stochastic volatility models, *Journal of Business and Economic Statistics* 12, 371–389.

Johansen, Soren, 1995, *Likelihood-based Inference in Cointegrated Vector Autoregressive Models* (Oxford University Press).

Judge, George G., R. Carter Hill, William Griffiths, Helmut Lütkepohl, and Tsoung-Chao Lee, 1988, *Introduction to the Theory and Practice of Econometrics* (Wiley).

Jungbacker, Borus, Siem J. Koopman, and Michel Van der Wel, 2011, Maximum likelihood estimation for dynamic factor models with missing data, *Journal of Economic Dynamics and Control* 35, 1358–1368.

Kadiyala, Krao, and Sune Karlsson, 1997, Numerical methods for estimation and inference in Bayesian VAR models, *Journal of Applied Econometrics* 12, 99–132.

Kalman, Rudolph Emil, 1960, A new approach to linear filtering and prediction problems, *Journal of Basic Engineering* 82, 35–45.

Kapetanios, George, Massimiliano G. Marcellino, and Fotis Papailias, 2014, Variable selection for large unbalanced datasets using non-standard optimisation of information criteria and variable reduction methods, Available at SSRN: http://ssrn.com/abstract=2444421.

——— , 2016, Forecasting inflation and GDP growth using heuristic optimisation of information criteria and variable reduction methods, *Computational Statistics and Data Analysis* 100, 369–382.

Karlsson, Sune, 2012, Forecasting with Bayesian VAR models, in Graham Elliott, and Allan Timmermann, ed.: *Handbook of Economic Forecasting, Volume 2 Part B* . pp. 791–897 (Elsevier).

Kelly, Bryan, and Seth Pruitt, 2013, Market expectations in the cross-section of present values, *Journal of Finance* 68, 1721–1756.

——— , 2015, The three-pass regression filter: A new approach to forecasting using many predictors, *Journal of Econometrics* 186, 294–316.

Koenig, Evan F, Sheila Dolmas, and Jeremy Piger, 2003, The use and abuse of real-time data in economic forecasting, *Review of Economics and Statistics* 85, 618–628.

Koenker, Roger, and Gilbert Bassett, 1978, Regression quantiles, *Econometrica* 46, 33–50.

Koop, Gary, M. Hashem Pesaran, and Simon M. Potter, 1996, Impulse response analysis in nonlinear multivariate models, *Journal of Econometrics* 74, 119–147.

Koop, Gary M., 2003, *Bayesian Econometrics* (Wiley).

——— , 2013, Forecasting with medium and large Bayesian VARs, *Journal of Applied Econometrics* 28, 177–203.

Kuzin, Vladimir, Massimiliano G. Marcellino, and Christian Schumacher, 2011, MIDAS versus mixed-frequency VAR: Nowcasting GDP in the Euro Area, *International Journal of Forecasting* 27, 529–542.

———, 2013, Pooling versus model selection for nowcasting GDP with many predictors: Empirical evidence for six industrialized countries, *Journal of Applied Econometrics* 28, 392–411.

Kvedaras, Virmantas, and Vaidotas Zemlys, 2012, Testing the functional constraints on parameters in regressions with variables of different frequency, *Economics Letters* 116, 250–254.

Kwiatkowski, Denis, Peter C.B. Phillips, Peter Schmidt, and Yongcheol Shin, 1992, Testing the null hypothesis of stationarity against the alternative of a unit root: How sure are we that economic time series have a unit root?, *Journal of Econometrics* 54, 159–178.

Leeper, Eric M., Christopher A. Sims, and Tao Zha, 1996, What does monetary policy do?, *Brookings Papers on Economic Activity* 1996, 1–78.

Lin, Jin-Lung, and Clive W.J. Granger, 1994, Forecasting from non-linear models in practice, *Journal of Forecasting* 13, 1–9.

Linton, Oliver, and Enno Mammen, 2005, Estimating semiparametric arch () models by kernel smoothing methods1, *Econometrica* 73, 771–836.

Litterman, Robert B, 1986, Forecasting with Bayesian vector autoregressions - five years of experience, *Journal of Business and Economic Statistics* 4, 25–38.

Ljung, Greta M., and George E. P. Box, 1978, On a measure of lack of fit in time series models, *Biometrika* 65, 297–303.

Lütkepohl, Helmut, 2007, *New Introduction to Multiple Time Series Analysis* (Springer).

———, 2012, *Forecasting Aggregated Vector ARMA Processes* (Springer).

Luukkonen, Ritva, Pentti Saikkonen, and Timo Teräsvirta, 1988, Testing linearity against smooth transition autoregressive models, *Biometrika* 75, 491–499.

MacKinnon, James G., 1996, Numerical distribution functions for unit root and cointegration tests, *Journal of Applied econometrics* 11, 601–618.

———— , Alfred A. Haug, and Leo Michelis, 1999, Numerical distribution functions of likelihood ratio tests for cointegration, *Journal ofAapplied Econometrics* 14, 563–577.

MacKinnon, James G., and Halbert White, 1985, Some heteroskedasticity-consistent covariance matrix estimators with improved finite sample properties, *Journal of Econometrics* 29, 305–325.

Malliavin, P., and M. Mancino, 2005, Fourier method for the estimation of volatilities, *Review of Financial Studies* 5, 387–409.

Marcellino, Massimiliano, 1999, Some consequences of temporal aggregation in empirical analysis, *Journal of Business and Economic Statistics* 17, 129–136.

Marcellino, Massimiliano G., 2004a, Forecast pooling for European macroeconomic variables, *Oxford Bulletin of Economics and Statistics* 66, 91–112.

Marcellino, Massimliano G., 2004b, Forecasting emu macroeconomic variables, *International Journal of Forecasting* 20, 359–372.

Marcellino, Massimiliano G., 2006, Leading indicators, in G. Elliott, C. Granger, and A. Timmermann, ed.: *Handbook of Economic Forecasting, Volume 1* . pp. 879–960 (Elsevier).

———— , 2016, *Applied Econometrics: An Introduction* (Bocconi University Press).

———— , and Christian Schumacher, 2010, Factor MIDAS for nowcasting and forecasting with ragged-edge data: A model comparison for German GDP, *Oxford Bulletin of Economics and Statistics* 72, 518–550.

Marcellino, Massimiliano G., James H. Stock, and Mark W. Watson, 2006, A comparison of direct and iterated multistep ar methods for forecasting macroeconomic time series, *Journal of Econometrics* 135, 499–526.

Mariano, Roberto S., and Yasutomo Murasawa, 2003, A new coincident index of business cycles based on monthly and quarterly series, *Journal of Applied Econometrics* 18, 427–443.

Mariano, Roberto S, and Yasutomo Murasawa, 2010, A coincident index, common factors, and monthly real GDP, *Oxford Bulletin of Economics and Statistics* 72, 27–46.

McCracken, Michael W., Michael Owyang, and Tatevik Sekhposyan, 2015, Real-time forecasting with a large, mixed frequency, Bayesian VAR, FRB St Louis Paper No. FEDLWP2015-030.

Mitchell, James, and Kenneth F Wallis, 2011, Evaluating density forecasts: Forecast combinations, model mixtures, calibration and sharpness, *Journal of Applied Econometrics* 26, 1023–1040.

Mittnik, Stefan, and Peter A. Zadrozny, 2004, *Forecasting Quarterly German GDP at Monthly Intervals using Monthly Ifo Business Conditions Data* (Springer).

Mizon, Grayham E., and Jean-Francois Richard, 1986, The encompassing principle and its application to testing non-nested hypotheses, *Econometrica* 54, 657–678.

Nelson, Daniel B., 1991, Conditional heteroskedasticity in asset returns: A new approach, *Econometrica* 59, 347–370.

Newey, Whitney K, and Kenneth D. West, 1987, A simple, positive semi-definite, heteroskedasticity and autocorrelation consistent covariance matrix, *Econometrica* 55, 703–708.

Newey, Whitney K., and Kenneth D. West, 1994, Automatic lag selection in covariance matrix estimation, *Review of Economic Studies* 61, 631–653.

Nunes, Luis C., 2005, Nowcasting quarterly GDP growth in a monthly coincident indicator model, *Journal of Forecasting* 24, 575–592.

Parzen, Emanuel, 1957, On consistent estimates of the spectrum of a stationary time series, *Annals of Mathematical Statistics* 28, 329–348.

Patton, Andrew J., 2011, Volatility forecast comparison using imperfect volatility proxies, *Journal of Econometrics* 160, 246–256.

——— , and Allan Timmermann, 2007, Properties of optimal forecasts under asymmetric loss and nonlinearity, *Journal of Econometrics* 140, 884–918.

Perego, Erica R., and Wessel N. Vermeulen, 2016, Macro-economic determinants of european stock and government bond correlations: A tale of two regions, *Journal of Empirical Finance* 37, 214–232.

Perron, Pierre, 1989, The great crash, the oil price shock, and the unit root hypothesis, *Econometrica* 57, 1361–1401.

Phillips, Peter C.B., 1986, Understanding spurious regressions in econometrics, *Journal of Econometrics* 33, 311–340.

———— , 1987, Time series regression with a unit root, *Econometrica* 55, 277–301.

———— , 1988, Multiple regression with integrated time series, *Contemporary Mathematics* 80, 79–105.

———— , 1991, Optimal inference in cointegrated systems, *Econometrica* 59, 283–306.

———— , and Bruce E. Hansen, 1990, Statistical inference in instrumental variables regression with i (1) processes, *Review of Economic Studies* 57, 99–125.

Phillips, Peter C.B., and Mico Loretan, 1991, Estimating long-run economic equilibria, *Review of Economic Studies* 58, 407–436.

Phillips, Peter C.B., and Pierre Perron, 1988, Testing for a unit root in time series regression, *Biometrika* 75, 335–346.

Phillips, Peter C.B., and Zhijie Xiao, 1998, A primer on unit root testing, *Journal of Economic Surveys* 12, 423–470.

Ploberger, Werner, and Walter Krämer, 1992, The CUSUM test with OLS residuals, *Econometrica* 60, 271–285.

Priestley, M.B., 1962, Basic considerations in the estimation of spectra, *Technometrics* 4, 551–564.

Psaradakis, Zacharias, and Nicola Spagnolo, 2006, Joint determination of the state dimension and autoregressive order for models with markov regime switching, *Journal of Time Series Analysis* 27, 753–766.

Rossi, Barbara, 2012, Advances in forecasting under instability, in Graham Elliott, and Allan Timmermann, ed.: *Handbook of Economic Forecasting, Volume 2 Part B* pp. 1203–1324. Elsevier.

Saikkonen, Pentti, 1991, Asymptotically efficient estimation of cointegration regressions, *Econometric Theory* 7, 1–21.

Schorfheide, Frank, and Dongho Song, 2015, Real-time forecasting with a mixed-frequency var, *Journal of Business and Economic Statistics* 33, 366–380.

Schumacher, Christian, 2016, A comparison of MIDAS and bridge equations, *International Journal of Forecasting* 32, 257–270.

Schwert, G. William, 1989, Why does stock market volatility change over time?, *Journal of Finance* 44, 1115–1153.

Sentana, Enrique, 1995, Quadratic arch models, *Review of Economic Studies* 62, 639–661.

Shephard, N, 2005, *Stochastic Volatility: Selected Readings* (Oxford University Press).

Sims, Christopher A, 1980, Macroeconomics and reality, *Econometrica* 48, 1–48.

———— , 1993, A nine-variable probabilistic macroeconomic forecasting model, in James H. Stock, and Mark W. Watson, ed.: *Business Cycles, Indicators and Forecasting* . pp. 179–212 (University of Chicago Press).

———— , and Tao Zha, 1998, Bayesian methods for dynamic multivariate models, *International Economic Review* 39, 949–968.

Smith, Aaron, Prasad A. Naik, and Chih-Ling Tsai, 2006, Markov-switching model selection using Kullback–Leibler divergence, *Journal of Econometrics* 134, 553–577.

Spanos, Aris, 1987, Error autocorrelation revisited: The AR (1) case, *Econometric Reviews* 6, 285–294.

Stock, James H., 1994, Unit roots, structural breaks and trends, in Daniel McFadden, and Robert F. Engle, ed.: *Handbook of Econometrics, Volume 4* pp. 2739–2841. Elsevier.

———— , and Mark W. Watson, 1999, A comparison of linear and nonlinear univariate models for forecasting macroeconomic time series, in Robert F. Engle, and Halbert White, ed.: *Cointegration, Causality, and Forecasting: A Festschrift in Honour of Clive W.J. Granger* pp. 1–44. Oxford University Press.

———— , 2002a, Forecasting using principal components from a large number of predictors, *Journal of the American Statistical Association* 97, 1167–1179.

———— , 2002b, Macroeconomic forecasting using diffusion indexes, *Journal of Business and Economic Statistics* 20, 147–162.

———— , 2005, Implications of dynamic factor models for var analysis, Discussion paper, National Bureau of Economic Research.

———— , 2006, Forecasting with many predictors, in *Handbook of Economic Forecasting, Volume 1* . pp. 515–554 (Elsevier).

———— , 2009, *Introduction to Econometrics, Second Edition* (Addison-Wesley).

Stoica, Petre, Torsten Söderström, and Benjamin Friedlander, 1985, Optimal instrumental variable estimates of the ar parameters of an arma process, *IEEE Transactions on Automatic Control* 30, 1066–1074.

Swanson, Norman R., and Halbert White, 1997, A model selection approach to real-time macroeconomic forecasting using linear models and artificial neural networks, *Review of Economics and Statistics* 79, 540–550.

Taylor, Stephen J., 2007, *Modelling Financial Time Series* (World Scientific Publishing).

Teräsvirta, Timo, 1996, Power properties of linearity tests for time series, *Studies in Nonlinear Dynamics and Econometrics* 1, 1–16.

———, 2006, Forecasting economic variables with nonlinear models, in Graham Elliott, Clive W. J. Granger, and Allan Timmermann, ed.: *Handbook of Economic Forecasting, Volume 1* pp. 413–457. Elsevier.

———, Dag Tjøstheim, and Clive W. J. Granger, 2010, *Modelling Nonlinear Economic Time Series* (Oxford University Press Oxford).

Theil, Henry, and Arthur S. Goldberger, 1961, On pure and mixed statistical estimation in economics, *International Economic Review* 2, 65–78.

Timmermann, Allan, 2006, Forecast combinations, in Graham Elliott, Clive W. J. Granger, and Allan Timmermann, ed.: *Handbook of Economic Forecasting, Volume 1* pp. 135–196. Elsevier.

Tsay, Ruey S., 2005, *Analysis of Financial Time Series* (Wiley).

Van Dijk, Dick, and Philip Hans Franses, 1999, Modeling multiple regimes in the business cycle, *Macroeconomic Dynamics* 3, 311–340.

Van Dijk, Dick van, Timo Teräsvirta, and Philip Hans Franses, 2002, Smooth transition autoregressive models - A survey of recent developments, *Econometric Reviews* 21, 1–47.

Wallis, Kenneth F., 1986, Forecasting with an econometric model: The ragged edge problem, *Journal of Forecasting* 5, 1–13.

Wallis, Kenneth F, 2005, Combining density and interval forecasts: A modest proposal, *Oxford Bulletin of Economics and Statistics* 67, 983–994.

Watson, Mark W., 1994, Vector autoregressions and cointegration, in Daniel McFadden, and Robert F. Engle, ed.: *Handbook of Econometrics, Volume 4* pp. 2843–2915. Elsevier.

West, Kenneth D., 1996, Asymptotic inference about predictive ability, *Econometrica* 64, 1067–1084.

———, 2006, Forecast evaluation, in G. Elliott, C. Granger, and A. Timmermann, ed.: *Handbook of Economic Forecasting, Volume 1* . pp. 99–134 (Elsevier).

White, Halbert, 1980, A heteroskedasticity-consistent covariance matrix estimator and a direct test for heteroskedasticity, *Econometrica* 48, 817–838.

————— , 2014, *Asymptotic Theory for Econometricians* (Academic Press).

Wold, Herman, 1966, Estimation of principal components and related models by iterative least squares, in Krishnaiaah P., ed.: *Multivariate Analysis.* Academic Press.

Wooldridge, Jeffrey, 2012, *Introductory Econometrics: A Modern Approach* (South-Western).

Zadrozny, Peter A., 1990, Forecasting US GNP at monthly intervals with an estimated bivariate time series model, *Federal Reserve Bank of Atlanta Economic Review* 75, 2–15.

Zellner, Arnold, 1996, *An Introduction to Bayesian Inference in Econometrics* (Wiley).

Subject Index

Author Index